The Chicano Studies Reader

AZTLÁN ANTHOLOGY SERIES

Las obreras: Chicana Politics of Work and Family, edited by Vicki L. Ruiz (2000)

The Chicano Studies Reader: An Anthology of Aztlán: 1976–2010, edited by Chon A. Noriega, Eric Avila, Karen Mary Davalos, Chela Sandoval, and Rafael Pérez-Torres (second edition, 2010; first edition, 2001)

I Am Aztlán: The Personal Essay in Chicano Studies, edited by Chon A. Noriega and Wendy Belcher (2004)

AZTLÁN ANTHOLOGY SERIES, VOLUME 2

The Chicano Studies Reader
An Anthology of Aztlán, 1970-2010

Edited by

Chon A. Noriega
Eric Avila
Karen Mary Davalos
Chela Sandoval
Rafael Pérez-Torres

UCLA Chicano Studies Research Center Press
Los Angeles
2010

10 09 08 07   3 4 5 6

Library of Congress Cataloging-in-Publication Data

The Chicano studies reader : an anthology of Aztlán, 1970-2010 / edited by
Chon A. Noriega ... [et al.]. -- 2nd ed.
     p. cm. -- (Aztlán anthology series ; v. 2)
 Includes bibliographical references and index.
 ISBN 978-0-89551-123-2 (paper : alk. paper)
 1. Mexican Americans. 2. Mexican Americans--Study and teaching (Higher)
I. Noriega, Chon A., 1961- II. Aztlán.
 E184.M5C458 2010
 973'.046872--dc22
                                    2010007121

⊗ The paper used in this publication meets the minimum requirements of the
American National Standard for Information Sciences—Permanence of Paper
for Printed Library Materials, ANSI Z39.48-1992.

UCLA Chicano Studies Research Center
193 Haines Hall
Los Angeles, California 90095-1544
www. chicano.ucla.edu

FORTY
YEARS OF
ETHNIC
STUDIES
AT UCLA

CONTENTS

Preface to the Second Edition   ix

The Dissension of Other Things   1
CHON A. NORIEGA

DECOLONIZING THE TERRITORY

Introduction   9
ERIC AVILA

Toward an Operational Definition of the
Mexican American   16
FERNANDO PEÑALOSA

Toward a Perspective on Chicano History   28
JUAN GÓMEZ–QUIÑONES

Los Desarraigados: Chicanos in the Midwestern Region
of the United States   76
GILBERTO CÁRDENAS

Recent Chicano Historiography: An Interpretive Essay   107
ALEX M. SARAGOZA

Chicano Cinema and the Horizon of Expectations:
A Discursive Analysis of Film Reviews in the Mainstream,
Alternative, and Hispanic Press, 1987–1988   170
CHON A. NORIEGA

Refiguring Aztlán   197
RAFAEL PÉREZ-TORRES

PERFORMING POLITICS

Introduction   223
KAREN MARY DAVALOS

Chicano Teatro: A Background   232
JORGE A. HUERTA

Folklore, Lo Mexicano, and Proverbs   248
AMÉRICO PAREDES

Mexican Muralism: Its Social-Educative Roles
in Latin America and the United States   257
SHIFRA M. GOLDMAN

A Perspective for a Study of Religious Dimensions
in Chicano Experience: *Bless Me, Ultima*
as a Religious Text   275
DAVID CARRASCO

Mexican American Home Altars: Toward Their
Interpretation   297
KAY TURNER

CONFIGURING IDENTITIES

Introduction   315
CHELA SANDOVAL

Chicanas and El Movimiento   325
ADALJIZA SOSA-RIDDELL

Unraveling America's Hispanic Past:
Internal Stratification and Class Boundaries   336
RAMÓN A. GUTIÉRREZ

Beyond Indifference and Antipathy: The Chicana
Movement and Chicana Feminist Discourse   351
DENISE A. SEGURA AND BEATRIZ M. PESQUERA

Chicana Identity Matters   371
DEENA J. GONZÁLEZ

Latino Performance and Identity   386
DAVID ROMÁN

REMAPPING THE WORLD

Introduction   405
RAFAEL PÉREZ-TORRES

Political Familism: Toward Sex-Role Equality
in Chicano Families   412
MAXINE BACA ZINN

Chicano Critical Discourse: An Emerging
Cultural Practice   428
ANGIE CHABRAM-DERNERSESIAN

Mapping the Spanish Language along a Multiethnic
and Multilingual Border   465
ROSAURA SÁNCHEZ

The Folklore of the Freeway: Space, Culture,
and Identity in Postwar Los Angeles 512
ERIC AVILA

Chicana/o Studies and Anthropology: The Dialogue
That Never Was 527
KAREN MARY DAVALOS

CONTINUING TO PUSH BOUNDARIES

Introduction
CHON A. NORIEGA 559

Illegal Status and Social Citizenship: Thoughts on
Mexican Immigrants in a Postnational World 561
ADELAIDA R. DEL CASTILLO

Gender, Order, and Femicide: Reading the Popular
Culture of Murder in Cuidad Juárez 581
STEVEN S. VOLK AND MARIAN E. SCHLOTTERBECK

"El destierro de los Chinos": Popular Perspectives on
Chinese-Mexican Intermarriage in the
Early Twentieth Century 615
ROBERT CHAO ROMERO

Prothesis, Surrogation, and Relation in
Arturo Islas's *The Rain God* 647
JOHN ALBA CUTLER

Spatializing Sexuality in Jaime Hernandez's *Locas* 673
JESSICA E. JONES

CONTRIBUTORS 703

INDEX 712

Preface to the Second Edition

This second edition of *The Chicano Studies Reader* commemorates the fortieth anniversary of *Aztlán: A Journal of Chicano Studies*, whose first issue was published in 1970, and of the UCLA Chicano Studies Research Center, which was established in 1969. It is dedicated to the many people who have worked on the journal and who have helped realize its contributions to Chicano studies and the Chicano community. Since its inception, *Aztlán* has been the product of many people who have dedicated themselves to its goals, especially founding editors Juan Gómez-Quiñones, Roberto Sifuentes, Reynaldo Macias, Deluvina Hernandez, and Teresa McKenna. Raymund Paredes guided *Aztlán* into the 1990s, establishing the journal's current cover design, which features the work of Chicana and Chicano artists. For the past fourteen years, I have been fortunate to follow in the footsteps of these scholars and to be able to contribute to the ongoing history of this journal as its current editor. For over a decade, Managing Editor Wendy Belcher was a crucial and dynamic force in helping to return the journal to a regular publishing schedule and re-establish our book publications program. I have no doubt that without her *Aztlán* would not have made it to the twenty-first century. Today, Rebecca Frazier continues her legacy, overseeing greatly expanded publication activities that include three book series, a media arts series, and regular policy briefs and research reports. We both owe a debt of gratitude to the staff and consultants who make *Aztlán* possible—David O'Grady, William Morosi, and Catherine S. Sunshine—as well as to the past and current editorial boards.

Raymund Paredes first raised the idea for this anthology and held preliminary meetings with faculty in the mid-1990s. I am grateful to the book's editorial team—Eric Avila, Karen Mary Davalos, Rafael Pérez-Torrez, and Chela Sandoval—for their hard work, thoughtful selections, and informed appreciation for the journal's history from 1970 to 2000. For this edition, Rebecca and I have culled five essays from the last ten years in consultation with other scholars. These essays, which appear as a separate section at the end, resonate with the four thematic clusters that organized the first edition.

The Dissension of Other Things

Chon A. Noriega

In Spring 1970, *Aztlán: A Journal of Chicano Studies* started publication as part of the newly created UCLA Chicano Studies Research Center. That first year was quite tumultuous, not just on campus, but across Los Angeles and the nation. The defining event would be the Chicano Moratorium Against the Vietnam War on 29 August 1970, a peaceful rally in East Los Angeles that ended in a deadly police riot, an event encapsulated by the police shooting and killing of journalist Ruben Salazar (Noriega 2000b). For many, that event marks the beginning of the end for the Chicano movement and the end of the beginning for Chicano studies. The two would be separated by a death, both actual and metaphorical, that, as Mario T. García notes, "silenced an expression of hope that American society would keep its promises" (1995, 35).

Social change is never easy, for, as Frederick Douglass noted in the nineteenth century, "Power concedes nothing without demand." But demand necessarily acknowledges power and thereby locates concessions within its authority. As such, concession can be a double-edged sword, cutting demand down to size, then fitting it into pre-established categories. And that was the situation facing the Chicano movement in 1970. Thirty years later, Chicano studies continues to struggle with this double-edged sword.

What happened in 1970—helped along by tear gas and police batons—signaled a crucial and profound shift from social movement to public institution, especially insofar as these tend to be antithetical terms within social theory. This shift is the moment of our own "memory crisis" in which the past became disarticulated from the present, becoming an object of historical study (see Terdiman 1993). In effect, the past died. Henceforth, the historian's method and research skills—and institutional moorings—would be required in order to locate and conserve memory.

But that death also served an important function within Chicano studies. As Michel de Certeau notes, "It is an odd procedure that posits death, a breakage everywhere reiterated in discourse, and that yet denies loss by appropriating to the present the privilege of recapitulating the past as a form of knowledge" (1988, 5). What makes the procedure especially odd is that the past becomes not only a form of knowledge—that is, abstract and rational—but a "remembered" knowledge that constitutes our innermost sense of individual-cum-social identity. If the past is no longer immanent within the present, we remember it as a formal knowledge that posits a death at the core of our being. This death is at once the origin of our genealogy and the sign of our historical alienation. Death becomes us. In a rhetorical and historiographic gesture exemplified by Rodolfo "Corky" Gonzales's *I Am Joaquin* (1967), we are and can only hope to become Joaquin (or someone else occupying his place), the namesake of an epic genealogy of conquerors and conquered, all long dead.

This "odd procedure" is intimately tied to power; and, for that reason, it is useful to reread the ambiguity in Douglass's aphorism: "Power concedes nothing without demand." If demand can wrench concessions from power—surely the founding ideal for Chicano studies—then power itself also *makes* demands as part of its concession. In this manner, radical demands for social equity became the more limited concession of affirmative action (see Skrentny 1996). Such moments create complicity—or what sociologists writing about political institutions often refer to as "ironies"—between those making demands and those who have the power to concede. Thus, by complicity, I am not talking about ethical choices but about the structural relations that subtend all social conflicts.

But we forget that part. In fact, we are obliged to do so, amnesia being the better part of identity.[1] As Benedict Anderson argues in *Imagined Communities*, "Having to 'have already forgotten' tragedies of which one needs to be 'reminded' turns out to be a characteristic device in the latter construction of national genealogies" (1991, 201). Remember the Alamo. But also remember Plymouth Rock. And remember them as something they were not in their own time: articulations of an "American" national identity. Such historiography is solemn and deadly earnest. It engenders the sense of a primordial and "deep, horizontal comradeship" amongst a people—in a word, nationalism—"that makes it possible, over the past two centuries, for so many millions of people, not so much to kill, as willingly to die for such limited imaginings" (7).

Chicano histories, too, have partaken of such imaginings: from the Aztecs to the Alamo itself, we are asked to "remember" something we have, by implication, "forgotten" about our own origins. Of course, Chicano nationalism lacks a state apparatus that controls the "means of violence and coercion" within a geographically bounded territory,[2] and so its articulations tend to be either cultural or part of a minority rhetoric within U.S. political discourse. But the overall structures of memory and amnesia within identity formation are the same.

Or can we tell another story about our relationship to the past? As Michel Foucault writes: "What is found at the historical beginning of things is not the inviolable identity of their origin; it is the dissension of other things. It is disparity. History also teaches how to laugh at the solemnities of origin" (1977, 142–143). Indeed, *can* Chicano studies laugh at the solemnities of origin and still maintain its original goals of social equity? Instead of Joaquin, can we be joking…?[3] I would argue that is precisely what we *must* do in order to achieve these goals. But how?

We can start with a different history for the field of Chicano studies, using *Aztlán: A Journal of Chicano Studies* as a case in point. From the first issue in spring 1970, *Aztlán* has been dedicated to scholarly research relevant to or informed by the Chicano experience. The journal has also always undertaken the even more difficult task of defining—or even deconstructing—that experience. Little could be taken for granted; and, in fact, great effort has been necessary in order to bridge the disciplinary border between the social sciences and the humanities and the sociopolitical border between the academy and the community. Why? Because we are *not* Joaquin. Internal differences—particularly of class, region, language, gender, and sexuality—have had a profound impact on the development of Chicano studies.

The first impact, seen most clearly in El Plan Espiritual de Aztlán (1969), was an attempt to "transcend" such "factions" as a political and organizational strategy within the Chicano movement. We remember this moment now as that of the old *veterano* counterpoised to the latter-day emergence of the new mestiza—one historical outlook supercedes another. But such an attempt could never be absolute in the first place; rather, it signaled that little could be taken for granted except the fact of internal differences. When looking at it in this light, one notices that El Plan Espiritual de Aztlán actually gives these internal differences the weight of historical fact, while transcending such "factions" remains entirely hypothetical as part of an overall call for nationalism and organized political action. Such an approach opens up a space for a more complex and dynamic historical narrative.

This rereading suggests something on the order of what Emma Pérez calls the "decolonial imaginary" (1999) and what Chela Sandoval calls "differential consciousness" (2000). History is a palimpsest and not just the story of the victors; and one does not undo the victor's history as much as weave one's writing into and around the other stories. Indeed, Pérez reveals the paradox that forgetting is itself another form of memory, ending her book with the phrase, "Forget the Alamo." To use "Forget the Alamo" as the battle cry of Chicana historiography is to point to the exclusions at work in the predominant history about the Southwest. But it also places the Alamo at the origins of the history or counter-memory that Pérez writes as an *alternative*. Indeed, Pérez is not alone in being "obliged" to forget the Alamo—such is the precondition for our national belonging. It is just that she then remembers other things in its place. Here—as with the above account of El Plan Espiritual de Aztlán—we find the dissension of other things at a point of historical origin. And laughter.

In this anthology, we bring together a selection of twenty-one essays drawn from the thirty-year print run of the journal. We do so with three different goals in mind: (1) to reprint some of the classic essays that have helped shape and influence Chicano studies; (2) to include work that suggests the broad disciplinary and thematic range of Chicano studies scholarship over the past three decades; and (3) to historicize the journal and the field in a different way that both engages and challenges previous paradigms.

It is with the latter goal in mind that we have grouped the selections into four sections, each with a critical introduction by one of the co-editors: "Decolonizing the Territory" (Eric Avila), "Performing Politics" (Karen Mary Davalos), "Configuring Identities" (Chela Sandoval), and "Remapping the World" (Rafael Pérez-Torres). After significant discussion, the editors rejected the usual categories that divide the social sciences from the humanities, and an implicitly male "politics" from gender and sexuality. Instead, we settled upon four broad themes that traverse these various approaches and their objects of study. Each theme at once reflects contemporary questions within the field and provides an organizing principle for scholarship since the 1970s. This two-fold action is important since it locates each essay within historical context while also suggesting some very specific continuities.

Rafael Pérez-Torres's conclusion about the last section stands in well for the anthology as a whole:

> The essays undo the ontological category of singular ethnic otherness that the term "Chicano" sometimes represents. They assume a critical position interrogating the relation between knowledge and power, between self and other, between margin and center. They contest the conditions that have allowed certain forms of knowledge to appear natural while others seem relegated to the realm of the exotic. Finally, they seek to redraw the boundaries that set up divisions between knowledge, action, and being.

That these essays span thirty years does not at all suggest that Chicano studies has remained the same. On the contrary, we can only begin to appreciate the history of the field when we take note of the specific ways in which Pérez-Torres's words apply to the different essays collected in this anthology.

In 1969, the founders of *Aztlán: A Journal of Chicano Studies* were graduate and even undergraduate students at UCLA, including: Juan Gómez-Quiñones, Deluvina Hernandez, Reynaldo Macias, Teresa McKenna, and Roberto Sifuentes. These and other students came together across disparate fields—history, sociology, education, English, Spanish, political science, and theater arts—as an extension of their involvement in the Chicano student movement and the early formation of Chicano studies. Over the next fifteen years, the founding editors would bring out an impressive range of scholarship that both shaped and legitimized a multidisciplinary field. Meanwhile, these scholars moved from student to professor, often taking up the necessary but daunting task of institutional reform, program development, and mentorship within the university. Today they are recognized as the founding generation of Chicano studies.

But rather than take this history as inevitable, it is important to look at the field's origins from the perspective of demand before it gave way to concession. For what is often forgotten is that we start with the dissension of *students* wanting to remember other things. Students have been and continue to be one of the major catalysts for change within the university. In a way, that is their job! For the professors, our job resides in the methods, sources, and practices of the academy. This book documents a field wherein the twain do meet. Therefore it is only fitting that I end by citing the undergraduate student whose paper taught—rather than reminded—me of this important lesson about the origins of the journal and the field it serves (Perez 2001).

Notes

1. See Benedict Anderson's discussion of being "obliged" to forget in his gloss of Ernest Renan's "Qu'est-ce qu'une nation?" (1991, 199–200).

2. As John A. Hall and G. John Ikenberry point out, "There is a great deal of agreement amongst social scientists as to how the state should be defined" (1989, 1).

3. In *Entelequia*, Ricardo Sánchez provides an extended parody of Gonzales's *I Am Joaquin*, using "joking" as the English-language pronunciation of "Joaquin." See my discussion of the poems and their film adaptations (2000a, chapter 1).

Works Cited

Anderson, Benedict. 1991. *Imagined Communities: Reflections on the Origin and Spread of Nationalism*. 2d ed. London: Verso.

de Certeau, Michel. 1988. *The Writing of History*. Trans. Tom Conley. 1975. New York: Columbia University Press.

Foucault, Michel. 1977. "Nietzsche, Genealogy, History." In *Language, Counter-Memory, Practice: Selected Essays and Interviews*, ed. Donald F. Bouchard. Trans. Donald F. Bouchard and Sherry Simon. Ithaca: Cornell University Press.

García, Mario T., ed. 1995. *Ruben Salazar, Border Correspondent: Selected Writings, 1955–1970*. Berkeley: University of California Press.

Hall, John A., and G. John Ikenberry. 1989. *The State*. Minneapolis: University of Minnesota Press.

Noriega, Chon A. 2000a. *Shot in America: Television, the State, and the Rise of Chicano Cinema*. Minneapolis: University of Minnesota Press.

———. 2000b. "Requiem for Our Beginnings." *Aztlán: A Journal of Chicano Studies* 25, no. 2 (Fall): 1–10.

Pérez, Emma. 1999. *The Decolonial Imaginary: Writing Chicanas into History*. Bloomington: Indiana University Press.

Perez, Mario R. 2001. "Building Monuments, and Naming Battlefields: The Early Years of Chicano Studies Through *Aztlán: A Journal of Chicano Studies*." unpublished manuscript.

Sandoval, Chela. 2000. *Methodology of the Oppressed*. Minneapolis: University of Minnesota Press.

Skrentny, John David. 1996. *The Ironies of Affirmative Action: Politics, Culture, and Justice in America*. Chicago: University of Chicago Press.

Terdiman, Richard. 1993. *Present Past: Modernity and the Memory Crisis*. Ithaca: Cornell University Press.

I.
Decolonizing the Territory

Decolonizing the Territory
Introduction

Eric Avila

The social movements of the 1960s shattered the myth of the university as an ivory tower. The militant demands for social change extended to the university, as social activists called upon campus administrators and faculty to implement programs of study that addressed the life experiences and collective histories of marginalized peoples in the United States, those who had been ignored by generations of scholars who worked within the established disciplines. At the same time, new intellectual developments began to illuminate the situated nature of knowledge, asserting that what we know is conditioned by who we are, and that our claims to "pure" knowledge are not untouched by deeper values and assumptions. This realization underscored the need for programs such as affirmative action, which attempted to implement a more diverse faculty, who could, theoretically, bring a greater sensitivity to and a deeper understanding of the group experiences of marginalized peoples. Today, the university's faculty is more diverse than ever, and the presence of ethnic studies and women's studies departments illustrates not only the legacy of the 1960s, but also the ongoing process by which the American university becomes more and more relevant to diverse histories and disparate cultures of the United States.

The struggle continues, however. For many, affirmative action has been a bitter pill to swallow since its inception in the early 1970s, and the vote to end affirmative action in California in the late 1990s is symptomatic of a larger rollback of some of the gains made during the 1960s. And the struggle to establish women's studies and ethnic studies on American campuses has always engendered bitter controversy, pitting students against administrators and faculty against each other. Indeed, it would be difficult to find one instance of the birth of an ethnic studies program without some public outcry of "favoritism" or "divisiveness." The issue, however, is more than mere favoritism. At stake in the establishment of ethnic studies and women's studies is the very nature of knowledge production. Dissatisfied with the inadequacy of existing paradigms and conventions that inform the course of study in the established disciplines, scholars working within ethnic studies and women's studies question the established canons of knowledge, seeking new theories and paradigms that better serve understudied groups of people.

Within the "contested terrain" of the university, Chicano studies has emerged in the past thirty years as its own territory upon the academic landscape. Chicano studies, born of more established disciplines, history in particular, is many things at once. As a product of the Chicano movement, Chicano studies reflects the impact of 1960s activism upon higher education and continues to replenish that legacy by illuminating the very inequalities that prompted the movement in the first place. As a mode of scholarly inquiry, Chicano studies explores the history and experiences of people of Mexican descent in the United States, drawing upon the methods and theories of multiple disciplines (political economy, cultural studies, historical analysis). And as a departmental program with its own set of majors, minors, and graduate students, Chicano studies, like its counterparts in ethnic studies and women's studies, provides an institutional space where scholars question disciplinary conventions, asking if they are relevant to the study of a people with a unique, but certainly not uniform, history and culture. As a fundamentally interdisciplinary program of study, Chicano studies affords some shelter from the disciplinary hierarchies that have structured the university throughout its history.

This section, "Decolonizing the Territory," presents a set of essays that reflect the efforts of Chicano scholars to distinguish Chicano studies from the purview of older disciplines, whose methods, theories, and assumptions have been identified as problematic to the study of marginalized peoples. The use of the word "toward" in the titles of the first two essays underscores the preliminary nature of initial forays into the field of Chicano studies. Despite their disciplinary origins, the essays reach out to a multidisciplinary audience, mapping out a tentative terrain upon which to explore the regional and historical variants of the Chicano experience, one that transcends the boundaries of any particular discipline. The following two essays, written after the initial establishment of Chicano studies, illustrate a moment of critical reflection within the field, calling for further elaboration upon the internal diversity of Chicano history and culture. The last two essays reflect the move toward "Chicano studies" during the 1990s, in which the rise of cultural studies, with its emphasis upon the discursive dimensions of identity formation, influenced the scholarly approach toward understanding the Chicano experience. Together, the six essays in this section provide a snapshot of some of the major changes that have shaped the evolution of Chicano studies.

"Decolonizing the Territory" begins with a sociologist's basic search for the contours of Mexican American identity. Fernando Peñalosa's essay, "Toward an Operational Definition of the Mexican American," seeks to ask the "right questions" about Mexican American peoples, urging scholars to locate not the typical or true nature of that identity, but rather to establish the range and variation of Mexican American identity across space and time. Thus, the author organizes his essay around a set of seven questions, each of which addresses a particular aspect of Mexican American identity and its relationship to other social groups.

Peñalosa's essay illustrates the tentative approach that some Chicano scholars adopted in their preliminary foray into the new field of Chicano studies. In contrast to the current perception that early Chicano academics of the post-1960s generation held a static and monolithic view of "the Chicano," Peñalosa calls into question many of the uncritical assumptions that informed the agenda of the early Chicano movement. For example, at a time when a regnant Chicano nationalism sought to establish Chicanos as a separate and monolithic social group, Peñalosa urges scholars to explore the extent to which Mexican Americans constituted an identifiable racial, ethnic, and cultural group and to identify the range of variation within each of those categories. Similarly, the author seeks to locate the multiple sources of Chicano culture, arguing that that culture is multidimensional and must be studied in terms of its "heterogeneous" nature. Finally, the essay identifies the regional and historical variants of Mexican American cultures, emphasizing divergent histories, generational differences, and regional variations among Mexican American subgroups living within the United States. By foregrounding these possible lines of inquiry, while simultaneously acknowledging the need for others, Peñalosa attempts to map some areas of future research, which would "help in the sociological definition of our subject population."

In the second essay of this section, historian Juan Gómez-Quiñones undertakes a similar task in regard to Chicano history. His seminal essay, "Toward a Perspective of Chicano History," attempts to identify the grounds for Chicano history and the significance of that history to the "self-definition of a people." Although Gómez-Quiñones notes the relationships between Chicano history and other fields of U.S. history, namely, nineteenth-century, twentieth-century, and western history, he emphasizes the important relationship between Chicano history and other disciplines, stressing the potential of Chicano history to cultivate "rigorous interdisciplinary research and innovative methods." By attempting to delimit the subject, approaches, periodization, and methods of Chicano history, the essay seeks to arm historians and scholars working within other disciplines for a "conceptual paradigm" to approach the study of the evolution of Chicano society over time. Gómez-Quiñones asserts the potential of Chicano history not only to reconceptualize the dominant framework of U.S. history, but also to revolutionize the role of history in society. By forging a union between history as a discipline and history as "action on behalf of a community in its struggle for survival," Gómez-Quiñones articulates the possibilities for a marriage between research and activism under the rubric of Chicano history.

Other historians subsequently added their own emphases to Gómez-Quiñones's call for a new history. The common view of Chicanos as a population confined to the U.S. Southwest prompted others to broaden this regional perspective, bringing the historical experiences of Chicanos and other Spanish-speaking people living in other regions of the United States within the scope of Chicano history. In a special issue of *Aztlán* devoted to the experiences of Chicanos living in the Midwest, Gilberto Cárdenas assessed the historical and contemporary conditions of Chicanos living in the U.S. Midwest in his article "Los Desarraigados: Chicanos in the Midwestern Region of the United States." The first part of the article offers a historical overview of the Chicano population in the Midwest, emphasizing migratory and employment patterns as a major explanatory framework. The second part of the article provides a description and analysis of some selected demographic and socioeconomic characteristics of the Spanish-speaking population, centering upon the cities of Detroit and Chicago. Cárdenas's regional approach underscores the internal diversity among Spanish-speaking peoples in the United States, accounting for regional differences within the many aspects of the Chicano experience.

Alex Saragoza probes deeper into the internal diversity of the Chicano experience in his essay "Recent Chicano Historiography: An Interpretive Essay." The essay offers a historiographical analysis of Chicano history, arguing that past formulations of the Chicano past have been inadequate and require a critical re-evaluation. The field of Chicano history, Saragoza argues, suffers from a reliance upon a problematic interpretation of the

Chicano past, one that reflected the ideological struggles of the 1960s. A "them-versus-us" vision of the Chicano past not only depended upon a set of dubious assumptions, but also minimized the internal diversity of the Chicano community in the name of group solidarity. In particular, Saragoza cites gender as a major challenge to the standard interpretation of Chicano history, which privileged race as the critical division between false notions of "us" and "them." Developments within the discipline of history, however, gave rise to an alternative vision of the Chicano past. Between the years of 1979 and 1984, a new generation of Chicano historians departed from overly ideological interpretations of Chicano history and opened the way to a more nuanced and complex understanding of that history. Their work illuminated the multiple ways in which Chicanos have been stratified throughout their history, by race, class, and gender. After a cursory survey of the issues raised in their research, Saragoza concludes by identifying new avenues for historical research and by encouraging Chicano scholars to continue exploring the complexities of the Chicano past.

The above essays were written from the perspective of social science, with its emphasis upon archival research, statistical analysis, and other methods used to measure the structural dimensions of the Chicano past and present. The "cultural turn" of the 1990s, however, to employ a crude chronology, opened new avenues of research for Chicano scholars who looked to the theories and methods emanating from cultural studies, with its emphasis upon the symbolic dimensions of identity construction and the production of meaning. Thus, "Chicano studies," as the field is presently described on most campuses, reflects the growing influence of scholars working within the humanities—literature, linguistics, and film studies—who explore "texts" and "discourse" in their investigation of Chicana/o identity and culture.

The following two essays reflect the foray into cultural studies that many Chicana/o scholars took during the past decade. In "Chicano Cinema and the Horizon of Expectations," Chon A. Noriega undertakes an analysis of film reviews for a spate of Chicano feature films that appeared in the late 1980s, which centered upon life in southern California barrios. Noriega contends that the critical reception of cultural texts such as films, that which constitutes the "horizon of expectations" that shape audience reception of film, is conditioned by the critic's position in society. Thus while "alternative" publications like the Spanish-language media celebrated the arrival of films such as *Born in East L.A.* and *La Bamba*, the non-Hispanic press discussed the same films within the context of social problems, reinforcing stereotypical depiction of Chicanos as a "problem" community, inundated with gangs, drugs, and crime. Noriega's essay dramatizes the point made by Richard Wright in his famous response to a reporter's question about the "Negro problem" in the United States, to which Wright responded, "There is no Negro problem. There is only a white problem." Indeed, the misrepresentation of a racial minority in the mainstream of American culture is a "white" problem, despite the enduring stereotype of Blacks and Chicanos as "problem" communities.

The final essay in this section marks an extension of the discursive emphasis within Chicano studies. In "Refiguring Aztlán," Rafael Pérez-Torres explores the contradictions and ambiguities implicit within the notion of Aztlán, the name of the mythic homeland that is "either dismissed as part of an exclusionary nationalist agenda or uncritically affirmed as an element central to Chicanismo." Surveying the various ways in which Chicano activists, artists, and scholars have deployed the notion of Aztlán—as a call to "brotherhood," a link to the indigenous past, a reminder of territorial conquest, a symbol of future glories, or as a metaphor for other kinds of oppression—Pérez-Torres argues against any fixed meaning of Aztlán. Rather, the multiple discourses surrounding the word reinforce the fragmented and hybrid nature of Chicana/o identity itself, revealing the numerous heritages and influences that bear upon the Chicana/o articulation of the self and its position within space and time. Pérez-Torres concludes that as an "empty signifier," Aztlán names not that which is or has been, but rather that which is ever absent—nation, unity, liberation. The power of Aztlán, therefore, lies in its ability to make these absences present in the face of oppressive power.

These essays do not reflect the sum of Chicana/o scholarship, but they do provide an overview of some of the changes that have occurred within the field since its inception in the early 1970s. They also reflect the expansion of the territory we know as Chicana/o studies, a space in which scholars explore the structural and symbolic dimensions of the Chicana/o experience and theorize about the spatial and historical intersections of race, class, gender, and sexuality. The variety of methods and approaches among the six articles demonstrate not the aimless search for a discipline, but rather the evolutionary, and highly interdisciplinary, process by which layers of knowledge build upon one another. As this volume will hopefully illustrate, the strength of Chicano studies lies in its very interdisciplinary nature, largely if not entirely removed from the exclusionary canons and social hierarchies that endure within more established disciplines.

For scholars teaching and writing within Chicana/o studies departments, today's struggle is one of legitimacy. The culture of the university breeds suspicion toward ethnic studies programs, reflecting and reinforcing the current move to dismantle ethnic studies and the efforts to re-establish the canon of "dead white males." The situation is disconcerting, but not hopeless. Enrollments in Chicana/o studies programs and other ethnic studies programs are growing, slowly but surely. This issue assumes a greater urgency in light of the growing numbers of non-European immigrants to American cities like Los Angeles, whose presence demands a more relevant curriculum in higher education and underscores the futility of trying to preserve the academic status quo. Like it or not, the decades that this volume spans mark only the beginning stages of the democratization of the university. As the articles in this volume illustrate, the process by which an oppressed group comes to know itself is crucial to that group's advancement. Knowledge, when used in the service of enacting change, is power.

Toward an Operational Definition of the Mexican American

Fernando Peñalosa

The sociological study of the Mexican American, until very recently almost the exclusive province of Anglo sociologists, is about to be launched into a new period of development that should certainly produce more fruitful, more realistic, and more relevant data and conclusions than have previously been forthcoming. Before we move into this new period, however, we would be well advised to map out somewhat more carefully the population we are going to study. In developing a relatively new field, it is not so important to attempt to produce immediately the right answers as it is to ask the right questions. If we ask simple questions, we may get simple and probably misleading answers, particularly since our subject is not at all simple, but exceedingly complex. Mexican Americans may constitute one of the most heterogeneous ethnic groups ever to be studied by sociologists. With reference to the scholarly study of the Mexican American, we would be well advised to stop trying to find the "typical" or "true," and seek rather to establish the range of variation. Generalizations extrapolated from the community in which a Chicano writer happened to grow up or that an Anglo sociologist or anthropologist happened to have studied can be particularly misleading.

It is furthermore essential that we avoid simplistic either-or types of questions, such as: Are Chicanos a people or not? Do they have a distinctive culture or not? Or, is there such a thing existentially as the Mexican American community or not? Realistically we are handicapped in attempting to answer these types of inquiries in which the alternatives are already implicitly limited by the question itself. A much more productive approach might be rather to consider prefixing our questions with a phrase such as "to what extent..." so that we ask to what extent do Mexican Americans constitute a stratum, possess a distinct subculture, etc.

From *Aztlan: A Journal of Chicano Studies* 1, no. 1 (1970): 1–12.

Scholars, both Chicano and Anglo, have furthermore spent countless hours debating the question of the correct name for our group, and then attempting to define the entity for which the supposedly correct name stands. Perhaps the time has come to move beyond terminological and definitional polemics to an examination of some of the dimensions along which we might explore our subject in an attempt better to understand its character.[1]

The method of procedure in this paper will be as follows. A series of questions will be asked about the Mexican American population. An attempt will be made to answer each one, based on the writer's admittedly limited perception of the current state of knowledge, and to point out some possible lines of future research along that dimension. Someday, when we have approximately adequate answers to the questions posed, we may have a more or less acceptable operational definition of the Mexican American. By way of overview, these questions will be discussed:

1. To what extent do Mexican Americans constitute a separate racial entity?
2. To what extent do Mexican Americans conceive of themselves as belonging to a separate ethnic group?
3. To what extent do Mexican Americans have a separate or distinct culture?
4. To what extent do Mexican Americans constitute an identifiable stratum in society?
5. To what extent is it realistic to speak of Mexican American communities?
6. To what extent are differences in historical antecedents reflected among Mexican Americans?
7. To what extent are regional socioeconomic differences significant among Mexican Americans?[2]

Let us then direct our attention to each of these questions in turn.

To What Extent Do Mexican Americans Constitute a Separate Racial Entity?

A goodly number of Mexican Americans and others are confused as to the biological nature of this particular group. An Anglo American may carelessly divide people into whites, Negroes, and Mexicans, or a Chicano may assertively speak of "La Raza."[3] The recently increasing use of the term "brown" similarly represents pride in the group's presumed racial distinctiveness, analogous not only to the Negroes' newly found blackness but also to "La Raza Cósmica" of José Vasconcelos. Although most Mexican Americans are of mixed Spanish, Indian (both southwestern and Mexican), and Negro descent, a large proportion are not physically distinct from the majority American population; hence the group as a whole cannot be characterized in terms of race.[4] "Race" is essentially furthermore a nineteenth-century notion that is rapidly becoming obsolete in physical anthropology and related disciplines. In any case, biological differences as such are no concern of the sociologist; only the ways in which notions of race influence people's behavior concern him. The topic of our discussion is therefore what social scientists refer to as socially supposed races. Regardless of whatever mythology may be involved, however, if the majority group considers Mexican Americans as a race, and insists therefore on continuing to treat them in a discriminatory fashion, then the consequences are nonetheless real: not only the deprivation and segregation, but as the progress of the Chicano movement has shown, racial pride. Not all the consequences of racism are necessarily negative.

Some historical perspective is needed here. With reference to color discrimination, Manuel Gamio noted in the 1920s that dark-skinned Mexicans suffered about the same type of discrimination as Negroes, but that medium-complected Mexicans were able to use second-class public facilities. Even light-brown-skinned Mexicans were excluded from high-class facilities, while "white" Mexicans might be freely admitted, especially if they spoke fluent English.[5] To what extent is this type of scale still applied in public facilities or in other areas of public and private life, and what social factors affect its application? Furthermore, we might well examine the extent to which differences in physical appearances are socially significant to Mexican Americans themselves. The fact that we live in a racist society, where the primary factor affecting a person's status and life chances has always been the color of his skin, means that it is unrealistic to attempt to sweep an unpleasant situation under the carpet and pretend it does not exist.

To What Extent Do Mexican Americans Conceive of Themselves as Belonging to a Separate Ethnic Group?

Tentatively, at least, we might characterize an ethnic group as a subpopulation that shares a common ancestry and that is distinguished by a way of life or culture significantly different in one or more respects from what of the majority of the population, which regards it as an out-group. Do Mexican Americans conceive of themselves in this manner? If they thus conceive of themselves, what is the degree of separateness perceived? It depends, of course, on whom you ask. But it may be hypothesized that answers would probably fall along a spectrum or continuum, of which it is not too difficult to identify three principal segments: those at the extremes, and one at or near the center.

These segments can be characterized according to varying self-conceptions and variations in self-identity. At one extreme are those who acknowledge the fact of their Mexican descent but for whom this fact constitutes neither a particularly positive nor a particularly negative value, because it plays a very unimportant part in their lives and their self-conception. At or near the middle of this putative continuum are those for whom being of Mexican ancestry is something of which they are constantly conscious and which looms importantly as part of their self-conception. Their Mexican descent may constitute for them a positive value, a negative value, or more generally an ambiguous blend of the two. At the other end of the continuum are those who are not only acutely aware of their Mexican identity and descent but are committed to the defense of Mexican American subcultural values, and strive to work actively for the betterment of their people. Tentatively I would like to suggest, without any implication as to their "correctness," that the terms "Americans of Mexican ancestry," "Mexican Americans," and "Chicanos" are sometimes used for those who closely resemble the three types suggested.

Research is needed to determine whether indeed such a continuum can be identified, and if so, what are the proportions of persons falling at various points along its length, and with what other social indices these positions are associated. Sample surveys would seem to be one of the most direct ways of attacking this problem.[6]

To What Extent Do Mexican Americans Have a Separate or Distinct Culture?

Mexican American culture or subculture, whatever its precise nature, composition, and structure, if such are even determinable, appears to be a product of multiple origins, as one would expect in light of its history. The focus of its synthesis and emergence is of course the barrio, and it is here and not toward Mexico that we must focus our primary attention. At the same time, we should not minimize differences between the way of life of Chicanos residing inside and of those residing outside the barrio.

Tentatively it may be suggested that the chief sources of Mexican American culture are four in number. First, there is the initially overriding but subsequently attenuated influence of what is usually called "traditional" Mexican culture, the way of life brought by most of the immigrants from Mexico during several centuries.[7]

Secondly, there is the initially weak but subsequently growing influence of the surrounding majority American culture. Mexican Americans are subject to approximately the same educational system and mass media of communication as are other Americans and participate to varying extents in the economic, social, intellectual, and religious life of the broader society. A careful comparison of the way of life of persons of Mexican descent in the United States with that of people in Mexico will help substantiate the notion that the former are first and foremost "Americans," and only secondarily "Mexican Americans."

A third source of influence upon Mexican American culture is class. The fact that the bulk of the Mexican American population has been concentrated at the lower socioeconomic levels of the society means that some aspects of Mexican American culture may have their source in behavior characteristic generally of lower-class people regardless of ethnic group. Thus, for example, the alleged relatively high crime rate (at least for certain types of crimes) among Mexican Americans can perhaps best be explained in terms of social class rather than ethnicity, as well as in terms of the relative youth of the group as a whole and differential law enforcement practices. Apart from the question of Anglo discrimination, insensitivity, and incompetence, Mexican American problems in education seem to be as much class problems as they are cultural problems. Educational studies comparing lower-class Chicano students with middle-class Anglos are as methodologically faulty as they are socially pernicious. Neither must it be forgotten that class discrimination is as real in this country as racial or ethnic discrimination.

The fourth source of influence on Mexican American culture results from the minority status of its bearers. The term "minority" is not properly a numerical concept (Chicanos outnumber Anglos in East Los Angeles), but rather a term suggesting that the group has less than its share of political, economic, and social power vis-à-vis the majority population and hence suffers from educational, social, occupational, and other economic disadvantages mediated through the processes of prejudice, discrimination, and segregation. Inasmuch as the concept of culture basically refers to the sum total of techniques a people has in coping with and adapting to its physical and social environment, there have been developed some special cultural responses among Mexican Americans to their minority status, as occurs among members of other minority groups. These responses may be viewed as very important components of the admittedly heterogeneous and ill-defined Chicano subculture. An obvious example of this sort of trait is the Chicano movement itself, which is both a response to the majority culture and society and an outstanding component of Chicano culture. But even here the matter gets complicated, for it is necessary to recognize that the movement has borrowed at least some of its goals, values, techniques, and strategies from both the black and Anglo civil rights movements.

It is suggested therefore that Mexican American culture is a multidimensional phenomenon and must be studied in terms of these four dimensions at least (there may be more), as well as in terms of its historical, regional, and ecological variants. It is highly unlikely that all the various strands will ever be completely unraveled and laid out neatly side by side for us to see, but neither must we lose sight of the heterogeneous origins of Mexican American culture, the nature of the varying continuing influences on it, and its continuously changing nature, as we seek to ascertain its differential dispersal, influence, and persistence among persons of Mexican descent in this country.

To What Extent Do Mexican Americans Constitute an Identifiable Stratum in Society?

A number of social scientists who have studied the relations between Mexican Americans and Anglo Americans in the Southwest have described these relations as being "caste-like."[8] That is, the nature of interethnic relations was said to bear some resemblance to the relations between castes in India and elsewhere. In the United States the situation that undoubtedly most closely resembles a color caste system is the traditional pattern of race relations in the South, with its supposedly superordinate white caste and subordinate Negro caste.

Although Mexican-Anglo relations have never been as rigid as black-white relations there may still have been a resemblance, particularly in certain communities, strong enough to characterize them as "semi-caste," "quasi-caste," or "caste-like." That is, there would be manifested a strong degree of segregation, blocking of entrance to certain occupations, political impotence, ritual avoidance, and taboos on intermarriage stemming from notions of "racial" or "color" differences. Intermarriage is an important criterion, for marriage implies social equality between partners. The idea that Mexicans and Mexican Americans are not whites was certainly more prevalent before the World War II period, or at least people expressed the idea more frequently without worrying whether or not anyone might take offense. The current situation in this regard is unclear.[9] It may be that the continuing low rate of intermarriage, the tacit or explicit superior-inferior nature of ethnic relations, and the concentration of Mexican Americans in certain jobs and their virtual exclusion from others mean that Mexican-Anglo relations still approximate a semi-caste system, although increasingly less so.

If Anglo-Mexican relations appear to be moving away from a caste basis to a class basis, and the evidence is definitely pointing in this direction, the internal stratification of the Mexican American population looms increasingly more important. With a few exceptions, our knowledge of Mexican American stratification has had to depend so far primarily on the rather impressionistic accounts of a handful of Anglo social scientists. We know that, generally speaking, Mexican American rural populations have less differentiated social class structures than the urban ones; that is, the status spread is greater in the city than in the country. We know some of the variables associated with socioeconomic status and self- and community perception. Much more, we do not know.

Impressionistic accounts and reworking of U.S. census data in the manner of the UCLA Mexican American Study Project have not been enough. Careful original sample surveys to study the interrelations of "objective" stratification variables as well as the study of the "subjective" perceptions by Chicanos of their own internal stratification systems are urgently needed. Only thus will the myth of the class homogeneity of the Mexican American population be thoroughly discredited and its heterogeneity adequately documented.

To What Extent Is It Realistic to Speak of Mexican American Communities?

One badly neglected area of research is the extent to which Mexican Americans have a feeling of belonging to an identifiable Mexican American community and the extent to which their participation in its organizations and other community activities enables us to identify leadership roles and a social structure as well as a body of sentiment. Regional and ecological considerations are of primary importance here. Degree of community feeling and participation undoubtedly varies among such places as East Los Angeles, Pomona, Tucson, Chicago, or Hidalgo County, Texas, to mention but a few. It varies between those who live in the barrio and those who live outside. Rural-urban differences are likewise significant. Rural Mexican Americans were never able to establish true communities in California, for example, because of Anglo pressures and because of the migratory work patterns of most of the people, according to Ernesto Galarza.[10] The range and variation of "communityness" must be empirically studied, not assumed a priori, both within populations and among a sample of different locales reflecting the differential impact of relevant regional and ecological variables.

To What Extent Are Differences in Historical Antecedents Reflected among Mexican Americans?

To a certain extent, this question foreshadows the succeeding one inasmuch as the principal regional variations have emerged because of different historical antecedents, and hence it is possible to separate analytically but not empirically the geographical and historical dimensions.

The Mexican American population in the United States from 1848 down to the present has been continually expanded and renewed by immigration both legal and illegal from Mexico—a continuously changing Mexico. Mexican immigrants who came, for example, before the revolution, during the revolution, shortly after the revolution, and more recently, came in each case from a somewhat different Mexico. Those coming in at the present time as permanent residents come for the most part from a Mexico vastly more industrialized, urbanized, modernized, and educated than the Mexico of our fathers or grandfathers. How well have immigrants from different periods of Mexico's history, and their children, fared in the United States? What have been the differential rates of mobility and/or assimilation? We should also raise questions about generational differences, and about the differential composition of Mexican American local populations in terms of their historical antecedents. How are these kinds of differences associated with significant social indices, rates of acculturation, and self-perception and self-identity variables?

To What Extent Are Regional Socioeconomic Differences Significant among Mexican Americans?

A number of Mexican American regional subcultures can probably be identified. The historical and geographical factors affecting the emergence of these subvarieties are of crucial importance in understanding their present nature. It is important to realize, for example, that the Hispanos of New Mexico and Colorado evolved their culture in isolated mountain villages fairly remote from Anglo civilization; that the Texas-Mexicans are not only concentrated along the border but are also located geographically in the South with its unique tradition of discrimination and prejudice; and that the Chicanos of Southern California have been caught up in a changing situation of rapid urban growth.

In all areas of the Southwest, the shift from rural to urban has been a highly significant trend. The overwhelming majority of southwestern Mexican Americans now live in urban areas. These Mexican American urban settlements have grown primarily through migration from the countryside, so that the bulk of the adult residents of those communities have not yet completely adjusted to urban life. The kinds of problems they face therefore are quite different from those they had to face in the small towns and rural areas from which they came. Simple agricultural skills are no longer enough for the security of employment. The kinds of job opportunities available are primarily industrial and increasingly require a high degree of either manual dexterity or intellectual skills or both. The needs of automation are furthermore constantly raising the level of skills required in order to compete successfully in the job market. So the urban Mexican American is pushed further and further away from pre-industrial skills, habits, and attitudes and directly into the modern industrial social order with all its complexities and problems.

At the opposite extreme, Mexican Americans in such a place as rural Texas score the lowest on all the social measures. It is in this area that the permanent residences of many migratory agricultural laborers are concentrated. There is perhaps less social differentiation of Mexican Americans here than in any other area of the Southwest, and the most vigorous preservation of so-called traditional Mexican rural culture.

The Spanish Americans, Hispanos, "manitos," or "mejicanos" are the descendants of the original racially mixed but Europeanized settlers of New Mexico and southern Colorado, when this area was under Spanish rule but administered and colonized from Mexico. Traditionally most of the

Hispanos lived in isolated rural areas and were economically and socially handicapped. In recent years, they have become increasingly urbanized as many have been forced off their lands by the more competitive Anglo farmers, or as mines were closed. Many Hispanos left New Mexico and Colorado during the World War II and postwar periods. Many came and continue to come to Southern California and other areas of high urbanization. Here we have another case of attempting to unravel the strands, as Chicano urban populations are increasing in heterogeneity with reference to interstate geographical origins. The sociological study of the Mexican American should include the systematic comparative examination of regional variants of the admittedly hard to define and identify Chicano culture and community (and not just a series of monographic reports, each one on a separate community), as well as the way in which these differences are being gradually obliterated in the urban milieu.[11]

In summary, seven questions were posed with reference to the Chicano population, some tentative answers given, and some areas for future research indicated. It is not the writer's intention to imply that a series of adequately documented answers to these questions would constitute the corpus of Chicano sociology. There are a number of other extremely important unmentioned questions and topics that are obviously part of such a sociology, such as those relating to family life, value systems, power relations, bilingualism, education, and many others. Rather, the explicit intention and hope is that the answers to these questions will help in the formulation of a sociological definition of our subject population before we tackle the multitude of difficult intellectual and social questions that lie ahead of us.

Notes

1. The terms "Mexican American" and "Chicano" are used here for convenience as equivalent and interchangeable, without any implication as to their "correctness" or the "correctness" of any other term or terms that might have been used in their place.

2. The careful reader will have detected that the writer's philosophical bias is strongly nominalistic, that is, he conceives of "culture," "community," "ethnic group," etc., not as "things," but rather as labels that refer to abstractions conjured up by the social scientist or others as a convenience in handling the data they are trying to understand. For example, the latest issue of *El Chicano*, a newspaper

published in San Bernardino, California, carries the headline "Mexican Community Demands Dismissal of Judge Chargin." This is a figure of speech, of course, inasmuch as if the community is indeed an abstraction, it cannot demand anything; only individuals or organized groups can demand.

3. Readers of this journal are undoubtedly acquainted with the fact that throughout the Spanish-speaking world Columbus Day is referred to as "El Día de la Raza," the word "raza" in this context referring to all persons of Hispanic culture, as it does in the motto of the National Autonomous University of Mexico: "Por mi raza hablará el espíritu." Nevertheless, in matters social, words mean what their users want them to mean.

4. See Marcus Goldstein, *Demographic and Bodily Changes in Descendants of Mexican Immigrants* (Austin: Institute of Latin American Studies, University of Texas, 1943), and Gonzalo Aguirre Beltrán, *La Población Negra de México 1519–1810* (México, D.F.: Ediciones Fuente Cultural, 1946).

5. Manuel Gamio, *Mexican Immigration to the United States* (Chicago: University of Chicago Press, 1930), 53.

6. The writer is currently carrying out a random-sample survey of the Mexican American population of San Bernardino, California, with reference to internal social stratification, self-identification, and perception of community and subculture. I hope that the results will throw some light on these questions.

7. The pitfalls of stereotyping in this area are very great, as so ably pointed out by Octavio I. Romano-V., "The Anthropology and Sociology of the Mexican Americans," *El Grito* 11 (fall 1968): 13–26.

8. Walter Goldschmidt, *As You Sow* (New York: Harcourt, Brace and Co., 1947), 59; Paul Schuster Taylor, *An American-Mexican Frontier, Nueces County, Texas* (Chapel Hill: University of North Carolina Press, 1934); Ruth D. Tuck, *Not with the Fist: Mexican-Americans in a Southwest City* (New York: Harcourt, Brace and Co., 1946), 44; Thomas E. Lasswell, "Status Stratification in a Selected Community" (Ph.D. diss., University of Southern California, 1953); Robert B. Rogers, "Perception of the Power Structure by Social Class in a California Community" (Ph.D. diss., University of Southern California, 1962); James B. Watson and Julián Samora, "Subordinate Leadership in a Bi-cultural Community," *American Sociological Review* 19 (August 1954) 413–21; Ozzie Simmons, "Americans and Mexican Americans in South Texas" (Ph.D. diss., Harvard University, 1952); William H. Madsen, *The Mexican-Americans of South Texas* (New York: Holt, Rinehart & Winston, 1964).

It may be argued that since the authors of all these studies are Anglos they may have had a slanted view of the situation, yet it should be understood they are reporting Anglo residents' perceptions of the social barriers they themselves have set up.

9. After the 1930 census, in which Mexicans were listed as a separate "race," persons of Mexican descent were subsequently put back into the "white" category largely because the Mexican American leaders of that time insisted Mexicans were "white." Similarly, the Chicano population is substantially the same as the 1950 and 1960 census category "White persons of Spanish surname." Understandably, therefore, the recent emphasis on "brown" and "La Raza" has some Anglos confused. With reference to the possible relevance of the caste model, it should be pointed

out that the nature of the discrimination against Chicanos has been primarily social rather than legal, as has been the case for blacks in the South.

10. Lecture in the University of California Extension Series "The Mexican American in Transition," Ontario, California, spring 1967.

11. One of the findings of the writer's "Spanish-surname" sample survey of Pomona was that in every case in which a household contained a "Spanish American" adult, that person was married to a "Mexican American." It may be hypothesized on the basis of this admittedly flimsy evidence that in urban Southern California, Hispanos are more likely to marry children or grandchildren of Mexican immigrants than they are other Hispanos because there are no real barriers between the two groups and the statistical odds are therefore against the endogamy of the smaller group. To what extent this may be true of other areas of the country it would be hazardous to guess.

Toward a Perspective on Chicano History

Juan Gómez–Quiñones

Clearly, Chicano history is an exciting field for the historian. Research in this field will provide insight into nineteenth- and twentieth-century América, particularly the West, from a vantage point often previously overlooked. Similarly, it will contribute to the comparative understanding of ethnic-minority history, within an international as well as a national framework. The field will be a test of the training and the standards of the scholar, because it will call for rigorous interdisciplinary research and innovative methodology. It is a field that is professionally wide open; there are sources to be discovered, and interpretations as well as a narrative to be defined. The most important aspect, however, for those who are Chicano, is that in writing the history they will contribute modestly to the heritage and self-knowledge of the community, and perhaps contribute a structural analysis for positive action on behalf of the community.

Conceptualizing Chicano history entails, at this stage, tentative norms on delimiting the subject, approaches, the literature, periodization, patterns, and methods. The phrase "tentative norms" is used purposely, for opinion on these areas is currently subject to debate; this essay is a contribution to the debate.

History, as reflective inquiry and informed analysis, is the analytical investigation of identified problems from the perspective of configurations present in contemporary society. It cannot be merely storytelling about the past. It is not the historian's task to attempt to describe what it is like to be a Chicano. The task is to describe those conditions, both social and historical, of which Chicano society is a product, and analyze how Chicano society has developed over time. These conditions are primarily the material aspects of life, i.e., technology, economics, and the division of labor (which affects the

28

development of race and class relations), family relations, the forms of the household, religious ideology and religious organization, political ideology and political organization. Therefore, Chicano history needs a conceptual paradigm of the functional society. The paradigm should reveal, historically, the interrelations between culture and economic role, group personality configurations, mechanisms of social control, and the accumulating weight of historical experiences—all of which form the historical context. With such a paradigm, one can begin to investigate the pressures, structural characteristics, and events that combine to produce the Chicano community of today. Such a paradigm would necessarily be based on an analytical framework of the economic-social context of the "New World" from the sixteenth through the twentieth century.

Delimitation

A central question in conceptualizing Chicano history is ascertaining those factors that set off this community from the larger society. There are eight factors that are important. The first is that the territory and the community are the result of a war and its legacy, socially and institutionally. The second, and very important, factor is that the Chicano community is set off racially from other sectors of the society. The third differentiating factor is the practice of racism and its impact as peculiar to the people of Mexican descent. The fourth differentiating factor is an area perceived as homeland which has had a continuing, numerous population. The fifth factor is the appearance of a syncretic culture. Sixth, there is intense conflict in a wide spectrum of areas. The seventh factor is that, economically, an overwhelming number of Chicanos have been laborers and have had comparatively low incomes. The eighth differentiating aspect is the prolonged subordination of the community. The combination of these factors determines that the history of the Chicano community has few analogies and has many significant differences from the histories of other identifiable groups in the United States.

The questions of designation, general approaches, and origins of the history are inter-related and problematic. The issue of the proper designation for the community has often been, given the gravity of its implications, controversial. A name has significance in defining self-perception, the perception of one's peers, the cultural heritage, and the larger society. If heightened ideological consciousness is involved, then the designation may have political ramifications. This controversy over nomenclature has been misinterpreted and overemphasized, especially by the sententious outside the community. It is a problem that has to be reckoned with, not dodged. The import that the proper designation has in terms of its psychological-ideological ramifications is usually overlooked. There has never been doubt as to the existence of consciousness in the community or the awareness of the most pressing needs facing it. There has been difference of opinion as to what image to project given racial attitudes in the larger society, and as to the methods employed to achieve desired common ends, hence polemics over the name.

Personally, I find the term Chicano to be preferable. Past various designations have had their special historical roots and meanings associated with particular geographical regions. The choice of Chicano is not in itself depreciatory of other designations. It is not new; it is an in-group term with connotations of peer fellowship usually reserved for working-class people and those of marked Indian descent. It has also been used to distinguish people of Mexican parentage born north of the border; and it also has been used with pejorative intent. Today, however, the acceptance of the term as the self-designation for the community is increasing. The preference for it can be argued on the grounds that it speaks to what is autochthonous as well as syncretic of the Chicano historical experience. It is a statement of self-assertion.

Chicano history is the experiences of the communities of peoples of Mexican descent (indio-mestizo-mulatto) within the United States. This situation is a result of the U.S.-Mexican War. The community has increased its numbers through natural growth, assimilation, and migration; but there is a past prior to the U.S.-Mexican War that must be taken into account in explaining the community's present diversity, geographic location, and cultural differentiation from United States and Mexican societies. Yet, to explore the past beyond 1848 entails confronting and understanding a bifurcated dynamic process. Its primary elements are the formation of the modern Mexican nation and the differentiation from it of its offshoot: the Southwest community of indio-mestizo-mulatto Spanish-speaking people.

The definition of the beginning of Chicano history is important. It is the chronological point of departure for the analytical inquiry of the history. To ascertain origins is difficult, subject to exaggerations that are meaningless and denials that are equivocating. Surrounding the problem are ahistorical notions on the one hand and projections into the past of a present condition conceived in static terms on the other. These notions involve the assertions that the community is a result of emigrations and has no historical legacy or roots beyond the twentieth century. There is also the claim that Chicano history begins with the dawn of creation. Only in meaningless terms can these assertions be maintained. The Chicano community is an ongoing process; it is, and has been, in the process of becoming. It must be analyzed dynamically and with keen attention to time.

Chicano history begins with the basic element for its continuity, permanent settlement in the Southwest by peoples from frontier communities of northern "New Spain." Most modern societies and subsocieties assume form in the interplay of political dislocation, economic transformation, social changes, and international wars, and through other general causal factors. The Chicano community of today is a result of a similar process. It is a process that has been in operation for several centuries. It is related to the processes of formation and expansion of the Mexican and the United States nations. It is also related to the formation of a regional culture and society that has been unified as a result of time, space, genetic makeup, culture, and common experience. In the total historical process, there is no clear benchmark other than the U.S.-Mexican War and even this is subject to local variations. Yet, the broader outlines are identifiable, as are the more specific periods. All of these may be viewed through contrasting approaches.

Approaches

There are four possible general approaches to Chicano history. The identification of these approaches, albeit boldly for the purposes of discussion, is a step toward crystallizing the design of Chicano history and toward unraveling hidden assumptions in its literature.

The historical experience of the community may be seen in a strictly autochthonous frame of reference and causation, in isolation from influences and factors from without the community. This approach asserts or assumes that those factors that have operated in determining the action and the character of the community are wholly internal to it. The second approach is premised on the conviction that the community and its individuals are undifferentiated from the larger society in any but insignificant details such as country of origin or surname. This involves the judgment that the historical experience of the community is one of a barely identifiable subcommunity of the larger society and that its historical record shares all patterns, influences, factors, and changes of the larger society. Further, this subcommunity has no more problems or accidents than those related to locality, class, and other special determinants also operating as differentiating variables upon other sectors of the larger society. A third approach proceeds from the assumption or judgment that the people of Mexican descent residing in the Southwest are a part of Mexican society, but outside the Mexican state, undifferentiated from peoples south of the border. Moreover, the values, influences, and forces that have determined Chicano historical action are those operating from México. A fourth approach is to view the Chicano people as distinct from Mexican society and as a distinct population within the United States occupying a geographical march in the U.S. political structure. In this approach, color, class, and culture determine that the Chicano is in a special relationship to the larger society. Accordingly, Chicano history and contemporary situation is best understood within the framework of colonial relations and patterns.

Only the fourth approach provides the basis to develop a thoroughly satisfactory and explanatory framework. The first three approaches limit and distort the reality of the Chicano experience. They impoverish analysis. A modified colonial framework allows us to relate factors that heretofore have been kept separate. For example, there are factors and forces active within the community that contribute to a dynamic that is peculiar to it. Some of these factors are the collective memory of its experience and its collective perception, among others. Certainly the Chicano community is within the larger context of U.S. society and it is organically a part of its intellectual climate and economy. On the other hand, there are influences and factors related to México that have impact upon the Chicano community, e.g., emigration and its ramifications, ideas, economics, and political events. The status of the Chicano community as a minority-territorial enclave is analogous to other colonial cases in different parts of the world. The aspects that this situation produces and the actions that it engenders are important in the historical formation of the community and in its historical patterns. Some of these aspects are the caste-like social-economic relations, institutional hostility and neglect, and movements of resistance and assertion. The complexity of the Chicano historical experience is one of the many reasons that make its historical analysis challenging.

The Literature

A pressing need for the historian is an assessment of the literature of relevance to the Chicano. The historiographical, like other aspects, is tenuous and problematic. Broadly defined, the historiographical material relevant to the history of the Chicano stretches from the writings concerned with settlement to yesterday's latest feature article or popular survey, and covers fields and areas other than history. Following a strict interpretation, a historiographical essay is presently premature because of the lack of general consciousness among writers of a history, and the relatively few titles, again by a strict definition, that may be considered as directly intended contributions to the history of the peoples of indio-mestizo-mulatto descent in the United States. Nonetheless, an evaluation of the material is needed, and it will be done in the following manner: first, general observations of the literature as a whole; second, observations on general surveys; third, a chronological review, from the colonial period to the present, of the literature that is contemporary to the period, and that is secondary; fourth, comments on recent literature in the social sciences and the arts; and fifth, tentative generalizations. The literature discussed will be selective of those titles that are best and/or most representative. The discussion will be limited to materials concerning the Chicano in the Southwest.[1]

Literature concerning the Chicano numbers around three thousand titles, distributed among books, pamphlets, and articles, as well as unpublished essays, doctoral dissertations, and master's theses. Many of these titles deal only in part with the Chicano. On the whole, all of the literature has at least some informational value and is invaluable as historical documentation of attitudes toward the Chicano in the United States. Just as clearly, the majority of this literature only provides a tentative basis for evaluating the historical process of the community. There are, however, a sufficient number of titles dealing with historical aspects for the establishment of a chronological framework and for the tentative explanatory generalizations. Explicitly, the task for historians is to write the history of the Chicano, and not to expend energy in denouncing or defending what has been written.

In reviewing the literature, one finds more historical writings on the nineteenth and earlier centuries than on the twentieth. There is a need, however, for complex and subtle analysis of the social, economic, and cultural facets of the Chicano. The twentieth century, though short on historical studies, has a substantial number of materials written by journalists, government researchers, and social scientists to aid the historian. The literature of the twentieth century also has contributions by educators, sociologists, anthropologists, economists, and political scientists, in that order. Literature on migration and rural labor (not labor history or economic history) is of the largest quantity. It is followed by what may be loosely called "sociocultural" literature, usually biased, dealing with family living modes, cultural values, and social "deviancy."

Chicano writers are far outnumbered by Anglos, and not surprisingly, given the historical reality of higher education for the Chicano community. Equally unsurprising is the general impression that some of the most scholarly and socially sensitive work has been done by Chicano and Mexican writers. It is an error to suppose that Mexican writers have had no interest in the Chicano; a respectable body of writing exists. In the 1960s, the number of total writings dramatically increased and in the last few years there has been a marked consciousness of writing within a field of Chicano studies. Concurrently, there have been attempts to crystallize definite conceptual, methodological, and ideological approaches. The increase is related to a greater interest in the Chicano on the part of scholars and the public, and is especially related to the presence of an organized Chicano sector on academic campuses and the fact that there now exist Chicano academic and artistic publishing outlets.[2]

Greatly facilitating the historian's task of exploring the possibilities created by the new dispensation are a number of general bibliographies.[3] The more complete and up-to-date bibliography is that of the Inter-Agency Committee on Mexican American Affairs.[4] It, however, emphasizes twentieth-century material and the researcher must use it with care because of its organization, its incompleteness, and its occasionally erroneous citations. More helpful to the general student seeking easy reference to a wide variety of titles in all disciplines are the selective and annotated bibliographies published by Stanford University and the Chicano Studies Center at San Diego State College.[5] The latter bibliography provides evaluations more in line with the thinking of Chicanos in Chicano studies while the former covers more titles and provides summaries rather than judgments. Because of the encompassing intent of the bibliographies, not many historical works are covered. For historians, the most welcome bibliography is that of professors Matt S. Meier and Feliciano Rivera, *A Selective Bibliography for the Study of Mexican American History* (San Jose: Spartan Bookstore, 1971).[6] As valuable as they are as preliminary efforts, no historian working in the field can wholly rely on the available references, for in each case titles have been overlooked and new materials are always being identified by researchers. Progress toward the identification of the extant literature is at this stage limited and preliminary. A fairly complete, reliable, annotated, well-indexed bibliography for Chicano history or literature on the Chicano in general, including primary and secondary sources, has yet to be compiled.[7]

GENERAL WORKS

A scholarly and current general history is not available on the Chicano, and it may be some time before a serious attempt can be undertaken.[8] There are gaps to be filled in the historical record, views and revisions to be tested, and a larger body of monographic literature must be available before a historian can, with some confidence, address himself to the effort. Still, early treatments have laid a foundation for Chicano history.

George I. Sánchez (1948) and Lyle Saunders (1950) made pioneering efforts to survey, even if briefly, the history of the "Spanish-speaking" in the Southwest.[9] Saunders acknowledged generously Sánchez's work. Both authors noted the importance of the historical roots of the twentieth-century community and emphasized the heterogeneity of the people and those factors, since at least 1900, affecting change within the Chicano community. Equally, they noted the problems of defining aspects of the population in order to deal with it historically. Significantly, Saunders pointed out the importance of the urbanization process. Another writer, Carey McWilliams, was in substantive agreement with Sánchez and Saunders but went far beyond.

In 1949, Carey McWilliams published a general historical survey, *North from Mexico: The Spanish Speaking People of the United States* (New York: Greenwood Press, 1968). It is the best general treatment of the Chicano and an admirable and sensitive accomplishment. McWilliams synthesized the existing literature, reinterpreted views, and contributed firsthand knowledge to the book. Most important, he implicitly defined, in large measure, the scope, unity, and major themes of Chicano history. He did this with sympathy and readability. Clearly, his subject engaged him. For him, history was a point of departure for dealing with today and facing tomorrow. What stands out is that McWilliams identified elements of change and continuity operating in the urban and rural sectors. He placed the chronology from Spanish explorations to World War II, stressing conflict, exploitation, and discrimination as themes, but he focused on Anglo-Chicano relations and slightly emphasized California in the twentieth century. He is at his best when dealing with the rural migrant workers. His judgment reflected the radical liberalism of the 1930s, and his style, eastern middlebrow journalism.

Some academic historians usually frown, if not snicker, at the book. It is faulted for its generalizations without substantiation, for the maddening absence of documentation, and for its occasional errors concerning time sequence, dates, names, and grammar; mediocre graduate students can always score points by singling these things out. It was also written by a non-professional historian. Worse, it is popular and seminal. The book is inconsistent in its presentation, perhaps because apparently its contents were determined by what was available or known to the author and by his own social interests. More importantly, McWilliams accepted several negative stereotypes and half-truths. There is condescension in the book. It also falls short when dealing with the Indian. Further, he does not fully understand Chicano processes and values. The book does have these shortcomings, but it will still be the point of historiographical departure.

Professor Manuel P. Servín, to fill the need for an updated survey, has provided *The Mexican Americans: An Awakening Minority* (Beverly Hills, Calif.: Glencoe Press, 1970). In his words, "this volume—a compilation of brief studies by authors in various disciplines and fields, is a historical work teaching in chronological order the racial, cultural, educational, economic, and political development of the Mexican American in the Southwest" (viii). The result is a patchwork of selections without perspective or unifying themes, despite the editor's introductory remarks to each section. One essay, that of Servín, "The Post–World War II Mexican American, 1925–1965: A Non-Achieving Minority," endeavors to survey a part of the history. It is disappointing; the overwhelming emphasis is on California. It has the most common clichés and it is quaintly apologetic. The governing explanatory thesis for understanding Chicano history is the attitudinal one of non-achieving values which is hardly of much currency among contemporary social scientists.

A more successful contribution is Wayne Moquin and Charles Van Doren, *A Documentary History of the Mexican American* (New York: Praeger, 1971). The editors endeavored to focus on unifying themes: urbanism, evolution of ethnic consciousness and, implicitly, inter-ethnic conflict. Chronologically, the volume spans from 1536 to 1970, divided according to periods. However, many of the sixty-five "documents" are about, not from, the Chicano, and the introductory remarks to the sections are not suggestive of the complexity of the history. Certainly, current research is going to bring to light additional documentary sources. The volume as a whole, however, is a positive contribution to the historiography.

The brief note of Jesús Chavarría, "A Précis and a Tentative Bibliography on Chicano History," *Aztlán* (spring 1970), is perhaps the most innovative and seminal work in sketching a chronological framework, suggesting themes and signal events. Though very brief, and suggestive rather than fully explanatory, it is the piece that is most expressive of the views of the younger Chicano historians. Unless the reader is fully conscious of the unidimensional treatment usual in the secondary literature and the emphasis on Anglo-Chicano relations, Chavarría's insight might be easily glossed over. Rather than lamenting on or engaging in polemics, he deals with Chicano history as a fact, not as a personal discovery. He sees three major periods: first, from pre-Western times to Mexican independence, as the roots; second, covering the 1821–1900 period, as the crucible; and third, the twentieth century as the full expression of consciousness. In each period he identifies themes and major characteristics and sees the culture as syncretic, paying attention to both Mexican influences and Anglo factors and emphasizing internal as well as external elements. He has boldly offered a series of insights that may well be the working assignments for a generation of scholars.

There is little that can be said in reviewing general histories of the West that should deal with the Chicano as a thread in the fabric of society.[10] General histories of the Southwest after the perfunctory section on Spanish explorers and the first contacts ignore, more often than not, the continuous Mexican presence.[11] The most positive manner of dealing with this literature is to identify some works that are useful in placing Chicano history in the western context. The representative romantic episodic treatments helpful in this regard are Erna Fergusson, *Our Southwest* (New York: Alfred A. Knopf, 1940) and Paul Horgan, *The Great River: The Rio Grande in North American History* (2 vols., New York: Holt, Rinehart and Winston, 1954). Ferguson has a sense of the contrast of Southwestern society; Horgan offers a broad view from prehistoric to present times and several interesting insights, such as his notion of the ebb and flow of lifestyles and cultures. Among the academic general treatments are Odie B. Faulk, *Land of Many Frontiers: A History of the American Southwest* (New York: Oxford University Press, 1968) and Eugene W. Hollon, *The Southwest: Old and New* (Lincoln: University of Nebraska Press, 1968). Faulk's view of the Southwest as a setting of acculturation is serviceable, and Hollen emphasizes the political and economic aspects of the Southwest. Nonetheless, both are characteristic of the literature that ignores or misunderstands the twentieth-century Chicano community. The best general historical framework is provided by the geographer D. W. Meinig in *Southwest: Three Peoples in Geographical Change, 1600-1700* (New York: Oxford University Press, 1971). He surveys four centuries of cultural-economic interaction emphasizing spatial relations, thus providing a dynamically complex context for viewing change over time. It represents an approach that will prove influential.

The historiography related to Chicano history is richest in dealing with the period of the sixteenth, seventeenth, and eighteenth centuries. Perhaps in this period, from the perspective of Chicano history, research is not as imperative as is a reexamination and reinterpretation of the available sources. This is not the case for the following period of Mexican independence, where new research must be undertaken as well as reinterpretations of the presently available sources. The historiographical legacy of the early period, however, cannot be taken at face value. It is seriously flawed by several distortions caused by the overemphasis on institutional administrative history and by the confusion caused by semantic imprecision in referring to this historical development as "Spanish." It is also marred by an undeniable racism.

1600 to 1800

The documentary literature on the early period is large. Most of the items pertain to administration. There are many printed collections containing documents, accounts, and biographical material of the early Spanish explorers and the Indio-Mestizo-Mulatto settlers. Among the more accessible and those containing a more varied sampling are: Frederick W. Hodge and T. H. Lewis, eds., *Spanish Explorers in the Southern United States, 1528–1543: The Narrative of Alvar Nunez Cabeça de VACA* (New York: C. Scribner's Sons, 1907); Herbert Eugene Bolton, ed., *Spanish Exploration in the Southwest, 1542–1706* (New York: C. Scribner's Sons, 1916); and Charles W. Hackett, ed., *Historical Documents Relating to New Mexico, Nueva Vizcaya and Approaches Thereto, to 1773* (3 vols., Washington, D.C., The Carnegie Institution of Washington, 1923–1937). Perhaps the earliest "historical" account is one written in meter and in the courtly tradition by Gaspar Pérez de Villagra in 1610, *History of New Mexico* (translated by Gilberto Espinosa, Los Angeles: Quivira Society, 1933). It is more romance inspired by exploration and pioneering than a trustworthy chronicle.

Hubert H. Bancroft and Herbert E. Bolton are the major contributors and founders of the secondary literature in this period.[12] A historian must begin and deal with them. Though in some aspects superseded by later work, dated, and with some errors, their work has stood the test of time. As is often the case for founders, the faults and narrowness of the disciples are not the rule in these works. Bolton focused on the "Spanish" period and Bancroft also covers the early centuries though is more valuable for the nineteenth century. Bancroft is best on California and offers a romantic, broad sweep of the early period in sections of *History of the Northern Mexican*

States and Texas (San Francisco: The History Co., 1886–1889), *History of Arizona and New Mexico, 1530–1888* (San Francisco: The History Co., 1889), and *History of California* (San Francisco: Wallace Hebbard Co., 1889). Bolton defined the field of "Spanish borderland history." He is the source for many of the basic interpretations and views, hence his books such as *The Spanish Borderlands* (New Haven: Yale University Press, 1921), merit scrutiny. His most substantial scholarship is *Texas in the Middle Eighteenth Century* (Berkeley: University of California Press, 1915). Representative of institutional histories, and one of the first attempts in the literature, is the racist and dated work of Frank W. Blackmar, *Spanish Institutions in the Southwest* (Baltimore: Johns Hopkins University, 1891). It slights economic-social history and sees institutions in a void.[13]

In contrast, Vito Alessio Robles provides excellent scholarship and interpretation that give an alternative view of the period, at least for Texas. He has done fine work on the expansion and development of the northern frontier in *Francisco de Urdinola y el norte de la Nueva España* (México, Imprenta Mundial, 1931), *Coahuila y Texas desde la consumación de la Independencia hasta el Tratado de Paz de Guadalupe Hidalgo* (México, D.F., 1945), and *Coahuila y Texas en la época colonial* (México, D.F., 1938).[14] Attractive to some, and interesting for a very marked nationalist bias, despite censure of Mexican policy, are the writings of Alfonso Teja Zabre and Alfonso Trueba.[15] The New Mexican Fray Angélico Chávez wrote a genealogical treatment that presents a proud view of frontier families and has several social insights concerning ethnic origins and the development of family ties.[16]

An alternative to traditional views of the frontier is one that emphasizes the formation of a syncretic culture and the socioeconomic factors at play in the expansion and development of the Mexican North. A seminal interpretation has been provided by Eric Wolf, published in a series of essays entitled "Ensayo de Formulación de la Nación," *Cuadernos Americanos* 4 (1953). There is implicitly a more dynamic view of the frontier period in Texas, New Mexico, and California in the works of Odie B. Faulk, *The Last Years of Spanish Texas, 1778–1821* (The Hague: Mouton and Co., 1964); Marc Simmons, *Spanish Government in New Mexico* (Albuquerque: University of New Mexico Press, 1968); and Cecil Alan Hutchinson, *Frontier Settlement in Mexican California: The Hijas-Padres Colony and Its Origins, 1769–1835* (New Haven: Yale University Press, 1969). Perhaps they are indicative of a shift in the interpretation of the period. The latest, and a very able, general synthesis of a now voluminous literature is that of John

Francis Bannon, *The Spanish Borderlands Frontier, 1513–1821* (New York: Holt, Rinehart and Winston, 1970). It is pegged on the Bolton framework and it demonstrates that a survey unleavened by new sources or different perspectives adds little to the literature, even if well done.

In understanding the nineteenth and earlier centuries, the historian is aided by the substantial growing body of literature. Yet, the historian is seriously hindered in his perception of the human element, and in particular from the Chicano viewpoint, in appreciating the historical reality of these centuries. One must adopt a critical position in dealing with the literature of the "Spanish borderlands," the assumption of the existence of a Spanish civilization in the Southwest, and the literature of the nineteenth century.

Naturally, history involves people and the forces that they as groups and individuals generate. Much of the abundant literature of the so-called "Spanish borderland" historiography is devoid of human content. Broad reading of it will leave the investigator vague about social-cultural developments. Granted, in many cases the focus of past historians was not social and cultural, but institutional in a legalistic sense. Yet, many generalizations concerning the Southwest disregard the limitations of this approach. The literature has information based on legal documents concerning administrative practice, architecture, laws (ideally operating), and economic trade, but there is relatively little as to the people, their values, and relations as they developed over time. Certainly, borderland literature can be looked at critically, revised, and supplemented.

Another element that often causes distortion in assessing the historical development of the community is the pernicious "Spanish myth." It probably originated as a result of an insufficiently sophisticated view of colonial New Spain and the social nature of its northern frontiers. It has also fitted racistly rooted mental gymnastics of Anglos and Spanish speakers alike.

The history of the Southwest is beclouded by assumptions of Spanish this and Spanish that. It is an unconscious reflection of racial bias. A common-sense evaluation would indicate that permanent settlement of the Southwest involved a frontier area twice or thrice removed from Spain and from the social-cultural baseline of a certain stage in the evolution of the Mexican colony. Settlement was carried on, in the majority, by indio-mestizo-mulatto settlers. Nonetheless, upon reviewing the literature, an individual of Mexican descent can speculate, understandably, about the probability of a Machiavellian conspiracy to deny the historical presence of ancestral kin. Probably less emotionally charged is the observation, based on analogous sociological and psychological phenomena, that the absurd fixation of the "Spanish myth"

treatment and a good survey. Vito Alessio Robles, previously mentioned, covers the period for Texas, as do Teja Zabre and Trueba for California. A judicious and sensitive view is offered by the fine Chicano scholar Carlos E. Castañeda in volumes that are much more than the title implies, *Our Catholic Heritage in Texas, 1519–1936*, (6 vols., Austin: Von Boeckman–Jones Company, 1936–1958). Justin Smith set the tone for writing on the period, and rationalized the Anglo-Texas view in the long accepted standard work on the Anglo takeover, *The Annexation of Texas* (New York: Baker and Taylor, 1911).[20] Perhaps the work most esteemed by Texans is that of Eugene C. Barker, the acknowledged authority on Anglo colonization. His work is indispensable and may be found in several books and many articles.[21] Though he does not escape the Texas bias, his work is often excellent scholarship. Bancroft's work and the works by Ralph E. Twitchell, *Leading Facts of New Mexican History*, (5 vols., Cedar Rapids, Iowa: Torch Press, 1911–1917) belong to the literature that is chronicle as well as source. Ray A. Billington's *Westward Expansion: A History of the American Frontier* (New York: Macmillan, 1949), and his later *The Far Western Frontier, 1830–1860* (New York: Harper and Brothers, 1956), are outstanding scholarly works that chronicle the motifs and events of expansion.[22] Recently David J. Weber has contributed an excellent monograph, *The Taos Trappers: The Fur Trade in the Far Southwest, 1540–1846* (Norman: University of Oklahoma Press, 1971), which employs Mexican documents and other primary materials to shed light on the economic penetration of New Mexico by Anglos.[23]

The U.S.-Mexican War is the decisive benchmark in Chicano history. The literature that surrounds it is the most abundant and the most controversial for any single event in Chicano history. A fine piece of literature as well as the best memoir from the Mexican side is José M. Roa Barcena's *Recuerdos de la Invasión Norte Americana, 1846–1848: por un Joven de Entonces* (1883; reprint, México, D.F.: Porrua, 1947). A highly personal account of events in México is that of José Fernando Ramírez, *Mexico during the War with the United States* (Columbia, University of Missouri, 1950), translated by Elliot B. Scherr and edited by Walter V. Scholes. Admirably, Albert Ramsey desired to make available the Mexican point of view. His failing was that he was not a good translator, as his collection of fifteen Mexican writers shows: *The Other Side, or Notes for the History of the War between Mexico and the United States* (New York, J. Wiley, 1850). Carlos E. Castañeda makes an excellent contribution in *The Mexican Side of the Texas Revolution* (Dallas: P. L., Turner CO, 1928). He edits and translates five narratives, including that of Santa Anna, relating to the Texas rebellion. The collection edited by Antonio Peña y Reyes, *Algunos documentos sobre el tratado de Guadalupe y la situación de México durante la invasión Americana* (México, D.F.: Publicaciones de la Secreteria de Relaciones Exteriores, 1930; recent edition, 1970), is indispensable to understanding the events and the thinking processes during the war and the Treaty of Guadalupe-Hidalgo.[24]

Mexican accounts show a greater appreciation for the larger causes of the war and exhibit amusement and disgust at the social manners of the Anglos. These writings are sardonically self-critical as opposed to the Anglo accounts, which are self-righteous and congratulatory. The collection that graphically captures the United States experience is George W. Smith's and Charles Judah's *Chronicles of the Gringos: The U.S. Army in the Mexican War, 1846–1849: Accounts of Eyewitnesses and Combatants* (Albuquerque: University of New Mexico Press, 1968), and Thomas D. Tennery's *Mexican War Diary of Thomas D. Tennery.* (Norman: University of Oklahoma Press, 1970). Fascinating are the "Mexican War Memoirs of Samuel E. Chamberlain," *Life Magazine* (23 July, 30 July, and 6 August 1956); also see Samuel E. Chamberlain, *My Confession* (New York: Harper, 1956). There are, of course, the pertinent parts of the memoirs of General Ulysses S. Grant, *Personal Memoirs* (Webster, 1886), and *Memoirs of Lieut.-General Scott, L.L.D.* (New York, Sheldon, 1864).

The secondary literature varies widely in quality. Standard treatments reflecting the respective national prejudice are presented by Bosch García, a conservative nationalist who emphasizes commercial rivalry and expansionism, and the parochial and self-righteous George L. Rives.[25] There are two studies that shed light on the controversial topics of the Alamo and Santa Anna. Miguel A. Sánchez Lamego, a Mexican military historian, has written a narrative of the Alamo campaign from the point of view of the victors, *Sitio y toma del Alamo, 1836* (México, D.F.: Militar Mexicana, 1966); and José C. Valadés has written a revisionist biography that tempers the previous negative judgment, *Santa Anna y la guerra de Tejas* (México, D.F.: Imprenta Mundial, 1936). General Mexican national histories by Justo Sierra and Vicente Riva Palacio, written close to the period, offer unusually interesting and judicious accounts.[26] The classic Anglo interpretation, and the one considered to be the definitive work, is Justin Smith's *War with Mexico* (New York: Macmillan, 1919). An excellent analysis that corrects some of Smith's assumptions is Albert K. Weinberg's *Manifest Destiny: A Study of Nationalist Expansionism in American History* (Baltimore: Johns Hopkins University Press, 1935). Other works that have not accepted the

Smith view and offer novel and illuminating accounts are Otis A. Single-tary, *The Mexican War* (Chicago: University of Chicago Press, 1960), and Glenn W. Price, *Origins of the War with Mexico: the Polk-Stockton Intrigue* (Austin: University of Texas Press, 1967).

The secondary literature on the conflict may be divided into four general interpretations. One places responsibility chiefly, though not exclusively, on individuals such as Polk and Santa Anna and can be found in the works of Glenn Price, Wilfred Calcott, Frank Hanighan, and others.[27] The second set of interpretations see the conflict as the result of class and self-interest. These may be identified as the Southern slaveocracy, western land-hungry sectors, and New England commercial entrepreneurs. These interpretations can be found in the writings of James Rhodes, William Dodd, and Norman Graebner.[28] Another group of writers such as Albert Weinberg, Justin Smith, Carlos Bosch García, and Gastón García Cantú emphasize national aggressiveness, expansionist motives, and racial atti-tudes as the key to understanding the war.[29] The literature may also be divided interpretively according to whether the blame is generally placed on México (Smith for example), or the United States (García Cantú). A recent addition to the field, *North America Divided: The Mexican War, 1846–1848*, by Seymour V. Connor and Odie B. Faulk (New York: Oxford University Press, 1971) indicates that the work of Singletary, Price, or García Cantú is not being generally endorsed and that Smith's view shows continuing acceptance.

The two lone Chicano historians who have dealt with the war, Ruiz and Castañeda, have, as editors, made scholarly and judicious contributions. Hopefully this will be the prevailing tradition.[30] The nineteenth century will be the bloodiest ground in the field of Chicano historiography. Much of the literature is influenced by the passion and guilt of the conflict; however, the archival material is large and there are diverse secondary insights that make reinterpretation possible.

1848 to 1900

The literature on the second half of the nineteenth century is among the best and most interesting, especially the source-chronicle-memoirs and the professional secondary treatments. In this period, there is an interesting variety, though limited in size, of writings from the Chicano community. The memoirs from this sector, as well as those of Anglos, have a tone of *temps perdu*. There is an underlying resentment and bitterness in the Chi-cano memoirs while those of the Anglos are optimistic and self-serving.

Anglo memoirs in reference to the "Mexicans" or "Spanish" are not as harsh or overtly hostile as during the war years. Rather, the racism is now leavened by a patronizing condescension.

A representative volume of the period is that of William Wetts Hart Davis: *El Gringo or, New Mexico and Her People* (Santa Fe: Rydal Press, 1938). While a valuable source, it is a priggish and condescending account of the subject. In comparison to other works of this literature, William Heath Davis's *Seventy-Five Years in California* (San Francisco: J. Howell, 1929) is a more objective and sympathetic insight into the society. Examples of a different kind are Edith M. Bowyer, *Observations of a Ranch-woman in New Mexico* (New York and London: Macmillan, 1898); Jenny Parks Ringgold, *Frontier Days in the Southwest; Pioneer days in old Arizona* (San Antonio: Naylor Company, 1952); J. Oscar Langford and Fred Gipson, *Big Bend: A Homesteader's Story* (Austin: University of Texas Press, 1952); and John Russell Bartlett, *Personal Narratives* (New York: D. Appleton and Company, 1856). All of these, in a left-handed manner, touch upon the "Mexican problem." The importance of the Chicano, especially economic, is implicitly evident in each of these works. The economic relationship is clear, Anglo owners on the one hand and Chicano workers on the other. It is clear the writers were unaware of their racism and oblivious to the strength and wherefore of the animosity and resentment of the Chicanos, which they periodically captured in their writings.

The descendants of the Mexican settlers have left a literature of these years that chronicles the events. The most ambitious are the *nuevo meji-canos*, Francisco de Thomas, *Historia popular de Nuevo México, desde su descubrimiento hasta la actualidad* (New York: American Book Company, 1896) and Benjamin M. Read, *Historia ilustrada de Nuevo México* (Santa Fe: Compania Impresora del Nuevo México, 1911). These are sensitive and noble efforts at interpretation. It must be remembered that by this time the Chicano community has been exposed to the racial and cultural prejudice of the United States and that some Chicanos slight or overlook what are considered to be the less acceptable aspects of their heritage. Though his accounts differ from lack of organization, Miguel A. Otero provides insight into the process of accommodation in politics in *My Life on the Frontier*, (2 vols., New York: Press of the Pioneers, 1935–1939), and *My Nine Years as Governor of the Territory of New Mexico, 1897–1906* (Albuquerque: University of New Mexico Press, 1940). Though overlapping into the twentieth century, there is the excellent book by Fabiola Cabeza de Vaca Gilbert on the life and trials of cattle ranging and sheep herding,

We Fed Them Cactus (Albuquerque: University of New Mexico Press, 1954). The Mexicano *californios* left unpublished manuscript material that is in several collections. The published material is José del Carmen Lugo, "Life of a Rancher," *Historical Society of Southern California* 32 (September 1950); Prudencia Higuera, "Trading with the Americans," in *California Heritage: An Anthology of History and Literature*, edited by John and Laree Caughey (Los Angeles: Ward Ritchie Press, 1962); Angustias de la Guerra Ord, *Occurrences in Hispanic California*, edited and translated by William Ellison and Francisco Price (Washington, D.C.: Academy of Franciscan History, 1956); and Guadalupe Vallejo, "Ranch and Mission Days in Alta California," *Century Magazine* 41 (1890).

The secondary literature of the middle and late nineteenth century is among the best. The relevant sections of the works of Castañeda, Bancroft, and Twitchell are among the most valuable. Though the latter two have been questioned because of their excessive footnotes and method of documentation, they are still indispensable. Twitchell, however, endeavors to equivocate and implicitly defend the Santa Fe Ring and the Republican Party, both active in land grant schemes. Though limited to the four territories of Utah, Colorado, Arizona, and New Mexico, a sound general survey of the period is available in Howard Roberts Lamar's *The Far Southwest, 1846–1912: A Territorial History* (New Haven: Yale, 1966).[31] Undoubtedly the best research and writing on sociocultural history in relation to Chicano history are Américo Paredes's *With His Pistol in His Hand* (Austin: University of Texas, 1958), and Leonard Pitt's *The Decline of the Californios: A Social History of the Spanish-Speaking Californios, 1846–1890* (Berkeley: University of California Press, 1966). Both are excellent interpretive analyses. Paredes, through the exhaustive use of ballads and printed material, chronicles the life of Gregorio Cortés. In so doing, Paredes depicts, sensitively yet with defiance, Chicano-Anglo relations in South Texas. Pitt focuses on the economic and social displacements of the wealthy californios with the underlying themes of oppression and continuity, but slights the Indian and poor mestizo. An approximation toward the study of an institution that has material on this period is Alexander M. Darley, *The Passionists of the Southwest: Or, The Holy Brotherhood* (Glorieta, N.M.: Rio Grande Press, 1968).[32] Robert D. Gregg and Clarence Clendenen deal with border conflict.[33] An example of the secondary literature that sees the people as quaint and picturesque is the sometimes sensitive, often maudlin, "classic," *The Land of Poco Tiempo*, by Charles Fletcher Lummis (Albuquerque: University of New Mexico Press, 1966).

1900 to 1945

In the literature of the twentieth century, some of the themes of the previous periods persist but the patina of nostalgia and romance is gone. Problems and themes are painfully contemporary; they include labor exploitation, discrimination, immigration, social disintegration, cultural conflict, and political oppression. Literature of direct importance is slight, but what exists is helpful. The historian for the twentieth century has the auxiliary aid of the large journalistic commentary as well as social science literature. Fortunately, signs indicate a brighter and richer future for the historiography.

The best identified statement of political tribulations and ideas are the writings of Alonso S. Perales, a leading figure in Mexican American politics; these include *El México-Americano y Politica del Sur de Tejas; Comentarios* (San Antonio, 1931), and *En Defensa de Mi Raza* (San Antonio: Artes Gráficas, 1937). The volume by Ernesto Hidalgo, *La Protección de Mexicanos en los Estados Unidos* (México, D.F.: Talleres Graficos de la Nacion, 1940), is a document in itself, as well as a survey of the problems of the Chicano from the Mexican perspective, with the special insight of a former consul. Also interesting in the same regard is the essay by Enrique Santibañez, *Ensayo Acerca de la Inmigración Mexicana en los Estados Unidos* (San Antonio: Clegg, 1930). The case histories compiled by the fine scholar Manuel Gamio in *The Mexican Immigrant: His Life Story* (Chicago: University of Chicago Press, 1931), present us with a record of the experiences and attitudes of Mexican immigrants.

The secondary literature is, in some cases, excellent, though it is not often written by historians. Only recently have historians become interested in the period. The anthropologist Manuel Gamio is outstanding on labor and immigration. He wrote a classic in methodology and analysis, *Preliminary Survey of the Antecedents and Conditions of the Mexican Immigration Population in the United States and the Formation of a Program for a Definite and Scientific Study of the Problem* (New York: Social Science Research Council, 1928). Equally scholarly and sympathetic are the works of Paul S. Taylor, *Mexican Labor in the United States* (Berkeley, 1928–1934), and *An American-Mexican Frontier: Nueces County, Texas* (Chapel Hill: University of North Carolina, 1934). They include excellent descriptive passages in economic and social conditions. A fair biographical and political study is that written by Alfred C. Córdova, *Octaviano Larrazolo: A Political Portrait* (Albuquerque: University of New Mexico Press, 1952). A Chicano classic that is partially historical in focus is *Forgotten People: A Study of New Mexicans* (Albuquerque: University of New Mexico Press, 1940), by George

I. Sánchez. Servín, as mentioned, has attempted to survey the history of the early twentieth century in his article, "The Pre–World War II Mexican American: An Interpretation," *California Historical Society Quarterly* 45 (December 1966). A group of younger historians has begun to contribute to the field in the area of immigration and labor history. Ronald López and Charles Wollenberg have reexamined the agricultural strikes of the late 1920s and 1930s.[34] Abraham Hoffman has examined the repatriations, and Solomon Jones, the Zoot-Suit Riots in Los Angeles during the Second World War.[35] These writers indicate the subject of interest to contemporary historians. None of them fully used Chicano materials and sources, although their research was professional. Revision and reinterpretation of these events will depend on the use of Chicano sources, an experience and opinion that is, as yet, untapped.

1945 to 1970

The historical material dealing with the post–World War II period is as sketchy as that dealing with the previous period. Again, for these years, there exist the supplementary materials of the other social sciences. Political scientists have written what may be judged as historical surveys, with special attention to post–World War II political developments in the Chicano community. Two examples are Ralph Guzmán's work, "Politics and Policies of the Mexican American Community," in *California Politics and Policies*, edited by Eugene Dvorin and Arthur Misner (Reading: Addison-Wesley, 1966); and Miguel David Tirado's article, "Mexican American Community Political Organization," *Aztlán* (Spring 1970). The Chicano historian Juan Martinez has contributed an essay reviewing politics and analyzing leadership, "Leadership and Politics," in *La Raza: Forgotten Americans*, edited by Julian Samora (South Bend: University of Notre Dame Press, 1966). Dealing with the Chicano in World War II and the Korean War is the proud and dignified *Among the Valiant* by Raul Morín (Alhambra, Calif.: Borden, 1966). The most outstanding work to date on this period is that of Ernesto Galarza, *Merchants of Labor* (Santa Barbara: McNally-Loftin, 1964), and *Spiders in the House and Workers in the Field* (South Bend: University of Notre Dame Press, 1970). The former is an account of the abuse of migrant workers at the hands of government and business and the latter relates the struggle of the National Farmworkers Union to gain recognition. In Galarza's work, the migrant worker is the central focus. He is active socially, economically, and politically, against an oppressive complex of forces that thwart his progress.

Though he is not a historian, and is a controversial individual to some people, the anthropologist Octavio Romano-V. has influenced the attitudes of Chicanos toward history and other social sciences. He has sharply criticized the ahistorical views and pejorative stereotypes of social science in "The Anthropology and Sociology of the Mexican Americans, the Distortion of Mexican American History," *El Grito* (fall 1968), and has called for viewing the Chicano through his own historical process and his own ideological tradition in "The Historical and Intellectual Presence of the Mexican American," *El Grito* (winter 1968). Moving from assertions of what ought to be in history to doing it is the pioneering project of Professor Carlos Cortés who, in "CHICOP," *Aztlán* (fall 1970) discusses the research and writing of local history.

Although dissertations are increasing, they are still often character-ized by a one-dimensional approach, that is, what the Anglo does to the Chicano. Among the more interesting dissertations in history are those of Juan Martinez, Richard Ulibarri, Robin Scott, and Abraham Hoffman; those outstanding in the allied fields are of Nostrand and Romano, followed by those of Thurston and Valadez.[36] Currently, two research projects that indicate much promise are those of Carlos Cortés and Arthur Corwin.[37] Felix Almaraz continues research on Texas, and the highly respected and popular Américo Paredes and his students work and develop materials for the social history of the lower Rio Grande. The interchange of ideas and the flow of research among Chicano scholars is presented in the two acknowledged leading journals, *El Grito* and *Aztlán*.[38] These projects and avenues, combined with the force of the movement and with the acceler-ating change in the values of the United States, will contribute to a rich literature on the history of the Chicano.

BIOGRAPHICAL LITERATURE

The published biographical material on ninteteenth- and twentieth-century figures is scanty.[39] It is often sensationalist and biased as well as poorly documented. Generally, the thesis efforts are slightly better. As a whole, the literature that exists, if critically used, provides for tentative hypotheses and typologies of leadership. The controversial José Bernardo Gutiérrez de Lara, who was active in the Mexican independence movement of 1813 in Texas, has been the subject of two endeavors. Neither Rie Jarratt in *Gutiérrez de Lara, Mexican-Texan* (Austin: Creole-Texana, 1949), nor Vidal Covian Martinez, in *Don José Bernardo Maximiliano Gutiérrez de Lara* (Ciudad

Victoria, México: 1967) places him in the perspective of the events and currents of his time. A better, though romantic, work is the biography on the Mexican California leader Mariano Guadalupe Vallejo by Myrtle M. McKittrick, *Vallejo, Son of California* (Portland, Ore.: Binford and Mort, 1944). Fortunately, there are manuscripts in which Vallejo and other Mexicanos of the period speak for themselves. When inspected and interpreted from the perspective of Chicano history, a different view of the attitudes and experiences of the victims of the Bear Flag Revolt emerges. There is a preliminary work on the first Mexican governor of California. Pio Pico, the last Mexican governor, is treated in two theses.[40] Juan N. Cortina, the resistance leader of the South Texas pueblos, is treated cavalierly in Lyman L. Woodman's *Cortina: Rogue of the Rio Grande* (San Antonio: Naylor, 1950). A more serious effort is Charles W. Goldfinch's *Juan N. Cortina, 1824–1892: A Reappraisal* (Brownsville, Texas: Bishop's Print Shop, 1950). Kyle Crichton collaborated with his subject and the result was *Law and Order, Ltd.: The Rousing Life of Elfego Baca of New Mexico* (Santa Fe, 1928). The California resistance figures, Joaquín Murrietta and Tiburcio Vásquez, are surrounded by controversy and myth. The most interesting works are those of Ralph Rambo and Richard Mitchell.[41] A suggestive and insightful perspective into these and other similar figures, their times, the function of their "myths," and the hostile literature on them may be that of "social banditry" as it occurs in situations of cultural stress, conflict, alienation, and colonial rule. The fascinatingly enigmatic priest-political leader Antonio José Martinez remains so despite Pedro Sánchez's *Memorias Sobre la Vida del Presbiterio Antonio José Martinez* (Santa Fe: Compania Impresora de Nuevo Mexico, 1903), and E. K. Francis's excellent "Padre Martinez, a New Mexican Myth," *New Mexico Historical Review* 31 (October 1956). The best biographical treatment is that of Alfred G. Córdova on the influential and skillful Octaviano A. Larrazolo, *The Prophet of Transition in New Mexico: An Analysis of His Political Life* (Albuquerque: University of New Mexico Press, 1954). Twentieth-century figures of national prominence such as César Chávez, Reies López Tijerina, and Henry B. González have been partially treated biographically.[42] Rather than stressing the sentimental, the sensational, or the scurrilous, future biography work would be more enlightening and relevant if the approach were comparative and functional.

SOCIAL SCIENCE LITERATURE

Indispensable to the historian for the twentieth century is the literature of other social sciences. However, it must be read and used critically, for the majority of it presents an ahistorical, culturally biased view.[43] Though it proves valuable because of the political facts that may be mined, perhaps its greater value lies in the sociocultural and economic insight that may be gleaned by contemporary historians. Certainly the studies are themselves documents on attitudes toward the Chicano. The more relevant social science studies are those that have been published since 1945.

Of the social sciences, political science literature is often the more valuable to the historian. One of the first, and still among the few book-length studies on community politics, is that of Sister Frances Jerome Woods, *Mexican Ethnic Leadership in San Antonio, Texas* (Washington D.C.: Catholic University of America, 1949).[44] What is of interest is the profile of politics that emerges for the period, the analysis of class, leadership recruitment, and her typology of leadership: those that are leaders vis-à-vis the Anglo community, those that hold leadership internally within the community, and lastly the self-interested exploiters. Although Woods engages in racial stereotypes, she does endeavor to approach the analysis with a focus on the internal process within the community. Ten years later, Scott A. Greer, in *Last Man In* (Glencoe, Ill.: Free Press, 1959), made a comparative analysis of Blacks and Chicanos in organized labor. This provided a perspective for an evaluation comparing Chicano labor relations in the 1930s to what they are currently. Greer, however, does not question some of the patterns he sees, that is, low organizational interest, dependency attitudes, and so forth. There are articles and dissertations written before 1965 that deal with Chicano politics. Most are of slight value. Since 1965, a new literature in political science, quantitative and analytical, has appeared, that sees politics from within the community: the writings of Ralph Guzmán, Miguel Tirado, José A. Gutiérrez, Carlos Ornelas, and Mario Barrera indicate probable future trends.[45] Young scholars such as Raymond A. Rocco and Carlos Muñoz are highly critical of their discipline.[46]

Sociologists have, for the most part, ill-served their discipline in regard to the Chicano.[47] Yet the literature is sizable and it contains information, though biased, on culture norms, family relations, health attitudes, intragroup relations, and much else that is of interest to historians.[48] The outstanding representative studies are those of Lyle Saunders (1954), Munro S. Edmonson (1957), and William Madsen (1964), as well as the Hispano Julian Samora (1967).[49] Although quantitative virtuosity is progressively accentuated in these works, the reader questions whether there has been significant improvement over Emory Bogardus. In effect, many of these studies emphasized elements of "Spanish" culture that were stereotyped, and one suspects that the research was organized in such a manner as to validate the assumptions. They also failed to recognize the diversity within the community, the elements of change or adaptation within the overall underlying continuities, or the different styles and mechanisms for carrying on activity that varied too markedly from Anglo norms or mechanisms.[50] Indicative, at least partially, of the more sensitive new directions within sociology is the work of Joan Moore, who has undergone change in her approach to the study of the "Mexican American." Increasingly critical of past analysis, she has turned to the paradigms of colonialism and has recently endeavored to relate historical patterns of oppression and conflict in order to shed light on contemporary social phenomena.[51] Fernando Peñalosa has written perceptively and raised many questions of relevance to historians.[52] The most interesting current work is that being carried on by Rodolfo Alvarez of Yale University, a dynamic and productive professor.[53] Clearly indicative of future work by the younger Chicanos are the writings of Nick Vaca as well as those of Deluvina Hernández and Jaime Sena Rivera.[54]

To point out the obvious, the school is one of the formative influences upon the child; and children become adults. The literature on education provides the facts and perspective for knowing the relationship of one institution, the school, to the community and for assessing some factors that eventually influence adult attitudes and behaviors. The literature is large. Avoiding polemics about educational methods or instruments, there are a few studies of particular significance to historians. The work of George Sánchez, which called for special educational programs in the 1920s and 1930s, is pioneering and sensitive.[55] A work that is nearly comprehensive of all the material up to 1948 is Lloyd S. Tireman's *Teaching Spanish Speaking Children* (Albuquerque: University of New Mexico Press, 1948). It highlights the major problems and patterns in schooling and stresses the need for reforms. It was to be 20 years before educators again began noting what Tireman and Sánchez had pointed out. An informative study, though not generally endorsed as to its assumptions or suggestions, is that of Herschel T. Manuel, *Spanish Speaking Children of the Southwest: Their Education and the Public Welfare* (Austin: University of Texas Press, 1965). Herschel is useful in that he surveys culture conflict, prejudice, language, poverty, and migration factors; he presents school and census statistics as well as biographical material, and includes a review of the literature. Particularly valuable is Thomas P. Carter's *Mexican Americans in School: A History of Educational Neglect* (New York: College Entrance Examination Board, 1970). Within a defined historical framework, Carter surveys the various factors related to education. His work is in effect a resource text. Generally, the literature on education has dramatically altered from the late 1960s, and currently reflects the Chicano community's discontent with methods and theories and obvious past failures.[56]

Economic studies would be of measurable help to historians; unfortunately, few economic studies are available. An early exploratory effort was that of Frederick Meyers, "Employment and Relative Earnings of Spanish Name Persons in Texas Industries," *Southern Economic Journal* 19 (April 1953). Though based on employer information, Meyers's article did provide data on job placement. The interest in economics has been in regard to income, employment, and lately, consumption. To date the major research has been done by Walter Fogel and Frank Mittlebach.[57] Fogel has statistically analyzed income distribution, educational correlation, and occupational status, importantly detailing regional variations and uneven progress. The data provided him with the profile from which to discuss levels of bitterness and frustration, especially those of the third generation. Mittlebach has looked at income distribution pegged to the 1960 census on a comparative framework with Chicanos, whites, and nonwhites. The most historically relevant and soundest work has been that of Fred Schmidt.[58] The discipline has not provided a theoretical approach with which to view the Chicano experience specifically.[59] For general approaches, Clark Kerr, Harry J. Gillman, and Gary S. Becher are useful, as is Dale Hiestrand.[60]

From a culturally nonpejorative psychology, one can expect much sensitive insight toward the understanding of Chicanos. As yet, the expectations exceed the results. There are a number of investigators in the field, and one can expect more in the future. Gartley E. Jaco, in an essay entitled "Mental Health of the Spanish-Americans in Texas," developed the proposition that the Spanish-surnamed population has a lesser rate of major psychoses because of the values and relations found among the group.[61] Dale V. Johnson and Melvin P. Stikes have attempted to test psychologically for cultural persistence in family attitudes.[62] Ari Kiev, in the book-length study *Curanderismo: Mexican American Folk Psychiatry* (New York: The Free Press, 1968), his tone partially perplexed and apologetic, analyzed folk healing practices through psychiatric as well as anthropological methods, and found them generally positive. The most interesting work is that of

Marvin Karno, Robert B. Edgerton, and other associates, who have tested the hypothesis of low incidence of neurosis and psychosis and found it untrue. They investigated social and cultural factors that "hide" mental illness, and have proceeded to investigate the "quality" of mental illness among Chicanos.[63] Their major papers are forthcoming. Horacio Fabrega and associates have done comparative work among Chicanos, Blacks, and Anglos, testing the variable of culture as it affects mental neurosis.[64]

There are, as yet, no significant critical studies and only a few published collections on Chicano art and literature.[65] There is considerable folklore material, poetry and fiction, for collection and critical analysis. The work of Chicano artists, except for that of New Mexico *santeros*, has not been made neatly available. As is obvious, there is relevance in the art for the historian, especially in the areas of folklore and fiction. These are documents on attitudes and events of particular value to the historian. Significantly, art had no place in the "major social science work on the Chicano," *The Mexican American People*, recently published.

Leo Grebler's book *The Mexican American People* (New York: The Free Press, 1970) is an interdisciplinary attempt at surveying the relations of Chicanos and Anglos in the Southwest in a comprehensive socioeconomic and political context.[66] It was intended and announced as the major social science work on the Chicano and it will probably be so received and used, to the detriment of innovative scholarship and of the community that will undoubtedly suffer the consequences of this book when its influence affects policy and programs.[67] The work is a high point in the social science literature on the "Mexican American" common to the 1940s and 1950s. Its usefulness to historians will lie in providing a skewed compendium on the population based on the 1960 census. Its drawback will be that the work will be a base from which to launch revisionist research. It is also an object lesson on the surprises that await a social scientist who proceeds without adequate background research, and what happens when the "variable" people are left out.

Ingeniousness is a hallmark of the book. At the outset the author informs us that the work is "unrestrained by specific sets of hypothesis," though the data collected and the analysis presented perhaps suggest otherwise. This attitude is enough to make the reader leery. Following, we learn that "assimilation potential" is the theme as well as the pervasive guiding norm of the work. Next, we learn that there has been a "discovery of Mexican Americans as a national minority," by John F. Kennedy, the work's researchers, the nation, and, not least, the "Mexican Americans" themselves. The staff's rigorous research suggested to them that in the "Mexican American" community and culture, diversity existed. That is, change and diversity were emerging. Further, the author daringly asserts that "the progress of the group will depend to some considerable extent on the speed with which the local institutions of the larger society provide Mexican Americans with access to opportunities," and 564 pages later "Mexican Americans ... are showing a growing potential for participating in the larger society." These statements suggest that the author's understanding of U.S. society is not much deeper than his grasp of the Chicano complexity. Perhaps the quaintest touch of all is that the researchers, in their opinion, met with apprehension in the community because of the scope of the study, its quantitative orientation, and because it transgressed the localism of leadership.[68]

The point is that the book must be dealt with and that the scholar must approach it critically. Criticism of the work is to be directed at its attitudes, assumptions, and implicit hypothesis, as well as its data and data collecting. When scholars not associated with the project examine the working hypothesis, the methodology, and especially the raw material of 1,552 interviews, the volume will fall into perspective.

THE MEXICAN LITERATURE

In conversation, one often hears that the lack of interest shown by Mexicans in regard to the Chicano is remarkable. The fact is that there exists a respectable, if limited, body of literature by Mexican writers relating to the Chicano; it is serious and popular, fictional and nonfictional.[69] Its patterns can be an interesting subject of study.

Early writings reflected concern and experience surrounding the Mexican-U.S. conflict, as well as memoirs of travels.[70] Interest in and analysis of the conflict continues as a subject for writers, though now it is placed within the larger framework of diplomatic relations and the historical pattern of border conflict and incursions.[71] The focus is generally México–United States relations and the Chicano is usually only mentioned because of spatial circumstance.

At the turn of the century the Mexican press reflected an interest in conditions of life for Chicanos and nationals in the Southwest.[72] This interest has continued to our day, as evidenced by books and journalistic reporting on the problem of emigration and the discrimination suffered by people of Mexican descent. By 1892, the newspaper *El Siglo* (25 April) pointed out that life in the United States, contrary to expectations, was not pleasant for Mexicans; they, as communities or individuals, could not be self-determinate and those who did not assimilate suffered. Especially galling were the mistreatment of Mexican schoolchildren, the "jail suicides," and the lynchings during the period 1906–1911.[73]

Major modern research was initiated by the work of Manuel Gamio (1930).[74] His implicit concern was the exodus from México. He wished to ascertain the factors involved in the migration, in order to lessen the impulse. For their time, his works were impressive scholarly studies that reached conclusions through statistical analysis, interviews, government reports, etc. Gamio emphasized an economic interpretation. He also noted Mexicans' distrust or dislike of Chicanos. Enrique Santibañez (1930) and Ernesto Hidalgo (1940) wrote on problems of emigration, emphasized exploitation and discrimination, and urged government action.[75] A more historical interest was shown in the colonial period. In 1931 and 1938 Alessio Robles published his major research project on the colonization of Northern New Spain.[76]

In the 1940s and 1950s interest was nearly exclusively focused on the bracero program and the illegal immigrant.[77] During these decades Mexican novelists also concerned themselves with the subject of the bracero and often were critical of the Mexican government's lack of zeal in protecting these workers. In their works, they developed the themes of discrimination and exploitation. Often in the nonfiction as well as fiction the Chicano was seen as a victim of the Anglo as well as an exploiter of his Mexican brethren.[78]

The 1960s and the 1970s saw a shift from the focus of the 1950s, and the development of a more marked historical perspective in approaching the problems of the Chicano community. In effect, a greater historical understanding of the contemporary situation and a stronger and more militant empathy with the Chicano exists. The journalists Manuel Mejida and Agustin Cue Cánovas were among the first to rediscover the plight of the New Mexican villagers and to see the problem in relation to historical factors.[79] With the impact of the Chicano movement, newspapers and periodicals began featuring articles on the Chicano by 1969.[80] In 1970 Agustin Cue Cánovas published a quasi-historical book on "el México olvidado."[81] The most recent survey of the contemporary Chicano community is that of Gilberto López y Rivas. He regards the situation as that of an exploited national minority.[82] Works by Mexican writers on the whole present a generally clearer profile of the Chicano situation in the U.S. than do the corresponding separate literatures written by Anglo Americans or Chicanos.

Toward Interpretation

The question of who produces the better historical presentations, a member of the group in question or an outsider, has been posed in relation to any number of societies, usually only providing material for inconclusive debate. The question is a false one. In addition, it has anti-humanist assumptions. Upon the presentation of the notion of a historiography on the Chicano, an obvious, if crude, idea is that "schools" may be definable on the basis of ethnicity. In surveying the literature based on pejorative stereotyping and empathy or the lack of it, there is no clear division along ethnic lines. However, judging by the degree of complexity perceived and the degree of internal dynamics recognized, there does appear a division more or less along ethnic lines. To date, Chicanos have been more sensitive to the heterogeneity of the community and more sensitive to the internal elements that determine its action or reaction in a given historical situation.

Tentatively, the literature and writers are divisible into two broad categories: those writers who view the community in a historical perspective as nonparticipants, and those who see it historically as participants. Although the student must be aware of this general division, it can hardly be a meaningful perspective for viewing the literature on Chicano history, for the present or the future. Perhaps more illuminating is to judge the literature by those frameworks and interpretations that generally perceive accommodation, mobility, and assimilation, and those that perceive conflict, exploitation, and syncretization when dealing with the politics, economics, or culture of the Chicano community. Yet, it must be pointed out that the literature does not provide the wealth or depth to discuss, at this time, interpretations of Chicano history.

More to the point, at this time, is an analysis of publications, research, and projects since 1965 that are conscious efforts in the field of Chicano history. In the last ten years outstanding works are those of Paredes, Pitt, and Galarza, all sharing certain commonalities.[83] Each of the authors rejected or simply ignored pejorative culture-bound stereotyping; if they were short of a fact or a rational explanation they did not take refuge in a racist's assertion. The studies were specific and amply researched; each presented the Chicano as active in a context of interplay involving social, economic, and cultural forces. These studies were sensitive and empathetic, and no less scholarly for it.

Recent general attempts indicate a greater sophistication with regard to the "Spanish-speaking" sector in southwestern society. These works acknowledge the importance of early formative factors, note the continuity between contemporary and historical situations, and emphasize the importance of plural interaction in the development of the Southwest. This is noticeable in the works of Rodman W. Paul, "The Spanish Americans in the Southwest," in *The Frontier Challenge*, edited by John G. Clark. (Lawrence: University of Kansas Press, 1971); D. W. Meinig, *Southwest: Three Peoples in Geographical Change 1600–1970* (New York: Oxford University Press, 1971); and Jack Holmes, *Politics in New Mexico* (Albuquerque: University of New Mexico Press, 1967). At the present time, these works are the exception and they hold out the possibility as well as perhaps indicate a growing trend in reconceptualization of history. The extant literature even permits a tentative identification of major periods and subperiods.

Periodization

Chicano history divides into two major periods, 1598 to 1848 and 1848 to 1971. The period prior to 1598 is in the field of ethnohistory. The years that run from the seventeenth to the twentieth centuries may be viewed in terms of a variety of major patterns: settlement, expansion, trans-acculturation, cultural development, institutionalization, political partisanship, inter-ethnic contact, cultural-economic conflict, resistance, and subordination. The three centuries are divisible into five recognizable periods: 1600–1800, settlement; 1800–1830, florescence; 1830–1848, conflict; 1848–1875, resistance; and 1875–1900, subordination. During these periods the basis for later land preference is demarcated, the claims to charter membership founded, a distinctive subculture elaborated, ethnic stereotypes defined, and the set of social-political-economic relations cast that are to govern between the Chicano people and Anglo society.

The period 1600–1800 has visible basic patterns although they vary in their specifics depending on locality. Indio-mestizo-mulatto settlers from the middle and lower sectors of the northern frontiers of "New Spain," because of preference, audacity, initiative, expansion of the cattle frontier, mining interest, and religious and state encouragement, established ranchos and pueblos in Tejas, Nuevo México, Arizona, Colorado, and Alta California. It was a period of intense hardship unknown to eastern nineteenth-century Anglo immigrants in the Southwest. It involved a testing of endurance, courage, and plain hard work. It was also a time of acclimatization and of refinement of suitable technology and institutions. Throughout the period, the population grew and the area of settlement expanded. Local communication networks functioned and the separate subregions maintained contact with central México. A process of transculturation and assimilation took place with the scattered indigenous tribes. In customs, values, technology, and economy the societal connection was closest to that of what is now northern México. This is a continuous factor through Chicano history, a point that deserves recognition and reflection.

1800–1830 is the period that appears as one of relative harmony and prosperity. The struggle for the independence of México, as well as the political partisanship that precedes, characterizes, and follows it, had reverberations in the Southwest. Ideological divisions developed in the communities reflecting the general lines of Mexican liberalism and conservatism. Subregional cultural lifestyles gained distinctiveness. There was greater economic wealth and continuing expansion. Class distinctions became more evident. Economic penetration by the Anglo was signaled by the opening of commerce through the Santa Fe Trail, the Pacific trade route, and the tentative Anglo settlements in the Tejas province. At this time, forces generated in the eastern seaboard colonies and from international developments determined that the Southwest was to be an area of clash and contest. U.S. consciousness of the Southwest became more acute, and the first interethnic contacts took place.

The period 1830–1848 is one of conflict and turmoil. Important issues were debated throughout the Mexican nation concerning the structure and ethos of the formal state organization. Concurrently, the administrative problems that resulted from the changeover from colonial to independent administration were acute. These issues and problems were present in the Southwest communities and partisan debate intensified. These internal matters coincided with the Anglo problem in the Southwest; one set became interrelated with the other. Issues surrounding Anglo settlement, trade, and the Anglo's obsession with Manifest Destiny culminated in a state of war between the United States and México. Irregular warfare carried on by local citizens against the Anglo preceded and followed the formal war action. In all areas there was resistance as well as accommodation to the Anglo. Military government was imposed first, later followed by civil administration. Despite the traumatic shock of the war and the corresponding transfer of State authority from México to the United States, the communities faced the situation taking positive steps. The process of displacement and subordination of the Chicano by the Anglo began. Ethnic and racial attitudes hardened and mutual derogatory stereotypes evolved.

1848–1875 is a period of resistance, both legal and extra-legal. As a reaction to the injustice practiced against individuals, partisan bands and leaders took up arms against Anglo authorities and civilians. Through politics, courts, and newspapers, Chicano spokesmen sought to protect the community's interest. There was also accommodationist self-interested maneuvering on the part of the remnants of the wealthier sectors. A preference for the Democratic Party was evident. Mexican migration continued and there was class-identifiable reverse migration to the Southwest. Social and cultural cohesiveness was maintained, although fragmentation and demoralization existed. Economic displacement of the Chicano occurred in all activities and areas, though the degree varied according to locality. The factors involved in the U.S. Civil War affected the Mexican community and, to a lesser degree, the Mexican-French conflict was also important.

The period 1875–1900 is one of marginalization: socially, politically, and economically. This process was formative to the Chicano community of the twentieth century. Major elements and components of the West's economic empire were affirmed, such as large-scale farming and cattle raising, the railroad transportation system, industrialized mining, and mass labor divided along caste lines. In all of these, the Chicano participated, contributed, and suffered. Social discrimination, cultural suppression, and economic displacement were aspects of the general situation. The proportion of Chicanos to Anglos sharply decreased, and barrios and *colonias* as a rule became isolated communities. Social characteristics associated with economic exploitation and social marginality were present in the community, and precursory labor and civic organizing appeared. In México the regime of the Porfiriato engineered a beginning industrialization and during its rule certain ideological developments took place; both developments influenced thinking and migration in the Southwest.

The twentieth century is part of the period 1848 to 1971. It has several major patterns and aspects: rural-urban dichotomy, urbanization, cultural synthesis and differentiation, development of consciousness, repression, conflict, intracommunity factionalism, and the quests for educational emancipation and political power. The majority of these are a continuation of those same elements visible in the late nineteenth century. Each represents a potential area of study. These historical patterns are visible in the four major contemporary problems of the community: political powerlessness, economic marginality, social fragmentation, and educational deprivation. There are five subperiods for the twentieth century.

The period 1900–1920 has two principal characteristics of formative importance; these are emigration and urbanization. Large numbers of migrants arrived from Mexico. The urban communities assumed central importance. Labor conflict was intense. The Chicano communities extended beyond the Southwest. Political activity was a continuation of that seen in the late nineteenth century. However, this political activity was divided; one type of activity was oriented toward the needs of the Chicano community. The Mexican Revolution had a major impact on the southwestern communities.

Intense repression and major labor and political organizing characterized 1920 to 1941. For the most part, it was a period of economic deprivation. Regional organization of the entrepreneurial and professional sectors developed on the basis of agreed ideological tenets. The political-ideological division was between those generally favoring assimilation and accommodation, and those favoring cultural plurality and political self-determination. An Anglo ideological-sociological view of the Chicano was defined. There was increasing fragmentation in the rural communities.

The years of World War II were in some aspects an interregnum; even so, three major developments took place. The severe loss of manpower affected social mores and relations within the family. Because of the demands of the war, caste-like relations were lessened in labor as well as in the Services, and the Chicano had access to technical training, the skilled labor market, and industrial unions. The third development was the definition of the lifestyle, language, and values of the *pachuco*.

From 1945 to 1965 was the period in which the Chicano community believed in participation, with minimum reservations, on the terms of the larger society. The disillusionment the Chicano community experienced was a factor in the politics of the later years of the period, and influenced the seminal beginnings of the movement. Even though the Chicano continued to enter the skilled labor market, there were larger numbers who were kept poor through discrimination, exploitation, and the colonial mechanism of selective and limited mobility. An economic and political elite crystallized and solidified. Large-scale political organizing with hitherto unprecedented strength was evident. Labor organizing lessened when compared with preceding periods. Explicit discrimination receded in some areas. Toward the end of the period, there was a reevaluation of earlier ideological tenets and the development of a new style of politics.

The years from 1965 to the present have as their most noticeable aspect *la reconquista*—the movement. It has affected jobs, culture, lifestyles, family relationships, and politics. A marked feature has been that cultural plurality and self-determination are, organizationally, the preeminent influencing factors within the community. The colonias have been subject to major systematic efforts seeking to bring about change in several institutions. The number of broken families and families in poverty increased even though greater numbers entered the professional class. Also, a dramatic revitalization of the arts took place during this period. What occurs in succeeding years is not solely dependent on either the larger society or the Chicano; it is a dialectical process.

On Methods

History, to be analytical, must be approached by asking questions, by posing a problem in an open-ended manner. Descriptive story-telling history has limited value, whereas conceptualized history has applicability and logical substance. Ideally, the research strategy of Chicano history should be to pose a question on an identified general process and to focus the research on a local or state case. Much can be derived from an imaginative exploration of published literature, but interpretations and a narrative designed to enjoy more than tentative validity will depend on discovery and reconstruction of sources. Valuable in this regard are, of course, the standard archival materials. Of great utility are the more novel methods: oral history, urban statistical analysis, and psychohistory.

Certainly there is a large volume of documentary material on the Chicano. Archives in México and the United States have material on Chicano affairs, particularly on legal cases (civil and criminal), political activity, and union organizing of the nineteenth and twentieth centuries. For the nineteenth century and earlier periods, research work is greatly facilitated. There are many archival collections. Some of these collections are on microfilm and often well catalogued and indexed. The late nineteenth and twentieth centuries are the problem periods. However, with adequate preparation and patience, fruitful work is possible at the Federal Record Centers and in the Archivo de la Nación in México as well as in other collections. Although there is no ready-made classification of material under "Mexican American," with names, specific dates, policy, or subject area, the effort to identify sources is not a despairing one for the scholar. The material, because it will be selective, demands that the historian organize it, supplement it, and think creatively concerning it.

Equally creative and responsible must be the use of another indispensable source, oral testimony and traditions.[84] These are of obvious importance in instances where written testimony is limited. However, historians have been rightly skeptical of much of what has been done under the auspices of "oral history projects." Too often, persons with more enthusiasm than training have recorded interviews without context, clear method, or standardized questionnaires, and have uncritically offered and accepted the results as "documents." The true result is a cluttering of endless hours of worthless or superfluous self-serving speech. Technique takes time to perfect, as does an adequate interview framework. Oral history cannot be merely recording of reminiscences. Both the average participant and the major figure of the particular process or event are valuable sources, but the interviews must be structured differently. In all cases each interview must be structured, and involve critical examination, but not be impersonal or inflexible. Clearly, it is best done by a social scientist and with adequate background preparation. Historians in the Chicano field have a responsibility to make possible and preserve the historical record. There is obvious urgency in this matter, for recent events as well as the more distant ones.

Developments in methods and sources within the last ten years in what is properly social history have led to "the new urban history."[85] These developments are of particular value to the study of Chicano history. Historians can now more systematically explore the societal process of urbanization through the use of quantitative data derived from census records, parish registrars, tax lists, and city directories, and the computerized analysis of them. It is the emphasis on the urbanization process that distinguishes it from traditional urban history. These recent developments will be of singular importance for they shed light on the process, allowing for fairly precise comparative evaluation of patterns of class stratification, occupational and residential mobility, community growth, family structure, and social adaptation. The amount and complexity of data calls for a theoretical interdisciplinary approach and data-processing methods. These new methods are not the panacea. Too often, for key social aspects of the Chicano, the data are absent or not sufficiently encompassing or detailed. The new methods are supplemental to other sources and are limited to that which can be counted. These methods, clearly, are also limited by the analytical bias of the investigator.

Psychohistory has much to contribute toward understanding motivation and values or why men act as they do.[86] Psychohistory refers to the application of psychoanalytical and psychological insights and theories to historical problems. It is the approach and method that most calls for demanding and lengthy preparation by the historian. It also calls for rigorous self-understanding by the practitioner. Psychohistory complements quantitative data and standard interpretive sources, through the suggestive illumination of an area too often slighted, the actions and historical patterns of the community itself. Especially needed in Chicano history are explanatory internal paradigms for the development of culture, the character of social mobilization, and leadership.

Conclusion

Chicano history is, and must continue to be, innovative. It is innovative because it calls for a reconceptualization of history and the role of history in society. This means the use of new methods of inquiry and a reconstruction and reinterpretation of available sources. Thus, it would chronicle a union of history as discipline and history as action on behalf of a community in its struggle for survival. It must be viewed critically because Chicano history is not an adjunct to U.S. Anglo history. It is not the listing of "important" names and contributions of "Mexican Americans" to the development of "this great country." Chicano history is not exclusively the relationship of the Anglo as oppressor and the Chicano as oppressed, but must realistically reflect the historical context of the Chicano community vis-à-vis other oppressed groups in U.S. society.

While the scholar's responsibility remains reflective inquiry and informed analysis, Chicano history involves more than the creation of a new discipline or area of study. The elaboration of new definitions and interpretations must be within the framework of the history of the community and must be the work of scholars from that community. It involves the self-definition of a people.

Notes

1. Though the Chicano is closely identified with the Southwest, the community is national. However, material on the Chicano outside the Southwest is scanty. Any generalization made concerning the Chicano, historically, in this region will be subject to correction as more is known about the evolution and character of the Chicano communities in the Middle West and the East.

2. Popular magazines and newspapers have, of course, existed for many years.

3. See Joseph A. Clark y Moreno, "Bibliography of Bibliographies Relating to Mexican American Studies," *El Grito* 3, no. 4 (summer 1970).

4. Inter-Agency Committee on Mexican American Affairs, *A Guide to Materials Relating to Persons of Mexican Heritage in the United States* (Washington, D.C.: U.S. Government Printing Office, 1969). See also the bibliography in Leo Grebler, et al., *The Mexican American People* (New York: The Free Press, 1970). A recent publication is the Cabinet Committee on Opportunities for Spanish Speaking People, *The Spanish Speaking in the United States: A Guide to Materials* (Washington, D.C., 1971).

5. Luis G. Nogales, ed., *The Mexican American: A Selected and Annotated Bibliography* (Stanford: Stanford University Press, 1971); and Ernie Barrios, *Bibliografía Aztlán: An Annotated Chicano Bibliography* (San Diego: Centro de Estudios Chicanos Publications, San Diego State College, 1971).

6. See also "Bibliography," *Journal of Mexican American History* 1 (fall 1970), originally published as *Mexican American History: A Critical Selective Bibliography* (Santa Barbara: Mexican American Historical Society, 1969).

7. As a result of current research through Quinto Sol Publications (Berkeley) and Aztlán Publications (Los Angeles), a complete listing of Chicano newspapers for the nineteenth and twentieth centuries will be available.

8. Recently a slew of brief surveys has appeared that is oriented to presenting the current situation of the Chicano community and its historical background. Leaning heavily on Carey McWilliams, they are intended for general and youthful audiences. Except for Rudy Acuña's *A Mexican American Chronicle* (New York: American Book Company, 1971), one can question their value even to youthful and general audiences since they perforce deal in stereotypes and patchy information. The following cannot be considered contributions to the historiography: Ernesto Galarza, et al., *Mexican Americans in the Southwest* (Santa Barbara: McNally & Loftin, 1969); Ruth Landes, *Latin Americans of the Southwest* (St. Louis: McGraw-Hill, 1965); Julian Nava, *Mexican Americans: Past, Present, Future* (New York: American Book Company, 1969); Ramón E. Ruiz and J. Tibbell, *South by Southwest* (Garden City, N.J.: Doubleday, 1969).

9. George I. Sánchez, "Spanish-Speaking People in the Southwest: A Brief Historical Review." Mimeograph report to the Advisory Committee for the Study of Spanish Speaking People, Austin, Texas, November 22, 1948. Later published in *California Journal of Elementary Education* 22 (November 1953). Lyle Saunders, "The Social History of the Spanish-Speaking People of Southwestern United States Since 1846," *Proceedings of the First Congress of Historians from Mexico and the United States* (México, D.F. Editorial Cultura, 1950); see also Manuel P. Servín, "The Pre–World War II Mexican American: An Interpretation," *California Historical Society Quarterly* 45 (December 1966). An updated version is "The Post–World War II Mexican-American, 1925–1965: A Non-Achieving Minority," in *The Mexican-Americans: An Awakening Minority* (Beverly Hills, Calif.: Glencoe Press, 1970).

10. For a geographical description and definition that is useful see Rubert Norval Richardson and Carl Coke Rister, *The Greater Southwest* (Glendale, Ill.: Arthur H. Clark, 1935).

11. For attempts at defining the region, see John Walton Caughey, "The Spanish Southwest," in *Regionalism in America*, ed. Merrill Jensen. (Madison: University of Wisconsin Press, 1952). Also, see the brilliant and insightful article by Burl

Noggle, "Anglo Observers of the Southwest Borderlands, 1825–1890: The Rise of a Concept," *Arizona and the West* 1 (summer 1959); and the sensitive essay by Cecil Robinson, "Spring Water with a Taste of the Land," *American West* 3 (summer 1966).

12. See John Walton Caughey, *Hubert Howe Bancroft* (Berkeley and Los Angeles: University of California Press, 1946) and John Bannon, *Bolton and the Spanish Borderlands* (Norman: University of Oklahoma Press, 1964).

13. See the following contributions to "borderland" history: Lillian E. Fisher, *The Intendant System in Spanish America* (Berkeley, 1929), and Herbert I. *Priestley, and José de Galvez, Visitor-General of New Spain* (Berkeley, 1916), are standard monographs. Works on the northern expansion of New Spain include John Lloyd Mecham, *Francisco de Ibarra and Nueva Vizcaya* (Durham, N.C., 1927); Philip W. Powell, *Soldiers, Indians, and Silver* (Berkeley and Los Angeles, 1952); and Alfred B. Thomas, *Teodoro de Croix and the Northern Frontier of New Spain, 1776–1783* (Norman, Okla., 1941). Biographies of the major missionary figures include *Rim of Christendom: A Biography of Eusebio Francisco Kino* (New York, 1936), by Bolton; and *The Life and Times of Fray Junipero Serra* (Washington, 1959), by Maynard J. Geiger.

14. See also the bibliography by Vito Alessio Robles, *Bibliografía de Coahuila: historia y geografía* (México, D.F.: Imprenta de la Secretaría de Relaciones Exteriores, 1927), and the recent article by Margarita Nolasco Armas, "Continuidad y cambio sociocultural en el norte de México," *América Indigena* 31 (April 1971).

15. Alfonso Teja Zabre, *Lecciones de California* (México, D.F.: Universidad Nacional Autónoma de México, 1962); and Alfonso Trueba, *California, Tierra Perdida*, 2 vols. (México, D.F.: Jus, 1958).

16. Fray Angélico Chávez, *Origins of New Mexico Families* (Santa Fe: Historical Society of New Mexico, 1954). Frances V. Scholes provides some social commentary; see "Civil Government and Society in New Mexico," *New Mexico Historical Review* 10 (1935); *Church and State in New Mexico, 1610–1650,* (Albuquerque: University of New Mexico Press, 1937), etc.

17. See Miguel Ramos Arizpe, *Report that Dr. Miguel Ramos de Arizpe, Priest of Bourbon, and Deputy of the Recent General and Special Cortes of Spain for the Province of Coahuila, one of the Four Eastern Interior Provinces of the Kingdom of Mexico, Presents to the August Congress on the Natural, Political and Civil Condition of the Provinces of Coahuila, Nuevo Leon, Nuevo Santander and Texas of the Four Eastern Interior Provinces of the Kingdom of Mexico,* ed. Nettie Lee Benson, (Austin: University of Texas Press, 1950).

18. Lansing B. Bloom, "Barreiro's 'Ojeada sobre Nuevo México'," *New Mexico Historical Review* 3 (January 1928). For a nostalgic recollection by the New Mexican Spanish Speaking, see Benjamin M. Read, "in Santa Fe during the Mexican Regime," *New Mexico Historical Review* 2 (January 1927).

19. Bernard de Voto, *The Year of Decision, 1846,* (Boston, 1943); Henry S. Foote, *Texas and Texans or Advance of Anglo Americans to the Southwest* (Philadelphia, 1841); Thomas E. Falconer, *Notes of a Journey through Texas and New Mexico* (London, 1842). See also *Letters and Notes on the Texan Santa Fe Expedition, 1841–1842* (Chicago, 1963); James J. Webb, *Adventures in the Santa Fe Trade, 1844–1847* (Glendale, Ill.: 1931); James O. Pattie, *The Personal Narrative of James O. Pattie,* ed. Timothy Flint (Chicago, 1930). Pike's account is in numerous

editions; see Stephen H. Hart and Archer B. Hulbert, eds., *Zebulon Montgomery Pike's Arkansas Journal* (Denver, 1932). The same is true of memoirs of Mexican California, though the reminiscences are deceptively sympathetic and patronizing and surely just as biased. This is the case for the standard sources: Alfred Robinson's *Life in California*, and Richard Henry Dana's *Two Years Before the Mast*; and to a lesser extent in the more hostile *Diary of Faxon Dean Atherton, 1836–1839*, ed. Doyce B. Nunis (San Francisco, 1969) and *Josiah Belden 1841 Pioneer his Memoirs and his Letters*, ed. Doyce B. Nunis (Georgetown, Calf., 1962).

20. A patchy effort with an inspirational title is Samuel H. Lowrie, *Culture and Conflict in Texas, 1821–1835* (New York: Columbia University Press, 1932).

21. Eugene C. Barker, *Life of Stephen F. Austin, 1793–1835* (Nashville: Cokesbury Press, 1925); and *Mexico and Texas, 1821–1835* (New York: Russell, 1963).

22. In my opinion, T. Villasana Haggard, "The Neutral Ground between Louisiana and Texas, 1806–1821" (Ph.D. diss., University of Texas, Austin, 1942) is still valuable.

23. A popular reappraisal of commerce is found in *The Santa Fe Trail* by Robert Luther Dufus (New York: Longman's Green and Co., 1930), and a well documented academic treatment is Max L. Moorehead's *New Mexico's Royal Road: Trade and Travel on the Chihuahua Trail* (Norman: University of Oklahoma Press, 1958).

24. Much confusion on the subject of the treaty may be avoided if one considers that the treaty as ratified by the U.S. Senate, the easily available version, is an amended copy of the original and that it is often published without the all-important protocol. See George P. Hammond, *The Treaty of Guadalupe Hidalgo, 1848* (Berkeley: Friends of the Bancroft Library, 1949); México, *Tratado de paz, amistad, limites y arreglo definitivo entre la República Mexicana y los Estados Unidos de América* (1948); and Hunter Miller, *Treaties and Other International Acts of the United States of America* (Washington, D.C.: U.S. Government Printing Office, 1942).

25. Carlos Bosch García, *Historia de las relaciones entre México y los Estados Unidos, 1819–1848* (México, D.F.: Universidad Nacional Autónoma de México, 1961); and George L. Rives, *The United States and Mexico, 1821–1848*, 2 vols. (New York: Charles Scribner, 1913).

26. Justo Sierra, *Evolución del pueblo Mexicano* (México, D. F.: 1940); and Vicente Riva Palacio, *México a traves de los Siglos*, 5 vols, (México, Barcelona, 1887–1889).

27. Glen W. Price, *Origins of the War with Mexico*; Wilfred H. Calcott, *Santa Anna: The Story of an Enigma Who Once Was Mexico* (Norman, Okla., 1936). See also Frank C. Hanighan, *Santa Anna: The Napoleon of the West* (New York, 1934). For contrast, see José Fuentes Mares, *Santa Anna: aurora y ocaso de un comediante* (México, D.F.: Jus, 1959).

28. James Ford Rhodes, *History of the United States from the Compromise of 1850*, vol. 1 (New York, 1892–1922); William E. Dodd, "The West and the War with Mexico," *Journal of the Illinois State Historical Society* 5 (July 1912); and Normal A. Graebner, *Empire on the Pacific* (New York: Ronald Press, 1955).

29. Albert K. Weinberg, *Manifest Destiny*; Justin Smith, *War with Mexico*; Carlos Bosch García, *Historia de los Relaciones Entre México y los Estados Unidos*; and Gaston García Cantú, *Las invasiones norte americanas en México* (México,

D.F.: Editorial Era, 1971). An excellent recent collection accompanied by a fine historiographical essay is Josefina Vásquez de Knauth, *Mexicanos y norteamericanos ante la Guerra del '47* (México, D.F.: SepSetentas, 1972),

30. In contrast to their work see the popular effort by Ruben Rendón Lozano, who argues that the Texas rebellion was one of liberty-loving peoples against a tyrannical central government: *Viva Texas: The Story of the Mexican-born Patriots of the Republic of Texas* (San Antonio and Houston: Southern Library Institute, 1936).

31. Interesting for views of the development of the Southwest, even if not especially pertinent to the Chicano, are Frederick L. Olmstead's *A Journey Through Texas: Or a Saddletrip on the Southwestern Frontier* (1857; reprint, New York: Dix Edward and Company, 1957), and F. R. Lubbock, *Six Decades in Texas*, ed. C. W. Raines (Austin, 1900).

32. The following work sees the Penitentes not only as a religious group but also as a social and political unit that functions as a defense mechanism: Dorothy Woodward, "The Penitentes of New Mexico" (Ph.D. diss., Yale University, 1935).

33. Clarence C. Clendenen, *Blood on the Border: The United States Army and the Mexican Irregulars* (New York: Macmillan, 1969); and Robert Danforth Gregg, *The Influence of Border Trouble on Relations between the United States and Mexico, 1876–1910* (Baltimore: Johns Hopkins Press, 1967).

34. Ronald W. López, "The El Monte Berry Strikes of 1933," *Aztlán* 1, no. 1 (spring 1970); Charles Wollenberg, "Conflict in the Fields," *California Monthly* (November 1968), and "Huelga, 1929 Style: The Imperial Valley Cantaloupe Workers' Strike," *Pacific Historical Review* 38 (February 1969).

35. Abraham Hoffman, "The Repatriation of Mexican Nationals from the United States during the Great Depression" (Ph.D. diss., University of California, Los Angeles: 1970); Solomon J. Jones, "The Government Riots of Los Angeles, June 1943" (master's thesis, University of California, Los Angeles, 1969).

36. Juan R. Martinez, "Mexican Emigration to the United States, 1910–1930" (Ph.D. diss. University of California, Berkeley, 1957); Richard O. Ulibarri, "American Interest in the Spanish-Mexican Southwest, 1803–1848" (Ph.D. diss., University of Utah, Salt Lake City, 1963); Robin F. Scott, "The Urban Mexican–American in the Southwest, 1932–1955" (Ph.D. diss., University of Southern California, 1969); Richard L. Nostrand, "The Hispanic-American Borderland: A Regional Historical Geography" (Ph.D. diss., University of California, Los Angeles, 1968); Octavio Romano, "Don Pedrito Jaramillo: The Emergence of a Mexican American Folk Saint" (Ph.D. diss., University of California, Berkeley, 1964); Richard G. Thurston, "Urbanization and Sociocultural Change in a Mexican-American Enclave" (Ph.D., diss., University of California, Los Angeles, 1957); Daniel Tapin Valdés, "A Sociological Analysis and Description of the Political Role, Status and Voting Behavior of Americans with Spanish Names" (Ph.D. diss., University of Colorado, Boulder, 1964).

37. See Carlos Cortés, "CHICOP: A Response to the Challenge of Local Chicano History," *Aztlán* 1, no. 2 (fall 1970). Professor Cortés has several publications forthcoming. Corwin is working on an extended study of immigration.

38. There are also the *Journal of Mexican-American History*; the *Journal of Mexican-American Studies*, and *Epoca*, as well as the journals oriented to contemporary events: *El Pocho Che*, *Magazin*, *Con Safos*, and *La Raza*.

39. For works dealing with figures of earlier periods see: Jessie B. Bailey, *Diego de Vargas and the Reconquest of New Mexico* (Albuquerque: University of New Mexico Press, 1940); George P. Hammond, *Don Juan de Oñate, Colonizer of New Mexico, 1555–1628* (Albuquerque: University of New Mexico Press, 1953); Alfred B. Thomas, ed., *Teodoro dé Croix and the Northern Frontier of New Spain, 1776–1783* (Norman: University of Oklahoma Press, 1941); and John U. Terrel, *Estevanico the Black* (Los Angeles: Westernlore Press, 1968).

40. Jessie Bromilow, "Don Pio de Jesús Pico" (master's thesis, University of Southern California, Los Angeles, 1931); Marion Smith, "Pio Pico" (master's thesis, University of California, Berkeley, 1928); and Raymond Morrison, "Luis Antonio Arguello, First Mexican Governor of California" (master's thesis, University of Southern California, Los Angeles, 1938).

41. Ralph Rambo, *Trailing the California Bandit Tiburcio Vásquez* (San José: Rosicrucian Press, 1968); Richard Mitchell, "Joaquin Murrietta: A Study of Social Conditions in Early California" (master's thesis, University of California, Berkeley, 1927). See also Robert Greenwood, "The California Outlaw, Tiburcio Vásquez," *Historical Society of Southern California Quarterly* 29 (September 1950); the dubious John R. Ridge [Yellow Bird, pseud.], *The Life and Times of Joaquin Murrietta* (Norman: University of Oklahoma Press, 1955); and Joseph Henry Jackson, *Bad Company* (New York, 1949). For a Mexican treatment see Ireneo Paz, *Joaquin Murrietta: His Exploits in the State of California* (Chicago, 1937); for a Chilean poetic approach, see Pablo Neruda, *Fulgor y muerte de Joaquin Murrietta* (Santiago: Zig-Zag, 1967). See also the forthcoming article by Carlos Cortés, "The Chicano Social Bandit as Romantic Hero," in *Symposium on Romanticism*, ed. Hugo Rodriguez Alcala and Robert Gleckner.

42. Peter Matthiesen, *Sal Si Puedes: César Chávez and the New American Revolution* (New York: Random House, 1969). This is the best available biography of a Chicano. However, even granting that a biography of a living person will be rudimentary, it leaves much to be desired. Reies Lopez Tijerina, obviously, is a mark for the sensationalist pundit, and despite surface empathy, the writings that deal with him are deleterious. He deserves much better. Especially appreciated would be a knowledgeable and empathetic analysis and appreciation of his ideological impact on the movement. Currently, the best work on Tijerina is that of Richard Gardner, *Grito* (New York: Bobbs-Merrill, 1970); see also Peter Nabokov, *Tijerina and the Courthouse Raid* (Albuquerque: University of New Mexico, 1969); and Michael Jenkinson, *Tijerina* (Albuquerque: Paisano Press, 1968). See Eugene Rodriguez, "Henry B. González, A Political Profile" (master's thesis, St. Mary's University, San Antonio, 1965). In all probability, a current work on González would be more critical.

43. For a highly critical review of some of this literature from the point of view of contemporary Chicano scholarship, see the seminal work of Octavio Romano-V., "The Anthropology and Sociology of the Mexican-American: The Distortion of Mexican American History," *El Grito* 2, no. 1 (fall 1968); see also Deluvina Hernández, *Mexican American Challenge to a Sacred Cow* (Los Angeles: Aztlán Publications, Chicano Studies Center, UCLA, 1970) which emphasizes the field of education; Raymond A. Rocco, "The Chicano in the Social Sciences: Traditional Concepts, Myths, and Images," *Aztlán* 1, no. 2 (fall 1970), which

emphasizes the field of political science. A most cogent and structured review of sociological and anthropological literature is the series of articles by Nick C. Vaca, "The Mexican-American in the Social Sciences, 1912–1970," *El Grito*, 3, no. 3 (spring 1970), and 4, no. 1 (fall 1970).

44. For an early analysis of Mexican American politics, see Douglas O. Weeks, "The League of United Latin-American Citizens. A Texas Mexican Civic Organization," *Southwestern Political and Social Science Quarterly* 10 (December 1929), and "The Texas-Mexican and the Politics of South Texas," *American Political and Social Science Review* 24 (August 1930).

45. Ralph Cortéz Guzmán, "The Political Socialization of the Mexican American Peoples" (Ph.D. diss., University of California, Los Angeles, 1970); Miguel David Tirado, "Mexican American Community Political Organization: The Key to Chicano Political Power," *Aztlán* 1, no. 1 (spring 1970); José Angel Gutiérrez, "La Raza and Revolution: The Empirical Conditions of Revolution in Four South Texas Counties" (master's thesis, St. Mary's University, San Antonio, 1968); and Mario Barrera, Carlos Muñoz, and Carlos Ornelas, "The Barrio as Internal Colony," *Urban Affairs Annual Review* 6 (1972), ed. Harlan Hahn..

46. Raymond A. Rocco, cited above; Carlos Muñoz, "Toward a Chicano Perspective of Political Analysis," *Aztlán* 1, no. 2 (fall 1970).

47. A sociologist who did much early work is Emory Bogardus. Among his works are: "The Mexican Immigrant," *Journal of Applied Psychology* 11 (1927); "Second Generation Mexicans," *Sociology and Social Research* 13 (1930); and "Racial Distance Changes in the United States during the Past Thirty Years," *Sociology and Social Research* 44 (1959). Typical sociological works for the 1920s are Helen S. Walker's "Mexican Journeys to Bethlehem," *Literary Digest* 77 (June 2, 1923) and "Mexican Immigrants as Laborers," *Sociology and Social Research* 13 (1930).

48. For a critique of this literature, see the Nick Vaca and Octavio Romano articles cited above.

49. Lyle Saunders, *Cultural Differences and Medical Care: The Case of the Spanish Speaking People of the Southwest* (New York: Russel Sage Foundation, 1954); William Madsen, *Mexican-Americans of South Texas* (San Francisco: Holt, Rinehart and Winston, 1964); Julian Samora and Richard A. Lamanna, *Mexican Americans in a Midwest Metropolis: A Study of East Chicago* (Graduate School of Business, University of California, Los Angeles, 1967).

50. For exceptions see the historically oriented and perceptive work of Clark S. Knowlton, "Patron–Peon Pattern among the Spanish-Americans of New Mexico," *Social Forces* 41 (October 1962), and "The Spanish Americans in New Mexico," *Sociology and Social Research* 45 (July 1961); see also Frances L. Swadesh, "The Alianza Movement of New Mexico: The Interplay of Social Change and Public Commentary," in *Minorities and Politics*, ed. Henry J. Tobias and Charles E. Woodhouse (Albuquerque: University of New Mexico Press, 1969).

51. Compare her earlier writings with those published since 1970: *Mexican Americans: Problems and Prospects* (Institute for Research on Poverty, University of Wisconsin Press, November 1966); "Social Class, Assimilation and Acculturation," in *Spanish Speaking People in the United States; Proceedings of the 1968 Annual Spring Meeting of the American Ethnological Society*, distributed by the University of Chicago

Press, 1968; "Colonialism, the Case of the Mexican American," *Social Problems* (spring 1970); and *Mexican Americans* (Englewood Cliffs, N.J.: Prentice-Hall, 1970).

52. Fernando Peñalosa, "The Changing Mexican American in Southern California," *Sociology and Social Research* 51, no. 4 (July 1967); "Social Mobility in a Mexican American Community," *Social Forces* 44 (June 1966); "Toward an Operational Definition of the Mexican American," *Aztlán* 1, no. 1 (spring 1970).

53. See Rodolfo Alvarez, "The Unique Psycho-historical Experience of the Mexican American," *Social Science Quarterly* 51, no. 1 (June 1971). His current work in progress is "The Evolution of a Distinctive Mexican American Culture: Prospects and Problems."

54. Deluvina Hernández, "La Raza Satellite System," *Aztlán* 1, no. 1 (spring 1970); and Jaime Sena Rivera, "Chicanos: Culture, Community, Role—Problems of Evidence and a Proposition of Norms, Toward Establishing Evidence," *Aztlán* 1, no. 1 (spring 1970).

55. In addition to his arguments on education in *Forgotten People: A Study of New Mexicans*, there is his early "Bilingualism and Mental Measures—A Word of Caution," *Journal of Applied Psychology* 18 (December 1934); "Concerning Segregation of Spanish Speaking Children in the Public Schools," occasional papers IX (Austin: University of Texas, December 1951); and "History, Culture and Education," in *La Raza: Forgotten Americans*, ed. Julian Samora (South Bend: University of Notre Dame, 1966), 1–26.

56. Leo Grebler's monograph, *The Schooling Gap: Signs of Progress* (Graduate School of Business, University of California, Los Angeles, 1967) is an example of how rigorous statistical analysis, in this case the 1960 census, date problems. The data were used even though the author and researchers agree that census data present serious deficiencies when used in research on Mexican American. The results may be amusingly misleading.

57. Walter Fogel, *Education and Income of Mexican Americans in the Southwest* (Graduate School of Business, University of California, Los Angeles, 1965); *Mexican Americans in Southwest Labor Markets* (Graduate School of Business, University of California, Los Angeles, 1967); and Frank G. Mittlebach and Grace Marshall, *The Burden of Poverty* (Graduate School of Business, University of California, Los Angeles, 1966). For generalization on these aspects see Clark Kerr, "The Balkanization of Labor Markets," in *Labor Mobility and Economic Opportunity*, ed. E. Wight Bakke, et al. (New York: Technology Press of the Massachusetts Institute of Technology and John Wiley and Sons, Inc., 1954), and same author, "Labor Markets: Their Character and Consequences," *Proceedings, American Economic Review*, 40 (May 1950).

58. Fred Schmidt, *After the Bracero: An Inquiry into the Problems of Farm Labor Recruitment* (Institute of Industrial Relations, University of California, Los Angeles); and *Spanish Surnamed American Employment in the Southwest* (Washington, D.C.: U. S. Government Printing Office, 1970).

59. For a satirical view of economic models see Raúl Fernández, "The Political Economy of Stereotypes," *Aztlán*, 1, no. 2 (fall 1970).

60. Harry J. Gillman, "Economic Discrimination and Unemployment," *American Economic Review* 55 (December 1964); Gary Becher, *The Economics*

Discrimination (Chicago: University of Chicago Press, 1957); and Dale Hiestrand, *Economic Growth and Employment: Opportunity for Minorities* (New York: Columbia University Press, 1964).

61. In Marvin K. Opler, ed., *Culture and Mental Health* (New York: Macmillan Company, 1959).

62. Dale L. Johnson and Melvin P. Stikes, "Rorschach and TAT Responses of Negro, Mexican-American, and Anglo Psychiatric Patients," *Journal of Projective Techniques and Personality Assessment* 29 (March 1965).

63. Marvin Karno, "The Enigma of Ethnicity in Psychiatric Clinic," *Archives of General Psychiatry* 20 (February 1969); Marvin Karno and Robert B. Edgerton, "Perception of Mental Illness in a Mexican American Community," *Archives of General Psychiatry* 39 (February 1968).

64. Horacio Fabrega, John D. Swartz, and Carole Ann Wallace, "Ethnic Differences in Psychopathology: Specific Differences with Emphasis on a Mexican American Group," *Journal of Psychiatric Research* 6 (1968); and Horacio Fabrega and Carole Ann Wallace, "Value Identification and Psychiatric Disability: An Analysis Involving Americans of Mexican Descent," *Behavioral Science* 13 (1968).

65. Cecil Robinson has written the major study of the image of México and the Mexican in Anglo literature over time, *With the Ears of Strangers: The Mexican in American Literature* (Tucson: University of Arizona Press, 1963). A recent collection ed. Antonia Castañeda Shular, et al., is *Literatura Chicano, Texto y Contexto* (Englewoods Cliffs, N.J.: Prentice Hall, 1972). A collection of short fiction about the Mexican American by Anglo and Chicano writers, with an informative introduction and a fairly selective bibliography, is the one ed. Edward Simmen, *The Chicano: From Caricature to Self-Portrait* (New York: Mentor, 1971). An outstanding collection of contemporary poetry and fiction is Octavio Romano, *El Espejo—The Mirror* (Berkeley: Quinto Sol Publications, 1969); for a prize-winning single-author collection see Tomás Rivera,—*Y No Se Lo Tragó La Tierra* (Berkeley, 1971). An influential poet is Alurista, *Floricanto en Aztlán* (Los Angeles: Aztlán Publications, Chicano Studies Center, University of California, Los Angeles, 1971). Among the Chicano novelists are: José Antonio Villareal, *Pocho* (New York, 1959); Raymond Barrio, *The Plum Plum Pickers* (Sunnyvale, Calif.: 1969); and John Rechy, *The City of Night* (New York, 1963) and *Numbers* (New York, 1967). For published folklore material see: Arthur L. Campa, "The Spanish Folksong in the Southwest," *Bulletin of the University of New Mexico* 4, no. 1 (1933); "A Bibliography of Spanish Folklore in New Mexico," *Bulletin of the University of New Mexico* 11, no. 3. (1930) and José Manuel Espinosa, "Spanish Folk Tales from New Mexico," *Memoirs of the American Folklore Society* 30 (New York: G. E. Stechert and Company, 1937); Gustavo Duran, *14 Traditional Spanish Songs from Texas* (Washington, D.C.: Pan American Union, 1942); Aurelio M. Espinosa, "Los Romances Tradicionales en California" in *Homenaie Ofrecido a Menendez Pidal* (Madrid: Librería y Casa Editorial Hernando, 1925) and Juan Rael, *Cuentos Españoles de Colorado y de Nuevo México*, 2 vols. (Stanford: Stanford University Press); George Keebler, *Santos: The Religious Folk Art of New Mexico* (Philadelphia: University of Pennsylvania Press, 1964); and *Antología del Saber Popular*, ed. Aguilar et. al. (Los Angeles: Aztlán Publications, Chicano Studies Center, University of California, Los Angeles, 1971). For an

introductory bibliography and historical review of Chicano theatre, see Jorge A. Huerta, "Chicano Teatro: A Background," *Aztlán* 2, no. 2 (fall 1971).

66. For a series of review articles on the volume, see the *Social Science Quarterly* 51, no. 1 (June 1971).

67. Recently I had occasion to visit the office of Vice President Johnson of the University of California and on his desk was a copy of Grebler. If this is the frame of reference for decisions on Chicano programs at this university, the results will be traumatic.

68. Fortunately, in this instance, the point of view of the other side, the Chicano community, is on record and available; see "An Evaluation and Critique of 'The Mexican American Studies Project,' a Ford Foundation Grant Extended to the University of California at Los Angeles," prepared by Manuel H. Guerra, Ph.D., and Y. Arturo Cabrera, Ed.D. (1966), prepared for the Education Council of the Mexican American Political Association. This critique raised objections to the research project in three general areas: philosophy and rationale, scholarship, and directorship. In the opening paragraph it states, "Those who address themselves to the Mexican American community often lack the legitimate objectivity which true scholarship demands. Either the frame of reference stems from a prosaic point of view which is outmoded and unrealistic or a patronizing sentimentalism which flirts with a new-colonialist attitude, or a racist complex."

69. Among popular depictions are: Jesús Topete, *Adventuras de un bracero* (México, D.F.: América, 1949); and Máximo Peón [*sic*], *Como viven los Mexicanos en Los Estados Unidos* (México, D.F.: Costa–Amic, 1966).

70. Some are: José M. Sánchez, *Viaje a Texas en 1828–1829* (México, D.F., 1939); José M. Roa Barcena, *Recuerdos*—(México, D.F., 1949); José F. Ramírez, *Mexico during the War with the United States* (Columbia, 1950).

71. Some are: Miguel Sánchez Lamego, *Sitio y Tomo del Alamo, 1836* (México, D.F.: 1966); Carlos Bosch García, *Historia de las relaciones entre México y los Estados Unidos, 1819–1948* (México, D.F., 1961); Alberto M. Carreno, *México y los Estados Unidos de América* (México, D.F., 1962); and Gastón García Cantú, *Las invasiones norte americanas en México* (México, D.F., 1971).

72. *El Siglo XIX, Diario del Hogar, El Tiempo,* and *El Imparcial, 1890–1912,* México, D.F.

73. See for example: in *Diario del Hogar,* "La expulsion de los niños Mexicanos en Texas" (August 8, 1910); in *El Tiempo,* "Bartolo López Mexicano condenado" (2 January 1911) and "El Linchamiento de Rodriguez" (27 January 1911).

74. Manuel Gamio, *El Emigrante Mexicano* (México, D.F., 1969); and *Mexican Immigration to the United States* (Chicago: University of Chicago Press, 1930; reprinted, New York: Arno Press, 1969).

75. Enrique Santibañez, *Ensayo acerca de la emigración Mexicana a Estados Unidos* (San Antonio, 1930); Ernesto Hidalgo, *La protección de Mexicanos en los Estados Unidos* (México, D.F., 1940).

76. Vito Alessio Robles, *Francisco de Urdinola y el norte de la nueva España* (México, D.F., 1931), and *Coahuila y Texas en la época colonial* (México, D.F., 1938); see also the work of Alfonso Teja Zabre, and Alfonso Trueba cited and that of Lino Gómez Canedo, *Primeras exploraciones y poblamiento de Texas, 1686–1694*

(Monterrey, México: Publicaciones del Instituto Technológico de Monterrey, 1968).

77. For example, see José Lázaro Salinas, *La emigración de braceros* (México, D.F., 1955); and Gloria R. Vargas y Campos, *El problema del bracero Mexicano* (México, D.F., 1964).

78. For an early novel see Teodoro Torres, *La patria perdida* (México, D.F., 1935); see also Luis Spota, *Murieron a la mitad del rio* (México, D.F., 1948) and José Revueltas, *Los motivos de Cain* (1957).

79. Agustin Cue Cánovas, "El Pueblo Olvidado" in *El Día* (23–27 May 1963); Manuel Mejida, "El Problema Moreno—Ocaso de los Hispanos Americano," in *Excelsior* (24–27 November 1967).

80. For example see *El Día* (26–27 November 1969); *Siempre* (14 May 1969); *El Día* (21 February 1970).

81. Agustin Cue Cánovas, *Los Estados Unidos y el México olvidado* (México, D.F., 1970).

82. Gilberto López Rivas, *Los Chicanos: Una minoria nacional explotada* (México, D.F., 1971).

83. These three authors have a clear consciousness that their writing is related to the larger historical perspective of indio-hispano-mestizo peoples in the Southwest. The question of the consciousness of the historian will be a crucial determinant in a future approach to a historiographical assessment of Chicano history. The works of Marc Simmons, *Spanish Government in New Mexico* (Albuquerque: University of New Mexico Press, 1968), and Alan C. Hutchinson, *Frontier Settlement in Mexican California* (New Haven: Yale University Press, 1969), and *The Mexican Government and the Mission Indians of Upper California* (Washington, D.C.: Academy of American Franciscan History, 1965) do present complexity and change in frontier society but these authors do not emphasize continuity of relations.

84. See Saul Penison, "Reflections on Oral History," *American Archivist* 28 (1965); Gould P. Colman, "Oral History—An Appeal for More Systematic Procedures," *American Archivist* 28 (1965); Robert K. Merton, "The Focused Interview," *American Journal of Sociology* 51 (1946); and James W. Wilkie and Edna Monzon de Wilkie, *México visto en el siglo XX: Entrevistas de Historia Oral* (México, D.F., 1969).

85. See Arthur M. Schlesinger, "The City in American Civilization," in *Paths to the Present* (New York, 1949); Eric E. Lampard, "American Historians and the Study of Urbanization," *American Historical Review* 67 (1961); Philip M. Hauser and Leo Schmore, eds., *The Study of Urbanization* (New York, 1965); and Stephen Thernstrom, "Reflections on the New Urban History," *Daedalus* (spring 1971).

86. See John Klauber, "On the Dual Use of Historical and Scientific Method in Psychoanalysis," *International Journal of Psychoanalysis* 49, no. 1 (1968); Besancon Alain, "Psychoanalysis: Auxiliary Science or Historical Method?" *Journal of Contemporary History* 3 (April 1968); Eric H. Erickson, "Psychoanalysis and On-going History: Problems of Identity, Hatred and Non-violence," *American Journal of Psychiatry* 122 (September 1965); Robert Jay Lifton, *History and Human Survival: Essays on the Young and Old, Survivors and the Dead, Peace and War and on Contemporary Psychohistory* (New York, 1970); and Peter Loewenberg, "The Psychohistorical Origins of the Nazi Youth Cohort," American Historical Review 76 (December 1971).

Los Desarraigados
Chicanos in the Midwestern Region of the United States

Gilberto Cárdenas

It has been a common, though incorrect assumption that Spanish-speaking peoples reside only in the five southwestern states (California, Texas, New Mexico, Colorado, and Arizona) or along the East Coast (New York, Connecticut, Pennsylvania, and New Jersey). Yet, according to the 1970 census, there are some 1.1 million persons of Spanish origin in the midwestern region of the United States (Illinois, Indiana, Iowa, Kansas, Michigan, Minnesota, Missouri, Nebraska, Ohio, and Wisconsin). Estimates by Chicano and Puerto Rican organizations go as high as 1.5 million.[1] Judging by the published literature, one would hardly know that Chicanos and other Spanish-speaking ethnic populations reside outside the Southwest or East Coast since the literature ignores the Midwest despite the availability of historical documentation on the subject. While the presence of Spanish speakers in the Midwest and Great Lakes states must be understood in a larger framework, it is itself the subject of a complex history that has yet to be written and understood. Since 1919, Spanish-speaking people have worked and settled in the Midwest. Many from the Southwest continue to migrate to the Midwest to work on a temporary and seasonal basis. As early as 1928, the single largest employer of Mexican labor anywhere in the United States was located on the southern shore of Lake Michigan (Taylor 1932). Mexican workers and their families have for decades contributed to the growth and development of key industries in the region such as railroads, steel, agriculture, and cement.

Michigan is the third-largest user of migrant agricultural laborers in the United States. In 1967–68 over 98,213 agricultural migrant workers were reportedly located in the state of Michigan. In the same year, over 214,381

From *Aztlan: A Journal of Chicano Studies* 1, no. 1 (1970): 1–12.

agricultural migrants were located in the Midwest and Great Lakes states (U.S. Congress 1969). In 1969, 23 percent of the hired farm workforce in the United States was located in the north central states (Department of Agriculture 1970). The majority of the Spanish-speaking ethnics permanently living or working in the Midwest, however, live in urban areas and are not engaged in agricultural occupations. Nevertheless, the farm labor situation has occupied an important place in the history of the Spanish speaking in the Midwest and continues to be a critical area of concern in terms of agricultural activity and settlement patterns (Cárdenas 1974). The more recent growth of the urban Spanish-speaking ethnic population is in part a result of large numbers of Spanish-speaking farmworkers who settle out of the migrant stream. While this process occurs in large cities such as Chicago and Detroit, it is particularly significant in numerous small and medium-sized cities such as Saginaw, Michigan; South Bend, Indiana; Racine, Wisconsin; and Davenport, Iowa.

Chicago, Illinois, has one of the largest concentrations of Chicanos in the United States. Chicago also has the highest concentration of Puerto Ricans of any city outside New York. There are large barrios in other midwestern cities such as Detroit, Michigan; East Chicago, Indiana; Kansas City, Missouri; Minneapolis and St. Paul, Minnesota; Cleveland, Ohio; and Milwaukee, Wisconsin. The employed workforce (Spanish-language) was heavily concentrated in industrial occupations (33 percent in the operative category). The urban setting, life experiences, and the urban family in the Midwest have not been adequately researched. Since 1915 the Spanish-speaking population in the Midwest has increased phenomenally. The Mexican population was 69,193 in 1930, more than doubled by 1960, and by 1970 it again increased by nearly three times (see table 1). For example, Faught, Flores, and Cárdenas (1975) reported that Chicago doubled or tripled, depending upon the indicator used. There was an increase of 181 percent (almost tripling) between 1960 and 1970 (22,975 in 1960 to 64,575 in 1970) for the foreign born whose mother tongue (i.e., the language spoken in the person's home when he/she was a child) was Spanish. Migration and immigration patterns and fertility rates indicate that the Spanish-speaking population in the Midwest will continue to grow at a phenomenal pace (see table 1).

This paper presents an overview of Chicanos in the Midwest. No attempt is made to provide a definitive or comprehensive analysis of Chicanos in the Midwest, a task that is needed but beyond the scope of this effort. This brief introduction will be followed by a critique of the literature and an analysis of the origins and significance of migration and settlement.

Table 1. Mexican Population in the Midwest

State	1850–1890*	1900	1910	1920	1930	1940	1950	1960	1970
				Mexican Foreign Stock					
Ohio	134	53	85	942	3,099	2,792	5,959	9,960	13,349
Indiana	98	43	47	680	7,589	4,530	8,677	14,041	18,325
Illinois	240	156	672	4,032	20,963	23,545	34,538	63,063	117,268
Michigan	127	56	86	1,333	9,921	9,474	16,540	24,298	31,067
Wisconsin	59	499	39	178	1,853	1,716	3,272	6,705	9,160
Minnesota	308	162	52	248	2,448	2,976	3,305	3,436	4,575
Iowa	75	29	620	2,650	2,760	3,959	3,973	3,374	4,546
Missouri	37	24	1,413	3,411	3,482	4,783	5,862	8,159	8,353
Nebraska	48	27	290	2,611	4,178	5,333	6,023	5,858	5,552
Kansas	126	71	8,429	13,770	12,900	13,742	13,429	12,972	13,728
Total	1,252	1,122	11,733	29,855	69,193	72,476	101,578	151,866	225,923

Source: U.S. Bureau of the Census, *Census of Population, 1850–1970,* Washington, D.C.
*1860 and 1870, no data available.

This is followed by a description of immigration and farm labor patterns and then by an analysis of some demographic and social characteristics of the population utilizing 1970 census data.

The term "Midwest" as utilized throughout this report corresponds to a ten-state area—Ohio, Indiana, Illinois, Michigan, Wisconsin, Minnesota, Iowa, Missouri, Nebraska, and Kansas—normally referred to by Chicanos and other Spanish-speaking people as a region in which they identify and in which others, in turn, identify Spanish-speaking people. Like the Southwest (Texas, Arizona, Colorado, New Mexico, and California), the Midwest does not entirely correspond to the regular regional divisions utilized by the U.S. Bureau of the Census, e.g., Northeast, North Central, South, and West (although a special subject report, *Persons of Spanish Surname,* covering the five southwestern states is published by the U.S. Bureau of the Census). Thus, when reference is made to the "Midwest," only those ten states mentioned above are included. With the exception of two states—North Dakota and South Dakota—the Midwest corresponds to the North Central region defined by the Bureau of the Census. The ten-state area defined as Midwest is also known in government circles (federal regional councils) as Region V and Region VII.[2]

Review of Literature: Conceptual Focus

Inadequate recognition and documentation of the history and life experiences of Chicanos in the Midwest is reflected in a dearth of scholarly research, a meagerness of educational curricula, and a lack of public policy.

Despite the recent upsurges in attention to minority group problems and the ethnic and cultural heritage of minority peoples, Spanish-speaking ethnic groups in the Midwest continue to be neglected and forgotten. There is hardly any mention and virtually no analysis given to their history and life experience in the Midwest in all of the important books, monographs, reports, and articles about the Spanish-speaking in the United States. Aside from past tendencies to exclude reference to Spanish-speaking people in the United States and from the more blatant effect of biased and distorted treatment in the literature when it was written, there still remains the tendency to treat Spanish-speaking people as a homogeneous ethnic group. However, Spanish-speaking ethnic groups are not homogeneous and are differentiated in many ways, such as in their historical and cultural conditions of social contact and varying relationships with the dominant society in the United States. In the Midwest, where all Spanish-speaking ethnic groups are substantially represented, these differences are especially significant. There is a need to make explicit the multicultural and multiethnic heritage of Spanish-speaking people. However, omission of their experiences in the Midwest, in most of the important literature on ethnic groups, suggests that few people are informed about its significance.

Since the literature available on Spanish-speaking people in the United States has mainly been on Chicanos, we have only to survey treatment of the Midwest in this literature to underscore our point and to clarify its dimensions. The UCLA Mexican American Study, one of the most ambitious studies of Chicanos to date, restricted its focus to Chicanos in the Southwest (Grebler, Moore, and Guzmán 1970). With the exception of one advance report by Samora and Lamanna (1967) there was virtually no attention given to the Midwest. The U.S. Commission on Civil Rights since 1970 has undertaken a mass study of the educational status of Mexican Americans (1971). With the exception of one table in the first report, the study and all six reports were based exclusively upon the Chicano experience in the five southwestern states. All of the fifteen books critiqued in John Womack Jr.'s feature article, "Who Are the Chicanos?" (1972) omitted reference and analysis of the Chicano experience in the Midwest and only covered the situation of Chicanos in the Southwest. Numerous other recent scholarly research and reports have been undertaken and published, yet have also omitted the Midwest (Galarza, Samora, and Gallegos 1970; Johnson and Hernández-M. 1970; Acuña 1972). The above-mentioned research efforts have made an impressive addition to the literature on Chicanos and have influenced the curricula produced and utilized in ethnic studies courses, particularly in Chicano studies. Moreover, these studies and reports along with others have been taken as authoritative sources that social scientists, educators, historians, and public officials have relied upon for interpreting the history and status of the Spanish-speaking. Public and private agencies have also used these studies as bases for the allocation of funds. The ethnic studies programs focusing on the Spanish-speaking that have been started or are in the process of development in colleges and universities throughout the Midwest tend to follow models developed in the Southwest and the East Coast. These programs, however, suffer from the unavailability of resource and reference materials documenting these groups' history in the Midwest.

Despite the omission of Spanish-speaking ethnic groups in the literature and curriculum materials frequently used in ethnic studies and related courses of study, various reports have been recently published, and in some cases empirical studies with a Midwest setting, focusing on a specific problem, have been produced (Taylor 1932; Humphrey 1943; Samora and Lamanna 1967; Choldin and Trout 1969; Weeks and Spielberg 1973; Lebeaux and Salas 1973; Shannon and Shannon 1974). However, a comprehensive review of this literature and an overall assessment of the situation in the Midwest is lacking.[3] A systematic attempt to compare and relate the Midwest experience with others requires that one depart from the exclusively regional experience and begin with a national approach. Through this approach it is possible to reconceptualize the history and cultural heritage of Spanish-speaking ethnic groups. It expands the scope of ethnic studies, and establishes a direct method of studying the Midwest. The Midwest experience is not simply an extension of the Southwest experience into the North (nor is it necessarily an extension of the East Coast Puerto Rican experience into the Midwest). A significant proportion of the Chicano population, for example, was born and raised in the Midwest and has never visited the Southwest. Yet, in terms of interregional migration, the study of Chicanos who left the Southwest at their destination points rather than their area of origin enhances our understanding of the southwestern experience and the reasons why people left. More often than not, research based in the Southwest only includes "survival" population samples. There are both theoretical (conceptual) and methodological problems pertaining to the study of Chicanos that must be further clarified and modified.

Including the Midwest in the analysis of Spanish-origin ethnic groups not only broadens the scope and focus of a particular group, but also gives the student of ethnic studies a concrete basis in which interethnic relations can be observed. Midwestern cities such as Chicago and Detroit as well as other smaller cities have long histories of ethnic experiences and remain as areas in which ethnic enclaves continue to vibrate. While the history of European ethnic groups (Polish, Italian, Hungarian) in these communities has been the subject of scholarly attention, it is only recently that Spanish-origin ethnics have received serious attention. While the much-criticized immigrant analogy approach may not be entirely applicable to the Chicano and Puerto Rican experience in the Southwest, some aspects of the model may be applicable in the Midwest. Similarly, the colonial model advanced by sociologists such as Blauner (1972), Barrera (1976), Moore (1970), and Rex (1973) may also be applicable to the Chicano experience. These questions remain theoretical and empirical problems that have heretofore not been raised with respect to the experience of Spanish-origin ethnic groups in the Midwest.

Mexican Immigration to the Midwest

Despite the settlement of Chicanos in the Midwest even before the turn of the century, it was not until the first large-scale recruitment and importation efforts in the 1910s that a Mexican presence became noticeable, particularly in Kansas City and Chicago. The increase in the Mexican population throughout the Midwest was largely due to increased industrial activity and agricultural development. The first significant increase of the Mexican population derived from settled Mexican immigrants in urban-industrial areas and seasonal agricultural workers from Mexico and Texas. The first groups were foreign-born Mexican stock. After World War II, the bulk of the workers and interregional migrants resettling in the Midwest were native-born Chicanos. In other words, prior to World War II, settlement was largely based on immigration from Mexico and (step) migration of persons of Mexican stock. After World War II, migration and settlement of Mexican persons in the Midwest, while still including Mexican immigrants, became a type of migration that could be characterized as "displaced migration," that is, of a more domestic (internal) character. Although we begin treatment with an analysis of immigration, the thesis of displacement as presented above suggests that Chicanos and Mexicanos can be properly considered *displaced refugees* and that their seasonal and regional mobility (migration) can be compared to that type of migration normally referred to as "depression migration," i.e., a type of migration that occurs during periods of great economic hardship such as that of the 1930s.

Unlike the Southwest, where Chicanos were originally native to the region and predated the appearance of the Anglo-European Americans, in the Midwest the *origins* of the Mexican population were entirely immigrant. In contrast to the Southwest-bound Mexican immigrant who worked or settled in an area contiguous to Mexico—an area previously ruled by Mexico, populated by Mexicans, and retaining cultural, physical, and climatic similarities to the areas of origin—the first waves of Midwest-bound Mexican immigrants were traveling longer distances to areas beyond the Southwest in which none of the above characteristics prevailed. The predominant industrial and other manufacturing-related employment and the urban settlement of Mexican immigrants to the Midwest more closely parallel the European immigrant pattern than the earlier patterns of immigration in the Southwest. The importance of ethnic succession and labor market segmentation of Chicanos in midwestern cities can be more fully understood by drawing from the concrete experiences of European immigrant laborers (aspects of the European immigrant model formulation).

Strong comparisons between Mexican and European immigration can be made with respect to settlement and employment patterns, particularly in midwestern cities. While the first large-scale movements of Mexicans to the Midwest involved both direct migration from Mexico to the Midwest and step migration (Mexico to Southwest, Southwest to Midwest), the direct migration was the main feature of these movements. Many of the midwestern-bound Mexican immigrants eventually made their way to the Midwest after having passed, worked, or lived in the Southwest. For purposes of this analysis, these migrants would be classified as seasonal workers who did not establish roots in the Southwest before settling in the Midwest. In many respects, this seasonal labor parallels the movement of European immigrants from the Atlantic Coast to the Midwest. (A major distinction, however, relates to the timing of migration, particularly with respect to economic development and entrepreneurship.) To this extent, then, such workers would be viewed as direct immigrants. In contrast are those seasonal workers who established roots in the Southwest, their descendants and native Chicanos who eventually left and settled in the Midwest. Thus, in terms of direct migration, the comparison with European immigration is most applicable.

Labor Migration

The distinguishing feature of all major Mexican migratory movements to the United States has been labor migration. The massive shifts and growth of the Chicano population in the United States has corresponded to the movement of Mexican labor to U.S. capital and the settlement of Mexican workers and their families in the centers or fringes of capitalist enterprises. The proletarian status of immigrant workers has been a dominant feature of labor migrants from Mexico since the first organized importation programs in 1917–1922.

One mobility opportunity relatively open to Mexican workers in the United States was geographic labor mobility. For the most part, this mobility, in terms of employment, was lateral rather than vertical. The territorial dispersion of Mexican laborers first within the Southwest and later throughout the entire United States was followed by the settlement of Mexican people in all the states in which they worked. Competition for Mexican labor among employers in the Southwest and later outside the Southwest arose because of the assumed labor demands of their industries, which for the most part was a demand for cheap and unorganized labor (Samora 1971). In the same manner that employment opportunities and recruitment efforts in certain industries were extended to Mexican nationals residing in Mexico, inducing their migration into the United States (legal, illegal, and temporary, etc.), employment opportunities and recruitment efforts were also extended to those settled in the Southwest. The process continued at the same time as competition for Mexican labor arose between southwestern and midwestern employers. The first, largest, and most significant mass migration of Mexican people occurred along the border, with Texas being the most important state. Later, migration shifted within Texas and was finally directed toward California (State of California 1930).

Gamio (1930) and Taylor (1932) described the process of recruiting and importing Mexican labor by the private sector during World War I and the post–World War I period. During the war, the U.S. government in conjunction with the private sector initiated a series of administrative maneuvers to import Mexican contract workers.[4] In the Midwest, contract workers were employed in railroad industries, manufacturing plants, stockyards, and the sugar beet fields. Admittedly less than 300,000 workers were imported through this work program in the period from 1917 to 1922, and while importation was mainly on a temporary basis, thousands of workers never returned to Mexico, while thousands more eventually made their way back to the United States after their contracts expired. The program provided the first major stimulus for the migration of Mexican workers to the Midwest. Midwestern employers who had utilized contract workers actively and illegally advertised and recruited workers from

Mexico during and after the operation of the program. Other employers who had not utilized contract workers during the program actively sought Mexican labor after the program was terminated and began recruiting in Mexico and in the Southwest. Throughout the congressional debates and public hearings on Mexican immigration and agricultural labor during the 1920s, midwestern employers and their representatives lobbied for the relaxation of immigration laws, assisted in preventing the enactment of restrictive legislation, and advocated on behalf of the importation of Mexican contract labor.[5]

The importation and employment of Mexican labor in the Midwest increased and expanded into other branches of industry and agriculture during the latter part of the war and extended into the post–World War I period because of the increase in war-related industrial activity, the steel strikes of 1919, the packinghouse strikes of 1921 (Chicago), and the substitution of Mexican labor power for European immigrant labor as a major supply of "cheap labor" in the agricultural sector. The structure of the Mexican population during the World War I and post–World War I period was largely determined by immigration. Using the Mexican foreign–stock population as an indicator, we find a large pattern of growth from 1910 to 1930. During this period the Mexican population grew from 11,733 to 69,193.

While the private employment practices of midwestern capitalists and the World War I government importation program stimulated the first major flow of immigrant workers, the Great Depression, the repatriation activities, and anti-alien sentiment stimulated a sizable reverse migration flow. Thousands of Mexican nationals were rounded up in places such as Chicago, East Chicago, and Detroit. Virtually "kicked out," Mexicans and their families (many of whom were American citizens) were either returned to Mexico through deportations, voluntary departure removal processes, or the Mexican-assisted repatriation program, or were forced to leave the cities on their own initiative for places unknown, some of them returning to Mexico.[6] The net change in the Mexican foreign-stock population in the Midwest during the decade of the 1930s was less than 4,000.

The importation of Mexican labor power to the Midwest was accelerated during World War II primarily through a combined process of step, drift, and contract labor migration and the internal movement of the resident Chicano population (northward). During the war, thousands of braceros were utilized in midwestern agricultural and railroad projects (Rasmussen 1951). Nearly all the states in the east north central region utilized bracero labor at one time or another, yet for the most part the midwestern states were not large users of bracero labor. Michigan, Nebraska, Minnesota, and Wisconsin were the largest users. As in the case of the World War I experience, after the termination of contracts many braceros returned to the Midwest either through legal means or illegally. Overall, the number of "lost" braceros who failed to return to Mexico was not as widespread in the Midwest as it was after World War I. Throughout the bracero program (1943–1947; 1951–1964), employers benefited from the supply of labor provided by a highly developed "underground" smuggling system linking Mexico's surplus labor, the southwestern labor pools, and midwestern industries (see table 2).

Table 2. Mexican Contract Workers Employed in the Midwest

Year	Total	Ohio*	Indiana	Illinois	Michigan	Wisconsin	Minnesota	Iowa	Missouri	Nebraska	Kansas
1943–1947	28,156	n.d.	436	1,083	7,486	4,817	5,288	4,211	n.d.	4,039	796
1952–1962	130,788	94	2,808	1,783	84,800	6,489	4,281	858	12,420	16,743	512
Total	158,944	94	3,244	2,866	92,286	11,306	9,569	5,069	12,420	20,782	1,308

Sources: 1943–1947: Rasmussen 1951, 226, table 8; 1952–1957: Hancock 1951, 20; 1958–1962: U.S. Congress, First Session, Washington, D.C.

Note: Data not found for 1951 and 1958. Data not available for Ohio.

During the Depression period and World War II, legal immigration was either curtailed through administrative devices or held to a trickle. While Mexican immigration steadily continued during the 1950s, 1960s, and 1970s, it has not been as prominent as it was before the Depression (Samora 1971). U.S. involvement in the Korean War and the Vietnam War enabled Mexican immigration to continue during an otherwise restrictive period. The passage of the Immigration and Nationality Act of 1965 has enabled Mexican immigration to the Midwest to continue at a slightly increased rate compared to the pre-1964 immigration.

Origins

A recurrent interest among observers of Mexican immigration to the Midwest has been the question of origins. The data on the origins of Mexican immigration during the 1920s reveal that the central plateau of Mexico accounted for 75 to 88 percent of the immigrants. Estimates on the northeastern region range from 9 to 21 percent. Migration from the west coast, southern and eastern regions was relatively insignificant. Recent data (Cárdenas 1974b, 1976b) indicate that the central plateau and northwest regions continue to constitute the major sources of immigration, yet the central plateau has

Table 3. Regional Origins of Mexican Immigrants to the Midwest

Region	1920s		1970s		
	Taylor	Gamio	Rosales	Cárdenas	Portes
Northeast	21.3	9.0	18.0	32.1	53.9
Central Plateau	74.8	88.3	80.0	60.7	43.9
West Coast	2.0	0.1	1.2	4.8	0
South and East	1.9	0.8	0	2.4	2.4
Total	100.0	100.0	100.0	100.0	100.0
	(N = 3,132)	(N = 3,366)	(N = 1,017)	(N = 109)	(N = 164)

Sources: Taylor 1932, 49, table 8 (Agency and Employer Records 1919-1930); Gamio 1930, 19, table XI (Illinois, Indiana, Michigan postal orders, February 1927); Rosales 1976 (South Chicago, Ill.; East Chicago, Ind.: 1920s); Cárdenas 1974a; Special tabulation for Gilberto Cárdenas, "Mexican Immigrants to Midwest: The Assimilation of Latin American Immigrants Study," directed by Alejandro Portes (1973).

declined relative to the northwestern region and the remaining regions have increased as source areas compared to the 1920s (see table 3).

UNDOCUMENTED MIGRATION

Undocumented Mexicans (workers without documents) have been apprehended in the Midwest since the early 1900s. Taylor (1932) reports specific efforts by the Immigration and Naturalization Service (INS) in the Chicago-Calumet region to apprehend Mexican undocumented workers during the 1920s. During the 1930s, large numbers of Mexicans were located and removed from midwestern agriculture and midwestern industrial centers.[7]

During Operation Wetback in 1954, thousands of Mexican aliens were apprehended in the Chicago Campaign.[8] The more recent efforts by the INS to apprehend the undocumented have been concentrated in the Chicago area. The campaigns, roundups, and raids conducted by the INS are greatly resented by Chicanos in the Midwest and elsewhere. The presence of the INS continues to provoke a "reign of terrorism" in Chicano communities in the Midwest. According to INS figures, in 1975 Mexicans constituted 62 percent (11,685) of the total number of persons apprehended in the Midwest (18,992). Compared to the proportion of Mexicans apprehended in the United States, 89 percent (766,600), the Midwest Mexican proportion was much lower (Department of Justice 1975, 1976).

In Chicago, however, which has the highest numbers of deportable undocumented Mexicans in the Midwest, the Mexican proportion (80 percent) approximates the U.S. proportion.

Undocumented Mexicans apprehended in the Midwest are not the "border runners" of the Southwest. Whereas 76 percent of all persons apprehended in the Midwest had been in the United States for one month or more, the remaining 24 percent were either caught at entry or within thirty days. In contrast, 26.8 percent of the undocumented outside the Midwest had been in the United States for one month or more and 74 percent were apprehended within thirty days. The impact of apprehension is particularly acute in the Midwest. In a recent survey, the majority of Midwest-bound Mexican immigrants surveyed had lived in the Midwest portion of the United States for more than three years prior to legal admission (Cárdenas 1976b). The implications of prior residence are further illustrated by the fact that 50 percent of the sample indicated that their eldest child was born in the United States. The vast majority of aliens apprehended in this region are caught while employed in industry[9] (see table 4).

Table 4. Deportable Aliens Located, by Length of Time Illegally in the United States, 1975

Area	Total	At entry	Within 72 Hours	4–30 days	1–6 months	7 months to 1 year	Over 1 year
Percent	100.0%	31.0%	26.2%	14.8%	16.1%	4.3%	7.6%
U.S. total	756,819	234,377	198,194	112,180	121,893	32,455	57,720
District	160,023	537	12,258	26,685	53,615	20,178	46,750
Sector	596,796	233,840	185,936	85,495	68,278	12,277	10,970
Midwest							
Cleveland	1,050	12	16	131	547	126	218
Chicago	10,833	1 412	1,000	3,826	2,050	2,544	
Detroit	4,691	871	359	555	1,453	619	834
Kansas City	1,229	-	90	359	391	171	218
Omaha	903	-	32	182	362	160	167
St. Paul	286	-	4	38	105	58	81
Grand Rapids	1,119	176	351	245	215	52	80
Total	20,111	1,060	1,264	2,510	6,899	3,236	5,142
	100.0	5.3	6.3	12.5	34.3	16.1	25.6

Source: U.S. Department of Justice, Immigration and Naturalization Service, *Annual Report 1975.*

RECENT MIGRATION

Illinois ranks third in receiving Mexican immigrants.[10] Cárdenas (1976b) found that slightly over 10 percent of all Mexican immigrants to the United States in 1973 reported a Midwest state as an intended place of residence. Of the midwestern-bound immigrants (Mexican) about 77 percent report Illinois as their intended state of residence. According to the INS, 62,205

Mexican immigrants admitted in fiscal year 1975 were intending to reside in the Midwest (Department of Justice 1975). This constituted about 12 percent of all Mexican immigrants admitted in 1975.

The following characteristics were found in the 1973 sample: 80 percent of the Midwest-bound Mexican immigrants had been employed in manual labor occupations. Over 50 percent of the sample reported that their main and, last occupation (and expected occupation) was in the semiskilled urban worker, skilled worker, or artisan category. Six percent reported a white-collar, professional, or academic occupation. About 57 percent reported that work was the main reason for coming into the United States, while 18 percent claimed education and 19 percent claimed family reunification as main reasons for coming to the United States. Less than 10 percent had earned more than $10,000 during the previous year, thus pointing to the relatively low earnings of immigrant workers in the North. The average earnings in 1972 for the sample studied were about $5,400 (Cárdenas 1976b).

One of the salient characteristics of the urban-industrial cities of the Midwest, particularly Chicago and Detroit, is the ethnic composition. Since 1957 Mexico has been leading in numbers of immigrations to Chicago. In 1957 the Mexican alien population ranked third behind the Polish and German; yet by 1973 it was ranked first in size. The INS figures show that 82,303 Mexican aliens resided in the Midwest in fiscal year 1975. About 74 percent of the Midwest aliens were reportedly residing in Illinois.

Today, as in the past, Mexican immigration to the Midwest has been to the city, and the settlement experience of Mexican immigrants has been largely an urban experience. Yet, while Mexican immigrants and their children constitute an unusually high proportion of the Mexican population in large urban areas, this segment is proportionally less significant in the many small and medium-sized cities in the Midwest. In Chicago and Detroit, for example, the Mexican immigrant population (Mexican foreign stock) stands out as the single most distinctive segment of the Mexican population. In contrast to the immigrant population, interstate and agricultural migrants are more evenly dispersed between rural and urban areas and between small and medium-sized and large cities throughout the Midwest. In the small and medium-sized cities, agricultural migrants, particularly from Texas, and other interstate migrants stand out as the single most distinctive segment of the Mexican population (numerically and socially).

MIDSTREAM MIGRATORY LABOR

Origins

While the dependency on migrant farm labor in American agriculture has decreased over the years due to mechanization, thousands of migrant farmworkers are still utilized in American agriculture. The largest group of migrant farmworkers in the United States is Chicano. For over fifty years Chicano farmworkers have been the backbone of the seasonal agricultural labor force (Cárdenas 1974b). Over the years, regular patterns of agricultural labor–related migration have emerged. One of the largest, the midstream, involves seasonal migration from Texas and Mexico to various states in the Midwest. Paralleling this flow of seasonal migration has been the migration of workers and their families who do not rejoin the migrant labor stream at the end of the Midwest harvest. These workers either remain in the agricultural related sectors of the midwestern economy or attempt to settle permanently in midwestern cities. Among the ranks of this group are farmworkers who are too poor to return to their home base (Cárdenas 1974b).

Mexican labor has been utilized in midwestern agriculture since 1917, when 21,000 workers were imported from Mexico under the authority of the Department of Labor. However, it was not until the latter part of the 1920s that farmers began to depend upon large-scale interstate migrant labor. Since that time, seasonal migration has increasingly become organized and Mexican labor has been the main source of recruitment. The availability of workers for midwestern agriculture declined as better alternatives for employment became available in the industrial sectors for local and European immigrant labor. Since alternatives to agricultural labor were not readily available for Mexican workers in Texas, they were forced to join the ranks of the interstate migrant stream. The day and casual labor in Midwest agriculture was eventually replaced by family labor as the ethnic composition of the workforce changed to predominantly Mexican labor. Migrancy did not just evolve naturally, nor was it simply a matter of traditional supply and demand functions. It was reasoned that the use of migrant labor would assure higher profits at minimum economic cost or social responsibility. It was thus necessary to preserve the conditions that would ensure an almost unlimited labor supply, restrict the mobility (labor market discrimination) of Mexican workers, keep wages to a minimum (in Texas wages are often below the level necessary for subsistence), and restrict the employment of Mexican workers to a seasonal, temporary, and periodic basis. As Vernon M. Briggs Jr. stated: "No one becomes a migrant farm worker if he has any possible alternative way of making a living — the work is physically demanding, it is poorly paid, and accordingly it attracts only those who have no options" (1973).

According to the most recent information from the U.S. Department of Agriculture, approximately 5.5 million farmworkers were employed on U.S. farms in July 1976 (Department of Agriculture 1976). About 40 percent, or 2.1 million, were hired workers. In July 1976, approximately 510,000 hired workers were employed in midwestern agriculture. This compares to 572,000 in July 1975 and 458,000 in July 1974.[11]

It is estimated that approximately 300,000 farmworkers migrate to the Midwest annually.[12] While the bulk of the migrant farmworkers in midwestern agriculture are Chicano, an indeterminate number are black and white workers from the South.[13]

In 1976 the composite wage rate for field and livestock workers was about $2.50 per hour (Department of Agriculture 1976).[14] This compares favorably to the $2.13 rate in July 1975 and $1.90 in 1974. While wage rates in midwestern agriculture are slightly better than in the South, they are not as high as in the West, nor are they improving commensurately with the gains in industry or the rate of profit in midwestern agriculture.[15] By these criteria, farmworkers continue to be exploited and the gap between the poor and the rich continues to grow. While the figures presented are based on estimates for all hired farmworkers, no information is provided that would show the proportion of the hired farm labor workforce who were seasonal workers or migrant workers. Also, the ethnic composition of the workers is not known.

The living and working conditions of Chicano migrant workers in midwestern agriculture continue to be nothing less than wretched (Reno 1970; U.S. Commission on Civil Rights 1975; U.S. Congress 1970). Midstream migrants probably live in worse housing than anywhere else where migrants work. One of the most revealing approaches toward describing the experiences of Chicano migrant farmworkers in the Midwest is to analyze the housing issue. A fundamental source of conflict between the workers and their employers centers on the conflict between property ownership and human rights. A relationship between the ownership of property and social enslavement in agriculture has been described by an observer:

> Traditionally, the growers who hire the migrants furnish the housing. This has been a point of irritation for both growers and migrants over the years. Growers complain that they are the only employers in the country who are required to furnish housing for their labor force. This contention is

often used to justify why stricter farm labor housing codes should not be enacted or actively enforced. Migrants complain that housing provided by growers is used as an unreasonable tool by their employer to gain an unfair bargaining position and control over their private lives. It is well documented that a large number of labor camps run by growers, groups of growers, or labor contractors often become virtual prisons for the employees and families who occupy them. (Reno 1970, 25)

The legal status of Chicano farmworkers in midwestern agriculture has been equally precarious. Excluded from most federal legislation protecting workers, farmworkers are also nearly categorically denied legal protection by state legislation.[16] Existing laws usually are too weak to really benefit farmworkers and very often are designed to protect the employer. Despite the militant protests by Chicano farmworkers and support groups through-out the Midwest, the wretched working and living conditions have not appreciably changed. The issue of farm labor continues to remain a major area of concern among Chicanos in the Midwest. The agricultural labor market has been subject to the near-total control and domination of farm-ers, growers, and agribusiness. By creating an abundant supply of workers and by preventing or otherwise thwarting government or union efforts to protect hired agricultural workers, employers undermined any opportunity for workers to gain anything more than subsistence wages.

With the enactment and implementation of the national seasonal and farmworker program (Title III-B of OEO), the number of settled-out Chicano migrants increased phenomenally in the Midwest (Faught 1974).[17] This, in turn, had important consequences in that the selective process of migration also influenced and bolstered the number of migrants settling out in the Midwest without assistance from the migrant programs. The steady growth of the Chicano population in small and medium-sized cities and rural and semirural areas in the Midwest has been directly related to these employment patterns. While it appears that his objective social position may be better off in the long run, the Chicano migrant, whether he remains in his home base state or whether he is located, retrained, or resettled, still finds himself at the bottom. As underemployed, wage-earning, or publicly assisted families, Chicano migrants more often than not fall into a vicious trap and become victims, joining the ranks of the consumer, store-buying, and debtor class of the ghetto and inner-city poor. Considering all factors, the policy and wisdom of administered or guided migration, manpower mobility, and resettlement programs, when administered by government officials and agencies, comes under serious question.

The resettlement of Chicanos from agriculture-related activities has greatly augmented the population of Chicanos in small and medium-sized cities throughout the Midwest (Choldin and Trout 1969; Price 1971; Faught 1974). Moreover, agriculture-related migration and resettlement has contributed greatly to a "Tejano" influence as a dominant factor within Chicano communities throughout these cities. In contrast, the impact of immigration from Mexico has remained a dominant influence in the large cities such as Chicago, Illinois; Kansas City, Missouri; Detroit, Michigan; and Gary, Indiana.

PROFILE OF THE POPULATION, 1970

Population

It has not been possible in the past to present an acceptable statistical profile of Chicanos in the Midwest because data were not available until reports from the 1970 census of the population were released. With the exception of impressionistic reports, case studies, and research findings based on samples taken in midwestern communities, there has not been any basis to present such a profile prior to the 1970 census of the U.S. population. While the Bureau of the Census used multiple indicators for enumerating the Spanish-speaking population, we shall restrict our analysis to data produced through the identifier "Spanish-origin population." This includes household data obtained from all persons who identified themselves as of Spanish origin. The classification "Spanish origin" includes persons of Mexican origin, Puerto Rican origin, Cuban origin, Central and South American origin, and "other" persons of Spanish origin.[18]

In 1970 there were 9,072,602 persons in the United States who reported that they were of Spanish origin (Bureau of the Census 1973a, 1973b). The Mexican-origin population (Chicanos) constituted half (50 percent) of the total Spanish-origin population in the United States, 78.6 percent in the Southwest (Texas, Colorado, New Mexico, Arizona, and California), and 35.8 percent in the Midwest.[19] Outside the Southwest and Midwest, the Mexican-origin population was proportionately smaller, constituting only 7.3 percent of the total Spanish-origin population, while Puerto Ricans and Cubans constituted over half the Spanish-origin population (56 percent). Over one-half (55.2 percent) of the Spanish origin population was living in the five southwestern states of California, Arizona, New Mexico, Colorado, and Texas; 11.5 percent were in the Midwest and 33.3 percent were living outside the southwest and midwest portions of the United States in 1970. While persons of Mexican origin were distributed throughout the United States in 1970, they were nevertheless numerically concentrated in the Southwest. While 86.9 percent of the Mexican-origin population were living in the Southwest, only 8.2 percent were living in the Midwest and less than 5.0 percent were living in the rest of the nation.

In 1970, the Spanish-origin population in the Midwest was slightly over one million persons. Illinois, with 393,204 persons of Spanish origin, was the top-ranking Midwest state in terms of Spanish-origin population size. Three other states had a Spanish-origin population larger than 100,000—Michigan, Ohio, and Indiana.

It is surprising that persons of Central and South American origin constituted the single largest group, 41.3 percent of the Spanish-origin population in the Midwest.[20] Ignoring the validity of the Central and South American count, it appears that in every state in the Midwest, the Mexican-origin population was the single largest group. The Mexican-origin population ranged from a high of 57.0 percent of the Spanish-origin population in Nebraska to a low of 20.6 percent in Ohio. The Mexican, Puerto Rican, and Cuban-origin populations in the Midwest are heavily concentrated in Illinois. Illinois accounts for 42.9 percent of the total Mexican-origin population, 65.2 percent of the total Puerto Rican population, and 63.4 percent of the total Cuban population in the Midwest in 1970. Persons of Central and South American origin and persons classified as "all other Spanish origin" were more evenly distributed in the Midwest.

Rural-Urban Residence

Over four-fifths of the total Spanish-origin population in 1970 were classified as urban, and the remaining as either rural nonfarm or rural farm (Bureau of the Census 1973). There were no significant differences by region. Despite the heavy urban concentration of the Spanish population throughout the United States, when comparing regions, the midwest Spanish-origin group is less urban by only 3.1 percent than the total Spanish-origin population in the nation. In light of the questions raised concerning the classification "Central and South American," it is interesting to note the high proportion of that group reportedly residing in rural areas throughout the Midwest. For example, in Indiana, 30 percent of the Central and South American population was rural. Persons familiar with the Spanish-speaking in Indiana would claim that this figure may be entirely incorrect.

Standard Metropolitan Statistical Areas: Chicago, Illinois and Detroit, Michigan

The Chicago, Illinois and the Detroit, Michigan standard metropolitan statistical areas (SMSAs) constituted the two largest concentrations of all persons of Spanish origin in the Midwest counted by the 1970 census of the population. While space does not permit comment on the historical significance of these two urban centers, it is possible to at least characterize the ethnic composition of the population.[21]

According to the 1970 census of the population, the total Spanish-origin population for the Chicago SMSA was 324,215. Persons of Mexican origin comprised 44.3 percent (143,659); persons of Puerto Rican origin comprised 26.6 percent; and other persons of Spanish origin including Cuban, Central and South American, and other Spanish-origin comprised 29.6 percent of the total. The city of Chicago ranks fourth in size of the Spanish-speaking population among U.S. cities. The Chicago SMSA reflected a comparable increase of foreign-born with Spanish mother tongue of 193 percent—from 27,273 to 80,004—almost a tripling of the 1960 population. Growth in this subgroup of the Spanish-speaking population is occurring mainly in the city, with an increase in Chicago of about 42,000, which is 70.2 percent of the change in the Chicago SMSA. It appears that the traditional concentration of immigrating groups within the city rather than in the urban fringe is clearly being maintained by the geographic settlement of the Spanish-speaking population in Chicago (Faught, Flores, and Cárdenas 1975). The city of Chicago has one of the largest concentrations of Chicanos in the United States and the highest concentration of Puerto Ricans of any city outside New York City.

In the Detroit SMSA there were a total of 66,585 persons of Spanish origin counted in the 1970 census of the population. Persons of Mexican origin comprised 40.0 percent of the total Spanish-origin population of Detroit, while the Puerto Ricans, Cubans, Central and South Americans, and other Spanish-origin comprised the remaining portion. Other SMSAs having large concentrations of persons of Spanish origin are the Gary-East Chicago–Hammond, Indiana SMSA; Kansas City, Missouri SMSA; Milwaukee, Wisconsin SMSA; Cleveland, Ohio SMSA; Lansing, Michigan SMSA; and St. Paul-Minneapolis, Minnesota SMSA.

Nativity and Parentage

About 85 percent of the Spanish-origin population in the United States were native born, while 15 percent were foreign born. The native population is defined as including persons of native *parentage* (61.5 percent) and persons of mixed or foreign parentage (29.9 percent) (Bureau of the Census 1973). In community areas of Chicago, Illinois where Chicanos are highly concentrated (Westside, Little Village, and South Chicago), the Spanish-language foreign-stock population was larger than the native stock. In Chicago's Westside, the Mexican foreign-stock constituted 66.6 percent of the population, and in South Chicago it constituted 61.6 percent. In these areas the natives of native parentage are outnumbered by the foreign-stock population. The numerical importance of the foreign-stock population is clearly reflected in the social and cultural milieu of the Chicano barrios in Chicago.

Migration

When utilizing the census publications one finds that interstate migration data on the Spanish-speaking are relatively lacking. Moreover, outside the Southwest, migration data are limited to state of birth of the native population, state of residence of the native population, and place of residence. Also, the 1970 published data are only available for the classification "persons of Spanish origin" without further designation (Mexican, etc.) (Bureau of the Census 1973).

Despite these limitations, the data provide a basis upon which migration (interregional, intraregional, interstate) can be crudely measured. Prior to the availability of the 1970 census data, it was not possible to even provide a crude measure of migration for the Spanish-speaking population in the Midwest.

Interregional Migration

About 97,936 native persons of Spanish origin who were living in the Midwest in 1970 were born in one of the five southwestern states. While this constitutes less than 10 percent of the total Spanish-origin population in the Midwest (1,042,843), it does constitute more than one-half (53.9 percent) of all native persons of Spanish origin who had migrated to the Midwest from a different region since birth (N = 181,822). The state of Texas accounted for 79,512, or 81.2 percent, of the southwestern migrants (N = 97,936). The Texas-born migrants were distributed throughout the Midwest but were highly concentrated in the northeast portion of the

Table 5. Interregional Migration: In-Migration from Southwest to the Midwest (State of Birth and State of Residence of the Native Spanish-Origin Population), 1970

State of birth	Total	State of residence									
		Midwest		Ohio		Indiana		Illinois		Michigan	
Texas	79,512	81.2	8,527	58.0	6,173	79.5	27,984	86.9	20,563	90.0
Colorado	5,068	5.2	122	1.2	466	6.0	1,040	3.2	662	2.9
New Mexico	4,235	4.3	469	4.7	97	1.3	916	2.8	325	1.4
Arizona	1,962	2.0	217	2.2	92	1.2	619	1.9	316	1.4
California	7,159	7.3	704	7.0	936	12.1	1,639	5.1	995	4.4
Total	97,916	100.0	10,039	100.0	7,764	100.0	32,198	100.0	22,861	100.0

State of birth	State of residence											
	Wisconsin		Minnesota		Iowa		Missouri		Nebraska		Kansas	
Texas	5,856	85.3	1,692	58.1	1,041	63.0	1,797	47.2	1,797	58.1	4,082	60.6
Colorado	260	3.8	399	13.7	260	15.7	662	17.4	347	11.2	850	12.6
New Mexico	250	3.6	181	6.2	104	6.3	493	13.0	581	18.8	819	12.2
Arizona	84	1.2	129	4.4	82	5.0	194	5.1	58	1.9	171	2.5
California	419	6.1	510	17.5	166	10.0	660	17.3	310	10.0	840	12.2
Total	6,869	100.0	2,911	100.0	1,653	100.0	3,806	100.0	3,093	100.0	6,742	100.0

Source: U.S. Bureau of the Census 1973a, tables 21 and 22 (State of Birth).

region, e.g., Ohio, Indiana, Illinois, Michigan, and Wisconsin (87.0 percent, N = 79,512) (see table 5).

In 1970 about 66,141 native persons of Spanish origin who were born in the Midwest were living in the Southwest. Of this group over one-half were living in the state of California (54.1 percent) while 30.3 percent were living in Texas.

Net Gain through Migration

Defining migration as the difference between (region) state of birth and (region) state of residence in 1970 on the basis of the available information, i.e. survival population in 1970, it appears that there was a net gain of 83,330 native persons of Spanish origin in the Midwest. This constitutes approximately 11 percent of the total native Spanish-origin population in the Midwest (N = 789,576). On these criteria the state of Illinois gained 34,490 persons, the highest single gain in the Midwest, while Michigan was relatively close behind with a net gain of 25,506 persons. Iowa, Missouri, Nebraska, and Kansas lost more persons than they gained. In analyzing the composition of the Spanish-origin population in the Midwest, the preceding analysis demonstrates the importance of migration. In determining the composition of the population we shall rely upon data compiled for the north central region (Midwest and North and South Dakota).[22] By dividing the

Table 6. Mobility Status of Native Population in Midwest, by Region, State of Birth, and Region of Residence, with Net Gain or Loss through Interregional Movement, 1970

Mobility status of U.S. native-born	Total Midwest	Ohio	Indiana	Illinois	Michigan	Wisconsin	Minnesota	Iowa	Missouri	Nebraska	Kansas
Total native population	789,576	105,359	97,361	243,231	126,870	50,922	32,746	16,805	51,478	17,962	46,842
Population born in state	706,246	88,686	83,803	208,741	101,364	45,323	31,762	21,042	55,157	21,268	49,100
Population born/living										12,219	31,304
in state	557,096	70,494	69,518	177,297	83,820	37,149	25,485	12,601	37,209		
Out-migration	149,150	18,192	14,285	31,444	17,544	8,174	6,277	8,441	17,948	9,049	17,796
Within region	50,681	5,211	6,139	9,835	4,308	3,191	1,853	3,943	8,990	1,779	5,432
Outside region	98,469	12,981	8,146	21,609	13,236	4,983	4,424	4,498	8,958	7,270	12,364
In-migration	232,480	34,865	27,843	65,934	43,050	13,773	7,261	4,204	14,269	5,743	15,538
Within region	50,681	4,058	6,905	13,632	6,145	3,897	2,498	1,860	5,602	1,469	4,535
Outside region	181,799	30,807	20,858	52,302	36,905	9,876	4,763	2,344	8,667	4,274	11,003
Net gain or loss										–3,306	–2,258
through migration	83,330	16,673	13,558	34,490	25,506	5,599	984	–4,237	–3,679		
Within		–1,153	846	3,797	1,837	706	645	–2,083	–3,388	–310	–897
Outside		17,826	12,712	30,693	23,669	4,893	339	–2,154	–291	–2,996	–1,361

Source: U.S. Bureau of the Census 1973a, tables 21 and 22 (State of Birth).

Note: It is not possible to factor out North and South Dakota from the published data utilized to determine the composition of the population. The Spanish-origin population in these states is small and does not contaminate the analysis. However, since we are not using the same data, this analysis is not precise.

total Spanish origin population in the north central region by residence and birth, we find that a very high proportion of the population (41.6 percent) could be classified as migrant, while only 58.4 percent were born in the region (see table 6).

The "migrant population" includes persons who were born in a different region in the United States; other native-born in the United Sates; those born in Puerto Rico and outlying area or foreign-born.

Socioeconomic Status: Occupation, Income, and Education

Both Chicago and Detroit are heavily industrialized. The concentration, location, and employment status of the Spanish-speaking population in these cities are greatly affected by the urban industrial complex. In small and medium-sized cities throughout the Midwest, the socioeconomic status (SES) of Spanish-speaking people also reflects the influence of urban-industrial factors. The remaining section of this profile will focus on occupational status, income, poverty status, and education. The analysis of SES will be based on published data generated through the identifier "Spanish Language" (S.L.).[23] Where possible, comparisons will be made with the white population (excluding S.L.) and the black population (see table 7).

Table 7. Occupational Distribution of Employed Spanish-Language Persons 16 Years and Older Compared with Other Persons in the Midwest and Great Lakes States, 1970

Occupational category	Total	White	Black	Spanish-language
	21,204,800	19,596,661	1,513,666	277,071
Professional, technical, managers, administrators, and kindred workers, except farm	22.0	22.3	10.4	15.0
Sales, clerical, and kindred workers	24.4	25.0	19.0	18.2
Craftsmen, foremen, and kindred workers	14.2	15.0	9.3	13.3
Operatives, including transport equipment operatives	19.0	18.3	28.0	33.0
Service workers, including private household workers	13.0	12.0	25.0	12.3
Laborers, except farm	4.3	4.0	8.0	8.0
Farmers, farm managers, farm laborers, and farm foremen	4.0	4.3	1.0	1.3

Source: Bureau of the Census 1970.

Occupation

Of the 277,071 persons of "Spanish-Language" who were employed in the Midwest in 1970, only 15 percent were in professional-technical, managerial, and administrative occupations. The bulk of the workers were sales and clerical workers (18.2 percent), or craftsmen and operatives (46.3 percent), and the remainder were service workers, laborers, and farm workers (21.6 percent). One-third of the S.L. employed population were in the operative category. This not only stands out as the single highest proportion among the S.L. population but also is comparably higher than the black population (28 percent) and the white population (18.3 percent). The extremes are most notable in the northeast portion of the Midwest and in portions of Chicago and Detroit.

Income

The gap between Spanish-language family income and white family income is not significant at the bottom level, particularly if the difference is compared to black families. More significantly, the gap is more pronounced if one compares the income of families receiving less than $10,000 and $10,000 or more. About 48 percent of white families received less than $10,000 compared to 56.5 percent of Spanish families and 65.8 percent of black families. White families receiving $10,000 or more averaged 52.1 percent, compared to only 43.5 percent of Spanish-language families and only 34.1 percent of black families. By these comparisons, Spanish-language

Table 8. Income of Families in Midwest, 1970

Income level	White N	%	Black N	%	Spanish-language N	%
Less than 4,999	1,958,580	16.24	304,463	30.32	30,649	17.39
5,000 to 9,999	3,816,944	31.65	355,983	35.45	68,869	39.08
10,000 to 14,999	3,601,426	29.86	222,611	22.17	48,661	27.62
15,000 +	2,682,852	22.25	121,146	12.06	28,025	15.90
Total	12,059,802	100.00	1,004,203	100.00	176,204	99.99

Source: Bureau of the Census 1970.

family income is greater than black family income, yet far below white family income. The differences are most extreme in the state of Illinois, where the median income of the Spanish-language population is 85.9 percent of the white population's ($8,032 compared to $9,351). However, in four states (Iowa, Minnesota, Missouri, Nebraska) the Spanish-language median income was greater than the white median income and in the case of Missouri it was nearly twice the median income of the black population (see table 8).

Poverty Status

Compared to the white population, the Spanish-language population is relatively poor on the basis of the percent age of families receiving public assistance income (Bureau of the Census 1970). While 2.35 percent of white families received public assistance in 1970, 3.16 percent of the Spanish-language families received public assistance. Yet, when compared to black families (10.9 percent), the Spanish-language fared much better. In 1970, 7.1 percent of white families fell below the poverty level, compared to 21.3 percent of black families and 11.6 percent of Spanish-language families. In Illinois, 7.0 percent of S.L. families received public assistance. Missouri represents the proportion of S.L. families receiving public assistance (3.6 percent). There were over 10,000 S.L. families in Illinois who were below the poverty level in 1970. The mean income for these families was only $2,218 and the mean income deficit was $1,868. Only 28.2 percent of these families received public assistance in 1970.

While nearly one-half of black families in poverty were receiving public assistance in 1970, slightly over one-quarter of S.L. families and slightly over one-tenth of white families received public assistance (see table 9).

Education

Data were available on the educational status of the Spanish-language population in the 1970 census for the number of school years completed by

Table 9. Poverty Status of Families and Persons in the Midwest, 1969

	White		Black		Spanish-Language	
Income level	N	%	N	%	N	%
All income level families	12,818,814		1,003,645		176,027	
Percentage receiving Public Assistance Income	301,850	2.35	109,308	10.89	5,557	3.16
Income less than poverty level families	906,889		214,112		20,450	
Percentage of all families		7.07		21.33		11.60
Percentage receiving public assistance	118,014	13.01	92,154	43.04	5,213	25.4

Source: Bureau of the Census 1970.

persons 25 years and older, by sex, and for the number of school years completed by persons 18 to 24 years of age. The Spanish-language population 25 years old and over in the Midwest ranks at the bottom in educational attainment. Over 42 percent of the Spanish-language population had no high school education compared to 33 percent for blacks and 26 percent for whites. The gap between the Spanish-language population and the white population is not as pronounced at the college level. Looking at the various states, we find that the gap is most extreme in Illinois, where nearly 50 percent of the Spanish-language population 25 years and over had no high school education in 1970, compared to 28 percent for whites and 35 percent for blacks. However, in Missouri, where the Spanish-language median school years completed was 12.2, the Spanish language population with some college education surpassed the college-educated white population by 7.5 percent[24] (see table 10).

Table 10. Educational Characteristics (Years of School Completed): Midwest Totals

Total persons	White		Black		Spanish-language	
25 years and over	N	%	N	%	N	%
No school years completed	247,691	0.9	39,738	1.9	17,869	5.4
Elementary	7,084,697	25.8	701,502	33.3	123,394	37.1
High school	14,539,108	53.1	1,127,066	53.6	136,390	41.0
College	5,517,165	20.2	236,183	11.2	55,386	16.6
Total	27,389,111	100.0	2,104,489	100.0	333,139	100.0

Source: Bureau of the Census 1970.

Conclusion

There is a fairly large amount of independent data on demographic, SES, and language characteristics that can be utilized in further understanding the Midwest experience and for drawing meaningful comparisons. The longitudinal studies of Shannon and Shannon (1973), the rural-to-urban migration study of Daniel Price (1971), and the workers in transition study of Choldin and Trout (1969) provide documentation and analysis of data that in many cases remain much more helpful in understanding the Chicano experience in the Midwest than the data provided by the census. While it was not possible to integrate the findings of the independent research into this chapter, their findings greatly augment the data base in which we may increase our understanding of the Chicano experience in the Midwest.

With a focus on the Chicano experience in the Midwest, hopefully the longstanding preoccupation with the Southwest experience will be broken down. Because of the tendency to neglect the Midwest experience, it will be necessary to give this region explicit attention. However, in the long run, the greatest contribution of the midwestern Chicano experience will be toward helping to establish a national Chicano identity. The vitality and persistence of Chicano communities outside the Southwest further suggest the continuity of internationality in the Chicano sociohistorical experience. While a national identity is greatly needed for research and policy purposes, the international identity is one that Chicano activists have long argued.

One of the distinctive features of La Raza in the Midwest is that all the major Spanish-speaking ethnic groups in the United States are substantially represented. In Mexico, the Southwest, the Northeast, or Puerto Rico, only one nationality is dominant, whereas in the Midwest the presence of each group is substantial. In Chicago, for example, the possibilities for coalition and integration are real as are the possibilities for rivalry and conflict. Indeed, it is still problematic how the diverse groups will work out their differences and commonalities in the barrios as well as how their numbers will translate in the political arenas. Certainly it would not be a mere reproduction of the Southwest experience.

Notes

1. Ricardo Parra, director of the Midwest Council of La Raza, University of Notre Dame, Indiana, conversation with author.

2. Geographical areas and classification:

Midwest	Census North Central Region	Federal Regional Council Areas
Midwest	East North Central	Region V
Ohio	Ohio	Ohio
Indiana	Indiana	Indiana
Illinois	Illinois	Illinois
Michigan	Michigan	Michigan
Wisconsin	Wisconsin	Wisconsin
Minnesota		Minnesota
Iowa		
Missouri	West North Central	Region VII
Nebraska	Minnesota	Iowa
Kansas	Iowa	Missouri
	Missouri	Kansas
	Kansas	Nebraska
	North Dakota	
	South Dakota	

3. See *Bibliography on La Raza in the Midwest and Great Lakes States* (Cárdenas 1976a).

4. See Proviso 9 of the Act of February 5, 1917, 39 Stat. 878.

5. See congressional hearings on agricultural labor and Western Hemisphere immigration 1921, 1926, 1928, and 1930.

6. See the following: Humphrey 1941; Kiser and Silverman 1973; Betten and Mohl 1973; Simon 1974; Spencer 1974.

7. Humphrey 1941; Kiser and Silverman 1973; Betten and Mohl 1973; Simon 1974; Spencer 1974.

8. U.S. Department of Justice, Immigration and Naturalization Services, *Chicago Operation*, Washington, D.C. 1954.

9. In the Southwest region about 90 percent are caught while seeking employment, less than 9 percent in agriculture, and less than 1 percent in industry.

10. California ranks first and Texas ranks second. (Bureau of the Census, *Subject Reports. Persons of Spanish Origin*. HA201 PC (2)-1C. Washington, D.C., 1973.)

11. U.S. Department of Agriculture, *Farm Labor*, Statistical Reporting Service, Washington, D.C., 1976. Farm employment represents the number of family and hired laborers working during the survey week. Hired workers include all persons working one hour or more for cash wages during the survey week. No comparable information was available on farmworker unemployment. Statistics on farmworkers for individual states are generally unavailable or severely limited. Limited data on farmworkers are available in the Census of Agriculture. The Employment Standards Division of the Department of Labor conducted a national study in 1972. Yet, because of the sampling techniques utilized in the survey, data are only reported for geographical regions, e.g., East, North Central, South, and West, of the United States. If one suspects the sincerity of government agencies in dealing with farmworker

problems, then it can also be expected that one would also be likely to question statistics gathered and compiled by government agencies. Related to the criticism of the accuracy and reliability of statistics on farmworkers are criticisms of the inadequacy of research designs to get at relevant information, e.g., unemployment, health, education, services, etc.

12. *Migratory Farm Workers: Number and Sex of Workers, Average Days Worked and Wages Earned, U.S., 1960–1972*, Rural Development Service. Based on data from enumerative sample surveys made by the U.S. Department of Commerce for the Economic Research Service.

13. The available data do not break down with the ethnic composition of the workers.

14. Hourly wage rates can be grossly misleading if they are not understood, and cannot be compared to industry. High unemployment (largely hidden), travel time, number of hours and weeks worked, etc. all contribute to the variability in gross income. A better indicator is total family income.

15. See Hightower (1972) for an excellent analysis of salient dimensions concerning agribusiness.

16. 29. U.S.C., S141-188; *et. seq.* 29 U.S.C. 213 (a) (b); 29 U.S.C. 213 (b) (12); 29 U.S.C. 213 (c) (1); 29 U.S.C. 213 (c) (2); 26 U.S.C. 3301 *et. seq.*, 26 U.S.C. 3401 *et. seq.*

17. A major effort of the Migrant Division of OEO was directed toward resettlement of farmworkers in northern cities. In many respects the availability of experienced farmworkers for midwestern agriculture was increased by OEO efforts. By augmenting the supply of "local labor," these efforts decreased the demand for and recruitment of interstate migrant labor.

18. For a detailed account of the procedures, limitations, and uses of the 1970 census data on the Spanish-origin population please refer to the following publications: U.S. Bureau of the Census, *Subject Reports: Persons of Spanish Origin*, HA201, PC (2)-lC (Washington, D.C., 1973); U.S. Bureau of the Census, *Persons of Spanish Ancestry, Supplementary Report, 1970 Census of Population*, PC (Sl)-30 (Washington, D.C., February 1973); U.S. Bureau of the Census, *Census of Population: 1970, Subject Reports Final Report: Persons of Spanish Origin:* PC (2)-1C (Washington, D.C., 1973); Josá Hernández, "Public Sources of Data and the Chicano Community," *Journal of Mexican American Studies* 1, no. 3 and 4 (spring/summer 1973): 123–29; Grebler, Moore, and Guzman, "Derivation of Data on Mexican Americans from the United States Census", appendix A, chapter 6, in *The Mexican American People* (New York: Free Press, 1970), 601–8; Hernández, et al., "Census Data and the Problem of Conceptually Defining the Mexican American Population," *Social Science Quarterly* 53, no. 4 (March 1973): 671–87); U.S. Bureau of the Census, *Persons of Spanish Origin in the United States: March 1972 and 1971*, Current Population Reports, Series P-20, No. 250 (Washington, D.C., April 1973).

19. Percentages are now shown; compiled separately.

20. Serious questions have been raised with respect to the accuracy of the 1970 census, particularly with respect to enumerating the Spanish-origin population. The U.S. Bureau of the Census, despite the allegations that it has undercounted the size of the Spanish origin population, has acknowledged that it has reason to believe that confusion about the category "Central and South American origin" may have led to an overcount of the Spanish-origin population, particularly in the Midwest and in the South. It seems that the United States Bureau of the Census would have to give very compelling reasons why, everything taken into consideration, the Spanish-origin population in the Midwest was actually overcounted. Note that it is also difficult to make a more accurate determination of the size of each ethnic group because of the confusion about the Central and South American–origin category. For reasons explained earlier in this paper there is strong indication that there is an overcount

in the category "Central and South American origin" due to the lack of clarity in doing the census for this question. Thus, persons of Mexican origin probably constitute the single largest Spanish-origin ethnic group in the Midwest. It is very doubtful if the proportion of the Central and South American origin population is as large as reported by the census publications. This clarification is also applicable to the case for each state in the Midwest.

21. Apart from the 1970 Census Tract Reports PHC (1)-43 and PHC (1)-58 for the Chicago and Detroit SMSAs, the two most recent publications are, respectively: Department of Development and Planning, *Chicago's Spanish-Speaking Population: Selected Statistics* (City of Chicago, Illinois, September 1973) and John R. Weeks and Joseph Spielberg, "The Ethnomethodology of Midwestern Chicano Communities," paper presented at 1973 annual meeting of the Population Association of America, New Orleans, Louisiana. These materials should be consulted for further up-to-date information about Chicago and Detroit.

22. It is not possible to factor out North and South Dakota from the published data utilized to determine the composition of the population. The Spanish-origin population in these states is small and does not contaminate the analysis. However, since we are not using the same data this analysis is not precise.

23. Persons of Spanish Language comprise persons of Spanish mother tongue and all other persons in families in which the head or wife reported Spanish as his or her mother tongue.

24. Median school years completed, 1970, Spanish-Language: Illinois 9.2; Indiana 10.5; Iowa 12.1; Kansas 10.9; Michigan 10.5; Minnesota 12.2; Missouri 12.2; Nebraska 11.0; Ohio 11.3; Wisconsin 10.5. Source: U.S. Bureau of the Census, *General Social and Economic Characteristics for States*, PC (1), 1970.

Works Cited

Acuña, R. 1972. *Occupied America: The Chicano's Struggle Toward Liberation*. San Francisco: Canfield Press.

Barrera, M. 1976. "Colonial Labor and Theories of Inequality: The Case of International Harvester." *Review of Radical Political Economics* (summer).

Betten, N., and R. Mohl 1973. "From Discrimination to Repatriation: Mexican Life in Gary, Indiana During the Great Depression." *Pacific Historical Review* 22, no.3 (August): 370–88.

Blauner, R. 1972. *Racial Oppression in America*. New York: Harper and Row.

Briggs, V. 1973. *Chicanos in Rural Poverty*. Baltimore: Johns Hopkins University Press.

Cárdenas, G. 1976a. *Bibliography on La Raza in the Midwest and Great Lakes States (1924 to 1976)*. Dept. of Sociology, University of Texas, Austin. Revised.

———. 1976b. "Profile of Midwest Bound Mexican Immigrants, 1973." Department of Sociology, University of Texas. Mimeo.

————. 1974a. "Socioeconomic and Language Characteristics of Proyecto Vencermos Student Population." Centro de Estudios Chicanos e Investigaciones Sociales, Inc.

————. 1974b. "The Status of the Agricultural Workers Center for Civil Rights." University of Notre Dame.

————. 1973. *Mexican Immigrant Population Chicago: Social, Economic and Language Characteristics*. Midwest Council of La Raza. University of Notre Dame.

Choldin, H. M., and G. D. Trout. 1969. *Mexican Americans in Transition: Migration and Employment in Michigan Cities*. Department of Sociology, Rural Manpower Center, Michigan State University.

City of Chicago. 1973. *Chicago's Spanish Speaking Population*. Department of Development and Planning.

Faught, J. D. 1974. *Social and Economic Conditions of the Spanish Origin Population in South Bend, Indiana. Report #1*. Centro de Estudios Chicanos e Investigaciones Sociales, Inc. University of Notre Dame.

Faught, J., E. Flores, and G. Cárdenas. 1975. *A Profile of the Spanish Language Population in the Little Village and Pilsen Community Areas of Chicago, Illinois and Population Projections, 1970–1980*. Centro de Estudios Chicanos e Investigaciones Sociales, Inc.

Galarza, E., J. Samora, and H. Gallegos. 1970. *Mexican Americans in the Southwest*. Santa Barbara, Calif.: McNally and Loftin.

Gamio, M. 1930. *Mexican Immigration to the United States*. Chicago: Univ. of Chicago Press.

Grebler, L., J. Moore, and R. Guzmán. 1970. *The Mexican American People*. New York: Free Press.

Hancock, R. H. 1951. *The Role of the Bracero in the Economic and Cultural Dynamics of Mexico*. Hispanic American Society, Stanford, California.

Hightower, J. 1972. *Hard Tomatoes, Hard Times*: A Report of the Agribusiness Accountability Project on the Failure of America's Land Grant College Complex. Cambridge, Mass.: Schenkman.

Humphrey, N. D. 1943. "The Migration and Settlement of Detroit Mexicans." *Economic Geography*. 19: 358–61.

————. 1941. "Mexican Repatriation from Michigan: Public Assistance in Historical Perspective." *Social Science Review* 15 (September): 497-513.

Johnson, H., and W. J. Hernandez-M. 1970. *Educating the Mexican American*. Valley Forge, Pa.: Judson Press.

Kiser, G., and D. Silverman. 1973. "Mexican Repatriation During the Great Depression," *Journal of Mexican American History* 3: 139–64.

Lebeaux, C. N., and G. Salas. 1973. *Latino Life and Social Needs Study of Detroit*. Detroit, Mich.

Moore, Joan W. 1970. "Colonialism: The Case of the Mexican-Americans." *Social Problems* 17 (spring): 463–72.

Price, D. O. 1971. "Rural to Urban Migration of Mexican Americans, Negroes and Angloes." *International Migration Review* 5: 281–91.

Rasmussen, W. D. 1951. *A History of the Emergency Farm Labor Supply Program*. Agricultural Monograph #13, U.S. Department of Agriculture, Washington, D.C.

Reno, L. 1970. *Pieces and Scraps*. Rural Housing Alliance, Washington, D.C.

Rex, J. 1973. *Race, Colonialism and the City*. London: Routledge and Kegan Paul.

Rosales, A. 1976. "Regional Origins of Mexicano Immigrants to Chicago." Paper presented at National Association of Chicano Social Scientists.

Samora, J. 1971. *Los Mojados: The Wetback Story*. University of Notre Dame.

Samora, J., and R. Lamanna. 1967. *Mexican Americans in a Midwest Metropolis: A Study of East Chicago*. UCLA Study Project Advance Report.

Shannon, L., and M. Shannon. 1973. *Minority Migrants in the Urban Community*. Beverly Hills, Calif.: Sage Publications.

Simon, D. T. 1974. "Mexican Repatriation in East Chicago, Indiana," *Journal of Ethnic Studies* 11 (summer): 11–23.

Spencer, L. 1974. "Exile and Union in Indiana Harbor." *Revista Chicano–Riqueña* 11 (winter): 50–57.

State of California. 1930. *Mexicans in California*. Governor Young Report, Sacramento.

Taylor, P. 1932. *Mexican Labor in the United States: Chicago and the Calumet Region*. Berkeley: Univ. of California Press.

U.S. Bureau of the Census. 1970. *General Social and Economic Characteristics for States*. PC(1). Washington, D.C.

U.S. Bureau of the Census. 1973a. *Subject Reports. Population* Vol. II, PC (2) 2A. State of Birth, Tables 21 and 22. Washington, D.C.

U.S. Commission on Civil Rights. Indiana State Advisory Committee. 1975. *Indiana Migrants: Blighted Hopes, Slighted Rights: A Report*. Chicago: Midwestern Regional Office, U.S. Commission on Civil Rights.

U.S. Commission on Civil Rights. 1971. *Mexican American Education Study*. Report #1. Washington, D.C.

U.S. Congress. 1970. *Senate Migrant and Seasonal Farmworker Powerlessness*. Senate Subcommittee on Migratory Labor and Public Welfare.

———. 1969. *Senate Report of the Committee on Labor and Public Welfare*.

———. 1941. "Report on the Migration of Mexican Labor from Texas to the Sugar Beet Fields." Interstate Migration Hearings, Part 5, 76th Congress, 3rd session, 1845–59.

U.S. Department of Agriculture. 1970–1976. *The Hired Farm Working Force: A Statistical Report*. Washington, D.C.

U.S. Department of Justice. Immigration and Naturalization Services. 1954. "Chicago Operation" (Operation Wetback). Washington, D.C.

———. Immigration and Naturalization Service. Various years. Annual Report. Washington, D.C.

Weeks, J., and J. Speilberg. 1973. "Ethnodemographic Studies of Midwestern Chicano Communities." Department of Anthropology, Michigan State University.

Womack, J. 1972. "Who Are the Chicanos?" *New York Review of Books 19*.

Recent Chicano Historiography
An Interpretive Essay

Alex M. Saragoza

AUTHOR'S NOTE: *Since the writing of this essay, the field of Chicano/a history has been marked by important advances, as evidenced in the works of George Sanchez, Vicki Ruiz, Douglas Monroy, David Guiterrez, Antonia Castaneda, Deena Gonzalez, Virginia Bouvier, Rudy Acuna, and Mario Garcia, among several others. Collections of Chicano historical writings have appeared to bring fresh perspective to the interpretation of Chicano/a history, as found, for example, in the recent anthology edited by Vargas Zaragoza. Studies of a comparative nature have been a welcome addition, as reflected, for instance, in Neil Foley's excellent treatment of workers and the cotton economy of east Texas, as well as Devra Weber's monograph on farm labor activism in the San Joaquin Valley of California in the 1930s.*

Nonetheless, despite impressive scholarly efforts over the last decade, there is still much pioneering work to be done on the gender, labor, social and cultural history of people of Mexican origin in this country. Furthermore, the era after 1940 remains largely absent of concerted attention by historians of comparative race and ethnic relations, with some notable exceptions, such as the provocative publication by Rudy Torres and Victor Valle on Los Angeles. Given the continuing and significant influx of Mexican immigrants to the United States since the 1960s, much more historical research is necessary to address adequately this tenacious, crucial question in Chicano history. More specifically, the post-World War II global economic shifts and their impacts on Mexican-origin people on both sides of the U.S.–Mexico border await serious historical examination. And studies that encompass other Latino groups and/or racialized communities would enrich the field as well. It can only be hoped that this collection will spur more research in the field of Chicano/a history, and equally, if not more important, encourage students to join the profession in this area of historical inquiry.

The intent of this essay is to assess Chicano historiography over the last decade as a means of interpreting the Chicano past. As a consequence, this essay will avoid the usual forms of the traditional historiographical account. Rather, the emphasis will be on major developments in the field

From *Aztlan: A Journal of Chicano Studies* 19, no. 1 (1988–1990): 1–77.

and their implications for the interpretation of the history of people of Mexican origin in the United States. In this essay I will argue that past formulations of Chicano historical experiences have been inadequate and require a critical reevaluation. Such an assessment is not coincidental. The conceptual moorings of Chicano history have been affected by recent shifts and debates in the broader field of American history, particularly the area of social history. Combined with other factors, this tense and at times fractious discussion holds important consequences for Chicano historiography and its direction, and thus requires an initial explication.[1]

In a recent publication on Chicano ethnicity, the authors make a highly suggestive comment on the difficulty of defining "Chicano culture":

> It is only through the study of the interrelationships of cultural, social, and structural factors in *historical perspective* [my emphasis] that a broad understanding of the nature of ethnicity and sociocultural change can be achieved.[2]

This observation appears at the conclusion of the book and reflects the continuing inadequacy of interpretive work on people of Mexican origin in the United States. For despite the flawed research of the authors of *Chicano Ethnicity*, the fact remains that the field of Chicano history has produced relatively few works since the initial tide of monographs of a decade ago.[3] The promise of Chicano history, touted by one of the first major reviews in 1976, has failed to bloom completely or as anticipated by its early proponents.[4]

Indeed, my reluctance to employ a more traditional approach in structuring this essay stems from the scarcity of scholarship on any particular topic, period, or subfield. Yet, the issue is much more than one of productivity. Basic questions of interpretation, analysis, and methodology continue to vex students of the Chicano past. In this light, Chicano history, I would argue, confronts an important, if not decisive turning point in its development. This turn in Chicano historical writing consists of several elements, and they merit brief mention.

The first issue is generally underestimated: the very small number of new scholars entering the field. As will be noted in this essay, the motivation of a group of academics in the wake of the Chicano movement of the 1960s contributed importantly to the conceptual origins and early production of Chicano history. With relatively few exceptions, such as Deena González, George Sánchez, and David Gutiérrez, the overwhelming majority of Chicano graduate students in the last decade have avoided academic careers generally, and specifically in history.

Thus, the "natural" constituency of Chicano historical research has yielded precious few professional practitioners. Furthermore, again with notable exceptions such as Sarah Deutsch, non-Chicano historians have generally not entered the field. Hence, even a cursory review of published articles and books on Chicano history finds sparse results; the citations of the recent scholarship section in the *Journal of American History*, for example, over the last several years reflect the paucity of Chicano-related publications. And when published, some of the work is derivative, narrow, and limited in scope.[5] The difference in the case of African American or women's history is an indication of the problems facing the writing of the Chicano past.

Second, it is clear that the place of Chicano history in the profession continues to be neglected. In spite of the efforts of certain individuals, such as Albert Camarillo, to promote greater appreciation of the Chicano experience at annual professional meetings, the attention accorded to Chicano issues in the profession remains truncated. In part, this lack of visibility in the profession stems from the points made above as well as perhaps other factors, for example, the insensitivity of program commit-tees, a reluctance on the part of Chicano scholars to submit papers or panel topics, and the virtual absence of established Chicano historians in the workings of the professional organizations. Nonetheless, the relative insignificance of Chicanos as subjects in the writing of American history raises several questions, and the issue is not related simply to professional visibility or to the number of titles of books and articles on Chicanos in the bibliographies of standard U.S. history texts. Instead, attention should be given to the *meaning,* for instance, of the publication of Elliott and Meier's book on Black historical scholarship: the continual entry of researchers into the field of Black history has been crucial to the explora-tion of new and different problems, infusing and enriching the debate over the interpretation of the African American experience.[6] More important, Chicanos and other peoples of color continue to be subordinated to and/or subsumed in the historical trajectory of Blacks. Questions of race, ethnicity, and even class and gender in American history remain often bounded by references to Blacks. The history of African Americans continues to be the essential reference point in the acknowledgment of race in U.S. history. Only a casual glance at the textbook indexes or tables of contents and survey materials is necessary to underscore the point.

This is not a plea, however, for textbooks merely to mention Chicanos more often, nor is my point to argue necessarily the uniqueness of the

Chicano experience. The key issue centers on the conceptualization of racism and its consequences. In this respect, even comparative studies remain few in number.

Ronald Takaki's *Iron Cages* represents a singular and admirable effort in the comparative history of racial and ethnic groups, but it focuses primarily on the nineteenth century.[7] Still, the centrality of the Black experience in American historical thinking seems to overwhelm considerations of the differences between African Americans and other groups, for example, Chicanos, in the interpretation of American history, broadly speaking.

Third, intrinsic to this problem was the propensity of social history (and its subfields such as urban, labor, family, and women's history) to focus its interpretive lens on geographic areas other than the West.[8] Thus, many of the main currents of American historical writing, especially those spawned by the "new social history," essentially left out Chicanos. Whereas the migration of Blacks from the South to industrializing cities in the East and Midwest made them an inherent dimension of the "new urban history," for example, Chicanos figured much less prominently in the incorporation of race into the historical writing and thinking about the industrialization of America (despite the efforts of certain Chicano historians to correct this tendency). Given the bias (understandable in many respects) of practitioners of the new social history to locate their research in the East or Midwest, Chicanos were subsumed in the application of ideas and concepts generated by research on Blacks or European immigrants, or both. The experiences of these two broad categories of analysis became implicitly if not explicitly the standard reference points to gauge the meaning of Chicano history.[9]

The combination of the scarcity of Chicano historians, the relative unimportance accorded to Chicanos in U.S. history, and the tendency of the "new history" to slight the West has made the field of Chicano history largely dependent—if only by default—on the interpretive aspects that undergirded the spate of books that appeared roughly from 1979 to 1984. These works included those by Albert Camarillo (1979), Mario Barrera (1979), Richard Griswold del Castillo (1979), Mario García (1981), Arnoldo De León (1982), Mauricio Mazón (1984), and Ricardo Romo (1983), among others. (See bibliography for full citations.) That initial generation of "Chicano" historical works reflected to a large extent the reigning questions of postconsensus historiography, that is, of the "new social history." The emphasis of the new social history centered on "ordinary people" and their capacity to sustain an identity before the onslaught of industrialization and its repercussions. Beginning in earnest in the 1960s, the debates and discussion engendered by the approach of the "new historians" resonated in the writing of Chicano scholars and their interpretive outlook.[10] The monographs on Chicanos that began to appear in the 1970s marked a sharpening of the debate over interpretation among Chicano scholars.

The shift in the work of Rodolfo Acuña illustrates the problematic of interpretation of the Chicano past. In the third edition of his popular text *Occupied America*, Acuña makes a significant concession: "The first edition [1972], influenced by the times and Third World writers such as Frantz Fanon, was angry, filled with moral outrage."[11]

In the fifteen-year span between his first and third editions, Acuña fails to explain the significance of the changes in his text. Rather, in his third edition, Acuña notes his "harsh criticism of the Chicano middle class vis-à-vis twentieth century urbanization and the ever increasing division of labor."[12] The emphasis on class difference in the third edition of *Occupied America* represents a major modification of the interpretive framework of Acuña's two earlier editions. It is also a less optimistic work. Acuña laments the unwillingness of the middle class to forge an alliance with the "lower classes" (his words) to effect social change since the 1960s. Instead, according to Acuña, increasingly "Chicanos raised in the more affluent, integrated communities take on the identification of the majority society. Thus physical separation and lack of knowledge of history and Mexican culture complete an alienation from the lower classes."[13]

While this observation contains several debatable assumptions, a key conceptual question emerges: Are the less affluent immune to the "majority society"? Or, put another way, does barrio residence lead necessarily to political awareness as well as a rejection of the "majority society"? And, are the two issues linked or are they mutually exclusive? The logic of Acuña's assumptions leads him to a significant conclusion. As Acuña states it, "LULAC and other Chicano organizations were often at the vanguard of social change [in the 1930s]—which is not true of Chicano organizations now."[14] For Acuña to "blame" the current Chicano middle class for such a situation, in my opinion, begs the question. The critical issue is, why the change? Acuña points to an answer: "A government policy that promotes the interests of the Chicano middle class at the expense of the poor has emerged."[15] And he also suggests a decline in nationalism "outside the barrio" as part of the problem. This conclusion fails to address the question of why middle-class Chicanos seem so vulnerable to such an alleged policy, or why there has been a decline in nationalism "outside the barrio." Nonetheless, by posing the question in such terms, Acuña raises (perhaps inadvertently) gritty, thorny issues consistent with the debates among American historians over agency, resistance, and protest.

Central to this debate is the issue of labor, or workers, of the so-called new labor history, perhaps the most vibrant subfield encompassed by the new social history, personified most visibly in the United States by Herbert G. Gutman and an able group of followers. Building on the ideas of E. R. Thompson, Gutman and others charted a distinctive course. As summarized by Mari Jo Buhle and Paul Buhle, this approach "redefined class as a *cultural*, [my emphasis] more than an economic, category and class consciousness as a collective expression not necessarily encompassed by such institutions as trade unions or political parties."[16] Understandably, such a view encouraged a perspective amenable to "Chicano" history as opposed to the history of working-class Chicanos. Or, as I will discuss below, the new social history facilitated a "them-versus-us" notion of the Chicano past.

Such an approach is no longer tenable, as Acuña suggests. Nonetheless, Acuña yearns for the viability of a collective sense of Chicano history. Tellingly, he states:

> The basic difference between now and the 1930s ... is that ... the majority of the members [of organizations such as LULAC], because of nationalism reinforced by extreme racism among Euroamericans, promoted the improvement of the lower classes ... and nationalism with all of its limitations has historically linked the various social classes.[17]

Acuña's lament over the lack of a Chicano consciousness—as opposed to a class consciousness—resonates with the dilemmas of the new labor historians. As one critic of the approach of Gutman and allied historians put it, "All of them agree that 'ethnic traditions, prior workplace cultures, community parades and celebrations' and other institutions like family and religion created 'solidarity' among the workers."[18] As John Patrick Diggins goes on to argue, such assumptions may be flawed.

Similarly, the assumptions of Chicano history, particularly the tendency to suggest a collective experience, require rethinking. As this essay will argue, class tensions and social rifts have marked the history of people of Mexican origin from the beginning, before the arrival of the gringo, *gabacho, yanqui,* or "Anglo." If American racism lessened such differences among Chicanos, it did not erase them. A sense of nationalism or group grievance may have attenuated class distinctions, but class cleavages endured. The implications of a basic bifurcation within the "Chicano community" over time clearly undermine the initial premises of Chicano historiography.

In this respect, the issue of gender also challenges the notion of a collective experience as a core element in the interpretation of the history of Chicanos. And here one must insist on the fundamental meaning of gender and history. As Joan Scott has observed on the relation of gender to labor history:

> If women as subject have increased in visibility, the questions raised by women's history remain awkwardly connected to the central concerns of the field. And gender has not been considered seriously for what it could provide in the way of a major reconceptualization of [labor] history … Still, the half-hearted attention to gender is dismaying. The relegation of this potentially radical concept to a set of descriptive social roles vitiates the theoretical interest and the analytic force feminist history could have.[19]

Thus, the incorporation of gender suggests more than mentioning Chicanas, regardless of the criteria. The inclusion of Chicana labor organizers in historical texts, for example, misses the point. Gender implies a major challenge to the writing of Chicano history, a challenge magnified by the points raised above.

As this review will argue, recent Chicano historical scholarship represents a departure from the conceptual origins of the field, that is, a reliance on a "them-versus-us" perspective of Chicano-Anglo relations. Recent works point to the fundamental diversity and complexity of the Chicano experience. As Sarah Deutsch has put it, "historians of the Chicano experience [have] moved to theories of cultural interaction rather than victimization."[20] Students of Chicano history have illuminated, as a consequence, the sources of differentiation within the Chicano community, past and present. More important, recent research confirms that issues of class, as well as race, represent critical factors in the interpretation of Chicano history. And, though work specifically on Chicanas remains rudimentary, gender questions clearly form a crucial dimension for the conceptualization of the Chicano past.

Them-versus-Us History

Given the origins of Chicano history, the shifts in its conceptualization become, in retrospect, understandable. Most of the major publications that appeared in the field in the late 1970s and early 1980s derived from dissertations researched and written at a distinctive moment in the development of "minority history." During the 1970s, the conjunction of the civil rights movement and fresh trends in American historiography, particularly the rise of the "new social history," moved historians to depict the evolution of American society "from the bottom up." This tendency influenced a generation of scholars, including most students of the Chicano past at the time. Thus, the intellectual roots of Chicano history were nourished by the profession's enthusiasm for labor, urban, family, and related historical fields that fell under the rubric of social history. Furthermore, the orientation of the practitioners of the new social history tended to be revisionist, critical of previous treatments of minorities, workers, and women.[21] This view within the profession facilitated (if not spurred) the emergence of Chicano history and its intrinsic disapproval of an assimilationist perspective on ethnic/ race relations in American history. As a result, the beginnings of Chicano history were by and large implicitly nationalist in origin. The nationalist currents among various minority groups paralleled the development of the new social history. This convergence between such trends in the profession and Chicano history was not without its biases. "Generally, American social historians have related their interest in ordinary people to a belief in at least semi-independent, identifiable sub-cultures that allow popular groups some independent basis for reaction to larger systems and processes," as Peter N. Stearns has observed.[22] Even in the study of workers, as Stearns and the labor historian David Brody have noted, most social historians eschewed an explicitly Marxist framework of analysis.[23] The nationalist impulse of the Chicano movement developed in an amendable context within the profession, therefore, and it engaged most younger Chicano scholars.[24]

This nationalistic bent formed an essential element in the underpinnings of much Chicano scholarship through the 1970s. The concept of racial conflict, or racism, complemented this premise and prompted a generalized acceptance of a Chicano-Anglo dichotomy, that is, a "them-versus-us" approach. From this primordial viewpoint, many Chicano scholars took their cues. The consequences were—and continue to be—significant. First, this approach tended to emphasize the separation and conflict that existed between the two groups by the very nature of the dichotomy. Second, and related to the latter point, the "them-versus-us" perspective minimized internal stratification and gender differences in the historical experience of Chicanos. Third, the conceptualization of Chicano history in such terms exaggerated the continuities in Chicano/Mexicano culture and obscured its discontinuities and variation. Fourth, a tendency toward local community studies inhibited a geographically comparative view.

As a consequence, the theme of victimization ran through much of the historical literature on Chicanos. Not surprisingly, occupational charts revealed the historic downward mobility of most Chicanos in the face of Anglo ascendancy. For those Mexicans who held property, landholding patterns after 1848 exposed frequent dispossession at the hands of venal Anglo lawyers, a racist judicial system, and corrupt politicians. To complete the picture, many stressed the resistance offered by Chicanos to their historical subjugation. The publication of Rodolfo Acuña's first edition of *Occupied America* culminated this trend through its use of the internal colonial "model," the quintessential victimization framework. Published originally in 1972, Acuña's landmark book greatly popularized the application of the concept of internal colonialism as an interpretive framework for a synthesis of the Chicano experience. By 1981, however, Acuña felt compelled to retreat from his facile acceptance of "internal colonialism" as an interpretive framework.[25]

This was not unique to Acuña, as the internal colonial model was found inadequate by several Chicano scholars by the time of the publication of the second edition of *Occupied America* (1981). Still, Acuña clung to the concept for the nineteenth century, as other Chicano intellectuals also remained tied to variations of the idea, such as labor segmentation theory. Yet, as Tomás Almaguer has shown convincingly, the colonial framework fails to explain adequately the experience of Chicanos in the nineteenth century, particularly for California.[26] For instance, the colonial framework did not explain satisfactorily the discrepancies in timing and character of Chicano resistance. Why the rise of the *gorras blancas* in the late nineteenth century in New Mexico as opposed to the solitary social banditry of Murrieta in California half a century earlier? Put another way, why the necessity in the nineteenth century of Texas Rangers to subdue the Chicano population in that state and the lack of a similar organization to accomplish the same goal in the same period in California? To be fair, as a textbook the first edition of *Occupied America* derived much of its information from the extant literature at the time that held similar conceptual notions. Nonetheless, despite Acuña's disclaimer, the "them-versus-us" character of *Occupied America* endured despite the pruning of the colonial framework in the second edition.

Between 1979 and 1984 over a half-dozen publications appeared that both affirmed and surpassed Acuña's popular text. The majority of these efforts (noted earlier in this essay) reflected the imprint of the currents gen-erated by the new social history of the 1960s and 1970s. Not coincidentally, urban history figured prominently in these works. Southern California, specifically Los Angeles, received deserved attention. Richard Griswold del Castillo, Albert Camarillo, and Ricardo Romo provided an excellent foundation to which historians of the City of Angels and its environs will remain indebted for years to come. Mario T. García's fine account of El Paso complemented Oscar Martinez's study of Ciudad Juárez. Arnoldo De León offered much valuable information with his works on Texas. Mauricio Mazón explored with exemplary originality the Zoot-Suit Riots of 1943, while David Weber produced an important book on the Mexican era of the Southwest, an accomplishment supplemented by Oakah Jones's contribu-tion on northern Mexico in the colonial period. These publications in numerous ways expanded our knowledge of the Chicano past and marked a maturation in Chicano-related historical writing.

While this tide of monographs documented the sources of the oppres-sion of Chicanos, they also showed the variation and nuances in the larger context of inequality that marked relations between Anglos and people of Mexican origin. The complexity and subtlety that characterized these new works implicitly discredited the colonial model's crude dichotomy (colonized and colonizer). And they undermined (albeit inadvertently) the nationalistic cast of "them-versus-us" history. Albert Camarillo, to cite an example, noted the tension that punctuated relations between U.S.-born Mexicans and immigrant Mexicanos in Santa Barbara. In a different vein, García's rendering of El Paso's Mexican community underscored the impor-tance of events in, and attachments to, Mexico. In contrast, De León's study on south Texas minimized the links between *tejano* society and Mexican culture and politics. Other examples may be cited, but the conclusion was clear: the conceptualization of Chicano history had to take into account the diversity of the Chicano experience from its beginnings.

If only indirectly, these monographs intensified the debate over the appropriate framework for understanding Chicano history. Influenced by the currents of the 1970s, these works reflected the common intellectual wellsprings of the authors. Several of these books, for instance, stressed themes of nationalism or ethnic pride. Romo and Camarillo, for instance, discussed at length the importance of the *mutualista* organizations that, to use Camarillo's words, "helped perpetuate Mexican culture, language, and cohesiveness in an otherwise foreign society."[27] García devoted an entire chapter to "border culture," and De León titled one of his chapters "culture and community." In each case, though the authors noted changes in the cultural character of the Chicano community, cultural maintenance was also emphasized—a key tenet of the Chicano movement of the 1970s. The incipient concern over ethnic identity among these scholars informed their view and interpretation of social and cultural expression. Furthermore, the anti-assimilationist tone of the new social history sanctioned the nationalistic posture of the Chicano history represented by the authors noted above.

Yet, despite their sensitivity to cultural continuities, these studies and their authors were faithful to their evidence. The neat cleavage between Chicano and Anglo failed to be so clear-cut in El Paso, Los Angeles, or south Texas. Mario García perhaps stated it best when he concluded:

> Consequently, a dialectical relationship existed between the immigrant's native culture and the attempt by American institutions and reformers to restructure earlier habits and instill a new urban-industrial discipline among the Mexicans. The eventual result: a Mexican border culture, neither completely Mexican nor American, but one revealing contrasting attractions and pressures between both cultures.[28]

In spite of a dual wage structure, segregation, and discrimination, sociocultural change took place in the border community. In brief, as a whole these works constituted a transition away from mere chronicles of victimization to a perspective open to nuance, subtlety, and complexity.

This shift, however, also made for certain dilemmas. Notably, there arose the problem of reconciling two distinctive yet interrelated dimensions over time *and* space: first, the apparent inequities of intergroup relations (Chicano and Anglo); second, the differences in intragroup relations (among Chicanos themselves). If class and race formed the axis of Chicano-Anglo relations, what impact did class and race have within the Chicano community? And, equally important, in what ways was gender to be taken into account to deepen our understanding of both intergroup and intragroup relations? Thus, the surge of published monographs from 1979 to 1984 served to underscore the need for, and contributed to the question of, the conceptualization of Chicano history.

The publication of a special issue of *Review* in 1981 indicated a clear departure from the internal colonial model and other forms of them-versus-us history. The *Review* edition gathered several papers that attempted to merge the issue of race with a class-informed analysis. Influenced also in part by the world-system concept of Immanuel Wallerstein, the articles in *Review* provided a scheme that encompassed geographic and economic variation in the Chicano experience as well as the salience of racial factors. They also acknowledged class differentiation within the Chicano community over time as well as a sensitivity to geographic considerations. The process of capitalist development in the United States, particularly in the Southwest, represented a critical element in the view emanating from the *Review* collection. Though the articles were relatively brief and limited in certain respects by a reliance on secondary sources, they nonetheless offered a different, admittedly schematic, perspective on Chicano history. In sum, despite their schematic quality, the *Review* articles' use of the world-system approach and their emphasis on class analysis added a provocative, fruitful dimension to the racial conflict/colonial "them-versus-us" frameworks of the past.

The thrust of the *Review* papers suggested another interpretation of the conflict between Anglos and Mexicans: a battle among competing economic and political interests. And, in a broader sense, the outcomes of the struggle revealed the disjunction between two countries with enormous differences in their relative levels of development. If cultural antagonism occurred, for instance, it magnified an essentially economic confrontation. Self-interest, for instance, pushed Miguel Otero of New Mexico, a member of the elite, toward assimilation with Anglos. Small landholders, in contrast, found that accommodation held little promise for them to maintain their holdings. The resultant gorras blancas, composed largely of small farmers, were fighting for their livelihood as much as, or more than, for the maintenance of their culture. In light of the approach embedded in the *Review* collection, the varying forms of resistance to Anglo encroachment reflected economic factors, geographic expansion, and race rather than simplistic, one-dimensional explanations, such as, cultural conflict.[29]

Structural Origins of Chicano Diversity

Capitalist development in the United States occurred in a series of fits and starts that leapfrogged certain areas and engulfed others at the same time. And the consequences, when analyzed carefully, failed to meet the easy generalizations of "them-versus-us" history. On several issues, for example, Richard Griswold del Castillo urged historians to "refine" their views on nineteenth-century California in order to "give an accurate picture of the complexity of the transformation of Spanish-speaking California's pastoral economy."[30]

The economy of Los Angeles, Griswold del Castillo noted, differed from that described in Albert Camarillo's study of Santa Barbara, whose economy was apparently decimated by the depression of the 1860s. On this point, Griswold del Castillo concluded that for Los Angeles "the process of property disenfranchisement was well underway *before the 1860s*" (my emphasis). And, he went on to argue that the "economic fortunes of the Angelenos followed a different trajectory from that of the landholders in the surrounding countryside."[31] The more rapid pace of the city's economic development, Griswold del Castillo proposed, accounted for the discrepancy.

Thus, even within adjacent areas, careful scrutiny found contrasting outcomes in the timing of capitalist penetration dominated by the new, non-Spanish-speaking population. Population distribution and growth in Texas, California, and New Mexico varied greatly and had significant implications for the Spanish-speaking communities of those areas. New Mexico, for example, held approximately two-thirds of the Mexican population of the Southwest at the time of the Mexican War. The majority of New Mexico's Hispanos were concentrated in the northern region of the province. In contrast, the Spanish-speaking population of California hugged the coast so that the land boom of the 1840s led to American immigrants being "geographically isolated from the Californios" in the Central Valley.[32] The substantial size and density of the New Mexican population conditioned the gradual entry of Americans *into the same area* as opposed to the initial geographic distance between the American and Mexican populations in California. The location, size, and density of the Mexican population in the two areas distinguished the impact of the "Anglo invasion": for New Mexico it meant a longer period of adjustment to, and defense against, American encroachment; for California, it facilitated the victory of the American immigrants.

As Weber's account of the Mexican frontier illustrates, demography and geography in Texas also figured prominently in the transition away from Mexican control. "*Tejano* oligarchs saw the economic growth in Texas … and their fortunes," Weber observes, "as inextricably linked to the well-being of the Anglo newcomers and their slave-based, cotton growing economy."[33] On the eve of the Texas revolt, *tejanos* were outnumbered ten to one, due in part to efforts of tejanos of the upper class to promote American immigration. Thus, the early geographic thrust of the American influx represented an extension of the spread of the South's cotton economy, and it inevitably edged toward areas occupied earlier by Mexican settlers. In brief, the interface between the spread of American capitalism into northern Mexico and its varying effects revealed basic differences in the demography, geography, and economy of the region.

In this light, Weber's account of the northern Mexican frontier provides an indispensable reference point to assess the repercussions of the
early interaction between the capitalist penetration of the United States
and the Southwest's Spanish-speaking population. The similarities *and
the variation* in that process make works concerning the period *before* U.S.
Mexican hostilities important to understanding the specific consequences
of annexation. In short, the evolving impacts of American rule were not
uniform in their timing, nature, or outcomes.

Responses to Subordination

Despite the diversity that marked the experience of Mexicans in the
post-1848 era, the process of subordination touched the lives of most
Spanish-speaking people. Though a few sustained their middling or upper-
class status, the bulk of such groups suffered downward mobility compared
to their previous place in society. Erosion or loss of landholdings, reduction
in opportunities, or the effects of institutional racism held consequences
for even the upper crust of Mexican rancheros, merchants, and artisans. In
certain areas such as California, the process of subjugation took place rapidly in the wake of the tremendous influx of Americans that overwhelmed
the small coastal settlements of the Spanish-speaking population. In
other regions, the shift in power, numerical superiority, and/or American
geographic expansion differed, such as in New Mexico. Consequently,
the responses by Mexicans varied given their status, resources, and ability
(or time) to respond to the seemingly unavoidable confrontation with
American domination and its consequences.

Most Mexicans, nonetheless, were or became laborers, ranch hands,
farmworkers, railroad crewmen, and the like. While regional variations
occurred, the vast majority of Mexican workers generally faced various forms
of economic discrimination: dual wage structures, job segregation, and racist
labor practices. Organized protest to these conditions took place, yet the work
on Chicano labor history prior to the 1920s suggests a rather paltry record
of strikes, unionization efforts, and overt labor actions. Further research on
Chicano workers in the 1848 to 1900 period may alter this impression. Still,
this apparent lack of labor activism demands explanation.

The answer appears complex and seems further complicated by the
arrival of Mexican immigrant workers. Mario García, for instance, in his
chapter on class, race, and labor in El Paso emphasized that the "Mexicans'
response to their conditions must be seen in light of their motives for

having left Mexico."[34] In García's view, "Mexicans tolerated their economic subordination" because a job in the United States made for a "significant improvement over their previous lower paying or unemployed positions in Mexico."[35]

This does not mean, as García went on to stress, "that Mexicans were incapable of struggling against exploitative conditions."[36] Clearly, there were forces that limited overt resistance, but one must also appreciate the specific circumstances of the Mexican, particularly the immigrant, worker. "To dip into the past for inspiring examples of struggle or the like is to write history backwards and eclectically," Eric Hobsbawm has written. Furthermore, such an approach, the eminent British historian adds, "is not a very good way of writing it [history]."[37] García's treatment of workers in El Paso underscores the wisdom of Hobsbawm's remarks and provides a lesson for students of Chicano labor history.

The historical rendering of Chicano workers, therefore, remains incomplete when reduced to obvious, organized forms of resistance. Rather, Chicano labor history must also take into account more subtle expressions of protestation. Particularly for Mexican labor between 1848 and the 1880s (when immigration accelerated substantially from Mexico), one must take into consideration the structures of power, authority, and economic necessity that forced many Mexican workers to avoid explicit confrontations with their employers (Anglo or Mexican). Instead, the seeming "passivity" of Mexican workers reflected a pervasive and often effective system of repression, compelling Mexican workers to indirect forms of protestation, for example, leaving their jobs, returning to Mexico or moving elsewhere, slowdowns, workplace "sabotage," and other forms of resistance. And the labor movement in the United States into the late nineteenth century held scant hope for Mexican workers for a number of reasons, not the least of which was the general racism that characterized early labor organizations. In sum, the responses of Mexicans to American domination in the post-conquest era contained an essential diversity, including among Mexican workers, whose protests ranged widely in form and magnitude.[38]

In light of the above, the conceptualization of the Chicano experience must be anchored in the extension and penetration of capitalist development in the West. Furthermore, it must be emphasized, several factors mediated the specific outcomes of the interaction between Mexicans and an expanding American economy: local economic structures, geographic location, proximity to the border, ethnic composition of the population, and the presence of Mexicans in the area as merchants, landholders, or political figures. In brief, the interface between Mexicans and the westward movement of American capitalism and its intrinsic racism reflected a variegated, complex process.

Yet, the process of subordination meant more than economic adversity and political disenfranchisement. The entry of Americans into the Southwest also altered in varying, and at times subtle, ways, notions of status, prestige, and identification. To take an example, David Montejano offers an insightful observation concerning south Texas in the late 1920s that merits lengthy quotation:

> In the Mexican counties, Anglos were always careful to make the critical distinction between the "high-status Spanish" and the mass of landless "half-breed" Mexicans ... The absence of a landed Mexican class in the farm areas, however, made such distinctions immaterial ... What this means ... is that Mexicans became a "race"—an inferior people—in areas where they constituted a landless community. The "Castilian" landowners as well as the small Texas Mexican middle class in the cities resented and challenged such stigmas. Not surprisingly, the identification of Mexicans as a distinct "race" became, like the question of political representation and civil rights, an important issue to be settled locally ... Mexican landownership basically settled the question of whether or not Mexicans would become defined and treated as "racial" inferiors.[39]

Thus, American economic expansionism also ushered in a constellation of ideas, values, socializing institutions, and ideological forces that sanctioned and promoted a racist social order.

The economic transformation and racism that marked American rule provoked diverse social and cultural responses among Mexicans, as new reference points arose to denote one's place in society. Segregation failed to provide an effective barrier to the cultural powers of capitalism. At best, the insular world of barrios slowed the entry, but not the ability of capitalism and its racist corollaries to corrode self-esteem, group identity, and cultural commonalities among Mexican communities. The resultant changes pointed to the ways in which the combination of racism and capitalism widened and/or stimulated differences within the Mexican community. As David Weber and others have shown, variations in status were present in the Southwest long before the "conquest." In Texas, for example, the distinctions within the tejano community were clearly visible, notwithstanding the generally racist climate that surrounded Mexican enclaves. As De León has noted in his description of tejano social life:

> Entertainment also reflected the social divisions that existed within the community ... *Tejanos* of means had their social clubs, private dances, and appreciated the literary works of Spain. They recognized their differences to the majority of the community and probably felt more comfortable interacting with other members of their ranking.[40]

But the introduction of American concepts of race (as opposed to those derived from Spanish colonialism) disrupted and then displaced the established notions of prestige and self-worth.[41]

For upper-class Mexicans, links with Americans through business dealings and/or intermarriage took place. And women, it should be noted, were not without choices as well, including exogamy. In New Mexico, for example, racist attitudes failed to block intermarriage, particularly between higher-status Mexicans and Anglos. Class differences, rather than strict considerations of race, influenced at times the calculations leading to interracial unions. On the other hand, class status failed apparently to dictate unions between Mexicans and Anglos, regardless of gender. Given the current evidence, predictable patterns or correlations involving class, gender, and marriage appear difficult to determine with any accuracy.

Nonetheless, the racist ideology toward Mexicans endured, creating a defensiveness within the Mexican community and a subtle pressure to conform to the precepts of being an "American." Some Mexicans were able to bridge the gulf of being "Mexican" and earn a measure of acceptance from "whites." But such "success" was often tied apparently to one's class position. If it was true, for instance, that "for many New Mexican women, a rise in social status accompanied marriage to an Anglo,"[42] the impact of the "white invasion" held repercussions for both class and racial relations within and outside the Mexican community.

Class position, it seems, had the potential of attenuating the consequences of race, since status among Americans pivoted primarily on economic determinants. Without wealth and its trappings, and stigmatized by their ethnicity (race), Mexicans found acceptance in the new dominant social order virtually impossible. Given the economic discrimination that took place against Mexicans, few attained sufficient wealth to gain easy access to non-Mexican society. Racism tended to polarize social relations between gringos and "greasers." Yet, even within barrios, colonias, and "Mextowns," internal differences usually lay beneath the veneer of homogeneity imposed by racist practices.

While some Mexicanos undoubtedly celebrated their social distance from Americans, others felt the discomfort of being "different," the sting of segregation and public rejection. Such feelings provoked perhaps attempts at conformity, and they may have led to a sense of alienation, frustration, and dislocation. For some, if not many, Mexicanos the awareness of racial distinction became a highly sensitive, emotionally laden issue. In this regard, the pioneering research of Genaro Padilla on autobiographical accounts offers insights into the responses of Mexicans to the development of a social and cultural world in the aftermath of conquest that essentially rendered them as "others."[43]

As the disparate evidence cited above suggests, by the 1990s Mexicans in the United States had responded in various forms to their encounters with an essentially racist economy and its socializing institutions. *This process was cumulative, complex, and subject to the conditions in which it took place.* The specific results, however, remain ambiguous as most works continue to employ an Anglo-Chicano dichotomy as the fundamental reference point of their analyses. Male-female relations, gender roles, childhood and adolescence, religion, popular culture, social networks, that is, the inner lives of Mexicanos, have escaped the concerted focus of the historical writings of the last ten years.

Periodization and Conquest

The historical literature on Chicanos under review has examined primarily the period before 1940. The reasons stem from several sources: (a) the assumption (implicit in the number of works on the period before 1930) that the era prior to World War II forms the foundations of inequality between Chicanos and American society; (b) the notion that the years between 1848 and the 1920s establish the conditions that push most Chicanos into the lower-income segments of society; (c) the overt and easily confirmed oppression of Chicanos during this period; (d) the conviction that the origins of the Chicano community derive from the aftermath of the U.S.-Mexican War. As this essay will argue, the 1930s represent a transition to a decisive period in Chicano history.

If this is the case, however, it raises the question of periodization, of the chronological construction of the Chicano past. In this regard, conditions in the northern reaches of New Spain (Mexico), that is, the Spanish borderlands, warrant attention in understanding the context for the interaction between Americans and Spanish-speaking settlers of that region prior to 1821. And Mexico's era of independence must not be ignored; one cannot comprehend Mexico's weakness and vulnerability to American expansionism without understanding the travail of the new nation in the aftermath of its struggle from Spanish colonialism. Finally, the social and cultural character of the Spanish-speaking settlers of northern Mexico before the U.S.-Mexican War cannot be separated from the legacies of Spanish colonialism.

In short, "Chicano history" begins before 1836, and certainly prior to 1848. Chicano historians err if they relegate the pre-1848 period to a perfunctory preface to the U.S.-Mexican War. The actual "conquest" commenced with the Texas revolt of 1836 and culminated with the signing of the Treaty of Guadalupe Hidalgo. In this respect, a full understanding of this period must extend beyond an emphasis on the sources of American imperialism. The underlying causes of Mexico's inability to defend its borders must also be examined, as well as the role of other foreign powers, especially England, in conceding U.S. territorial expansionism.

The postconquest era reflected the consolidation of American domination and the structural incorporation of the Southwest into the U.S. economy, signaled by the completion of the transcontinental railroad (1869). This process took place with wide variations in timing and specific consequences given the context of the locality involved. In my opinion, the years from the 1880s to the 1920s mark a distinctive period in the postconquest era owing to two key elements. First, the period witnessed the hardening of the structures of subordination that eclipsed the remnants of the "Spanish" population, symbolized by the virtual disappearance of the landed elite of preconquest society. Second, the four decades following the railway linking of the East and West accelerated dramatically the absorption of the Southwest into the rapid spread of industrial capitalism. Hence, the general economic development of the West intensified the demand for cheap labor, generating an increasing migration of Mexicans to the region. This latter trend was furthered by the particular conditions in Mexico that induced migration to the United States, including the social consequences of massive foreign investment in the neighboring country.

These two elements formed the basis of the distinction between immigrants and the Spanish-speaking population that derived from the preconquest era. More important, this basic bifurcation in the Mexican/ Spanish-speaking communities of the Southwest occurred despite the similar treatment accorded to both groups by American rule. As a consequence, the discrete public character of the nonimmigrant "Spanish" population diminished, though many of them maintained a private, distinctive sense of identification, that is, Spanish-American. Furthermore, a "leveling" of class differences took place as a result of the process of subordination. Nevertheless, stratification and social hierarchies—including patriarchical attitudes—persisted within Chicano communities. Moreover, in social and cultural terms the arrival of increasing numbers of immigrants changed in many respects the ethos of Spanish-speaking communities in the United States, given the specific context of the area and the cultural characteristics of the immigrant population, for example, their regional origins and their attendant rituals, customs, food, religion, etc.

It should be emphasized that a thin base of evidence underlies this chronological sketch. Large gaps of knowledge remain. Much of the extant literature evokes the victimization and/or resistance of Mexicans as a consequence of the conquest. As a result, certain topics have been slighted with important methodological implications, such as the tendency to minimize the significance of stratification within Chicano communities.

Future research must cast a wider net in order to capture a more complete picture of the Chicano experience from the late 1700s to the 1920s.

As noted earlier, it seems that for most Chicano historians the years from 1836 to the 1920s create the foundations of Chicano inequality. Thus, recent Chicano historiography suggests, if only indirectly, that the Great Depression years represent a pivotal time, as they precipitated a sharp intensification of anti-Mexican sentiment and the dissipation of a thirty-year surge in Mexican immigration.[44] The question remains, however, whether the period after the New Deal signifies an extension of previously established historical patterns, or whether 1940 marks a distinct stage in the Chicano experience.

Modern Chicano History: Problems and Issues

The contemporary era has drawn much less attention, but the few works on the post-1940 period raise key questions for the conceptualization of Chicano history. Three basic issues appear to hold particular importance for the more recent past of Chicano communities: first, the ramifications of American culture and ideology; second, the implications of structural changes in the U.S. economy; third, the effects of recurring immigration from Mexico. These three factors contribute significantly to the increasing differentiation that marks the present Chicano community. Moreover, I would argue, these three broad themes lead to thorny historical problems as well as specific areas of need in Chicano historiography.

CULTURE AND IDEOLOGY

World War II represented a rare moment when the social distance between Anglos and Mexicans diminished before the exigencies of an external threat.[45] The war and its patriotic repercussions pervaded the country and reached deeply into barrios as the calls for unity and victory momentarily softened racial barriers. In this sense, wartime meant an enormous common experience that touched virtually the entire spectrum of the Chicano community. Nonetheless, this common experience failed to stem the growing differentiation among Chicanos. Rather, it served to reveal the community's fragmentation and to crystallize a singular group, that is, the so-called Mexican American generation. "These 'new' Mexican Americans or members of the 'Mexican American generation' increasingly saw themselves as closer to United States conditions," Mario García has concluded, and "especially the more middle class members of this generation sought full integration and achievement of the 'American Dream.'"[46] In this respect, the variation of the Mexican population apparently continued and multiplied in the post–World War II era, with important consequences.

Mauricio Mazón's *The Zoot-Suit Riots* offers a telling confirmation of these changes in the fabric of the Chicano community, changes generated in part by the deepening spread of American culture and ideology. Mazón not only describes the now familiar story of the scapegoating of Mexicans in wartime Los Angeles, but he also uses the Zoot-Suit Riots as a means of understanding American society at a tense historical moment. More significant for our purposes, Mazón's analysis contains incisive observations on the meaning of the zoot-suiter for Mexican Americans. Mazón's discussion on this point reveals the extent to which pressures of conformity had penetrated the Mexican American community. In this regard, Mazón stresses the importance of the criminal stigma associated with Mexican American youth and that "among those who expanded on the deficits of Mexican adolescence were both Mexican and Mexican American writers."[47]

Complementing Mazón's views, Mario García has examined the Coordinating Council for Latin American Youth of Los Angeles in the 1940s. As the group's name implies, the organization strove to rehabilitate the image if not the behavior of Mexican American young people. Taking into account Mazón's conclusions, we can detect a thread of defensiveness running through the activities of the Council: the concern for reforming youth, the promotion of education, the drive for youth employment, criticism of the "bad" press on Mexican American youth, and a stress on being Americans "first." Looked at differently, the work of the Council revealed an attempt to eliminate those aspects of barrio youth that brought a negative light to people of Mexican descent. By implication, this group was aware that its own status was conditioned (and threatened) by "other" Mexicans, in this case, *pachucos*, youth gangs, and Mexican American juvenile delinquents. While the efforts of the Council were commendable, and even courageous at times, they also reflected in part the desire of this group to "blend in," to be accepted, and to take on the responsibility of minimizing those "bad" elements in the community that jeopardized the acceptance of Mexican Americans into the mainstream of American society.[48]

The coupling of García's examination of the Council with Mazón's comments yields an understanding of the Mexican American generation and its formation in the context of American cultural and ideological currents. In this regard, as Gilbert González has shown, young Mexican women were particular targets of "Americanization" schemes since the early 1900s.[49] And one must assume that such efforts achieved a certain measure of success. Thus, as Mario García's seminal study on the Mexican American generation has concluded:

> By the 1930s the political climate among Mexicans, especially the children of immigrants, began to change ... Coming of political age during the reform period of the New Deal and experiencing the patriotic idealism generated by World War II, Mexican Americans expected more from American life than immigrants. For Mexican Americans, there was no going back to Mexico ... They hungrily pursued the American dream.[50]

Nonetheless, class continued to figure importantly in the definition of the Mexican American generation. Based on García's description, much of this group (though not all) was of middling status.

The tie between class and the integrationist viewpoint of this sector of the Mexican American population finds further confirmation in Manuel Peña's *The Texas-Mexican Conjunto*. A merger of social history, anthropology, and ethnomusicology, Peña's study shows the connection between socioeconomic variation in the Mexican community of south Texas and its musical expression. Peña, an anthropologist with a sensitivity to historical change, illustrates how class differences over time generated a new style of music (*orquesta*) that was distinct from the working-class origins of another style, *conjunto*. Peña calls attention to this divergence among tejanos, and he locates its sources in the urbanization and "class differentiation" of the post-Depression years. In short, social mobility, Peña's study suggests, tended to create or exacerbate divisions among Chicanos.

If certain segments experienced social mobility, one consequence was a fracturing of the Chicano community. Yet this divisiveness was not merely economic in origin, but ideological as well. As Peña notes, much of the tejano working class "remained far less accessible to American culture than the emerging middle class, a fact that played a prominent role in the ideological rift between the two classes."[51] The integrationist bent of this tejano middle class corresponds to their disdain for conjunto music and their search for a musical style that signified their disassociation from "them." Apparently, then, the rise in mobility among certain elements of the Mexican American population made them more susceptible to the inroads of cultural forces that valued conformity and that engendered a style commensurate with a higher economic status. In this case, the tejano middle class attempted to deflect the racism against Mexicans generally by distancing themselves from their poorer brethren, that is, by espousing pluralism and affecting a behavior that confirmed their distinct class positions.

Such a conclusion for Chicanos elsewhere, however, rests on skimpy evidence, and generalizations elude much specificity. As García has proposed most forcefully, there appears to be a basis for the emergence of a certain ideological generation in the aftermath of the Great Depression years. To what extent this Mexican American generation reflected wider changes among Chicanos as a whole remains unclear. Peña's work suggests the importance of class cleavages. But Guadalupe San Miguel's study on educational reform in Texas points to the ability of Mexican Americans to forge an effective alliance with working-class tejanos.[52] It may be that Chicanos, regardless of class status, could agree to fight racism and discrimination, but perhaps for differing reasons.

The battles against school segregation in the 1940s and 1950s indicated a heightened sense of ethnic consciousness and assertiveness among Chicanos, yet such expressions of opposition to racist practices failed to represent necessarily a common ideology, only perhaps an acknowledgment of a common enemy. While poor tejanos may have worked to confront racism by the side of their Mexican American counterparts, such cooperation may have been based on different aims. For working-class tejanos, the fight against discrimination may have expressed overtly their everyday struggles against racist institutions and employers. For tejano Mexican Americans, desegregation may have expressed their determination to be accepted by Anglo society and their embrace of American ideals of opportunity and equality. As Peña's work suggests, working-class tejanos may have been much less sanguine than their idealistic Mexican American counterparts;

they may have also been much more discerning and less inclined toward the assimilationist overtones of Mexican American rhetoric.[53]

On the other hand, working-class Chicanos were not entirely immune to the influence and effects of American culture, including its impacts on family life, gender roles, and sexuality. As one study has argued, as early as the 1920s Mexican immigrants confronted the cultural changes among their children in the face of an emergent consumerism and the entry of women into the workforce.[54] Such generational differences seem to have accelerated "in the wake of social changes emanating from war mobilization and mass migration during World War II," including among urban Chicano youth. The resultant "cultural interactions," as George Lipsitz has demonstrated, in "the postwar years brought radically new social formations that encouraged the development of alternative forms of cultural expression."[55] As Lipsitz goes on to show, the changes and shared experiences among poor whites, Blacks, and Chicanos in East L.A. housing projects led to the origins of a distinctive mix in the musical preferences of Chicano youth, leading to the emergence of Chicano rock and roll.[56]

In short, even class similarities failed to reflect necessarily cultural or ideological consensus. Conjunto music coexisted with Ritchie Valens and *La Bamba*; at the same time, the implacable defender of farmworkers, Ernesto Galarza, worked in the midst of the reformist idealism of LULAC and G.I. Forum. Nevertheless, as expressed by the Mexican American generation, class appeared to play a forceful role in the cultural and ideological formation of the Chicano community as the Cold War era ended.

The U.S. Economy and Chicanos after World War II

The concern over status among the Mexican American generation reflected its mobility and the people's desire to accelerate their socioeconomic ascent. The American economy underwent a momentous period of growth because of the particular situation in the world economy during and following World War II, especially in the Southwest where most of the Chicano population was concentrated. The flux created by wartime meant job openings, even for the underemployed Chicana population, jobs that had been difficult if not impossible to acquire before 1940. The postwar boom sustained this greater degree of opportunity for Chicanos; thousands took advantage of their veteran's benefits to gain access to better jobs. Many acquired or enhanced their middling status, furthering the distinctive place of the Mexican American generation in Chicano communities. (It was often this segment in particular and its offspring that were poised by the 1960s to benefit from the Great Society and War on Poverty programs of the Johnson years.)

As the 1960s wore on, however, signs of change in the structure of the U.S. economy appeared that held adverse consequences for most Chicanos. Though it is beyond the scope of this essay to discuss the origins and consequences of this shift in detail, a brief sketch may suffice.[57] First, the now well-recognized process of deindustrialization began to take effect, and the mismanagement of the American economy served to worsen the slide of the United States in comparative terms. Second, the cumulative effects of decades of discrimination and institutional racism meant that most Chicanos were ill-prepared for an economy where higher skills were required for mobility. As a consequence, many Chicanos continued to fall into the rapidly expanding secondary labor market, characterized by low wages and limited possibilities for advancement. Thus, the mobility of the two decades after World War II waned for working-class Chicanos in the 1970s, as the costs of poor schooling in particular became more painfully apparent for an expanding and large proportion of the Chicano population, that is, the Chicano "working poor." Third, the number of jobs in the secondary labor market (the so-called service sector) accelerated through the 1970s and into the 1980s. Meanwhile, the contraction of relatively highly paid (and often unionized) industrial jobs continued.

Hence, in the 1970s and into the present, many working-class Chicanos confronted a ceiling to their mobility. The residue of past racism, especially educational neglect, coupled with the changes in the American economy, exacerbated the disparities among Chicanos as well as between Chicanos and American society as a whole. While a small segment of Chicanos achieved notable gains in income and job status, most Chicanos experienced either modest gains or downward mobility.

Fourth, these shifts in the economy took place with particular force (and volatility) in the so-called Sun Belt, including the Southwest. Consequently, the concentration of the high-tech industry and the well-paid sectors of the service economy in the Southwest, especially California, paralleled a similar growth in the same region's low-paid secondary labor market. While the Southwest has generally avoided the harshest problems of the Rust Belt, the region has not been untouched by the consequences of an American economy losing ground to other industrialized nations, notably Japan.[58] Fifth, the combination of a declining

American economy and the fiscal conservatism of the 1980s had especially negative consequences for cities. Again, while the Southwest escaped the trenchant blight of eastern cities, the level of urbanization of the Chicano population spelled an intensification of the problems faced by inner-city, poor Chicanos: bad schools, inefficient public transportation, housing woes, and the growing suburbanization of labor. Many of these problems had their origins in federal, state, and local policies that extended back at least to the 1950s. The social costs of these policies (or lack of them) fell disproportionately on the urban poor, including large proportions of the Chicano population. And rural Chicanos remained among the poorest segments of American society.[59]

The effects of this process have yet to be fully assessed and its long-term consequences are a realm beyond the hand of the historian. It appears, nonetheless, that the burdens were (and continue to be) especially difficult for poor Chicano youth in the contemporary era because of the overwhelming presence of a culture at odds with the daily realities of impoverished young people. In a consumer culture, a crucial confrontation for the poor often occurs during adolescence: a critical moment when sexual, social, and cultural aspects of identity frequently converge with particular intensity. The wider society with its culture of consumption has sustained ideals and views of self-worth that have made the poor aware of their difference—a difference magnified by the constant racial imagery propagated by the mass media.[60]

The cumulative cost, particularly it seems since the 1960s, has been a deepening alienation among the poorer segments of the Chicano population, especially youth. Without the resources to acquire the trappings of status defined by a consumer culture they can neither ignore nor escape, poor Chicanos have often turned to alternative, and at times socially unacceptable, forms of expression: increasingly, it appears, self-validation and self-esteem among poor young Chicanos reflect a sharp sense of frustration and/or disillusion. The numbers of Chicanos in gangs, youth detention facilities, prisons, and rehabilitation centers of various sorts appear to be growing. The historical basis of this phenomenon, however, continues unexplored. The recent work of Martin Sánchez-Jankowski, Joan Moore, Ruth Horowitz, and James Diego Vigil documents primarily the contemporary outcomes of a historical process for significant segments of the Mexican-origin population.[61]

The question remains: Is this a new, distinctive turn in Chicano social history? *Pelado, pachuco, cholo* and related terms have had over time distinctive meanings in Chicano communities, that is, they have been

historically specific. The term *pachuco*, for instance, is not chronologically synonymous with low rider: in the 1940s few pachucos had cars for
cruising. Such terms possessed a subtle but significant meaning, as they
were often ascribed pejoratively to a particular stratum of the Chicano
community. This specific social vocabulary reflected a distinctive segment
with discernibly different modes of dress, vernacular, rituals, and notions
of status. Moreover, many Chicanos tended to associate pachucos, cholos,
zoot-suiters, and others similarly defined with crime, drug abuse, and related
"bad" behavior. Nonetheless, the historical analysis of this thread in the
social fabric of Chicano social life has been largely ignored by students of
the Chicano past. (In contrast, Chicano literature has given much attention to such groups.) To put the issue more provocatively, were such groups
indicative of the formation of a Chicano "underclass," to use the term
coined by the Black sociologist William J. Wilson?[62] If so, are the historical causes of this Chicano "underclass" the same as for Blacks, assuming
the validity of Wilson's analysis? Note should be made here that Wilson's
argument is historically grounded, emphasizing the structural shifts in the
economy and the social consequences of discrimination, particularly for
Black males.

On the surface, the evidence suggests that a Chicano "underclass"
does exist. But the specific characteristics assigned to the term beg an
important question: Is this a new development in Chicano social history?
The scattered evidence past and present suggests that there has been a
pivotal turn in Chicano social life since the 1960s for a particular segment
of Chicano communities. Still, despite the long tradition of attention to
Chicano delinquency, the historical analysis of the intersection of poverty,
prejudice, and economic change remains essentially undone.[63]

Similarly, there has been scant historical research on female-headed
households, teenage pregnancy, or single motherhood.

Again, there has been a surge of publications and research on this issue
recently (owing in part to the "underclass" debate). Nevertheless, the question
for the historian is whether teenage pregnancy, for instance, represents a different meaning in the contemporary era compared to the past. Clearly, teenage
pregnancy occurred among Chicanos. The crux of the issue, however, centered
on the marriage of the young woman. Apparently, social pressures were such
that most men felt compelled, or were compelled, to marry the young woman.
This seems to have changed—but if so, when and why? Or, stated differently,
young men evidently appear in recent times to be much less compelled to
marry women that they have impregnated than was the case in the past. On

the other hand, it may be that young pregnant women exercise much greater choice in the decision whether to marry or not than was the case in the past. While recent studies give us an understanding of this issue in contemporary terms, we have few historical benchmarks at this time to examine with much viability the causes and consequences of this apparent change.[64]

In sum, the social common ground among Chicanos has, it seems, lessened substantially. Class differences have been compounded by generational change, cultural variations, attitudinal diversity, and differing notions of ethnic ideology. In part, this social differentiation suggests change endogenous to the Chicano community (e.g., immigration from Mexico). But this further fracturing of the Chicano community also reflects the pressures of American culture and ideology, such as the social imperatives of consumerism, the strong ageism of U.S. popular culture, and the persistence of Cold War conservatism.[65]

The key issue remains, nonetheless, the long-term effects of low socioeconomic status and its consequences. The combination of persistent poverty and the impact of American culture and ideology has, it appears, distanced a growing proportion of Chicanos, especially youth, from other Chicanos. As a result, the meaning of these differences reflected (and continue to do so) a deepening fragmentation of notions of identification among Chicanos. As one scholar found recently, for example, in a California high school:

> Mexican-descent students have multiple identities in which symbols, stereotypes, and styles assume great significance. Among these students, maintaining separate identities as "Mexican," "Mexican American," "Chicano," or "cholo" appears to be important in their lives at school. These labels are emblems that carry meaning both to those who so name themselves and to outside observers.[66]

In this study, the author goes on to note the particular problem of those students whose identity as "Chicanos" or "cholos" leads to a "forced-choice dilemma: they must choose between doing well in school or being a Chicano [or cholo]."[67] The author concludes that for such groups their identity at school represents an "oppositional process":

> The construction of this identity is thus at once a product of both *historical exclusion and structural subordination* [my emphasis] imposed by the dominant group, and a vehicle used by the oppressed group to resist structured inequality.[68]

These differences among Chicano high school students mirror, therefore, the outcomes of historical changes within and outside the Chicano community.

More important, the consequent stratification and differentiation has led, it seems, to a furthering of the social rifts among Chicanos, where the resultant boundaries have created differing notions of self in the context of American society *and* the Chicano community.

The Impact of Immigration

Immigration represents a fundamental source of the continuing differentiation within the Chicano community. The insights provided by Romo, García, and Camarillo into an earlier period, for instance, should not be lost on students of the post–World War II era of Chicano history. Those works suggest the importance of continuing waves of immigrants and their interaction not only with American society, but with established enclaves of previous Mexican immigrants as well.[69]

Immigrants generally differ upon arrival from their American-born counterparts; and the *recién llegado* should remind historians of the different ways of "seeing" self and society in the Chicano experience in specific times and places. In this sense, immigration adds a dimension to Chicano communities, such as a renewal of their "Mexicanness." Yet, the historian's analysis of the meaning of immigration must be construed carefully, especially regarding questions of culture, identity, and ideology. As the anthropologist Renato Rosaldo warns, "cultures themselves never are sealed by impermeable membranes, but instead they are always in process, borrowing and lending across their porous boundaries, and inventing ever new scenes and combinations of scenes."[70]

Mario García's essay on the varying meaning of the border over time for Mexicans in the United States affirms Rosaldo's contention. García's examination of the border as a symbol, however, goes further. He argues for a framework involving three distinct eras: the immigrant era (1900–1930), the Mexican American era (1930–1960), and the Chicano era (1960–1970). By focusing on the border as a reference point, García illuminates the changing relationship between Mexico and Mexicans in the United States. In this regard, García concentrates on the views of certain figures and intellectuals of Mexican origin in the United States. His explication of their work and of his chronological scheme suggests a useful, enlightening framework for the ideological analysis of the Mexican immigrant experience in the United States.[71] Neglected in this otherwise excellent essay, on the other hand, are the Mexican immigrants who continued to arrive during the last two of García's "eras." The author, it is important to emphasize, has captured essentially one dynamic or dimension of the Mexican experience in the United States: that of the Mexican immigrant era and its offspring.

As a whole, the Mexican immigrant experience of the last forty years or so remains largely unexamined. The few works on braceros, for instance, tend to chronicle primarily their exploitation as workers. In this respect, Dennis Valdés's excellent monograph on agricultural workers in the Midwest adds importantly to our knowledge of Mexicano workers in a geographic area often neglected by Chicano history. Valdés's valuable study is enhanced by its inclusion of Puerto Rican immigrant workers and its careful analysis of the development of agribusiness in that region and its implications for farm labor. Moreover, the extraordinary work of Erasmo Gamboa, *Mexican Labor and World War II*, represents a fresh examination of the braceros, as he delves sensitively into the daily lives of Mexican nationals as well as the more familiar story of the harsh working conditions confronted by Mexicano laborers. And, like Valdés, Gamboa locates his study in an area (the Pacific Northwest) often ignored by Chicano-related historical writings. More important, the works by Gamboa and Valdés underscore the need to examine the braceros, and those Mexican workers who followed, as part of another immigrant generation distinct from that earlier generation suggested by Mario García and others. [72]

This post-1940 generation of Mexicanos and their experience of adjustment, including the process of cultural change, continue to be slighted by historians. On this point, Rosaldo offers an important insight: "The key questions of cultural reproduction involve the means by which communities ... perpetuate themselves through time, as dynamic constellations and not static entities."[73] García's essay on the frontera demonstrates Rosaldo's dictum for a specific cohort of the Mexican-origin community in the United States, but not necessarily for the immigrants after 1940. The historical rendering of the immigrant—who came with the bracero program, who overcame "Operation Wetback" and the termination of the bracero program in 1964, and who continued to arrive thereafter—awaits an author. Significantly, this neglect suggests a persistent flaw in Chicano scholarship: the tendency to underestimate the importance of continuing immigration, including the complexities of Chicano-Mexicano relations in the formation of Chicano communities since World War II. And, though the controversy over contemporary immigration has fueled prodigious amounts of research, it sustains a preoccupation with economic considerations and an aversion for understanding the Chicano-Mexicano dimensions of Mexican immigration.[74]

The works of Rodolfo de la Garza, one of the very few Chicano scholars studying the topic, represent the general failure of Chicano scholarship to illuminate the nature and consequences of immigration.[75] For example, de la Garza paints recent immigrants as essentially apolitical, though events in Mexico contradict the premises of de la Garza's conclusions. The upsurge of oppositional movements in the 1988 Mexican elections clearly refutes the notion that most poor Mexicans avoid politics or are incapable of political expression. And in 1989, for the first time in sixty years, the dominant party in Mexico was forced to concede a governorship to an opposition party. Furthermore, in the small rural community of Watsonville, California, a coalition involving a large number of recent immigrants successfully challenged in court the method of local elections in order to assure greater representation for the Mexican-origin, primarily poor, community of the town.[76] Other instances of such political cooperation have taken place, undermining de la Garza's observations on immigrant-Chicano political relations. Indeed, his depiction of the immigrant has much more to do with the failure of Chicano organizations than with the underlying political character of recently arrived Mexicanos.

De la Garza compounds his error by misreading the past. He argues, for example, that concerns over status underlined the opposition of Mexican Americans to immigration in the 1940s and 1950s. On this point, he disregards the work of Ernesto Galarza, who opposed the abuse of braceros by employers, not the immigrants themselves. (Galarza was an immigrant himself.) Thus, the extent and causes of anti-immigrant sentiment among Mexican Americans were much more complex than de la Garza admits.[77] Moreover, de la Garza's reading of Mexicanos and Mexico contributes to the misunderstanding of this issue. For instance, he suggests that the "complete reversal" of policy by the Mexican government after 1940 concerning the "well-being of Mexican-origin people in the United States" was tied to anti-*pocho* views in Mexico.[78] This mistaken interpretation reaches a low point with his explication regarding the tensions between Mexicanos and Chicanos by the 1960s. Adequate research would have easily demonstrated that the tensions between Chicanos and Mexicanos extended back to the nineteenth century, rendering his conclusion misleading at best: "By the 1960s, then, these two populations had become sufficiently different that Mexican immigrants could no longer expect to be welcomed by Mexican Americans as they had been a century earlier."[79]

De la Garza's misinformed history and his insufficient knowledge of Mexico lead him to a misreading of the meaning of Mexican immigration.

Specifically, he fails to discuss the frequent inability and/or unwillingness of Chicano organizations to address the concerns of Mexican immigrants with much imagination or sensitivity. While de la Garza is quick to ascribe the problem to the attributes of immigrants, he eschews a substantive analysis of Chicano organizations and their inability to understand the recién llegados, including their political potential. Given de la Garza's stature in the field of Chicano studies, it is especially disheartening to find in the late 1980s the persistence of such shallow analyses on Chicano-Mexicano relations, past and present. In short, de la Garza's writings on this topic indicate the general impoverishment of Chicano scholarship on immigration, particularly Chicano-Mexicano relations.[80]

The sum of the previously cited works, especially those of Mazón, García, Peña, and Griswold del Castillo, implies a continuing if not widening diversity among Chicanos after the Depression years. In this process, it appears that World War II represents a watershed in the periodization of the Chicano experience. The current evidence, though sketchy, points to three factors in particular that influence the Chicano community in the post-1940 era: the deepening impact of American culture and ideology; the variation produced by the differential incorporation of Chicanos into a structurally changing American economy; and recurring immigration from Mexico. The combination of these effects leads, it seems, to a further fragmentation of the Chicano community into increasingly distinct segments. Nonetheless, it must be emphasized, these processes of differentiation have been framed by the legacies and outcomes of an enduring racism, however subtle, and by the consequences of class differences among Chicanos.

The Uses of Chicano History

Chicano historical writing began with a disposition to interpret the past as a group experience, to seek commonalities rather than divisive elements. As recent scholarship has shown, such premises were questionable and, to a considerable extent, misleading. Differences among Chicanos understandably, if not predictably, surfaced in the definition of the political goals of Mexicano/Mexican American/Chicano organizations in the past and into the present. In fact, recent works provide the historical basis for the divergent political directions that punctuated the so-called Chicano movement from the 1960s to the present. The unity to which early Chicano writers appealed was not necessarily grounded in the past.

Given the political context in which Chicano scholarship originated, the search for common historical threads paralleled the search for a means to organize Chicanos into a viable and coherent political force. Activists in this sense "used" history as an ideological base for concerted action. Among many examples borrowed for political purpose, the most accomplished and reasoned was undoubtedly the work by Mario Barrera, *Race and Class in the Southwest*. Plumbing an extensive secondary historical literature, Barrera proposed a "class-differentiated colonial perspective" that fused appropriate elements of internal colonialism, Marxism, and labor segmentation theory. Aware of the differentiation within the Chicano community, Barrera nonetheless argued in a key passage that a common ground existed "*based on the common experience of discrimination*" (my emphasis).[81]

Still, Barrera admits that the "various Chicano subordinate segments have certain interests in common, their colonial interests, and certain interests in opposition, their class interests."[82] More important, Barrera acknowledges that the "segmentation line has been weakening at least since the Second World War."[83]

And, he proceeds to state that the persistence of the trend "will mean that class divisions will become more salient as Chicanos become more integrated into the non-subordinate part of the labor force."[84] Hence, despite certain commonalities in the Chicano experience, class differences suggest tenuous ground for solidarity and unified political action. Barrera's work, therefore, supplies a provocative, but ultimately incomplete analysis. His preoccupation with the structural aspects of the Chicano experience underestimates the apparent class and ideological divisions that sustain the distance between and among segments of the Chicano community from the 1960s to the present.[85]

In this light, one cannot escape the conclusion that the "Chicano movement" encompassed, in fact, several movements, overlapping at times, yet frequently in contrast. As Carlos Muñoz's new study shows, even among the "Chicano" student elements, sharp differences arose at the height of the so-called *movimiento*[86] (not unlike the differences that surfaced among other minority-based social movements). Thus, as Muñoz demonstrates, the accomplishments of the so-called movimiento not only were constrained by its "Anglo" opposition, but the internal ideological dissension among Chicanos also played a role—a dissension rooted in the historic differences within the Chicano community. For example, Muñoz distinguishes the views of the "Mexican American" generation of the 1940s and 1950s from those of their counterparts of the late 1960s and early 1970s, who tended to reject the moderate reformism of their predecessors. Yet, as Muñoz points out with poignant irony, the "Chicano movement" fragmented in part because of divergent political influences, regional differences, and class distinctions despite the nationalist rhetoric that punctuated the movimiento. This conclusion resonates with the revealing, highly personal description provided by Ignacio García of the rise and fall of La Raza Unida party.[87] In short, the ideological rifts among Chicanos in the 1960s and 1970s reflected the political consequences of a historical process, where the patriotism of World War II and Cold War conservatism produced a distinct ideological context for "Mexican Americans"; this context changed radically with the 1960s, leading to a basic difference between "Chicanos" and "Mexican Americans."[88] The resultant differences represented a major obstacle to the development of a progressive political project capable of embracing the diversity among people of Mexican origin. Law enforcement agencies, federal programs, political parties, and local and state institutions exploited this weakness in various ways (deliberately and inadvertently) to frustrate the efforts at unity by radical Chicano organizations.[89] Thus, Muñoz's work advances our understanding of the difficulties facing Chicano political efforts, particularly among more radical, youth-based organizations.

On the other hand, the political history of the post-1940 period for Chicanos rests on a handful of disparate studies leaving substantial issues unclarified. In this regard, Juan Gómez-Quiñones has written a dense, yet informative political history, but much of his narrative covers familiar ground.[90] The monograph yields few significant new insights as most of the points raised appear in the studies of other Chicano scholars, such as Mario García, Carlos Muñoz, Rodolfo Acuña, Mario Barrera, and Ignacio García. While Muñoz and others have supplied portraits of the Chicano movement and its limitations, there are no comparable studies of Chicano political initiatives covering the period since the 1970s. As one study on Black and Hispanic struggles for political incorporation put it:

> Although these findings do tell us much of the reason why minorities in some cities mobilized, entered coalitions, and gained incorporation more strongly than others, they do not "explain" why minorities mobilized in the first place.[91]

The recent work of Felix Padilla, on Mexican American and Puerto Rican coalitions in Chicago, suggested that programs of political incorporation promoted a broadly based sense of ethnic political consciousness.[92] In a similar vein, one study found that:

> Hispanic leaders were politicized and brought into the electoral arena by
> their experience with demand-protest, with federal programs of the six-
> ties and early seventies, and with the establishment of community-based
> organizations to influence or to run such programs.[93]

Thus, incorporation conceivably held the capacity to raise the political
consciousness, *and* to facilitate the cooptation, of Chicano leaders, as well
as to undermine more radical Chicano organizations.[94]

In the absence of further historical research, however, the political
expression of Chicanos since World War II will remain pieces of a larger
puzzle. Nonetheless, it is important to note that a them-versus-us perspective of the Chicano past invited a false sense of historical solidarity among
Chicano activists of the 1960s and 1970s. The scholarship of the last decade
contradicts such a simplification of Chicano history. In this light, to insist on
a crude nationalist approach to Chicano political organizing is a rejection of
the past and its lessons.

New Directions for Historical Research

Recent Chicano historiography, in spite of its strengths, reveals certain shortcomings that must be addressed by students of the Chicano past. Four key areas
of need can be identified. First, as this review demonstrates, there is an urgent
need for research on Chicanas. Most of the studies under review include women
in their examination of occupational patterns, labor relations, and other areas
related to employment. Still, the deeper questions of male-female relations,
family, child rearing, and the like remain often unexplored. More than a
function of the scarcity of sources, this neglect also indicates a major dilemma
facing the field of women's history. Several years ago, Gerda Lerner pointed
to the problem of conceptualizing women's history where issues of class and
race would not be ignored. More specifically, Jacqueline Jones, in her history
of Black women, remarks disconcertingly that women's history continues "for
all intents and purposes race-specific in its narrow conception of historical
changes as they affected women's work."[95]

Clearly, historians must begin to explore this dimension of the Chicano experience in a way that is sensitive to the critical place of women
in the formation of the Chicano community without losing sight of the
differentiation that apparently occurred among women themselves.[96]
Patricia Zavella, for example, has pulled together several threads of inquiry
to offer a rich, provocative essay on women affected by the recent "Sun
Belt industrialization" of Albuquerque, New Mexico. Though the author

(an anthropologist) focuses on the familial impacts, the study incorporates various elements of economic history, local change, age difference, labor experiences, and types of work. Despite the small scale of the work, Zavella nonetheless supplies a textured portrayal of the lives of women adapting to large-scale structural and social change.[97]

On the other hand, the distinction between women's history and family history must be drawn. Given the dearth of Chicano social history, one must applaud the publication of Richard Griswold del Castillo's *La Familia: Chicano Families in the Urban Southwest, 1848 to the Present*. The sweep of his work will make it a reference point for future historians. As such, the work will surely provoke debate over the author's methodology and his substantial reliance on modernization theory (mistakenly in my opinion) to inform his analysis and conclusions.[98] Regardless of one's view of Griswold del Castillo's effort, the fact remains that the history of women must not be confused with that of the Chicano family.

Indeed, when driven by distinct theoretical arguments, Chicana history can be seen in a vastly different light. Antonia Castañeda, in an insightful and landmark essay focusing on Spanish-Mexican women on the frontier, expresses clearly the larger question facing Chicana history and deserves lengthy citation:

> The threads of Spanish-Mexican women's history run throughout these sources. *What is missing is an approach to the history of the frontier that integrates gender, race, and culture or class as categories of historical analysis* [my emphasis]. An integrative ethnohistorical approach would enable us to examine women's roles and lives in their societies of origin, as well as to describe and interpret how conquest changed their lives and restructured economic and social relationships not only between the sexes but also among persons of the same sex .... But it is premature to generalize about women and race relations, intermarriage and assimilation on the frontiers of expansion. We have not yet done the research.[99]

Castañeda's observations, I would argue, apply to the history of Chicanas beyond the frontier era. As a consequence, the lack of research on Chicanas and of an adequate approach to the complexity of their lives hinders substantially a full understanding of the Chicano experience. Until this shortcoming is addressed, Chicano history will remain essentially incomplete.

The complex historical questions generated by gender underscore the second area that historians need to explore carefully, namely, the role of immigration, of recién llegados, in Chicano history, particularly in the post-1940 era. In this respect, the relationships between new immigrants and previous generations of immigrants represent an important focus of analysis. The work of Patricia Zavella is again instructive on this point.[100] In her study on female cannery workers, the variance and occasional tensions between Mexicanas and Chicanas surface frequently in her portrait of their work experience. In this sense, Zavella echoes a point made nearly sixty years ago by Manuel Gamio in his pioneering research on Mexican immigrants in the United States published in 1931.[101] In brief, Chicano historians must acknowledge more so than before the continuing significance of immigration for a full understanding of the Chicano experience. As noted earlier in my comments on the work of Rodolfo de la Garza, Chicano scholarship in this regard continues to be inadequate. Fortunately, recent works on immigration, by Douglas Massey and coauthors Alejandro Portes and Robert Bach in particular, provide a number of useful insights for students of Chicano history since 1940.

Immigration suggests a third area of concern for Chicano history, that is, the impact of American culture and ideology on the Mexican origin community. On this point, the current discussion among historians of the influence of advertising, the mass media, fashion, consumerism, and related issues holds important possibilities for examining the sources, as well as the consequences, of the ideological variation among Chicanos, particularly after 1940.[102] As noted earlier, a recent essay by George Lipsitz illustrates how the widespread sociocultural consequences of World War II and its aftermath engendered a distinctive milieu in Los Angeles that witnessed the emergence of new forms of cultural expression, including the appearance of "Chicano" rock and roll.[103] By placing his discussion of the appearance of Chicano rock and roll within the larger cultural context of the time, Lipsitz enriches greatly our understanding of this historical period and its social impacts on Chicano youth and its musical expression. Furthermore, as Manuel Peña's work exemplifies, historians must not lose sight of the manifestations of "counter ideology" among Chicanos, without falling prey to romanticizing such expressions.

This last point underscores the necessity of taking into account the specific texture of American society, a fourth area of need in Chicano history. The recent wave of Chicano historical scholarship has tended to concentrate on certain geographic areas or cities. As a result, the interface between Chicanos and broad trends in the U.S. economy, polity, and culture possesses a disparate quality, given the diversity of the Chicano community. For example, in *Protest Is Not Enough*, the authors examine communities in northern California to assess the impact of the political incorporation of Latinos in the 1960s and 1970s. The utility of their observations and conclusions for other cities with sizable Latino populations, in light of the historical differences between Oakland, California and San Antonio, Texas, for instance, is subject to much debate, in my opinion.[104]

Thus, historians must make an effort to break the parochial bent that has characterized Chicano historical writing. And, as Erasmo Gamboa and Juan García show in two informative articles, students of the Chicano past have concentrated on the Southwest, neglecting other geographic areas.[105] (Indeed, a crucial but neglected area of research is the historical geography of the Chicano population.) To put it briefly, Chicano history would be enormously improved by work that compares different geographic areas in the context of political, economic, and social currents in American history.

The Challenge of Future Chicano Historical Research

An important, if not critical, challenge faces future Chicano historical research: its capacity to ask different questions of the Chicano past, to bring a fresh perspective to the relations between people of Mexican origin and non-Mexicans, as well as relations among people of Mexican descent. In his forthcoming book on marriage and honor in New Mexico from the 1600s to the 1950s, for instance, Ramón Gutiérrez weaves a variety of historical threads to produce a textured, illuminating analysis of social life in New Mexico from 1690 to 1846.[106] His use of concepts from other disciplines enriches his discussion and contributes importantly to his sensitive and probing explanation of a complicated social process. Gutiérrez's examination encompasses parent-child relations, patriarchy, class considerations, religion, and economic change providing a compelling argument for the changes in the institution of marriage in pre-1846 New Mexico. The wide range of Gutiérrez's approach (Spanish colonial history, early Mexican historiography, medieval notions of honor, race relations, and feminism, among others) and his mastery of various historical sources (demography, archival research, court testimony, travelers' accounts, etc.) mark his research as a major advance in the writing of Chicano history.

If Gutiérrez's book represents a fresh example for early Chicano history, the work of David Montejano offers a similar case of a more contemporary nature. In his deservedly highly praised, award-winning book, *Anglos and Mexicans in the Making of Texas, 1836–1986*, Montejano emphasizes the changes wrought by the impact of capitalism primarily on south Texas, leading to shifts from a ranch to farm, and then to an urban-industrial economic order.[107] Thus, Montejano brings to his analysis a conceptual framework anchored in a structural approach that recognizes the fundamental racism that attended the capitalist development of south Texas. His insightful argument gains much force from his attention to local political and economic characteristics, as he persuasively points out the significance of landownership patterns and county politics in the expression of class and race relations. Montejano's approach offers an important lesson to historians through his careful linking of local conditions and class and race relations to larger economic forces.

In both cases, Montejano and particularly Gutiérrez have enhanced their analyses by their ability to utilize an interdisciplinary approach and to cross subfields within the discipline. More important, Gutiérrez's research represents a powerful corrective to the tendency in early Chicano history to minimize the importance of the period before the "Anglo takeover," in contrast to the apparent eagerness to document the travail of Mexicans after 1846 in the Southwest in earlier works by Chicano historians. Furthermore, Gutiérrez reveals the dynamic, diverse nature of the Spanish-speaking communities of New Mexico—and one can assume some degree of generality elsewhere—before the arrival of "Anglos." Significantly, Gutiérrez's analysis demonstrates the links and interaction between larger socioeconomic forces and community life in terms of personal values and behavior. As such, it is a mature, pathbreaking, landmark work in Chicano history.

Less comprehensive though no less significant, Montejano's excellent work constitutes a forceful refutation of them-versus us history. His rendering of class and race relations in Texas yields a nuanced, convincing portrait of the evolution of Mexican and Anglo relations. Nonetheless, for all of their formidable attributes, the works by Gutiérrez and Montejano are not without shortcomings. Montejano has suggested, for example, the applicability of his framework to the Southwest as a whole. Instead, it appears that Montejano offers a fine study from which to understand the differences between South Texas and other parts of the region. For instance, Montejano correctly stresses the unevenness of capitalist development, yet his notion of a "peace structure" is compromised precisely because of the variation in the capitalist penetration of former Mexican territory.[108] According to Montejano: where the Mexican population remained a sizable population, the new authorities generally sought to establish a "peace structure." Under this arrangement, the Mexican settlements were usually allowed limited representation in the new government, but authority relations were structured so that in no instances would Mexicans stand over Anglos.[109]

Outside of a very few pockets of settlement, the Southwest in 1848 was marked by the lack of "sizable Mexican populations." The Jim Crow–like "peace structure" depicted by Montejano held for south Texas, in part because of the density and particular characteristics of the rural tejano population and the attendant social setting of the area. In California, the pattern of relations differed considerably. Hence, a basic difference—rather than the similarities—in the trajectory of the experience of Chicanos in Texas and California is greatly clarified by Montejano's explication of class and race relations in south Texas.[110]

The work of Gutiérrez and Montejano (as well as that of others) indicates a transition, an advance in Chicano historical scholarship that will sharpen the debate over interpretation and conceptualization. Significantly, Chicano historians are not alone in grappling with this dilemma. It may reflect to some degree the larger problem of historically interpreting contemporary America. As Alan Brinkley observed on this issue a short time ago, "historical scholarship [on twentieth-century America] has become fragmented, compartmentalized, diffuse."[111] In a recent issue of the *Journal of American History*, a discussion regarding synthesis in the writing of U.S. history provoked widely divergent responses. Particularly important, the notion of agency, of the capability of individuals to respond to the power of larger political economic and ideological forces, was a key point of debate. This questioning of a basic tenet of the new social history has crucial implications for the construction of Chicano history.[112]

Chicano historians, like most other minority scholars, have focused on the origins of subordination, locating them primarily in the intersection of racism and capitalism. This has led to three general concerns to document the capacity of Chicanos to resist their subordination: political underrepresentation, economic inequity, and social inequality. Yet the costs of subordinate status over a long period of time contain elements less easily discerned than the results of electoral campaigns, unemployment figures, income distribution charts, or housing statistics. It is important to recognize the process of subordination and its capacity to penetrate the lives of individuals. In his analysis of Chicano autobiographies, Genaro Padilla has argued that "cultural denial" has occurred in the past as well as the present. Thus, as Padilla goes on to note, "Richard Rodriguez ... is by no means the first Chicano autobiographer who has publicly disaffiliated himself from his culture in order to assume the mask of the 'middle class'

American."[113] In this light, students of the past must come to grips with the fact that Chicanos "can share a kind of half-conscious complicity in their own victimization."[114] Complicity, or consent, in this sense contradicted the binary essentialism of nationalist Chicano historical writing and its narrow construction of subordination. "In this view," as Rosa Linda Fregoso and Angie Chabram have noted, "Chicano identity was a static, fixed, and one-dimensional formulation. It failed to acknowledge our historical differences in addition to the multiplicity of our cultural identities as a people." Fregoso and Chabram go on to conclude: "This representation of cultural identity postulated the notion of a transcendental Chicano subject at the same time that it proposed that cultural identity existed outside of time and that it was unaffected by changing historical processes." As a consequence, Fregoso and Chabram insist, correctly in my opinion, that "critical points of difference were often overlooked. These critical points of difference and the experience of rupture and discontinuity also shape our identities in decisive ways, for instance, the heterogeneous experiences of migration, conquest, and regional variation."[115]

In this light, Richard Rodriguez's autobiographical work, *Hunger of Memory*, becomes a telling historical document: evidence of that complicity, I would argue, not unknown or unique in the history of people of Mexican origin. Rather, we must acknowledge that Chicanos may participate in maintaining a political and social order that serves to legitimate their domination.[116] Such a view is at odds with the perspective that has characterized much of the writing of Chicano history, and more generally, much of American social history in the last two decades. I would go further: to stress the overt oppression of Chicanos, and/or their explicit resistance to it, leads only to a partial view of the past and to an incomplete understanding of the historical effects of racism, sexism, and capitalism.

In this respect, historians of the Chicano experience can learn much from the observation of Linda Kerber regarding women's history: "To continue to use the language of separate spheres is to deny the reciprocity of gender and society, and to impose a static model on a dynamic relationship."[117] In a similar vein, Linda Alcoff, citing Teresa de Lauretis, has argued

> that an individual's identity is constituted with a historical process of consciousness, a process in which one's history is interpreted or reconstructed by each of us within the horizon of meanings and knowledges available in the culture at given historical moments ... Consciousness, therefore, is never fixed, never attained once and for all, because discursive boundaries change with historical conditions.[118]

Alcoff continues by emphasizing the "positionality" of women that "makes her identity relative to a constantly shifting context, to a situation involving others, the objective economic conditions, cultural and political institutions and ideologies." Alcoff, however, is quick to stress that her notion of identity is not determined "solely by external elements," where the "woman herself is merely a passive recipient of an identity created by these forces."[119] From this perspective, agency remains in the making of history, in which "Chicano" may mean "to take up a position within a moving historical context and to be able to choose what we make of this position and how we alter this context."[120] Such a view of the Chicano experience allows for a Gregorio Cortez and a Richard Rodriguez; Cortez chose explicit resistance and Rodriguez perhaps represents the "spectacle of the cultural 'other' trying various means of transformation into [an] American."[121] This supple view of the Chicano past departs from the essentialism of them-versus-us history and sustains the significance of agency in the making of Chicano history. Understanding the "horizon of meanings" and "context" in a full sense becomes, in my view, an important task for future Chicano historical inquiry.[122]

Summary and Conclusion

Utilizing recent historical scholarship, this essay has emphasized the fundamental diversity of the Chicano experience, a diversity complicated by an expanding American capitalism and its attendant cultural forces, including its pervasive racism. I have argued that the post-Depression era witnessed an acceleration of an antecedent differentiation because of a widening class structure in the Mexican-origin community, and as a result of the pressures exerted by an increasingly penetrative hegemonic order. This hegemonic order (which I have proposed here, based, I admit, on a small number of texts) has exacerbated if not created sources of divisiveness over time. It appears, for example, that the presence of a persistent racist ideology and the spread of a consumer culture have extended and deepened the cleavages among Chicanos with diverse consequences, including a wide range of self-identification.

The resultant variation in self-perceptions has implied political distinctions as well as social and cultural diversity. And this process of differentiation has been furthered by the recurring and varying impacts of immigration from Mexico. Consequently, these rifts in the Chicano community have intensified with time, sharply evident in the debates over the direction and purpose of Chicano political efforts. Given the diversity of the Mexican-origin population in the United States and their specific circumstances, the history of their responses has understandably lacked uniformity.

The contemporary Chicano community and its differences reflect, therefore, the diverse ways in which people of Mexican descent have responded to their conditions over time. This obviously sketchy interpretation of the significance of recent Chicano historical scholarship remains, of course, to be confirmed, modified, or disproven by further research.

Politics has surrounded the writing about ethnicity and race in the United States, and this has certainly been the case for Chicano historiography. For those who wish to learn from the past to inform their politics, Chicano history offers caution, but not despair. The commonalities in the Chicano experience have waned; historians cannot refashion the past to vindicate political purpose or need. For activists, the diversity among Chicanos—history argues—must be the linchpin of any political strategy or project. The fracturing of the Chicano movement stands as testimony to the absence of a stable, trenchant common ground among people of Mexican descent. The inherent political appeal of "good guys versus bad guys" history will continue: John Chávez's account of the notion of a "lost land" (or Aztlán) among Chicanos illustrates this point, and several other works could be cited.[123]

Nevertheless, the historical literature of the last few years suggests the complexity of the Chicano experience. To press history to yield essentially an epic of heroes, victories, gallant resistance, and labor militancy blurs the everyday struggles of working Mexican men and women to sustain their dignity in a world that has taken a great deal, including, at times, their sense of self. The outcomes of those struggles, it seems, represent the basis of the Chicano past and present.

Notes

This essay is a revised and expanded version of an article that appeared in *Ethnic Affairs* 1 (fall 1987): 24–6Z. I would like to acknowledge the aid of Lilly Castillo-Speed, head librarian of the Chicano Studies Library at the University of California at Berkeley. I am also indebted to Kent Wilkinson for research assistance for this essay, and to Magali Zúñiga, Ana Coronado, and Rosa Johnson.

Note to the reader: Citations have been abbreviated. Complete publication data are included in the bibliography.

1.   1. For an introduction to this change, see the responses to the article by Leon Fink in a "roundtable" discussion in the *Journal of American History* 75, no.1 (June 1988): 115–61, passim. See also the excellent essay by Ira Berlin on the evolution of the field of social history as personified by its most celebrated proponent, Herbert O. Gutman, in Gutman, *Power and Culture: Essays on the American Working Class*, 3–69.

2.   2. Susan Keefe and Amado Padilla, *Chicano Ethnicity*, 195.

3.   3. Keefe and Padilla, despite their statement, failed to acknowledge the historical works available either in their text or in their references that may have helped to explain Chicano ethnicity. For a reference on publications, see Matt Meier, *Bibliography of Mexican American History*.

4.   4. See Juan Gómez-Quiñones and Luis Arroyo, "On the State of Chicano History: Observations on Its Development, Interpretations, and Theory, 1970-1974," 155–85.

5.   5. For example, articles continue to appear on the land grant issue despite the fact that relatively few Mexicans held title to large grants prior to the U.S.-Mexican War. See the articles by Ebright, Engstrand, Knowlton, Oppenheimer, Tyler, and Vassberg as examples of work that essentially builds on previous research and modes of inquiry.

6.   6. See John Hope Franklin, "Afro-American History: State of the Art," 162–73.

7.   7. In Ronald Takaki's *Iron Cages*, he emphasizes the hegemonic power of American political and economic forces, using key figures of the past to make the point. The comparison, then, is from the "top down" rather than actually analyzing relations among racial/ethnic groups.

8.   8. Patricia Nelson Limerick, *The Legacy of Conquest*, especially the introduction, offers a biting assessment of "western history" in the context of the larger field of American history. See also Richard White, "Race Relations in the American West."

9.   9. Howard Rabinowitz, "Race, Ethnicity, and Cultural Pluralism in American History," in Gardner and Adams, *Ordinary People*, 23–49.

10. Ibid.

11. Rodolfo Acuña, *Occupied America*, 3d ed., ix.

12. Ibid., A.

13. Ibid.

14. Ibid.

15. Ibid.

16. Mari Jo Buhle and Paul Buhle, "The New Labor History at the Cultural Crossroads," 151.

17. Acuña, *Occupied America*, 3d ed., A.

18. John P. Diggins, "The Misuses of Gramsci," 143. See also Diggins, "Comrades and Citizens: New Mythologies in American Historiography," 614–38.

19. Joan Scott, "On Language, Gender and Working-Class History," 1–2.

20. Sarah Deutsch, *No Separate Refuge*, 6.

21. Rabinowitz, "Race, Ethnicity, and Cultural Pluralism in American History."

22. Peter N. Stearns, "Toward a Wider Vision," in *The Past Before Us*, 21.

23. Peter N. Stearns and David Brody, "Workers and Work in America: The New Labor History," in *Ordinary People*, 139–159

24. These characteristics of Chicano writings were largely reactive in nature and in this regard paralleled a similar element in the works by Blacks, feminists, Asian Americans, and Native Americans. For a discussion of this issue relating to women's history, see Gerda Lerner, *The Majority Finds Its Past: Placing Women in History*, 145–59.

25. Rodolfo Acuña, *Occupied America: A History of Chicanos*, 2d ed., 1981. In his preface, Acuña states: "I have reevaluated the internal colonial model and set it aside as a useful paradigm relevant to the nineteenth century but not to the twentieth." Acuña, in explaining the change in his subtitle, notes that it was done as "a reaction to the paradigm rut that so many Chicano scholars have fallen into!" (vii). It should be noted that Acuña's use of the internal colonial model did not necessarily reflect the definition developed by the key proponents of the framework, e.g., Robert Blauner in *Racial Oppression in America*.

26. Tomás Almaguer, "Ideological Distortions in Recent Chicano Historiography," 7–28.

27. Albert Camarillo, *Chicanos in a Changing Society: From Mexican Pueblos to American Barrios in Santa Barbara and Southern California*, 1848–1930, 154.

28. Mario T. García, *Desert Immigrants: The Mexicans of El Paso, 1880–1920*, 231.

29. For a largely cultural interpretation, see Robert J. Rosenbaum, *Mexicano Resistance in the Southwest*, 12. It seems that Rosenbaum overreached his analysis, for his discussion of New Mexico tends to be much deeper and more refined than his examination of other areas. Similarly, his use of "peasantry," based to a large extent on Eric Wolf's characterization, seems forced.

30. Richard Griswold del Castillo, *The Los Angeles Barrio, 1850-1890: A Social History*, 3Z.

31. Ibid., 47.

32. David J. Weber, *The Mexican Frontier, 1821–1846: The American Southwest under Mexico*, 206.

33. Ibid., 176.

34. García, *Desert Immigrants*, 106.

35. Ibid.

36. Ibid., 107.

37. Eric Hobsbawm, "Labor History and Ideology," in *Workers: Worlds of Labor*, 375. Much of Hobsbawm's work on labor history generally warns of attempts to constrict labor history to specific movements, labor leaders, or work actions. Indeed, he stresses other forms of resistance, e.g., in working-class culture. See his excellent collection of essays, *Workers: Worlds of Labor*. Finally, as an example of the indirect forms of resistance by workers, one should note the example concerning a Mexican immigrant worker in David Montgomery's *Workers' Control in America: Studies in the History of Work, Technology, and Labor Struggles*, 44

38. Juan Gómez-Quiñones and David Maciel note in *Al norte del Río Bravo: pasado lejano (1600–1930)*: "Las diferencias en la población se debían a condiciones objetivas tales como las influencias locales específicas y las diferencias en las relaciones de tenencia de la tierra" 80.

39. David Montejano, "Is Texas Bigger than the World-System?" 620–3.

40. Arnoldo De León, *The Tejano Community, 1836–1900*, 185.

41. See Ramón Gutiérrez, "Changing Ethnic and Class Boundaries in America's Hispanic Past," in Chan, *Social and Gender Boundaries*, in the United States, 37–53.

42. Darliss A. Miller, "Cross Cultural Marriages in the Southwest: The New Mexico Experience, 1846–1900," 341. For a different conclusion, see Dysart's "Mexican Women in San Antonio, 1830–1860: The Assimilation Process." For an analysis of perceptions of male-female reactions in Texas, see Arnoldo De León, *They Called Them Greasers: Anglo Attitudes toward Mexicans in Texas, 1821–1900*, especially chapters 2 and 4.

43. Genaro Padilla, "The Recovery of Chicano Nineteenth-Century Autobiography," 286–306.

44. It should be noted that the 1930s—the FDR/New Deal years—mark a major break in American history. Most Chicano historians seem to conform to this historical framework. Periodization schemes after 1940 are more difficult to pinpoint—a reflection of the dilemma facing American historians for the post-FDR era. Whether and to what extent American history-based time schemata work for Chicano history awaits further research. For a general formulation of this problem of research and periodization, among other issues, see Bernard Bailyn, "The Challenge of Modern Historiography."

45. See Raúl Morin, *Among the Valiant*, cited in Mauricio Mazón, *The Zoot-Suit Riots: The Psychology of Symbolic Annihilation*, 65.

46. See Mario T. García, "Mexican Americans and the Politics of Citizenship: The Case of El Paso," 187–8.

47. Mazón, *The Zoot-Suit Riots, The Psychology of Symbolic Annihilation*, 113.

48. Mario T. García, "Americans All: The Mexican American Generation and the Politics of Wartime Los Angeles, 1941–1945," 278–89.

49. Gilbert González, "The Americanization of Mexican Women," in Chan, *Social and Gender Boundaries in the United States*, 55–79.

50. Mario T. García, *Mexican Americans: Leadership, Ideology, and Identity, 1930-1960*, 15–6. For a sketch of one of the most important figures of the Mexican American generation and his views, see Ricardo Romo, "George I. Sánchez and the Civil Rights Movement: 1940–1960." It should be noted that this generation contained certain inconsistencies in its views, particularly the tension between its assimilationist tendencies and its respect for Mexican culture and the Spanish language. On this point, see San Miguel's description of LULAC, in *"Let All of Them Take Heed,"* 67–74 For an overview of World War II and its aftermath, see John P. Diggins, *The Proud Decades: America in War and Peace, 1941–1960*. And Mario T. García has just published his long-awaited study of Mexican American leaders, *Mexican Americans: Leadership, Ideology, and Identity, 1930–1960*.

51. Manuel H. Peña, *The Texas-Mexican Conjunto: History of a Working*

Class Music, 138.

52. Guadalupe San Miguel Jr., *"Let All of Them Take Heed": Mexican Americans and the Campaign for Educational Equality in Texas, 1910–1981*, especially chapters 4–6.

53. For an excellent view of the post–World War II era, see Lary May, ed., *Recasting America: Culture and Politics in the Age of the Cold War*; also Diggins, *The Proud Decades*.

54. John D'Emilio and Estelle Freedman, *Intimate Matters: A History of Sexuality in America*, 194–201.

55. George Lipsitz, "Land of a Thousand Dances," in May, *Recasting America*, 269.

56. It should be emphasized that the appeal of traditional Mexican music continued in part because of the persistence of Spanish-language media in the United States.

57. This discussion is based on several works, notably Paul Kennedy's *The Rise and Fall of the Great Powers*, especially chapter 7. This issue has been the subject of much recent comment; unfortunately, the implications of this process for Chicanos have been scantily addressed. The so-called Sun Belt growth augurs well, some might argue, for Chicanos, given their concentration in the Southwest. Recent statistics, however, continue to show disproportionately high dropout rates for Chicano youth, with corresponding consequences. Thus, the opportunities generated by Sun Belt relocation of industries do not necessarily portend well for Chicanos as a whole, though many of the service-related jobs will likely continue to grow, with Chicanos unfortunately well represented. For a summary of the change in the American economy, see Robert Reich, *The Next American Frontier*.

58. For a specific analysis of the rise of the service sector and the industrialization in California, see Michael Teitz and Phillip Shapira, *Growth and Turbulence in the California Economy*.

59. For a national view, see Refugio Rochin, *Economic Perspectives of the Hispanic Community*; on California specifically, see University of California, *The Challenge: Latinos in a changing California*.

60. Richard Griswold del Castillo, *La Familia: Chicano Families in the Urban Southwest, 1848 to the Present*, 13Z.

61. See Joan W. Moore, *Homeboys: Gangs, Drugs and Prison in the Barrios of Los Angeles*; Ruth Horowitz, *Honor and the American Dream: Culture and Identity in a Chicano Community*; Martin Sánchez-Jankowski, *City Bound: Political Attitudes among Chicano Youth*; James Diego Vigil, *Barrio Gangs: Street Life and Identity in Southern California*.

62. See William J. Wilson, *The Declining Significance of Race*. In his recently published work on gangs, James Diego Vigil uses the term "underclass" without qualification, and Rodolfo Acuña, in his third edition of *Occupied America*, has titled the second "The Cementing of an Underclass." In this sense, they use the term with the same apparent definition established by Wilson.

63. No major work has been written on long-term economic changes and their impact on Chicanos in light of the differentiated groups in the Chicano community, i.e. immigrants, second-generation, etc. A recent article by Marta

Tienda and C. Matthew Snipp, "Mexican American Occupational Mobility," attempts to assess job mobility affected by generational change. As the authors put it: "New Chicano workers actually 'disinherit' the advantages of family background, but they are not immune from its disadvantages; Chicanos from lower status families enter lower status occupations. In short, Chicanos do not benefit from family background but they suffer its liabilities" (371). The conclusions of Tienda and Snipp are highly important, but they reflect a "snapshot" of a historical process without a consideration, for instance, of regional differences. Historians must begin to complement the work of Tienda and others on this issue. More important, Chicano scholars must assess the sources of the differences and similarities for Chicano and Anglo workers. Tienda and Snipp note, for example, certain degrees of congruence in the mobility of Anglo and Chicano workers (577). See also Jeremiah Cotton, "More on the 'Cost' of Being a Black or Mexican American Male Worker."

64. Rochin, *Economic Perspectives of the Hispanic Community*, 6.

65. For a discussion of consumerism and its impact on culture and ideology, see the essays ed. Richard Wightman Fox and T. J. Jackson Lears in *The Culture of Consumption: Critical Essays in American History, 1880–1980*.

66. Maria Eugenia Matute-Bianchi, "An Ethnographic Study of Mexican Descent Students in a California High School," in Chan, *Social and Gender Boundaries in the United States*, 90.

67. Ibid., 92.

68. Ibid.

69. The interaction between native-born and foreign-born Mexicans remains largely unstudied by historians. This question is complicated by the diversity among native-born Mexicans, but how this has played out over time continues relatively unexplored. On this issue, see Lawrence W. Miller, Jerry L. Polinard, and Robert D. Wrinkle, "Attitudes toward Undocumented Workers: The Mexican American Perspective." Note that the authors stress the importance of class among the factors that influence the attitudes of native-born Mexicans as opposed to those born in Mexico.

70. Renato Rosaldo, *Assimilation Revisited*, 10–1.

71. Mario T. García, "La Frontera: The Border as Symbol and Reality in Mexican American Thought." This scheme receives full treatment in García's *Mexican Americans*; see especially chapters 1 and 12.

72. Dennis N. Valdés, *Al Norte: Agricultural Workers in the Great Lakes Region, 1917–1970*; Erasmo Gamboa, *Mexican Labor and World War II. Braceros in the Pacific Northwest, 1942-1947*. Gamboa, "Braceros in the Pacific Northwest: Laborers on the Domestic Front, 1942–1947." On the initial immigrant generation, see García, *Mexican Americans*, especially chapter 1, for a further explication, including the comments of others. On the significance of Mexican immigration during and after World War II to contemporary patterns of Mexican migration to the United States, see Douglas Massey et al., *Return to Aztlán: The Social Process of International Migration from Western Mexico*, 43–106.

73. Rosaldo, "Assimilation Revisited," 10–1.

74. A review of articles and monographs on Mexican immigration is beyond the scope of this essay, but even a cursory glance at recent research clearly shows

little work on Chicano-Mexicano relations.

75. See, for instance, Rodolfo de la Garza's introduction to *Mexican Immigrants and Mexican Americans*, and his article in the same collection, "The Impact of Mexican Immigrants on the Political Behavior of Chicanos."

76. Paule Cruz Takash and Joaquin Avila, *Latino Political Participation in Rural California*.

77. De la Garza, introduction to *Mexican Immigrants and Mexican Americans*, 6.

78. Ibid.

79. Ibid., 7. For example, Camarillo notes the tensions between old-time residents of Santa Barbara and Mexican immigrants when they began to arrive in the late nineteenth century.

80. For an excellent analysis of the binational aspects of immigration in the contemporary cultural context, see Roger Rouse, "Mexican Migration and the Social Space of Postmodernism." For two recent, excellent works on migration, see Alejandro Portes and Robert Bach, *Latin Journey*, and Massey et al., *Return to Aztlán*.

81. Mario Barrera, *Race and Class in the Southwest: A Theory of Racial Inequality*, 216.

82. Ibid.

83. Ibid., 217.

84. Ibid., 217–8.

85. Mario Barrera seems to acknowledge the incompleteness of his analysis in *Race and Class in the Southwest* when he states: "Thus the Chicano situation is complex in terms of interests, and it is not surprising that Chicano political patterns have somewhat of a shifting nature ... It is familiar to most informed observers, and frequently creates political dilemmas" (216).

86. Carlos Muñoz, *Youth, Identity, Power: The Chicano Movement*.

87. Ibid. See especially chapters 1 and 3. Also see Ignacio M. García, *United We Win*, 218–32.

88. Ibid., especially chapter 2. See Mario Barrera, "The Historical Evolution of Chicano Ethnic Goals: A Bibliographic Essay." Barrera's schemata, though useful, seems to underestimate the continuation of certain trends throughout Chicano history. Thus his division into three broad eras tends to simplify a very complex process. Barrera emphasizes the contradiction between two basic goals in Chicano political organizations: "communitarian" as opposed to "egalitarian" goals. For a more complex analysis of the contemporary era, and in my estimation, a very useful one, see Michael Omi and Howard Winant, *Racial Formation in the United States*. They stress three major contending factions among minority social movements of the 1960s and 1970s and into the present. Also see, for a distinctive view, Felix Padilla, *Latino Ethnic Consciousness: The Case of Mexican Americans and Puerto Ricans in Chicago*. Omi and Winant provide an examination that holds important considerations for students of Chicano politics. More historical research must be done to see whether the analysis of Barrera, or of Omi and Winant, is applicable or accurate in light of the diversity among Chicano political actions past and present.

89. Muñoz, *Youth, Identity, Power*, especially chapter 6.

90. See Juan Gómez-Quiñones, *Chicano Politics: Reality and Promise*,

1940–1990. For example, the 1970s and 1980s witnessed a large increase in Latino elected officials, but there has been no major study of this process. In Rufus Browning, Dale Rogers Marshall, and David H. Tabb, *Protest Is Not Enough*, the conclusions are limited by the geographic constraints of the study.

91. Browning, Marshall and Tabb, *Protest Is Not Enough*, 135.

92. Felix Padilla, *Latino Ethnic Consciousness*, 8.

93. Browning, Marshall, and Tabb, *Protest Is Not Enough*, 125.

94. See Isidro Ortiz and Marguerite Marin, "Reaganomics and Latino Organizational Strategies," in Chan, *Social and Gender Boundaries in the United States*.

95. Jacqueline Jones, *Labor of Love, Labor of Sorrow: Black Women, Work and the Family from Slavery to the Present*, 7. On the issue of women and history, see Anne Firor Scott, "On Seeing and Not Seeing: A Case of Historical Invisibility." Also see Lerner's fine essays in *The Majority Finds Its Past*. It should be noted that Chicanas continue to be neglected by feminist historians, their considerations subsumed under immigrant or Black women's experiences. Jones's work on Black women finds no parallel for Chicanas. Lamentably, perhaps the best work on working women fails to address in any substantive way—as opposed to its treatment of Black women—the situation of Chicanas; see Alice Kessler-Harris, *Out to Work: A History of Wage-Earning Women in the United States*. To her credit, Sara Evans's new survey of women's history in the United States acknowledges Chicanas as a separate group. Still, the difference with Black women in this regard is reflected in Evans's index, where a comparison with the citations for Black women indicates the paucity of research on Chicanas. See Sara M. Evans, *Born for Liberty: A History of Women in America*.

96. For an example of this distinction, see the collection of essays ed. Vicki Ruiz and Susan Tiano, *Women on the U.S.-Mexican Border*.

97. Patricia Zavella, "The Impact of 'Sun Belt Industrialization' on Chicanas."

98. Griswold del Castillo, La Familia. In his section on the theories that underlie his approach, he discusses modernization theory, with particular emphasis on Barbara Laslett's "theory of family history in relation to the economy" (7). To add a sociocultural or, more precisely, a psychological dimension to his analysis, Griswold del Castillo incorporates Mark Poster's approach, a fusion of Marxist and Freudian concepts. It should be emphasized that Griswold del Castillo's study is based on a family history approach—an approach that has raised a contentious debate between family historians and feminist historians. For a powerful critique of Griswold del Castillo's methodology, see Helen Lara-Cea's paper presented at the Conference of the National Association for Chicano Studies, Salt Lake City, Utah, April 1987. The feminist literature on the historical construction of gender is vast and beyond the scope of this essay. For an excellent introduction, see Judith L. Newton, Mary P. Ryan, and Judith R. Walkowitz, *Sex and Class in Women's History*.

99. Antonia I. Castañeda, "Gender, Race, and Culture: Spanish-Mexican Women in the Historiography of Frontier California," 16. For a similarly valuable view on these issues, see Aida Hurtado, "Reflections on White Feminism," and Alvina E. Quintana, "Challenge and Counter-Challenge: Chicana Literary Motifs," in Chan, *Social and Gender Boundaries in the United States*. In varying ways, the authors distinguish differences in the views of Chicanas and white feminists, as well

as among Chicanas. As Quintana notes, "Looking at literature as the articulation of history or as ethnographic documentation of culture and female experience effectively opens the door to a new kind of interdisciplinary, but more importantly, intergenderal (a form that takes into account both male and female ideas) approach to knowledge" (203).

100. Patricia Zavella, *Women's Work and Chicano Families: Cannery Workers of the Santa Clara Valley*.

101. Manuel Gamio's classic work on the Mexican immigrant, *The Mexican Immigrant: His Life-Story* (1931), noted this issue long ago, thus the history of this question is a lengthy one. For example, in rural areas, one must consider the impact of immigrants on resident farmworkers. The political complexities of immigrants in the Chicano community add yet another consideration for historians. One should note, for instance, Mario García's observations concerning El Paso at the turn of the century: "The continued influx of immigrants after 1920 not only expanded roles for Mexican Americans as mediators between the newcomers and local government but also reminded American politicians of the political importance of El Paso's Mexican population" (*Desert Immigrants*, 171). Whether and to what extent such patterns occurred elsewhere and after 1940 remains largely unstudied by historians. For a consideration of such issues, see Evan Anders, *Boss Rule in South Texas: The Progressive Era*.

102. Space does not allow a deeper discussion of this issue, but the concept of hegemony underlies much of this discussion. The works inspired by Gramsci's notion of hegemony have multiplied rapidly in recent years. For a summary of their significance within the context of American history, see the excellent article by T. J. Jackson Lears, "The Concept of Cultural Hegemony: Problems and Possibilities." Tomás Ybarra-Frausto and José Cuéllar, among others, have been studying the basis and meaning of the cultural expression of cholos, lowriders, Chicano graffiti, and other forms in order to understand their political significance. But such studies are essentially contemporary in focus rather than historically grounded—another challenge for historians. See Michael Fischer, "Ethnicity and the Post-Modern Arts of Memory," in Clifford and Marcus, *Writing Culture*.

103. Lipsitz, "Land of a Thousand Dances," 269.

104. See, for example, Felix Padilla's notion of "situational Latino ethnicity," in "On the Nature of Latino Ethnicity." Also see the critical view of Raphe Sonenshein, "Biracial Coalition Politics in Los Angeles."

105. Erasmo Gamboa, "Mexican Migration into Washington State: A History, 1940–1950"; Juan R. García, "Midwest Mexicanos in the 1920s: Issues, Questions, and Directions." Note should also be made of the article by Boswell and Jones on the geographical characteristics of the Mexican-origin population. One interesting outcome of this tendency to concentrate on certain regions has been the imbalance in works available to researchers for comparative purposes. Texas has drawn much attention; see Arnoldo De León, "Tejano History Scholarship: A Review of the Recent Literature," and *Ethnicity in the Sun Belt: A History of Mexican Americans in Houston*. In California, Albert Camarillo has published an able text, *Chicanos in California: A History of Mexican Americans in California*, There are no comparable works for other areas. For a collection dealing with an area in the Midwest, see

James B. Lane and Edward J. Escobar, *Forging a Community: The Latino Experience in Northwest Indiana, 1919-1975*.

106. Ramón Gutiérrez, *When Jesus Came, the Corn Mother Went Away: Marriage, Conquest and Love in New Mexico, 1500–1846*.

107. David Montejano, *Anglos and Mexicans in the Making of Texas, 1836–1986*.

108. Ibid., 317.

109. Ibid.

110. See Tomás Almaguer, "Ideological Distortions in Recent Chicano Historiography."

111. Alan Brinkley, "Writing the History of Contemporary America: Dilemmas and Challenges," 124. For further discussion on this point with relevant works cited, see Thomas Bender, "Making History Whole Again," 1, 42–3. Also see Thomas Bender, "Wholes and Parts: The Need for Synthesis in American History," and the response that it elicited, "A Round Table: Synthesis in American History," in *Journal of American History* 74, no.1 (June 1987): 107–30.

112. See the "roundtable" discussion regarding Leon Fink's article on the Knights of Labor in the *Journal of American History* 75, no.1 (June 1988): passim.

113. Padilla, "The Recovery of Chicano Nineteenth-Century Autobiography," 302–3.

114. T. J. Jackson Lears, "The Concept of Cultural Hegemony: Problems and Possibilities," 573.

115. Rosa Linda Fregoso and Angie Chabram, "Chicana/o Cultural Representations: Reframing Alternative Critical Discourses," 205–6.

116. Lears, "The Concept of Cultural Hegemony," 573.

117. Linda Kerber, "Separate Spheres, Female Worlds, Woman's Place," 38.

118. Linda Alcoff, "Cultural Feminism versus Post-Structuralism," 425.

119. Ibid., 433–4.

120. Ibid., 435.

121. Genaro Padilla, "The Recovery of Nineteenth-Century Chicano Autobiography," 302. See the interesting case of being "Spanish" in New Mexico by Philip Gonzales, "Spanish Heritage and Ethnic Protest in New Mexico: The Anti-Fraternity Bill of 1933."

122. Sara Evans, in her *Born for Liberty*, notes the need for feminist historians to extend their vision and recognize the diversity among women: "Then, and only then, can we understand how these stories, so diverse among themselves, affected and transformed the dynamic interplay of public and private life in our past and how the experience of women in America actively shaped the broader history that we, women and men, all claim our own" (6). It seems to me that Evans's view holds important implications for Chicano history as well.

123. John R. Chávez, *The Lost Land: The Chicano Image of the Southwest*. For an analysis of the Chicano that maintains a highly nationalistic cast, see Alfredo Mirandé, *The Chicano Experience: An Alternative Perspective*.

Bibliography

BOOKS

Acuña, Rodolfo F. *Occupied America: A History of Chicanos.* 3d ed. New York: Harper & Row, 1988.

————. *A Community under Siege: A Chronicle of Chicanos East of the Los Angeles River, 1945–1975.* Los Angeles: Chicano Studies Research Center Publications, University of California, 1984.

————. *Occupied America: A History of Chicanos.* 2d ed. New York: Harper & Row, 1981.

————. *Occupied America: The Chicano's Struggle toward Liberation.* San Francisco: Canfield Press, 1972.

Allsup, Carl. *The American G. I. Forum: Origins and Evolution.* Austin: Center for Mexican American Studies, University of Texas, 1982.

Anders, Evan. *Boss Rule in South Texas: The Progressive Era.* Austin: University of Texas Press, 1982.

Barrera, Mario. *Race and Class in the Southwest: A Theory of Racial Inequality.* Notre Dame Ind.: University of Notre Dame Press, 1979.

Bernstein, Barton J. *Towards a New Past: Dissenting Essays in American History.* New York: Random House, 1969.

Blauner, Robert. *Racial Oppression in America.* New York: Harper & Row, 1972.

Browning, Rufus P., Dale Rogers Marshall, and David H. Tabb. *Protest Is Not Enough: The Struggle of Blacks and Hispanics for Equality in Urban Politics.* Berkeley: University of California Press, 1984.

Camarillo, Albert. *Chicanos in California: A History of Mexican Americans in California.* San Francisco: Boyd and Fraser, 1984.

————. *Chicanos in a Changing Society: From Mexican Pueblos to American Barrios in Santa Barbara and Southern California, 1843-1930.* Cambridge: Harvard University Press, 1979.

Chan, Sucheng, ed. *Social and Gender Boundaries in the United States.* Lewiston, N.Y.: Edwin Mellen Press, 1989.

Chávez, John R. *The Lost Land: The Chicano Image of the Southwest.* Albuquerque: University of New Mexico Press, 1984.

Cohen, Stephen S., and John Zysman. *Manufacturing Matters: The Myth of the Post-Industrial Economy.* New York: Basic Books, 1987.

Cruz Takash, Paule, and Joaquin Avila. *Latino Political Participation in Rural California.* Davis: California Institute of Rural Studies, 1988.

Daniel, Cletus E. *Bitter Harvest: A History of California Farmworkers, 1870–1941.* Ithaca: Cornell University Press, 1981.

De la Garza, Rodolfo, and Harley L. Browning. *Mexican Immigrants and Mexican Americans: An Evolving Relation.* Austin: Center for Mexican American Studies, University of Texas, 1986.

De León, Arnoldo. *Ethnicity in the Sun Belt: A History of Mexican Americans in Houston.* Houston: Mexican American Studies Program, University of Houston, 1989.

————. *The Tejano Community, 1836–1900.* Albuquerque: University of New Mexico Press, 1985.

————. *They Called Them Greasers: Anglo Attitudes toward Mexicans in Texas, 18211900.* Austin: University of Texas Press, 1983.

D'Emilio, John, and Estelle Freedman. *Intimate Matters: A History of Sexuality in America.* New York: Harper & Row, 1988.

Deutsch, Sarah. *No Separate Refuge: Culture, Class, and Gender on an Anglo-Hispanic Frontier in the American Southwest, 1880–1940.* New York: Oxford University Press, 1987.

Diggins, John P. *The Proud Decades: America in War and Peace, 1941–1960.* New York: W. W. Norton, 1988.

Evans, Sara M. *Born for Liberty: A History of Women in America.* New York: The Free Press, 1989.

Fox, Richard Wightman, and T. J. Jackson Lears, eds. *The Culture of Consumption: Critical Essays in American History, 1880–1980.* New York: Pantheon Books, 1983.

Gamboa, Erasmo. *Mexican Labor and World War II: Braceros in the Pacific Northwest, 1942–1947.* Austin: University of Texas Press, 1990.

Gamio, Manuel. *The Mexican Immigrant: His Life-Story.* Chicago: University of Chicago Press, 1931.

García, Ignacio M. *United We Win: The Rise and Fall of La Raza Unida Party.* Tucson: University of Arizona Press, 1989.

García, Mario T. *Mexican Americans: Leadership, Ideology, and Identity, 1930–1960.* New Haven: Yale University Press, 1989.

————.*Desert Immigrants: The Mexicans of El Paso, 1880–1920.* New Haven: Yale University Press, 1981.

Gardner, James B., and George Rollie Adams, eds. *Ordinary People and Everyday Life: Perspectives on the New Social History.* Nashville: American Association for State and Local History, 1983.

Gómez-Quiñones, Juan. *Chicano Politics: Reality and Promise, 1940–1990.* Albuquerque: University of New Mexico Press, 1990.

Gómez-Quiñones, Juan, and David Maciel. *Al norte del Río Bravo: pasado lejano (1600–1930).* Mexico City: Siglo XXI Editores, 1981.

Griswold del Castillo, Richard. *La Familia: Chicano Families in the Urban Southwest, 1848 to the Present.* Notre Dame, Ind.: University of Notre Dame Press, 1984.

————. *The Los Angeles Barrio, 1850–1890: A Social History.* Berkeley and Los Angeles: University of California Press, 1979.

Gutiérrez, Ramón A. *When Jesus Came, the Corn Mother Went Away: Marriage, Conquest and Love in New Mexico, 1500–1846.* Stanford: Stanford University Press (in press).

Gutman, Herbert G., *Power and Culture: Essays on the American Working Class.* Ed. Ira Berlin. New York: Pantheon, 1987.

Handlin, Oscar. *Truth in History.* Cambridge, Mass.: Belknap Press, 1979.

Hobsbawm, Eric. *Workers: Worlds of Labor.* New York: Pantheon Books, 1984.

Horowitz, Ruth. *Honor and the American Dream: Culture and Identity in a Chicano Community.* New Brunswick, N.J.: Rutgers University Press, 1983.

Jones, Jacqueline. *Labor of Love, Labor of Sorrow: Black Women, Work and the Family from Slavery to the Present.* New York: Basic Books, 1985.

Kammen, Michael, ed. *The Past Before Us: Contemporary Historical Writing in the United States.* Ithaca: Cornell University Press, 1980.

Keefe, Susan E., and Amado Padilla. *Chicano Ethnicity.* Albuquerque: University of New Mexico Press, 1987.

Kennedy, Paul. *The Rise and Fall of the Great Powers: Economic Change and Military Conflict from 1500 to 2000.* New York: Random House, 1987.

Kessler-Harris, Alice. *Out to Work: A History of Wage-Earning Women in the United States.* New York: Oxford University Press, 1979.

Lane, James B., and Edward J. Escobar. *Forging a Community: The Latino Experience in Northwest Indiana, 1919–1975.* Chicago: Cattails Press, 1987.

Lerner, Gerda. *The Majority Finds Its Past: Placing Women in History.* New York: Oxford University Press, 1979.

Limerick, Patricia Nelson. *The Legacy of Conquest: The Unbroken Past of the American West.* New York: W. W. Norton, 1987.

Los Angeles Times. *Southern California's Latino Community.* Los Angeles: The Los Angeles Times, 1983.

Maciel, David. *Al norte del Río Bravo: pasado inmediato (1930–1981).* Mexico City: Siglo XXI Editores, 1981.

Massey, Douglas, Rafael Alarcón, Jorge Durand, and Humberto González. *Return to Aztlán: The Social Process of International Migration from Western Mexico.* Berkeley: University of California Press, 1987.

May, Lary, ed. *Recasting America: Culture and Politics in the Age of the Cold War.* Chicago: University of Chicago Press, 1989.

Mazón, Mauricio. *The Zoot-Suit Riots: The Psychology of Symbolic Annihilation.* Austin: University of Texas Press, 1984.

McDowell Craver, Rebecca. *The Impact of Intimacy: Mexican-Anglo Intermarriage in New Mexico, 1821–1846.* El Paso: Texas Western Press, 1982.

Meier, August, and Elliott Rudwick. *Black History and the Historical Profession, 1915–1980.* Urbana: University of Illinois Press, 1986.

Meier, Matt S. *Bibliography of Mexican American History.* Westport, Conn.: Greenwood Press, 1984.

Meining, D. W. *Southwest: Three Peoples in Geographical Change, 1600–1970.* New York: Oxford University Press, 1971.

———. *Imperial Texas: An Interpretive Essay in Cultural Geography.* Austin: University of Texas Press, 1969.

Merk, Frederick. *History of the Westward Movement.* New York: Alfred A. Knopf, 1978.

Mirandé, Alfredo. *The Chicano Experience: An Alternative Perspective.* Notre Dame, Ind.: University of Notre Dame Press, 1985.

Montejano, David. *Anglos and Mexicans in the Making of Texas, 1836–1986.* Austin: University of Texas Press, 1987.

Montgomery, David. *Workers' Control in America: Studies in the History of Work, Technology, and Labor Struggles.* New York: Cambridge University Press, 1979.

Moore, Joan W., et al. *Homeboys: Gangs, Drugs and Prison in the Barrios of Los Angeles*. Philadelphia: Temple University Press, 1978.

Muñoz, Carlos. *Youth, Identity, Power: The Chicano Movement*. London: Verso Press, 1989.

Newton, Judith L., Mary P. Ryan, and Judith R. Walkowitz, eds. *Sex and Class in Women's History*. Boston: Routledge and Kegan Paul, 1983.

Omi, Michael, and Howard Winant. *Racial Formation in the United States, from the 1960s to the 1980s*. New York: Routledge and Kegan Paul, 1986.

Padilla, Felix M. *Latino Ethnic Consciousness: The Case of Mexican Americans and Puerto Ricans in Chicago*. Notre Dame, Ind.: University of Notre Dame Press, 1985.

Peña, Manuel H. *The Texas-Mexican Conjunto: History of a Working Class Music*. Austin: University of Texas Press, 1985.

Polenberg, Richard. *One Nation Divisible: Class, Race, and Ethnicity in the United States Since 1938*. New York: Penguin Books, 1980.

Portes, Alejandro, and Robert L. Bach. *Latin Journey: Cuban and Mexican Immigrants in the United States*. Berkeley: University of California Press, 1985.

Reich, Robert B. *The Next American Frontier*. New York: Penguin Books, 1984.

Rochin, Refugio I. *Economic Perspectives of the Hispanic Community*. San Antonio: Tomás Rivera Center, 1988.

Romo, Ricardo. *East Los Angeles: History of a Barrio*. Austin: University of Texas Press, 1981.

Rosenbaum, Robert J. *Mexicano Resistance in the Southwest*. Austin: University of Texas Press, 1981.

Ruiz, Vicki L. *Cannery Women/Cannery Lives: Mexican Women, Unionization, and the California Food Processing Industry, 1930–1950*. Albuquerque: University of New Mexico Press, 1987.

Ruiz, Vicki L., and Susan Tiano, eds. *Women on the U.S.-Mexico Border: Responses to Change*. Boston: Allen and Unwin, 1987.

Sánchez-Jankowski, Martin. *City Bound: Political Attitudes among Chicano Youth*. Albuquerque: University of New Mexico Press, 1986.

San Miguel Guadalupe, Jr. *"Let All of Them Take Heed": Mexican Americans and the Campaign for Educational Equality in Texas, 1910–1981*. Austin: University of Texas Press, 1987.

Scott, James C. *Weapons of the Weak: Everyday Forms of Peasant Resistance*. New Haven: Yale University Press, 1985.

Takaki, Ronald T. *Iron Cages: Race and Culture in Nineteenth-Century America*. New York: Alfred A. Knopf, 1979.

Teitz, Michael B., and Phillip Shapira. *Growth and Turbulence in the California Economy*. Morgantown: Regional Research Institute, West Virginia University, 1989.

University of California, SCR 43 Task Force. *The Challenge: Latinos in a Changing California*. Berkeley: University of California, Office of the President, 1989.

Valdés, Dennis N. *Al Norte: Agricultural Workers in the Great Lakes Region, 1917–1970*. Austin: University of Texas Press, 1990.

Vigil, James Diego. *Barrio Gangs: Street Life and Identity in Southern California.* Austin: University of Texas Press, 1988.

Weber, David J. *Collected Essays.* Albuquerque: University of New Mexico Press, 1989.

————.*The Mexican Frontier, 1821–1846: The American Southwest under Mexico.* Albuquerque: University of New Mexico Press, 198Z

————. ed. *New Spain's Far Northern Frontier: Essays on Spain in the American West, 1540–1821.* Albuquerque: University of New Mexico Press, 1979.

Wilson, William J. *The Declining Significance of Race: Blacks and Changing American Institutions.* Chicago: University of Chicago Press, 1980.

Zavella, Patricia. *Women's Work and Chicano Families: Cannery Workers of the Santa Clara Valley.* Ithaca: Cornell University Press, 1987.

ARTICLES

Acuña, Rodolfo. "La Generación de 1968: Unfulfilled Dreams." *Corazón de Aztlán* 1 (January–February 1982): 6–7.

Alcoff, Linda. "Cultural Feminism versus Post-Structuralism: The Identity Crisis in Feminist Theory." *Signs* 13, no.3 (spring 1988): 405–36.

Almaguer, Tomás. "Ideological Distortions in Recent Chicano Historiography: The Internal Model and Chicano Historical Interpretation." *Aztlán: A Journal of Chicano Studies* 18, no.1 (spring 1987): 7–28.

Arreola, Daniel D. "The Mexican American Cultural Capital." *Geographical Review* 77 (January 1987): 17–34.

Bailyn, Bernard. "The Challenge of Modern Historiography." *American Historical Review* 87 (June 1982): 1–24.

Barrera, Mario. "The Historical Evolution of Chicano Ethnic Goals: A Bibliographic Essay." *Sage Race Relations Abstracts* 10 (February 1985): 1–48.

Bender, Thomas. "Wholes and Parts: Continuing the Conversation." *Journal of American History* 74, no.1 (June 1987): 123–30.

————. "Wholes and Parts: The Need for Synthesis in American History." *Journal of American History* 73, no.1 (June 1986): 120–36.

————. "Making History Whole Again." *New York Times Book Review*, 6 October 1985, 1, 42–3.

Boswell, Terry, and Diane Mitsch Bush. "Labor Force Composition and Union Organization in the Arizona Copper Industry: A Comment on Jiménez." *Review* 8 (summer 1984): 133–51.

Boswell, Thomas D., and Timothy C. Jones. "A Regionalization of Mexican Americans in the United States." *Geographical Review* 70 (January 1980): 88–98.

Breines, Winifred. "Whose New Left?" *Journal of American History* 75, no.2 (September 1988):528–45.

Brinkley, Alan. "Writing the History of Contemporary America: Dilemmas and Challenges." *Daedalus* 13 (summer 1984): 121–41.

Bruce-Novoa, Juan. "History as Content, History as Act: The Chicano Novel." *Aztlán: A Journal of Chicano Studies* 18, no.1 (Spring 1987): 29–44.

Buhle, Mari Jo, and Paul Buhle. "The New Labor History at the Cultural Crossroads." *Journal of American History* 75, no.1 (June 1998): 151–7.

Camarillo, Albert. "Observations on the 'New' Chicano History: Historiography of the 1970s." SCCR Working Paper No. 1. Stanford: Stanford University Center for Chicano Research, 1984.

Carrillo, L., and T. A. Lyson. "The Fotonovela as a Cultural Bridge for Hispanic Women." *Journal of Popular Culture* 17 (winter 1983): 59–64.

Castañeda, Antonia I. "Gender, Race, and Culture: Spanish-Mexican Women in the Historiography of Frontier California." *Frontiers: A Journal of Women's Studies* 11, no.1 (1990): 8–20.

Chacón, Ramón D. "Labor Unrest and Industrialized Agriculture in California: The Case of the 1933 San Joaquin Valley Cotton Strike." *Social Science Quarterly* 65 (June 1984): 336–53.

Cotton, Jeremiah. "More on the 'Cost' of Being a Black or Mexican American Male Worker." *Social Science Quarterly* 66 (December 1985): 867–85.

De la Garza, Rodolfo, and Adela I. Flores. "The Impact of Mexican Immigrants on the Political Behavior of Chicanos: A Clarification of Issues and Some Hypotheses for Future Research." In *Mexican Immigrants and Mexican Americans: An Evolving Relation*, ed. Harley L. Browning and Rodolfo de la Garza. Austin: Center for Mexican American Studies, University of Texas, 1986.

De León, Arnoldo. "Tejanos and the Texas War for Independence: Historiography's Judgement." *New Mexico Historical Review* 61 (April 1986): 137–46.

———. "Tejano History Scholarship: A Review of the Recent Literature." *West Texas Historical Association Yearbook* 61 (1985).

De León, Arnoldo, and Kenneth L. Stewart. "Lost Dreams and Found Fortunes: Mexican and Anglo Immigrants in South Texas, 1865–1900." *Western Historical Quarterly* 14 (July 1983): 191–310.

Deutsch, Sarah. "Women and Intercultural Relations: The Case of Hispanic New Mexico and Colorado." *Signs* 12, no.4 (Summer 1987): 719–39.

Diggins, John P. "The Misuses of Gramsci." *Journal of American History* 75, no.1 (June 1988): 141–5.

———. "Comrades and Citizens: New Mythologies in American Historiography." *American Historical Review* 90 (June 1985): 614–38.

Dinwoodie, David H. "Indians, Hispanos, and Land Reform: A New Deal Struggle in New Mexico." *Western Historical Quarterly* 17 (July 1986): 291–323.

Durán, Tobias. "Francisco Chávez, Thomas B. Catron, and Organized Political Violence in Santa Fe in the 1890s." *New Mexico Historical Review* 59 (July 1984): 291–310.

Dysart, Jane. "Mexican Women in San Antonio, 1830–1860: The Assimilation Process." *Western Historical Quarterly* 7 (October 1976): 365–75.

Ebright, Malcolm. "Spanish and Mexican Land Grants and the Law." *Journal of the West* 27 (July 1988): 3–11.

Engstrand, Iris H. W. "California Ranchos: Their Hispanic Heritage." *Southern California Quarterly* 67 (fall 1985): 281–90.

Fink, Leon. "The New Labor History and the Powers of Historical Pessimism: Consensus, Hegemony, and the Case of the Knights of Labor." *Journal of American History* 75, no.1 (June 1988): 115–36.

————. "Relocating the Vital Center." *Journal of American History* 75, no.1 (June 1988): 158–61.

Firor Scott, Anne. "On Seeing and Not Seeing: A Case of Historical Invisibility." *Journal of American History* 71 (June 1994): 7–21.

Fischer, Michael M. J. "Ethnicity and the Post-Modern Arts of Memory." In *Writing Culture: The Poetics and Politics of Ethnography*, ed. James Clifford and George E. Marcus. Berkeley: University of California Press, 1986.

Fox, Richard Wightman. "Public Culture and the Problem of Synthesis." *Journal of American History* 74, no.1 (June 1988): 113–6.

Franklin, John Hope. "Afro-American History: State of the Art." *Journal of American History* 75, no.1 (June 1988): 162–73.

Fregoso, Rosa Linda, and Angie Chabram. "Chicana/o Cultural Representations: Reframing Alternative Critical Discourses." *Cultural Studies* 4, no.3 (October 1990): 203–12.

Frisbie, W. Parker, Frank D. Bean, and Isaac W. Ebertstein. "Recent Changes in Marital Instability Among Mexican Americans: Convergence with Anglo Trends?" *Social Forces* 58 (June 1980): 1205–1220.

Gamboa, Erasmo. "Braceros in the Pacific Northwest: Laborers on the Domestic Front, 1942, 1947." *Pacific Historical Review* 56 (August 1987): 378–98.

————. "Mexican Migration into Washington State: A History, 1940–1950." *Pacific Northwest Quarterly* 72 (July 1981): 121–31.

García, Juan R. "Midwest Mexicanos in the 1920s: Issues, Questions, and Directions." *Social Science Journal* 19 (April 1982): 89–99.

García, Mario T. "La Frontera: The Border as Symbol and Reality in Mexican American Thought." *Mexican Studies/Estudios Mexicanos* 1, no.2 (Summer 1985): 195–225.

————. "Americans All: The Mexican American Generation and the Politics of Wartime Los Angeles, 1941–1945." *Social Science Quarterly* 65 (June 1984): 278–89.

————. "Mexican Americans and the Politics of Citizenship: The Case of El Paso, 1936." *New Mexico Historical Review* 19 (April 1984): 187–204.

García, Philip, and Lionel A. Maldonado. "America's Mexicans: A Plea for Specificity." *Social Science Journal* 19 (April 1982): 9–24.

Gleason, Philip. "Americans All: World War II and the Shaping of American Identity." *Review of Politics* 43 (October 1981): 155–185.

Gómez-Quiñones, Juan, and Luis Arroyo. "On the State of Chicano History: Observations on Its Development, Interpretations, and Theory, 1970–1974." *Western Historical Quarterly* 7 (April 1976): 155–85.

Gonzales, Philip B. "Spanish Heritage and Ethnic Protest in New Mexico: The Anti-Fraternity Bill of 1933." *New Mexico Historical Review* 61 (October 1986): 281–99.

Gonzalez, Gilbert G. "The Americanization of Mexican Women and Their Families during the Era of De Jure School Segregation, 1900–1950." In *Social and Gender Boundaries in the United States*, ed. Sucheng Chan. Lewiston, N.Y.: Edwin Mellen Press, 1989.

———. "Interamerican and Intercultural Education and the Chicano Community." *Journal of Ethnic Studies* 13, no.3 (fall 1985): 31–53.

Graham, Otis L., Jr. "Uses and Misuses of History in the Debate Over Immigration Reform." *The Public Historian* 8, no.2 (Spring 1986): 41–64.

Grandjeat, Yves-Charles. "Conflicts and Cohesiveness: The Elusive Quest for a Chicano History." *Aztlán: A Journal of Chicano Studies* 18, no.1 (spring 1987): 45–58.

Gratton, Brian, F. Arturo Rosales, and Hans De Bano. "A Sample of the Mexican-American Population in 1940." *Historical Methods* 21, no.2 (Spring 1988): 80–7.

Gutiérrez, Ramón A. "Changing Ethnic and Class Boundaries in America's Hispanic Past," in *Social and Gender Boundaries in the United States*, ed. Sucheng Chan. Lewiston, N.Y.: Edwin Mellen Press, 1989.

———. "Unraveling America's Hispanic Past: Internal Stratification and Class Boundaries." *Aztlán: A Journal of Chicano Studies* 17, no.1 (Spring 1986): 79–102.

———. "Honor Ideology, Marriage Negotiation, and Class-Gender Domination in New Mexico, 1690-1846." *Latin American Perspectives* 12, no.1 (winter 1985): 81–104.

Hennessy, Alistair. "The Rise of the Hispanics I: Chicanos." *Journal of Latin American Studies* 16 (May 1984): 171–94.

Hurtado, Aida. "Reflections on White Feminism: A Perspective from a Woman of Color." In *Social and Gender Boundaries in the United States*, ed. Sucheng Chan. Lewiston, N.Y.: Edwin Mellen Press, 1989.

Hurtado, Aida, and Carlos H. Arce. "Mexicans, Chicanos, Mexican Americans, or Pochos... ¿Qué somos? The Impact of Nativity on Ethnic Labeling." *Aztlán: A Journal of Chicano Studies* 17, no.1 (spring 1986): 79–101

Jameson, Frederic. "Postmodernism, or the Cultural Logic of Late Capitalism." *New Left Review* 146 (July/August 1984): 53–91

Joll, James. "Business as Usual." *New York Review of Books*, 26 September 1985, 5–6, 8, 10.

Kerber, Linda K. "Separate Spheres, Female Worlds, Woman's Place: The Rhetoric of Women's History." *Journal of American History* 75, no.1 (June 1988): 939.

Knowlton, Clark S. "The Mora Land Grant: A New Mexican Tragedy." *Journal of the West* 27 (July 1988): 59–73.

Lears, T. J. Jackson. "Power, Culture and Memory." *Journal of American History* 75, no.1 (June 1988): 137–40.

———. "The Concept of Cultural Hegemony: Problems and Possibilities." *American Historical Review* 90 (June 1985): 567–93.

Limón, José E. "Legendary Metafolklore and Performance: A Mexican-American Example." *Western Folklore* 42 (July 1983): 191–208.

Lipsitz, George. "Land of a Thousand Dances: Youth, Minorities, and the Rise of Rock and Roll." In *Recasting America: Culture and Politics in the Age of the Cold War*, ed. Lary May. Chicago: University of Chicago Press, 1989.

———. "The Struggle for Hegemony." *Journal of American History* 75, no.1 (June 1988): 146–50.

Lotchin, Roger W., and David J. Weber. "The New Chicano History: Two Perspectives." *History Teacher* 16 (February 1983): 219–47.

Lowry, Sharon K. "Mirrors and Blue Smoke: Stephen Dorsey and the Santa Fe Ring in the 1880s." *New Mexico Historical Review* 59 (October 1984): 395–409.

Matute-Bianchi, Maria Eugenia. "An Ethnographic Study of Mexican Descent Students in a California High School." In *Social and Gender Boundaries in the United States*, ed. Sucheng Chan. Lewiston, N.Y.: Edwin Mellen Press, 1989.

Metzgar, Joseph V. "Guns and Butter: Albuquerque Hispanics, 1940–1975." *New Mexico Historical Review* 56 (April 1981): 117–39.

Miller, Darliss A. "Cross Cultural Marriages in the Southwest: The New Mexico Experience, 1846–1900." *New Mexico Historical Review* 57 (October 1982): 335–53.

Miller, Lawrence W., Jerry L. Polinard, and Robert D. Wrinkle. "Attitudes toward Undocumented Workers: The Mexican American Perspective." *Social Science Quarterly* 65 (June 1984): 482–494.

Montejano, David. "Is Texas Bigger Than the World-System?" *Review* 4 (winter 1981): 620–3.

Morrisey, Marietta. "Ethnic Stratification and the Study of Chicanos." *Journal of Ethnic Studies* 10 (winter 1983): 71–99.

Musoke, Moses S., and Alan L. Olmstead. "The Rise of the Cotton Industry in California: A Comparative Perspective." *Journal of Economic History* 42 (June)

Myres, Sandra L. "Mexican Americans and Westering Anglos: A Feminine Perspective." *New Mexico Historical Review* 57 (October 1982): 317–33.

Nostrand, Richard L. "The Century of Hispano Expansion." *New Mexico Historical Review* 62 (October 1987): 361–86.

Omi, Michael, and Howard Winant. "By the Rivers of Babylon: Race in the United States, Part One." *Socialist Review* 13 (November–December 1983): 35–68.

Oppenheimer, Robert. "Acculturation or Assimilation: Mexican Immigrants in Kansas, 1900 to World War II." *Western Historical Quarterly* 16 (October 1985): 429–48.

Ortiz, Isidro D. "Chicano Urban Politics and the Politics of Reform in the Seventies." *Western Political Quarterly* 37 (December 1984): 564–77.

Ortiz, Isidro D., and Marguerite V. Marin. "Reaganomics and Latino Organizational Strategies," in *Social and Gender Boundaries in the United States*, ed. Sucheng Chan. Lewiston, N.Y.: Edwin Mellen Press, 1989.

Padilla, Felix M. "On the Nature of Latino Ethnicity." *Social Science Quarterly* 65, no.2 (June 1984): 651–64.

Padilla, Genaro, M. "The Recovery of Chicano Nineteenth-Century Autobiography." *American Quarterly* 40 (September 1988): 286–306.

Painter, Nell Irvin. "Bias and Synthesis in History." *Journal of American History* 71, no.1 (June 1987): 109–115.

Pike, Frederick. "Latin America and the Inversion of United States Stereotypes in the 1920s and 1930s." *Americas* 42 (October 1985): 131–6Z.

Postol, Todd. "Reinterpreting the Fifties: Changing Views of a 'Dull' Decade." *Journal of American Culture* 8 (summer 1985): 39–45.

Poyo, Gerald E., and Gilberto M. Hinojosa. "Spanish Texas and Borderlands Historiography in Transition: Implications for United States History." *Journal of American History* 75, no.2 (September 1988): 393–416.

Quintana, Alvina E. "Challenge and Counter-Challenge: Chicana Literary Motifs." In *Social and Gender Boundaries in the United States*, ed. Sucheng Chan. Lewiston, N.Y.: Edwin Mellen Press, 1989.

Rapp, Rayna, Ellen Ross, and Renate Bridenthal. "Examining Family History." In *Sex and Class in Women's History*, ed. Judith L. Newton, Mary P. Ryan, and Judith R. Walkowitz. Boston: Routledge and Kegan Paul, 1983.

Redding, Jay Saunders. "The Negro in American History," in *The Past Before Us: Contemporary Historical Writing in the United States*, ed. Michael Kammen. Ithaca: Cornell University Press, 1980.

Reich, Michael. "The Economics of Racism." In *Problems in Political Economy: An Urban Perspective*, ed. David M. Gordon. Lexington, Mass: D. C. Heath, 1977.

Review 4 (winter 1981): 453-636. Special number on Chicano labor and unequal development. (Journal of the Fernand Braudel Center, State University of New York at Binghamton.)

Rogin, Michael. "Kiss Me Deadly: Communism, Motherhood, and the Cold War Movies." *Representations* 6 (spring 1984): 1–36.

Romo, Ricardo. "George I. Sánchez and the Civil Rights Movement: 1940-1960." *La Raza Law Journal* 1, no.3 (Fall 1986): 342–6Z.

Rosaldo, Renato. "Assimilation Revisited." SCCR Working Paper No. 9. Stanford: Stanford University Center for Chicano Research, 1985.

Rosenzweig, Roy. "What Is the Matter with History?" *Journal of American History* 74, no.1 (June 1987): 117–22.

Rouse, Roger. "Mexican Migration and the Social Space of Postmodernism." Paper presented at Center for U.S.-Mexican Studies, University of California at San Diego.

Schoen, Rober, and Lawrence E. Cohen. "Ethnic Endogamy Among Mexican American Grooms: A Reanalysis of Generational and Occupational Effects." *American Journal of Sociology* 86 (September 1980): 359–66.

Scott, Joan W. "On Language, Gender, and Working-Class History." *International Labor and Working-Class History* 31 (Spring 1987): 1–13.

Sonenshein, Raphe. "Biracial Coalition Politics in Los Angeles." *PS* 19 (summer 1986): 582–90.

Stearns, Peter N. "Toward a Wider Vision: Trends in Social History." In *The Past Before Us: Contemporary Historical Writing in the United States*, ed. Michael Kammen. Ithaca: Cornell University Press, 1980.

Thurow, Lester C. "Losing the Economic Race." *New York Review of Books* 27 September 1984, 29–31.

Tienda, Marta, and C. Matthew Snipp. "Mexican American Occupational Mobility." *Social Science Quarterly* 65 (June 1984): 364–80.

Towes, John E. "Intellectual History after the Linguistic Turn: The Autonomy of Meaning and the Irreducibility of Experience." *American Historical Review* 92 (October 1987): 879–907.

Tyler, Daniel. "Ejido Lands in New Mexico." *Journal of the West* 27 (July 1988): 24–35.

Vassberg, David E. "The Spanish Background: Problems Concerning Ownership, Usurpations, and Defense of Common Lands in 16th Century Castile." *Journal of the West* 27 (July 1988): 12–23.

Weber, David J. "John Francis Bannon and the Historiography of the Spanish Borderlands: Retrospect and Prospect." *Journal of the Southwest* 29 (winter 1987): 331–63.

Wells, Miriam J. "Power Brokers and Ethnicity: The Rise of a Chicano Movement." *Aztlán: A Journal of Chicano Studies* 17, no.1 (Spring 1986): 47–78.

———. "Social Conflict, Commodity Constraints, and Labor Market Structure in Agriculture." *Comparative Studies in Society and History* 23 (October 1981): 679–704.

White, Richard. "Race Relations in the American West." *American Quarterly* 38, no.3 (1986): 396–416.

Woolsey, Ronald C. "Rites of Passage? Anglo and Mexican-American Contrasts in a Time of Change: Los Angeles, 1860-1870." *Southern California Quarterly* 69 (summer 1987): 81–101.

Wright, Erik Olin, and Bill Martin. "The Transformation of the American Class Structure, 1960–1980." American Journal of Sociology 93, no.1 (July 1987): 1–29.

Zavella, Patricia. "The Impact of 'Sun Belt Industrialization' on Chicanas." SCCR Working Paper No. 7. Stanford: Stanford University Center for Chicano Research, 1984.

Chicano Cinema and the Horizon of Expectations

A Discursive Analysis of Film Reviews in the Mainstream, Alternative, and Hispanic Press, 1987–1988

Chon A. Noriega

> But even the smallest smoke signal can mark the way on the road out of
> the cinema barrio and toward Mama's dream of el Norte.
>
> —Richard Corliss, "Born in East L.A"

Between summer 1987 and spring 1988, Hollywood released four films that depicted aspects of the Chicano experience: *La Bamba* (1987), *Born in East L.A.* (1987), *The Milagro Beanfield War* (1988), and *Stand and Deliver* (1988). These films were seen as part of a new phenomenon, a hybrid called "Hispanic Hollywood." According to several mainstream periodicals, the Hispanic directors, producers, and writers who made these films had escaped the "cinema barrio" of their alternative production companies and entered the mainstream, bringing positive, yet popular images with them.

Yet we may question what these films did, in fact, represent: "authentic" portrayals of the Chicano experience, or Hollywood success stories featuring, incidentally, Chicano characters? Upon considering the films' diverse audiences within the United States, several answers or "readings" are revealed. In an attempt to move Chicano film criticism toward a theory of reception as integral to the production of meanings, I will examine the aesthetic discourse of film reviews, interviews, and feature articles in the mainstream, alternative, and Hispanic press. It is here that each film first reveals itself as a multiple text, since each publication offers a different interpretation, one that either reflects, anticipates, or attempts to influence the expectations of its readership.

From *Aztlan: A Journal of Chicano Studies* 1, no. 1 (1970): 1–12.

Reception and Discourse

Chicano cultural and historical studies have long turned to Spanish-language newspapers in order to reconstruct Chicano perceptions of events since the U.S.-Mexican War. In fact, in one of the first essays on Chicanos and film, José Limón brings such a historical approach to his examination of Mexican American reception of the silent "greaser" films of the 1910s.[1] The focus, however, is not on audiences per se, but on the role of the press in contributing to a public discourse on reception. In this period, the Spanish-language press of South Texas, if not of other regions, published editorials and organized boycotts of movie theaters.

Building on the film scholarship of Carlos Cortés, I will examine the multiple receptions within the aesthetic discourse on Chicano feature films that can be found in the popular press of the late 1980s. Cortés argues that the image the viewer sees on the screen depends on the pre-established context of the "societal curriculum" (family, peer groups, neighborhoods) and "total media curriculum" (newspapers, magazines, television) that "educate" the viewer.[2] The media curriculum that interprets and evaluates films plays a significant role in providing a context within which to receive the projected images and narrative. In particular, Cortés cites film reviews and newspaper columns as the "fragmentary evidence" available to the film historian attempting impact analysis, but he fails to recognize or utilize these sources as an important discourse in their own right. Nonetheless, Cortés's concept of the "total media curriculum" allows for multiple readings and challenges the primacy of the text, since "film does not operate alone."[3]

In the model that Cortés outlines, a film does not exist as a pristine text, but in mediation with media coverage and audience expectations. Likewise, in "Colonialism, Racism, and Representation: An Introduction," Robert Stam and Louise Spence provide a contextual framework for reception: "We must be aware ... of the cultural and ideological assumptions spectators bring to the cinema. We must be conscious, too, of the institutionalized expectations ... which lead us to consume films in a certain way."[4] While Cortés does not discuss the various receptions possible within such a framework, Stam and Spence suggest the three levels of reception that Stuart Hall delineates in "Culture, the Media and 'the Ideological Effect.'"[5] Hall argues that the formal properties of a text construct a "preferred" reading. The audience, however, can produce an alternative reading that is either "negotiated" with or "oppositional" to the "preferred" one. The fact that Stam and Spence, among others, refer to these two readings as "aberrant," however, reveals the extent to which these film critics privilege a determinate or "fixed" text over its multiple inscriptions within multiple social contexts.[6] The use of the word "aberrant" derives from a semiotics-based criticism, which maintains the uniqueness of a "closed text," even when social context and the processes of reception are taken into account. Thus, for example, while Umberto Eco places the word aberrant in quotation marks, he nonetheless argues for the "unadulterable specificity" of the text.[7]

The notion of reception outlined above, however, assumes that the "preferred" reading expresses itself in a universal language accessible and constant across the social spectrum. Ethnic and other distinct audiences, then, who somehow fail to grasp or engage the "preferred" meaning are not seen as active participants who utilize the strategies of various "interpretive communities,"[8] but as "aberrant" readers who miss the point. Such a theoretical position puts too much emphasis on the unmitigated power of the cinema, and on the film critic who somehow escapes its "ideological effect." As Barbara Klinger notes,

> Despite substantial differences in theoretical perspectives … the spectator has tended to fall into perfect correspondence with the narrative and visual operations specific to a textual system. As a result, the entire film/spectator interaction is rendered as fixed and universal, effectively sealing it off from social contingencies.[9]

While Klinger examines intertextual "digressions" in which the viewer's individual interaction with the text exceeds the narrative proper, the social contingencies she mentions above have a cultural dimension as well.

Above all, the concept of the "preferred" reading raises the question as to who will determine what is preferred in the text. In the case of Chicano (and other ethnic) films, the "preferred" reading has often been defined by those aspects—mostly formal—that Anglo American critics and reviewers understand. In other words, critical reception masks itself as textual operation, often with the result that the bicultural text is attributed a monocultural signification. And, since the ethnic text appears to have the formal coherence of Swiss cheese, it is all too easily reduced to its content or "message." But rather than conceptualize reception in terms of adherence to or aberrance from a reformed notion of the fixed text (as multicultural), it proves more useful at this point to consider the ways in which reception determines the text or image.

The film reviews for *La Bamba* provide a striking instance of such difference in the reading of an ethnic-coded sign.[10] In the issue over whether actor Lou Diamond Phillips, a Filipino-Hawaiian, resembled a Chicano, reviewers disagreed on whether the real Ritchie Valens himself looked Chicano. Several noted that Valens looked like a bull and had obvious "Indian heritage" that made him "look so cool" (*Village Voice*; *Time*; *Video*). The fact that Valens looked Indian and Phillips did not was cited as something "you can see ... in any photo" (*Village Voice*). In most reviews, however, including those in the Hispanic press, neither Valens nor Phillips elicited comments over the "authenticity" of Chicano representation. But the reviewer in the *Los Angeles Times* saw another Valens altogether in claiming that "part of his appeal was how un-Latin he looked, with his freckles." The same photo elicited three different images: Indian, Chicano, Anglo.

In order to create a theoretical space for such difference in reception, I position Cortés's societal and media "curricula" within reception theorist Hans Robert Jauss's concept of the "horizon of expectations," which he defines as "the sum total of reaction, prejudgments, verbal and other behavior that greet a work upon its appearance."[11] The "horizon of expectations" provides the context within which viewers receive a film and can be divided into two broad categories: expectations derived from the film itself (style, genre, director, and stars); and the aesthetic discourse on film. Though the latter often mediates or defines the former, little research has been done on how the aesthetic discourse on film prefigures consumption.[12]

While film critics do have an impact on readers and each other,[13] most studies tend to reduce the nature of that impact to a comparison of popular tastes and critical opinion, which assumes that one can compare a quantity (audience attendance) with a quality (critical opinion). The fact that a person attended a film—whatever his or her reaction—is taken as a vote in favor of the film. Other studies have audiences rate films and compare the results to critics' ratings.[14] The focus of these studies is an overall evaluation—excellent, fair, or poor—that reduces the significance of the film to a question of purchase value.[15] Still, the impact of the aesthetic discourse on film can be described in general terms: "It tends to establish the critical vocabulary and frames of reference used not only by reviewers, but by film audiences as well."[16]

Overall, thirty publications were tracked. For the sake of analysis, I have divided these into nine categories: mainstream news/opinion, alternative news/opinion, Hispanic news/opinion, trade journals, aesthetic/entertainment, women, religious, educated/elite, and gossip (see appendix).[17] Some publications could legitimately belong to several classifications: for example, *Cineaste* is a film magazine (aesthetic) with a

Marxist orientation (alternative); and although the editorial board claims otherwise, the journal could be considered academic, given its contributors. The Chicano/Hispanic publications include the middle-of-the-road bilingual monthly magazine *Americas 2001* and the Spanish-language daily newspaper *La Opinión* (Los Angeles), as well as two bilingual newspapers, the Marxist *Unidad/Unity* (Oakland) and progressive *El Tecolote* (Mission District, San Francisco), which are published weekly and monthly, respectively.

In examining the aesthetic discourse, I will not attempt to posit an actual impact because too many variables would be involved: readers often subscribe to or read several publications, so the potential impact would depend upon an almost infinite number of combinations. Instead, the emphasis will be on what gets said where and for what (broadly defined) readerships. Also important is what does not get said, since—as film critic Roger Ebert argues— "critics can have the greatest impact by ignoring work."[18] Given the scope of the article, I limit the analysis to the two prominent issues that arose in the press: the response to the four films as a new development or cycle within the American film industry, and the use of the "barrio" as the dominant metaphor or framework for understanding these films.

Hispanic Hollywood

In its review of *La Bamba*, *Newsweek* did not evaluate the film per se, but the incipient phenomenon the film's success seemed to promise: "Hispanic Hollywood." The phrase soon gained currency as a shorthand for the half-dozen films in production and "more than twenty-five projects featuring Hispanic themes ... floating around Hollywood."[19] Few reviews, however, examined or defined "Hispanic Hollywood," except to cite the relative increase in Hispanic films, directors, and stars.

The discussion of "Hispanic Hollywood" as an economic or social phenomenon took place within the context of the news/general interest, business, or industry publications: *Advertising Age*; *Newsweek*; *Time*, in a special issue on Hispanic culture; *Americas 2001*, in a special issue on "Latinos in Hollywood"; *Americas*, an inter-American publication of the Organization of American States; and *Variety*, in its annual "Focus on Latin American and U.S. Hispanic Markets."[20] In addition, the *Los Angeles Times* and *New York Times* published six articles on *La Bamba* that explained the trend in terms of a "new" Hispanic market that Hollywood was "testing."[21] Finally,

Pat Aufderheide, senior editor of the socialist weekly newspaper *In These Times*, examined the forces at work in these films in her extended review of *Stand and Deliver* in *Mother Jones*.

The dominant explanation for the production of these films—called Hispanic although all four films were about Chicanos—was demographic factors coupled with the realization that Hispanics constituted a viable and distinct market that Hollywood could learn to target. According to market studies, the Hispanic population (estimated at 25 million) resembled the peak audiences of the 1930s and 1940s, who went to the movies on a regular basis (rather than to see a specific film) and as a family. Since the Hispanic population was concentrated in major urban areas, studios could reach the large Spanish-speaking audience with fewer dubbed or subtitled prints and a smaller, regional promotion campaign.[22]

La Bamba, with a record seventy-seven Spanish-language prints and a "Hispanic theme," was widely reported as the "first real test of the Hispanic market for American films."[23] Hollywood's recurrent "discovery" of the Hispanic market is, of course, a source of amusement and frustration among Chicanos. To its credit, *Advertising Age* recalled the "discovery" and "test" of the Hispanic market that accompanied *Zoot Suit* (1981), also directed by Luis Valdez.[24] *La Bamba* would earn nearly $60 million in the United States, with the return on advertising costs twice as high for the Hispanic market as for mainstream audiences. Columbia Pictures allocated 5 percent of its 1,250 prints and a $6 million advertising budget to the Hispanic market, which accounted for 10 percent of the national population and of the overall box office gross.[25]

La Bamba and the more modest, but nonetheless profitable, films *Born in East L.A.* and *Stand and Deliver* generated excitement in the press because Hispanic demographics and the Hollywood profit motive seemed to resolve racial conflict overnight without accommodation on either side. Studio heads reiterated that their desire to make a profit had no racial bias. *La Bamba* was presented as a "noble experiment" that would either prove that the Hispanic market and Hispanic films were profitable or fail and be forgotten.[26] While Hollywood often nurtures a star or theme through several failures in the hopes that a niche or market can be developed, industry executives did not afford Hispanic efforts the same opportunity. *Variety* alone—due to its function as a trade journal concerned with economic developments—noted that contradiction in an article titled "Hispanic Mart Promises B.O. but Studio Pursestrings Tight."[27] The resolution, however, was limited to a mutual economic exploitation that left racial attitudes unchallenged. *Variety* provided the clearest, and perhaps crudest, example of this line of thinking in the title of Peter Besas's article cited above: "Crossovers Vie for Megabuck Tortilla: Latinos & Anglos Seek to Break Ethnic Barriers."

Cuban American Ramón Menéndez, writer and director of *Stand and Deliver*, implicitly challenged the myth of demographics promulgated in the press, wherein the discovery and cultivation of a growing, untapped "market" leads to social change: "The [Hispanic] actors, directors and producers are in place. The real problem is the lack of powerful Hispanic executives."[28] Menéndez's remarks shifted the terms of the discussion on "Hispanic Hollywood" from one of Hispanic consumption to a consideration of the conditions of production for ethnic filmmakers. Still, Menéndez and the Chicano filmmakers subscribed to the Hollywood profit motive as a mechanism that could be used for cultural negotiation. Luis Valdez expressed the rationale behind his use of the "universal themes" of Hollywood cinema:

> I want to be part of the mainstream—as myself. What that requires is communicating artistically images and feelings society-at-large can understand.... We can stay in our barrios and pour our venom into our little community newspapers or teatros but we are not going to create substantial change until we get into the mainstream.

Richard "Cheech" Marin saw *Born in East L.A.* as a mainstream film that used comedy to raise social issues and make a profit, likening himself to Charlie Chaplin.[29] Despite this apparent change from an alternative to mainstream film practice, the same appeal to or strategic use of "universal themes" characterizes the manifestos of radical, alternative Chicano filmmakers of the 1970s, as the Chicano movement shifted its political discourse from cultural nationalism to internationalism.[30] Publications that promoted liberal causes or social change, however, tended to criticize the directors' efforts to fit into the mainstream, although Aufderheide implied that the films constituted an initial negotiation between Hispanic filmmakers and non-Hispanic Hollywood.[31]

Overall, the mass media placed the new "Hispanic Hollywood" within a historical context briefly described as a period of "limited roles" and "negative stereotypes." The vague sense of past racism isolated the new films from historical processes of reception, resistance, and production, which added weight to the explanation that the production of these films was driven by demographics. *Newsweek* alone provided a broader context for the appearance of these films when it mentioned the possible conflict with the Mexican film industry that supplies Spanish-language theaters in the United States.

Time, Americas, and *Americas 2001* were the only publications to offer brief historical overviews of Chicano or Hispanic representation in Hollywood cinema. In *Americas,* a publication of the Organization of American States, even the stereotypes the article alludes to are upbeat and innocuous: "mariachis" and "beautiful señoritas."[32] Given its political alignment, it is logical that *Americas* would repress material that might recall or evoke anti–United States sentiment.

Richard Corliss in *Time* presents a three-paragraph historical overview that contrasts the current difficult situation in which Hispanic filmmakers work with a benign past: "In the old days things were almost better," because, unlike other minorities, Hispanics were portrayed as such positive figures as the "Latin lover" and "camp goddess." As with *Americas, Time* begins its history after the silent "greaser" films and ignores the bandido and buffoon stereotypes that coincide with the Latin lover. Corliss states that Hispanics were not represented on the screen between the 1950s and 1970s, and then implicates liberal Hollywood and Blacks, a group that became the subject of social problem films and, later, "blaxploitation" films. Unfortunately, he fails to mention that social problem films about Blacks were pivotal in the demise of the Black independent production companies of the previous three decades.[33] In any case, numerous social problem, historic message, and especially Western films have depicted Chicanos and Mexicans since the 1930s.[34]

Corliss's selective history reinforces the notion that minorities contend with each other in a zero-sum game, wherein one racial or ethnic group's gain is another's loss. Corliss also uses the dubious statement about a "liberal" Hollywood in order to bolster his conservative message that Hispanics must assimilate with the mainstream. Ironically, the period he cites as liberal is notable for its Production Code censorship, and for the House Committee on Un-American Activities investigations that made it dangerous to be a liberal in Hollywood.

In turning from Hollywood representation to the more recent period of Chicano self-representation, Corliss describes the Chicano feature films of the late 1970s and early 1980s as "arthouse fodder … [that] … staggered under the weight of their liberal messages." The Chicano directors and producers who made these films—which are by no means "art-house fodder" but include social melodramas, *rasquache* or underdog seriocomedies, and coproductions with Mexico—are hidden behind a liberal-elite facade, summed up in the phrase "guilty connoisseurs." Corliss in effect substitutes a stereotyped liberal white audience for the actual agents who arose out of the Chicano movement of the 1960s. Likewise, he negates the Chicano audiences who saw these films, characterizing Chicano film history as a liberal-conservative drama in which Hispanic filmmakers face an "imposing" conflict between fine art and popular culture. In other words, the "cinema barrio" has to do with fine art and good (liberal) intentions—not the Chicano experience—while *El Norte* has to do with a "commercially appealing story line," not the Chicano experience.

In *Americas 2001*, Antonio Ríos-Bustamante challenges the selective history presented in *Time* and *Americas*. He examines the "Latin/Latina lover" as both a positive and negative image. While Corliss applauds the female "Mexican spitfires" as able to "explode" their roles with "wit and pizzazz," Ríos-Bustamante links Lupe Veléz's typecast career as the "Mexican spitfire" to her suicide. He also cites the recurrent "greaser" stereotype that began with silent films, and details the protests and negotiations that took place in the studios—with Mexican actors such as Dolores Del Rio and Ramon Novarro—and in the Spanish-language newspapers, especially *La Opinión*.

Despite a rich history of Chicano representation and resistance, the mainstream publications presented a selective history or context for the new wave of Chicano-produced films. Often it was a context that minimized Chicano agency, in order to play out a political drama well suited to the racial issues and subtexts of the presidential campaign then dominating the news. When Chicanos were the focus, the emphasis was on a passive "market" that could be "exploited," rather than on the Chicano filmmakers and professional organizations and their two-decade struggle to bring their stories before the American public.

The Barrio

Given the lack of historical awareness in the mainstream press, reportage on Chicanos continues to position them as the most "localized" ethnic group.[35] Such an act is more ideological than demographic, since it "localizes" the discourse on Chicanos to barrio issues, excluding Chicanos from the reportage and debates on "mainstream" and "national" issues.

La Bamba, *Born in East L.A.*, and *Stand and Deliver* are set in East Los Angeles, while *The Milagro Beanfield War* is set elsewhere in the Southwest.

But in contrast to the conventional depictions, these films attempt to redefine or reconceptualize the stereotyped "ethnic" spaces, especially through the use of genre. In place of the usual western, conquest, or gang film, these new films use the American "success" genre, comedy, and—in the case of *The Milagro Beanfield War*—reverse the terms of the conquest film.[36] Film reviewers, however, did not cite or question past and present instances of "localized" Chicano images. That these films were about the barrio was a given, although how each reviewer translated or understood barrio ("neighborhood" or "slum") varied, and with it the reviewer's assumptions about the Chicano experience as film narrative. While I had expected to discover significant differences across ideological as well as ethnic lines in the press, such was not the case. With few exceptions, Anglo reviewers or publications confined Chicanos to a barrio slum, while Hispanic reviewers or publications identified the barrio community as the starting point for Chicanos' placement within the national culture.

Because each film evokes different issues in the press about the barrio, I will approach the aesthetic discourse one film at a time in order of release before drawing some general conclusions. An analysis of the cultural codes, cinematic structures, and ideologies that inform these texts is the subject of other studies. For now, I will preface each section with a brief plot summary.

LA BAMBA. Luis Valdez's *La Bamba* is the biography of 1950s rock 'n' roll star Ritchie Valens (né Ricardo Valenzuela), who died at the age of seventeen in the same plane crash that killed Buddy Holly in 1959.

The Chicano/Hispanic newspapers *La Opinión* and *Unidad* hailed *La Bamba* as a realistic portrayal of the barrio. Realism, however, was evaluated through a complex set of cultural and aesthetic criteria. *La Opinión* argued that *La Bamba* "desborda cualquier clasificación que se le quiera dar anticipadamente" (exceeds all anticipated classifications): "simple crónica," musical, and "una historia sobre las gentes del barrio" (a story about the people of the barrio). Likewise, the characters were described as "seres auténticos, llenos de contradicciones, pero reales" (authentic, full of contradictions, but real). *Unidad* added that the film evokes "una justa medida de realismo de lo que es vivir como latino, con todo su color, emoción y hasta toque de lo sobrenatural" (a fair measure of realism about Latino life, with its color, emotion and a little bit of the supernatural). These reviews emphasized Valens's ethnic environment and the structural movement from north to south rather than the expected one *al norte*. But, in the attention to the interplay between Chicano and "mainstream" codes, the reviews stop short of an ethnic essentialism, and reveal instead how the film exceeds a singular classification. As *Unidad* noted, Valens moves closer to his ethnic roots—Mexico and "La Bamba"—at the same time that he enters the mainstream: "El filme trata con la búsqueda de identidad, y también del éxito" (The film depicts the search for both identity and success).

The Hispanic press saw *La Bamba* as a pivotal Chicano film in which the Chicano themes "adquieren, por primera vez, características verdaderamente universales" (acquire, for the first time, truly universal characteristics) (*La Opinión*). As *Americas 2001* explained, *La Bamba* depicted the "daily struggles ... [that] ... exist in every family." As a result, *La Bamba* was most often compared to *East of Eden* (1955), because both films depict the struggle between a "good" and a "bad" brother. The universal themes were not believed to compromise the Chicano experience—with its unique culture that includes a little bit of the supernatural—but instead to provide an entry point for non-Hispanic audiences.[37]

El Tecolote, on the other hand, faulted *La Bamba* as an American success film that superimposes an individualist and assimilationist ideology upon the Chicano community and its culture. The untold story of the barrio or "our house ... in shambles" includes poor education, job discrimination, the new immigration law, and English-only initiatives. Rather than emphasize Chicano "organizing and struggle," Columbia Pictures and Luis Valdez exploited a market with a film that offered a "momentary surge of cultural pride."

The mainstream newspapers found *La Bamba* realistic in its depiction of barrio details, but not life. The *Los Angeles Times* cited the "authentic details of migrant worker camps and cracker-box San Fernando Valley homes," but added that "there must have been a crunch somewhere as one culture accommodated another, and a lot of that is gone." Most reviewers criticized Valdez for shaping "facts into fable" (*Time*). *La Bamba* represented "mythmaking," historical "hocus-pocus" (*New Yorker*), "mystical inflation" (*Rolling Stone*), and even a "soapy ethnic melodrama verging on camp" that begs the question, "Is any of this true?" (*Video*). The *Village Voice* noted that "Southern California's Mexican culture—with its own early rock and roll—hardly exists on film."

Reviewers objected to "Ritchie's denial of his roots and total buy-in to the American dream" (*Variety*) and believed that the film should have emphasized his subjective experience as a Chicano (also *Glamour*). These reviews were similar to the one in *El Tecolote* in their criticism of "mainstream dreamers" in the barrio. As *New Yorker* critic Pauline Kael explained: "He can be the pride of the Latino community (and still be innocuous enough to be liked by the larger public). The picture is a hangover from the fifties: he's a credit to his ethnic group."

While these criticisms appear to be similar in nature, their contexts are disparate. *El Tecolote* serves a barrio audience, while the other publications are directed at an audience that is for the most part uninformed and unaffected. Also, in the issue after the review, *El Tecolote* provided a forum for Valdez to respond to these criticisms in a lengthy interview.[38] In this respect, Pat Aufderheide's review in *In These Times* stands out from others in the non-Hispanic press, as do her subsequent reviews. Even though often critical, she is careful to locate *La Bamba* within Valdez's career since the agit-prop "actos" of El Teatro Campesino in the mid-1960s, and can see the often problematic relationship between Chicano culture and an ostensibly "universal" postwar youth culture. In short, Aufderheide brings to her reviews an awareness of the Chicano experience, both aesthetic and social, perhaps due to her background in Latin American cinema.

The other Anglo reviewers criticize the film as "myth" without a corresponding recognition of the "truth" from which Valdez is said to have turned, a "truth" already identified here as a "localized" discourse and selective history.[39] This process in the mainstream and alternative press will become even more apparent on considering *Stand and Deliver*.

BORN IN EAST L.A. Richard "Cheech" Marin's directorial debut and first film without Tommy Chong is based on his popular music video (1985) of the same title. A lesser-known fact about the video and film is that both are based on a newspaper account about a Chicano born in East L.A. who was deported to Mexico in 1984. *Born in East L.A.* lampoons the Simpson-Rodino Immigration Act and California's English-only initiative, while it alludes to Depression-era "repatriation" and the 1950s Operation Wetback, which together deported over three million "Mexicans," many of whom were either born in the United States or were legal immigrants. With few exceptions, however, the film did not receive coverage outside the Hispanic press, except in Latin America.

Most non-Hispanic periodicals explained that *Born in East L.A.* attempts to create sympathy for "wetbacks."[40] But while the non-Hispanic reviews defined the narrative movement as from Tijuana to the U.S. border, *La Opinión* envisioned the movement from the point of view of "un típico muchacho del Este de Los Angeles" (a typical guy from East L.A.) as he is wrongly deported. That shift in perspective is captured in its headline, "De las calles del barrio a la frontera mexicana" (From the streets of the barrio to the Mexican border). In an earlier review, *La Opinión* described the film's premier in East L.A. to emphasize the congruence between film and barrio: "Hacía mucho tiempo que el público de origen hispano de la ciudad de Los Angeles no veía una película con la que se sintiera identificado" (It has been a long time since the Hispanic-origin people of Los Angeles have seen a film with which they could identify).

Unidad identified the crucial distinction the film makes between East Los Angeles (Chicanos) and Tijuana (illegals). Rudy Robles (Marin), a third-generation Chicano who does not speak Spanish, neither sympathizes with illegal aliens (including his cousin) nor understands the extent to which American society views him as more Mexican than American. It is only when Robles is deported that he begins to change his point of view. Thus the film targets East Los Angeles as well as mainstream society. *La Opinión* emphasized a similar dual-audience message, although it did not mention Rudy's initial equivocation: He is a victim, "la singular representación de una tragedia colectiva" (the singular representation of a collective tragedy).

Born in East L.A. ends with Robles and several hundred Mexicans and "OTMs" (INS-speak for Other Than Mexican) overwhelming the U.S. border to the sound of Neil Diamond's "America." The *Los Angeles Times*, which found the film better than *La Bamba*, felt that there was "nothing cynical or satirical" about the scene: "You don't have to be a WASP to love your country, warts and all" (also *Variety*). *Cineaste*, however, thought that the ending was "politically naive in that it perpetuates the myth of boundless opportunities for illegal aliens in the U.S.," and gave no credence to Marin's response in its interview: "America is the land of opportunity, however it may temper that opportunity with persecution and discrimination."[41] What no reviewer mentioned was the fact that Robles and the illegal aliens crossed the border not into the United States per se, but into East L.A.—the barrio—via the sewer system. Though cited as the film's funniest scene, the ending recalls the dangerous and fatal border crossing in *El Norte* (1983). Robles even brings a Salvadoran *novia* with him, so that their implied marriage symbolizes the impact of recent Salvadoran refugees on barrio life and culture.[42]

THE MILAGRO BEANFIELD WAR. Based on the 1974 novel by John Nichols, *The Milagro Beanfield War* is about an unemployed Chicano who resists developers' efforts to turn his town into a resort when he diverts state-controlled water to cultivate a beanfield on his dead father's land. The film was directed by Robert Redford and coproduced by Moctesuma Esparza, who owned the movie rights to the novel.

Because of Redford's star status, location in *The Milagro Beanfield War* took on significance not as a real place, but as a symbolic one: "merry black-and-white moral landscape" (*America*); and "Redfordland ... a dream of liberal community" (*Time*). Most reviewers identified the film as a "progressive fairytale" (*Guardian*) that ranged from "white liberal guilt" (*American Spectator*) to "wishful thinking" (*Newsweek; Commonweal*).

The conservative *American Spectator* criticized the Chicano characters as unrealistic liberal stereotypes: "They're one dimensional icons of noble poverty, courtesy of the cliché-infested, liberal-guilt-ridden imagination of a rich white movie star." Surprisingly, liberal and middle-of-the-road periodicals also objected to the film's reversal of the terms of the conquest narrative, so that the "noble peasant" now triumphed over "gringo indignities" (*Village Voice; New Republic; New York*). The liberal Catholic periodicals *America* and *Commonweal* even aimed some self-criticism at their earlier "1960s liberalism" with its "naive optimism" in the efficacy of "good intentions," which the film revived.

The more mainstream (and conservative) periodicals—*Newsweek, People*, and *Time*—also cited Robert Redford's liberal intentions, but nonetheless promoted the film as a "feel good fable" with either positive or subtle stereotypes. *Time*, which on the one hand locates the film in "Redfordland," even began its review with a paean to Redford's style, but in the process reduced the Chicano characters to little more than landscape:

> The kiss of two fine brown faces is silhouetted by an orange sunset. Night falls, and there's a rope of rainbow in the sky; a frosted moon smiles behind a scrim of mist. Nature has rarely gone to the movies in starker, more glamorous clothes.

The unnamed characters in this passage are reduced to color. The passive voice further denies their role as participants, so that they become instead components in an aesthetic experience of "Nature." The passage links the "brown faces" to the "frosted moon" through facial actions (kiss, smile) and color (brown, frosted, or white).

Because *The Milagro Beanfield War* was identified with Redford and his particular brand of Hollywood liberalism, reviewers often cited the influence of film genres, rather than some historical referent. Pat Aufderheide criticized that tendency, locating the problem in the film itself, which she argued "refers more to other movie conventions than it does to the texture of the experience and culture of its subjects" (*In These Times*). Given the mishmash of styles, genres and, for Aufderheide at least, Latin American accents, the

183

introduction of "magic realism" was seen as inappropriate: "When Gabriel García Márquez deals in magic realism, every whimsical idea is tied to a hard one" (*Los Angeles Times*; also *Village Voice*). The violence comes too late and proves harmless, although *America* pointed out that other reviewers underemphasize the "threatened and actual violence" in the film.[43]

The Hispanic press, however, identified *The Milagro Beanfield War* with Chicano history, rather than with Redford's "passionate humanism" (*Time*) or Hollywood genres. *Unidad* put the film into a political perspective: "The first major movie to take up the issue of the theft and struggle for Chicano lands in the Southwest." *La Opinión* called *The Milagro Beanfield War* "un 'milagroso' filme que nos recuerda el orgullo de nuestro origen" (a "miraculous" film that reminds us of the pride of our origins), and, in an earlier review, identified that pride with "la lucha contra la adversidad y el materialismo" (the struggle against adversity and materialism).[44]

Seen within the context of Chicano culture, "magic realism" did not detract from the film, but instead helped it become a poetic "monumento a la identidad hispana en Norteamérica" (monument to Hispanic identity in North America).[45] Thus the film was seen as pivotal in the history of "magic realism" and its dissemination to North America. Like *Unidad*, *La Opinión*'s reviewer thought that the film would educate non-Hispanics, though it placed even greater emphasis on the film's impact on Hispanic pride, telling its readers to see the Spanish version: "Disfrútela y recuerde que nuestra herencia hispana es lo más valioso que tenemos" (Enjoy the film and remember that our Hispanic heritage is our most valuable possession).

Clearly, then, the faults identified within the mainstream or Anglo press must be seen not as absolute shortcomings inherent in the text, but as perceived ones particular to the viewer and his or her cultural-political-class nexus.

STAND AND DELIVER. *Stand and Deliver* is, in the familiar advertisement lingo, "based on the true story" of Jaime Escalante, a math teacher at Garfield High School in East Los Angeles who gained national attention in 1982 when eighteen of his students passed the advanced placement exam in calculus. The Educational Testing Service accused the students of cheating, forcing them to take the exam again. Like *Born in East L.A.*, the film was inspired by newspaper accounts and takes place in the present-day East Los Angeles barrio.

The non-Hispanic press described the barrio as a problem space, while the Hispanic press described the barrio as "nuestra comunidad" (our community), a place with pride and achievement despite institutional racism and neglect. Religious, Marxist, liberal, and conservative publications alike referred to the barrio as an impoverished "environment": "gang-plagued, predominantly Hispanic" (*Christian Century; Newsweek*); "poor people and slums" (*Nation; People; Cineaste; Guardian; New York*); "drugs, joblessness, and early pregnancy" (*Christianity Today*); and a "war zone" (*Los Angeles Times*). Often Garfield High was treated as the representative "inner-city school," described as a "mess" (*Village Voice*) that perpetuated "an underclass programmed to fail" (*Time*), or "cycles of poverty and degradation" (*Commonweal*).

While these descriptions suggest a social criticism, most often it was the barrio community itself that was seen as holding back the students. In explaining the problems students faced, reviewers cited "the absence of competent parents and teachers" (*Village Voice*); gangs, "thoughtless and irresponsible parents," and "demoralized teachers" (*Glamour*); and "peer and home pressures" (*El Tecolote*) that explain "why barrio kids have a hard time doing their homework" (*New York Times*). The solution was likewise found within the barrio in either a "barrio hero" (*Time; Newsweek, Christianity Today*) or in the realization that "seeming limitations of environment and resources are only artificial barriers that can be overcome with hard work and the right attitude" (*Variety*).

Three publications—religious (evangelist), Hispanic (progressive), and alternative (Marxist)—cited broader explanations for the crisis in inner-city schools like Garfield. *Christianity Today* explained that "socioeconomic class [and not race] is the biggest predictor of academic success." The review thus revealed "hard work and the right attitude," which the Escalante character called *ganas* (desires), to be social constructs rather than individual attributes. The somewhat Marxist analysis, however, becomes subsumed under the evangelist paradigm, wherein the "visionary" teacher initiates students to the "Quest." *El Tecolote*, which cited "peer and home pressures," and the *Guardian* rejected the "barrio hero" or "individual-warrior-for-his-people" and "hard work" as solutions, especially given racism and "economic inequalities." The film, however, was seen as the site of multiple ideological positions, rather than as the producer of a singular "ideological effect." For example, despite the film's perceived conservative message and emphasis on Escalante rather than on the students, both reviews recommended the film "because it shows Latinos as people, not stereotypes."

Although most reviews discussed the film's narrative weaknesses and the social impact that was said to compensate for them, few considered whether *Stand and Deliver* challenged usual film conventions about the barrio. In fact, the discourse in the mainstream and alternative press often segregates questions of ethnic content from questions of filmic form, as though the two had nothing to do with each other. In a rare exception, Pat Aufderheide argued that *Stand and Deliver* shatters the division between message and entertainment, which "only works if there isn't human experience on either side of the dichotomy" (*In These Times*). She concluded that the film makes it "impossible to forget that you're watching people divided by class, ethnicity, language and gender." While *El Tecolote* and the *Guardian* made similar claims about the characters as socially defined, other reviewers identified the characters as individuals who transcend both an impoverished barrio and film narrative.

The review in *The Nation* revealed the conceptual blind spot common to most non-Hispanic reviewers who address the issue of Hollywood form and ethnic content. The review cited as a challenge to the conservative Hollywood formula "the mere notion of using poor people and slums as something other than a battleground between cops and drug peddlers." The unironic use of "poor people and slums" to describe an ethnic community, however, belies the reviewer's subsequent criticism that the film "leaps over ... any fresh knowledge or insight." In effect, the reviewer's desire for "fresh knowledge" is revealed to rest upon a rather stale assumption that conflates race with socioeconomic status.

On the other side of the political fence, *Newsweek* quoted Director Menéndez on his efforts to dispense with "expected clichés" and depict instead "the Latino experience." The review then undermined his point about stereotypes through its own gratuitous use of "expected clichés." Garfield, though described as a "mecca for barrio kids" who want to be educated, cannot escape a reference to "the inevitable gang jackets." The statement makes manifest the assumption that gangs are "inevitable" in (and particular to) the barrio. The review continued to develop the gang subtext in the last paragraph, which contains Menéndez's statement about the absence of clichés such as "bloody gang fights." A contrapuntal heading in boldface promises: "Gang fights." The heading could have read "No gang fights," reinforcing the point of the paragraph. Instead, the headline writer used "expected clichés" to draw attention to the last paragraph. The only other phrase in boldface is the title in the first paragraph, so that at first glance the reader sees *Stand and Deliver* and Gang fights, with the body of the review positioned in between.

Time, which described the Chicanos in *The Milagro Beanfield War* as landscape, further objectified Chicanos in its review of *Stand and Deliver*.

The review opened in dramatic fashion with three words: "Drugs, rape, murder." Because these social problems were unsuited to nature metaphors, the review turned to a cinematic one: "inner-city school life can be a recurrent horror movie." The review then described "a barrio hero" who solved these problems on the screen and in real life. While *Stand and Deliver* is based on a true story, neither drugs, rape, nor murder ever figure in the actual or depicted events. Rather than place the film within an appropriate genre, *Time* instead treated the barrio experience as an all-too-predictable and violent film genre.

Since the Hispanic press did not see the barrio as a problem space (but as a cultural space with achievements, problems, and so on), reviews emphasized the film's role as the most realistic and positive communal portrait to date. *La Opinión* praised *Stand and Deliver* as an authentic representation of "el tipo de vida que se desarrolla en medio de las abigarradas y coloridas calles del Este de Los Angeles" (the kind of life that unfolds along the diverse and colorful streets of East Los Angeles). This did not mean, however, that the reviewer pulled his punches on aesthetic or political shortcomings: "estríctamente cinematográfico, *Stand and Deliver* no es un filme deslumbrante"; and "en el filme de Menéndez ese grave hecho [de la educación en los Estados Unidos] sólo aparece ligeramente insinuado" (on strictly cinematographic grounds, *Stand and Deliver* is not a dazzling film; and in Menéndez's film this serious fact [of poor education] is only lightly insinuated).[46] In its description of the urban landscape, *Americas 2001* located Garfield High "comfortably behind Whittier Blvd... in the heart of East Los Angeles." The review then described how Garfield is perceived within the community: first for its "classic rivalry" with another high school, then later for its college-bound graduates. In a historical note, the reviewer added that "ten years ago, Garfield was known for its absenteeism and its youth gangs."

The few non-Hispanic publications that historicized the school's actual problems placed them in 1982, the year in which the film takes place (*Mother Jones*; *Los Angeles Times*; *New York*). Escalante, however, began teaching at Garfield High in 1974, and five students first took the AP exam in 1979.[47] Former students and Escalante himself also explain that, unlike the film, there were no gang members or *cholos* in the class; in fact, most students were already college-bound.[48] It is telling, then, that several reviewers complained that the gang problem is not emphasized enough in the film and that Escalante's success seems "too easy" (*Glamour, Variety; Village Voice; New York*).

In *New York*, David Denby complained that "Victory comes too easily, without enough resistance and backsliding. And what kids! They have to be among the tamest, sweetest ghetto teens in history." Denby, like Richard Corliss in *Time*, conjured up a history he didn't need to document, since—like any prejudice—it is already well known: "ghetto teens" are wild brutes. When Denby compared *Stand and Deliver* to Dennis Hopper's gang film *Colors*, he concluded that "the violent, despairing *Colors* is the one that has the ring of *truth*" (emphasis mine). This is, after all, the "truth" about Chicanos in Los Angeles that reaches him in New York through the news and entertainment media. These were the expectations on the horizon of the film's mainstream release.

Conclusion

The most obvious and significant breakdown that occurs within the publications, and one that obviates all other differences, is the one between the Hispanic and non-Hispanic press. Liberal non-Hispanic publications often relied on the same outsider's assumptions about the barrio that characterized the conservative publications. The barrio was a problem space, denied a history, culture, and separate point of view, not to mention internal complexity. That assumption manifested itself first and foremost in the mistranslation of barrio as "slum," rather than the more appropriate "neighborhood." As a result, the films were often discussed in the context of social problems, rather than in the context of cultural identity or even film history.

The differences between the Hispanic and non-Hispanic press signal a debate over the boundaries of ethnic expression, a debate that centered on the question of "authentic" versus "universal" film narratives. Non-Hispanic publications often denounced the imposition of universal values upon Chicano culture, a stance that seemed to be patronizing at best, since these same publications were active in the maintenance of the "mainstream" or a "universal" discourse. In *La Opinión* and other Chicano publications, the universal themes were not seen as an imposition on Chicano culture, but as a mechanism for increasing bicultural understanding through viewer identification with the film's plot and characters. Furthermore, Chicano viewers were seen as active participants who brought their experiences to bear upon these films. In this manner, Chicano directors and reviewers seemed to identify Chicano cinema as an effort to expand the non-Hispanic "horizon of expectations," thus changing the very nature of those "universal" values.

If the Chicano feature films had indeed "crossed over" into the Hollywood mainstream, their success held the potential to complicate the authentic/universal dichotomy with its distinct boundaries between center and margin, dominant and ethnic. The non-Hispanic press, however, often responded to these films with silence. *The Reader's Guide to Periodicals* listed just one review for *Born in East L.A.* And while it also listed fifteen reviews for *The Milagro Beanfield War*, the fact that most dealt with Robert Redford and his celebrity was itself a form of silence, since Chicano issues were not addressed. *Time* revealed a third kind of silence in its objectification of Chicano characters as either nature (landscape) or culture (horror films). In these reviews, Chicano issues often became a convenient foil in defense of traditional liberal and conservative politics. Thus, for the most part, the non-Hispanic reviews served to maintain and reinforce the "critical vocabulary and frames of reference" of the dominant culture.[49]

It is perhaps too early to tell whether "Hispanic Hollywood" as such will continue and whether these films have changed the "horizon of expectations." Additional research is needed to discern the interpretive communities that are active in constructing meaning, that reveal the text to be a process and not a product. In so doing, film scholars must be careful not to displace that horizon with their own set of expectations. But, above all, as scholars, reviewers, and filmgoers alike look to the "horizon of expectations" beyond the "cinema barrio," it is important to ask: Whose expectations? Whose barrio?

Appendix

Film reviews, listed by publication type

Source	La Bamba	Born in East L.A.	Milagro Beanfield War	Stand And Deliver
Mainstream news/opinion				
Newsweek	1		1	1
Time	1		1	1
U.S. News & World Report	1			
Los Angeles Times	1	1	1	2
New York Times	2	1	1	2
Alternative news/opinion				
Guardian		1	1	
In These Times	1		1	1
Mother Jones				1
The Nation				1
Village Voice	1		1	1
Hispanic news/opinion				
Americas 2001	1			1
La Opinión	2	3	3	2
El Tecolote	1			1
Unidad	1	1	1	1
Trade journal				
Variety	1	1	1	1
Aesthetic/entertainment			1	
American Film				1
Cineaste			1	
Horizon			1	
Rolling Stone	1			
Women				
Glamour	1		1	1
Vogue			1	
Religious				
America			1	
The Christian Century			1	1
Christianity Today				1
Commonweal			1	1
Educated/elite				
New York			1	1
New Yorker	1			
The New Republic			1	
The American Spectator			1	
Gossip				
People Weekly		1	1	1

Notes

I am grateful to Tomás Ybarra-Frausto and Kathleen Newman for their invaluable advice and support. I would like to thank Henry Breitrose, Gabrielle James Forman, David Maciel, Mary Louise Pratt, Renato Rosaldo, and Virginia Wexman for their comments on earlier drafts of this essay.

1. José Limón, "Stereotyping and Chicano Resistance: An Historical Dimension," *Aztlán: International Journal of Chicano Studies Research* 4, no. 2 (fall 1973): 257–70. Reprinted in *Chicanos and Film: Representation and Resistance*, ed. Chon A. Noriega (Minneapolis: University of Minnesota Press, 1992), 3–17.

2. Carlos E. Cortés, "Chicanas in Film: History of an Image," in *Chicano Cinema: Research, Reviews, and Resources*, ed. Gary D. Keller (Binghamton, N.Y.: Bilingual Review/Press, 1985), 96–7. See also Carlos E. Cortés, "The Societal Curriculum: Implications for Multiethnic Education," in *Education in the 80s: Multiethnic Education*, ed. James A. Banks (Washington, D.C.: National Education Association, 1981), 24–32; and Carlos E. Cortés, "The Greaser's Revenge to Boulevard Nights: The Mass Media Curriculum on Chicanos," in *History, Culture, and Society: Chicano Studies in the 1980s*, ed. National Association for Chicano Studies (Ypsilanti, Mich.: Bilingual Press/Editorial Bilingue, 1983), 125–40. Stuart Hall and Hans Robert Jauss make similar points about the education role of the media and the external factors that affect a text's reception. Stuart Hall, "Culture, the Media, and the 'Ideological Effect'," in *Mass Communication and Society*, ed. James Curran, Michael Gurevitch, and Janet Wollacott (London: Edward Arnold, 1977), 340–1; and Hans Robert Jauss, *Toward an Aesthetic of Reception*, trans. Timothy Bahti (Minneapolis: University of Minnesota Press, 1982), 41.

3. Carlos E. Cortés, "Chicanas in Film: History of an Image," in Keller, *Chicano Cinema*, 96.

4. Robert Stam and Louise Spence, "Colonialism, Racism, and Representation: An Introduction," *Screen* 24, no. 2 (1983). Reprinted in *Movie and Methods*, vol. 2, ed. Bill Nichols (Berkeley: University of California Press, 1985), 646–7.

5. Hall, "Culture," 344–6.

6. Stam and Spence, "Colonialism, Racism, and Representation," 646–7.

7. Umberto Eco, *The Role of the Reader* (Bloomington: Indiana University Press, 1979), 10, 49.

8. Stanley E. Fish, *Is There a Text in This Class? The Authority of Interpretive Communities* (Cambridge: Harvard University Press, 1980), 322; Julianne Burton, "Marginal Cinemas and Mainstream Critical Theory," *Screen* 26 no. 3 (1985): 18–21.

9. Barbara Klinger, "Digressions at the Cinema: Reception and Mass Culture," *Cinema Journal* 28, no.4 (summer 1989): 3–4.

10. Rather than footnote the seventy-plus film reviews used in this essay, I will cite the publication title in parentheses within the text. This is done to aid the reader and to give visual emphasis to the publications as discursive arenas in which certain types of reviews appear. The citations for the film reviews are listed by film in the bibliography at the end of the essay.

11. Jauss, *Toward an Aesthetic of Reception*, 3–45.

12. Robert C. Allen and Douglas Gomery cite just one study on the role of nonfilmic events in the production of meaning (*Film History: Theory and Practice*

[New York: Alfred A. Knopf, 1985], 257). For two recent studies that examine the aesthetic discourse of film reviews and reportage, see Janet Staiger, "Securing the Fictional Narrative as a Tale of the Historical Real," *South Atlantic Quarterly* 88, no.2 (spring 1989): 393–413; and Chon A. Noriega, "Something's Missing Here! Homosexuality and Film Reviews during the Production Code Era, 1934–1962," *Cinema Journal* 30, no. 1 (fall 1990): 20–41.

13. John W. English, *Criticizing the Critics* (New York: Hastings House, 1979), 74–88.

14. English, *Criticizing the Critics*, 126; Bruce A. Austin, "Critics' and Consumers' Evaluations of Motion Pictures: A Longitudinal Test of the Taste Culture and Elitist Hypothesis," *Journal of Popular Film & Television* 10, no. 4 (1983): 156–67.

15. The above remarks are based on an examination of the following annotated bibliographies: Bruce A. Austin, "Film Audience Research, 1960–1980: An Annotated Bibliography," *Journal of Popular Film & Television* 8, no. 2 (1980): 53–60; Bruce A. Austin, "Film Audience Research, 1960–1980: An Update," *Journal of Popular Film & Television* 8, no. 4 (1981): 57–9; and Bruce A. Austin, "Research on the Film Audience: An Annotated Bibliography, 1982–1985," *Journal of Popular Film & Television* 14, no. 1 (1986): 33–9.

16. Allen and Gomery, *Film History*, 90.

17. Sources were gathered from the *Reader's Guide to Periodicals*, *Alternative Press Index*, *Chicano Periodical Index*, *New York Times*, *Los Angeles Times*, and *Variety*.

18. Quoted in English, *Criticizing the Critics*, 110.

19. Review of *Stand and Deliver* in *Mother Jones*. In the same period, directors Richard "Cheech" Marin and Luis Valdez, among others, also attempted to "cross over" into network television, an area even less receptive than the film industry. See Richard Zoglin, "Awaiting a Gringo Crumb," *Time*, 11 July 1988, 76; Bradley S. Greenberg and Pilar Baptista-Fernández, "Hispanic-Americans: The New Minority on Television," in *Life on Television: Content Analysis of U.S. TV Drama*, ed. Bradley S. Greenberg (Norwood, N.J.: Ablex Publishing, 1980), 3–12.

20. See the review of *La Bamba* in *Newsweek*; Richard Corliss, "Born in East L.A.: Hollywood Can Be a Tough Town for Non-Anglos," *Time*, 11 July 1988, 66–7; Antonio Ríos-Bustamante, "Latinos in the Hollywood Film Industry, 1920–1950s," *Americas 2001*, January 1988, 6–12; Omar G. Amador, "Latin Lovers, Lolita and *La Bamba*," *Americas*, July–August 1988, 2–9; Wayne Walley, "La Bamba Wakes Up Hollywood: Hispanic Market Potential Pondered," *Advertising Age*, 10 August 1987, 41; Peter Besas, "Crossovers Vie for Megabuck Tortilla: Latinos and Anglos Seek to Break Ethnic Barriers," *Variety*, 23 March 1988, 43; and Amy Dawes, "Hispanic Mart Promises Big B.O. But Studio Pursestrings Tight," *Variety*, 23 March 1988, 86.

21. Geraldine Fabrikant, "Campaign Propels *La Bamba*," *New York Times*, 13 August 1987, sec. 4, 19; Patrick Goldstein, "MTV La Bamba—Adman's Coup," *Los Angeles Times*, 26 July 1987, sec. C, 90–91; Aljean Harmetz, "Hollywood Gamble en Español," *New York Times*, 18 July 1987, sec. 1, 9; Don Snowden, "La Bamba Party 'Classic Hollywood,'" *Los Angeles Times*, 20 July 1987, sec. 6, 5; Victor Valle, "Ritchie Valens Film Boosts Prospects of Dubbing, Subtitles," *Los Angeles Times*, 24 July 1987, sec. 6, 1; and Victor Valle, "La Bamba May Change Film Marketing," *Los Angeles Times*, 29 July 1987, sec. 6, 1.

22. Until 1986, studios limited subtitled releases to the big-name action features of Chuck Norris, Sylvester Stallone, and so on. When Universal Studios released a dubbed version of Steven Spielberg's animated feature *An American Tail* (1986), however, the one theater that exhibited it earned the second-highest gross for theaters nationwide.

23. Harmetz, "Hollywood Gamble en Español."

24. Walley, "*La Bamba* Wakes Up Hollywood."

25. Fabrikant, "Campaign Propels *La Bamba*"; Valle, "Ritchie Valens Film"; review of *La Bamba* in *Newsweek*.

26. Harmetz, "Hollywood Gamble en Español."

27. Dawes, "Hispanic Mart Promises Big B.O."

28. Corliss, "Born in East L.A." 67.

29. Luis Valdez, "An Artist Who Has Blended Art and Politics," interview, *El Tecolote*, October 1987, 9; Luis Valdez, "Luis Valdez habla sobre *La Bamba*," interview, *La Opinión*, 24 July 1987, sec. 3, 1; Richard "Cheech" Marin, interview, *Americas 2001*, June–July 1987, 18–21; Richard "Cheech" Marin, "Cheech Marin, un personaje nació en el Este de los Angeles," interview, *La Opinión*, 23 August 1987, sec. PDA, 5 and Richard "Cheech" Marin, "Cheech Cleans Up His Act," interview, *Cineaste* 16, no. 3 (1988): 34–7.

30. For reprints of manifestos by Cine-Aztlán, Francisco X. Camplis, and Jason C. Johansen (of the Chicano Cinema Coalition), see Noriega, *Chicanos and Film*, 275–307.

31. Reviews of *The Milagro Beanfield War* and *Stand and Deliver* in *The Nation*. See also reviews of *La Bamba* in the *New Yorker* and *El Tecolote*. There is no consensus on how to interpret "basic capitalism" or the profit motive as a force within the Chicano community. Carlos Cortés outlines a "Chicano Media Action Program" that puts the onus upon Chicano consumers to use the commercial media to their own advantage. Chicanos need to "vote with their feet" for Chicano filmmakers, because "support brings money, and money can mean better Chicano films in the future." Cortés applies the same formula to other Chicano media, wherein an increased audience would increase advertising revenue and "provide the financial base for greater social activism" (Cortés, "The Greaser's Revenge," 136–9).

32. The relationship between the Chicano audiences and media, however, is not a direct one, since the media must cater to advertisers (who want a suitable forum for their ads) and studios (which want to reach mass audiences) in order to obtain the needed funds and—in the case of movies—distribution. See, for example, Luis F. Plascencia's examination of the impact of advertisers on *Low Rider Magazine*, "Low Riding in the Southwest: Cultural Symbols in the Mexican Community," in National Association for Chicano Studies, *History, Culture, and Society*, 141–76.

33. Amador, "Latin Lovers, Lolita and *La Bamba*," 2.

34. Donald Bogle, " 'B' Is for Black," *Film Comment* (September–October 1985), 34.

35. See Keller, "The Image of the Chicano"; Chon Noriega, "Citizen Chicano: The Trials and Titillations of Ethnicity in the American Cinema, 1935–1962," *Social Research: An International Quarterly of the Social Sciences* 58, no. 2 (summer 1991): 413–38; Charles Ramírez Berg, "Bordertown, the Assimilation Narrative and the Chicano Social Problem Film," in Noriega, *Chicanos and Film*,

29–46; and Arthur G. Pettit, *Images of the Mexican American in Fiction and Film* (College Station: Texas A&M University Press, 1980).

36. See Arthur G. Pettit's discussion of "localized" portrayals of Mexican Americans in the introduction to his book *Images of the Mexican American in Fiction and Film*.

37. For a critique of the role reversal in ethnic portrayal, see Linda Williams, "Type and Stereotype: Chicano Images in Film," *Frontiers* 5, no. 2 (summer 1980): 14–17. Reprinted in *Chicano Images in Film*, ed. Don Cardenas and Suzanne Schneider (Denver: Denver International Film Festival, 1981); and Keller, *Chicano Cinema*, 59–63.

38. *U.S. News and World Report* also identified the film as both Chicano and "universal" in appeal.

39. Valdez, "An Artist Who Has Blended Art and Politics."

40. For an account of the mythological substructure of *La Bamba* and its relationship to Luis Valdez's mythopoetics since the Chicano Movement, see Victor Fuentes, "Luis Valdez, Hollywood y Tezcatlipoca," *Chiricu* 5, no. 2 (1988): 35–9; and "Chicano Cinema: A Dialectic Between Voices and Images of the Autonomous Discourse Versus Those of the Dominant," in Noriega, *Chicanos and Film*, 207-17.

41. *People; Variety; New York Times.* The *Los Angeles Times* was the only mainstream periodical to identify the dual theme: "the second-class nature of American citizenship for ethnic minorities and the desperate situation in which illegal aliens find themselves."

42. Marin, "Cheech Cleans Up His Act."

43. For recent scholarship on *Born in East L.A.*, see Rosa Linda Fregoso, "*Born in East L.A.* and the Politics of Representation," *Cultural Studies* 4, no. 3 (October 1990): 264–80; Chon A. Noriega, "Cafe Orale: Narrative Structure in Born in East L.A.," *Tonantzin* 8, no. 1 (February 1991): 17–18; and Eduardo Tafoya, "*Born in East L.A.*: Cheech as the Chicano Moses," *Journal of Popular Culture* 26, no. 4 (Spring 1993): 123–29.

44. Reviewers did not consider the implications behind the protagonist's shooting of his old neighbor, Amarante Córdova. The final scene, however, can be read as Córdova's death: he is seen walking down the road toward home, when the Coyote Angel suggests a shortcut across a field, and the two jump over a fence and disappear. In the previous scene, Córdova had just regained consciousness in the hospital, but was in no condition to be released, let alone walk.

45. This statement undermines the generalizations in the mainstream press and sociological studies that equate ethnic middle-class status or aspirations with material gain and the loss of cultural identity.

46. Jorge Luis Rodríguez, "Los santos en el celuloide americano," *La Opinión*, 26 March 1988, 1–2.

47. See also the review in *Unidad*.

48. Kim Hubbard, "Beating Long Odds, Jaime Escalante Stands and Delivers, Helping to Save a Faltering High School," *People Weekly*, 11 April 1988, 57–8; Aljean Harmetz, "Math Stars in a Movie," *New York Times*, 20 March 1988, sec. 2, 21.

49. Harmetz, "Math Stars in a Movie"; Victor Valle, "Real-Life Flashbacks to 'Stand, Deliver,'" *Los Angeles Times*, 17 March 1988, sec. 6, 1.

50. Allen and Gomery, *Film History*, 90.

Bibliography

Reviews Listed by Film

La Bamba

Americas 2001. September/October 1987, 7. Consuelo Preciado.
El Tecolote. September 1987, 11–12. Víctor Martínez.
Glamour. August 1987, 200.
In These Times. 22 July–4 August 1987, 19. Pat Aufderheide.
La Opinión. 22 July 1987, sec. 2, 1. Juan Rodríguez Flores.
Los Angeles Times. 24 July 1987, sec. 6, 1. Sheila Benson.
Newsweek. 17 August 1987, 66–7. Jennifer Foote.
New Yorker. 10 August 1987, 71–2. Pauline Kael.
New York Times. 24 July 1987, sec. 2, 23. Janet Maslin.
Rolling Stone. 13 August 1987, 13. Anthony DeCurtis.
Time. 17 August 1987, 62. Richard Corliss.
Unidad. 12 October 1987, 12. Maggie Cardenas.
U.S. News & World Report. 10 August 1987, 48–9. John Podhoretz.
Variety. 20 May 1987, 16. Cart.
Video. February 1988, 64. Scott Isler.
Village Voice. 28 July 1987, 64. R. J. Smith.

Born in East L.A.

La Opinión. 22 August 1987, sec. 6, 1. Juan Rodríguez Flores.
La Opinión. 23 August 1987, PD, 5. Juan Rodríguez Flores.
Los Angeles Times. 24 August 1987, sec. 6A. Kevin Thomas.
New York Times, 24 August 1987, sec. 3, 14. Caryn James.
People Weekly. 14 September 1987, 14. Tom Cunneff.
Unidad. 12 October 1987, 12. Maggie Cardenas.
Variety. 26 August 1987, 15. Cart.

The Milagro Beanfield War

America. 2 July 1988, 19. Richard Blake.
American Film. March 1988, 26–31. Jill Kearny.
American Spectator. June 1988, 40–1. Bruce Bawer.
Christian Century. 27 April 1988, 433–4. Dean Peerman.
Commonweal. 22 April 1988, 244–5. Tom O'Brien.
Glamour. April 1988, 210. Stephen Schaefer.
Guardian. 13 April 1988, 17. Dan Cohen and Ann Gael.
Horizon. March 1988, 14–16. Stephen Schaefer.
In These Times. 22 April–3 May 1988, 20. Pat Aufderheide.
La Opinión. 2 March 1988, sec. 2,1. Juan Rodríguez Flores.

La Opinión. 26 March 1988, sec. 3,1–2. Jorge Luis Rodriguez.
La Opinión. 27 March 1988, sec. PD, 3. Juan Rodríguez Flores.
Los Angeles Times. 18 March 1988, sec. 6,1. Sheila Benson.
Nation. 30 April 1988, 619. James Lardner.
New Republic. 18 April 1988, 30–1. Stanley Kauffman.
Newsweek. 28 March 1988, 67–9. David Ansen.
New York. 11 April 1988, 113. David Denby.
New York Times. 18 March 1988, sec. 3, 17. Vincent Canby.
People Weekly. 4 April 1988, 10. Peter Travers.
Time. 28 March 1988, 74. Richard Corliss.
Unidad. 11 March 1988, 9. Lorena Corea and Venustiano Olguin Jr.
Variety. 16 March 1988, 14. Cart.
Village Voice. 29 March 1988, 80. David Edelstein.
Vogue. March 1988, 64. Luisa Valenzuela.

STAND AND DELIVER

Americas 2001. November/December 1987, 12–14. Rena Muro.
El Tecolote. April 1988, 13. Carlos Alcalj.
Christian Century. 27 April 1988, 434. Dean Peerman.
Christianity Today. 2 September 1988, 61. Stefan Ulstein.
Cineaste. 16, no.4 (1988): 52–4. Alice Cross.
Commonweal. 3 June 1988, 341–2. Tom O'Brien.
Glamour. May 1988, 215–6. Joy Gould Boyum.
Guardian. 8 June 1988, 12. S. E. Anderson.
In These Times. 6–12 April 1988, 20–1. Pat Aufderheide.
La Opinión. 13 March 1988, sec. PD,3. Juan Rodríguez Flores.
La Opinión. 2 March 1988, sec. 2,1. Juan Rodríguez Flores.
Los Angeles Times. 29 March 1988, sec. 6A. Charles Champlin.
Los Angeles Times. 10 March 1988, sec. 6A. Sheila Benson.
Mother Jones. April 1988,24–6. Pat Aufderheide.
Nation. 30 April 1988, 618–9. James Lardner.
Newsweek. 14 March 1988, 62. Jack Kroll.
New York. 18 April 1988,100–3. David Denby.
New York Times. 20 March 1988, sec. 2,21. Janet Maslin.
New York Times. 18 March 1988, sec. 3,14. Janet Maslin.
People Weekly. 18 April 1988, 10. Tom Cunneff.
Time. 4 April 1988, 77. Richard Corliss.
Unidad. 25 April 1988, 5. Ed Gallegos.
Variety. 17 February 1988, 22. Cart.
Village Voice. 29 March 1988, 80. David Edelstein.

Refiguring Aztlán

Rafael Pérez-Torres

One image central to Chicano/Chicana intellectual and social thought has been the figure of Aztlán. Too often, the name of this mythic homeland is either dismissed as part of an exclusionary nationalist agenda or uncritically affirmed as an element essential to *chicanismo*. In refiguring Aztlán, we move toward a conceptual framework with which to explore the connections between land, identity, and experience. Significantly, these connections become centrally relevant as the political, social, and economic relationships between people and place grow ever more complicated and fluid. The problems posed by Aztlán as a site of home and dispossession represent the types of discursive engagements many different constituencies have, in their own idiom, undertaken. Beyond the dynamic issues posed by the questions of national origin—one in four people living in California today, for example, was born outside the U.S. national border—are the issues of shifting genders and sexualities, the interrogation of national identification, and the investigation of indigenous ancestry, all areas interrogating the relation between locality and identity.

Within a Chicana/o context, Aztlán as the mythic Aztec homeland has served as a metaphor of connection and unity. During the nearly thirty years of its modern incarnation, Aztlán has come to represent a nationalist homeland, the name of that place that will at some future point be the national home of a Chicano people reclaiming their territorial rights. It has also come to represent the land taken by the United States in its nineteenth-century drive to complete its manifest destiny. The current controversy over border control in the Southwest is, then, but the latest battle in the retaking of Aztlán, a retaking represented by the migration and immigration of Latinos to the United States through both legal and extralegal means. Aztlán also stands as an index within Chicana/o cultural production as the grounds of contested representations: a site of numerous resistances and affirmations.

These multiple significances of Aztlán indicate its durability. Locating the source of this durability, naming that which energizes it, forms one of the central tropes in discussions of Aztlán. The present essay is no exception. It seeks to trace some of the historical, literary, and intellectual discourses on the meanings of Aztlán. The object is not to conclude that one of these discourses serves to better describe or locate Aztlán. Rather, I argue that at stake is not so much the worth of Aztlán as cultural/critical signifier as its role in shifting the horizon of signification as regards Chicano/a resistance, unity, and liberation. As the following discussion serves to illustrate, Aztlán remains significant precisely because it functions as an empty signifier. I briefly elaborate this point at the close of the essay.

To call Aztlán an empty signifier is not to say that the term is vacuous or meaningless. On the contrary, if anything, Aztlán is overly meaningful. From a historical perspective, for example, three moments of contestation are evoked in the naming of Aztlán: the Spanish invasion of the Aztec Empire, the appropriation of Mexican lands by the United States in the nineteenth and early twentieth centuries, and the immigration to (or reconquest of) the U.S. Southwest by Mexicanos and Central Americans in the contemporary era. But to be fair, for many in the Chicano "community," Aztlán signifies little; it is the political, social, and cultural Chicano/a elite of a particular stripe for whom Aztlán resonates as an icon imbued with some historical meaning. Five hundred years of European presence in the Americas is contested by an assertion of the indigenous, by an affirmation of native civilizations, by the recollection of Aztlán.

Even though it does not quite add up as a political or cultural metaphor, the lure of Aztlán seems irresistible to the Chicano intelligentsia. The term inevitably calls up difficulties in relation to itself, difficulties that lead the reclamation of Aztlán to take on numerous forms. From a literary and cultural critical position, Daniel Alarcón argues that Aztlán can best be understood as a palimpsest, as "a trope that allows a more complex understanding of cultural identity and history" given that "Aztlán has been used to obscure and elide important issues surrounding Chicano identity, in particular the significance of intracultural differences" (1992, 35–36). Cherríe Moraga has rearticulated the nationalist concerns associated with Aztlán, expanding its metaphorical qualities to reconnect it to different forms of social struggle. Thus Aztlán as a metaphor for land stands as an overdetermined signifier: "For immigrant and native alike, land is ... the factories where we work, the water our children drink, and the housing project where we live. For women, lesbians, and gay men, land is that physical mass called our bodies. Throughout Las Américas, all these 'lands' remain under occupation by an Anglo-centric, patriarchal, imperialist United States" (1993, 173). From a sociological position, Mario Barrera describes Aztlán as a locus of difficulty, the site of struggle for Chicano equality and community. This struggle forms the catalyst driving Chicano political activism and, consequently, the engine leading to an accelerated assimilation "seen most dramatically in the overwhelming loss of fluency in Spanish by the third generation [of Mexican immigrants ... but also seen] in the trend toward residential dispersion and the rising rate of intermarriage" (1988, 5).[1] I, too, elsewhere have argued that Aztlán has shifted from signifying a homeland to signaling a complexity of multiple subjectivities called the borderlands.[2]

Each of these positions regarding Aztlán is limited in its scope and can be contested at numerous turns. Viewing Aztlán as a place of *mestizaje*, of multiple and simultaneous subjectivities, elides the way in which notions of the borderlands change depending on their contextualization: whether from a historiographic, sociological, cultural, or ethnographic position. Arguing that assimilation is the problematic result of political engagement erases the de-indigenization undergone historically by mestizos and overlooks the dynamic sociocultural contributions made by continuous migration and immigration to the United States. To recast Chicano nationalist concerns within a larger framework of indigenous rights does not fully address the historical and cultural specificities enacted within different localities of political struggle. Understanding Aztlán primarily as a trope does little to address the specificities of Aztlán as a contestation of power.

Aztlán and the Plan

In large part, the elusive and powerful quality of Aztlán as a signifier has to do with the history of its production. Aztlán was introduced to Chicana/o discourse with "El Plan Espiritual de Aztlán," drafted in March 1969 for the Chicano Youth Conference held in Denver, Colorado. The question in regard to "El Plan Espiritual de Aztlán" is how it enacted Chicano/a self-affirmation and determination. Aztlán marks a matrix where at least two seemingly contradictory strands of Chicano thought meet. On the one hand, the term "Chicano/a" signifies an identification with struggles for change within or the transformation of socioeconomic and political systems that have historically exploited Mexicans and people of Mexican ancestry. The focus along this trajectory is on the transformation of material conditions, on gains in a real economic and political sense.[3] On the other hand, the term "Chicano/a" identifies a subjectivity marked by a heritage and culture distinct from and devalued by Euro-American society. The interplay between these two meanings of the term Chicano/a is complex and not at all resolved. Although the claims for Chicano cultural agency have been to a greater or lesser degree effective, their translation into social empowerment has been largely unsuccessful. This tension between the social and cultural polarities within Chicana/o activism is made evident in the various articulations of the term Aztlán.

Aztlán as a signifier marking the completion or return of the Chicano to a homeland suggests both cultural and social signification.[4] As the representation of place, Aztlán makes claims to a political and economic self-determination not dissimilar to those asserted by indigenous populations throughout the world. As a symbol of unity, Aztlán indicates a type of cultural nationalism that is distinct from—though meant to work hand-in-hand with—social activism. The sense of a double signification resounds in "El Plan Espiritual de Aztlán":

> Brotherhood unites us and love for our brothers makes us a people whose time has come and who struggle against the foreigner "Gabacho," who exploits our riches and destroys our culture. With our heart in our hands and our hands in the soil, We Declare the Independence of our Mestizo Nation. We are a Bronze People with a Bronze Culture. Before the world, before all of North America, before all our brothers in the Bronze Continent, We are a Nation, We are a Union of free pueblos, We are Aztlán. (1972, 403)

Against the Euro-American, the *gabacho*, the plan condemns he who "exploits our riches" and simultaneously "destroys our culture." These two spheres in which violence occurs are—within the logic of the plan—equitable but not identical. One represents the riches of land and labor, commodities within sociopolitical and economic systems of exchange. The other manifests self-identity and cultural independence. The tension between cultural and political autonomy makes itself felt in the image of the Chicano community as at once affirming culture ("With our heart in our hands") and nation ("and our hands in the soil"), both coming together in the formation of a "Mestizo Nation." What this nation consists of—beyond the essentializing and vague vision of a "Bronze People" with a "Bronze Culture" forming a "Union of free pueblos"—remains unspoken.

There are those who want to claim Aztlán as the embodiment of a successful unity between the cultural and political. As a student of both religious studies and legal discourse, Michael Pina argues that Aztlán represents the successful union of the spiritual and social:

> On one level Chicano nationalism calls for the re-creation of an Aztec spiritual homeland, Aztlán; on another, it expresses the desire to politically reconquer the northern territories wrested from Mexico in an imperialist war inspired by American "Manifest Destiny." These two mythic narratives merged to form the living myth of Chicano nationalism. This myth spanned the diachronic chasm that separates the archaic contents of cultural memory from the contemporary struggle for cultural survival. (1989, 36)

In effect, Pina argues that the evocation of Aztlán bridges "the diachronic chasm" between past indigenous identity and contemporary social activism as well as spanning the gap between cultural and political agency. Rather than evoke a bridge beyond history, I would argue that Aztlán reveals the discontinuities and ruptures that characterize the presence of Chicanos in history. Although it evokes a Chicano homeland, Aztlán also foregrounds the construction of history within a Chicano context. The difficult articulation of Chicano/a history—a history that speaks of dispossession and migration, immigration and diplomacy, resistance and negotiation, compromise and irony—remains ever unresolved.

Aztlán and the Diaspora

Aztlán can at times be articulated as a rather quaint dream, a fantastical delusion:

> Through Aztlán we come to better understand psychological time (identity), regional makeup (place), and evolution (historical time). Without any one of these ingredients, we would be contemporary displaced nomads, suffering the diaspora in our own land, and at the mercy of other social forces. Aztlán allows us to come full circle with our communal background as well as to maintain ourselves as fully integrated individuals." (Anaya and Lomelí 1989, iv)

Despite such assertions, in action Aztlán marks less a wholeness than a heterogeneity of the subject position Chicana/o in terms of identity, geography, history, psychology, spirituality, and nationality. It is impossible to ignore the nomadic role Chicanos and Mexicanos have played within a diasporic history of the United States.

While invoking the diasporic in relation to the Chicano/Mexicano, one might want to tread lightly. From a political scientific perspective,

201

William Safran argues that the concept of diaspora should be expanded to include more than that segment of a people living outside their homeland. His focus is primarily on the contemporary diaspora of "third world" people into Europe. He suggests that the term be applied to expatriate minority communities whose members share a memory of, concern with, and desire for a return to their homelands. As such, Safran notes—in a move that resonates with the conclusions drawn by Mario Barrera—the "Hispanic (or Latino) community in the United States has not generally been considered a diaspora. The Mexican Americans, the largest component of that community ... are assimilating at a steady pace." More importantly, for the purposes of his argument, Safran argues that "Mexican Americans do not cultivate a homeland myth ... perhaps because the homeland cannot be easily idealized. The poverty and political corruption of Mexico (which is easy enough to observe, given the proximity of that country) stand in too sharp a contrast with conditions in the United States" (1991, 90). This is quite a reversal of that favorite Mexican saying: "Poor Mexico. So far from God and so close to the United States." Given the means of mass communication and relative ease of international travel, it is not clear how the physical closeness of Mexico to the United States significantly affects the comparative de-idealization of it as a homeland in the minds of its diasporic population. More centrally, Mexico —as a national or cultural icon—does at many levels remain significant for most individuals self-identified as Chicano or Mexicano or Mexican American.

More to the point, the evocation of the diasporic or nomadic indicates that there is no one ideal subject that encapsulates the multiplicity of Chicano/a subjectivities. One cannot assert the wholeness of a Chicano subject when the very discourses that go into its identity formation—be they discourses surrounding the mutability of gender identity, sexuality, class and cultural identification, linguistic and ethnic association—are incommensurably contradictory. It is illusory to deny the nomadic quality of the Chicano/Mexicano community, a community in flux that yet survives and—through survival—affirms its own self.

This is not to dismiss either the political significance of Aztlán or the social relevance of "El Plan Espiritual." The plan does—owing much to Frantz Fanon—articulate an ambitious (if ambiguous) nationalism suggesting that the spiritual longing and physical needs of the subaltern "native" are inexorably bound together. Although Fanon argues in *The Wretched of the Earth* that the immediate effects of a cultural nationalism are difficult to gauge—"I am ready to concede that on the plane of factual being the past existence of an Aztec civilization does not change anything very much in the diet of the Mexican peasant today"—he goes on to argue that "this passionate search for a national culture which existed before the colonial era finds its legitimate reason in the anxiety shared by native intellectuals to shrink away from that Western culture in which they all risk being swamped" (1968, 209). By Fanon's argument, the search for an "other" space proves not to be simply an escape from the present. On the contrary, since colonial processes wish to impose rule upon the past as well as the present and future of a colonized people, the quest for a past proves to be a great act of resistance and self-affirmation: "The native intellectuals, since they could not stand wonderstruck before the history of today's barbarity, decided to go back further and to delve deeper down; and, let us make no mistake, it was with the greatest delight that they discovered that there was nothing to be ashamed of in the past, but rather dignity, glory, and solemnity" (210). The affirmation of a glorious past becomes the condemnation of a repressive present.

Evoking a similar sentiment, "El Plan Espiritual de Aztlán" declares:

> In the spirit of a new people that is conscious not only of its proud historical heritage, but also of the brutal "Gringo" invasion of our territories: We, the Chicano inhabitants and civilizers of the northern land of Aztlán, from whence came our forefathers, reclaiming the land of their birth and consecrating the determination of our people of the sun, declare that the call of our blood is our power, our responsibility, and our inevitable destiny. (1972, 402–403)

The plan hearkens back to the "forefathers" as a basis for reclamation, a tenuous position at best given the diverse indigenous past of actual Chicanos. The plan, though influenced by Fanon's thought, strikes wide of the mark in relation to Fanon's final point about national culture:

> A national culture is not a folklore, nor an abstract populism that believes it can discover the people's true nature. It is not made up of the inert dregs of gratuitous actions, that is to say actions which are less and less attached to the ever-present reality of the people. A national culture is the whole body of efforts made by a people in the sphere of thought to describe, justify, and praise the action through which that people has created itself and keeps itself in existence. (1968, 233)

In evoking the quaintly and faintly recalled past, the plan fails to clearly articulate that which has best served Chicanos and Chicanas in the preservation of self. It does, however, help highlight a sense of historical consciousness—"the brutal 'Gringo' invasion of our territories"—that forms a central trope in Chicano/a cultural criticism. History, after all, has proved to the Chicano that U.S. society has no patience or respect (when it has time to take notice at all) for people of Mexican ancestry, U.S. citizens or not. Employing Aztlán as signifier, Chicano activists, artists, and critics constantly write and rewrite history.

The invocation of ancestry by the plan reclaims a position and a heritage that lays claim to integrity and agency. This claim suggests, through the "call of our blood," an essentialized and biologically determined nationalism that proves finally untenable. So problematic is this essentialization that, a decade after the plan, the poet Alurista felt compelled to defend it in his explanation of Chicano cultural nationalism. Alurista was—along with Rodolfo "Corky" Gonzales—one of the plan's drafters and masterminds. Luís Leal notes in "In Search of Aztlán" that "before March, 1969, the date of the Denver Conference, no one talked about Aztlán. In fact, the first time that it was mentioned in a Chicano document was in 'El Plan Espiritual de Aztlán,' which was presented in Denver at that time. Apparently, it owes its creation to the poet Alurista who already, during the Autumn of 1968, had spoken about Aztlán in a class for Chicanos held at San Diego State University" (Leal 1981, 20). As a principal player in the articulation of Aztlán, Alurista in 1981 argues that the plan "clearly stated that 'Aztlán belonged to those who worked it' (not only Xicano workers) and that no capricious frontiers would be recognized—an important point which, in the fervor of an exclusivist narrow nationalism, was quickly overlooked" (1981, 25). Alurista disavows what could be interpreted as the most exclusivist elements of nationalism evident in the plan. At the same time, he insists upon a type of transnational "nationalism," a cultural nationalism distinct from the "exclusivist narrow nationalism" of strict political delineation.

This distinction helps explain the tension between two (ultimately contradictory) veins of Chicano "nationalism" strongly influential in subsequent movements of cultural and political identification. Aztlán variously seems to signal a rationally planned nationalist movement and a mythopoetic cultural essence. Although the drafters of the plan, after Fanon, seem to view a cultural nationalism as simultaneous with a political nationalism, Aztlán came to be the hotly disputed terrain on which either one or another type of nationalism was ostensibly founded. Elyette Labarthe, discussing the development of Aztlán, notes the importance of these disputes in the early development of Chicano self-identity: "On one side an oracular voice crackled over that of reason, on the other side a dispassionate voice piped up above that of the inspired poet, but could not quite blot it out" (1990, 79). Militant factions in the Chicano movement, Labarthe points out, viewed Alurista's nationalism as a hollow and romanticized vision that subverted real claims to Aztlán, real political-nationalist interests. The tensions between the locally political and the universally cultural form one series of the fault lines that run through the terrain of Chicano cultural articulations.

Aztlán and Nation

Jorge Klor de Alva implies that this rupture between cultural and political nationalisms influenced the breakdown of leadership among Chicano communities. With the eye of an anthropologist, he notes:

> On one side are leaders with a humanist bent, often schooled in literature or fine arts, who tend to focus on cultural concerns while emphasizing the cultural autonomy of the individual. Their naive cultural nationalism is ultimately too chauvinistic to promote the unification efforts needed to overcome the divisive forces of monopoly capitalism and the seductiveness of modern fragmenting individualism. On the other side are those primarily trained in the social sciences, whose research is delimited by a preoccupation with economic and political issues, and whose eyes are fixed on social structures and the work force. The radicals among them disparage the importance of culture and nationalism while focusing primarily on the significance of class. (1989, 137)

Although Klor de Alva goes on to elaborate that this schema is "deceiving in its simplicity," it nevertheless reflects a distancing between "two valuable and necessary camps" (138). The schisms between "the political" and "the cultural" within Chicano discourses run deeply. They spread out over a larger historical and geographic terrain not divided neatly into camps like "political" versus "cultural," or "historical" as opposed to "mythical." The fissures involved in Chicano nationalist claims derive from a number of different historical sources: the nationalist movements—American Indian and Black—current in the political climate of the late 1960s; the Third World struggles for national sovereignty of the 1950s; the "nationless" status of Chicanos who, after fighting in World War II, returned to a country where they were still considered foreigners in the 1940s; the institutionalization, following the Mexican Revolution, of Mexican national culture in the 1920s and 1930s; the usurpation of Mexican territorial rights in 1848;

the continuous migrations of Mexicans before, during, and after the U.S.-Mexican War; the struggle for Mexican independence from Spain begun in 1810. All these form influential trajectories that cross at the matrix of Chicano nationalism.

The influence of the Mexican Revolution on Chicano thinking in particular should not be minimized. As Leal and Barrón note, "Immigration from Mexico to the United States from 1848 to 1910 was negligible. After 1910, however, and especially during the critical years of the Mexican Revolution (1913–1915), which coincided with the outbreak of World War I and the consequent expansion of American industry and agriculture, large numbers of immigrants crossed the border" (1982, 20). The influences on the economic and social conditions of Chicano life in the United States certainly changed as a result of the revolution. Not the least of these changes was the backlash against Mexicans that came—among other times—in the 1920s.[5]

The indigenism so valued by Chicano cultural discourses clearly draws its influence from the construction of postrevolutionary Mexican nationalism. Thus events following the Mexican Revolution—especially the institutionalization of "revolutionary" ideology—have significantly influenced the articulation of Chicano/a identification. The affirmation of native roots in the cultural identification of the Mexican begins with José Vasconcelos's service as minister of education under President Alvaro Obregón (1920–1924). Other movements toward Chicano empowerment are prefigured in the Mexican postrevolutionary world as well. In the politico-cultural realm, one finds a strong conflict between Mexican intelligentsia who wish to ally themselves with an international Marxism and those seeking to discover the true character of Mexico. Samuel Ramos undertook *Profile of Man and Culture in Mexico* in 1934 as a personality study of Mexico, and Jorge Cuesta's anthology of modern Mexican poetry from 1928 serves as an investigation into the meaning of Mexican cultural tradition. Octavio Paz notes: "They both reflect our profound desire for self-knowledge. The former represents our search for the intimate particulars of our nature, a search that was the very essence of our Revolution, while the latter represents our anxiety to incorporate these particulars in a universal tradition" (1985, 162). Of course the work of Paz himself has been extraordinarily influential, both as an affirmative point of reference and a sore point of rejection. Of Mexico, Paz argues: "Ever since World War II we have been aware that the self-creation demanded of us by our national realities is no different from that which similar realities are demanding of others. The past has left us orphans, as it has the rest of the planet, and we must join together in inventing our common future. World history has become everyone's task and our own labyrinth is the labyrinth of all mankind" (173). The embrace and rejection of the type of universalism that so interests Paz in this passage (and throughout his writing) forms a strong trajectory in the movement of Chicano cultural construction.

These strong intellectual and cultural associations with Mexico, according to Genaro Padilla, arise from a profound sense of disconnection experienced by Chicana/o writers and thinkers. They have, Padilla argues,

> a nostalgia for the Mexican homeland, especially as it has been imagined in that mythical realm of Aztlán. This impulse has manifested itself intensely in the last two decades, a period during which the Chicano, feeling deeply alienated from the foster parent United States, wished to maintain a vital spiritual link with Mexico, the model of language, culture and social behavior. This explains, in part, why Chicano cultural nationalists not only appropriated the pre-Columbian mythology of Mexico, but also its Revolutionary heroes—Benito Juárez, Emiliano Zapata, Pancho Villa—and affected a kinship with Mexico's common people and their history. (1989, 126)

While the longing described in Padilla's discussion might best seem to apply within a New Mexican cultural context, the kinship his argument asserts as central does inform the construction of Chicano cultural nationalism across the nation, especially as regards a nationalist alliance to progressive economic, social, and political agendas. What specific course those agendas should take—and the role that the culture should play in relation to those agendas—forms part of the discontinuity apparent in the realm of Aztlán.

Aztlán stands as that region where the diverse political, geographic, and cultural concerns gripping the Chicano imagination meet. Alurista, as we have seen, views Aztlán as a sign whose referent is unproblematically present. From Alurista's view, the conflation of a nation and a culture seems to provide no tension. Thus, he can assert that Chicano literature "is a national literature, and will have to reflect all the levels that our nation implies, all that IS our people" (Bruce-Novoa 1980, 284). Aztlán as a Chicano nation, from this perspective, stands as an ontological certainty. The literature that will emerge from it will reflect the same nationalist concerns as any other national literatures. There is a curious elision of nation, literature, and people in Alurista's configuration of Aztlán. The term comes to represent not just the fact of sovereignty, but the fact of existence, the very being that is the Chicano—a reflection of the essentializing moves manifested by this strain of Chicano cultural articulation, an essentialization that Alurista seems elsewhere to speak against.

In "In Search of Aztlán," Luís Leal looks upon the idea of Aztlán, and the Plan Espiritual specifically, from a more historical perspective. He traces the effects and traditions of Aztlán, most particularly by documenting "the rebirth of the myth in Chicano thought" (1981, 20). "El Plan Espiritual de Aztlán" forms an important document and turning point in the articulation of Chicano consciousness. In it, Leal argues, the Chicano "recognizes his Aztec origins" as well as "establishes that Aztlán is the Mexican territory ceded to the United States in 1848" (20). The plan articulates the affirmation of origins, both indigenous (though reified in the form of the "Aztecs") and nationalist. He goes on to note that "following one of the basic ideas of the Mexican Revolution, it recognizes that the land belongs to those who work it," making explicit the connection between Aztlán and the cultural history that enables its articulation. Leal's comments thus point toward the historical loci and salient components that make up the discursive practices associated with Aztlán. This historical perspective quickly dissolves in his essay into something else.

Leal concludes with the admonition "whosoever wants to find Aztlán, let him look for it, not on the maps, but in the most intimate part of his being" (22). His discussion, which begins as a historical project, turns into a rhetorical one. Aztlán ceases to exist except as a vague search for spiritual centering. Sylvia Gonzales makes a similar discursive move six years before Leal, eliding the historical ground of Aztlán with an essential and ultimately romantic notion of universal "culture." In her essay "National Character vs. Universality in Chicano Poetry," Gonzales begins by articulating a sociohistorically bound notion of Aztlán: "In recognition of our oppression, the Chicano people ...searched for identity and awareness as a group, as a nation within a nation. This became the cultural, psychological, philosophical and political nation of Aztlán" (1975, 15). Aztlán thus represents a contested, resistant site. Not specifically bound to a geographic reclamation, Aztlán in Gonzales's view is a discursive construction arising out of political necessity. However, her argument quickly moves from a project of political resistance to one of eschatological dimensions. Her vision of Aztlán leaves a messianic vision of cultural universality: "The world awaits the appearance of a disciple capable of propounding the message, interpreting the underlying language of their work, which has already been proscribed. That disciple will have to be a priest, a magician or a poet" (19). This articulation of Aztlán moves from issues of self-determination to a dream of cultural salvation.

Lines of Flight

In the end, the terrain termed Aztlán comes to represent both specific geographic locales and the means of a counterdiscursive engagement. In either case its efficacy in terms of political-institutional transformation remains questionable. When compared with the other plans marking El Movimiento, "El Plan Espiritual de Aztlán" does not leave as distinct a political legacy. Elyette Labarthe argues that the power of "Aztlán" lies in its imaginative conceptualization of Chicano unity: "The socioeconomic debate was to be awarded a spiritual dimension and a dynamism that were sadly lacking. The symbol of Aztlán had the power to legitimize the struggles, to cement the claims. It was a compensatory symbolic mechanism, fusing poetico-symbolic unity to sociocultural concerns. The Chicanos who were divided by history, found in it an ancestral territory and a common destiny" (1990, 80). Its compensatory function served to make it a lasting image. But, as a compensatory strategy, its political effects proved less than prepossessing.

Finally, as the arguments by Gonzales and Leal indicate, the function of Aztlán was to pronounce a minority position that staked claims for legitimacy through a cultural and ancestral primacy. In immediate terms, however, as Juan Gómez-Quiñones argues, the plan "was stripped of what radical element it possessed by stressing its alleged romantic idealism, reducing the concept of Aztlán to a psychological ploy, and limiting advocacy for self-determination to local community control—all of which became possible because of the plan's incomplete analysis which, in turn, allowed its language concerning issues to degenerate into reformism" (1990, 124). The political vagueness of the plan allowed it to dissipate its energies along the small fault lines of numerous cultural discourses. And this dispersal, although causing tremors in the cultural terrain of Euro-American society, did little to shake the walls and bring down the structures of power as its rhetoric so firmly proclaimed.

Aztlán as a supposed "common denominator with the claims to the *vatos locos, pochos, pachucos, cholos* and other *mestizos*" (Labarthe 1990, 80) fails. Purportedly invoked as a politically unifying metaphor, Aztlán becomes something quite different. Although politically and ideologically vague, "El Plan Espiritual de Aztlán" does help establish the discursive habits by which Chicano culture asserts its autonomy. Aztlán thus forms not a national but a critical region for El Movimiento. At its most efficacious moments, it comes to represent a cultural site by which to express pride in origins and heritages. The investigation of the past, the reclamation of history, the pride of place embodied in Aztlán manifests itself in the idea of chicanismo.

The poet José Montoya explains: "*chicanismo* is a basic concept which embodies both the Indio and the Spanish aspects of our heritage. As Chicano people we now accept the Indio side of our heritage. We somehow never had too much of a problem with our Hispanitude one way or the other. But to be considered an Indio!" (1986, 25). The mestizaje of Montoya's exclamations forms a nexus of cultural and personal identity that first gained currency in the nationalist movements of postrevolutionary Mexico. Although the impetus for the celebration of *indigenismo* emerges from the nationalist discourses of Mexico, hegemonic views on race and culture die long and agonized deaths. Despite the ideological valorization of mestizaje, the racism present in both U.S. and Mexican societies certainly circulates in the "Mexican American" communities. In a North American context, this means that the members of these communities are under pressure to assimilate particular standards—of beauty, of identity, of aspiration. In a Mexican context, the pressure is to urbanize, modernize, and Europeanize. Which is to say that in order to belong to larger imagined communities of the nation—particularly in the United States—"Mexican Americans" are expected to accept anti-indigenous discourses as their own.

In this respect, Aztlán has allowed for a subjectivity that reclaims the connection to indigenous peoples and cultures. Although it does not offer a viable political platform that would allow for a reclamation of a nation, it has in varied ways provided an alternate national consciousness. It has in problematic ways allowed for another way of aligning one's interests and concerns with community and with history. This may prove to be the most lasting legacy of Aztlán. In crystallizing a sense of rightful place and identity, it has sought to enable a newfound agency. Though hazy as to the precise means by which this agency will emerge, Aztlán has valorized a chicanismo that reweaves into the present previously devalued lines of descent.

These lines of descent do not come to us without problematic implications. Reimaginings of the past—Mexican, indigenous, Aztec, pure—are understood as true. Their revivification can, however, only be enacted through their manifestation in a conflicted present. Aztlán thus becomes a terrain of discontinuity, of disjuncture. An infatuation with tradition and the "native" represents the type of fetishization of Aztec and Mayan themes and icons critiqued by Jorge Klor de Alva: Chicanos "have consistently emphasized the form over the content of native ideology and symbolism by oversimplifying both to the point of caricaturing the intricate and enigmatic codes that veil the meanings of the original texts" (1986, 24). While an infatuation with historical "accuracy" is of course suspect, so, too, an easy manipulation of cultural iconography must be critiqued. In this regard, Daniel Alarcón's redeployment of Aztlán as a palimpsest is very instructive. Aztlán as a cultural/national symbol represents a paradox: it seeks to stand as a common denominator among Chicano populations, yet it divides rather than unifies; it maintains cultural traditions while promoting assimilation into Anglo-American culture; it affirms indigenous ancestry while simultaneously erasing the very historical, cultural, and geographic specificity of that ancestry. Consequently, Alarcón astutely maintains: "Unless Aztlán is understood in all of its layers, all its complexity, it will never be an attractive model to the diverse culture its leaders seek to encompass within its borders, borders that have been and will continue to be fluid" (1992, 62). Aztlán represents not a singular homeland, but rather borderlands between sites of alliance.[6] The borderlands mark a site of profound discontinuity between regions delimiting racial, sexual, gender, and economic identities.

To think of Aztlán as a signifier of the borderlands does not negate its historical significance. It still reaches out to the geography of the American Southwest and attempts to represent its distinct material qualities. Yet, it is also true that conceptions of the borderlands refute Aztlán as a fixed entity. Partly, the refutation of the nationalist dreams of the Chicano movement results from the conflicted message in which revolutionary rhetoric articulated what quite quickly became reformist demands. These reformist positions ultimately offered neither genuine self-determination nor universal liberation. Partly, the refutation of nationalist demands is because Latinos, as the fastest growing minority in the United States, have, in a sense, already reclaimed the Southwest. Partly, there remains the unshakable belief that the Southwest was never lost. Thus Aztlán as borderlands marks a site that both belongs to and has never belonged to either the United States or Mexico.

The tumultuous histories informing constructions of the U.S. Southwest mark the impossible interstices between imagination and history. In its negative recollection of repressive social forms, Aztlán as signifier marks how historically grounded Chicano consciousness is. This historical perspective serves to acknowledge the fluid mending and blending, repression and destruction of disparate cultures making up chicanismo. A tempestuous sense of motion therefore marks that region termed the "borderlands." Neither a homeland, nor a perpetuation of origin, the borderlands allude to an illimitable terrain marked by dreams and rupture, marked by history and the various hopes that history can exemplify. The borderlands represent the multiplicity and dynamism of Chicana/o experiences and cultures. It is a terrain in which Mexicans, Chicanos, and mestizos live among the various worlds comprising their cultural and political landscapes.

Sergio Elizondo, among others, seeks to give voice to the idea of the borderlands. He discusses a relationship to land that Chicano/a culture has often sought to express:

> We understand now the Border between the United States of America and the Estados Unidos Mexicanos; now we would do well to consider that Borderlands might be a more appropriate term to designate the entire area over which the Chicano people are spread in this country. In so doing, we would come also to understand that the mere physical extension between the U.S.-Mexico border and, let us say, Chicago, is a fact of human dispersion, and not a diaspora of the Chicano people. It is not static for us, but rather it has always been a dynamic and natural motion motivated by laws and processes common to all cultures. Our migrations north of the old historical border have extended the geography and social fabric of Aztlán northward in all directions; we have been able to expand our communal life and fantasies. (1986, 13)

Elizondo speaks to a number of the issues that emerge as central to the Chicano cultural imagination. The problematization of heritage and tradition, the relation between Chicano cultural and social experiences, the significance of land and nation, the expansion of "homeland" and "fantasies," all inform the various movements of contemporary Chicano culture. It is interesting that Elizondo suggests the movement of Chicanos through the United States is "motivated by laws and processes common to all cultures." The desire to make Chicana/o identity "universal" still finds a voice. Nevertheless, Elizondo's statement indicates that the notion of Aztlán has given way to a broader and more diverse vision of Chicano cultural terrain. This cultural terrain expands the realm of desire for Chicanas/os, moving it as it does across the entire face of the United States and beyond; but it also closes a chapter on Chicano cultural identity. No longer grounded exclusively in the Southwest or border region, the borderlands expand the territorial claims of Chicanos. Elizondo portrays this expansion as simply the extension of "the geography and social fabric of Aztlán." His conceptualization does not address at all what that sign "Aztlán" signifies.

As with the articulations of Chicano nationalism, Elizondo's view of Aztlán fails to perceive the multiplicity and discontinuity evident in the histories and geographies encompassed by the signifier "Aztlán." The discussion to this point should serve to indicate that as a place, or even as a unifying symbol or image, any fixed significance ascribed to Aztlán erases the vast differences that inform the terms "Chicana" and "Chicano." The histories of Mexicans in this country are marked by a series of tensions and ruptures—cultural, linguistic, political, sexual, economic, and racial—that cut across bounded terrains, that cut across ways in which one can and cannot call one's location "home." The interstitial becomes the liminal where the living between becomes a way of moving through such definitions as Other, native, foreign, gringo, pocho, etc. The performance artist Guillermo Gómez-Peña addresses the multiplicity that makes up identity in the borderlands:

> My "identity" now possesses multiple repertories: I am Mexican but I am also Chicano and Latin American. At the border they call me *chilango* or *mexiquillo*; in Mexico City it's *pocho* or *norteño*; and in Europe it's *sudaca*. The Anglos call me "Hispanic" or "Latino," and the Germans have, on more than one occasion, confused me with Turks or Italians. My wife Emily is Anglo-Italian, but speaks Spanish with an Argentine accent, and together we walk amid the rubble of the Tower of Babel of our American postmodernity. (1988, 127–28)

The identities Gómez-Peña exposes lead to a decentering of subjectivity accompanied by loss—of country, of native language, of certainty. But this leads as well to gain: a multifocal and tolerant culture, cultural alliances, "a true political conscience (declassicization and consequent politicization) as well as new options in social, sexual, spiritual, and aesthetic behavior" (129–30).[7] The desire to rediscover a homeland within the current climate of Chicano culture coexists with a much more complex and extensive reclamation. Demands for home are made simultaneously with calls for a reclamation of all that is cast between, all that is devalued by other nationalist identities. An interstitial Chicano culture traces "lines of flight," movements toward deterritorialization.[8] Chicana/o writers and critics most powerfully enable this type of cultural configuration as they have sought to articulate the deficiencies of a nationalism that presumes the centrality of heterosexual male subjectivity. Their experiences suggest a textured and multifaceted sense of self.

Hybrid Worlds

In this context, no Chicana author is associated with the borderland more than Gloria Anzaldúa. Caught between the worlds of lesbian and straight, Mexican and American, First World and Third World, Anzaldúa's writing seems to exemplify and reflect the condition of the interstitial and liminal—of being simultaneously between and on the threshold. In the poem "To Live in the Borderlands Means You," the speaker visits the various characteristics of the borderlands. The title reads as the first line of the poem, a device immediately signaling a transgression of borders and marking the thematics of the poem. The title also allows for a shifting in syntactical meaning. Taken alone the title signals a conflation between the "you" the title addresses and the borderlands of which it speaks. Melding into the poem, the title also signals the mestizaje inherent in the borderlands:

> To live in the Borderlands means you
> are neither hispana india negra española
> ni gabacha, eres mestiza, mulata, half-breed
> caught in the crossfire between camps
> while carrying all five races on your back
> not knowing which side to turn to, run from.
> (1987, 194)

The borderlands in the poem become a zone of transition and not-belonging. You are not Hispanic, Indian, black, Spanish, or white, but mestiza. Identity emerges from the racial, cultural, and sexual mixture. It is a land of betrayal where "*mexicanas* call you *rajetas*" and "denying the Anglo inside you / is as bad as having denied the Indian or Black." A mestizaje of linguistic and sexual identity emerges in the borderland as well: "*Cuando vives en la frontera* / people walk through you, the wind steals your voice, / you're a *burra* [donkey], *buey* [mule], scapegoat / ... / both woman and man, neither— / a new gender." The poem's interlingual expression and evocation of interstitial spaces represents the power of transgression. The borderlands do not represent merely a cultural or national transgression. As the imagery evoked by the poem suggests, sexual and gender identities give way before the transformative forces of a true mestizaje. To live in the borderlands means transgressing the rigid definitions of sexual and racial, national and gender definitions.

The battles of the borderlands finally are fought on a ground in which enemies are not without. In the borderlands "you are the battleground / where enemies are kin to each other; / you are at home, a stranger, / the border disputes have been settled / the volley of shots have shattered the truce." There is a discontinuity inherent in the borderland. From this perspective, Elizondo is right in conflating Aztlán with the borderland; they meld one into the other as regions of rupture where self and other perpetually dance around and through one another.

Although one enemy remains—the homogenizing elements of society that seek to erase any trace of "race," the mill that wants to "pound you pinch you roll you out / smelling like white bread but dead"—these enemies do not stand wholly without. These are the lessons internalized through the racism and violence that mark the borderlands. The borderlands represent a home that is not home, the place where all the contradictions of living among and between worlds manifests itself. Anzaldúa articulates the difficulties and problems inherent to this realm of discontinuity. Not offering a vision of another land as the utopian hope for peace or justice, all the poem can offer is advice on how to negotiate through the ruptured terrain of the borderlands: "To survive the Borderlands / you must live *sin fronteras* / be a crossroads." To live without borders means that the subjectivity to which Anzaldúa's poetry points constantly stands at the intersection of various discursive and historical trajectories. The crossroads that subjectivity becomes allows as well for the self to venture down various roads, follow trails that lead across numerous—often discontinuous, often contradictory, often antithetical—regions: European, Indian, Mexican, American, male, female, homosexual, heterosexual. The quest suggested by Anzaldúa's sense of the borderlands is not toward a fixed or rigid identity. The Chicana/o becomes a fluid condition, a migratory self who reclaims not merely the geographic realm of Aztlán. Instead, Chicanos/as come to be seen as transfiguring themselves—moving between the worlds of indigenous and European, of American and Mexican, of self and other.

Filling the Void

The transformation of "Aztlán" from homeland to borderlands signifies another turn within Chicano/a cultural discourse. It demarcates a shift from origin toward an engagement with the ever-elusive construction of cultural identity. As the U.S.-Mexican border represents a construction tied to histories of power and dispossession, the construction of personal and cultural identity entailed in any multicultural project comes to the fore in Chicana/o cultural production. The move represents at this point a liberating one that allows for the assumption of various subject positions. The refusal to be delimited, while simultaneously claiming numerous heritages and influences, allows for a rearticulation of the relationship between self and society, self and history, self and land. Aztlán as a realm of historical convergence and discontinuity becomes another source of significance embraced and employed in the borderlands that is Chicana/o culture.

The tendency in these figurations and refigurations of Aztlán recast it variously as an ontological reality or an epistemological construction. Aztlán thus is repositioned and refigured as a shifting, and thus ambiguous, signifier. Ambiguity suggests—problematically—a sense of equivalence. Rather than think of Aztlán as ambiguous signifier, we might consider it "empty," a signifier that points, as Ernesto Laclau argues, "from within the process of signification, to the discursive presence of its own limits" (1996, 36).[9] This shift does not help us fix the significance of the term Aztlán. It does, I hope, help sketch some ideas that unravel the bind to which the continued discussions of Aztlán attest. There can be two explanations why we have not, so to speak, arrived at Aztlán. On the one hand, the plan to get to Aztlán—representing nation, unity, liberation—has not been adequately articulated as yet. (This implies that the proper configuration of Aztlán is still to be enacted at some future utopian date.) Or, on the other hand, all the different articulations of Aztlán are equally valid and so we each live our own little atomized Aztlán. The first position is obfuscatory, the second hopeless. Both run counter to that which Aztlán seeks to name.

As an empty signifier, Aztlán names not that which is or has been, but that which is ever absent: nation, unity, liberation. The various articulations of Aztlán have sought to make these absences present in the face of oppressive power based on: racial grounds and the Chicano emergence from the indigenous; historico-political grounds and the struggles over land most clearly indexed by the U.S.-Mexican War of 1846–1848; economic grounds represented by the exploitation of laborers and most specifically farmworkers; sexual and gender grounds formed by the colonization of female and queer bodies; and cultural grounds invoked by references to indigenous, folk, and popular arts. Whatever its premise, the term "Aztlán" consistently has named that which refers to an absence, an unfulfilled reality in response to various forms of oppression.

This does not help us understand why the signifier Aztlán has so haunted Chicano/a critical thought. Perhaps the ways in which Aztlán has been used in contestations of power explain something of its sustained attraction. The discourses surrounding Aztlán present themselves as the incarnation of the term: the articulation of unity, of nation, of resistance to oppressive power. Each articulation offers its particular understanding of Aztlán as its fulfillment. This is precisely the reason that Aztlán never adds up. As a sign of liberation, it is ever emptied of meaning just as its meaning is asserted, its borders blurred by those constituencies engaged in liberating struggles named by Aztlán. This simultaneous process of arrival and evacuation does not mark a point of despair, nor in describing it do I mean to disparage Aztlán. On the contrary. We cannot abandon Aztlán, precisely because it serves to name that space of liberation so fondly yearned for. As such, it stands as a site of origin in the struggle to articulate, enact, and make present an absent unity. Aztlán is our start and end point of empowerment.

Notes

1. This argument of linguistic loss is complicated by the resurgence of interest in the learning and use of Spanish by second- and third-generation Mexicans. See Gonzales (1997).

2. See especially chapter 3 of my book *Movements in Chicano Poetry*, "From the Homeland to the Borderlands, the Reformation of Aztlán." There is an implied teleological argument in that discussion I now reject. Consequently, the present essay attempts to draw upon, elaborate, and clarify my previous analysis. The incisive comments offered by the readers of the journal *Aztlán* have helped me greatly in this venture and I thank them. All errors, misrepresentations, and slips of logic remain stubbornly mine.

3. Here one finds a dichotomy. As Juan Gómez-Quiñones notes, Chicano leaders of the 1960s were impeded by the contradictions between their assertive, often separatist, rhetoric and their conventional reformist demands involving educational reform and voter registration drives (1990, 141–6).

4. Thus Douglas Massey and his associates (1987) draw upon the signifier to name their study of transnational Mexican migration *Return to Aztlán*.

5. See Acuña (1988, 130–43) and Ralph Guzmán (1974, 21–22) for examples of Euro-American reactions and ensuent legislation to "stem the tide" of Mexican immigration.

6. In this respect we might think of Chela Sandoval's discussion of U.S. feminists of color in the 1970s. She notes that feminists of color began to identify common grounds upon which they formed coalitions across boundaries of cultural, racial, class, and gender differences. Their position in the borderlands of feminism enabled a crossing across difference, a recognition of sameness amid difference, a recognition of other countrywomen and countrymen living in a similar and sympathetic psychic terrain. The differences between these men and women—differences signifying struggle, conflict, asymmetry, differences implying dislocation, dispersal, disruption—were never erased. Rather, a fuller process of recognition occurred (1991, 11).

7. Of course, this articulation is complicated by Gómez-Peña's privileged position as a member of an international artistic elite capable, economically and politically, of crossing borders with relative ease.

217

8. The term "line of flight" from Deleuze and Guattari (1983, 1986) is meant to suggest escape from binary choices. The line of flight is formed by ruptures within particular systems or orders. It allows for third possibilities—neither capitulation to regimes nor unconditional freedom from them. The line of flight is a way out, a means of changing the situation to something other.

9. Laclau's discussion of empty signifiers has helped me think through some of the thorny dilemmas set in motion by the various articulations of Aztlán. While I sympathize with his political project, I do not fully ascribe to his view that modern democracy will begin as "different projects or wills will try to hegemonize the empty signifiers of the absent community" (1996, 46). His analysis of the empty signifier itself, however, I find insightful.

Works Cited

Acuña, Rodolfo. 1988. *Occupied America: A History of Chicanos*. 3rd ed. New York: Harper & Row.

Alarcón, Daniel Cooper. 1992. "The Aztec Palimpsest: Toward a New Understanding of Aztlán, Cultural Identity and History." *Aztlán* 19, no. 2 (1992): 33–68.

Alurista. 1981. "Cultural Nationalism and Xicano Literature During the Decade 1965–1975." *MELUS* 8 (summer 1981): 22–34.

Anaya, Rudolfo A., and Francisco Lomelí, eds. 1989. *Aztlán: Essays on the Chicano Homeland*. Albuquerque: Academia/El Norte Publications.

Anzaldúa, Gloria. 1987. "To live in the Borderlands means you." In *Borderlands/ La Frontera: The New Mestiza*, 194–95. San Francisco: Spinsters/Aunt Lute.

Barrera, Mario. 1988. *Beyond Aztlán: Ethnic Autonomy in Comparative Perspective*. Notre Dame, Ind.: University of Notre Dame Press.

Bruce-Novoa, Juan. 1980. *Chicano Authors: Inquiry by Interview*. Austin: University of Texas Press.

Cuesta, Jorge. 1928. *Antología de la poesía mexicana moderna*. Mexico: Contemporaneos.

Deleuze, Gilles, and Félix Guattari. 1975. *Kafka: For a Minor Literature*. Translated by Dana Polan. Minneapolis: University of Minnesota Press.

———.1972. *Anti-Oedipus: Capitalism and Schizophrenia*. Translated by Robert Hurley, Mark See, and Helen R. Lane. Minneapolis: University of Minnesota Press.

Elizondo, Sergio D. 1986. "ABC: Aztlán, the Borderlands, and Chicago." In *Missions in Conflict: Essays on U.S.-Mexican Relations and Chicano Culture*, ed. Renate von Bardeleben, 13–23. Tübingen: Gunter Narr Verlag.

"El Plan Espiritual de Aztlan." 1972. First presented at the Chicano Youth Conference in Denver, Colorado, March 1969. In *Aztlan: An Anthropology of Mexican American Literature*, ed. Luis Valdez and Stan Steiner, 402-406. New York: Knopf.

Fanon, Frantz. 1961. *The Wretched of the Earth*. Translated by Constance Farrington. New York: Grove Press.

Gómez-Peña, Guillermo. 1988. "Documented/Undocumented." Translated by Rubén Martínez. In *The Graywolf Annual Five: Multi-Cultural Literacy*, ed. Rick Simonson and Scott Walker, 127–34. St. Paul: Graywolf Press.

Gómez-Quiñones, Juan. 1990. *Chicano Politics: Reality and Promise, 1940–1990*. Albuquerque: University of New Mexico Press.

Gonzales, John M. 1997. "Relearning a Lost Language." *Los Angeles Times*, 26 May 1997.

Gonzales, Sylvia. 1975. "National Character vs. Universality in Chicano Poetry." *De Colores* 1 (1975): 10–21.

Guzmán, Ralph. 1974. "The Function of Anglo-American Racism in the Political Development of Chicanos." In *La Causa Política: A Chicano Politics Reader*, ed. Chris F. García, 19–35. Notre Dame, Ind.: University of Notre Dame Press.

Klor de Alva, J. Jorge. 1989. "Aztlán, Borinquen and Hispanic Nationalism in the United States." In *Aztlán: Essays on the Chicano Homeland*, ed. Rudolfo Anaya and Francisco Lomelí, 135–71. Albuquerque: Academia/El Norte Publications.

———.1986. "California Chicano Literature and Pre-Columbian Motifs: Foil and Fetish." *Confluencia* 1 (spring 1986): 18–26.

Labarthe, Elyette Andouard. 1990. "The Vicissitudes of Aztlán." *Confluencia* 5 (spring 1990): 79–84.

Laclau, Ernesto. 1996. "Why Do Empty Signifiers Matter to Politics?" In *Emancipation(s)*. 36-46. New York: Verso.

Leal, Luís. 1981. "In Search of Aztlán." Translated by Gladys Leal. *Denver Quarterly* 16 (fall): 16–22.

Leal, Luís, and Pepe Barrón. 1982. "Chicano Literature: An Overview." In *Three American Literatures*, ed. Houston A. Baker Jr., 9–32. New York: Modern Language Association.

Massey, Douglas S., Rafael Alarcón, Jorge Durand, and Humberto González. 1987. *Return to Aztlán: The Social Process of International Migration from Western Mexico*. Berkeley: University of California Press.

Montoya, José. 1986. "Chicano Art: Resistance in Isolation 'Aquí Estamos y no Nos Vamos.'" In *Missions in Conflict: Essays on U.S.-Mexican Relations and Chicano Culture*, ed. Renate von Bardeleben, 25–30. Tübingen: Gunter Narr Verlag.

Moraga, Cherríe. 1993. "Queer Aztlán: The Re-formation of Chicano Tribe." In *The Last Generation*, 145–74. Boston: South End Press.

Padilla, Genaro. 1989. "Myth and Comparative Cultural Nationalism: The Ideological Uses of Aztlán." In *Aztlán: Essays on the Chicano Homeland*, ed. Rudolfo Anaya and Francisco Lomelí, 111–34. Albuquerque: Academia/El Norte Publications.

Paz, Octavio. 1985. *Labyrinth of Solitude*. Translated by Lysander Kemp, Yara Milos, and Rachel Phillips Belash. New York: Grove Press.

Pérez-Torres, Rafael. 1995. *Movements in Chicano Poetry: Against Myths, Against Margins*. New York: Cambridge University Press.

Pina, Michael. 1989. "The Archaic, Historical and Mythicized Dimensions of Aztlán." In *Aztlán: Essays on the Chicano Homeland,* ed. Rudolfo Anaya and Francisco Lomelí, 14–48. Albuquerque: Academia/El Norte Publications.

Ramos, Samuel. 1962. *Profile of Man and Culture in Mexico.* Austin: University of Texas Press.

Safran, William. 1991. "Diasporas in Modern Societies: Myths of Homeland and Return." *Diaspora* 1, no. 1 (1991): 83–99.

Sandoval, Chela. 1991. "U.S. Third World Feminism: The Theory and Method of Oppositional Consciousness in the Postmodern World." *Genders* 10 (1991): 1–24.

II.
Performing Politics

Performing Politics
Introduction

Karen Mary Davalos

Since the 1960s social movements, Chicana/o studies has traced the connection between art and politics. Sensitive to the call for empowerment,
this research has focused on practices, institutions, and cultural products in
which the artistic goals are inseparable from the political goals. Chicano/a
scholars have documented those artists directly involved in promoting
cultural identity and political self-determination, the cultural products that
convey a message of political protest and action, and the arts institutions
that function as advocates for their communities. The essays in this section
are part of this project, but they are also something more.

The contributors document the performing and visual arts as well as
the literature and everyday speech acts throughout Greater Mexico, "all
the areas inhabited by people of a Mexican culture—not only within the
present limits of the Republic of Mexico but in the United States as well"
(Paredes 1976, xvi). No one article is about politics, the strategy of power,
control, or position, but together the arts that they document serve to
enact resistance to the U.S. social hierarchy by creating and procuring a
new subject-position, Chicanos/as. The theatrical expressions, proverbs,
murals, literature, and home altars discussed in these essays constitute an
"oppositional praxis" that Chela Sandoval describes in her definition of
oppositional consciousness (1991; 1998, 362). They are the public space
of political expression, the tactical positions, in which Chicanos/as not
only envision but name, "read, renovate, and make signs on behalf of the
dispossessed" in order to liberate the subordinated. Performing politics,
therefore, is the open aesthetic engagement, a cultural product, that aims
to "equalize power" by acting, speaking, painting, writing, designing, and
praying the position of Chicanos/as (Sandoval 1998, 359-62).

223

This section is primarily devoted to "representations of working-class and women's cultural forms and practices" (Fregoso and Chabram 1990, 206). These cultural forms and practices emerge from the margins but claim a central space in U.S. history, society, and culture. However, they do not aim for a singular site or territory. The "aesthetic works" of oppositional consciousness are "marked with both disruption and continuity; as well as by immigrants, diasporas, border crossings, and by politics, poetics, and procedures" (Sandoval 1998, 362). For instance, Chicano/a muralists draw on and acknowledge a Mexican heritage, strengthening a transnational cultural aesthetic; and they also transform or reject Mexican social hierarchies and symbols, confirming instead the differences between el norte and el sur. Similarly, home altars in East Austin, Texas, recirculate the icons and symbols of the Roman Catholic Church, and they subvert the official religious authority of the church by making sacred space within a private home but also among household items, including the television and the dresser (Turner 1986). In general, the performance of a political stance maneuvers between, within, and against the nations of Mexico and the United States, the cultures of Spain and Mesoamerica, and the ideologies of assimilation/accommodation and separatism.

While the content of each essay describes and analyzes the "performative" of an oppositional consciousness of Greater Mexico, the essays themselves are also a performance of a differential stance (Butler 1990). In short, if we consider the writing styles and interpretive strategies of the essays, then the authors are also procuring Chicano/a politics. Their work is self-consciously "organizing resistance, identity, praxis, and coalition under contemporary first world, late-capitalist cultural conditions" by writing for and against the canons of theater history, folklore, literature, religion, and art history (Sandoval 1998, 358). This oppositional consciousness is performed on several levels. First, the essays are a challenge to the univocal method of conventional and hegemonic disciplines, and some challenge the traditional disciplines by working across bodies of knowledge and intellectual canons. For instance, Carrasco uses the history of religion, theology, literature, and cultural geography to understand manifestations of the sacred. Paredes draws on folklore, sociolinguistics, cultural anthropology, and performance theory to analyze proverbs. In Huerta's essay, the interdisciplinary method produces an urgency, a writing style that draws on the immediacy of journalism, the descriptive method of ethnography, and the romanticism of a new-found subjectivity.

Second, some essays are outright transgressive and work against disciplinary boundaries. For example, Paredes, Goldman, and Carrasco are not simply concerned with interpreting Mexican proverbs, Mexican murals, or Chicano literature, respectively. They are each critical of the authority that conventional approaches have within academia, the privileges that such conventions grant by claiming universality, and the interpretive and ideological results of those conventions. As Renato Rosaldo has said about Paredes's writing style, in his hands the critique is a skillful attack that shifts in mode and tone. Using gentle humor, the voice of reason, and irony with an edge (Rosaldo 1985, 408), Paredes explains that other interpretations of Mexican proverbs are based on poor research techniques, ineffective methods, and bias. Turner and Carrasco write as if they are keenly aware of the limitations of disciplinary methods. Both commit a significant portion of their essays to substantiating the premise for the analysis, as if to acknowledge that the study of Chicanos/as requires a new framework and point of reference. Carrasco directly challenges Christian theology and identifies it as a culturally specific understanding of truth and the sacred, developing in Chicano/a studies a skepticism toward claims of neutrality, objectivity, and universality. Taking Paredes's critique one step further, he argues that the claims of universality function to normalize a social hierarchy in which Chicanos/as are near the bottom and (Christian) Euro-Americans are at the top. All of the essays call to our attention the importance of understanding the context and production of knowledge, contributing to Chicano/a studies' commitment to disclosure and experiential knowledge in producing social change.

Although the essays are arranged chronologically, my discussion places them thematically and with an attention to the development of Chicano/a studies. First, I examine Américo Paredes's essay on Mexican proverbs because it introduces the oppositional stance of the authors. The work of Jorge Huerta and Shifra M. Goldman comes next because they examine art forms that are specifically a performance of politics. Goldman's essay is also important because she develops Chicano/a studies pedagogy. The contributions by Kay F. Turner and David Carrasco complete the section with an attention to faith and the sacred. Both essays are significant in the development of Chicana/o studies because they investigate a somewhat marginalized topic: religion. In addition, Turner's essay is dramatically different from the others for two reasons: (a) she analyzes the cultural representations of women and (b) she explores the private space of performing politics. Contributing to a major unfolding in Chicano/a studies, Turner's work is a complement to what has become a central point of analysis: the intersection of gender, race, and culture—to which Turner adds faith. As noted above, Carrasco's essay complements Paredes's deconstruction of objectivity and thus it is a fitting bookend to the section. Overall, the thematic arrangement helps to illuminate connections and disjunctures in the field.

Américo Paredes's paper was originally a talk delivered to an American studies group in San Antonio, Texas, in 1970. It certainly has all of the qualities of a performance and theatrical satire. The essay begins with a definition of folklore as the history of the subaltern, clarifying almost immediately the position and the performance of the new politics. He then turns to a deceptively simple story about folklorist J. Frank Dobie and his interpretation of the expression *No te dejes*. Dobie's work is Paredes's springboard into a critical analysis of conventional research methods and the problems of bias. In turn he offers his own interpretations of dozens of *dichos*, the short and complete phrases that express a useful thought or lesson in a particular context, and he posits another more effective methodology.

Moreover, he argues that words are not transparent facts and people do not always say what they mean. Meanings are not "lying on the surface to be picked up by the most casual observer," particularly the social scientist. He reminds us that some speech-acts are a performance that is meant to entertain, and they may involve humor, satire, and deception (all of which Paredes employs in his writing). Finally, dichos are used in specific contexts by a speaker who communicates from a particular position in society. Mexicans, Paredes implies, may utter dichos, sing *corridos*, weave legends, and convey beliefs as a form of protest, as social critique of their oppressor. Although only suggestive in this essay, the body of his research confirms this analysis (see especially Paredes 1958). Social scientists, he warns, must understand this position, their relationship to the people they study, and the language before they attempt to interpret the folklore of Greater Mexico.

Whereas Paredes challenges the work of other social scientists, Jorge A. Huerta documents a theater movement that is "yet to be named" but that "concerns 'Los Teatros de Aztlán.'" This opening statement is significant in the development of Chicano/a studies. The theater of Chicanos/as is indeed named, as Huerta has indicated, since they are of Aztlán, the mythical homeland of Chicanos/as. Unlike Paredes, who constructs a disciplinary subject not confined by geopolitical boundaries or periodization that matches the formation of nations and thereby functions as a precursor to diaspora and border studies, Huerta contributes to the invention of Chicanos/as as distinct from those Mexicans *del otro lado*. Huerta articulates one of the authoritative premises in Chicano/a studies by referring to Aztlán and confines his subject to a new theater movement in the United States.

He also introduces an important construction of Mexican Americans that recognizes spatial and temporal depth by arguing that the theatrical expressions of Chicanos are a "continuation of centuries of theatrical expression" from preconquest civilizations, colonial Spain, and New Spain, to the frontier of Mexico. This articulation of Chicanos/as as a people with roots in pre-Columbian times, or indigenous historical continuity, is a tactic in "strategic essentialism" that functions to legitimate representations of the traditional and acknowledge the ability to survive U.S. social hierarchies (Danius and Jonsson 1993). According to Huerta, El Teatro Campesino is one example of this historical trajectory, but it performs a new direction that emerged after 1965.

For Huerta, the date marks a watershed of political and social activity that gave Chicano theater its form, function, and subject. Huerta documents the growth of El Teatro Campesino under Luis Valdez and his work with the United Farmworkers Organizing Committee in Delano, California. He described a theater based on the lived experiences of field workers, migrants, and union organizers—the subaltern of the San Joaquin Valley. He reports the initial projects and the rapid pace at which *teatros*, professional organizations, workshops, and conferences developed out of the need to enact or perform the collective experience of Chicanos/as. His description outlines what Yvonne Yarbro-Bejarano (1986) and Tomás Ybarra-Frausto (1991) identify as *rasquachismo*, an ambiguous and slippery sensibility "we use to speak to each other among ourselves" (Ybarra-Frausto 1991, 155). By employing rasquachismo as a theatrical method, Chicanos/as "subvert and turn ruling paradigms upside down"; it is an aesthetic tool of oppositional consciousness (155). It literally performs the subaltern position and calls into question the norms of society, including the presumptions and racial stereotypes surrounding Chicanos/as and the unspoken privileges that function to maintain social inequalities.

Shifra M. Goldman's essay is an art historical analysis of the Mexican mural renaissance and its influence in the Americas. Unlike the other essays in this section, Goldman is primarily concerned with an elite set of artists (*los tres grandes*), who nonetheless take up an art form that defies private consumption and occupies public space in the name of *la gente*. According to Goldman, Mexican muralism was an art of advocacy and it performed the politics of indigenism (Diego Rivera and David Alfaro Siqueiros), hispanism (José Clemente Orozco), and *mestizaje* (Rufino Tamayo and Orozco).

In general, she documents the performance of revolutionary Mexico, the enactment of a new vision for mestizos and indigenous civilizations, and the establishment of a position that supports working-class interests. Mexican peasants and laborers appeared as human subjects, not as exotic or passive people. The leaders of the Mexican mural movement may not have agreed on national or international issues but they nonetheless brought a new subjectivity to public space and made it possible for Mexicans and Chicanos to acknowledge their indigenous heritage and identity.

The second topic of her essay is the Chicano mural movement, and here the scope of her essay is instructive. Similar to Huerta and Paredes, Goldman envisions a cultural space that works across geopolitical borders, but she is more attuned to difference, discontinuity, and ambiguity. She recounts the stylistic and thematic influence of Mexican muralism on Chicano arts, particularly the emphasis on recovery of an indigenous heritage. However, she traces the ambiguous results of a transnational cultural expression. For instance, Goldman is critical of the romanticism and ahistoricism of Chicano visual and performing artists, including Luis Valdez; although I would suggest we read these as the result of a creative sensibility that seeks "alliance with other decolonizing movements for emancipation" (Sandoval 1991, 4) and therefore may shuttle across borders and "between meaning systems in order to enact the 'strategic essentialism' necessary for intervening in power on behalf of the marginalized" (Sandoval 1998, 359).

Finally, her essay is an argument of pedagogy. First, murals have transformative power in the classroom. She explains the advantages of using art to making course material more accessible in sociology, history, and political science classrooms. According to Goldman, art as an instructional tool is valuable in these disciplines because it is a window to experiential knowledge. In many ways the pedagogical lesson of the essay is its strength. She explores the educational role of Mexican and Chicano murals, contemplating the mural's ability to convey historical information, contemporary problems, and new perspectives. Murals serve to educate the public and help to reconfigure how people think about history and their condition. Murals are popular education in public space, and their location in the public domain provides an advantage. They can perform a new ideology and help to bring about social change. Further contributing to the development of Chicano/a studies, Goldman posits that in order to study murals, or art in general, it is important to consider when, for whom, and from what position it was created. In short, she reminds art historians, cultural critics, and artists that they tend to equate their assessment of artistic practices with the practices themselves, not acknowledging how their own constructions are mediated and constrained by political economies and nationalism. Although she does not address how this consideration should function in other disciplines, her work supports developments in Chicano/a studies that deconstruct how we form research questions and the boundaries we invent for the field.

Kay F. Turner's essay is based on ethnographic research in East Austin, Texas, and is an interpretive analysis of home altars. Focusing on the spiritual and artistic composition of home altars, she argues that they visually contribute to the cultural aesthetic of connectedness that is integrated in the design, form, and content of home altars. Mapping how connectedness comes into being, Turner untangles what might appear to the uninitiated as an unorganized collection of candles, pictures, religious statues, political figures, family heirlooms, and flowers. Each item, she contends, is assembled and arranged according to familial and sacred relationships and establishes a connection between the living and the dead, between a human family and the celestial family. Breaking down the dichotomy between the sacred and the profane, home altars are powerful sites of oppositional consciousness in that they bring into existence a new space-time continuum.

Elder Chicanas are at the center of this practice, and Turner's attention to Mexican American women advances our understanding of the performance of politics in ways that the other contributors in this section cannot. By documenting the work of Chicanas as human agents, Turner supports Chicano/a studies' commitment to experiential knowledge and the significance of gender as it intersects with race and culture. Although she is merely suggestive in her feminist analysis, Turner is operating with the modes and tools of U.S. Third World feminist consciousness (Sandoval 1991). The altar-makers possess knowledge about the world, they are cultural specialists who articulate collective systems of meaning and relations, and they have the power to bring together seemingly disparate things.

That is, their creative abilities and spiritual vision are a form of power that connects various domains—the sacred and the profane, the personal and the universal—instead of opposing these domains. Furthermore, the altar-makers operate in multiple social arenas that may have competing interests. The women are parishioners, workers, citizens, and mothers, and in the mode of U.S. Third World feminist consciousness, they shuttle between these identities and positions, at times mediating between them. As Turner argues, this women-generated power that emerges from continuity and relatedness makes the private performance of politics crucial to new forms of social critique.

229

David Carrasco enters into dialogue with Turner on the significance of sacred relationships and spiritual connectedness, although his approach is fundamentally comparative. His focus is the religious creativity in *Bless Me, Ultima*, Rudolfo A. Anaya's classic novel about Antonio Luna y Márez and his conflictive community in New Mexico. Exploring the religious dimensions of the text, Carrasco finds several manifestations of the sacred, specifically sacred landscapes, sacred humans, epiphanies, apparitions, and revelations. His work is guided by the premise that an interpretation of religious phenomena must be based on its own reality, or referent, and not on a so-called standard or norm of Christianity. This framework becomes a jumping-off point for his challenge to neutrality and objectivity. Furthermore, he argues that although religious expressions may involve rationality, they cannot be reduced to social, psychological, or rational functions. In this argument he implicates the tendency of Chicano/a studies to maneuver around the study of religion or to explain it as a "mask of oppression." Here he continues the internal critique of Chicano/a studies that Goldman initiates in her essay and questions how the blueprint for Chicano/a studies, "El Plan de Santa Barbara," could omit the study of religious structures.

Carrasco finds that the religious creativity in *Bless Me, Ultima* contains two general religious patterns: the sacredness of the landscape and the presence of sacred specialists. Both are important to understanding Chicano/a lived experience because, in his view, the sacred is equivalent to power. Thus, by performing the sacred, an "expression of the powerful, the valuable, the wonderful, and the terrifying," Antonio and Ultima, as well as other Chicanas and Chicanos, can experience a form of power that is organically their own. I infer from his argument about the novel and his criticism of Chicano/a studies that it is ironic that a discipline dedicated to the liberation of the dispossessed shows a "lack of interest" in all forms of power, particularly a form of power that is relatively untouched by, or at least outside of, the realm of the socially dominant.

Carrasco has enacted a new position for Chicano/a studies and thereby performs a political stance that parallels and resonates with Anaya's classic novel. Rafael Pérez-Torres's interpretation of Anaya is useful for understanding this performance. Carrasco "signals an aesthetic practice that crosses archaic modes of expression with a modern narrative form. In this aspect, his work reveals a central discontinuity that can serve as a focus for political critique" (Pérez-Torres 1995, 280, n. 31). It is a political critique of the limitations of Chicana/o studies, how it circumscribes its subject, and its resistance to acknowledging that which does not match its subject.

Through his writing, Carrasco embodies the discontinuity of oppositional consciousness and serves to further develop a Chicano/a studies that shifts from authenticity and similarity to a complex and multifaceted vision of its own subject.

References

Butler, Judith. 1990. *Gender Trouble: Feminism and the Subversion of Identity*. New York: Routledge.

Danius, Sara, and Stefan Jonsson. 1993. "An Interview with Gayatri Chakravorty Spivak." *Boundary 2* 20, no. 2: 24–50.

Fregoso, Rosa Linda, and Angie Chabram. 1990. "Chicana/o Cultural Representations: Reframing Alternative Critical Discourses." *Cultural Studies* 4, no.3: 203–12.

Paredes, Américo. 1976. *A Texas-Mexican Cancionero*. Urbana: University of Illinois Press.

———. 1958. *With His Pistol in His Hand*. Austin: University of Texas Press.

Pérez-Torres, Rafael. 1995. *Movements in Chicano Poetry: Against Myths, Against Margins*. New York, NY: Cambridge University Press.

Rosaldo, Renato. 1985. "Chicano Studies, 1970–1984." *Annual Review of Anthropology* 14: 405–27.

Sandoval, Chela. 1998. "Mestizaje as Method: Feminists-of-Color Challenge the Canon." In *Living Chicana Theory*, ed. C. Trujillo, 352–70. Berkeley: Third Woman Press.

———. 1991. "U.S. Third World Feminism: The Theory and Method of Oppositional Consciousness in a Postmodern World." *Genders* 10 (spring): 1–24.

Turner, Kay. 1986. "Home Altars and the Arts of Devotion." In *Chicano Expressions: A New View in American Art*, ed. I. Lockpez, 40–48. New York: INTAR Latin American Gallery.

Yarbro-Bejarano, Yvonne. 1986. "The Female Subject in Chicano Theatre: Sexuality, 'Race' and Class." *Theatre Journal* 38, no. 4: 389–407.

Ybarra-Frausto, Tomás. 1991. "Rasquachismo: A Chicano Sensibility." In *Chicano Art: Resistance and Affirmation, 1965-1985*, ed. R. Griswold del Castillo, T. McKenna, and Y. Yarbro-Bejarano, 155–62. Los Angeles: Wight Art Gallery, University of California, Los Angeles.

Chicano Teatro
A Background

Jorge A. Huerta

AUTHOR'S NOTE: *This was my first publication, written almost thirty years ago during my first year of doctoral studies at the University of California, Santa Barbara, in the spring of 1971. The article was the result of my initial forays into the university library to find whatever I could about the roots of Chicano theatre. As noted in the article, I found little in print about Chicano theatre other than several reviews and brief articles as well as one anthology of actos by the Teatro Campesino. Information about the many Chicano teatros that were active in the late 1960s and early 1970s was nil. In contrast, many sources dealt with Pre-Columbian ritual drama, Mexican colonial drama, and Spanish religious folk theatre. I knew then that I had entered an area of academic research that was wide open.*

Today, I can proudly point to many books, articles, dissertations, critical anthologies, CD-ROMs, videos, films, and web sites, all attesting to the continuing vibrancy of what we came to call the Chicano Theatre Movement. Numerous plays and collections of plays are being published and produced. Classes on Chicano theatre are taught in colleges and universities throughout the country. Chicano theatre has reached beyond our borders, with plays produced and papers presented to international audiences. And major university presses are publishing theoretical studies of Chicana and Chicano theatre.

TENAZ, the national coalition of teatros I wrote about in this article, had just been formed and grew into a major force within the Chicano Theatre Movement, promoting the dissemination of plays, newsletters, workshops and festivals for more than twenty years. Although TENAZ does not exist as it did back then, many active teatristas and teatros first became involved in theater through that important organization. I am proud of what TENAZ became and even prouder that Chicano theatre continues to thrive, albeit under different circumstances. While the initial teatros were composed of students and community activists in 1970, today there are Chicana and Chicano theatre artists working in everything from student teatros to professional companies. Fortunately, as the many recent studies of Chicana and Latina playwrights attest, many more women are writing, directing, and performing now.

Current theatre is still being generated by what we started in 1971. Luis Valdez remains the most visible of the original teatristas, but past members of his company are active as well. In a tradition that recalls nineteenth- and early-twentieth-century Mexican theatre troupes in Aztlán, the Teatro Campesino is now guided by the children of Teatro Campesino members. In other parts of the country, the children of the teatristas of the 1970s are now adults generating their own teatros.

I would like to think that this first overview of contemporary Chicano theatre was a touchstone for the many other scholars, critics, and teatristas who began to emerge over

From *Aztlan: A Journal of Chicano Studies* 1, no. 1 (1970): 1–12.

the next decades and who continue to investigate and critique this ever-evolving artistic and political movement. There was much to research in 1970 and there continues to be a need for historical explorations into Chicano theatre. As an artist/scholar, I have had the joy and frustration of attempting to create teatro while also writing about its continuing evolution.

The purpose of this article is to present a little-known and often unrecognized theater movement that is presently occurring in the United States, particularly the Southwest. This movement, yet to be named, concerns "Los Teatros de Aztlán," and is a continuation of centuries of theatrical expression and a reflection of social and political life and thought. Los Teatros de Aztlán are Chicano theater groups concerned with the education and politicization of the Chicano as well as the enlightenment of all the other groups that compose the American fabric. Theater as a novel form of creative expression is not new to the Chicano, but is firmly rooted in the indigenous as well as the Spanish and African heritage of the Americas.

Some ancient Mexican codices survived the planned destruction by the Spaniards, and we have records of life before the conquest. Most of the drama was a combination of recital, song, dance, and music. The ceremonies were frequent and long. Spectators watched, responding freely, often being involved in the dialogue.[1] The Maya, another highly sophisticated people to the south of Teotihuacán, also had dramatic presentations. A script of the Maya ritual drama, *Rabinal Achí*, has survived, allowing us a close look at their dramatic presentations. Francisco Monterde, in his Spanish translation of this ballet-drama, presents us with an account of Maya theatrical practice before Cortés:

> Entre los Mayas de Yucatán habia tambien espectáculos teatrales, con cierto predominio del ademán sobre la palabra, y estrechamente ligado a la música.[2]

This play has survived through the centuries. In 1825, the Catholic Church condemned it. However, it was again performed in 1856.

The Spaniards had as part of their theatrical experience the heritage of the Roman stage, classical poetry such as that of Seneca, and the people's theater. Almost as soon as the Spaniards gained control of Indian lands theatrical performances were presented. The Catholic Church used the liturgical drama, then so popular in Spain, to propagandize the people.[3] Thus, the religious drama of medieval Spain was transported to the Americas. Riva Palacios writes:

In the famous festival of Corpus Christi at Tlaxcala [México], in 1538, an elaborate "auto" was given, the subject being the sin of Adam and Eve. This "auto" was performed by native converts, for whom it had been translated into their own language.[4]

Oscar G. Brockett defines the "auto" thusly:

The auto sacramental combined characteristics of the morality and cycle plays. In it, human and supernatural characters mingled with such allegorical figures as Sin, Grace, Pleasure, Grief, and Beauty. Stories could be drawn from any source, even completely secular ones, so long as they illustrated the efficacy of the sacraments and the validity of church dogma.[5]

On 30 April 1598, on the river just below El Paso, the first Spanish-language play known to have been acted in what is now the United States was performed. Herbert E. Bolton tells us that the play was "an original comedy written by Captain Farfan on a subject connected with the conquest of New Mexico."[6] This predates by sixty-seven years the first English play recorded as acted in the area, and by eight years the French masque performed in Acadia in 1606.[7]

Mary Austin reported that when Oñate and his settlers had crossed the Rio Grande and reached the junction of that river with the Chama River, they celebrated the occasion with a play entitled *Los Moros y Los Cristianos*. This play was carried throughout the Americas by the Spanish armies. It depicts the conquest of a Moorish city by the Spaniards and the subsequent conversion of the Moors to Christianity.[8]

The Golden Age of Spanish literature ended about 1680, and Spanish theater declined, never really regaining the prominence it once had. The missionaries to Nuevo México, Colorado, Texas, and California brought liturgical drama with them, again using this important propagandizing tool. One of the best known of these religious plays is *Los Pastores*. It was brought from Spain and performed in Mexico City in 1526.[9] Various versions of this play survive today. Charles Basil Martin writes that "of the 119 known manuscripts of this one play, 95 are found in New Mexico."[10] The play has been continually performed in the Southwest. Some records of its productions include performances in Colorado, about 1880,[11] and San Rafael, New Mexico, 1899,[12] to mention only two.[13]

Nineteenth- and twentieth-century theater in Mexico, as attested by several bibliographies and histories of theater, is not difficult to follow. However, for the Southwest this is not the case. George MacMinn's book *The Theatre of the Golden Era in California* serves to illustrate this point.

At the old Pacific capital [Monterrey] the Spanish-Californians were still expressing their own dramatic instincts in a very lively manner at the time of the American occupation in 1846 …

The children's drama of Adam and Eve … was "got up by one of our most respectable citizens, who for the purpose converted his ample saloon into a mimic opera house." At the same time, by Lawrence's account, a Spanish troupe was presenting an entertainment at the house of Señor Rafael González … In 1844, says Lawrence, a party of Mexicans was giving a tightrope and legerdemain performance in the corral of Señora Bonifacio.[14]

In his last reference to Mexican theater, MacMinn states that in Los Angeles "there had been a theater of *some sort* in which the Mexicans and native Californians of the place amused themselves …"[15] (emphasis mine). A theater of "some sort" indeed! Mexican drama seems to have been approached by the Anglo critic as some sort of inane diversion—a children's play. Undoubtedly, this "children's play" is the same Adam and Eve that the Spaniards brought with them from Spain in the sixteenth century, but probably because he did not speak the language, the contemporary observer thought it was some sort of children's play.

Of course, brief mention of Mexican and Spanish theatrical activity is made in some publications, but only enough information seems to be available to prove that Spanish-speaking drama was occurring, and this information is slight outside of New Mexico. Much research is needed on the theater of the Spanish-speaking communities outside of New Mexico. In New Mexico, by the nineteenth century, troupes began to form and traveled from town to town performing a repertoire of religious plays. By the late 1840s these traveling troupes began to subside and instead of touring, began to stay in their own towns, vying for a play to call their own.[16] To be sure, it has been within the last forty years that critics have realized the significance of the New Mexican folk drama.[17]

There are records of acting companies and entertainments traveling from México to Santa Barbara throughout the period of 1769–1894.[18] A close study of Los Angeles's Spanish-language newspapers will reveal theatrical activity dating from the nineteenth century.

There is still much research needed in Chicano theatrical activity during the present century. There are records of Mexican *carpas y maromeros* touring Aztlán to entertain as well as comment upon the sociopolitical scene. More research will undoubtedly reveal some interesting notes about the theatrical history of the Chicano during this period.

Contemporary Chicano Theater

The year 1965 marks a new direction in Chicano theater. As part of the organizing activities of the United Farmworkers Organizing Committee, the Teatro Campesino was formed by Luis Miguel Valdez. Born to a migrant farm working family in the San Joaquin Valley, Valdez underwent the usual sporadic education given to migrants. Unlike the majority of our people, however, Valdez managed to graduate from high school, and even won a scholarship to San Jose State College. He studied biology, but was really interested in playwriting. After two years of dissecting various anatomies, Valdez changed majors to English, enrolled in many drama courses, and read all the plays he could.

During his sophomore year in San Jose, Valdez wrote a one-act play entitled "The Theft." This play won him a school prize, a production of the play by the San Jose Theater Guild, and much-needed confidence. During the next two years he worked on his first full-length play, "The Shrunken Head of Pancho Villa." He directed it for the Northwest Drama Conference at San Jose State, but felt it needed much revision. He then joined the San Francisco Mime Troupe in 1964. "When I discovered the Mime Troupe," says Valdez, "I figured if any theater could turn on the farmworker, it would be that type of theater—outside, that lively, that bawdy."[19] Valdez worked with the Mime Troupe until the *huelga* broke out in 1965. He went to Delano to see if he could start a teatro. Everyone liked the idea, so in November 1965 the Teatro Campesino began.

Valdez relates what happened at the first meeting of the new group:

> I talked for about ten minutes, and then realized that talking wasn't going to accomplish anything. The thing to do was do it, so I called three of them over, and on two hung "Huelgista" (Striker) signs. Then I gave one an "Esquirol" sign and told him to stand up there and act like an "Esquirol"—a scab. He didn't want to at first, because it was a dirty word at that time, but he did it in good spirits. Then the two Huelgistas started shouting at him, and everybody started cracking up. All of a sudden people started coming into the pink house from I don't know where; they filled up the whole kitchen. We started changing signs around and people started volunteering, "Let me play so and so," "Look, this is what I did," imitating all kinds of things.[20]

From that first meeting on, exciting *actos* began to emerge. An acto can be defined as a short, improvised scene dealing with the experience of its participants—a conversation between a boss (*patrón*) and his worker-striker (*huelgista*); a situation involving a Chicano and the sociopolitical forces around him. These forces may be manifested in a school teacher, probation officer, etc. "We could have called them 'skits,'" says Valdez, "but we lived and talked in San Joaquin Spanish (which has a strong Tejano influence) so we needed a name that made sense to the Raza."[21]

The acto is certainly not new, nor is it uniquely Chicano in form. Other radical theater groups such as the San Francisco Mime Troupe and the Bread and Puppet Theater use a type of acto. A Chicano acto, however, is one that deals solely with Chicano experiences and is in the Chicano language. As in other radical or sociopolitical groups, the acto should:

> Inspire the audience to social action. Illuminate specific points about social problems. Satirize the opposition. Show or hint at a solution. Express what people are feeling.[22]

Since the acto is arrived at through improvisation, Valdez feels that "the reality reflected … is thus a social reality."[23] The acto often employs group archtypes, which Valdez believes "symbolizes the desired unity and group identity through Chicano heroes and heroines. One character can thus represent the entire Raza, and the Chicano audience will gladly respond to his triumphs or defeats."[24] Thus, what may seem like overexaggeration to an Anglo audience is to the Chicano a true representation of his social state and, therefore, reality.

The Teatro Campesino began with the *huelga*, and its members were all farmworkers. When Valdez asked the actors to improvise a situation that might occur in the field, these actors had lived that experience and knew only too well its outcome. About a month after its inception, the group was invited to perform at Stanford University. Although the presentation was somewhat rough, it was well received, and Valdez realized the potential for spreading the news about the strike to the urban areas of California.[25]

The Teatro began touring the cities to raise money for the huelga, and returned each week for the union meetings. The group began to feel separated from the huelga because of the heavy touring schedule. They then curbed the traveling to outside areas, limiting their performances to campesino audiences. They played wherever they could, sometimes on the very boundaries of a nonunion ranch.

Valdez had discovered very early in working with the Teatro that comedy was its best asset

> not only from a satirical point of view, but from the fact that humor can stand up on its own … We use comedy because it stems from a necessary situation—the necessity of lifting the morale of our strikers … This leads

us into satire and slapstick, and sometimes very close to the underlying tragedy of it all—the fact that human beings have been wasted in farm labor for generations.[26]

During early 1967, Valdez said, "The most characteristic thing about the Teatro as a theater group is that we are dedicated to a very specific goal—the organization of farmworkers."[27] From this goal and activity, the group moved to a new stage. Valdez points out that:

> The strike in Delano is a beautiful cause, but it won't leave you alone. A Cause is a living, breathing thing. It's more important to leave a rehearsal and go to the picket line. So we found we had to back away from Delano ... to be a theatre. That was a very hard decision to make, very, very hard. Do you serve the movement by being just kind of halfassed, getting together whenever there's a chance, hitting and missing, or do you really hone your theatre down into an effective weapon? Is it possible to make it an effective weapon without being blood-close to the movement?[28]

The Teatro left Delano and the union to establish El Centro Campesino Cultural in Del Rey, California. In a rundown building in this small rural town, the Teatro conducted workshops, art classes, guitar lessons, Teatro rehearsals, and performances. They moved again in 1970, and now occupy a converted restaurant in Fresno.

The Teatro Campesino has had a very impressive existence. Almost since its inception, the critical acclaim has been favorable. In 1966 the *San Francisco Chronicle* said it was "vital, earthy and alive theater."[29] In July 1967 the *Wall Street Journal* called them "a tough act to follow."[30] The following month, on their way from the Newport Folk Festival to the Senate Subcommittee on Migrant Labor, the Campesino was at the Village Theatre, Greenwich Village, pleasing and surprising audiences. "They expect us to be farmworkers, which to them means stupid and ignorant. They're always surprised to find we speak good English," said Augustin Lira, the Teatro's former guitarist and composer.[31] During the "Obie" Awards for the 1967–1968 season, the Campesino won a special citation "for creating a worker's theater to demonstrate the politics of survival."[32]

By June 1969, the Teatro Campesino received international recognition when it participated in the Théâtre des Nations in Paris. When the group performed at the Inner City Cultural Center in Los Angeles in September 1969, Dan Sullivan, drama critic for the *Los Angeles Times*, wrote:

> Their rambunctious sketches go back to the very roots of theatre, and beautifully fulfill the twin tasks the medium has always set for itself: to

delight and instruct. And in that order … They hold up their heads as proudly as they want all Chicanos to, and when they make a white [sic] audience laugh, it is not by being peon-cute but by being superior farceurs.[33]

And in October 1970, Sullivan, again very impressed, wrote:

Is there anywhere a group of actors more in touch with themselves and the basic realities of life than these? A board and a passion is almost literally all they have to offer, yet the results make most big-city theater seem skimpy …

They have more fun on stage than anybody and communicate it. Yet they are talking about serious matters—what it means to be a Chicano right now and what it should mean.[34]

By 1968 other teatros began to emerge, inspired by the efforts of the Teatro Campesino. Danny Valdez, Luis's younger brother, formed El Teatro Urbano in San Jose, and Guadalupe Saavedra helped in the formation of El Teatro Popular de la Vida y Muerte in Long Beach, California. Aware of the need to help each other in the formative stages, the Teatro Campesino sponsored a "Festival de los Teatros" in Fresno in May 1970.

This first festival was important in the development of the Chicano teatro movement. There were approximately fifteen groups represented, one of which was Los Mascarones of Mexico City. As a result of the festival an exchange of ideas and style took place between the teatros of Aztlán and México.

The most vital question for Chicano teatros was: "Where do we get material to work with?" Some of the work that was performed showed much promise, and the participants returned with a renewed hope for their particular groups, eager to share what they had learned at the festival with their communities. An important point that was stressed was the need for the teatros to share their material. If an acto works in Texas, it should be successful anywhere in Aztlán.

Teatro Campesino began publishing the first journal of teatro Chicano during the summer of 1970. The publication, entitled *El Teatro,* included "Notes on Chicano Theater" by Valdez, as well as exercises and ideas for the development of a teatro. This publication was sent out to all interested groups and individuals in an effort to make the public aware of the current phenomenon called teatro.

The Second Annual Festival of Teatros was held during spring break of 1971 at Cabrillo College in Aptos, California, near Santa Cruz. This second festival was much better organized than the first, and lasted for an entire week. Participating teatros came from as far away as Mexico City and Seattle. During this eventful week teatros performed in surrounding Chicano communities, and workshops were held to help the groups in various teatro techniques: voice, movement, pantomime, songs, and playwriting.

This second festival reflected the development of each group. A key note of the conference was the need for better communication between the teatros. Valdez suggested that the directors of each group attend a directors' conference in Fresno the following weekend in order to begin a more successful means of communication.

The first directors' conference included representatives from eight groups. This meeting turned out to be a historic date in the history of Chicano theater, for it was then that a coalition of teatros called TENAZ, El Teatro Nacional de Aztlán, was formed. The directors agreed to have quarterly conferences. The first two TENAZ workshops were to be held during the months of July and August 1971. All teatros were invited to send participants to work in the Campesino's second theater, La Calavera de Tiburcio Vásquez in San Juan Bautista.

While Danny Valdez toured the Teatro Campesino through the midwestern United States, Luis worked with TENAZ members developing new material and preparing a program of one-act plays and *corridos*. The Teatro Campesino had held a playwriting contest and the two best plays, *Celebration* and *Encounter*, written by Luis Navarro of East Los Angeles, were prepared for performance. The workshop also premiered a new form of Chicano dramatic expression, the corridos. The corrido is a dramatized version of such old corridos as "Rosita Alvarez" and "Cornelio Vega." While the guitarist sings, actors in stylized makeup and simple costumes pantomime the message, sometimes actually speaking the lines from the song.

The two workshops proved very successful. The final products of this artistic endeavor were given a professional billing at the Inner City Cultural Center in Los Angeles from 16 to 26 September 1971. Divided into three separate programs, the Fiesta de los Teatros proved once again the continuing genius of Luis Valdez, and also impressed the critics with the ability of the actors to recreate the essence of good theater just like any other professional group.

The most important feature of the Los Angeles run is that the first six performances were TENAZ productions. Members of seven different teatros participated in the program, making it the first attempt at a national Chicano theater. Valdez and the Teatro Campesino were again invited to the Théâtre des Nations in Paris this May and June. Valdez hopes to take a TENAZ production to Paris, sharing this new coalition with the rest of the world.

The future of Los Teatros de Aztlán is very bright. The critical acclaim and the audience reactions seem to point to a true sense of pride in the Chicano as an artist, technician, actor, and writer. Unlike Anglo American Broadway theater, the members of teatros are not concerned with "stardom." What matters to the Chicano in a teatro is that a message be understood. It seems that those sixteenth-century missionaries have been replaced by a new religion and new apostles equally, if not more, fervent in their purpose. Los Teatros de Aztlán are filling an essential role in the Chicano struggle for identity, justice, and liberation.

Notes

1. Willard C. Booth, "Dramatic Aspects of Aztec Rituals," *Educational Theatre Journal* 18 (December 1966): 427.

2. Francisco Monterde, prologue to *Rabinal Achi: Teatro Indigena Pre-Hispánica* (México: Ediciones de la Universidad Autónoma, 1955), x. "Among the Mayas of Yucatán, there were also theatrical spectacles, with a certain disdain of the spoken word, and tightly bound to the music." My translation.

3. M. R. Cole, "Los Pastores," *Memoirs of the American Folklore Society* 9 (1907): xi. See also Carlos E. Castañeda, "The First American Play," *Catholic World*, January 1932.

4. Palacios as cited in Cole, "Los Pastores," ix. See also: William A. Hunter, "The Calderonian Auto Sacramental," in *The Native Theatre in Middle America* (New Orleans: Tulane University, 1961), 118; and Willis Knapp Jones, *Behind Spanish American Footlights* (Austin: University of Texas Press, 1966), 463.

5. Oscar G. Brockett, *History of the Theatre* (Boston: Allyn and Bacon, 1968), 197.

6. Herbert E. Bolton, *The Spanish Borderlands* (New Haven: Yale University Press, 1921), 127.

7. Winifred Johnson, "Early Theater in the Spanish Borderlands," *Mid-America* 13 (October 1930): 127, 131.

8. Mary Austin, "Spanish Manuscripts in the Southwest," *Southwest Review* 19 (July 1934): 404.

9. Jones, *Spanish American Footlights*, 460.

10. Charles Basil Martin, *The Survivals of Medieval Religious Drama in New Mexico* (Ph.D. diss., University of Missouri, 1959; Ann Arbor, Mich.: University Microfilms, Mic. 59-5645), ii.

11. Edwin B. Place, "A Group of Mystery Plays Found in a Spanish-Speaking Region of Southern Colorado," *University of Colorado Studies* 18, no. 1 (August 1930): 1.

12. Cole, "Los Pastores," xxviii.

13. Martin's dissertation makes an excellent study of the ten extant New Mexican medieval dramas, including performances. Martin, *Survivals*, 16 ff.

14. George P. MacMinn, *The Theatre of the Golden Era in California* (Caldwell, Idaho: Caxton, 1941), 24.

15. Ibid., 26.

16. Sister Joseph Marie McCrossan, *The Role of the Church and the Folk in the Development of the Early Drama in New Mexico* (Philadelphia: University of Pennsylvania, 1948), 95.

17. Enough significance has been given to New Mexican Spanish folk drama to warrant two doctoral dissertations. See the Bibliography.

18. See Tallant Smith's very interesting and informative master's thesis, "History of the Theatre in Santa Barbara 1769–1894" (University of California, Santa Barbara, 1969).

19. Beth Bagby, "El Teatro Campesino: Interview with Luis Valdez," *Tulane Drama Review* 11, no. 4 (summer 1967): 73.

20. Ibid., 74–5.

21. Luis Valdez, "Notes on Chicano Theater," *El Teatro* (fall 1970): 6.

22. Ibid.

23. Ibid.

24. Ibid.

25. Bagby, "Interview with Luis Valdez," 76.

26. Ibid., 77.

27. Ibid., 79.

28. Sylvie Drake, "El Teatro Campesino: Keeping the Revolution on Stage," *Performing Arts*, September 1970, 59–60.

29. Ralph J. Gleason, "Vital, Earthy and Alive Theater," *San Francisco Chronicle*, 4 May 1966.

30. John J. O'Connor, "The Theatre: Shades of the Thirties," *Wall Street Journal*, 24 July 1967.

31. "Actos: Teatro Campesino, a theatrical part of the United Farmworkers Organizing Committee," *The New Yorker*, 19 August 1967, 23–5.

32. "Worker's Theater Leads Obie Winners," *New York Times*, 28 May 1968.

33. Dan Sullivan, "Chicano Group at ICCC," *Los Angeles Times*, 27 September 1969, 9.

34. Dan Sullivan, "El Teatro Campesino in Halloween Program," *Los Angeles Times*, 1 November 1970.

Selected Bibliography

PRECOLUMBIAN DRAMA

Balty, Elizabeth Chestley. *Americans Before Columbus.* New York: Viking, 1951.

Bayle, Constantino. "El Teatro Indígena en América." *Lectura* 52 (15 June 1946): 219.

Booth, Willard C. "Dramatic Aspects of Aztec Rituals." *Educational Theatre Journal* 18 (December 1966): 421–8.

Caso, Alfonso. *The Aztecs, People of the Sun.* Norman: University of Oklahoma Press, 1958.

Cid Pérez, José, ed. *Teatro Indio Precolombino: El Gueguense, o Macho Ratón; El Varón de Rabinal.* Madrid: Aguilar, 1964.

Horcasitas Pimental, Fernando. "Piezas Teatrales en Lengua Nahuatl: Bibliografía Descriptiva." *Boletín Bibliográfico de Antropología Americana* 11 (1948, issued in 1949): 154–64.

Icaza, Francisco A. de. "Origines del Teatro en México." *Boletín de la Real Academia Española* (Madrid) 2, no. 6 (February 1915).

Irving, T. B. "Three Mayan Classics." *University of Toronto Quarterly*, October 1950.

Rabinal Achi: Teatro Indigena Pre-Hispánica. Prologue by Francisco Monterde. México: Ediciones de la Universidad Autónoma, 1955.

Sahagún, Bernardo de. *General History of Things of New Spain.* 3 vols. Santa Fe: School of American Research, 1950.

Torres-Rioseco, A. "Teatro Indígena de México." In *Ensayos Sobre la Literatura Latinoamericana*, 7–26. Berkeley: University of California Press, 1953.

Villacorta, José Antonio. "Rabinal Achi, Tragedia Danzada de los Quiches." *Anales* 17 (1942): 352–71.

MEXICAN DRAMA: XVITH THROUGH XIXTH CENTURIES

Alegre, S. J., and Francisco Javier. *Historia de la Compañía de Jesús en Nueva España.* México: D. Carlos María de Bustamante, 1841.

Arróm, José Juan. *Historia del Teatro Hispanoamericano Epoca Colonial.* México: Ediciones de Andrea, 1967.

Autos y Coloquios del Siglo XVI. Prologue and notes by José Rojas Garcidueñas. México: Universidad Nacional Autónoma de México, 1939.

Ballinger, Rex Edward. *Los Origines del Teatro Español y sus Primeras Manifestaciones en la Nueva España.* México, 1951.

Castañeda, Carlos E. "The First American Play." *Catholic World*, January 1932, 429–37.

———. "Los Manuscritos Perdidos de Gutiérrez de Luna." *Revista Mexicana de Estudios Históricos* 2, no. 5 (September/October 1928).

Cid Pérez, José. "El Teatro de América de Ayer y de Hoy." *Boletín* no. 16 (March 1947): 2–13.

Hunter, William A. "The Calderonian Auto Sacramental." In *The Native Theatre in Middle America*, ed. Gustavo Correa, et al., 105–201. New Orleans: Tulane University, Middle America Research Institute, 1961.

Jiménez Rueda, Julio. "La Edad de Fernández Eslava." *Revista Mexicana de Estudios Históricos* 2, no. 3 (May/June 1928).

Johnson, Harvey Leroy. *An Edition of "Triunfo de los Santos" with a Consideration of the Jesuit School Plays in Mexico Before 1650.* Philadelphia, 1941.

Maria y Campos, Armando de. *Representaciones Teatrales en la Nueva España (Siglos XVI al XVIII).* México: Colección La Máscara, 1959.

Monterde, Francisco. "Pastoral and Popular Performances: The Drama of Viceregal Mexico." *Theatre Arts Monthly*, no. 22 (1938): 597–602.

Olavarria y Ferrari, Enrique de. *Reseña Historia del Teatro en México,1538–1911.* 3d. ed. 5 vols. México: Editorial Porrua, 1961.

Perea de Rivas, S. J., Andrés. *Crónica y Historia Religiosa de la Provincia de la Compañía de Jesús.* México, 1896.

Rojas Garcidueñas, José J. *El Teatro de Nueva España en el Siglo XVI.* México, 1935.

Torre, Revella José. "El Primer Dramaturgo Americano." *Hispania* 24 (1941): 161–70.

MODERN MEXICAN DRAMA

Bach, Marcus. "Los Pastores." *Theater Arts* 24 (April 1940): 283–8.

Canton, Wilberto L. *Teatro Breve.* México, 1968.

Covarrubias, Miguel. "Slapstick and Venom." *Theatre Arts Monthly*, August 1938, 587–97.

Crow, J. H. "Drama Revolucionario Mexicano." *Revista Hispánica Moderna* 5 (1939): 20–31.

Lamb, Ruth S. *Bibliografía del Teatro Mexicano del Siglo XX.* Claremont, Calif.: Claremont Colleges, 1962.

Lamb, Ruth S., and Antonio Magaña Esquivel. *Breve Historia del Teatro Mexicano.* México: Ediciones de Andrea, 1958.

Monterde, Francisco. *Bibliografía del Teatro en México.* México: Monografías Bibliográficas Mexicanas, 1934.

Nomland, John Barrington. "Contemporary Mexican Theatre 1900–1950." Ph.D. diss., University of California, Los Angeles, 1957.

Novo, Salvador. "Chaos and Horizons of Mexican Drama." *Theatre Arts Monthly*, May 1941.

Theatre Arts Monthly 22, no. 8 (August 1938). Entire issue devoted to modern Mexican drama.

LATIN AMERICAN DRAMA

Arróm, José J. "Raíces indígenas del teatro americano." *Selected Papers of the XXIXth International Congress of Amercanists*, 299–305. Chicago: University of Chicago Press, 1952.

Correa, Gustavo, et al. *The Native Theatre in Middle America.* New Orleans: Tulane University, Middle America Research Institute, 1961.

Englekirk, John E. "El Teatro Folklórico Hispanoamericano." *Folklore Américas* 17 (June 1957): 1–36.

Hills, Elijah Clarence. "The Quechua Drama Ollanta." *Romanic Revue* 5 (1914): 127–76. Also in *Hispanic Studies* (Stanford University), 1929, 47–105.

Holmes, Henry Alfred. *Spanish America in Song and Story.* New York: Henry Holt and Co., c. 1932.

Jones, Willis Knapp. *Behind Spanish American Footlights.* Austin: University of Texas Press, 1966.

———. *Breve Historia del Teatro Latino Americano.* México: Ediciones de Andrea, 1956.

Pasquariello, Antonio M. "The Entremés in 16th-Century Spanish America," *Hispanic American Historical Revue* 32, no. 1 (February 1952): 44–58.

Rosenbach, A. S. W. "The First Theatrical Company in America." *Proceedings of the American Antiquarian Society* 48 (1939): 300–10.

Torre, Revello José. "Orígines del teatro en HispanoAmérica." *Cuaderno de Cultura Teatral,* no. 7 (1937): 49.

Ureha, Pedro Henriquez. "El Teatro en América durante la época colonial." *Cuaderno de Cultura Teatral,* no. 3 (1936): 9–50.

DRAMA IN THE SOUTHWEST

Austin, Mary. "Spanish Manuscripts in the Southwest." *Southwest Review* 19 (July 1934): 401–9.

———. "Folkplays of the Southwest." *Theatre Arts Monthly,* August 1933, 599–606.

———. "Native Drama in New Mexico." *Theatre Arts Monthly,* August 1929, 564–7.

———. "Native Drama in Our Southwest." *The Nation* 124 (20 April 1927): 437–40.

Campa, Arthur. *Spanish Religious Folk Theater of the Southwest.* 2 vols. Albuquerque: University of New Mexico, 1934.

———. "Religious Spanish Theatre in New Mexico." *New Mexico Quarterly,* February 1931.

Carson, William G. B. *The Theater on the Frontier.* Chicago: University of Chicago Press, 1932.

Cole, M. R. "Los Pastores." *Memoirs of the American Folklore Society* 9 (1907).

Curtis, F. S. Jr. "Spanish Folk-Poetry in the Southwest." *Southwest Review* 10 (January 1925): 68–73.

Englekirk, John E. "The Source and Dating of New Mexican-Spanish Folkplays." *Western Folklore* (Berkeley, Calif.) 16, no. 4 (October 1957): 325–55.

———. "Fernando Calderón en el teatro popular nuevo-mexicano." *Memoria del Segundo Congreso Internacional de Catedráticos de Literatura Iberoamericana,* 227–40. Berkeley, Calif., 1949.

———. "Notes on the Repertoire of the New Mexican Spanish Folk-theater." *Southern Folklore Quarterly* 4 (1940): 227–37.

Espinosa, Aurelio M. "Los Comanches." *University of New Mexico Bulletin* 1, no. 1 (1907): 5–46.

Espinosa, Aurelio M., and J. Manuel. "The Texans: A New Mexican-Spanish Folkplay." *New Mexico Quarterly Review* 13 (autumn 1934): 397–408.

Gallegly, Joseph. *Footlights on the Border*. The Hague: Mouton, 1962.

Johnson, Winifred. "Early Theater in the Spanish Borderlands." *Mid-America* 13 (October 1930): 121–31.

Lea, Aurora Lucero-White. *Literary Folklore of the Hispanic Southwest*. San Antonio: Naylor Co., 1953.

MacMinn, George P. *The Theatre of the Golden Era in California*. Caldwell, Idaho: Caxton, 1941.

Martin, Charles Basil. *The Survivals of Medieval Religious Drama in New Mexico*. Ann Arbor, Mich.: University Microfilms, 1959.

McCrossan, Sister Joseph Marie. *The Role of the Church and the Folk in the Development of the Early Drama in New Mexico*. Philadelphia: University of Pennsylvania, 1948.

Place, Edwin B. "A Group of Mystery Plays Found in a Spanish-Speaking Region of Southern Colorado." *University of Colorado Studies* 18, no. 1 (August 1930): 1–8.

Schaeffer, L. M. *Sketches of Travels in South America, Mexico, and California*. New York: James Egbert, 1860.

Smith, Tallant. "History of the Theatre in Santa Barbara 1769–1894." Master's thesis, University of California, Santa Barbara, 1969.

Stoddard, Charles Warren. *In The Footprints of the Padres*. San Francisco: A. M. Robertson, 1902.

Tully, Marjorie F., and Juan B. Rael. *An Annotated Bibliography of Spanish Folklore in New Mexico and Southern Colorado*. Albuquerque, University of New Mexico Press, 1950.

Twitchell, R. E. "The First Community Theatre and Playwright in the U.S." *Museum of New Mexico and the School of American Research* (Santa Fe) 16 (15 March 1924): 83–7.

Teatro Campesino

"Actos: Teatro Campesino, a theatrical part of the United Farmworkers Organizing Committee." *New Yorker*, 19 August 1967, 23–5.

Alvarez, Felix, and José Rendón, eds. *El Teatro*. Fresno, Calif.: El Teatro Campesino Cultural. Two issues published, summer and fall 1970.

Bagby, Beth. "El Teatro Campesino: Interview with Luis Valdez." *Tulane Drama Review* 11, no. 4 (summer 1967): 70–80.

Drake, Sylvie. "El Teatro Campesino: Keeping the Revolution on Stage." *Performing Arts*, September 1970, 56–62.

"El Teatro Campesino to Perform." *San Francisco Chronicle*, 12 February 1971, 45.

Gleason, Ralph J. "Vital, Earthy and Alive Theater." *San Francisco Chronicle*, 4 May 1966.

"Guerrilla Drama: productions of the San Francisco Mime Troupe, Bread and Puppet Theater, and California's Teatro Campesino." *Time*, 18 October 1968, 72.

Jones, David R. "Farm Labor: Viva el Picket Sign." *New York Times*, 30 July 1967.

Kushner, Sam. "Comment: Campesino Culture." *People's World*, 4 May 1968.

"New Grapes: El Teatro Campesino performs for migrant farmworkers," *Newsweek*, 31 July 1967, 79.

O'Connor, John J. "The Theatre: Shades of the Thirties." *Wall Street Journal*, 24 July 1967.

San Francisco Mime Troupe. "Radical Theater Festival." 1968.

Steiner, Stan. *La Raza: The Mexican Americans*, chap. 24, 324–38, 228–9. New York: Harper Colophon, 1970.

———. "Cultural Schizophrenia of Luis Valdez." *Vogue*, 15 March 1969, 112–3.

Sullivan, Dan. "El Teatro Campesino in Halloween Program." *Los Angeles Times*, 1 November 1970.

———. "Chicano Group at ICCC." *Los Angeles Times*, 27 September 1969, 9.

Valdez, Luis Miguel. "Notes on Chicano Theater." *El Teatro* (El Teatro Campesino Cultural, Fresno, Calif.), summer and fall 1970.

———. "El Teatro Campesino." *Ramparts*, July 1966.

"Worker's Theater Leads Obie Winners." *New York Times*, 28 May 1968.

OTHER TEATROS

Loper, Mary Lou. "Barrio Theater Run on Shoestring." *Los Angeles Times*, 7 February 1971, E4.

"Teatro Portrays Cultural Injustices." *El Popo* (MEChA, San Francisco Valley State College) 2, no. 4.

OTHER SOURCES CONSULTED

Anda, José de. "Mexican Culture and the Mexican American." *El Grito* 3, no. 1 (fall 1969): 42–8.

Grebler, Leo, Ralph Guzmán, and Joan W. Moore. *The Mexican American People: The Nation's Second Largest Minority*. New York: The Free Press, 1970.

McWilliams, Carey. *North from Mexico*. New York: Greenwood Press, 1968.

Samora, Julian, ed. *La Raza: Forgotten Americans*. Notre Dame, Ind.: University of Notre Dame Press, 1966.

Steiner, Stan. *La Raza: The Mexican Americans*. New York: Harper and Row, 1970.

Willett, John. *Brecht on Theatre*. New York: Hill and Wang, 1964.

———. *The Theatre of Bertolt Brecht*. New York: New Directions, 1964.

Folklore, Lo Mexicano, and Proverbs

Américo Paredes

The definition of *lo mexicano* has preoccupied Mexican philosophers on both sides of the border. This almost undefinable essence, making a Mexican or a Mexican American what he is, has been described in a number of ways. Another concept that has been given varying definitions is folklore. I will not attempt to define lo mexicano this evening, but I will make a stab at identifying folklore. For our purposes folklore may be described as "the unofficial heritage of a people." Defined in this way, folklore becomes especially important to minority groups, especially to groups that speak a language different from that of the majority. In such cases the national culture is the "official" culture, expressed in the majority language, while the minority culture becomes a "folk" culture, expressing itself in its own language.

In other words, folklore is of particular importance to minority groups such as the Mexican Americans because their basic sense of identity is expressed in a language with an "unofficial" status, different from the one used by the official culture. We can say, then, that while in Mexico the Mexican may well seek lo mexicano in art, literature, philosophy, or history—as well as in folklore—the Mexican American would do well to seek his identity in his folklore. If the Mexican American will not do it, others will do it for him, as they have done in the past. North Americans have sought clues to the Mexican character (both north and south of the border) by studying the Mexican's folklore. Let me give you an example, from the pen of a man who is considered by some as one of our greatest folklorists, J. Frank Dobie.

In 1957 Mr. Dobie published a little article called "Br'er Rabbit Watches Out for Himself in Mexico."[1] The article analyzed a folktale collected in Mexico about a rabbit who outwits a series of animals stronger than him, fixing things so each animal is killed by a successively stronger

From *Aztlan: A Journal of Chicano Studies* 1, no. 1 (1970): 1–12.

one, while the rabbit profits from each encounter. "The tales people tell reveal the tellers," Mr. Dobie stated. And he went on to conclude that this tale showed how ruthlessly competitive Mexicans were. Their philosophy of life was expressed in the saying, "No te dejes." Mr. Dobie, with the help of an American businessman living in Mexico City, described this philosophy as a desire to get ahead of everybody else without any regard for ethics or fair play. His American friend told about a Mexican friend of his who was sending his son to study in the United States. The Mexican friend had been raised by his own father according to the philosophy of "No te dejes." But then he had gone to college in the United States, where a professor told him on the first day of class, "You are here to acquire knowledge, but you must never forget the principle of fair play... Success is something more than just getting ahead of everybody else." This had been a revelation to the Mexican friend. Now he wanted his son to go to school in the United States, "where the idea of fair play is in the air," instead of letting him be educated in Mexico, where his mind would be warped by the "no te dejes" philosophy.

One can easily see the truth of Mr. Dobie's analysis of the Mexican character. Compared to North Americans, we Mexicans are a ruthless, aggressive, and extremely pragmatic people. That is why the center of world industry and finance is in Mexico City. That is why North Americans have to go begging hat-in-hand to the Mexican government for economic aid; and why North American business and industry is run by Mexicans who own villas in Florida and work in office suites in New York City, from which vantage point they can make casual assessments of the North American character. Need we say more? Perhaps not, except to note—somewhat sadly—that this was written not by some right-wing reactionary but by the leading Texas liberal of his time, a man who still is one of the father figures for the white liberals of this state.

Obviously there is something lacking in Mr. Dobie's interpretation since it is contradicted rather than supported by data from other sources. This is not to say that his little story may not tell us a great deal about the way Mexicans think and feel. The feelings and attitudes expressed in folklore, however, are not always lying on the surface to be picked up by the most casual observer. Finding them may require not only patience and wisdom but some real knowledge of the people and their culture. Compounding the problem is the matter of texture or complexity in such genres as folk narrative. There is such a wealth of elements in a folktale (plot, characters, setting, diction, performing style), that the "message" may be hard to spot. It may even be argued that the whole intricate structure is meant to entertain rather than to instruct, so that looking for a "message" is beside the point.

Still, there are many folktales—especially stories about animals—in which a dominant idea or "message" is clearly expressed, usually in a short and terse form; for example, "No te dejes," or "Un bien con un mal se paga." Such phrases exist independently, as proverbs. *Refranes*, we would call them in bookish Spanish, but our people call them simply *dichos*—sayings. Dichos are simple little things, if one compares them with the complexities of a folktale that may take a whole night in the telling. But they are not devoid of structure by any means, even if it takes just a single breath to utter them. Take, for example, the "true" proverb, as it is called by folklorists—a dicho that is always a complete statement, a sentence. It is also a complete little poem, using the same kinds of effects that are found in other poetry. One of the simplest poetic effects, and one of the oldest, is balanced structure—the balancing of the two parts of the dicho on either side of a center, like two weights on an old-fashioned type of scales, for example: "Arrieros somos / y el camino andamos." This is the same type of structure used in the Old Testament, in the Psalms: "The Lord is my shepherd; / I shall not want."

Contrast may be added to balanced structure, and the effect is even more pleasing to one's sense of form. Notice how in the following dichos two words are contrasted against each other: "Mucho ruido / y pocas nueces." "A buena hambre / no hay mal pan." A more familiar effect is the use of rhyme, as in most poetry we know: "Cada oveja / con su pareja." "A Dios rogando / y con el mazo dando." Some dichos use alliteration, the repetition of the first sounds of words—a poetic adornment more commonly found in the Germanic languages than in Spanish: "rough and ready," for example. Assonance, the matching of the vowel sounds at the end of phrases, is much more common in Spanish. In the following dicho, both assonance and alliteration are used: "Quien da pan a perro ajeno / pierde el pan y pierde el perro."

Another kind of dicho is known as a "proverbial comparison." It is not a complete sentence but a phrase beginning with the word *como* (like): "Como agua pa' chocolate," "Como calcetín de a nicle," "Como el que chifló en la loma." Dichos of this kind usually have stories behind them, stories everybody knows, so that when somebody says, "I was left there like the man who whistled on the hill" everybody knows just how the speaker was left—holding the bag.

The use of dichos or proverbs is extremely old. Proverbs are found in the Old Testament, but some of them go back to earlier civilizations in Egypt and Mesopotamia. It has been said that proverbs are "the wisdom of many and the wit of one." They are the "wit of one" because it was some one person, at some particular time and place, who put the thought of each proverb into just the right words. And they are the "wisdom of many" because they are supposed to express the feelings and attitudes of whole groups of people rather than just the feelings of an individual poet. They should be useful then in analyzing the character of a people. The "thought" or "message" of each proverb is clear.

Working on the assumption that people do accept their own proverbs as containing wisdom, and that they quote them as expressive of their values, some anthropologists have attempted, if not to establish the "Mexican character," at least to identify important values held by specific Mexican groups, through the analysis of their proverbs. "As a man's speech mirrors his thoughts, so do a people's proverbs reflect dominant attitudes and patterns," we are told.[2] Folklorists of the old school have objected to this use of dichos. Proverbs, say the old-fashioned scholars, are not only ancient but universal. All nations, for example, have believed that you tend to resemble the people you associate with. In English you say, "Birds of a feather flock together" and in Spanish you say, "Dime con quien andas y te diré quien eres," but the result is the same. These sayings tell us nothing about people today; they only tell us what somebody probably thought many, many years ago. People keep repeating proverbs out of habit, that is all. Furthermore, proverbs are often contradictory. Take a famous pair of proverbs in English: "Look before you leap" and "He who hesitates is lost." They advise you to do opposite things, so how can you believe that proverbs really mean anything?

Now, there was a time when most people believed that folklore was colorful but meaningless. Mexicans, for example, sang their *corridos* because they were happy (or drunk, perhaps). It was a quaint habit of theirs, inherited from their forefathers; but they did not mean anything by it. Today, we no longer accept the idea that there is no meaning at all to the way people behave. Telling dichos, narrating stories, and singing songs are all forms of behavior. If people persist in telling their children, generation after generation, "El que con lobos anda, a aullarse enseña," they must mean something by it. This certainly makes sense, but then, why are so many dichos contradictory?

"Entre menos burros, más olotes," the Mexican will say. "The fewer donkeys, the more corncobs." In other words, the fewer there are to share, the more there will be to go around. But the same person will also say, "Más vale pobre que solo"—"It's better to be poor than to live alone." Share what you have with others, even if there isn't much to share. There is another very Mexican dicho commenting on how difficult it is to change what is to be: "El que nace pa' tamal, del cielo le caen las hojas." If you're born to be a *tamal*, heaven will send you the cornshucks. So why try to be something else? Talk about the fatalistic Mexican, sleeping against an adobe wall in the sun! But the same people who use that dicho also have another one that says, "Todo cabe en un jarrito, sabiéndolo acomodar." That is to say, nothing is impossible. So where is our fatalistic Mexican now?

It seems that we are right back where we started from. How can dichos have any real meaning if they support both sides of the same question? Social scientists, however, are resourceful people. They point out—and rightly—that dichos do not contain absolute truths. They are not a set of rigid rules telling us exactly how to behave at all times. Instead, they are a storehouse of good advice, to be used according to specific situations. Obviously, people will have recourse to dichos that give all kinds of advice, depending on their mood and the situation they are in. But they do have sets of dominant values, which will be expressed in their choice of proverbs. The question then is, "What proverbs do people prefer?" What we need—to borrow from the physical sciences—is quantitative analysis. Mr. Dobie's error was in trying to deduce the Mexican character from one Mexican folktale, which included one Mexican dicho. What must be done is to take a large number of dichos, since they do offer typical advice, and see what percentages are derived from them. We would get a small percentage that give advice contradicting the actual values of the people, while the greater proportion will reflect a people's actual values and behavior.

Scholars are beginning to do precisely that. They collect all the dichos told by a Mexican or a Mexican American group and analyze them according to the values expressed. Their results are extremely instructive. In all cases, it has been found by our Anglo social scientist friends that the great majority of Mexican dichos fall into easily recognizable groups. Preponderant are dichos such as the following:

"¿A dónde ha de ir el buey, que no ha de seguir arando?" Where can the ox go that he will not have to plow? (Where can a poor man go, that he will not be given the hardest kind of jobs for the lowest pay?)

"El perro que come huevos, aunque le quemen el pico." You can't make a dog stop stealing eggs, even if you burn his mouth. (You can't change human nature. Things are the way they are going to be, and change is impossible.)

Others on the same theme:

> "El que ha de ser barrigón, aunque lo fajen." "El que nace pa' tamal, del cielo le caen las hojas." "El que tiene más saliva, traga más pinole." "Quien da pan a perro ajeno, pierde el pan y pierde el perro." "Un bien con un mal se paga." "Vale más mal conocido, que mejor por conocer."

Now, if you put these very popular Mexican dichos together and analyze them, you come up with the following picture of the Mexican:

1. He is quietistic.
2. He takes a fatalistic attitude toward life.
3. He is interested in the present or the past rather than in the future.
4. He is not interested in change.

So there we are again, with the usual stereotype of the Mexican—a much more familiar one than that of the ruthless, aggressive self-server Mr. Dobie talks about. We have ended up again with the peon, asleep with his back against an adobe wall, his ragged serape wrapped around him, and his hat over his eyes.

If we object that this is not a true picture, the social scientists will tell us we are being emotional and subjective about the whole thing. We are too close to it to really know what is going on. They, on the other hand, have applied an objective kind of analysis; and this is the picture their figures give them. If proverbs are a guide to the accepted behavior of a group, then the attitudes most frequently expressed in proverbs are those most highly valued by the group. And the majority of Mexican proverbs reflect a sense of fatalism and a resistance to change. So there you are—if you believe in figures. And we will have to admit—whether we like it or not—that any conclusions reached on the basis of a couple of hundred Mexican proverbs (where the message comes through loud and clear) are more convincing than Mr. Dobie's diametrically opposed conclusion based on one story accompanied by one dicho, "No te dejes."

But does the message come through loud and clear? Do the words we say always mean what they seem to mean? Let us return to Dobie and his Mexican Br'er Rabbit, with its picture of the Mexican as living in a ruthless, dog-eat-dog society, while the North American believes in fair play. There is no doubt that in the United States the idea of fair play is always uppermost in our minds. Teachers and preachers are always expounding on the subject; yet, we live in a highly competitive society, where making it is a high goal, and where nice guys always come in last.

Our answer is obvious, of course: principles that are honored more in the word than in the deed must be enunciated over and over again, in hopes that they will "take." If all the peoples in the world were one big, happy family, we would not have to spend so many, many words extolling the brotherhood of man. Dichos, proverbial or otherwise, may indicate social situations that are the opposite of what the dichos express. A reason for this may be an awareness, conscious or unconscious, that we are not living up to certain ideals we have set up for ourselves. Among the greatest exponents of fair play and good sportsmanship have been the British. This was not back during the Middle Ages, or during the Renaissance when English ships were challenging the might of Spain. It was in relatively recent times, when Britannia ruled the waves, when the British were building an empire at the expense of weaker peoples who were conquered and exploited without too much attention to such silly things as sportsmanship and giving your opponent a fair shake. Rudyard Kipling, himself the poet of imperialism, puts the whole thing into words when writing about the way British troops cut down spear-wielding Sudanese with their Martini-Henry rifles: "We sloshed you with Martinis, and it wasn't hardly fair." Fair play, indeed!

"No te dejes," then, may represent a desired state of affairs; but it does not tell us too much about what people actually do. We do not, therefore, know what the expression really means to the people who use it. We can find its true meaning only if we know how and when it is used. Words of themselves have no meaning; their meaning is given to them by the particular context in which they are used. So to study verbal content without a thorough knowledge of performance context is a futile exercise indeed. But nobody knows this better than the social scientists who should know all there is to know about studying social data in context. Social scientists, however, are not exempt from the human failing of not practicing what they preach. Those who run a quantitative analysis on hundreds of proverbs are still making the same mistake Frank Dobie made when he drew his conclusions from only one, except that they disguise their error with a lot of figures. They still are analyzing groups of words outside their context.

Let us take as an example a dicho mentioned earlier, "El que nace pa' tamal, del cielo le caen las hojas." No doubt, it owes a great deal of its currency to the fact that it is a nice little poetic construct. It says what it has to say so very well, and in the fewest words possible. Yet, it would be difficult to find a choicer expression of all the weaknesses Mexicans are accused of having. What fatalism! What supreme distrust of the future! What an eloquent statement of the futility of any effort to improve ourselves!

But let us reconstruct a typical situation where this particular dicho may be used. A young man—let us say—is being persuaded by a parent or by an older friend to take a certain course of action. The advice may be, "Try harder to do a good job"; or "Stand up for your rights, you are being cheated"; or "Demand what is your due"; or some similar bit of advice requiring action or change. The young man, however, does not respond. He is timid, or lazy, or just unconvinced. He would rather leave things as they are. Finally, the older person becomes exasperated, and he may say, "¡Ah, es por demás hablar contigo! ¡El que nace pa' tamal del cielo le caen las hojas!"

Nobody aware of the situation would even dream that the speaker means what his words seem to say. He is not counseling inaction or resistance to change, on the grounds that we will be what we are born to be and that is all we'll ever be. On the contrary, he is making a final attempt to goad his hearer into action by shaming him with this proverb. Far from advising that we accept things as they are, the proverb is a harsh call to action. It means exactly the opposite of what it says. But our field collector, avidly filling his little notebooks with Mexican dichos, rarely encounters such situations. He works with informants. He asks his informants for dichos; they tell him some dichos, and he enters them in his little notebook.

Proverbs may mean the opposite of what they say in still another fashion. The statements they make may give voice to bitter protest about the situations they portray. They express not the speaker's personal scale of values but his idea as to the values of his oppressors. It may be worthwhile to take another look at the great number of Mexican proverbs dealing with injustice, cruelty, and inequality—not as expressions of acceptance but as forms of social protest. It is ironic that they should be persistently interpreted as quietistic fatalism. Then, when the limits of human endurance are reached, when violence erupts, we do not know what to blame it on. And we must have recourse to still other stereotypes about the Mexican—such as machismo—in attempting an explanation.

I have been interested this evening in using proverbs as examples of what has been done, and what may be done, in using folklore to understand lo mexicano, because proverbs seem so simple, with such little possibility of being misunderstood. If explanations can be so far off the mark with proverbs—which seem to be all "message"—this is even truer of the more complex forms of folklore, such as legends, corridos, customs, or beliefs. We must know the situation in which this folklore is performed; and we must know the language and the people as well.

Notes

This talk was delivered by Dr. Américo Paredes to an American studies group in San Antonio, Texas in 1970.

1. J. Frank Dobie, "Br'er Rabbit Watches Out for Himself in Mexico," *Mesquite and Willow*, TPSP 27(1957): 113–7.

2. Joseph Raymond, "Attitudes and Cultural Patterns in Spanish Proverbs," *The Americas* 11 (1954): 57–77.

Mexican Muralism
Its Social-Educative Roles in Latin America and the United States

Shifra M. Goldman

Mexican muralism was originally created to play a social role in the post-revolutionary period of modern Mexico. It was clearly an art of *advocacy*, and in many cases it was intended to change consciousness and promote political action. (Whether or not it succeeded is a matter for sociological investigation.) Its other role was educative: to convey information about the pre-Columbian heritage (in the 1920s, a new and revolutionary concept); to teach the history of Mexico from the conquest to independence; and to deal with national and international problems from the reform to the contemporary period.

Since the muralists undertook to address a mass, largely illiterate audience in the 1920s, they chose a realistic style (often narrative) that would serve, as in the Renaissance, as a "painted book," and they contracted to paint their murals in accessible public buildings—government buildings, markets, schools, etc.

The argument for teachers today is that Mexican murals can still be used in an educative manner in schools. The same is true for the murals of other Latin American artists and for the Chicano murals of the 1970s, which were influenced by the Mexicans. However, some words of caution are necessary concerning the *method* of using art to teach other subjects in another time and another cultural framework.

First, artists are *not* historians. Some, like Diego Rivera, were encyclopedic in their research for the painted images they produced. Nevertheless, two points must be kept in mind: (a) the advocacy position already mentioned—meaning the interpretative function of the artist with his material according to his personal politics and ideology; and (b) the poetic license

From *Aztlán: A Journal of Chicano Studies* 13 (1982): 111–133.

that accompanies even the most "objective" presentation of the facts.

Second, a historical perspective is necessary. *When* a particular mural was painted is important since the issues and attitudes toward them have certainly changed with time. It is also important to consider *where* and *for whom* a mural was painted, especially when different national, regional, and local issues and attitudes are addressed. I would argue that *all* art viewing is more meaningful and emotionally stimulating when considered within its historical and cultural context. I hold the still unpopular view that understanding and enjoyment of art is time- and culture-bound. The enduring works are those reinterpreted for each society's needs; the original context is invariably lost in a short time or across any distance. Art—except on a formal, decorative level perhaps—is neither eternal nor universal; it functions in a time-space continuum and is assigned a new meaning in a new framework.

These cautionary suggestions can work advantageously in an educational situation. Art—particularly that being considered here, which is especially accessible because of its original purpose—can be used, as novels and films are, in history, sociology, or political science classes. Art becomes accessory to the facts and theories; it gives a human dimension and a personal point of view. Most important, art provides insight into the complexities of the time as interpreted by an individual artist or an artistic group.

An idea can appear in one time framework serving a given historical function, then reappear later transformed and charged with new meanings and implications. For example, the image of the Mexican revolutionary leader Emiliano Zapata had one meaning for José Guadalupe Posada, a Mexican engraver during the early revolutionary period; he was sympathetic, but at times satirical of a contemporary. For Diego Rivera, at a later date, Zapata represented the promises of the Mexican Revolution for agrarian reform and land distribution. Rivera treated Zapata as a historical heroic figure (he was assassinated in 1919 before Rivera returned from his European studies). For contemporary Mexicans in the United States, Zapata has become deified and sacrosanct. He has left history and become an abstract symbol. The fact that city-born youths from large urban ghettos in the United States transform a Mexican peasant leader into a hero image for their aspirations gives insight into the contemporary Chicano dynamic. Zapata has since been supplemented by more contemporary and relevant hero models: César Chávez, Che Guevara, and Rubén Salazar.

Indigenism

Diego Rivera in 1921 painted the first mural of what has become known as the Mexican Mural Renaissance. Many of his murals precisely depict the great Indian civilizations that existed before the Spanish conquest. Rivera, one of the earliest Mexicans to appreciate and collect pre-Columbian artifacts, carefully researched the history, culture, and art forms and represented them with great accuracy and detail. Poetic license and substitutions of motifs and images can, however, be found in his paintings. After the Mexican Revolution Rivera was concerned with two issues, and these determined his artistic themes: the need to offset the contempt with which the conquistadores had viewed the ancient Indian civilizations; and the need to offset the anti-mestizo and anti-Indian attitudes of the European-oriented ruling classes during the Porfiriato (the dictatorship of Porfirio Díaz). Mestizo and Indian peasants formed the basic fighting forces of the revolution, and their economic needs were to be addressed on the political plane. The role of the arts was to restore understanding of and pride in the heritage and cultures that the concept of Spanish superiority had subverted. Postrevolutionary *indigenista* philosophy appeared in the work of writers, musicians, filmmakers, sculptors, and painters as a facet of Mexican nationalism. In an advocacy position, the early indigenistas tended to glorify the Indian heritage and vilify that of the Spaniards as a means of rectifying a historical imbalance and advancing certain political ideas.

The *tres grandes* (Big Three) of the Mexican mural movement did not all agree in their interpretations of the indigenous heritage. Rivera idealized the Indian past as seen in his depiction of the Toltec god Quetzalcoatl in the National Palace mural. Except for the small Indian group engaged in warfare at the lower left of the painting, all is peace and harmony. This contrasts with the realities of the ancient past, especially the conflicts of empire-building cultures like the Olmec, Teotihuacano, Toltec, Maya, and Aztec, whose warring activities are reflected in their arts. Rivera shows ancient civilization almost without conflict: ideal and utopian like a lost Golden Age.

José Clemente Orozco had a very different view of history. He was a *hispanista*. As his paintings and writings make evident, he opposed Indian glorification, ancient or modern. However, in his Dartmouth College mural he did add one ancient Indian to his pantheon of heroes: Quetzalcoatl. Orozco depicted him as a statesman, educator, and promoter of the arts and civilization who, according to legend, was eventually exiled by the restored clergy of older gods he had replaced, and sailed away on a raft of serpents. It is curious that Orozco chose a mythological figure whom legend described as having been white-skinned, bearded, and blue-eyed—the very antithesis of the dark-skinned, dark-haired Indians. Orozco's heroes were often of Greek origin (Prometheus, the Man of Fire) or Spanish (Cortés, Franciscan monks, or the criollo Father Hidalgo), or were allegories of spirituality, education, human rationality, or rebellion. He did heroize modern Indian/mestizo leaders such as Felipe Carrillo Puerto, Benito Juárez, and Zapata. For him, these—like Quetzalcoatl—were the exceptional men who stood above the crowd.

The notion of a white hero/god as savior and civilizer of dark-skinned peoples is not unique to Orozco. More recently the idea has been promulgated by diffusionist anthropologist Thor Heyerdahl in books on the Ra reed vessels he sailed from Africa to the New World in an attempt to prove that the ancient Egyptians brought pyramids and mathematics to the indigenous peoples of the Americas. Ironically, the Egyptian civilization evolved in an African context, and the Egyptians themselves can certainly not be classified as "white," although the hierarchy of Western civilization that rests on the Egyptian-Greek-Roman foundation has "sanitized" Egypt by conceptually separating it and its history from that of black Africa. Thus Orozco's Quetzalcoatl and Heyerdahl's Egyptians both underline a European ethnocentricity.

Rivera and Orozco again illustrate their dichotomy in differing treatments of the ancient Aztecs. Rivera's mural of the marketplace Tlatelolco is an encyclopedic presentation of the multiple products, services, activities, and personages to be seen at the great Aztec marketplace. Presided over by an enthroned official, all is calm and orderly in the market. In the background is a topographical view of the Aztec capital city Tenochtitlan, with its pyramids, plazas, palaces, and canals. The painting gives no hint of Aztec imperialism, which the market symbolizes. Tribute and sacrifice victims were brought to Tenochtitlan from the subject peoples.

Orozco, on the other hand, took a critical stance. He often painted the brutality and inhumanity of ancient Indian sacrifice. Aztec culture for Orozco was cruel, bloodthirsty, and barbaric. In Dartmouth, he illustrates a scene of priests holding a victim's body from which a priest is about to tear out the heart. Spanish conquest was also cruel and bloodthirsty, according to Orozco's images, but it brought the redeeming quality of a higher level of civilization and of Christianity, which Orozco compared favorably to the ancient religions in his Hospicio Cabañas epic mural cycle.

Clearly neither Diego Rivera's unqualified indigenista idealization of Indian cultures nor Orozco's hispanista condemnation of Indian barbarism reflects historical accuracy. What teachers can extract from these representations are the modern interpretations of the past that accurately reflect a clash of ideologies in revolutionary and postrevolutionary Mexico.

Many of Rivera's murals show that his indigenism was not just historical. It was intimately tied to the interests of modern Indians and mestizos who had been exploited and abused not only during the 300 years of the conquest, but by large landowners, the Catholic Church, and commercial enterprises during the independence period up to the Mexican Revolution. Two of the most important planks of the 1917 Mexican Constitution dealt with agrarian reform and the rights of labor unions. Thus Rivera's mural in the Hospital de la Raza deals with modern medical treatment by the Social Security system as well as the medicinal practices of the indigenist past. Presided over by Tlazolteotl, goddess of creation, the earth, fertility, and carnal love, and recreated from the Codex Borbonicus, the indigenous section is an excellent index for teaching this aspect of pre-Columbian culture. The modern section shows medical care available to contemporary Mexicans who are both Indian and mestizo. But even this aspect has been idealized; the greater portion of the Mexican people today are not covered by Social Security, and thus care is not the norm, but the aspiration.

David Alfaro Siqueiros, youngest of the tres grandes, took a different approach to indigenist themes. He did not recreate archeologically accurate visions of the ancient world but used the indigenous motifs as allegories or metaphors for contemporary struggles. In two heroic images of Cuauhtemoc, the last of the Aztec emperors becomes a symbol for heroic resistance against invaders across time. These murals were painted in 1941 and 1944, during the period of World War II; they were meant to indicate that even overwhelmingly powerful forces could be defeated through resistance. *Death to the Invader* has reference to the invading Axis powers in Europe and Asia while *Cuauhtemoc Against the Myth* refers to the myth of Spanish invincibility. Though the original Cuauhtemoc was killed, Siqueiros shows him conquering the Spaniards. Not the historical Cuauhtemoc, but the symbolic one is important.

Mestizaje

The conquest brought the mingling of the races; it produced the mestizo who is referred to as the fusion of the Indian and the Spaniard. Actually *mestizaje* in Mexico (as in other American countries such as Venezuela, Colombia, Brazil, the Caribbean countries, and the United States) included intermixture with Africans who were brought in as slaves after the decimation of the Indians. Though modern murals do not often deal with this aspect, the colonial period produced a whole series of paintings that carefully delineated the various crossings with appropriate names for each caste.

Rufino Tamayo in *Birth of Our Nationality* treats the merging of two peoples in a poetic manner. His large Picassoesque horse of the conquest with a multi-armed figure on its back (the Spaniard) is framed by a Renaissance column on one side (European civilization) and a pre-Columbian moon/sun symbol on the other. Amid broken blocks of buildings (the destroyed Indian civilizations), an Indian woman gives birth to a child that is half red and half white. Deep rich color and the mythic quality of the figures give a mysterious and dream-like quality to the event. It is non-narrative; fixed in time like a fable from the past that has eternal verity.

Orozco deals with mestizaje in terms of known historical personages, Cortés and Malinche. Malinche (Malintzin, or Doña Marina) was a Nahuatl and Maya-speaking Indian woman who became Cortés's guide and translator and helped him conquer the imperial Aztecs. She was also his mistress; their son represents the mestizaje of the upper classes, the descendents of Spaniards and Indians who were often incorporated into the Mexican ruling class. In Orozco's image, the two nude figures—like the Adam and Eve of Mexican nationality, as Octavio Paz considers them—are seated together and are of equal size. White and brown color and European and Indian features are accentuated for contrast. Their hands are clasped in union, however Cortés is obviously dominant: his foot (and their union) rests on the fallen body of an Indian.

Rivera approaches the same theme in a more historical narrative, and in an accurate vein that is neither poetic nor exalted. Within the context of the armed conflict of the conquest, he picks out a small detail in which an anonymous Spanish soldier rapes an anonymous Indian woman. For the vast majority, this is how much mestizaje occurred.

Revolutionary History

Among the educative concerns of the Mexican muralists were a reordering and revision of Mexican history from a revolutionary point of view. Like Mexican American scholars and artists today, who are revising U.S. history by mandating the inclusion of Mexicans, Mexican Americans, and

Native Americans as the original occupants and the bearers of culture, so did Mexican intellectuals and artists in the 1920s challenge the European-oriented historical view. History did not begin with the "discovery" of the Americas by Spaniards or Englishmen; they were simply the latest comers who chose, on the whole, to ignore or disparage the millennia of cultures and civilizations that had preceded them. By the same token, the Mexican muralists did not choose to represent Mexican history as a succession of colonial aristocrats or postindependence rulers, but as a series of insurgencies and revolutions by the Mexican people and their leaders against colonizers and dictators.

The central portion of Rivera's epic mural at the National Palace recreates conflicts from the conquest to the revolutions of 1810 and 1910. Though his theme is conflict, movement and violence are only in the conquest scenes; the later periods are presented in a static manner with a dense cubistically composed piling-up of human forms, many of them historical portraits in shallow space. Porfirio Díaz can be seen surrounded by his *científicos*, military men, and the clergy. Behind him are the haciendas of Mexican landowners and the buildings of the Pierce Oil Company of London, a reference to foreign capital exploiting Mexican natural resources during the Díaz dictatorship. The revolutionary opposition appears on the other side; among them are Pancho Villa, Zapata, Felipe Carrillo Puerto, members of the Serdán family who fired the first shots of the 1910 Mexican Revolution, Ricardo Flores Magón, Francisco Madero, and caricaturist José Guadalupe Posada.

Siqueiros's treatment of the same subject also shows the alliance between Porfirio Díaz, the Mexican upper class, and the military, but in a more dynamic composition that openly confronts the ruling with the working class. His theme is a particular historical event: the 1906 strike by Mexican workers against the Cananea Consolidated Copper Company located in Sonora, Mexico, and owned by a North American, William Greene, known as the "copper king of Sonora." This event was one of several believed to have triggered the Mexican Revolution.

International Issues

The Mexican mural movement (which has been represented here only by the tres grandes, but which had a large following) did not limit itself to national issues; its view was international in scope. In the 1920s, Rivera and Siqueiros were members of the Mexican Communist Party. They had an unreserved admiration for the Soviet Union, whose revolution occurred seven years after Mexico's. Rivera's views later underwent a major change when his friendship with Leon Trotsky and his anti-Stalinism grew. However, he and Siqueiros remained strong advocates of socialism—not an uncommon phenomenon in the 1920s and 1930s. Orozco was an iconoclast; he was critical but not unsympathetic in these early years. The contrasting views of Rivera and Orozco in the mid-1930s are instructive.

Rivera's *Man at the Crossroads* was originally painted in Rockefeller Center, New York, under the sponsorship of Nelson Rockefeller. The inclusion of Lenin's portrait was too upsetting for Rockefeller and the tenants of the center. The mural was covered and then destroyed, so Rivera repainted it in the Palace of Fine Arts in Mexico City. Surrounding the central motif of a Russian workman at the controls of the universe are the worlds of capitalism (soldiers with gas masks, unemployed strikers attacked by the police, the rich gathered around festive tables) and of socialism (joyous youth, Lenin as a symbol of world brotherhood). In this mural, Rivera reflects the realities and horrors of World War I, which were still fresh in memory, and the Great Depression, during which the mural was painted. Nevertheless, Rivera applies the same utopian vision that informed his treatment of indigenist themes to this new work. By 1933 Lenin was dead, and Trotsky, after disagreements with the Stalin government, had been exiled. The only indication of this rift is the pointed inclusion of Trotsky's portrait and the exclusion of Stalin's beside the figures of Marx and Engels in the socialist half of the mural.

Orozco's New York murals of the same period feature three heroic leaders with their followers: the assassinated Maya governor of Yucatan, Felipe Carrillo Puerto; the deceased Lenin; and the Indian leader Mahatma Gandhi in his confrontation with British imperialism. With Gandhi was one of the few women Orozco placed in a heroic light, Madam Sarojini Naidu. Though Carrillo Puerto and Lenin occupy similar spaces and elevation in the mural, individualized followers surround Carrillo Puerto while Lenin appears above robotized masked soldiers with ranks of sharp bayonets. Through this subtle difference, Orozco could heroize the individual without necessarily accepting the society he constructed. This illustrates Orozco's philosophy in general: he distrusted masses of people and looked in a Nietszchean manner to individual supermen for social reform or salvation.

After Siqueiros returned to Mexico from the Spanish Civil War, he painted a complex mural on the walls, windows, and ceiling of a staircase in a trade union building. For him, the world scene looked bleak. Spain had been the proving ground for nazi and fascist militarism; the civil war presaged World War II. While the Axis consolidated its power in Europe and Asia, the Western nations adhered to a "neutrality" and appeasement policy, which brought down the Republican government in Spain and allowed Hitler access to European conquest. Siqueiros had no sympathy for either the Axis or the Allies. Beneath a huge steel-plated eagle/dive bomber in his mural is an anthropomorphic machine that turns human blood from war victims into gold coins (profits from munitions on both sides). On one side are the British, French, and U.S. allies; on the other are the Japanese, German, and Italian. On the left wall, a parrot-like demagogue waves a fiery torch while masses of soldiers march; on the right, as a symbol of opposition, is a powerful figure of the people's resistance.

For U.S. historians and teachers, Siqueiros's mural highlights a moment in time that tends to be overlooked in the subsequent unity of World War II: the period between the fall of Spain to Franco in 1939 and the attack on Pearl Harbor in 1941 that finally brought together the United States, the Soviet Union, England, France, and many other countries (including Mexico) against fascism. For artists, the mural is a fascinating study of the new artistic technology developed by Siqueiros (synthetic paints, spray gun application on a wall, documentary photography incorporated into painting) and new formal methods (filmic movement on a static painted surface, illusionistic destruction of architectural space, creation of a containing "environment"). Many of these means presage artistic directions explored in the United States in the 1960s.

For all their power and command of pictorial means, Rivera's and Orozco's methods and expression were far more traditional, though all three shared revolutionary social content. Perhaps this is one reason why Rivera and Orozco were the major influences on U.S. and South American artists until World War II, and Siqueiros was the most admired and copied by the U.S. street mural movement of the 1960s and 1970s.

Before leaving Mexican terrain, one must note that issues and attitudes are changed and reinterpreted with time. In the aftermath of the Mexican Revolution, the muralists and other cultural workers were aware of the need to create a new formal and thematic language in the interests of social change. New aspects of history were to be emphasized, new heroic figures given prominence, and new views of social relationships advanced. This language would reflect political concepts that emerged from the revolutionary process: agrarian reform, labor rights, separation of church and state, Mexican hegemony over natural resources, defense against foreign economic penetration, and literacy and education for the masses.

Sixty years have passed since the termination of the Mexican Revolution. The Mexican state, economy, political structure, and international role have changed. Much revolutionary oratory has become rhetoric in the speeches of government functionaries. Younger generations of artists have reexamined and are revising concepts of the traditional heroes. For example, two murals on revolutionary themes face each other in a salon of the National History Museum in Chapultepec Park, Mexico City. One, by Jorge González Camarena, is a mannered, heroized portrait of Venustiano Carranza, revolutionary general and early president of Mexico. Carranza at one stage fought against Zapata and was responsible for his assassination. Zapata had accused him of deceit and hypocrisy for preaching and not practicing agrarian reform. Directly opposite the Camarena mural is one by a much younger artist, Arnold Belkin. He confronts the Carranza portrait with one of Zapata and Pancho Villa derived from a famous Casasola photograph. The irony of the placement has not escaped Belkin. In addition, the figures of Zapata and Villa have the flesh stripped away as if the artist intends to demythologize them as well as Carranza.

In a similar vein is Felipe Ehrenberg's easel painting/collage of Carranza and Zapata. In it Carranza appears twice: once as a general with the Mexican flag substituted for his face as though his true features are hidden behind his patriotism, and again as president where he is superimposed over the body and face of Zapata. Carranza destroyed the man, but he absorbed his legendary aura. Beneath each figure is a ruler to take anew the measure of history and mythology.

The Mexican muralists accepted the role (as Jean Franco said in *Modern Culture of Latin America*) of "guide, teacher and conscience of [their] country" and produced an art that played a social role. The very choice of means—muralism—underscores their consciousness of this role since the technique and form is public and not conducive to the expression of subjective or introspective material. It served the needs of the time objectively. It created a new plastic language, a new ideology, and a new iconography. For the first time, the anonymous peoples of Mexico appeared in art, not as quaint or exotic subjects for genre paintings, but as heroes taking control of their own destinies: Orozco's villagers marching off to the revolution; Rivera's masses of farmers receiving the divided lands of the great estates; Siqueiros's workers creating unions in order to benefit from the riches of their own lands. With them are the leaders who aligned with them or came from their own ranks.

The Caribbean and South America

The 1920s, a period of reassessment and reevaluation of European values, followed the devastation and slaughter of World War I. Until then, these values had been considered the acme of civilization. Europeans (and some Latin Americans) turned to Dada, a self-mocking, iconoclastic movement that questioned existing mores, customs, and the nature of culture itself. The Americas, from the United States to South America, turned inward upon their own resources in an exuberant expression of nationalism and regionalism and sought values indigenous to their own continent. In the United States, this took a politically isolationist form and resulted in an artistic celebration of varied regions of the nation known as Regionalism. Among African Americans from the Caribbean, Brazil, and Harlem came the celebration of "negritude" and the search for a national identity. In Mexico, Guatemala, and the Andean area, nationalism took the form of indigenism—ancient and modern—tied to contemporary social reform. Artists and writers sought to cut their dependence on European models and develop their own artistic vocabulary and themes; they naturally turned to the Mexican muralists, particularly Rivera, who was known internationally, for inspiration. Many traveled to Mexico to study. However, with the exception of U.S. artists who worked in Mexico and assisted with, or studied, the murals done by Rivera, Orozco, and Siqueiros in many cities of the United States during the 1930s, few artists had the opportunity to do murals. The social conditions, including government commissions and support, conducive to monumental public art existed only in Mexico and in the United States of the New Deal. In other areas, relatively few murals were executed, and no opportunity existed for a national mural movement as in Mexico. Primarily, the Mexican influence can be seen in easel paintings, sometimes monumental in size. To my knowledge, no thorough study of modern Mexican influence on Latin American art has yet been compiled; a similar study of the Mexican influence in the United States has only just gotten underway. At this stage, any conclusions must be tentative. Nevertheless, stylistic, thematic, and some documentary evidence exists on Mexican influence in South America and the Caribbean.

Two easel paintings by Cuban artists illustrate this influence. Abela's *Guajiros* and Carreño's *Sugar Cane Cutters* deal with rural workers. Abela's work is similar to Rivera's in its use of stocky, simplified, and static figures and Carreño's is influenced by Siqueiros stylistically and in the use of Duco, an automobile lacquer that Siqueiros adapted to fine art use in the 1930s.

267

Cândido Portinari, universally recognized as Brazil's greatest modern artist, was among several young artists in the 1930s committed to dealing with Brazilian social problems and contemporary life. His large painting *Coffee* brought him international recognition. The use of space, the simplification of figures, compositional devices, and the exaggeration of bodily proportions show Rivera's influence. Portinari painted many important murals at the Ministry of Education in Rio de Janeiro, the Library of Congress in Washington, D.C., the Pampulha Church in Belo Horizonte, Brazil, and the United Nations. He continued to paint sugar and coffee workers, slum dwellers, Negroes, mulattos, whites, Indians, and other typically Brazilian subjects. *Burial in a Net* is part of a series of paintings dealing with a terrible drought in northeastern Brazil during the 1940s; it has elements of Picasso as well as the tragic expressiveness of Orozco.

In 1933, Siqueiros visited Buenos Aires where, assisted by several local artists, he painted an experimental mural called *Plastic Exercise*. Among the artists was Antonio Berni, whose huge oil paintings such as *Unemployment of 1935* express his social realist concerns and is indebted to Siqueiros. In 1946 Berni was one of a group of artists who did frescoes in an arcade in Buenos Aires (the others were Colmeiro, Urruchua, Spilimbergo, and Castagnino). Berni's monumental images in his two murals at this location owe a debt to Orozco and to the Italian Renaissance. Muralism, however, did not flourish in Argentina. There were no opportunities to do murals. As Berni stated in 1979, no revolution had taken place and there was no interest in public art. The immense size of his canvases seems to express a frustration with the lack of walls.

In Peru, with a larger Indian population, Mexican indigenism and social realism flourished. In 1922 José Sabogal visited Mexico, where the impact of the muralists turned him into an ardent indigenist and nationalist. His influence produced a school of painters, among them Teodoro Nuñez Ureta who shows the distinct influence of Orozco in his *Transmission of the Seed* and that of Siqueiros in *Allegory of Production and Work*. Nuñez's heroic treatment of indigenist and working-class themes places him in the social realist tradition of the Mexican School.

César Rengifo of Venezuela has been a social realist since the 1930s. He did one tile mural in Caracas on an indigenous theme; but realistic public art had few patrons in Venezuela. One exception is the case of Héctor Poleo who studied mural painting in Mexico in the late 1930s. He was influenced by Rivera, and executed a mural for the new University City in Caracas. Since the 1950s, geometric abstraction and kineticism have dominated Venezuelan art; these thoroughly cosmopolitan art forms reflect the urban-industrial development of Caracas that resulted from the discovery of large oil deposits in 1938 and 1973. Both Poleo and Rengifo dealt with the desolate life of the rural hinterlands (in contrast to the capital city, Caracas) primarily in easel paintings such as Rengifo's *Settlement of Peons* and *What the Petroleum Has Left Us: Dogs*.

Chicano Muralism of the 1970s

Between the 1940s and the 1960s, public muralism in the United States suffered an eclipse. The New Deal art projects were terminated in the 1940s, and artists turned to other pursuits for the duration of World War II. In the complacent, prosperous, and individualistic 1950s—overshadowed by the Cold War and McCarthyism—introspective easel painting flourished, dominated by abstract expressionism. New York became the art capital of the world and centralized arbiter of taste in the United States. Critics fulminated against "narrative, propagandistic" art and attacked "literary content" in painting. Representational art in general faced lean times. Art history was revised as the Mexican School, South American social realism, U.S. Regionalism, and New Deal art were written out of the history books. Only in the mid-1970s have these movements been reassessed and reintegrated into art history as a number of authors began to publish books on the New Deal and as regional exhibitions of New Deal art took place. The issue of regionality in art, of the validity of artistic pluralism in the United States, and of resistance to the absolute dominance of New York's establishment over the nation has now come into focus.[1]

One of the key factors promoting this new decentralizing of artistic focus, reevaluating of the 1930s, and burgeoning interest in the art of Latin America and Latinos in the United States is the street mural movement of which Chicano muralism has played a quantitative and qualitative part. The outdoor muralists turned to the Mexicans as an important source of knowledge, technique, concept, style, and inspiration. Nowhere was this more culturally important than among Chicanos, for whom the recovery of Mexican muralism was part of a larger recovery of heritage and identity after a century of deliberate deculturalization by the dominant society. Looking at this last statement with a finer lens, however, research still in its initial stages suggests that the deprivation of Mexican models for Mexican American artists is only two decades old, and applies to those artists who came to their calling during the hegemony of abstract expressionism or the "art for

269

art's sake" dictums of the art schools. The process of revitalizing the work of the Mexican muralists (as well as of younger artists) in the United States and making it available to artists of the 1960s and 1970s was the result of efforts by Chicano studies programs and mural groups in the Southwest and Midwest, and the establishment of alternative Chicano cultural structures that researched and disseminated information about Mexican art.

In this brief consideration of Chicano muralism as influenced by the Mexican mural movement, there are examples of the transformation of themes that were important to the Mexicans at an earlier date and that were charged with new meanings and implications within the context of contemporary Chicano concerns. For example, the initial cultural-nationalist phase of Chicano consciousness in the mid-1960s produced a wave of neo-indigenism like that of the Mexicans in the 1920s but with certain important differences. First, the Americanist indigenism of the 1920s was part of an isolationist-nationalist wave following World War I. It was not necessarily exercised by the indigenous peoples themselves but by intellectuals on their behalf. Present neo-indigenism has made links with people of color throughout the developing Third World, and it is being promoted by the affected groups: Chicanos, Puerto Ricans, and Native Americans. Second, Rivera's indigenism responded to a largely agricultural nation where the landless or small farmers, Indian and mestizo, made up a great part of the population, and where agrarian reform was a major plank of the revolution. Though Chicanos in the Southwest also have a large rural or semirural population, and the unionization struggles of the United Farm Workers were a focal point in the development of Chicano culture, this agrarianism exists in a highly industrialized country where even agriculture is a big business. Therefore, little probability exists that Chicanos would or could be the small farmers the Zapatistas aspired to be.

One of the earliest and strongest proponents of neo-indigenism was Luis Valdez of Teatro Campesino. He drew upon his interpretation of pre-Columbian religion to provide a non-European spiritual base for Chicano life. However, Valdez turned to this source at the point when he began to address urban Chicanos as well as farmworkers. He himself was urbanized through long residence in big California cities. The same is true of Chicano poets Alurista of San Diego and Rodolfo "Corky" Gonzales of Denver, important figures in the popularization of neo-indigenism.

Another point of differentiation was the exclusively pre-Columbian focus of the cultural-nationalist phase; the fraternity between mestizo Chicanos and Native Americans based on a commonality of "race" and oppression within the Anglo-dominated society did not occur until later. Mexico, on the other hand, has been a mestizo and Indian nation since the conquest; indigenism in the 1920s served to emphasize that national fact. Mestizos and Indians were the majority, not the minority, and artists addressed their present problems.

Two Chicano murals, one from Los Angeles and the other from Denver, are taken directly from pre-Columbian sources; they are copied uncritically without concern for historical context. Charles Félix recreates in color a sacrifice scene from a ballcourt relief sculpture at El Tajín, Veracruz. Sánchez reproduces the single figure of the goddess Tlazolteotl—the same used as a central figure by Rivera in his Hospital de la Raza mural on ancient and modern medicine. Rivera related pre-Columbian to modern medicine as a continuum, the patients being Indians of the past and present. The murals by Félix and Sánchez are essentially decorative and unselective about content—surely Félix did not intend to glorify human sacrifice.[2]

La Mujer, an enormous collectively painted mural in Hayward, California, uses a variety of motifs that mingle the pre-Columbian with contemporary urban problems. The central female figure with tripartite head and powerful out-thrust arms is adapted from Siqueiros's 1944 *New Democracy* in the Palace of Fine Arts, Mexico City. On one side of the Hayward mural are the evils of the big city: contaminated food, arson, violence in the streets, drug abuse, and others. One of the great arms holds a destructive hammer over these scenes. The other arm terminates in a wheel incorporating the four elements; the Puerto Rican, Mexican, Cuban, and Pan-African flags; and peace symbols of the Native American. Pre-Columbian figures intertwine with death and destruction on the left, and with corn, peace, and growth on the right. Thus the indigenous motifs are selectively chosen and thematically enhancing.

Another elaboration of this kind that creatively adapts motifs and formal elements from indigenous sources and the Mexican muralists is *Song of Unity* in Berkeley, California. Its point of departure is contemporary social song (called *nueva canción* in Latin America) in North and South America, and therefore its central motif is a double image of eagle and condor. The mural has an irregular billboard-like cutout surface. One side of the mural pictures North American musicians and songwriters like Daniel Valdez, Malvina Reynolds, and jazz musicians; the other side features the peoples of Latin America, particularly the Andean Indians. All the figures are dramatically foreshortened in space and seem to thrust from the surface in a manner typical of Siqueiros's paintings. Also adopted from Siqueiros's sculpture-painting technique is the dominant figure of the mural which is modeled three-dimensionally and projects in relief from the surface. This is an image of Chilean songwriter Victor Jara, who was killed by the military junta during the fall of the Allende government in 1973. His severed hands continue to play a guitar, while the peoples of South America with their regional instruments march through his transparent mutilated arm.

In Houston, Texas, muralist Leo Tanguma painted an enormous mural called *Rebirth of Our Nationality*. A Chicano man and woman emerge from a large red flower which rests in a bleak landscape on a platform of skulls. They are under the banner "To Become Aware of Our History Is to Become Aware of Our Singularity." From either side, brown-skinned figures, who represent the multiplicity of Mexican peoples and the complexity of their history and struggles in Mexico and the United States, drive toward the central inspiration of their rebirth. The dramatic thrust of the composition and the violent expressionism of the figures owe a debt to Siqueiros and Orozco, whom the artist has long admired. The social responsibility of the artist to his community is a philosophy Tanguma derived from Siqueiros, whom he met personally. Marcos Raya of Chicago has borrowed figures from Orozco and the major composition of Rivera's *Man at the Crossroads* for his mural *Homage to Diego Rivera*. He has substituted Mayor Daly of Chicago for the central figure of the worker in the original mural and surrounded him with images of corruption and violence.

Chicano murals exist in all states of the Southwest, as well as the Midwest/Great Lakes region. California has more than a thousand, scattered in cities and some rural areas. Texas has murals in Austin, San Antonio, Houston, Crystal City, El Paso, and other locations. No single style unites them; their commonality, to the degree that it exists, derives from thematic factors and what might be called "the Chicano point of view," a difficult thing to define and one that, even now, is undergoing transformation. Their commonality derives from life experiences common to Chicanos living in the United States during the second half of the twentieth century; those Mexicans who are expressing a growing awareness of their long history on both sides of the present border. Murals also include the process of redefining and changing that history, and education has played no small role in that process.

Notes

This paper is derived from a lecture given as part of the Arts and Music of Latin America for Pre-College Educators Conference, Institute of Latin American Studies, University of Texas, Austin, April 1980. Slides of all the artworks cited in the chapter are available at the UCLA Chicano Studies Research Center Library.

1. Three issues of *Art in America* reflect this new consciousness: the July–August 1972 special issue on the American Indian; the May–June 1974 issue dealing with public art, women's art, and street murals (hitherto an "invisible" category) across the country; and the July–August 1976 "Art Across America" issue whose cover is dominated by Texas artist Luis Jiménez's sculpture, and whose perspective is epitomized by Donald B. Kuspit's article "Regionalism Reconsidered."

2. An interview with Félix by a former student revelaed that the artist was metaphorically addressing local gang warfare.

Art Works Cited

Diego Rivera, *Totonac Civilization*, 1950–51. 2nd floor, National Palace, Mexico City.

Rivera, *Feather Arts*, 1945. 2nd floor, National Palace, Mexico City.

Rivera, *The Ancient Indigenous World*, 1929–30. Staircase, National Palace, Mexico City.

José Clemente Orozco, *Coming of Quetzalcoatl*, 1932–33. Baker Library, Dartmouth College, Hanover, New Hampshire.

Rivera, *Great Tenochtitlan*, 1945. 2nd floor, National Palace, Mexico City.

Orozco, *Ancient Human Sacrifice*, 1932–33. Baker Library, Dartmouth College, Hanover, New Hampshire.

Orozco, *The Spanish Conquest of Mexico, 1938-39*. Hospicio Cabañas, Guadalajara, Mexico.

Rivera, *Ancient and Modern Medicine*, 1952–54. Lobby, Hospital de la Raza, Mexico City.

David Alfaro Siqueiros, *Death to the Invader*, 1941. Mexican School, Chillán, Chile.

Siqueiros, *Cuauhtemoc Against the Myth*, 1944. Presently at the Tecpan of Tlatelolco, Mexico City.

Rufino Tamayo, *Birth of Our Nationality*, 1952. Palace of Fine Arts, Mexico City.

Orozco, *Cortés and Malinche*, 1926. National Preparatory School, Mexico City.

Rivera, *History of Mexico: The Conquest*, 1929–30. Staircase, National Palace, Mexico City.

Rivera, *History of Mexico: The Present*, 1929–30. Staircase, National Palace, Mexico City.

Siqueiros, *Revolt Against the Porfirian Dictatorship*, 1957–65. National History Museum, Mexico City.

Rivera, *Man at the Crossroads*, 1934. Palace of Fine Arts, Mexico City.

Orozco, *Struggle in the Occident and the Orient*, 1930–31. New School for Social Research, New York.

Siqueiros, *Portrait of the Bourgeoisie*, 1939. Electricians Union, Mexico City.

Jorge González Camarena, *Venustiano Carranza*, 1967. National History Museum, Mexico City.

Arnold Belkin, *La Llegada de los Generales Zapata y Villa Al Palacio Nacional el 6 de Diciembre de 1914*, 1979. National History Museum, Mexico City.

Felipe Ehrenberg, *Carranza and Zapata*, 1979. Easel painting/collage.

Eduardo Abela, *Guajiros*, 1942. Oil on canvas.

Mario Carreño y Morales, *Sugar Cane Cutters*, 1943. Duco on wood.

Cândido Portinari, *Coffee*, 1935. Oil on canvas.

Portinari, *Burial in a Net*, 1944. Oil on canvas.

Antonio Berni, *Unemployment*, 1935. Oil on canvas.

Berni, *mural*, 1946. Galería Pacífico, Buenos Aires.

Teodoro Nuñez Ureta, *Transmission of the Seed*, 1958. Oil on canvas.

Nuñez, *Allegory of Production and Work*, 1958. Ministry of Agriculture, Lima.

César Rengifo, *Settlement of Peons*, 1956. Oil on canvas.

Rengifo, *What the Petroleum Has Left Us: Dogs*, 1963. Oil on canvas.

Charles Félix, *Sacrifice Scene from El Tajín*, 1973. Estrada Courts Housing Project, Los Angeles.

Alfred Sánchez, *Tlazolteotl*, 1973. Denver.

Rogelio Cárdenas and Brocha de Hayward, *La Mujer*, 1978. Hayward, California.

Ray Patlán, Osha Neumann, O'Brien Thiele, Anna DeLeon, *Song of Unity*, 1978. La Peña Cultural Center, Berkeley, California.

Leo Tanguma, *Rebirth of Our Nationality*, 1973. Continental Can Co., Houston.

Marcos Raya, *Homage to Diego Rivera*, 1973. Chicago.

A Perspective for a Study of Religious Dimensions in Chicano Experience

Bless Me, Ultima as a Religious Text

David Carrasco

AUTHOR'S NOTE: *I wrote this essay on Rudolfo Anaya's wonderful novel* Bless Me, Ultima *because I was deeply concerned that Chicano studies as a multidisciplinary academic and community enterprise did not take seriously the diverse religious dimensions of Mexican American history, society, and culture. At the time, I was engaged in an intense discussion with the cultural anthropologist Jose Cuellar (since then aka Dr. Loco) about the diversity and depth of religiosity in Chicano life. My work with Mircea Eliade intensified my earlier interest in novels as imaginative worlds full of symbols, myths, and initiation rites. And while a graduate student at Chicago, I had spent two years in the mission of the Niño Fidencio, a curandero/espiritista whose ecstatic trances initiated me into the mestizaje of Mexican religiosity. So, while attempting to learn from and contribute to Chicano studies I was invited to lecture at University of California, Santa Barbara, in Cuellar's classes. I chose the dramatic relationship between Antonio and the curandera Ultima as my focus and laid out the patterns of sacred space and the sacred human that I believed motivated the plot and its meanings. Cuellar encouraged me to submit the work to Aztlán and I was thrilled when it was accepted. Since then I have continued my interest in the religious dimensions of novels and creative literature by writing on Carlos Fuentes's* Old Gringo, *Gloria Anzaldua's* Borderlands/La Frontera, *and working with and teaching about Toni Morrison and her astonishing novels. A few years after this article's publication in Aztlán, it was slated to appear in an Anaya Reader but was dropped from the list at the last moment. I'm sure the editors had good reasons, but it indicated again how the diverse and complex religious dimensions of Chicano life—indigenous, folk, Catholic, Protestant—were not considered areas of primary importance in Mexican American academic work. It has been very heartening to hear from a new generation of Chicano and Latino scholars that this essay was one inspiration among many that helped them to focus on pentitentes, curanderismo, pilgrimages, Cesar Chavez, chicanismo, and other Raza realities, and to interpret them as, in part, religious realities. It is an honor to be*

From Aztlán: A Journal of Chicano Studies 13 (1982): 195–221.

included in this valuable anthology of Aztlán's outstanding articles. I thank Aztlán, Jose Cuellar, and of course Rudolfo Anaya.

> "There are many gods," Cico whispered, "gods of beauty and magic, gods of the garden, gods of our own backyards—but we go off to foreign countries to find new ones, we reach to the stars to find new ones."[1]

This research is intended to encourage Chicano students and scholars to study and interpret the religious meanings and structures of Chicano life. First, I must describe the general orientation in which I work, an orientation known in the United States as the History of Religions.[2] More specifically, I will outline several hermeneutical principles articulated by the Chicago School of the History of Religions, present part of the approach I take toward religious experiences and expressions, and show this approach in action by focusing on passages depicted in the Chicano classic, Bless Me, Ultima.[3]

Passages from Bless Me, Ultima represent a few religious dimensions characteristic of and perhaps fundamental to Chicano experience. As a historian of religion, fascinated by the way in which human beings experience and express their sense of the sacred powers in their lives, I will discuss two religious dimensions of Chicano life reflected in the novel: (a) the dimension of the sacred landscape, and (b) the dimension of the sacred human being. In the first case I will pay special attention to powerful parts of the novel's natural landscape, such as the "presence of the river"; the golden carp who is described as a god; and the energies embedded in the hero's name, Antonio Luna y Márez. In discussing the sacred human, the focus is on Ultima's powers for dealing with supernatural forces and the dynamic relationship she has with Antonio. This relationship results in Antonio's initiation into the world of sacrality known to Ultima and his discovery that "the tragic consequences of life can be overcome by the magical strength that resides in the human heart." This study will illustrate the pattern of spiritual transformation that Antonio experiences under Ultima's guidance and in his dreams. Within this transformation, Antonio discovers magical strength within himself.

Christian Theology as a Limiting Discipline

My approach to the Chicano experience and Bless Me, Ultima is not as a Christian theologian. The theological approach, whether articulated by a theologian or a social scientist influenced by Judeo-Christian concepts and categories, tends to view the tremendous variety of religious phenomena in human experience, or even in Mexican and Chicano experience, by explicitly or implicitly measuring them against the beliefs, doctrines, teachings, and values of the Christian religion, usually judging them as inferior or degraded religious elements. This approach uses Christian categories of spirituality, value, morality, and truth as a powerful NORM, to establish the acceptability and even superiority of Christianity while marking other religions as inferior and sometimes evil. For the student attempting to understand not just the Christian view of God but the human experience of divine powers and beings, such an approach can limit and distort our understanding of the spiritual universe(s) within the Chicano community. Such an approach also inhibits our rigorous intellectual and emotional understanding of the Chicano community's many dimensions and richness. The Christian-centric orientation of most Chicano studies is a serious problem. Although the intellectual opportunities of Chicano students have been expanded, they are still shy and defensive about examining the religious realities (Euro-American and indigenous) of Chicano history and culture. A more humane and humanistic approach is necessary but difficult to cultivate.

Let me illustrate how the Christian-centric approach has limited our understanding of our Indian ancestors as creative human beings. When the Spanish conquistadors arrived in Anahuac, they were impressed by the crosses present in different parts of Indian society, and immediately thought that some Christian contact had preceded them. They were even more impressed by stories they heard in various places about an ancient Indian lord named Quetzalcoatl, "the Feathered Serpent," also called Topiltzin Quetzalcoatl, "Our Young Prince, the Feathered Serpent," who had been a great religious and political leader centuries earlier. The indigenous tradition told how this man-god preached with great authority, invented new rituals of sacrifice, possessed the power to go into ecstasy and visit heaven, and built the magnificent city of Tollan. In response, a debate broke out among Spanish authorities and mendicants. They played great intellectual and theological games with this tradition and tried to fit it within the Christian view of the world. One group argued that this story was evidence of pre-Hispanic demonic influences in New Spain, and these influences had misled the Indians into their terrible idolatry; this justified the conquest and missionization of the Indians. But another group saw this tradition as evidence of pre-Hispanic redeeming contact from the Christian religion suggesting that God had prepared the way for their great conquest and conversion. Some theologians claimed that Moses, or perhaps

Jesus, and certainly Saint Thomas had visited the Indians centuries before, spreading the truths of the Old and New Testament, and that Quetzalcoatl was not really an Indian genius or hero but a foreign missionary. That is, he was like the Spaniards! The application of the Christian theological view of history allows no room for the consideration of Indian creativity, Indian genius, Indian imagination or spirituality. My point is not that these Christians were bad people, for surely there were good and bad people among them. My point is that the aggressive use of a particular religious worldview to define the nature and value of another religious tradition does damage to an understanding of the "objects" of this exercise, in this case the Indians.

Chicano studies has generally obscured the significance of religious dimensions of Chicano life through its captivity by the Christian worldview or its inability to appreciate the intertwining of religious meanings with all of Chicano history. Consider the lack of interest in religious structures expressed in, for example, *El Plan de Santa Barbara* or even in the recent Chicano newsletter *La Red*. These two different statements of present-day Chicano scholarship reflect the fact that not just the "faithful" but even Chicanos who consider themselves "not religious" lack a methodology to investigate, criticize, and understand Catholic traditions and folk religious practices. (The reasons for this lacuna in academic programs would be a fascinating study in itself.)

The historian of religions aligns himself more closely to the position developed in an illuminating debate between the novel's hero Antonio and his friend Florence. The debate concerns the existence and cruelty of God in their lives. Antonio hears Florence challenge him:

> "My mother died when I was three, my old man drank himself to death, and," he paused and looked toward the church which already loomed ahead of us. His inquiring, angelic face smiled. "And my sisters are whores, working at Rosie's place ... So I ask myself," he continued, "how can God let this happen to a kid. I never asked to be born. But he gives me birth, a soul, and puts me here to punish me. Why? What did I ever do to Him to deserve this, huh?"

Antonio's mind is pushed by his friend's blunt questions to consider the absence of God, and he begins to see a new possibility about the nature of divine beings as he responds:

> "My father says the weather comes in cycles," I said instead, "there are years of good weather, and there are years of bad weather—"
> "I don't understand?" Florence said.

Perhaps I didn't either, but my mind was seeking answers to Florence's questions.

"Maybe God comes in cycles, like the weather," I answered. "Maybe there are times when God is with us, and times when he is not. Maybe it is like that now, God is hidden. He will be gone for many years, maybe centuries." I talked rapidly, excited about the possibilities my mind seemed to be reaching.

"But we cannot change the weather," Florence said, "and we cannot ask God to return—"

"No," I nodded, "but what if there were different gods to rule in his absence?" Florence could not have been more surprised by what I said than I. I grabbed him by the collar and shouted. "What if the Virgin Mary or the Golden Carp ruled instead of ... !" (188-90)

Understanding Homo Religiosus

The History of Religions as a discipline works from the conviction that religious experiences and the religions that form around them can be understood if they are approached (a) as an area for scientific inquiry, and (b) in relation to the endless variety of human expressions that appear to have a religious nature. The historian of religions examines many accounts of human encounters with God and attempts to understand the distinctiveness of these experiences and the common underlying patterns.[4] These patterns reveal a human desire and quest to transcend human limits and to participate in sacred realities and structures. Alan McGlashan has noted, "There is strong archaeological evidence to show that with the birth of human consciousness there was born, like a twin, the impulse to transcend it."[5] That is, religion is a part of human nature.

This research does not presuppose the God-human relationship but examines the endless claims and accounts of humans who tell how their lives have been interrupted, impressed, blessed, cursed, and determined by manifestations of a sacred nature and quality. This work begins with the accounts of how humans see, feel, hear, smell, and think about the divine forces in their lives and attempts to see what these accounts tell about the human mode of being. Perhaps the reality of God is witnessed in these accounts. But our primary concern is understanding the human being and not believing or disbelieving in his god.

To illustrate a partial curriculum developed under this approach, listed here are some areas of inquiry into religious traditions where I have done research. I have studied the various types of sacred kingship in Burmese Buddhism;[6] primitive religious structures such as the Trickster;[7] the Master of the Animals;[8] the ecstasy of the Shaman;[9] and the role of religious symbols in the rise of man's great invention—the city,[10] with special focus on the coincidence of city and symbol in pre-Columbian Mexico.[11] I have spent time analyzing the dynamics of religious movements such as cargo cults and crisis cults,[12] and the methodological problems involved in studying all these areas.[13] From this journey through the religious worlds of other men I have developed a perspective that led me, when I came upon *Bless Me, Ultima* and other Chicano texts, to be as impressed by the presence of an "archaic consciousness" in Mexican and Chicano life as I am by the presence of Catholic or Protestant consciousness. And Chicanos are basically Catholic! Neither the Western nor the indigenous religious traditions within Chicano life have been seriously looked at by Chicanos from the history of religion viewpoint.

These intellectual experiences and journeys into the spiritual universes of significant others produced in me an awakening that human beings, popularly referred to as Homo sapiens (in the context of certain Chicano scholars, it is Homo chicano) need to be understood as Homo religiosus. That is, human beings appear to be "wired" for religion. It is almost as though in the makeup of human life there is a religiogram, a program that insures that human beings will develop religious movements and traditions, texts, and rituals. This persistence for religion is reflected in the novel when Antonio is driven to great confusion about his communion experience ("only emptiness"), and asks his father, "Papa, can a new religion be made?" Certainly, new religions are made every day somewhere on this planet.

Respecting Powerful Data

In *Religion in Essence and Manifestation*, the Dutch phenomenologist of religion Gerardus Van der Leeuw gives this definition of religion:

> Religious experience, in other terms, is concerned with a "Somewhat." But this assertion often means no more than that this "Somewhat" is merely a vague "Something"; and in order that man may be able to make more significant statements about this "Somewhat," it must force itself upon him, must oppose itself to him as being Something Other. Thus the first affirmation we can make about the Object of Religion is that it is a highly exceptional and extremely impressive "Other."[14]

This simple but strange statement is a helpful place to begin our approach to the religious dimensions of *Bless Me, Ultima*, because it reflects one part of the methodological position taken by historians of religion. In short, it states that religions begin or are characterized by manifestations, epiphanies, apparitions, revelations of strange forces that humans perceive as "highly exceptional and extremely impressive" Otherness. These experiences are familiar; for example, Moses at the Burning Bush, Saul on the Road to Damascus, Juan Diego passing by Tepeyac, or Reyes López Tijerina's prophetic dreams. The methodological position states that religious expressions must be respected and appreciated for their peculiar intentionality if they are to be understood. Van der Leeuw has demonstrated that religious representations, myths, dreams, apparitions, and rituals will not be adequately understood if they are reduced to social, psychological, or rational functions. Scholars who follow this approach explain religion by saying that it is really not religion, but something else like a system of social cohesion, an expression of infantile trauma, a mask for oppression. Religions may involve all these things. But they are something more, and the history of religions seeks to illuminate the inner structures and meanings of religious phenomena.

This approach of respecting the intended and often obscure meaning of religious data has been expanded by Mircea Eliade, who summarizes our task through a comparison of religion with works of art.

> Works of art, like "religious data," have a mode of being that is peculiar to themselves; they exist on their own plane of reference, in their particular universe. The fact that this universe is not the physical universe of immediate experience does not imply their nonreality ... A work of art reveals the meaning, only insofar as it is regarded as an autonomous creation: that is, insofar as we accept its mode of being-that of an artistic creation—and do not reduce it to one of its constituent elements (in the case of a poem, sound, vocabulary, linguistic structure, etc.) or in to one of its subsequent uses (a poem which carries a political message or which can serve as a document for sociology, ethnography, etc.)
>
> In the same way, it seems to us that a religious datum reveals its deeper meaning when it is considered on its plane of reference, and not when it is reduced to one of its secondary aspects or its contexts.

And, Eliade continues, the history of religion must work "to bring out the autonomous value—the value as spiritual creation" of all religious movements and expressions.[15]

To make this method more relevant, when Antonio and Cico beheld the golden carp as a miraculous being, some insight can be gained by approaching it as a religious manifestation, an extremely impressive "other," rather than by quickly insisting that the fish is not a miraculous being but an object of fantasy that functioned to create social cohesion among bored children. As in most religions, the golden carp does have a social function and it may be a psychological projection—much of religion does invoke projection—but the golden carp, the owl of Ultima, the Juniper tree, the presence of the river will be better understood and point more directly to a Chicano mode of being in the world if approached as manifestations of power in Antonio's life, as expressions of the sacred, by which I mean the powerful, the valuable, the wonderful, and the terrifying.[16]

Hierophany and the Sacred Landscape

To clarify what I mean by "experiencing the sacred," let us turn to a term that has been utilized by Mircea Eliade, "hierophany." This word means simply "manifestation of the sacred." In Eliade's view, all religions are based on hierophanies or dramatic encounters that human beings have with what they consider to be supernatural forces manifesting themselves in natural objects. These manifestations transform those objects into power spots, power objects, wonderful trees, terrifying bends in the river, sacred animals. The stones, trees, animals, or humans through which a hierophany takes place are considered valuable, full of mana, things to be respected and revered. Human beings who feel these transformations in their landscape believe that a power from another plane of reality has interrupted their lives. Usually, they respond with a combination of great attraction and great fear. Their lives are deeply changed because of this encounter with numinous places.[17] The three following examples of hierophany illustrate this important notion. One is from Sioux religion; one is from a "high" religion, Islam; and the third relates to the origins of Chicano culture—the conquest of Mexico.

In Joseph Epes Brown's *The Sacred Pipe*, White Buffalo Cow Woman gives the sacred pipe to the Oglala Sioux. According to their mythic traditions, many winters ago two Lakota braves were out hunting when "they saw in the distance something coming towards them in a very strange and wonderful manner." The strange and wonderful "something" (to emphasize Van der Leeuw's phrase) turned out to be a very beautiful woman bringing them the sacred pipe. When she arrived at the tribal village and met the chief and the elders, she presented her gift, exhorting "Behold this and always love it." She produced the pipe miraculously and told how each intricate part of its structure and decoration represented some part of the cosmos where the Sioux dwelled. She announced that this object of stone and wood is a sacred force that will insure the continuity of tribal existence. The visitation ended when the sacred woman stated:

Behold what you see. Behold this pipe. Always remember how sacred it is, and treat it as such, for it will take you to the end. Remember, in me there are four ages. I am leaving now, but I shall look back upon your people in every age and at the end I shall return.

The "wakan" or sacred woman walks away, turning three times into a buffalo of different colors.[18]

This story initiates the account of the seven rites of the Sioux and is a brilliant example of hierophany. All of the sacred rites revolve around the sacred pipe that appeared to the tribe through the coming of the sacred woman who showed them their destiny. She repeatedly orders them, "Behold, behold," alerting them to this hierophany, this gift from a sacred being.

A similar revelation gave birth to the religion of Islam. W. Montgomery Watt's chapter "The Call of Prophethood" describes the events surrounding the origins of this great religion. He also notes that Muhammad, the founder of Islam, was previously a caravan agent who experienced periods of doubt and despair.

On one of the barren rocky hills in the neighborhood there was a cave where he sometimes went for several nights at a time to be alone and to pray and meditate. During these solitary vigils he began to have strange experiences. First of all there were vivid dreams or visions. Two in particular stood out as being of special significance. In the first visitation there appeared to him a glorious Being standing erect high up in the sky near the horizon; then this strong and mighty One moved down towards him until he was only two bow-shots or less from him, and communicated to him a revelation, that is, some passage of the Quran.

This mighty being interrupts Muhammad in his moments of meditation and commands him to become his spokesman. The relevant passage reads:

Recite
In the Name of thy Lord, who created—
Created man from a blood clot.[19]

One tradition tells that Muhammad resisted this strange appearance, protesting his inability to change his life, and the Being began to choke him in order to impress him with the reality of his situation. Again, we have an example of a powerful manifestation of a sacred reality to a human being who is impressed, opposed to, and eventually overcome by the other reality. In the Sioux example, the gift of the sacred pipe embodied the reality. In the Muslim case, the gift of the sacred book, the Quran, and the prophethood of Muhammad contained the reality.

The hierophany of the Virgin of Guadalupe caused one of the turning points of Mexican history. According to Mexican traditions, in 1531 a Christianized Indian was walking near the hill of Tepeyac, which had been the site of the Aztec shrine to the mother goddess, when he heard beautiful music.[20] As he sought out the source of this melody, a lovely lady speaking in Nahautl appeared to him. Astounded by this glimmering figure, he listened as she commanded him to visit the palace of the archbishop of Mexico at Tlatelolco and told him that the Virgin Mary, "Mother of the true God through whom one lives," wished a sacred shrine to be built at the site of the apparition so she could "show and give forth all my love, compassion, help, and defense to all the inhabitants of this land … to hear their lamentation, and remedy their miseries, pain and sufferings." The archbishop was not persuaded by this story from an Indian commoner. Then the Virgin displayed her powers and intentions more directly. She led Juan Diego to a site where roses were blooming out of season and commanded him to arrange them in a cloak. As Juan Diego unfolded his cloak in the presence of the archbishop, the roses fell to the ground and the image of the Virgin appeared on the cloak. The Mexican people came to life through this event and the site became the new spiritual center of colonial Mexico.[21]

In each of these three examples, human beings claim that some sacred being came into their lives and manifested "highly exceptional and extremely impressive Otherness," bestowing on their lives sacred values, meanings, and blessings. And the objects through which the manifestations took place became "numinous centers" in their new world. Eliade has written extensively about the "axis mundi." By axis mundi, he means a point in the environment that becomes the "center" of the vertical and horizontal cosmos as a result of a hierophany. The place or object is appreciated as the point of communication between the human community and the world of the gods.

The Sacred Human

In the history of religions, we find endless accounts of sacred specialists. These are individuals who have developed a profound knowledge of the sacred realities that guide their particular communities. They have also acquired sophisticated and ecstatic techniques that enable them to confront, utilize, and even evoke spiritual forces. This knowledge is usually transmitted to them by older sacred specialists, religious *virtuosos*, who were their teachers during a period of suffering and growth. Such a pattern of transmission is referred to in the case of Ultima, who tells Antonio on her deathbed:

> "I was taught my life's work by a wise old man, a good man [referred to elsewhere as "el hombre volador"]. He gave me the owl and said the owl was my spirit, bond to the time and the harmony of the universe ... My work was to do good, ... I was to heal the sick and show them the path of goodness. But I was not to interfere with the destiny of any man." (247)

The most archaic sacred specialists we know were shamans. I am suggesting here not that Ultima and Antonio are shamans, but that their relationship reflects some characteristics of the initiation scenario typical of shamanic ecstasy. In this regard, we are witnessing in Anaya's novel a Chicano variation of an archaic pattern of spiritual creativity; what I would call the lyrics of Chicano spirituality.

The pattern of shamanic ecstasy includes (a) sensitive and troubled individuals who (b) receive sacred knowledge through fantastic dreams and visions plus formal instructions under the (c) guidance of a great shaman (la Grande) during which the initiate (d) forms relationships with helping spirits, usually in the form of animals, that enable the seeker to (e) grasp a deep truth and techniques that enable him to renew contact with that wisdom and (f) obtain the powers to heal varieties of sickness and attack and kill enemies.

This pattern of initiation usually involves a great ordeal, sometimes experienced during a sickness that takes the novice close to death and introduces him to the terrors of finitude and spiritual forces. During this ordeal, which often includes ecstatic dreams, the hero is tested. He is symbolically killed and reborn into the vocation of singer, healer, and poet. This ordeal involves face-to-face encounters with terrible monsters, scenarios of chaos that may include visualizing the dismemberment and destruction of one's own body, community, and cosmos. For instance, in some shamanic ecstasies, the would-be sorcerer is confronted with his own skeleton, completely stripped of skin and hair and organs.[22] This total crisis emerges into a new integration of the self and the acquisition of sacred knowledge which is to be used to benefit the community. This is the meaning and purpose of much religious ecstasy. The novel reflects some of these characteristics.

Antonio's Sacred Landscape

The setting for Antonio's growth is a magical landscape overflowing with manifestations of religious power. In the hero's name and the qualities attributed to his name are reflected the Chicano respect for powerful earthly and heavenly places. He is Luna y Márez, moon and sea. Anaya's portrayal of these names shows that the Chicanos in the story do not regard them as simple, natural objects but as powers that influence the boy's life from birth. From one side he descends from the people of the "earthly sea," "people who hold the wind as brother," and his character is full of the spirits of this sea. From the other side he carries the blood and the spirits of the people of El Puerto, who are "steady, settled" and "hold the earth as brother." The influence of these realities is vividly portrayed in his first dream where he flies (like a shaman) back to the place and time of his birth. There he witnesses a struggle almost to the death of relatives from both sides of his family who wish to take the afterbirth and bury it in the llano or in the valley. A vigorous argument develops, and at the critical moment when death is about to appear, Ultima cries, "Cease ... I pulled this baby into the light of life, so I will bury the afterbirth and cord that once linked him to eternity. Only I will know his destiny" (6).

Throughout the novel this conflict charges the boy's waking and dreaming life while the secret of his destiny obsesses him. Ultima, in another dream, hints to him the solution to his agony caused by the struggle of these forces. He dreams of another argument, this time between his mother, who descends to a lake on the glowing moon, and his father, who stands on a corpse-strewn shore. They argue about his nature and destiny, causing an excruciating pain to sear through his body while he sees the forces of doom descend upon him. Again, Ultima appears and cries:

> Cease! ... The sweet water of the moon which falls as rain is the same water that gathers into rivers and flows to fill the seas. Without the waters of the moon to replenish the oceans there would be no oceans. And the same salt waters of the oceans are drawn by the sun to the heavens, and in turn becomes again the waters of the moon ... The waters are one, Antonio ... You have been seeing only parts. (113)

This stunning dream scenario shows the antagonistic relationship of the powers in his life and hints at the great message of his initiation.

Sacred space appears again in the scenes near the river. The river flowing through Antonio's world is not just a water source, but a presence, a manifestation of some "other" power. In his dreams a "goddess," *la llorona*, guards the river. On one occasion the "great presence of the river" evokes his curiosity about his destiny. Ultima and Antonio are walking by the river, which was

> silent and brooding. The presence was watching over us. ... "Ultima," I asked, "why are they [the Lunas] so strange and quiet? And why are my father's people so loud and wild?" She answered, "It is the blood of the Lunas to be quiet, for only a quiet man can learn the secrets of the earth that are necessary for planting ... they are quiet like the moon—And it is the blood of the Márez to be wild, like the ocean from which they take their name, and the spaces of the llano that have become their home."

They sat in silence, pondering these relationships, and the river manifested itself to them:

> The silence spoke, not with harsh sounds, but softly to the rhythm of our blood. "What is it?" I asked, for I was still afraid. "It is the presence of the river" Ultima answered. I held my breath and looked at the giant, gnarled cottonwood trees that surrounded us. Somewhere a bird cried, and up on the hill the tinkling sound of a cowbell rang. The presence was immense, lifeless, yet throbbing with its secret message. "Can it speak" I asked and drew closer to Ultima, "If you listen carefully" she whispered.... (38)

There are many similar power spots in Antonio's world: the bend in the river that is an evil place, the Juniper tree that is the scene of a murder, and a forked Juniper under which Ultima's owl is buried. During the curing of the Tellez house, Ultima tells the adults to let Antonio go and gather branches from a Juniper tree. "Let Tony cut it, he understands the power in the tree." And, of course, Ultima's owl, which is her spirit, is a classic spiritual helper found throughout the shamanic lifestyle. But our attention is drawn to the amazing figure of the golden carp. Antonio's companion Cico takes him to the secret spot where the golden carp appears. The scene exudes the quality of mystery and sacrality that appear in the form of this amazing animal. The text bustles with power.

> We sat for a long time, waiting for the golden carp. It was very pleasant to sit in the warm sunshine and watch the pure waters drift by.... Then the golden carp came. Cico pointed and I turned to where the stream came out of the dark grotto of overhanging tree branches. At first I thought I must be dreaming. I had expected to see a carp the size of a river carp ... I rubbed my eyes and watched in astonishment.
> "Behold the golden carp, Lord of the waters—" I turned and saw Cico standing; his spear held across his chest as if in acknowledgement of the presence of a ruler.

The huge, beautiful form glided through the blue waters. I could not believe its size. It was bigger than me! And bright orange! The sunlight glistened off his golden scales. He glided down the creek with a couple of smaller carp following.

"The golden carp," I whispered in awe. I could not have been more entranced if I had seen the Virgin, or God Himself. The golden carp had seen me.... I could have reached out into the water and touched the holy fish.... I felt my body trembling as I saw the bright golden form disappear. I knew I had witnessed a miraculous thing, the appearance of a pagan god, a thing as miraculous as the curing of my uncle Lucas. And I thought the power of God failed where Ultima's worked. And then a sudden illumination of beauty and understanding flashed through my mind. This is what I had expected God to do at my first holy communion. If God was witness to my beholding of the golden carp then I had sinned. I clasped my hands and was about to pray to the heavens when the waters of the pond exploded. (104-5)

In a sense, this episode says it all. The boys are awestruck by the appearance of a "holy fish" whose coming is announced as was the buffalo woman announced to the Sioux: "Behold, the golden carp." The impact is deep, reverent and frightening, both attracting and repulsing the young Antonio. His picture of heavenly beings is garbled and intensified by the appearance of a "miraculous thing." Sacrality has appeared to him in his blood, in the river that flows by his town, and in the golden carp that is lord of the waters.

Initiation into Sacred Knowledge: Death and Rebirth

To restate my description of the sacred human, power manifests itself to a human being who acquires insight into and techniques to deal with the sacred. This individual, touched deeply by sacred forces, passes through an initiatory process under the guidance of a religious virtuoso. He may participate so directly in the world of the sacred that he comes to represent a living hierophany. The shamanic paradigm outlined earlier illustrates a religious paradigm for the Chicano experience.

Ultima appears, as her name suggests, to be completely in touch with the ultimate powers of the universe. She can heal and apparently kill using her magical force. A dynamic relationship exists between the *curandera* and Antonio and the initiatory process, which runs throughout Antonio's life. In the initiation process, Antonio becomes a new person; he acquires new and special knowledge of not only Ultima and the forces of his world, but of himself. This new knowledge (superior to the knowledge of his family's members) emerges through powerful personal experiences highlighted by religious ecstasies. As in shamanic or archaic mystical initiations, Antonio is taught wisdom through (a) transmission of information about herbs, genealogy, and myths, (b) dream messages that reveal the world of spirits and cosmic forces that dismember and reintegrate him and his world, and (c) direct encounters with spirits while working as Ultima's helper and apprentice. In the last two types of instruction, a valuable lesson is forced into his consciousness. This lesson, which reflects the pattern of spiritual death and rebirth, is revealed in magnificent dream and waking scenarios of lyric and ecstatic quality.

The novel begins with Ultima's appearance in Antonio's life. Her arrival at the Márez home is not just another important event in his life, but a new beginning, a birth of awareness:

> When she came the beauty of the llano unfolds before my eyes, and the gurgling waters of the river sang to the hum of the turning earth. The magical time of childhood stood still, and the pulse of the living earth pressed its mystery into my living blood. She took my hand and the silent magic powers she possessed made beauty from the raw, sun baked llano, the green river valley, and the blue bowl which was the white sun's home. My bare feet felt the throbbing earth and my body trembled with excitement. Time stood still, and it shared with me all that had been, and all that was to come....
>
> Let me begin at the beginning. I do not mean the beginning that was in my dreams and the stories they whispered to me about my birth, and the people of my father and mother, and my three brothers,—but the beginning that came with Ultima. (7)

Ultima's arrival opened up the magical powers of his environment, the beauty of the land, the songs of the river, the mystery of the earth, and the magical force within a human being. His life trembles at her presence and he is reborn. The trembling is a physical reaction to Ultima's presence; this is seen in the first encounter between the two.

> I looked up into her clear brown eyes and shivered. Her face was old and wrinkled, but her eyes were clear and sparkling, like the eyes of a young child.
>
> "Antonio" she smiled. She took my hand and I felt the power of a whirlwind sweep around me. Her eyes swept the surrounding hills and through them I saw for the first time the wild beauty of our hills and the magic of the green river. My nostrils quivered as I felt the song of the mockingbirds and the drone of the grasshoppers mingle with the pulse of the earth. The four directions of the llano met in me and the white sun shone on my soul. The granules of sand at my feet and the sun and sky above me seemed to dissolve into one strange, complete being. (11)

The boy experiences himself as a trembling center of some new power. The four winds meet in him, the sounds of the world fill his being, and his depths are warmed by the sun. The intimation that Ultima is related to his whole being is communicated to him in his first dream, already discussed, where Ultima announces her secret knowledge of his destiny.

Antonio is allowed to address her by her name, "Ultima," while the others are symbolically separated from her by the use of "Grande." Ultima reciprocates this familiarity when she announces, "I knew there would be something between us." Indeed, it is a "powerful something" which quickly takes on the form of instruction and a secret alliance between the two. As the story progresses, Ultima manifests her powers and knowledge to him in nocturnal and daylight encounters. Soon after her arrival, Antonio witnesses the midnight killing of Lupito by the river, and he rushes home in terror ("the horror of darkness"), cutting and bruising himself along the way. Heartened by the watchful presence of Ultima's owl, the boy arrives home to find Ultima waiting for him and knowing what he has witnessed. She gives him her potion, which miraculously heals his wounds during the night and makes him realize, "There was a strange power in Ultima's medicine." As time passes, Antonio becomes aware that these "strange powers" penetrate deeper than his cuts and bruises and that he is "growing up and changing" through the magic of Ultima. This change and growth intensifies through the teachings of Ultima. The great curandera takes Antonio on her hunts for herbs and transmits her knowledge to him, carefully and systematically. He learns the details of the medicinal plants, to imitate her walk, to acknowledge the spirits that inhabit the plants. He feels that "my soul grew under her careful guidance."

> Ultima and I continued to search for plants and roots in the hills. I felt more attached to Ultima than to my own mother. Ultima told me the stories and legends of my ancestors. From her I learned the glory and the tragedy of the history of my people, and I came to understand how that history stirred in my blood.
>
> I spent most of the long summer evenings in her room. We talked, stored the dry herbs, or played cards. (115)

Ultima shows him the twisted dolls on her shelf, which represent her magical combat with the Trementina family, and he begins to realize the dangers involved in her way of life. She gives him her scapular full of "helpful herbs," something she has carried since childhood. Now, he has become part of the terrible combat of spiritual forces. Later, this sacred object protects him from Tenorio's attempt to kill him.

Antonio's initiation into the world of magical regeneration develops dramatically in two episodes: the curing of his uncle Lucas and the magnificent dream of the apocalypse of the world. Although this initiation has numerous other stages, these two events are outstanding. In the first event, Antonio is put through a cycle of sickness and healing as he assists Ultima with a cure. In the second, he witnesses the decay, destruction, and regeneration of the earth in his dream. Both give him messages about the ultimate meaning of life.

During the healing of Lucas, a three-day ordeal, Antonio acts as a spiritual conduit. Earlier, when Ultima accepted the challenge to cure Antonio's uncle, Ultima announces that she needs a helper and that it is "necessary" for Antonio to face the ordeal ahead with her. He accepts without fear for his life or reputation. Ultima states that she will have to "work the magic beyond evil, the magic that endures forever," for "forty dollars to cheat la muerte." Next, the two spiritual warriors prepare the room where this cure will take place. Outside, Ultima's owl guards them by attacking the barking hungry coyotes, spiritual helpers of the Trementina sisters. As the curing proceeds, Antonio, exhausted, falls into a trance and becomes a double of his bewitched uncle. Captured in a "deep stupor," he is unable to take his eyes off his uncle.

> I was aware of what happened in the room but my senses did not seem to respond to commands. Instead I remained in that waking dream. I saw Ultima make some medicine for my uncle, and when she forced it down his throat and his face showed pain, my body too felt pain. I could almost taste the oily hot liquid. I saw his convulsion and my body too was seized with aching cramps. I felt my body wet with sweat. I tried to call to Ultima but there was no voice, I tried to move but there was no movement. I suffered the spasm of pain my uncle suffered and these alternated with feelings of elation and power.... I felt that somehow we were going through the same cure.... He was across the room from me, but our bodies did not seem separated by the distance. We dissolved into each other, and we shared a common struggle against the evil within, which fought to repulse Ultima's magic. (92-93)

This merging of identities marks his full participation in the magical combat. The combat culminates when Antonio drinks the sacred blue *atole* and vomits up a poisonous green bile. Almost immediately, Lucas emits a horrible series of screams, and through a contorted face, he vomits the evil green bile and a huge ball of hair, "hot and steaming and wiggling like live snakes." Antonio has experienced a terrible familiarity with death and a swooning reprieve. But afterward, he is still only partially aware of the meaning of this overwhelming event. Much later in a dream, the Trementina sisters tell him what his role was. In a scene of diabolic hullabaloo, the sisters dance around him and cry, "Hie, Hie, through your body went the spell that cured Lucas, and your name lent strength to the curse that took one of us from the service of our Master. We will have our vengeance on you" (166).

In this dream, the religious pattern of decay, destruction, dismemberment, and regeneration is most vividly communicated to Antonio. The dream overflows with images of cosmic forces, human monsters, murder, and rebirth. It is like a Hieronymus Bosch painting turned into sound and motion. I cannot begin to interpret the entire dream but will merely comment on four phases that may represent stages in the ecstatic acquisition of knowledge.

(1) After Antonio witnesses the murder of Narciso under the Juniper tree, he feels himself drowning in the "awful power" of his "ocean of pesadilla." The nightmare's first sequence represents his spiritual crises. He enters into a pleading, screaming argument with God about forgiveness for his brother and Narciso, and punishment for Tenorio. He is told by a "roaring" God that God's power cannot be reduced to his "personal whims" and that God will forgive even Tenorio, though he is a murderer. Antonio feels utterly lost and sinful.

(2) In his nightmare, Antonio encounters the Trementina sisters, who have cast an evil spell on the world. Following this Antonio sees himself "withering away ... A long, dark night came upon me in which I sought the face of God, but I could not find Him ... In front of the dark doors of Purgatory, my bleached bones were laid to rest." This image of reduction to his bones represents, in religious terms, the disintegration of one's being.

(3) Next, his home is set afire and his family burned to death. His cosmos is disintegrating. Ultima's owl is killed, and the curandera, now powerless, is beheaded by a mob that drinks and bathes in her blood before driving a stake through her heart and burning her. The golden carp is cooked in the fires of Ultima's ashes and eaten. Then the entire earth crumbles.

> There was a thundering of the earth and a great rift opened. The church building crumbled, and the school collapsed into dust and the whole town disappeared in the chasm. A great cry went up from the people as they saw crashing tumultuous waters fill the dark hole.

The disintegration of life continues as

> the people looked upon each other and they saw their skin rot and fall off. Shrieks of pain and agony filled the air, ... the walking dead buried their sleeping dead ... disease and filth throughout. In the end no one was left. (167-68)

Here we have a Chicano apocalypse in which the hero is reduced to bones, the curandera of goodness ripped apart and cremated, the divine fish skinned and eaten, and the earth transformed into a black hole! It is the ultimate "meltdown"! It is a return to the cosmic womb of nothingness.

(4) But nothingness in religious terms is also the potential source of new life. Out of nothingness come regenerative powers. And in the shamanic imagination, new life cannot emerge unless there has been a death. And so the dream continues to carry us into the completeness of Ultima's teachings and religious wisdom.

> Evening settled over the land and the waters. The stars came out and glittered in the dark sky. In the lake, the golden carp appeared. His beautiful body glittered in the moonlight. He had been witness to everything that happened, and he decided that everyone should survive, but in a new form. He opened his huge mouth and swallowed everything, everything there was, good and evil. Then he swam into the blue velvet of the night, glittering as he rose towards the stars. The moon smiled on him and guided him, and his golden body burned with such beautiful brilliance that he became a new sun in the heavens. A new sun to shine its good light upon a new earth. (168)

This dramatic nightmare carries, at the dream ecstasy level, a heightened sense of the message that comes to Antonio toward the end when he is working in El Puerto. He has seen more of Ultima's curing power, experienced the failure of holy communion, witnessed the death of his companion, Florence. The secret message of Ultima's teachings and his dreams comes to the consciousness level. The message states plainly and directly the pattern of death and rebirth, decay and regeneration. During a memorable conversation with his father he thinks,

> Take the llano and the river valley, the moon and the sea, God and the golden carp—and make something new, I said to myself. That is what Ultima meant by building strength from life. "Papa," I asked, "can a new religion be made?"

And then later, Antonio tells us,

> The rest of the summer was good for me, good in the sense that I was filled with its richness and I made strength from everything that had happened

to me, so that in the end, the final tragedy could not defeat me. And that is what Ultima tried to teach me, that the tragic consequences of life can be overcome by the magical strength that resides in the human heart. (237)

Antonio articulates, at the level of his waking life, the knowledge that the integration of his diverse and conflicting elements and the cultivation of sacred forces within a human being can lead to a life full of blessings. This was the gift of Ultima and it is a form of religious wisdom.

In this research, I have demonstrated how the Chicano classic *Bless Me, Ultima* contains two general religious patterns that are important in the understanding of Chicano experience. These patterns are the sacrality of the landscape and the shamanic relationship between Antonio and Ultima. My approach as a historian of religions led me to place this discussion within the scope of the methods and discoveries of the comparative study of religions. This leads us away from viewing Chicano life from within the norms of Christian ethics and experience. It allows us to consider the specific character of Chicano experience and imagination within a general understanding of religious creativity. This creativity is similar to what Mircea Eliade calls an "archaic consciousness," a consciousness that is concerned with the reintegration of primordial forces of the land and the magic of human consciousness. I hope this approach to the novel can enrich our perspective for the study of religious dimensions in Chicano culture.

Notes

1. Rudolfo A. Anaya, *Bless Me, Ultima* (Berkeley, Calif.: Quinto Sol Publications, 1972), 227. This and subsequent quotations from *Bless Me, Ultima* are from this edition.

2. History of Religions is an outgrowth of the attempts to establish a Religionswissenschaft or science of religion in a number of European universities in the nineteenth century. For a short history of this movement and the present state of the art, see Charles H. Long, "The History of the History of Religions," in *A Reader's Guide to the Great Religions*, ed. Charles J. Adams (New York: Free Press, 1965). As Joachim Wach noted concerning this discipline, "The term 'science of religion' (Religionswissenschaft) was used to denote the emancipation of the new discipline from philosophy of religion and especially theology." See *The Comparative Study of Religions* (New York: Columbia University Press, 1958), 3.

3. This essay is intended as an introduction of a complex approach to understanding human culture. Therefore, I am not presenting a full picture of the methods utilized by the historian of religions. The emphasis here is placed on the phenomenological approach to religious data, as articulated by Gerardus Van der Leeuw and Mircea Eliade. Most historians of religions are also concerned with the history of religious manifestations and elements: the context in which religions appear, the uses made by elites and folk communities, the development and degradation of religious symbols and myths, the interaction between the sacred and all other dimensions of a society. Charles H. Long articulates the underlying methodological concern that I have attempted to reflect. Long writes in his article, "Primitive Religion":

> Though Van der Leeuw's work is permeated by a general theory of "religious dynamism," he does relate every mode of the religious consciousness and behavior to an objective form of the world, whether this form be a structure of nature or of human community. This kind of transition is completed in the work of Mircea Eliade. In a certain sense Eliade moves towards the objectivity and neo-positivism of Levi-Strauss, but instead of understanding the human consciousness as a purely intellectual structure, Eliade tends to see human consciousness as a locus for the intellectual and imaginative ordering of the world. (Adams, *Great Religions*, 11)

4. A succinct statement of this approach appears in Joseph M. Kitagawa's Centennial article where he notes, "I am conscious of the two important foci of the discipline of History of Religions, namely, the unity and continuity of the religious experience of man on the one hand, and the integrity and autonomous character of particular religious traditions, on the other." "One Hundredth Anniversary Celebration," *The Criterion*, fall 1969, 14.

5. Loren Eiseley, *The Unexpected Universe* (New York: Harcourt Brace Jovanovich, 1969), 172.

6. See such important works concerning this problem as Emanuel Sarki-syanz, *Buddhist Backgrounds of the Burmese Revolution* (The Hague: Martinus Nijhoff, 1965); Michael Mendelson, *Samgha and State* (Ithaca: Cornell University Press, 1975); and Htin Aung, trans., *Burmese Monk's Tales* (New York: Columbia University Press, 1966).

7. Paul Radin, *The Trickster: A Study in American Indian Mythology* (New York: Schocken Press, 1973).

8. A. E. Jensen, *Myth and Cult Among Primitive Peoples* (Chicago: University of Chicago Press, 1963).

9. Mircea Eliade, *Shamanism: Archaic Techniques in Ecstasy* (Bollingen Foundation, 1964).

10. 10. See Mircea Eliade, *The Myth of the Eternal Return* (New York: Pantheon Books, 1959), and the outstanding comparative work by Paul Wheatley, *The Pivot of the Four Quarters: A Preliminary Enquiry into the Origins and Character of the Ancient Chinese City* (Chicago: Aldine Press, 1971).

11. Walter Krickeberg, *Las Antiguas Culturas Mexicanas* (Mexico: Fondo de Cultura Económica, 1964).

12. Kenelm Burridge, *Mambu* (New York: Harper and Row, 1970); and Peter Worsley, *The Trumpet Shall Sound* (New York: Schocken Books, 1970).

13. 13. Mircea Eliade, *The Quest* (Chicago: University of Chicago Press, 1969).

14. Gerardus Van der Leeuw, *Religion in Essence and Manifestation* (New York: Harper and Row, 1963), 23.

15. Eliade, *The Quest*, 7.

16. Eliade's description of "sacred" is as follows: the sacred is equivalent to a power, and, in the last analysis, to reality. The sacred is saturated with being. Sacred power means reality and at the same time enduringness and efficacy. Eliade, *The Sacred and Profane* (New York: Harcourt, Brace, and World, 1959).

17. For an overview of sacred places, see Mircea Eliade, *Patterns in Comparative Religions* (New York: Meridian Books, 1972).

18. Joseph Epes Brown, *The Sacred Pipe* (New York: Penguin Books, 1977). Concerning the term "wakan," Joseph Brown writes, "Throughout this work I shall translate the Lakota word wakan as 'holy' or 'sacred' rather than as 'power' or 'powerful' as used by some ethnologists. The latter term may be a true translation, yet it is not really complete, for with the Sioux, and with all traditional peoples in general, the 'power' (really the sacredness) of a being or a thing is in proportion to its nearness to its prototype; or better, it is in proportion to the ability of the object or act to reflect most directly the principle or principles which are in Wakan-Tanka, the Great Spirit, who is One" (3-4).

19. W. Montgomery Watt, *Muhammad: Prophet and Statesman* (New York: Oxford University Press, 1976), 19.

20. I am utilizing the account of Father Virgilio Elizondo, "Our Lady of Guadalupe as a Cultural Symbol: The Power of the Powerless," *Concilium*, 1977.

21. For a brilliant account of the impact of this tradition on Mexican national consciousness, see Jacques La Faye, *Quetzalcoatl and Guadalupe: The Origin of Mexican National Consciousness* (Chicago: University of Chicago Press, 1975).

22. The persistence of this tradition was made vividly clear to me one day in the summer of 1973 in Pilsen, the largest Chicano barrio in Chicago, where I saw a sign painter with a tattoo of the Virgin covering his entire back.

23. For accounts of this kind of ecstasy experienced in many cultures, see especially the chapter "Initiatory Sicknesses and Dreams," in Eliade, *Shamanism*, 33-66.

Mexican American Home Altars
Toward Their Interpretation

Kay Turner

AUTHOR'S NOTE: *When I wrote this article, published as a Research Note in Aztlán almost twenty years ago, I was a graduate student in folklore at the University of Texas. Under the tutelage of Américo Paredes I was just beginning my formal exploration of Mexican American women's home altars in South Texas and this, my first effort at academic publishing, was an attempt to share my initial thoughts on the subject. Those thoughts, re-read in the year 2000 with some self-critique, nonetheless contain the seeds of my theoretical perspective on women's home altars, a perspective that has carried my work forward on the subject for the past two decades. For this anthology, I have rewritten and rearranged the article only for purposes of clarity. Because it was, to my knowledge, the first article published on Mexican American women's home altars, it stands in this book as a historical artifact of the early years of Chicano scholarship, an era rich in the discovery and analysis of new or long-overlooked Mexican contributions to American culture.*

In the years since writing this piece, I have continued my research interests in women's personal devotional arts. My interpretive frame shifted from folk art analysis—the perspective given here—to feminist aesthetics in my dissertation "Mexican American Women's Home Altars: The Art of Relationship" (University of Texas, 1990). The dissertation reflects an expanded fieldwork base (from Austin to Laredo) and, perhaps most important, records portions of in-depth interviews accomplished over a ten-year period with a number of altar makers—my teachers in the tradition—whom I came to know well and greatly admired. Social and behavioral aspects of the altar making tradition (especially as it relates to mothering and to women's developed allegiance with the saints and aspects of the Virgin Mary) are documented and analyzed in detail in the dissertation.

Over the past two decades I also have documented and studied women's altars representing other traditions—Afro-Caribbean, Sicilian, Wiccan, lesbian, and more—in settings throughout the United States. The results of my broader treatment, which also contains material from my dissertation, was recently published in book form as Beautiful Necessity: The Art and Meaning of Women's Altars (New York and London: Thames and Hudson, 1999). I invite readers of this article to pursue my other works; they bring to fruition the seeds that were planted here.

This research contributes toward the interpretation of a tradition among Mexican American women: the creation and maintenance of altars in the home.[1] Called *altarcitos* (personal altars) by their makers, these intimate devotional sites filled with religious images, family photos, candles, flowers, and mementos testify to a long-standing tradition of Catholic women's religious practice aimed particularly at creating and maintaining beneficial relationships between the earthly family (relatives, friends, and community) and the heavenly family (God, Christ, the Virgin Mary, and the saints). Home altars aesthetically model the necessity of good relationships and interconnection; they are a dynamic kind of folk art purposefully concerned with communication between a woman and her divine allies. A study of making altarcitos was carried out in the spring of 1979 by four graduate students in folklore at the University of Texas. In addition, they produced a videotape, "Home Altars: A Women's Tradition," for airing on a public access cable television channel in Austin, Texas, the site of the research project. Though altarcitos are considered by their makers to be contiguous with public altars in the Roman Catholic Church, home altars are distinctive because they represent a private, and most important, a creative source of religious experience. Previous to the Texas-based research project presented here, I had observed domestic altars in Mexico, Guatemala, southern Italy, New Mexico, New Jersey, and New York City. None was exactly like another, yet all made use of similar materials and, cross culturally, the same set of relations among materials was visibly present.

The four female consultants who figure centrally in this research are members of the same Catholic church and have lived in the same East Austin barrio for decades. They speak Spanish almost exclusively and maintain a tradition of home altar making which has been passed most usually from mother to daughter. Subsequent study of the Mexican American altarcito tradition will address in detail the ethnographic basis of the research, including full-length portraits of the altar makers and their individual sense of style in creating the sites.

In the semiological sense, altarcitos are richly significant in the way they visually and artistically model an ideal of good, productive relationships between various distinct domains (secular/sacred; material/spiritual; earth/ heaven). In fact, the home altar may be most inclusively defined as a personal, iconic representation of the power of relationship.[2] Additionally, the home altar is an instrument for the perpetuation of productive relationships because it marks the site where communication (the active means of establishing and maintaining relationships) between deities and humans takes place.

Though several modes of interpretation (e.g., sociolinguistic or historical) might productively be used to explore the meaning of home altars, I prefer initially to see them within the largest frame of meaning that addresses their essentially visual-material presentation. This frame is the folk art aesthetic. Clifford Geertz, concerned with developing a semiotics of art, has suggested the provocative idea that "to study an art form is to explore a sensibility, that such a sensibility is essentially a collective formation. ... [art forms] materialize a way of experiencing, bring a particular cast of mind out into the world of objects, where men can look at it" (1976, 1478). What the home altar visually (semiotically) contributes to the experience of Mexican American life is a religiously based folk aesthetic of connectedness: the sacred sense of family or community.

Feminists exploring women's traditional art forms have noted their networking properties. The term draws on cross-culturally encountered traditional understandings of women as inventors and primary practitioners of the cultural arts that are fundamentally concerned with linking like and/ or unlike materials together: material arts such as quilting and cooking, and social arts such as negotiation and mediation. Altar makers who, in a bricolage mode, combine a variety of images from diverse domains—personal and universal, religious and secular—creatively portray the networking principle as a religiously inspired ideal that can be individually interpreted within the bounds of the altar tradition.

The aesthetic of connectedness or networking evidenced in the altar-making tradition is unmistakably an integrated artistic (i.e., imagistically portrayed) and social (i.e., behaviorally realized) ideal of relation and interrelation. In this sense, home altars and their makers can be looked upon as a source for further understanding the role Mexican American women play in facilitating human relationship and interrelationship in the context of the family and the community. Though I dislike separating these two interdependent realms—art and behavior—for the sake of this theoretical analysis I will primarily focus on the visual-artistic composition of the home altar. I make minimal reference to ephemeral social behavior, which obviously requires extended treatment. In presenting the following material as a research note, I am interested for now in responses that would corroborate or criticize my presentation of home altars as religious folk art; for future expansion of this research I am interested in those respondents who might enlarge the social behavioral interpretation of home altars and their makers.

The theoretical underpinnings of my interpretation are grounded in a recent concern for the development of a more adequate conception of ethnoaesthetics. A number of scholars in the fields of anthropology, folk-lore, and art history have contributed to my initial thinking about altar aesthetics. I introduce—but only briefly—some of their core ideas, ones that have particularly stimulated my interpretation. I find useful Robert Plant Armstrong's sense of aesthetics as "*affecting things* and *events*, which are those cultural objects and happenings … in any given culture … accepted by those native to that culture as being purposefully concerned with potency, emotions, values, and states of being or experience" (1971, 3–4). I would also cite Johannes Fabian and Ilona Szombati-Fabian's provocative recon-sideration of certain constituents of folk art analysis, especially repetition, imitation, and triviality, as "cultural diagnostics" capable of demonstrating "the degree to which the production of images has come to express a com-munal or societal consciousness" (1980, 279). The home altar is filled with "affecting things" that give expression to a woman's religious and societal consciousness. Furthermore, I find useful the Fabians' criticism of Geertz's ideational conception of the relation between art and culture:

> A conception of culture as semiosis alone … may describe the nature of relationships between things cultural but it does not really address the problem of their genesis or, more precisely, of their production. In other words, we feel that we can only go along with Geertz's postulate that connections between art and society are "ideational" if ideation is seen as a practical activity, a mode of production. (258)

The *production* of *productive relationship* is the "practical activity" that drives the art of the altar. And this is accomplished through the altar maker's lifelong repetition of aesthetic processes—the visual art of image assembly and the verbal art of prayer—she considers to be ultimately pragmatic in achieving the benefits of devotion. The Fabians also present an excellent model for the study of folk art materials as these materials imply "totalities," that is, as they mediate and give access to "total contexts (urban life style, economics, a certain aesthetic sensibility, and, indeed, a kind of conscious-ness or world view)" (268).

The way that folk art products, such as home altars, give rise to "totalities" underscores folklorist Michael Owen Jones's disdain for the preoccupation with the question of whether or not any particular phenom-enon is folk art. Such preoccupation assumes that

> there are distinguishing features and consistent criteria for making this attribution, when in fact the process of conceptualization is intuitive, the standards variable, and the bases elusive. What distinguishes folkloristics

as a field of study is not so much a data base that can or should be labeled folklore or folk art but a method comprising questions, hypotheses, and models emphasizing and examining behavior. (1980, 330)

Even without the inclusion here of detailed data, I suggest that the study of home alters and their makers could provide an eloquent model of the relation between folk art and behavior. The home altar is never a mere display of objects; any understanding of the tradition requires an immersion in its context: the life, faith, beliefs, attitudes, hopes, and dreams of it maker.

Finally, George Kubler's concept of "real and virtual intersections" (Fleming 1974, 158–59) in the study of artifacts and art forms constitutes another motivation for my study of home altars. Kubler's "real intersections" are defined by Fleming as the demonstrable relations between artifacts and other cultural subsystems. With regard to home altars, we can evaluate them for real parallels that they exhibit with other systems such as the family.

Virtual intersections on the other hand are "noncausal, unprovable but possible correspondences and conformities between artifacts [or, I believe, art products] and cultural constructs" (1974, 159). In Kubler's own words virtual intersections "exist as possibilities, and it is in them that we can hope to discover some latent system of relations far more instructive than those revealed by the study of real problems" (1969, 8–9). The analysis of home altars points to possible virtual intersections concerning, for example, generative principles at work in other types of women's traditional art making such as quilting and cooking.

Analysis

Folklorists use the term *community* as a core concept for capturing people's capacity for identification with and support of each other. We distinguish the use of the word community in two ways. The first is territorial; the concept thus refers to a shared context of location, historically or currently. Generally, this sense of community as territory is local: the town, the village, the neighborhood, the parish, perhaps the region, are the loci of study. The second usage of community by folklorists is most relevant to this study; it is what Gusfield has termed the *relational* usage, and points to the *quality* or character of human relationships without necessary reference to location (1975, xvi). The two uses are not exclusive; rather, a major thrust of folkloristic studies within territorial bounds has been toward the examination of how communities achieve or diminish relations and identities through the use of traditional means: song, storytelling, art making, and so on.

Folklorists have always been concerned with the creation of art as an essential act of both literally and expressively circumscribing the community. The folk artist most clearly distinguishes her/his concern by achieving a larger identity through the work; in effect, the work will be burdened with this concern. In a sense, the folk artist sets aside individuality with the hope of representing a communal ideal in the execution of a piece. This is never to imply that folk artists do not express themselves fully; folk art is never a mere replication of tradition. But folk artists are generally concerned with the social interactive meaning of art. Folk artists contribute to and help maintain a sense of community, a unified quality of relationship. The making of folk art is, therefore, participatory, continuous through a history, as well as systemic and subject to transformation as the community of which it is a sign changes, or the artist, as a member of the community, perceives the need to initiate change.

Henry Glassie has said that the pleasure of folk art is "in the pleasure of the esoteric and traditional." The joy of the "esoteric and traditional" is encountered in the community, for in the community face-to-face (similarly *mask-to-mask* and *image-to-image*) interrelationship is essential. People come together around a central identity that they uphold through a sharing of symbols, for example names, images, implements, and sacred territories. Any traditional community exhibits this flow between symbolic and social relations.

Vitalizing community symbols are both historical (they persist and change through time) and unconscious as well. Their unconscious function is best understood in the sense that the materials of myth, religion, and art have to do with the formation of inner, spiritual, or psychic attitudes. The development of an inner attitude, a way of looking at the whole of life, is the first work of the community. The closed circle has often been used to symbolically designate community; the life view (or ethos) rises from that sense of enclosure, which, for the community, is the ineffable sense of holding together.

Of course, communities are rarely isolated; they intersect and affect each other. And any person may simultaneously hold membership in several communities. For example, the consultants for this study are, at once, communicants of a church parish, citizens of Texas, members of the greater Mexican cultural group, and mothers of extended families. The religious folk art tradition they express in the creation of altars serves to unify the separate but interdependent communities in which these women participate. Still, their primary sense of community derives from the profane, sacred, actual, and metaphorical meanings of the family. The family is the first community out of which others are created. If home altars are an iconic representation of the power of relationship, and power as relationship, it is blood relations that serve to model all others. Because the family is a bodily manifestation of the power of connection, perhaps no one knows the importance of this power as deeply as the one who makes it possible: the mother, whose umbilical cord connected to the child, is the most archaic sign of relation.

History of Home Altars

There is very little extant historical material on the keeping of home altars in Western Roman Catholic tradition. It is not a form of religious expression officially recognized by the Roman Catholic Church. Because it has been predominantly a women's tradition in a male-dominated church, and certainly because of its remarkable similarity and probable historic link to the pagan practice of maintaining house gods, women's domestic altar making—a globally encountered folk tradition of the Roman Catholic faith—is denied any formal history by the institution that indirectly makes it possible.

Available documentation dates the construction of religious altars (in general) to long before the Christian era began. Edmund Leach classifies the altar as a threshold between this world and the other (1976, 86). The most archaic altars were made of earth or piles of stone to mark an encounter between a person and the gods. According to Bolle's short history of altars in the *New Catholic Encyclopedia*, an altar is "a place designated by custom or tradition for the presentation of sacrifices or other offerings to superhuman beings (God, ancestors, etc.) *which reveals and guarantees communication with the other world*" (1967, 343, emphasis added). From earliest times, good communication between heaven and earth was made possible at the altar site; this same purpose of communication motivates the building of home altars today.

The first Christian altar was the table on which Jesus celebrated the Last Supper. The Christian altar's original association with feeding and nourishment is continuous with the pagan tradition of sacrifice or "eating the gods" at the altar. Food symbolism and physical nourishment are ancient signs and acts indicating communication with the gods. This becomes relevant in considering that the oldest altars are a central representation of the powers of earth, its fruitfulness and abundance and its archetypal designation as feminine. Bolle says:

> This idea [that the altar is a representation of earth] is at the heart of all altar symbolism. Hence the most archaic altars are made of earth or natural stone, which stands for the earth. ... The earth symbolism is never totally abandoned, even when altars become larger and even elaborate structures. The Roman temples had elevated altars for celestial deities and low altars or excavations in the earth for chthonic deities. ... Among the Indo-Europeans generally the hearth (deified as Vesta in Rome) appears to be the prototype of the altar. (343)

In current Mexican American home altar making, the original themes of nourishment and earth power are reiterated still, albeit more diffusely, abstractly. The home altar remains a site for the promotion of a maternal ideology based in generation and regeneration, principles originally associated with Mother Earth.

Though there is as yet no direct documentation to prove so, I suggest that the old Roman and Greek traditions of hearth worship and propitiation of household gods (*lares* and *penates*) were never fully obliterated by Christianity but rather incorporated and preserved in covert practice. Contemporary observation shows that home altars are maintained today by women in Greece and Italy as well as Spain. It seems possible that the current Mexican American tradition evolved from the early Christian era, spread from Italy to Spain, was eventually brought here from Europe during the period of conquest, and was then assimilated with preconquest Mexican traditions of keeping home altars.

Some documentary evidence from the major chroniclers of the conquest reports that household shrines were kept by indigenous peoples. For example, Landa (1937, 56–57) states that near or under their beds Mayan women on the Yucatán Peninsula maintained personal idols dedicated to Ixchel, the goddess of the moon, fertility, and childbirth. Considering the many syncretic "coincidences" (see Wolf 1959) that facilitated the conquest, it seems likely that Catholic Spaniards encountered indigenous home altars in Mesoamerica, and that as time went on, the images of the old Mexican gods and goddesses were supplanted by those of Christ, the Virgin Mary, and saints.[3]

Women's Altars and the Power of Relationship

The Mexican American altars I studied in East Austin are each composed bricoleur-style by the matriarch of the family. She is a folk artist par excellence in her commitment to creatively expressing, through an assemblage of images, a belief in sustaining the ultimate vitality of the family and community. Altar items are accumulated over time yet each one resonates to all others; the combination and association of images increases the power of any particular piece. The most important objects on the altar are statues of the Virgin and saints, which comprise, in effect, a women's version of her holy family. The most prominent statue on altars observed in Austin was that of Our Lady of Guadalupe, the Great Mother of Mexico, one from whom the spiritual sense of Mexican community is received. Other statues encountered frequently in Texas Mexican American altars included St. Anthony, petitioned to find lost things and to make good love matches; Santo Niño de Atocha, an elaborately enthroned and regally crowned variation of the infant Jesus; the Sacred Heart of Jesus, a central image of kinship, the home, and sacrifice; and assorted statuary of other aspects of the Virgin, including Our Mother of Mt. Carmel, Our Lady of the Miraculous Medal, and most significantly La Virgen de San Juan de los Lagos (Our Lady of St. John of the Lakes), whose origin is in Mexico and who is widely venerated in Texas.

According to Ouspensky, the images or icons of the saints and Jesus and Mary are theologically based on the Incarnation, suggesting that Christianity is not only the revelation of the Word of God, but also of the bodily Image of God disclosed in the God-Man, Jesus:

> Accordingly the liturgical tradition of the Orthodox Church connects the icon with the earthly life of Christ, with His image "made without hands." The image ... is above all Christ Himself, ... revealed "in the temple of His body." His icon is an authentic testimony of His Incarnation. (1967, 324)

The body is a central metaphor for relationship—only in the body and through the body do humans come into relation with others. That home altars are populated primarily with body images is an indication of the essential desire to bring spiritual and physical, sacred and profane realms together through incarnation—a reliance on the body as the chief source of knowing and being known.

As well, votive candles, flowers, and *milagros* are found, without exception, on all the East Austin altars. *La vela prendida*, or the ever-burning candle, symbolizes the light of faith, that active acknowledgement of relationship between the human and the divine. Moreover, candles remind us of the origin of altars as hearths, a root metaphor for domesticity and the feminine. Additional candles are lighted to establish relation between a saint and a particular person in need; that the relationship has been prayed for and achieved is symbolized by the light of the candle. By nature of its burning, energy-expending glow the candle perfectly represents the heat and dynamism of an ongoing relationship between, for example, the Virgin of Guadalupe and one of her daughters on earth. The relative instability and fleetingness of relationship is marked by the burning, wavering flicker, too. These relationships between home and heaven must be kindled and rekindled again as time goes on, but nothing represents them as present and vitalizing the way the votive candle does. One of our consultants, Sra. Zapata, besides keeping several votive candles on her altar, also maintains an electric lamp that is never turned off; this eternal light is in keeping with her desire to remain in constant personal relation with the power of what she calls the *corte celestial* (the celestial court), which is all the saints on her altar.

Milagros (or ex-votos) are tiny (1-by-1/2 inch) amulet-like sculptures made of brass, tin, nickel, and sometimes silver or gold in the shape of an arm, leg, hand (all body parts are represented), cow, car, house, child, man, or woman. These offerings comprise miniature replicas of the physical, especially the bodily aspects of the world, which are subject to the fate of damage, injury, or other misfortune. If a leg is arthritic, a prayer is made and a leg-shaped milagro is hung on a favorite saint with the hope of gaining relief. Milagros are also presented as gifts exchanged for answered petitions. In the use of milagros, a symbolic relation is drawn between the macrocosmic, actual world of bodies and the microcosmic, iconic-symbolic world of bodies. The small, tin image of a hand, for example, as sympathetic analog of a real hand is considered a true representation to the saint of a particular locus in need of healing relation. Milagros are *thing* or *place* or especially *bodily* specific in terms of what they represent, again a fine example of the dominant sensibility expressed in the altar tradition: that blessing or grace is received through the powerful communication achieved in recognizing correspondences between the symbolic and the actual, between images of the body and real bodies, between heaven and earth.

Ancestral and present-day family photographs are almost always found on the Austin altars. Sometimes propped against a statue, often stuck inside the edge of a framed picture of the Virgin, these pictures are an obvious demonstration of the relation the altar maker assigns between her family and the heavenly family. Sra. Pérez has hung an heirloom, hand-colored photograph of her mother and father at the same level as a gilded, flower-encircled painting of Our Lady of Guadalupe. Both mothers look down protectively from the walls onto the small, meticulously kept altar below.

To see kinship pictures enmeshed with images of the celestial family is to see the full meaning of the altar as a simultaneous sacred and artistic site. For in both religious experience and artistic expression we expect to experience the interlocking of cosmos and history, of space and time. This breaking down of orders and dichotomies, the two families united as one at the altar, is the essence of art and the sacred.

Other items included in the composition of an altar are more idiosyncratic and vary from maker to maker according to taste and personal symbolic sense. Often flowers (plastic and real), shells, and stones are generously distributed about. Of course, the Virgin is associated with flowers; the rose is the flower of Guadalupe so one expects to find roses on a Mexican American altar. Additional displays of nature imagery suggest a more diffuse but necessary sense of abundance.

Altars, especially women's domestic altars, have, since prehistory, addressed the desire for fertility and fruitfulness. They have been sites of special identification with earth-derived (feminine archetypal) powers. A necessary prerequisite to achieving the *ideal* of power as relationship is a state of receptivity sought at the altar site. The earth has long symbolized the receptivity that enables fertility and reproduction. That fruits of the earth, flowers, and shells are present on Mexican American altars is a visual sign of their makers' receptivity to power that they believe will insure productive, harmonious living.

In contrast to, but always in relation with, the images of saints and the Virgin, one finds pictures or statues of political figures on or near the altar. In the United States, the martyred Kennedys are seen as directly analogous to the saints who died for their faith, and pictures of the two brothers are occasionally in evidence. The presence of other state figures, including the current president or even local politicians, suggests the altar is a site where sacred and secular powers are symbolically represented as being in relation even though religious dogma and state law preserve their strict and generally separate domains.

The most idiosyncratic pieces on the altar are also usually the most anomalous. As might be expected, the most necessary items, such as sacred statuary, are centrally located while oddities are given their place on the periphery. Comprising an utter carnival of varicolored, varivoiced objects one would think abnormal on an altar table, they are nevertheless repeatedly encountered, especially at the edges of a display. These unusual "icons" include stuffed animals, bottles of buttons, travel souvenirs, knickknacks, teacups—the conceivable and, more likely, the inconceivable. Yet, in understanding the altar as an iconic assemblage that signifies the power of relationship, it is perfectly appropriate that this power should embrace items that formally do not fit the scheme. Crucial to the ideal of relationship are continuity and inclusion, the conscious attempt to draw together people, places, things, and institutions that do not necessarily function in terms of each other.

In addition, the inclusion of seemingly anomalous objects on the altar makes a specific claim that altar making is not ultimately rule-bound. As bricoleur, the altar maker clearly maintains her creative independence in assigning highly personal and idiosyncratic symbols to the altar. In so doing, the microcosmic view of the world realized at her altar becomes even more dramatically *her* view, of the sacred and secular worlds and their connection.

Her view is promoted and affirmed on a daily basis through specific acts of devotion. At the site of her altar, usually sitting in a chair or sometimes kneeling, a woman makes petition to her favored saints through prayer (*rezos promesas, mandas*) and praise (*oraciones, alabanzas*). The altar is the place where active mediation between heaven and earth is accomplished. If the home altar stands as a visual representation of the desire for relationship, it is the use of ritual and language there that fulfills the altar tradition's potential for actually achieving the benefits of relationship. The altar is a visual model of shared power between a women and her divine allies, but, most important, it is an instrument for the mediated exchange of that power.

Meditation is at the heart of all activity that takes place at the home altar. Women facilitate relationship and interrelationship through mediation. Almost all communicative activity at the altar site is dedicated to the facilitation of relationship through a religiously derived mode of mediation: intercession. The Virgin Mary is the primary model of the power of intercession. Just as She is asked by all the Austin altar makers to intercede between them and God for their needs, so they as mothers will be asked to intercede in any of a number of cases where family or other social relationship has fallen apart: between father and son, for example, the mother is often the only one who can carry a message of need or a request for permission. Mediation and networking recommend a horizontal, earth-bound, spreading out and crossing of boundaries to insure the life-flow of relationship between structurally opposed domains. This is in contrast to the rigidity of hierarchical, vertically structured institutions. These domains, though we tend to think of them as discontinuous (son vs. father, public vs. private, church vs. home, heaven vs. earth) are, in fact, continuous. Mediation, networking, and intercession perpetually reaffirm this continuity. Women, as mediators, collapse the formal barriers to relationship by emphasizing a cyclically based dialogue between seemingly discrete entities. All the women we came to know through the altars project insisted that *asking* is the necessary counterpart of *answering* just as *giving* is the complement of *receiving;* they are aspects of the same cycle, a cycle propelled effectively by mediation and networking. As Sra. Pescina told us so many times: "El pedir es fuerza, el dar es voluntad" (One asks because of need, one gives because one wishes).

In a recent paper entitled "Is Female to Male as Nature Is to Culture?" (1974), Sherry Ortner proposes a new meaning of woman as mediator. In conventional structuralist and sociohistorical terms, nature (the feminine and the female) and culture (the masculine and the male) oppose each other, placing women essentially outside the demesne of culture. This is the basis for other structural oppositions, most notably the domestic/public split: domesticity, associated with women and children, is opposed to polity, the public powers associated with male authority. But, according to Ortner, women, as the instrumental figures in the domestic sphere actually occupy "an intermediate position between culture and nature" (84). She goes on to say that:

> intermediate may have the significance of "mediating," i.e. performing some sort of synthesizing or converting function between nature and culture.... The domestic unit—and hence woman, who in virtually every case appears as its primary representative—is one of culture's crucial agencies for the conversion of nature into culture, especially with reference to the socialization of children. (84)

What the study of home altars clearly points to is a need to fully reassess the meaning and function of the domestic sphere on its own terms as a crucial but different *cultural* domain. Ultimately, the domestic altar is a woman's instrument for "converting" non-relation into relation, and this carries the sense of converting nature into culture, especially because women inherit the tradition from their mothers and use the tradition as mothers to fortify family life and assure the healthy and productive socialization of their children.

Viewed as a kind of women's folk art, the Mexican American home altar exemplifies a particular aesthetic of connection and relation which the artist Miriam Schapiro has aptly called *femmage* (Meyer and Schapiro 1978, 68–69). Femmage is the term Schapiro applied to the process that seems evident in so much of women's domestic art making, the process of collecting and creatively assembling odd or seemingly disparate elements into a functional, integrated whole.[4] Essentially, femmage is the art of "making something out of nothing" and in this sense, both metaphorically and literally, resonates with the most basic of female biological functions: intrauterine creation of the child—the making of *someone* out of nothing. In the making of the home altar, femmage is the process of assembling a powerful association of images, a family of images that synthesizes and projects the fundamental social and spiritual values of the family: nurturance, relationship, and a sense of place.

Gregory Bateson believes that the attainment of grace is sought through any art. For him all art is a "particular sort of partly unconscious communication" and an invitation to engage in interface communication between conscious and unconscious realms (1972, 138). Using Freud's sense of unconscious communication as *primary process*, Bateson says that it is mainly carried out through metaphor and image (139). The highest purpose of art (an essentially unconscious phenomenon), then, is to aid consciousness in realizing "an inevitable fact":

> that mere purposive rationality unaided by such phenomena as art, religion, dream, and the like, is necessarily pathogenic and destructive of life; ... life depends upon interlocking *circuits* of contingency ... love can survive only if wisdom (i.e., a sense or recognition of the fact of circuitry) has an effective voice. (146)

The traditional Mexican American altar maker—the wise women—has long been visually and verbally articulating Bateson's claim.

Notes

1. The domestic altar-making tradition is not *exclusively* a women's practice; however, the tradition is most often performed and maintained by women. In my research thus far I have never encountered a man who kept an altar and prayed there regularly. I am extremely interested in hearing from *Aztlán* readers who can address the male dimensions of home altar use. [Twenty years later, I am still convinced that folk Catholic altars are *primarily* a woman's religious art form].

2. *Iconic* has both religious and semiotic definitions that may be usefully applied to the primary objects found on the altar. In the Peircian sense of iconic (1940) the relation between signifier and signified manifests a "community of some

quality": a similarity or fitness of resemblance proposed by the sign to be understood by the receiver. The home altar is an iconic, visual presentation of the meaning of relationship itself, the fitness to be recognized being the necessary equivalence between the domestic family, the community family, and the heavenly family. In Christian religious tradition the icon (actually a likeness of God, Christ, Mary, or the saints in media such as sculpture or painting) is a testimony to the relation between God and man and of man's life in God. "The icon is a visible expression of the patristic formula: God became Man in order that man may become god" (Ouspensky 1967, 324). The icon does not truly present Divinity; it indicates through symbolic pictorial language, the participation of believers in divine life.

3. Much of my research on the early history of home altars in Mexico remains to be done. The work of archaeologist K. V. Flannery is highly suggestive in regard to preconquest domestic altars. His discovery of home altars in a Formative Stage (1300 B.C.) settlement near Oaxaca yields the earliest evidence I know of the tradition. [See my dissertation [1990] for an extensive bibliography on the ancient history of domestic alters.]

4. Miriam Schapiro derived the term femmage from the names of techniques such as decoupage, collage, assemblage, and photomontage, all of which have in common the act of assembling diverse elements or images to create a single, new artistic statement.

Work Cited

Armstrong, Robert Plant. 1971. *The Affecting Presence*. Urbana: University of Illinois Press.

Bateson, Gregory. 1972. *Steps to an Ecology of the Mind*. New York: Chandler.

Bolle, K. W. 1967. "Altar: Historical Background." In *New Catholic Encyclopedia*. Vol. A. New York: McGraw Hill & Co.

Fabian, Johannes, and Ilona Szombati-Fabian. 1980. "Folk Art from an Anthropological Perspective." In *Perspectives on American Folk Art*, ed. Ian Quimby and Scott Swank. New York: W. W. Norton.

Flannery, Kent V. 1976. "Contextual Analysis of Ritual Paraphernalia from Formative Oaxaca." In *The Early Mesoamerican Village*, ed. K. V. Flannery. New York: Academic Press.

Fleming, E. McClung. 1974. "Artifact Study: A Proposed Model." In *Winterthur Portfolio* 9, ed. Ian M. G. Quimby. Charlottesville: University Press of Virginia.

Geertz, Clifford.1976. "Art as a Cultural System." *Modern Language Notes* 91: 1473–99.

Gusfield, Joseph R. 1975. *Community: A Critical Response*. New York: Harper & Row.

Jones, Michael Owen. 1980. "L.A. Add-Ons and Re-Dos." In *Perspectives on American Folk Art*, ed. Ian Quimby and Scott Swank. New York: W. W. Norton.

Kubler, George. 1969. "Time's Perfection and Colonial Art." In *Spanish, French, and English Traditions in the Colonial Silver of North America*. Winterthur, Del.: Winterthur Museum.

Landa, Friar Diego de. 1937. *Relación de las cosas Yucatán*. Translated by William Gates. 1566. Baltimore: The Maya Society. Reprint: New York: Dover Publications, 1978.

Leach, Edmund. 1976. *Culture and Communication*. London: Cambridge University Press.

Meyer, Melissa, and Miriam Schapiro. 1978. "Waste Not, Want Not." *Heresies* 4:66–69.

Ortner, Sherry. 1974. "Is Female to Male as Nature Is to Culture?" In *Women, Culture and Society*, ed. Michelle Rosaldo and Louise Lamphere. Stanford: Stanford University Press.

Ouspensky, L. 1967. "Icon." In *New Catholic Encyclopedia*. Vol. 1. New York: McGraw Hill & Co.

Peirce, Charles. 1940. *Selected Writings*. New York: Harcourt Brace Jovanovich.

Wolf, Eric. 1959. *Sons of the Shaking Earth*. Chicago: University of Chicago Press.

III.
Configuring Identities

Configuring Identities
Introduction

Chela Sandoval

In previous chapters we looked at how Chicana and Chicano scholarship has sought to decolonize lands, histories, and politics. Indeed, Chicano/a scholarship has been directed toward the decolonization of identity itself. But what does it mean to say this? How have we gone about disinhabiting, recultivating, and reoccupying who we are, what we have become? How much in control are we of the identities we express? These are the questions we face in the twenty-first century, questions to which there are changing answers. The following essays a) track Indian, Spanish, mestizo/a, Chicano/a, and Latino/a identities as they reconfigure over history, b) examine the transformations of these identities as they respond to state and global power apparatuses, and c) describe identity as a political survival strategy. Each article argues that to "decolonize the territory" of identity—to act, or "perform," not just to ensure survival, but to bring peace and justice to the social world—means that one must examine one's own identity, how it has been constructed, and what ethical and moral purposes it serves or does not serve. This self-awareness can be thought of as a heightened and radical *conciencia de sí*: a consciousness in part comprised of the ability to transform identity, and the willingness to do so when required by ethical imperatives. The scholars we have selected for this section on "configuring identities" are all thinkers who have taken on the task of trying to understand what emancipatory identities for Chicano/as and Latino/as look like and feel like. How do these identities, as we asked in section 2, "perform," or enact, their liberation?

One of the great Chicana intellectual activists of the late twentieth century confronted these questions in her 1973 manifesto entitled "Chicanas and El Movimiento." Adaljiza Sosa Riddell lays the groundwork on

"Configuring Identities" when she describes the emotional, intellectual, and political beings who performed Chicano/a politics during the 1960–1973 period. Her argument is that Chicano and Chicana activists must have the courage to examine their own gender identities. In this sense, Sosa Riddell sees identity on its most fundamental level as negotiable, as a survival strategy that one can self-consciously reconfigure in order to bring about egalitarian changes. Her article is a call to action for Chicano activists to develop political compassion and solidarity with Chicana feminism, understood as an expansive politics capable of uplifting the entire community. To treat "Chicanas as an integral, not subordinate, part of the group we call Chicanos," she writes, must be one of the goals of the movement. Of all the important issues Chicanos and Chicanas face in the 1970s, she continues, "that of La Chicana" remains "the most problematic."

This problem that becomes a tragedy, in Sosa Riddell's view, is that Chicanos describe and define their "very being and existence" in terms of the conditions and values that were "imposed upon them by their colonizers and neocolonizers." As a result, she continues, our peoples have accepted into their everyday lives, into their very identities, "externally imposed stereotypes about Chicanas." These historically constructed gender and sex stereotypes constrain everyone, Sosa Riddell writes—but especially Chicanas. Until these stereotypes are recognized—and released—clashes over Chicana roles will persist unabated among our peoples such that "the Chicana" will continue to "feel guilty about what she is." Sosa Riddell's claim is that this is how Chicanas remain the most "direct heirs" of the subjugation of all our peoples to the Spanish, to Catholic imperialism, and then to Anglo conquest. Sosa Riddell's 1973 essay posits the following questions: In what ways are women subjugated within Chicano/a cultures, and why? What does it mean to be sexually subordinated? What does it mean to be subordinated by gender? In what ways are Chicanos also subjugated by gender stereotypes? By sex stereotypes? In what ways do sex and gender stereotypes restrict, control, or empower identities differently? What are the human and social changes that would be necessary to bring about "Chicana liberation," as well as more just social and human orders?

In 1973, Sosa Riddell wrote that if we do not answer these questions, Chicanos will not only continue to perpetuate the stereotypes and the very conditions those stereotypes support, but also will "be guilty of intensifying those conditions and their negative results" for all people. Adaljiza Sosa Riddell's essay is about how majoritarian stereotypes construct and affect identity for everyone, and it asks what kinds of relationships these constructed identities are creating, and will create ... in love, in sexual relations, in friendships, in community relations. The question of identity, then, not only for Sosa Riddell, but for all the scholars in section 3, becomes the problem of how we can go about transforming structures of domination and subordination both inside and outside of ourselves; and how these transformations can bring about new identities capable of supporting egalitarian change—not only for Chicanos and oppressed peoples understood as a generalized, singular group, but specifically for Chicanas, women, and children: the liberation from sex/gender stereotypes for us all. Sosa Riddell reminds us that flexibility of identity is necessary in order for us to engage such revolutionary processes. She exhorts us to remember that what is "Chicano exists in [a] diversity of truths, which poses a problem for analysts who would like to define once and for all what Chicano culture consists of." Indeed, when one has been colonized or subordinated, then it is all the more important to find the courage to examine one's own sense of identity, and to commit to whatever processes are necessary to transform that construct in the interests of more egalitarian and humane relationships: only then can the world itself be changed.

The question of *Qué somos?*—What are we?—reverberates throughout Chicano/a scholarship. The next article, written in 1976 by Ramón Gutiérrez, confronts this question by tracking the figuration of Chicano/a, Latino/a, and indigenous identities over time, histories, cultures, religions, circumstances, and geographies. Gutiérrez unravels "America's Hispanic Past" by showing us the ways in which that history is shot full of "internal stratification and class boundaries." What he identifies are the lines of force that have resulted in *many* different kinds of identities—many different kinds of "Chicano/as." Two important ideologies are challenged by Gutiérrez's article. First, that U.S. Hispanic, Spanish, Mexican, mestizo/a, and indigenous populations comprise one homogenous immigrant group, and second, that immigration scholarship can generalize about the impact of immigration on identity.

Several decades before the Pilgrims landed at Plymouth Rock, Spanish colonizers had already settled in the Southwest. Gutiérrez explains that they brought with them a strong *conciencia de sí*, consciousness of the self. He then tracks the history of this consciousness as it travels and transforms across time, incidents, and identities, in order to demonstrate how our "selves" are complexly and dynamically constructed. Gutiérrez begins by showing that when the fifteenth-century European colonizers of the U.S. Southwest arrived, they identified, by custom, according to the Spanish region where they were born. But in their confrontation with radical difference—that is, with indigenous populations—these colonizers immediately gathered up their own regional differences into a single unity—becoming "Spanish"—in order to construct that infamous binary opposition between themselves, *los españoles,* and the other, *los indios.* In the following three hundred years of contact, cohabitation, and marriage between these groups, however, this binary opposition became kaleidoscopically compounded. Gutiérrez's article asks the reader to watch these transforming identities as they are expressed through majoritarian labels such as *gente sin razón* and *gente de razón, californios, tejanos, nuevo mexicanos, mestizos, castizos, mulatos, genízaros, lobos, coyotes,* Mexicanos, Latinos, Indians, Latin Americans (as in the tejano organization LULAC), Mexican Americans, or "the Spanish."

When Spanish colonization was replaced with another colonization, however, new historical and social powers kaleidoscopically reconfigured once again how these populations would see themselves. The new Anglo American conquerors of the Southwest were unable to perceive distinctions among the diverse peoples they encountered, who, in their eyes, "all looked alike, dressed alike, spoke Spanish, and were fanatic Catholics." Gutiérrez shows us how this Anglo American perception economized all diversity into a single difference—that of "Mexican"—while erasing all others. By the mid-twentieth century, however, this phase too was challenged and replaced. With another manifold refiguration of identities came new names to describe them, including "American Indian," "Chicano," and "Chicana." These labels, once utilized to insult people holding "out-group" status, Gutiérrez writes, were reappropriated to became signs of "self-determination and ethnic militancy."

Gutiérrez implies that the fifteenth-century colonizer's need to view society as "hierarchically ordered" according to identity status is a conditioned need that continues to penetrate colonizer and colonized identities, even as these identities transform over time. Gutiérrez's 1976 hope is that Chicano/as recognize that the ways they identify themselves, and the ways they come to be identified by others, are power-filled and transformable social processes. What must go along with the renaming "Chicano/a," he believes, is the recognition that all identities are shot through with power. Like Sosa Riddell, who argues that what is "Chicano exists in [a] diversity of truths," Gutiérrez makes the point that there is no identity that can be understood as a "fixed and static entity." Rather, he writes, identity "ebbs and flows as history itself unfolds."

Nearly twenty years after the publication of Adaljiza Sosa Riddell's 1973 manifesto, Chicana sociologists Denise Segura and Beatriz Pesquera demonstrate that the aims of Chicana feminism have not yet been integrated into Chicano politics. Their 1992 article, "The Chicano Movement and Chicana Feminist Discourse," shows how this breach has resulted in the proliferation of Sosa Riddell's Chicana feminism into matrixes of possibility, potentiality, and viewpoints. Segura and Pesquera schematize these many Chicana feminisms into three primary categories: (a) Chicana liberal feminism, which advocates gender and race equality—and so, they write, "is not likely to emphasize the struggle against all forms of patriarchy"; (b) Chicana insurgent feminism, which "critiques inequality by race/ethnicity, class, gender, and sexual orientation," and calls for "revolutionary change to end all forms of oppression"—including homophobia; and (c) Chicana cultural nationalist feminism, which articulates a "feminist vision within the ideological rubric of *la familia*." This last mode of politics, they explain, struggles toward "justice and gender equality" while at the same time "adhering to and maintaining" traditional Chicano/a cultural forms.

These three forms of feminist politics differ in relation to the kinds of identities and politics for which they aim. Nevertheless, these modes of Chicana feminist politics are similar, Segura and Pesquera write, for they all express a "collectivist orientation" that is "grounded in the material condition" of Chicano/a peoples. Moreover, each feminist ideology arises in response to the "multiple sources" of Chicana oppression. There are two shared questions that further unite differing Chicana feminist ideologies. The first is how to go about resolving the tension that exists between their collective desires to end the subordination of Chicanas, on the one side, and Chicano cultural nationalism on the other, which Segura and Pesquera describe as continuing to "advocate racial/ethnic unity against Anglo American domination while idealizing traditional Chicano culture." The second question is just as important: How to go about resolving the tensions between Chicana feminisms and U.S. hegemonic feminisms, which stress "female unity against patriarchy." Both Chicano cultural nationalist and hegemonic feminist politics are skewed, Segura and Pesquera argue, the first in favor of race and ethnicity, the second in favor of gender. Neither is able to address "the unique situation of Chicanas," they write, whose very "life chances are dependent" upon the links between class, race/ethnicity, sex, and gender, and who similarly "share a physical, cultural, and material vulnerability to the dicta of men." For these reasons, they state, all Chicana feminisms are allied in a shared search "for an alternative discourse," one that can "integrate the eradication of patriarchy in the Chicano community, within a struggle against race/class domination."

Segura and Pesquera believe that a "union between nationalist and feminist" ideologies is possible, but only through what they describe as a "unique feminism" that is grounded in the experiences of people who are both "women and members of oppressed minority groups and classes." The Chicana feminism they propose would recognize all Chicana feminist expressions as tactics that can be "unified," they hope, when enacted through a coalitional method. Ongoing Chicano/a scholarship has described this method further as a process of "radical mestizaje" or as a "differential *conciencia de la mestiza*." What Segura and Pesquera have provided is a schema by which to understand the ethical and political implications of Chicano and Chicana politics in their patriarchal and feminist forms, whether these are manifested as integrationist, revolutionary, supremacist, nationalist, separatist, or as *la conciencia de la mestiza*.

The vision and passion of Sosa Riddell, Gutiérrez's use of historiography as method for tracking and unraveling Chicano/a and Latino/a identities, and Segura and Pesquera's commitment to generating more effective modes of feminist political consciousness are woven together in 1997 by Chicana historian Deena González. "Chicana Identity Matters" is based on the premise that all peoples access meaning according to how they have been gendered, sexed, raced, classed, and categorized. For González, then, "identity" is a corporeal, substantive construct that "matters." That is, identities are materially affected by the social world, but identities also tangibly affect that world. González argues that Chicana identities "matter" in specific ways.

This three-part article discusses (a) the general problem of identity, (b) the social creation of the identity "Chicana" in the Southwest, and (c) the new "transnational, transmigratory, first world cultural polyglot" identities produced by urban, lesbian Chicanas during the late twentieth century. Citing Gloria Anzaldúa, who writes that to be Chicana is to be "an image/that comes and goes/clearing and darkening," González demonstrates that being "Chicana" has always been problematized as "an identity in waiting, as an incomplete act." But this does not mean, she states, that Chicanas "do not know who we are." Rather, she continues, the irony is that Chicanas should "suffer the accusation that we know too much who we are, have too much identity." This is a paradoxical identity that is both too much and too little, and thus difficult to recognize and name: a situation that has resulted in Chicanas being made "invisible or absent in the academy."

Like Sosa Riddell, Gutiérrez, Segura, and Pesquera, González reminds us that from the beginning of Spanish contact, the search for identity has hinged on questions of status and social location. In those days "identity cards" were common, and dominant categorizations regulated one's access to individuality and choice in marriage. González points out that in this era claiming conquistador heritage was a better survival strategy than to claim mestizo or indigenous ethnicity. She then demonstrates how residual and "lingering" racial, cultural, class, and sexual tensions continue to operate as active structures around which identities are constructed. The label "Chicana" has been deployed as a means to challenge these structures, and is used, González writes, as a way to define Spanish-speaking women in any area presently considered a territory of the United States. Yet what must be remembered in deploying this label, González reminds us, is that there are no "true" Chicanas: for "if we have learned anything about authenticity," she continues, "and the power of authenticating, it is that such differentiations proceed along contrary lines historically and contemporarily."

The search for a liberatory sense of identity and secure homeland for U.S. "Chicano/as" was taken up forcefully during the late twentieth century, González writes, by urban, lesbian Chicanas such as Gloria Anzaldúa, Cherríe Moraga, Emma Pérez, and Alicia Gaspar de Alba, who have been distinguishing "identities in the multiples." It is among this recent generation of self-identified Chicanas, González writes, that "more fluid identities" are located. Indeed, the radical *conciencia de sí*, or political self-consciousness in the writings of both Anzaldúa and Pérez, embraces mestiza pasts that are "more blurring rather than less." So, too, Gaspar de Alba locates the term "Chicana" as an identity that can be assumed around "blurred linguistic borders." Whereas Moraga, González argues, privileges blood, color, or geography in identifying who is "Chicana," Anzaldúa, Pérez, and Gaspar de Alba establish an "ethnicity of the borderlands," which functions similarly to Anzaldúa's *la conciencia de la mestiza*. This conceptual "space," González asserts, is capable of one day allying Latino/a, Hispanic, Chicana, Native, Euroamerican, Third World, and/or transgendered others. It is a space of "reunification," she continues, a place Emma Pérez terms a *sitio*, and which is brought into being through a specific process I call "the methodology of the oppressed." Here, in this sitio, writes González, is the location of survival and homecoming for which all Chicano/as long.

All the articles we have read in sections 1, 2, and 3 of this volume demonstrate how "identity" is a major political concern for Chicano/as and Latino/as. David Román takes our investigation one step further in his 1997 article "Latino Performance and Identity." Román defines "performance" not only as theater, but as the many individual and social roles that citizen-subjects enact in their everyday lives. Román points out that it has often been "politically efficacious for people from distinct cultural backgrounds and ideological positions" to meet and organize under singular labels for identity, like "Chicano" and/or "Latino," even though such labels draw together, as if they are one, *many* different nationalities, ethnicities, races, cultural backgrounds, languages, genders, sexualities, and classes. The problem in using terms such as Chicano or Latino to solidify a collective and individual political identity that can resist majoritarian institutions, Román believes, is that this process of naming can make invisible the ways in which identity is also and foremost a flexible site of potentiality, struggle, and historical negotiation. The political problem is that in order to accomplish the political goals for which the terms "Chicano" or "Latino" were invented, other aspects of identity are dangerously sublimated—aspects such as gender, race, and sexuality. This is a political and identity paradox, and is one reason why many have chosen to understand the labels "Chicano/Latino" not as an identity, but as a process—that is, as a method comprised of shifting political *performances* in relation to power. One important outcome of engaging this method of performance politics—of differential and radical mestizaje politics—has been the development of what David Román terms a "necessary theater."

This Latino/a and Chicano/a "necessary theater" calls up varieties of identities through self-conscious performance. According to Román, necessary theater insists on the visibility and "coherence of Latino/Chicano identity even as it refuses to stabilize that identity as any one image, role, stereotype, or convention." Román explains how Latino/a, Puerto Rican, Cuban, and Chicano/a performance artists such as Guillermo Gómez Peña, Carmelita Tropicana, Luis Alfaro, Coco Fusco, Aliana Troyano, and Culture Clash each address identity, in any number of ways, by showing how it is both empowered and constrained by our various cultures. Their performances provide a variety of effects, Román writes: they can be oppositional to the practices of dominant Anglo culture or reflections of shattered identity in relation to exile or immigration, or demarcations of "new areas of Chicano sociality." Performances might locate participants as "border-subjects in a transglobal economy," or they may ask the spectator to locate and perform their own positionality. Sometimes, performances reinforce a type of cultural nationalism that, Román points out, "collapses all Latino experience into a unified heterosexual male subject by failing to account for the differences among Latino/as." But in other cases, he writes, "performances critique heteronormativity and the masculinization of traditional Chicano politics." Necessary theater posits such problematics as: how does one enact what it is to be female, to be "Latina," and when doing so, for whom is one performing, and for what reasons? What possible social and performative identities are available and/or useful to Latinos/as and Chicano/as who live in the midst of human suffering, class oppression, and turmoil? How can stereotypes of Chicano/as and Latino/as produced by Hollywood be challenged or used? These questions of aesthetics and politics can be answered in many different ways, but necessary theater performances always are arranged in order to demonstrate how both the stabilization as well as the reconfiguration of identities within our own cultures are inescapable activities.

What we can say about the radical performance theater of Chicano/as and Latino/as is this: like the potential dynamics of identity itself, necessary theater is comprised of self-conscious performances that are influenced by the immediate reality in which they unfold, at the same time that they also transform that very reality. In this sense these performances are "live," as in Román's example of *Día de los Vivos*, a Chicano/a-Latino/a performance piece that shapes and reshapes the actor's identity in the very act of performing it. This theater expresses the radical *conciencia de sí*, the *sitio* where many differential possibilities that are linked to the methodology of the oppressed can be enacted. Román's idea of Latino/a and Chicano/a identities in performance embodies the movement of meaning itself—and represents a new definition of the term "Chicano/a" as a process that can extend across and through all colonial boundaries.

This other definition of Chicano/a that reaches across colonial sex, gender, historical, cultural, language, class, geographic, political, and intellectual boundaries—across the category of the human itself—has been deployed by each of the scholars in this section as they grapple with what it means to be "indigenous," "Chicano/a," "Hispanic," and/or "Latino/a." Each essay extends beyond usual notions of what we are, and how we identify, in order to propose something else. This "something else" moves beyond the usual sex/gender binary of male/female, as well as all identity stereotypes. What each article adds up to is something that moves within, between, and through Chicano and Chicana politics, transforming everything it touches. This method of radical mestizaje can perhaps be indicated as Chicanisma: the politics of Chicanas.

After having read the articles in this section, where do you think we are today in relation to identity, to decolonizing the territory of identity, and to performing the politics of identity? How do our understandings of these processes empower us to reconfigure the world?

Chicanas and El Movimiento

Adaljiza Sosa-Riddell

AUTHOR'S NOTE: *When the first edition of the* Chicano Studies Reader *was published in 2001, I noted that the words in my 1974 article were constrained, cautious, content to stay within the boundary lines of cultural nationalism. Was this a misguided effort to preserve ethnic/racial unity? Probably, I did intend to promote Chicano Movimiento unity, but I was not misguided. I intended to convince the broader community outside of the Chicano community that they too share the burden of oppression. To the Chicano community, I was pleading for it to take another look, longer and deeper than before, and to acknowledge their own complicity with negative gender stereotypes and the anguish these things cause. Finally, my plea was for more research, the use of our own voices, to create an extensive body of literature speaking with our own voices, a literary heritage that could never be completely destroyed. Again, there was more left unsaid than was said. It seems I too hid behind the smoke and mirrors of our existence.*

What then would I change? I would first change the title to: Chicanas en el Movimiento. *One two-letter word seems so inconsequential, changing* and *to* en. *Yet I remember many long, heated arguments: Should we write in Spanish or English or caló? Should we provide articles in various languages? Should we use side-by-side translations, or could we mix all words in a new form of "spanglish"? Was this Chicano Spanish?*

Beyond this unresolved issue of language(s), I would move to a more definitive and clearer discussion of what Chicanas had been to el movimiento precursors, their leadership roles in many aspects of el movimiento. In more recent research projects, I have discovered a multi-dimensional grid of political activities, somewhat of a fourth and fifth dimension. I have also concluded that las mujeres were often much more radical then their male counterparts, especially when they confronted patriarchal control of their own sexuality. Why were we so afraid of speaking to our realities? Were we afraid of being used as a weapon to hurt our future generations? Or was it because we did not want to be labeled agringadas? Nor did we enjoy being called traitors. Recalling my first Malinche poem, "Como duele," I understand now my inner voice: whatever name you call me, or acts you accuse me of, it all hurts, and hurts deeply. I have committed my life to re-creating a better, more just, non-oppressive world for la raza, la indigena, los mestizos, our gente, and nuestras y nuestros paisas. Would not this new world for Chicanas y Chicanos be a better world for all?

From *Aztlán: A Journal of Chicano Studies* 5, nos. 1 and 2 (1974): 155–165.

The Chicano movement is the all-encompassing effort to, on the one hand, articulate and intensify the Chicano existence, and on the other hand, to articulate and alleviate the suffering that has accrued to Chicanos precisely because of that existence.[1] Of the important issues it faces, that of las Chicanas is perhaps the most problematic. Ordinarily, when the issue of Chicanas is raised, whether by Chicanos, by Chicanas, or by those outside of the Chicano context, the concern is with the status and role of Chicanas within the Movimiento in general, within specific activist organizations, and within Chicano society. This is particularly unfortunate because expression of interest in Chicanas thus inspires a defensive attitude on the part of Chicanos included within any of those categories. These defensive Chicanos are not too different from the Mexican Americans who, in the early days of the newly articulated Movimiento, defended the status quo situation either because they had invested so much time and energy into attaining a certain status within it or because they had reasoned, along with the Anglo social scientists, that there was something innately wrong with the Mexican culture that resulted in the conditions within which the Chicano existed in the United States.

The tragedy of this situation is simply an extension of the all-too-familiar syndrome under which Chicanos have suffered. Chicanos are induced to define and describe their very being and existence in terms of external constraints and conditions imposed upon them by their colonizers or neocolonizers. Thus, what we have is the acceptance of certain externally imposed stereotypes about Chicanas acting as a restraint upon actions or suggestions for changes among Chicanas; actions and changes that would not conform to the stereotypes or act to destroy the stereotypes.

Many of the stereotypes have been equated with aspects of Mexican-Chicano culture. Social scientists describe la Chicana as "ideally submissive, unworldly, and chaste," or "at the command of the husband, who [keeps] her as he would a coveted thing, free from the contacts of the world, subject to his passions, ignorant of life."[2] Social scientists also describe "machismo" as a masculinity syndrome particularly attributable to the Latin male, and thus by extension to the Chicano male. These attitudes are echoed by Chicanos themselves in such contexts as the song "The Female of Aztlán," by la familia Domínguez: "Your responsibility is to love, work, pray, and help ... the male is the leader, he is iron, not mush," and by statements such as those made at the Denver Chicano Youth Liberation Conference in 1969 emphasizing that the role of la Chicana in the movimiento was to "stand behind her man."[3] More problematic, however, are the large numbers of Chicanas and Chicanos who have come to accept these descriptions and syndromes as part of their daily lives.

Obviously these stereotypes have little meaning to those who have lived the reality of the Chicano existence. Within each of our memories there is the image of a father who worked long hours, suffered to keep his family alive and united, and struggled to maintain his dignity. Such a man had little time for concern over his "masculinity." Certainly he did not have ten children because of his machismo, but because he was a human being, poor, and without "access" to birth control. We certainly remember mothers and sisters who worked in the fields or at menial labor in addition to doing the work required at home to survive. Submissiveness, chastity, and unworldliness are luxuries of the rich and/or nearly rich. Machismo is a myth propagated by subjugators and colonizers who take pleasure in watching their subjects strike out vainly against them in order to prove themselves still capable of action. The following billboard sign in Los Angeles was certainly not written by any Chicano:

MACHO
Join the LAPD

The term macho is not applied to the Anglo society itself.[4] Chicanos are faced with stereotypes of themselves that are standards they are goaded into emulating, and expected to achieve in order to be accepted by the dominant society, the colonizers. Strenuous efforts to achieve these externally imposed goals may thus result in excesses that can then be blamed, by outsiders, on cultural traits. Conversely, failure to achieve them can result in the same syndrome, that is, a view of a culture as somehow inferior and inflexible. Thus, to talk about change becomes a very real threat to Chicanos who wish to retain what they have defined as their culture. The stereotypes, the acceptance of stereotypes, and the defensive postures adopted by "culturalists" become the problems for Chicanos striving to bring about some changes, rather than the problems being defined as they more adequately could be, in terms of external forces.[5] Chicano activists, in turn, tend to define the changes they wish to see in internal terms rather than external terms, so that we see articles written by Chicanas with such titles as: "¡Machismo No! ¡Igualdad, Si![6] The clashes thus continue unabated over Chicana roles, and the Chicana continues to feel guilty about what she is, or is not, doing for her people and to and for her man. The important point is that Chicanos have had and continue to have very little control over their self-images, cultural awareness, and self-definition.

In order to comprehend adequately the pervasiveness of the external restraints that operate upon the quality of the Chicana existence it is necessary to evaluate the earliest descriptions of women in the societies of the valley of México. These early descriptions were provided by either Spanish conquerors or Spanish male settlers.[7] In either case, the Spanish role was one of imposition upon, first, the native local cultures, and second, the individuals within that local group. What these early chroniclers described was the world as they saw it, through Spanish eyes, much as Anglo social scientists "see" Chicano barrios today. The Spanish chroniclers were not wholly concerned with describing local customs prior to the conquest itself. In most cases, what was described was a situation already changed under the impact of a brutal and thorough conquest. The women of México had never been exploited in the same manner and to the same degree that they were during the conquest. Exploitation of contemporary Chicanas begins in a very real sense with the Spanish conquest, regardless of what conditions were among the native peoples prior to the conquest.

Two other conditions render the descriptions of native customs provided by the conquering peoples unreliable. There was not one native group with its unique customs, but a multitude of native groups.[8] Thus, descriptions that consider all native groups as one entity should be immediately suspect. The Spanish conquerors, whether soldiers, settlers, or priests, were all themselves products of the Judeo-Christian tradition. This tradition has been often and well described in terms of its racist and sexist attitudes. The effect of this combination of attitudes is that in word and in deed, the Spaniards relegated the native woman, and later the mestiza, to the lowest position in the structured society that came to dominate México.

The social structure for females in the conquered nation of México paralleled that of the overall population based upon race. The Spanish-born residents of México were at the top of the socioeconomic ladder, followed by the Mexican-born criollos, with the mestizos and the natives lumped together at the bottom. However, when individuals from the "bottom" group were able to resemble the other two classes, by being light-skinned and adopting their way of life, that is, by assimilating, they were allowed to form a third class. This class was between the criollos and the Indians and mestizos who looked like and lived like their Indian ancestors.

The Catholic Church is as responsible for the Conquest of México as the Spanish soldiers, and is part and parcel of the Judeo-Christian tradition. It not only dealt with the natives as subjects, but with the women as subjects of the subjects and the subjugators. The Spanish Catholic Church, an institution of conquest, thus stands as a guardian and perpetrator of an ancient tradition whereby women were unequal to, and in need of the constant surveillance of, men, preferably white Catholic men. The social structure of Mexican society, and that of all the other lands conquered by the Spaniards, reflected the views of the Catholic Church on women and on native peoples. The Spanish woman, being white and Catholic, was often considered as religious, sacrosanct, pure, somehow like the Virgin Mary, untouched and untouchable, the ideal woman, wife, and mother. The mestizas and the native women were regarded as heathens, women in need of redemption, loose women, thus women who could be exploited without fear of punishment.

The Indian and mestizo men saw quickly the need to protect their women. The women responded to this blatant abuse by the conquerors by staying out of public view, because public meant being exploited, being raped. Women were, current female chauvinism notwithstanding, most vulnerable because of their unique childbearing ability. In this situation the women were given no choice. The men themselves could not be effectively protective of the women when they themselves were subject to enslavement, torture, and death. Thus the new race was born, and this is a reality with which Chicanas and Chicanos must live.

The sexism and racism were translated in México, as they were in the United States, into mechanisms of domination by those in control over the political system. The Spanish also dealt with the Indian and mestizo males separately and distinctly from the Indian females and mestizas. Whether or not Indian females and mestizas were the subjects of the Indian males and mestizos is not primarily relevant to the Chicana condition because Chicanas are the direct heirs of the subjugation of the women of the valley of México by the Spanish conquerors. What is important is that the Indian male and mestizo were unable to act as intermediaries for the women with the Spanish power structure, even when they attempted to do so. The indigenous peoples of México and the mestizos became economic and political objects of the Spaniards and the Indian females and mestizas became the sexual objects of the conquerors. Changes in the power structure throughout the years between the conquest and the Mexican Revolution of 1910 did not substantially alter the situation.

The migration of Mexicans in large numbers to the areas north of the Río Bravo did not mark an end to this colonization experience. It simply meant that Mexicano-Chicanos, having internalized a past colonial experience, added a second one to their existence. Since they were largely from the working classes of Mexican society, and were Mexican, they came into the U.S. economic and political system at the lowest stratum. The females were dealt with only through the males until they attempted to compete for jobs. It was when Chicanas began to seek work outside of the family groups that sexism became a key factor of oppression along with racism. Chicanas were more readily hired for farm work when they were with their husbands and children, thus forming, or being required to form, a working unit. When Chicanas operated outside of this context, they were relegated to other positions of menial labor. Chicanas have suffered through both experiences and now suffer from two apparently contradictory stereotypes. This contradiction was described by Gracia Molina de Pick:

> Las mujeres somos tradicionalmente presentadas en una doblez, que por una parte nos hace gozar con el sufrimiento diciendo además que somos víctimas de nuestra cultura, mártires de nuestros hombres, excesivamente supersticiosas, fanáticas, sucias, perezosas, tontas, aparatos de reproducción, y sonrientemente resignadas, sin ninguna vida interior, emocional o intelectual. Pero también somos las mujeres seductoras, voluptuosas, sensuales, pasionales, immorales, en suma, la representación de la aventura sexual más provocadora.[9]

This contradiction of roles serves a dual purpose. First, it removes all blame for the social problems of Chicanos from the dominant society, placing it upon Chicanas themselves. Second, it serves to keep Chicanas preoccupied with their apparent "shortcomings," so as to keep them from looking outward. Chicanas, then, can be blamed by the Anglo society and its institutions for not being good mothers, for not keeping their families together, for working instead of staying home, or, conversely, for being too oriented to their families, for having too many children, for not working, for staying home.

Statistics compiled on California by the U. S. Equal Employment Opportunity Commission indicate the following situations (see table 1)[10]. First, of the total Spanish-surname employees, 68 percent are male and 32 percent are female. This percentage breakdown is not unlike that of the state's general population. Spanish-surname females do not stay at home any more nor less than women in the general population. It would seem ethnicity is the most important factor working against Chicanas as against Chicanos in general. The ratio of women to men appears to be 1 to 1 (see table 1).

Figure 1. Spanish-Surname White Collar Workers by Category and Sex

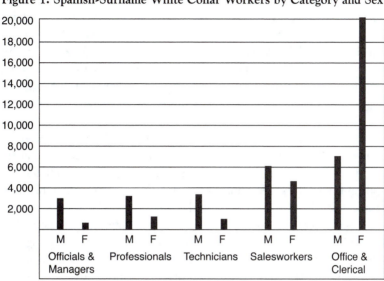

Table 1. California Spanish-Surname Employment by Sex and Job Category

	Total Population Employment - 1970*		Total Spanish-Surname employment - 1967**		White Collar Spanish Surname Employment - 1967**		Blue Collar Spanish Surname Employment - 1967**	
Sex	Number	%	Number	%	Number	%	Number	%
Male	5,285,220	63.4	167,721	68.6	25,519	47.4	123,682	75.8
Female	3,053,273	36.6	74,469	31.4	28,278	52.5	39,533	24.2
Total	8,338,493	100.0	237,190	100.0	53,797	100.0	163,215	100.0

*United States Bureau of Census. United States Department of Commerce, Detailed Characteristics, California, Table 164.
**United States Equal Employment Opportunity Commission, California Section, 1967, Table 5.

However, if we look at a detailed breakdown of white-collar employment, we see in addition to ethnicity, sex mitigates against Spanish-surname females achieving certain positions within the category (see fig. 1). The highest proportion of females in the white-collar category is in office and clerical work. Since Chicanos are not doing the majority of hiring, it is the dominant Anglo society that is responsible for such ratios in the hiring of Spanish-surname males and females.

Nonetheless, some Chicanas perceive that it is the Chicano (male) who keeps them from attaining professional status. Linda Aguilar writes:

"I have found that a Chicana has a better chance of being employed by an Anglo if she seeks any type of administrative position than by a Chicano."[11] This may very well be the case in the experience of Ms. Aguilar, but how often do Chicanas encounter Chicanos (males) in positions of administrative responsibility who are called upon to review them for hiring or promotion? This position can lead one to ignore important facets of our oppression. Chicanas may come to believe that the external realities are caused by the internal conditions rather than the other way around. This is a dimension of being colonized, that is, coming to believe in one's own reference group as inferior to the dominant group.[12] For the Chicana, racism is added to sexism and the result is the same manipulation, exploitation, and control by the superordinate group. Chicanos, being part of the situation, can also be expected to express themselves in similar ways. Therefore, there is the very real possibility that, were there more Chicanos (males) in positions of administrative responsibility, they would be biased against Chicanas to a greater extent than Anglo males, for whatever reasons. It is this double oppression that we may ignore if we blame only Chicano males for the problems of Chicanas.[13]

Chicanos and Chicanas and the Movimiento must now address themselves to these realities. If Chicanos act in such a way as to ignore the condition of double oppression under which Chicanas suffer, they are not only perpetuating the stereotypes and the conditions that those stereotypes support, but they are also guilty of intensifying those conditions and their negative results. We should articulate specific proposals and goals that relate to the Chicana and should direct ourselves to relieving some of the unique burdens that the dominant society places upon the Chicana, thus separating her from her male counterpart.

Many Chicanas find the women's liberation movement largely irrelevant because more often than not it is a move for strictly women's rights. While women's rights advocates are asking for a parity share of the "American" pie, Chicanas (and Chicanos) are asking for something other than parity. The end desired by Chicanas is the restoration of control over a way of life, a culture, an existence. For a Chicana to break with this goal is to break with her past, her present, and her people. For this reason, the concerns expressed by Chicanas for their own needs within the Movimiento cannot be considered a threat to the unity of the Movimiento itself.

One of the questions to which Chicanos should be addressing themselves is: What goals within the Movimiento can be constructed to relate to Chicanas in particular? If we recognize the external imposition of much of what defines and delineates the conditions for Chicanas, then it is obvious there must be a special effort to remove some of these unique burdens. La Malinche's situation symbolizes the problems that face Chicanas as they attempt to deal with the dominant Anglo society. She was, after all, as much a victim of the conquest and of Cortés as she was one of the keys to the conquest. La Chicana is not only placed in a status below the Chicano (male), but in a category apart vis-à-vis the dominant society. That division is manipulated and exploited to further control Chicanos. To end the division by including Chicanas as an integral, not subordinate, part of the group we call Chicanos, is to also diminish the ability of outside groups to manipulate and exploit us. This should be one of the goals of the Chicano Movimiento.

Notes

1. The term Chicano will be used throughout this paper in the generic sense, inclusive of male and female, unless otherwise specified or used in companionship with Chicana.

2. The first example is from Arthur Rubel, "The Family," in *Mexican-Americans in the United States*, ed. John H. Burma (New York: Shenkman, 1970), 214. The second example is from Alfred White, "The Apperceptive Mass of Foreigners as Applied to Americanization: The Mexican Group," Master's thesis, University of California, 1923, 31.

3. The Denver Chicano Youth Liberation Conference was held in 1969 and one workshop that dealt with the question of Chicanas issued the statement that Chicanas do not want to be liberated. This is akin to saying that Black slaves loved their masters, and worse, saying this with pride.

4. Various authors have come to realize that machismo operates as much, if not more, in the dominant society. I.F. Stone in *The New York Review of Books* (18 May 1972) entitles his article "Machismo in Washington."

5. Culturalists in this paper are defined as those who wish to preserve certain aspects of the Chicano existence. Sometimes the concern with preservation of cultural characteristics becomes simply a status quo position, as if cultures never change. At other times, culturalists border on traditionalists, that is, those who wish to go back to an earlier era, as if in that era "culture" was somehow pure and unadulterated by contact with Anglo society. The reality for the Chicano is that the contact has already occurred, and much of what was his past was no better than his present. The Chicano, then, exists in that diversity of truths that poses a problem for analysts who would like to define once and for all what Chicano culture consists of.

6. Lionila López Saenz, "¡Machismo, No! ¡Igualdad, Si!" *La Luz*, May 1972.

7. The two most famous chroniclers of the native societies were Bernal Díaz del Castillo, a soldier, and Fray Bernardino de Sahagún. Fray Sahagún's interest was in preserving knowledge of the history of the conquest and of the civilizations that existed before the conquest. Yet, by the time he began his chronicles, the conquest was well established.

8. The word "group" is used here instead of "tribe" because of the connotation, which appears to this writer as a negative one, attached to the concept of tribe. A tribe is somehow inferior in the level of social development compared to contemporary groupings. This distinction is, to me, unacceptable, and certainly inapplicable to the type of social structures extant in the valley of México on the eve of Cortés's arrival in México.

9. Gracia Molina de Pick, "Reflexiones Sobre el Feminismo y la Raza," *La Luz*, August 1972, 58.

10. All statistics utilized are available from the U.S. Equal Employment Opportunity Commission. The data on California are for 1968.

11. Linda Aguilar, "Unequal Opportunity and the Chicana," *La Luz*, September 1972, 52.

12. Robert Blauner in describing internal colonialism includes this aspect of being colonized in his definition of racism. See Blauner, ed, *On Racial Oppression in America* (New York: Harper & Row, 1972).

13. The term "double oppression," herein used, refers to how this dominant Anglo society places Chicanas in categories and positions that deny them a modicum of dignity both because they are Chicanas and because they are females. Secondly, Chicanos, echoing the values of the dominant majority, often seek to confine Chicanas further.

Works Cited

Aguilar, Linda. "Unequal Opportunity and the Chicana." *La Luz* 1, no. 5 (September 1972): 52.

Blauner, Robert, ed. *On Racial Oppression in America*. New York: Harper & Row, 1972.

Molina de Pick, Gracia. "Reflexiones Sobre el Feminismo y la Raza." *La Luz* 1, no. 4 (August, 1972): 58.

Montiel, Miguel. "The Social Science Myth of the Mexican-American Family." In *Voices*, ed. Octavio Roman-V. Berkeley, Calif.: Quinto Sol Publications, 1971.

Rubel, Arthur. "The Family." In *Mexican-Americans in the United States*, ed. John H. Burma. New York: Shenkman, 1970.

Saenz, Lionila López. "¡Machismo, No! ¡Igualdad, Si!" *La Luz* 1, no. 2, (May 1972): 19–24.

Shedd, Margaret. *Malinche and Cortez*. New York: Doubleday, 1971.

Stone, I. F. "Machismo in Washington." *New York Review of Books*, 18 May 1972, 13–14.

U.S. Equal Employment Opportunity Commission. *California Section, 1967*. U.S. Government Printing Office, Washington, D.C.

Vaillant, George C. *La Civilización Azteca*. México: Fondo de Cultura Económica, 1960.

White, Alfred. "The Apperceptive Mass of Foreigners as Applied to Americanization: The Mexican Group." Master's thesis. University of California, Davis, 1923.

Unraveling America's Hispanic Past
Internal Stratification and Class Boundaries

Ramón A. Gutiérrez

There is a tendency in historical and sociological literature to describe the Spanish/Mexican–origin population of the United States as a homogeneous group. The prevalent assumption about this population is that it is a national immigrant group experiencing structural assimilation at the macro level via market integration, and acculturation at the micro or personal level through exogamous marriage, English language mastery, and participation in the dominant political institutions.[1] Assimilation theorists who have studied the immigrant experience in the United States have generally assumed that Mexicans, like other ethnic groups before them, would eventually forsake their initial cultural conservatism in the United States, gradually blending into that big cauldron of stew—"the melting pot"—called America, first as hyphenated Americans (e.g., Mexican-Americans, Italian-Americans, Polish-Americans, Afro-Americans, etc.) and someday as full participants in American middle-class culture. This essay challenges this traditional wisdom by examining the internal stratification of the Spanish/Mexican–origin population in the United States. Far from being a homogeneous group, the Hispanic population of the Southwest is complexly stratified and is defined by a variety of historically constituted social boundaries. My intent here is to show that how people define themselves and are defined by others is a dynamic process. Cultural identity is not a fixed and static entity; rather it ebbs and flows as history itself unfolds. My hope is that the findings presented herein will serve as a corrective to the immigration literature that is founded on the assumption that it knows what the core

336

features of Mexican immigrant culture are and how those features, regardless of regional, class, and generational differences, are somehow miraculously transformed into American middle-class culture.

The Hispanic ethnic past in the United States is a long one. Several decades before Jamestown was founded and the Pilgrims landed at Plymouth, Spain's citizens had already established permanent settlements on soil that would become part of the United States. The colonization of the Kingdom of New Mexico (then encompassing roughly the current states of New Mexico and Arizona) was launched in 1598.[2] Texas's first Spanish settlements date from 1691; and the settlement of Alta California began with the founding of San Diego in 1769. The Kingdom of New Mexico, Texas, and Alta California were all situated at the northern edge of Spain's empire, isolated from each other, surrounded on all sides by hostile Indians, and too distant from the major centers of Spanish culture in central Mexico for frequent communication. What developed in each of these provinces over the centuries were distinct regional subcultures that were Iberian in form, but thoroughly syncretic in content due to prolonged contact with local indigenous cultures. National consciousness, and by this I mean identity as a citizen of a nation-state, was weakly developed among the colonists Spain initially dispatched to settle the Southwest. What common identity they did share was religious; they were Christians first and foremost. The fervor of their religious sentiment had been forged during Spain's reconquest, those years of warfare between 711 and 1492 when the Moors occupied the Iberian Peninsula. In these years the Christian monarchs rallied their populations behind the standard of the cross to push the forces of Islam back into Africa. What victories they won were won in the name of Christianity.[3]

Next in importance to the identity of these colonists was the *patria chica*, the "small fatherland," or region of origin. Each of Spain's kingdoms had a well-developed *conciencia de sí*, or self-consciousness. After men and women proclaimed themselves Christians, they boasted of being Aragonese, Catalans, Leonese, Galicians, Castilians, and so on. It should come as no surprise that the word the Indians of the southwestern United States first used to describe their European overlords was *Castilla*, meaning Castile. Though the Indians understood little of what Spain's soldiers told them, they did nonetheless repeatedly hear the soldiers call themselves *castellanos*, announce that the Indians were subjects of Castilla, and declare that the king of Castilla was their new lord. Gaspar Peréz de Villagrá, who participated in the 1598 conquest of New Mexico and in 1610 commemorated those feats in his *Historia de la Nueva México,* writes that the Indians at Acoma Pueblo "called to me, crying, Castilian! Castilian! ... Zutacapan [their chief] asked me if more Castilians followed me and how long before they would arrive."[4]

The colonists' identification with Spain's various regions was gradually lost in the Southwest, but not their habit of identifying with the region in which they lived. The literary evidence indicates that by the beginning of the nineteenth century residents of the Kingdom of New Mexico were calling themselves *nuevo mexicanos,* those in California were referring to themselves as *californios,* and those in Texas called themselves *tejanos.*

The Spanish conquest of America brought together men from different regions and by so doing helped to shape a common experience and cultural identity. Men who had never before really identified as Spaniards now came to think of themselves as such in cultural terms, particularly when confronting indigenous cultures as overlords. By calling themselves Spaniards or *españoles* the colonists in the Southwest acknowledged that their culture and social institutions were of Iberian origin and thus quite different from those of the Indians. Three hundred years of contact between these two groups through intermarriage and cohabitation in a common ecological zone would radically transform what it meant to be *español* and *indio,* but that story is beyond our scope here.[5]

The españoles who colonized the Southwest were extremely status conscious and viewed society as hierarchically ordered by a number of ascriptive status categories based on race, legitimacy of birth, occupation, citizenship, and religion. Whenever anyone came before a legal tribunal, whether civil or ecclesiastical, the judge was always eager to determine the person's *calidad* or social status, for punishment was meted out differentially according to one's status. Thus legal dockets always began with a formulaic statement to the effect that *Fulano de tal* "es de calidad mestizo, obrero, hijo legitime de tal y tal y Christian nuevo" (John Doe's social status is mestizo, laborer, the legitimate son of so and so, and a New Christian). A person's racial status was derived through the biological criteria outlined in the *Régimen de castas* or Society of Castes, that artifact of Spanish purity-of-blood statutes that attempted to measure one's genealogical proximity to socially tainted peoples by scrutinizing qualities of blood. In Spain even remotely impure blood derived from Jews, Moors, and other heretics disqualified a person from high honorific posts. In America contact with Indians and Black slaves was deemed equally undesirable. To describe the various racial groups created through miscegenation in America, an elaborate legal-racial vocabulary was devised. A mix between a Spaniard and an Indian produced a *mestizo*; a Spaniard and a mestizo produced a *castizo*; a Spaniard and a Black begat a *mulato*, and so on.[6]

Of equal importance in every local status hierarchy was whether one worked with one's hands or not. The assumption was that Blacks toiled because of the infamy of their slavery. With Indians, they worked because of their vanquishment by a superior power. Racial status was similarly adduced from one's legitimacy or illegitimacy of birth. The legal scholar Juan de Solórzano y Pereira in his *Politica indiana* maintained that illegitimates were:

> those born of adulterous or other illicit and punishable unions, because there are few Spaniards of honor who marry Indian or negro women; this defect of birth makes them infamous, at least *infama facti*, according to the weighty and common opinion of serious scholars; they carry the stain of different colors and other vices.[7]

Throughout the colonial period illegitimacy was seen as an indecent and shameful mark because of its association with mixed racial unions. Finally, to differentiate Christians of peninsular origin from those recently converted to the faith, the categories "Old Christian" and "New Christian" were widely used. To call someone a "New Christian" was to recognize his indigenous ancestry and therefore his infamy or low status in the status hierarchy.

All of these categories that defined a person's calidad were intricately related. In fact, a person's social standing in a community was a public summation of these various measures. We see this very clearly in social action. The fiercest fighting words one could utter were slurs that impugned a person's total social personality—his race, his ancestry, and his position in the division of labor. On 3 June 1765, for example, we hear about the fight in Albuquerque between Eusebio Chávez and his father-in-law, Andrés Martín. Chávez beat Martín with a large stick and dragged him by his hair, leaving Martín's arm badly bruised, his chest covered with black and blue welts, his scalp swollen out of shape, and his hair completely tangled and caked in blood. The reason: Martín had called Chávez a "perro mulato hijo de puta" (mixed-blood dog son-of-a-bitch). One insult, perhaps, would have been enough; but by calling Chávez a dog, Martín implied that he was less than human. He also added that Chávez was a mixed blood, and if truly a son of a bitch, he was undoubtedly illegitimate. Martín had thus combined three statuses to insult Chávez.[8]

Another social distinction that deserves mention here is the legal category that was widely used in the Southwest during the colonial period, and particularly in California: *gente de razón*, literally "people of reason," or rational beings. There is a great deal of confusion among contemporary scholars as to whom this category encompassed and what precisely it meant. The category is best understood by looking at its opposite, that is, *gente sin razón*, "people lacking reason," or irrational persons. The Holy Office of the Inquisition concocted this legal distinction to protect the Indian from prosecution for heretical ideas. The Indians were gente sin razón, mere children lacking the rational faculties to understand dogmas of faith. Everyone else was deemed gente de razón and could be punished by the Inquisition for acts judged heretical. With the demise of the Inquisition the term gente de razón remained current as a way of classifying the non-Indian population of an area.

The word *genízaro*, which appears in New Mexico at the beginning of the eighteenth century, was another term employed to refer to a specific class of Indians in Spanish society. The genízaros were primarily Apache and Navajo Indians enslaved during Spanish raids, and secondarily Pueblo Indians who abandoned their indigenous towns or were exiled from them for some transgression. Approximately 4,000 genízaros entered New Mexican society during the eighteenth century. For most of that and the following century they were considered marginals because of their slave, ex-slave, or outcast status.[9] They spoke a distinctive broken form of Spanish, were residentially segregated, married endogamously, and shared a corporate identity, living together, said Fray Carlos Delgado in 1744, in great unity "como si fueran una nación" (as if they were a nation).[10] In 1776, Fray Atanasio Domínguez described the genízaros as "weak, gamblers, liars, cheats, and petty thieves." This caricature survived, for today when New Mexicans say "No seas genízaro," they mean "Don't be a liar."

Other folk classification systems also existed among Spain's colonists in the Southwest. Españoles referred to half-breeds as *lobos* and *coyotes*, denoting a mixture between a Spaniard and an Indian. With both of these labels, the mixed-blood individual was portrayed as a low species close to an animal. Lobo and coyote were maintained in the common parlance over the centuries and today are used to refer to persons who are a mix of Anglo and Mexican.

There can be no doubt that the Indians the Spanish conquered and dominated had a linguistic arsenal of their own to describe the Europeans. I have searched for this lexicon but have only had slight success. The evidence I encountered comes from the Pueblo, the Yaqui, and the Mayo Indians. All three Indian groups were impressed by the sacrament of baptism and devised words to describe the Spaniards that made reference to this sacrament. Among the Pueblo Indians the Spaniards were called "wet-heads" because of the water poured on a person's head at baptism. For similar reasons the Yaqui and Mayo Indians called the Spaniards "water-fathers" and "water-mothers."[12]

As Mexican independence approached in 1821, other status categories came into use. Residents of the Southwest did at times employ the *peninsular* and *criollo* categories to differentiate españoles (i.e., persons born in Spain) from *españoles mexicanos* (i.e., persons of Spanish origin born in Mexico). At the beginning of the nineteenth century the only persons in the Southwest who could genuinely claim peninsular Spanish origin were the priests, and it is among them that one sees the peninsular/criollo categories applied most rigorously. For the rest of the population of New Mexico, Texas, and California little seems to have changed as a result of Mexico's independence from Spain. One does not find a rapid increase of people calling themselves *mexicanos*. The category does appear in the 1830s but is used by a very small number of people. In New Mexico, for example, only about 5 percent of all individuals who married legally during 1830–1839 claimed they were mexicanos. The rest still preferred to call themselves españoles.[13]

There were nonetheless forces of change operating in Hispanic society in the Southwest that would radically transform it after 1821. Internally, the increased level of economic activity in the Southwest fostered by the Bourbon monarchs in the 1770s, and meant to safeguard the area and integrate it into larger marketing centers in northern Mexico, shattered the traditional bonds of society. With the rise of wage labor and the growth of a large landless peasant class, the status system based on ascription slowly gave way to one based on achievement. International rivalries, large-scale migration, and other political events also helped to change the nature of society. In 1836 Texas won its independence from Mexico through revolution. A decade later the rest of the Southwest was ceded to the United States as a result of the U.S.-Mexican War of 1846–1848. As a new political order was established and people moved back and forth across the Rio Grande, and west across the Great Plains, a new conception of society emerged. Just as when colonists from various parts of Spain first arrived in the Southwest and defined themselves culturally as Spaniards vis-à-vis the Indians, so too after 1848 did settlers from various parts of the United States define themselves as Anglos and Americans when confronted with Mexicans and Indians.

From the moment *americanos* entered the Southwest, the Mexican population residing there concocted a variety of ethnic terms for the invaders. There were names for the americanos that focused on the peculiarities of their skin, eye, and hair color, and the size of their feet. Thus we find in the folklore: *canoso* (gray-haired), *colorado* (red-faced), *cara de pan crudo* (bread-dough face), *ojos de gato* (cat eyes), *patón* (big foot). Other Spanish ethnic labels for the Americans were the result of difficulties with and misunderstandings of the English language. The word gringo comes from the corruption of the first two words in a song the Mexican soldiers heard the Texas rebels singing at the Alamo. The first two lyrics to the prairie song, "Green Grows the Grass," were heard by Mexicans as "grin gros," and finally gringos. Because the americanos loved cabbage in their diet they were called *repolleros*. And because of their penchant for chewing tobacco they were called *masca tabacos*.[14]

Of course, Anglos were themselves quite adept at calling the Mexican-origin populace names too. From the Mexican diet come such derogatory terms as "greaser," "grease-ball," "goo-goo," "pepper-belly," "taco-choker," "frijole guzzler," "chili picker," and for a woman, "hot tamale." From the word "Mexican" evolved slurs such as "mex," "meskin," "skin," and "skindiver."

When the Anglos entered the Southwest, much as when the Spaniards entered in 1598, they saw few distinctions among the residents of their newly conquered territory. Certainly long-standing cleavages of the sort described above existed. In addition, the long-established Spanish residents of the area clearly saw themselves as different from Mexican immigrants who started to cross the border in large numbers after 1848, and particularly after 1880. But to the conquerors of the land, people were either Americans, Mexicans, or Indians. The United States had won the territory from Mexico through war; thus the most appropriate term for the population in the Southwest seemed to be Mexican. Through American eyes the residents of the area all looked alike, dressed alike, spoke Spanish, and were fanatical Catholics; therefore they were all Mexicans. And the deep-seated racial prejudice among americanos against Blacks was easily transferred to persons of Spanish origin due to their swarthy skin color.[15]

To counter the tendency among Americans to refer to all residents of the Southwest as Mexicans, the long-standing population of the area employed old ethnic categories in new ways. By so doing the Hispanic population that had resided in the Southwest since before 1848 wanted to clearly differentiate itself from the constant flow of lower-class Mexican immigrants. In addition, they wanted to clearly establish that they were Spaniards of white European ancestry and not of a mixed Indian, and therefore inferior, background.

Since the massive influx of immigrants into California after the 1848 gold rush radically transformed the ethnic mix of the state, let us begin with a discussion of its ethnic dynamics. The californios, the colonists who settled the area first under Spain's control, then after 1821 under Mexico's control, and finally after 1848 under the control of the United States, were faced with the arrival of numerous Mexican nationals who came to strike it rich in the mines. The californios referred to these immigrants as mexicanos because they were indeed Mexicans. Anglos, however, saw no apparent physical or cultural differences between the californios and the mexicanos, and so referred to both of them as Mexicans.

To counter this perception and to clearly differentiate themselves from the recent lower-class immigrant, the californios increasingly referred to themselves as "Spaniards," and insisted that other English speakers do the same. This tendency was particularly strong at the old Spanish pueblos, at Santa Barbara, San Fernando, Los Angeles, and San Francisco.[16]

But the sheer number of Mexican immigrants entering California from 1848 on drastically dissipated the californio population. The first "good" statistics on Mexican immigration to the United States start with the decade 1911–1920. Mexican immigration to the United States then totaled 219,000, representing approximately 20 percent of all immigrants to the United States. From 1921 to 1930, the official number more than doubled, reaching 459,287. In that decade, Mexicans were the largest group, representing close to 10 percent of the national total. Most of these immigrants went to California and so increasingly after the 1920s the terms "Mexican" and "Mexican American" became prominent and "Spanish American" totally disappeared.

Ethnic identity in New Mexico was similarly shaped by population dynamics and a new political order. But here the process of redefining the ethnic boundaries did not begin until after World War I. Unlike California where the californios were quickly outnumbered by Mexican immigrants, in New Mexico the native Spanish speakers retained their cultural identity as españoles or Spaniards. When faced with the arrival of Mexican immigrants in the 1920s and 1930s they referred to themselves as "Spaniards" or "Spanish Americans." Some went so far as to claim that they were the direct descendants of conquistadors who had colonized the region in 1598 and that over the centuries they had maintained their bloodlines free of any taint with inferior races. Of course, this was more fiction than fact. Most of the people who settled New Mexico were racially mestizos and few, if any, after three hundred years of miscegenation could claim "pure" Spanish ancestry. But whatever the ideology, it served primarily to avoid being called Mexican.

If we examine the linguistic context in which ethnicity was defined, we see the logic of their defensive ethnic ideology. When Arthur L. Campa in the 1950s asked long-time New Mexican residents in Spanish what their ethnicity was, most responded, "Soy mexicano" (I am Mexican). When he asked the same individuals what they liked to be called in English, they responded, "Spanish American." Campa then asked in Spanish, What do you call a person from Mexico? "Mexicano de México" (Mexican from Mexico). In English such a person was simply a "Mexican" because "Mexican ... is the most used when someone is being rude ... Example—'dirty Mexican'." Another woman echoed these sentiments: "I'd rather not be called Mexican because of the stereotype remarks that are associated with it. Such as lazy, dirty greaser, etc."[17]

Part of the New Mexicans' hostility to the term "Mexican" stems from its association with Mexico and Mexican nationals. New Mexico was always marginal to Spanish imperial politics and just as isolated from Mexico City. This fact prompted one man to state:

> My identity has always been closer to Spanish as an ethnic group and for that reason I consider myself Spanish ... but the civil laws under which I live and which make me proud are American ... being from northern New Mexico the only connection I have with anything Mexican is as a tourist and not as my national origin.[18]

Erna Fergusson has argued that "Spanish American" came into popular use in New Mexico after World War I to counter the Anglo perception that soldiers who called themselves in Spanish "mexicanos" were aliens from another country. Nancie González agrees that the term "Spanish American" emerged in response to an upsurge of prejudice and discrimination against Spanish speakers during the 1920s.[19]

The ethnic categories employed by tejanos or Texans of Spanish/Mexican origin require more explanation. One would assume that, as with the californios and nuevo méxicanos, they too would elect to be called Spanish or Spanish Americans when differentiating themselves from recent Mexican immigrants in the 1920s and 1930s. They did not. Instead they called themselves latinos and "Latin Americans." History provides some, but not all, of the rationale. When the tejanos joined forces with the American settlers of Texas to form their own independent republic in 1836, they clearly rejected their Mexican identity. Faced with the same prejudice that the Mexican immigrants suffered in the 1920s, the tejanos insisted on being called "Latin Americans" in polite English-speaking company. Obviously they did not want to be called "Mexicans" or "Mexican Americans." Why they rejected "Spanish" and "Spanish American" is as yet unknown. Whatever the reason, by 1929 the first major civil rights group in Texas was named the League of United Latin American Citizens.[20]

Survey data collected by Leo Grebler between 1965 and 1970 found that in San Antonio, the self-use of the label latino was positively associated with income. The higher one's income, the greater the preference for being called a latino; the lower one's income, the greater the incidence of calling oneself mexicano.[21] Michael Miller replicated Grebler's study in 1976 among South Texas high school students and found that virtually no one called himself a Latin American, latino, Mexican American, or mexicano. The preference among these students was for *chicano*, thus exposing the strong generational undercurrents in ethnic identity.[22]

Among other areas that had a native core of settlers who considered themselves culturally "Spaniards," Arizona too experienced the same Spanish/Mexican tension when confronted with massive immigration. One of the first civic organizations in Arizona during the early twentieth century was the Spanish American Alliance of Tucson. But again, given the rapid influx of Mexicans into the area with the development of irrigation agriculture, "Mexican" and "Mexican American" rapidly gained ascendancy here too.[23]

The tension between Spaniards and Mexicans created in the Southwest by the arrival of Mexican immigrants was couched in broad cultural terms as a basic class tension and usually as a generational rift. I turn now to explicit in-group terms that differentiated the Hispanic population by class.

Pocho is perhaps the most popular of these terms. It refers to a lower-class individual who has assimilated middle-class habits. There is a folksong that captures the meaning of pocho well:

Los pochos de California
no saben comer tortilla
porque solo en la mesa
usan pan con mantequilla.

(The "pochos" of California
Don't know how to eat tortillas
For at mealtime on the table
All they serve is bread and butter.)[24]

Another class-based term is *chicano*. There are several possible origins for the word. Researchers at the Center of Hispanic Linguistics at the Universidad Nacional Autónoma de México in Mexico City believe that the word is a *pochismo* (a corruption) created through the linguistic process of metathesis, whereby the order of letters in a word is reversed. They maintain that chicano possibly comes from *chinaco*, which means "tramp" or "guttersnipe," and changing *c* for *n* results in chicano.[25]

Tino Villanueva, taking a slightly different linguistic approach, has sought the origins of chicano in the speech play between adults and small children. Many adults employ "baby talk" with their infants, shortening words and exaggerating those that a child has difficulty pronouncing. Thus when a child cannot pronounce the name Eugenio it is shortened to Cheno; Mauricio becomes Wicho; and Socorro becomes Choco. In each of these examples a shortening of the name and the addition of "ch" produced the nickname. Similarly, Villanueva argues, the word chicano comes from *meshicas*, the ancient Aztec tribe that settled the Valley of Mexico. Meshicas slowly corrupted to meshica, shicanos, and finally chicanos. Curiously enough, numerous informants associated the word chicano with children. One woman said that she wanted to be called "Mexicana and not Chicana" because "the true meaning of Chicano is small boy—coming from the word *chico*—meaning small." Professor Carlos A. Rojas, emeritus professor of Spanish at Fresno State University, also believed that chicano stemmed from chico, which means "young one" or "small one."[26] In each of these explanations of the word chicano the implication is that the power dynamics in the parent/child relationship becomes the model for upper/lower-class relations in the Hispanic community.

Leaving the origins of the word chicano aside, we find that the word has always been a derogatory term for lower-class Mexicans. One informant said he disliked being called a chicano because "people ... mean a lower class of people." Another interviewee stated his objection to the term: "This word to me is equal to 'chicanery' or 'surumato' and is insulting." A *surumato*, incidentally, is a rough lower-class Mexican immigrant. Michael Miller found in his survey of South Texas youth that a negative relationship existed between socioeconomic status and the use of the word chicano as an ethnic self-referent. Only teenagers of recent immigrant origin preferred it.[27]

José Limón maintains that the word chicano as a derogatory in-group term has two meanings: (a) a person of dubious character, and (b) a recent immigrant of lower-class standing. The word is used folklorically as in-group banter and social self-affirmation in the face of widespread discrimination. A Black calling another Black a "nigger," or an Italian calling another Italian a "wop," is light-hearted banter. Thus is the case when a chicano tells another, "No seas chicano." If an out-group member used any of these terms they would be considered racist and their use of the word an explicit attempt to humiliate. So with chicano. Among members of one's social group it was social self-affirmation. Survey data bear this out. One New Mexican said that among his friends he wished to be called a chicano, but at school he always insisted on being called a "Spanish American."[28]

Militant and politically conscious Mexican-origin residents of the Southwest in the early 1960s embraced this term of out-group insult and in-group banter as a sign of self-determination and ethnic militancy. There is no doubt that chicano was popularized to establish a genealogical tie to a militant, warrior Aztec past. Some Hispanics objected to the use of the word chicano because, as one woman stated, "All my life I claim myself Spanish-American. Chicano to me is like someone who is radical." Studies by Metzgar and by Gutiérrez and Hirsch found that the use of chicano was inversely related to age. The younger one was, the greater the likelihood of consciously identifying as a chicano. Older individuals preferred terms such as Mexican, Mexican American, Latin American, and Spanish American.[29]

The meaning the word chicano acquired in the 1960s is well stated in the following poem:

> La palabra Chicano es un reproche,
> Una angustia con algo de esperanza ...
> Es un reto, quizás una bandera,
> El estandarte terco de una raza ...
> La palabra Chicano es una flecha
> Y el arco es el aliento de una raza.
>
> (The word Chicano is a reproach,
> An anguish with something of a hope ...
> It is a challenge, perhaps a banner,
> The stubborn standard of a race ...
> The word Chicano is an arrow
> And the bow is the inspiration of a race.)[30]

I have tried to show in these few pages that the peculiarities of Spain's colonization of the Southwest led to the development of three regional subcultures located in the Kingdom of New Mexico, in Texas, and in California. In each of these provinces the Hispanic residents interacted with indigenous populations and as a result, devised various ways of defining themselves and the other. When Spain and Mexico controlled the Southwest, society was complexly stratified by ascriptive status hierarchies based on race, religion, occupation, and legitimacy of birth.

With the development of a market economy and the proliferation of capitalist relationships of production, status was increasingly achieved and decreasingly ascribed. The ethnic confrontations created by the Texas revolution, the U.S.-Mexican War, the gold rush, and finally the large-scale immigration of Mexican nationals into the United States starting in the 1880s profoundly transformed the ways in which the long-established Hispanic residents of the Southwest defined themselves and those with whom they shared numerous cultural affinities. When faced with an assault on their social standing by Mexican immigrants, the Hispanic residents of the Southwest repeatedly returned to their oldest identity as Spaniards or Spanish Americans. In addition, new terms were brought into the ethnic vocabulary to clearly delineate those boundaries within the Hispanic community that had developed along class, age, generational, national, and political lines. My object in describing all of these ethnic and class categories has been to debunk the persistent assumptions about the monolithic characteristics of the Spanish/Mexican–origin population in the United States. Once this is recognized perhaps we will be able to move beyond the facile application of European immigrant models to that history. By saying all of this I do not deny that assimilation and acculturation have taken place, and that these processes are indeed powerful explanatory tools; rather, I sound a cautionary note. If we do not begin our studies of the past with a thorough understanding of the basic cleavages that divided society, we are doomed to wrong conclusions, and particularly if we propose that our driving aspiration has been to reach Anglo American middle-class goals.

Notes

1. The classic statements of this perspective are Milton M. Gordon, *Assimilation in American Life: The Role of Race, Religion, and National Origin* (New York: Oxford University Press, 1964), and Leo Grebler, Joan Moore, and Ralph C. Guzmán, *The Mexican American People: The Nation's Second Largest Minority* (New York: Free Press, 1970).

2. Saint Augustin in Florida was founded in 1565. I did not mention this town in the text as the first Spanish settlement in the United States because the focus of this essay is the Southwest.

3. Américo Castro, *The Spaniards: An Introduction to Their History* (Berkeley: University of California Press, 1971), 1–94.

4. Gaspar Pérez de Villagrá, *History of New Mexico*, trans. Gilberto Espinosa (Alcalá, 1610; reprinted, Los Angeles: The Quivira Society, 1933), 173. See also Aurelio M. Espinosa, "El desarrollo de la palabra *Castilla* en la lengua do los indios Hopis de Arizona," *Revista de Filología Española* 22 (1935): 298–300.

5. The details of contact between Spaniards and Indians can be found in Ramón A. Gutiérrez, "Marriage, Sex and the Family: Social Change in Colonial New Mexico, 1690–1846" (Ph.D. diss., University of Wisconsin, 1980).

6. Magnus Morner, *Race Mixture in the History of Latin America* (Boston: Little, Brown, & Co., 1967).

7. Quoted in Verona Martínez-Alier, *Marriage, Class and Colour in Nineteenth-Century Cuba* (London: Cambridge University Press, 1974), 83–4.

8. Spanish Archives of New Mexico, reel 9, frames 789–820.

9. Fray Angélico Chávez, "Genízaros," in *Handbook of North American Indians*, vol. 9, ed. William C. Sturtevant (Washington, D.C.: Smithsonian Institution, 1979), 198–201; Steven M. Horvath, "The Social and Political Organization of the Genízaros of Plaza de Nuestra Señora de los Dolores de Belén, New Mexico 1740–1812" (Ph.D. diss., Brown University, 1979); David M. Brugge, *Navajos in the Catholic Church Records of New Mexico 1694–1875*, Research Report no. 1 (Window Rock, Ariz.: The Navajo Tribe, 1968), 30.

10. Archivo General de la Nación (México): Historia 25–25:229.

11. Fray Atanasio Domínguez, *The Missions of New Mexico*, trans. Eleanor P. Adams and Angélico Chávez (1776; reprinted, Albuquerque: University of New Mexico Press, 1956), 259.

12. Elsie C. Parsons, "Tewa Mothers and Children," *Man* 24 (1924): 149; Edward H. Spicer, *The Yaquis: A Cultural History* (Tucson: University of Arizona Press, 1980), 22–3; N. Ross Crumrine, *The Mayo Indians of Sonora: A People Who Refuse to Die* (Tucson: University of Arizona Press, 1977), 69.

13. Gutiérrez, "Marriage, Sex and the Family," 145-6.

14. Américo Paredes, "The Problem of Identity in a Changing Culture: Popular Expressions of Culture Conflict Along the Lower Rio Grande Border," in *Views Across the Border: The United States and Mexico*, ed. Stanley R. Ross (Albuquerque: University of New Mexico Press, 1978), 68–94.

15. Raymund A. Paredes, "The Mexican Image in American Travel Literature, 1831–1869," *New Mexico Historical Quarterly* 1 (1977): 5–29; Deena Gonzáles, "The Spanish-Mexican Women of Santa Fe: Patterns of Their Resistance and Accommodation, 1820–1880" (Ph.D. diss., University of California, Berkeley, 1986); John R. Chávez, *The Lost Land: The Chicano Image of the Southwest* (Albuquerque: University of New Mexico Press, 1984); Phillip A. Hernández, "The Other Americans: The American Image of Mexico and Mexicans, 1550–1850" (Ph.D. diss., University of California, Berkeley, 1974); Susan R. Kenneson, "Through the Looking Glass: A History of Anglo-American Attitudes Toward

the Spanish-American and Indians of New Mexico" (Ph.D. diss., Yale University, 1978); Jack D. Forbes, "Race and Color in Mexican-American Problems," *Journal of Human Relations* 16 (1968): 55–68; Manuel Gamio, *Mexican Immigration to the United States* (Chicago: University of Chicago Press, 1930), 129, 209.

16. Leonard Pitt, *The Decline of the Californios: A Social History of the Spanish-Speaking Californians, 1846–1890* (Berkeley: University of California Press, 1966), 53, 157, 174, 188, 204, 259, 267, 309; Arthur L. Campa, *Hispanic Culture in the Southwest* (Norman: University of Oklahoma, 1979), 5.

17. Joseph V. Metzgar, "The Ethnic Sensitivity of Spanish New Mexicans: A Survey and Analysis," *New Mexico Historical Review* 49 (1974): 52.

18. Ibid., 60.

19. Erna Fergusson, *New Mexico: A Pageant of Three Peoples*, 2d. ed. (New York: Knopf, 1964), 218; Nancie González, *The Spanish-Americans of New Mexico: A Heritage of Pride* (Albuquerque: University of New Mexico Press, 1969), 80–81.

20. Richard Norstrand, "Mexican American and Chicano: Emerging Terms for a People Coming of Age," *Pacific Historical Review* 42, no. 3 (1973): 396.

21. Grebler, Moore, and Guzmán, *The Mexican American People*, 386–87.

22. Michael V. Miller, "Mexican Americans, Chicanos, and Others: Ethnic Self-Identification and Selected Social Attributes of Rural Texas Youth," *Rural Sociology* 41 (1976): 234–47.

23. Gamio, *Mexican Immigration to the United States*, 133.

24. Campa, *Hispanic Culture in the Southwest*, 5.

25. Ibid., 7.

26. Tino Villanueva, "Sobre el término 'chicano'," *Cuadernos Hispano-Americanos* (1978): 387–410; Metzgar, "Ethnic Sensitivity of Spanish New Mexicans," 59; Nostrand, "Mexican American and Chicano," 398.

27. Metzgar, "Ethnic Sensitivity of Spanish New Mexicans," 55, 72; Miller, "Mexican Americans, Chicanos, and Others," 241.

28. José Limón, "The Folk Performance of 'Chicano' and the Cultural Limits of Political Ideology," in *And Other Neighborly Names*, ed. Richard Bauman and Roger Abrahams (Austin: University of Texas Press, 1980), 197–225; Metzgar, "Ethnic Sensitivity of Spanish New Mexicans," 66.

29. Metzgar, "Ethnic Sensitivity of Spanish New Mexicans," 51; Armando Gutiérrez and Herbert Hirsch, "The Militant Challenge to the American Ethos: 'Chicanos' and 'Mexican Americans,'" *Social Science Quarterly* 53 (1973): 830–45.

30. Campa, *Hispanic Culture in the Southwest*, 7.

Beyond Indifference and Antipathy
The Chicana Movement and Chicana Feminist Discourse

Denise A. Segura and Beatriz M. Pesquera

> Chicana feminism means working toward the liberation of Chicanas from the indifference of the women's movement, the antipathy among Chicanos/Latinos, and the fulfillment of their own dreams and capacities.
>
> —Faculty member, age 49

Feminism as an ideology and a movement has developed in response to women's need to overturn their historical subordination to men. By and large, the public discourse on feminism has been demarcated by white feminist scholars. Increasingly, women of Color,[1] both heterosexual and lesbian, are challenging the relevance of American feminism and the American women's movement of the 1960s and 1970s for evading varying, often competing interests among women.[2] They posit instead a unique feminism grounded in their experiences as women and as members of oppressed minority groups and classes.

In this article we explore the form and content of feminist discourse among a selected group of Chicanas[3] in higher education. We argue that their articulations of feminism reveal tension between Chicano cultural nationalism and American feminism. The ideology of Chicano cultural nationalism advocates racial/ethnic unity against Anglo American domination and idealizes traditional Mexican/Chicano culture.[4] Feminism, in the broadest sense, calls for female unity against patriarchy (a system of male domination and female subordination) in traditional cultural patterns. Each perspective is skewed in favor of race/ethnicity or gender. Neither addresses the unique situation of Chicanas whose life chances mirror the intersection of class, race/ethnicity, and gender. Chicana feminism reverberates with the dialectical tension between their lives and the ideological configurations that dichotomize their experiences and exploit their political loyalties.

We begin our analysis by examining Chicanas' perspectives of the American women's movement and the Chicano movement of the late 1960s and early 1970s. This sets the stage for our analysis of the rise of the Chicana movement and contemporary Chicana feminist discourse among a selected group of 101 Chicanas in higher education. This study elucidates the social context of Chicana feminism while contributing new evidence on the diverse expressions of feminism in the United States.

The American Women's Movement and Chicanas

The contemporary American women's movement emerged during the 1960s and evolved into two major branches—the "women's rights" branch and the "women's liberation" or "left" branch.[5] The women's rights branch concentrated on programs that would integrate women into the mainstream of American society.[6] The women's liberation branch, in contrast, called for a radical restructuring of society that would eliminate patriarchy, the system of male control and domination of women.[7] Although both branches of the women's movement advocated on behalf of women, the issues of women of Color were often overlooked.[8]

The Chicana movement developed during the late 1960s. Organizationally, it shared some of the characteristics of the "left" or women's liberation branch of the women's movement. Chicanas formed caucuses within Chicano movement organizations, started various groups to advocate a feminist agenda, began consciousness-raising groups, and organized conferences on *la mujer* [women]. Within the women's movement these activities often led to a separatist politic. When Chicanas engaged in these activities, however, they did not always articulate a separatist ideology or organizational strategy. When women formed Chicana organizations, they justified their actions under the rubric of the Chicano movement. They insisted they were not "separate" but simply more focused on issues of *la mujer*, thereby strengthening the movement.

This stance makes sense if we consider that Chicanas' political consciousness is grounded in a fundamentally different reality than that of white feminists. Conquered in 1848, economically and culturally subordinated to Anglo American domination, Chicanas and Chicanos share a collective identity. Because of the historical racial/ethnic antagonisms between Anglos and Chicanos, Chicanas often feel a closer affinity to their Chicano brothers than to their feminist sisters. At the same time, Chicanas share a physical, cultural, and material vulnerability to the dicta of men.

While Chicana activists recognized their gender-based oppression, they usually rejected the ideology of separatism and tried to find ways of integrating their concerns within Chicano movement organizations.[9] These attempts were usually resisted by Chicano male activists, and to a lesser degree by some women. Therefore, Chicana activists committed to integrating gender into the race/class politic organized separate groups that responded to their needs as women and as members of a historically exploited racial/ethnic group and class.

Caught between the ideological pull of racial/class unity and their subordination within the male-dominated Chicano left, Chicana activists articulated the seemingly contradictory position of advocating unity while forming separate organizations. Ideologically Chicanas adopted a "united front" stance. Adelaida del Castillo, editor of *Encuentro Femenil*, a Chicana feminist journal, voiced this perspective in 1974:

> We're not a separatist movement, that would be suicidal. We as Chicanas and Chicanos are oppressed. We're not going to ally ourselves to white feminists who are part of the oppressor. I mean, that would be a contradiction. It also hurts when Chicano men don't recognize the need for this specialization which is called "Chicana Feminism."[10]

Del Castillo rejected the politics of advancement advocated by the women's movement as a reform that would not change the social reproduction of inequality based on race/ethnicity, class, and gender. This perspective predominated among Chicanas of the late 1960s and early 1970s.[11]

Cultural Nationalism and Chicanas

Chicanas' critique of American feminism and the women's movement took shape during the heyday of Chicano cultural nationalism.[12] Ideologically, this perspective identified the primary source of Chicano oppression in the colonial domination of Mexican Americans following the annexation of northern Mexico by the United States after the U.S. Mexico War of 1846–48.[13] As part of the process of colonial domination, Chicanos had limited access to education, employment, and political participation. Thus, race/ethnicity rather than individual merit defined the life chances of

Mexican Americans. Cultural differences between Anglos and Mexicans became the ideological basis that legitimized the unequal treatment and status of Mexicans in the United States.[14] In the Anglo American ideology, Mexicans were viewed as intellectually and culturally inferior.

Cultural nationalist ideology countered this pejorative perspective by celebrating the cultural heritage of Mexico in particular, indigenous roots, *la familia*, and political insurgency.[15] Politically, cultural nationalism called for self-determination including the maintenance of Mexican cultural patterns, culturally relevant education, and community control of social institutions.[16] The term "Chicano" arose as the symbolic representation of self-determination.[17] It conveys a commitment to struggle politically for the betterment of the Chicano community. Cultural nationalism became modified during the 1970s to incorporate a class analysis.[18] An analysis of gender as a base of oppression was and continues to be subsumed in the "larger" struggle against race- or class-based domination.[19]

Cultural nationalism idealized certain patterns associated with Mexican culture (e.g., Spanish-English bilingualism, communalism, familism). Chicano movement groups often organized around the ideal of la familia. Any critique of unequal gender relations within the structure of the family was discouraged. Chicanas who deviated from a nationalist political stance were subjected to many negative sanctions including being labeled *vendidas* (sell-outs), or *agabachadas* (white-identified). Once labeled thus, they became subject to marginalization within Chicano movement organizations. Martha Cotera points out that even the label *feminista* was a social control mechanism:

> We didn't say we were feminists. It was the men who said that. They said, "Aha! Feminista!" and that was a good reason for not listening to some of the most active women in the community.[20]

The severity of these sanctions rendered feminism an anathema to be avoided at almost any cost.

The ideological hegemony of cultural nationalism was exemplified in the first official position taken by the Chicana caucus at the 1969 National Chicano Youth Conference in Denver, Colorado: "The Chicana woman does not want to be liberated."[21] This official statement belies the heated debate on gender oppression voiced by Chicana feminists that day.[22] While this debate was dropped from the official record, it acted as a catalyst to spur women to militant action to challenge the hegemonic sway of cultural nationalism.

Chicana writings and organizational activities of this period resounded with frustration over patriarchy in the Chicano movement. Chicanas formed such groups as Hijas de Cuauhtémoc and founded alternative publications including *Encuentro Femenil* and *Regeneración*. For their organizations and publications, Chicanas adopted names rooted in Mexican revolutionary heritage. Hijas de Cuauhtémoc, a feminist organization founded in 1910 in Mexico City, opposed the dictatorship of Porfirio Díaz.[23] *Regeneración* was the official journal of the Partido Liberal Mexicano, a progressive Mexican political party.[24] These quintessential images of revolutionary struggle provided Chicanas with a means to frame their local agendas within a larger critique of race, class, and gender domination.

Chicanas sought various ways to reconcile their critique of male domination within the Chicano community to the Chicano movement agenda. Numerous conferences on la mujer reverberated with tension between cultural nationalism and feminism-and whether or not a union between these ideologies was possible.

At the 1971 Conferencia de Mujeres por la Raza in Houston, Texas, an ideological debate on "Chicana liberation" split participants into two opposing camps: "loyalists" and "feminists." Loyalists viewed Chicanas who called themselves feminists as allies of a middle-class women's movement that advocated individualistic upward mobility rather than struggle against racial/class domination. Feminists, in contrast, argued that the struggle against male domination was central to the overall Chicana/o movement for liberation.[25] Anna Nieto-Gómez, a prolific Chicana feminist writer of the late 1960s and early 1970s, articulates this position:

> What is Chicana feminism? I am a Chicana feminist. I make that statement very proudly, although there is a lot of intimidation in our community and in the society in general against people who define themselves as Chicana feminists. It sounds like a contradictory statement, a *Malinche* statement—if you are a Chicana you're on one side, if you're a feminist, you must be on the other side. They say you can't stand on both sides—which is a bunch of bull.[26]

At the Houston conference, participants engaged in a hostile debate on reproductive rights. Loyalists argued that reproductive rights including birth control and abortion threatened la familia. They accused women who failed to support this position of betraying Chicano culture and heritage. Feminists, in turn, declared "Our culture hell!" and by advocating a feminist agenda, sought to demystify the romanticization of Chicano culture which justified Chicanas' subordinate position.[27] Alma García argues that the loyalist position continues to influence Chicanas' political consciousness.[28] It organizes oppression hierarchically, she claims, assigning primacy to the struggle against racial, ethnic, and class domination. Within this formulation, feminism is nonrelevant and divisive to the "greater" Chicano struggle.

Early Chicana feminism viewed oppression as the simultaneous product of racial, class, and gender subordination. Chicana feminists expressed a high level of frustration with both the Chicano movement and the women's movement. They argued that freedom from racial/class oppression would not eliminate sexual oppression. Similarly, freedom from sexual oppression would not eliminate oppression on the basis of race/ethnicity and class.

The extent to which Chicana feminists have adhered to American feminist ideologies is uncertain.[29] To gain insight into this issue we explore the views of a group of Chicanas in higher education. Based on their written responses to a mail survey, we discuss how the historical concerns of the Chicana/o community and feminism inform contemporary Chicana feminist discourse among these women. Specifically, we analyze the relationships among the Chicano movement, the American women's movement, and the emergence of Chicana feminism. We end with a typology of the emergence of Chicana feminism.

The Women of MALCS

In 1988 we mailed a questionnaire to women on the mailing list of MALCS (Mujeres Activas en Letras y Cambio Social), an organization of Chicana/ Latina women in higher education. The organization's charter and activities demonstrate familiarity with Chicana concerns, a feminist orientation, and sensitivity to cultural concerns.

MALCS was founded in 1983 by Chicana faculty and graduate students as a support and advocacy group and a forum for sharing research interests. The founding declaration of MALCS states:

> We are the daughters of Chicano working class families involved in higher education. We were raised in labor camps and urban barrios, where sharing our resources was the basis of survival.... Our history is the story of working people—their struggles, commitments, strengths, and the problems they faced.... We are particularly concerned with the conditions women face at work, in and out of the home. We continue our mothers' struggle for social and economic justice.[30]

Drawing upon a tradition of struggle, MALCS members document, analyze, and interpret the Chicana/Latina experience in the United States.

A total of 178 questionnaires were mailed; 101 were completed and returned for a response rate of 57 percent. The questionnaire asked women to discuss their perceptions of the major features of the contemporary American women's movement, the major concerns of Chicanas today, and the extent to which the women's movement and feminist theory have addressed the needs of Chicana women. The questionnaire also contained a series of closed-ended questions about the respondents' familiarity with writings on the women's movement, their involvement with "feminist" and "women's" activities, and their socioeconomic status.

Nearly all who replied were associated with institutions of higher learning as faculty members (38.6 percent), graduate students (25.7 percent), undergraduate students (8.9 percent), or professional staff (8.9 percent). Eleven women were employed outside a university setting, and seven provided no information on their employment or education.

The women's ages ranged from 22 to 65 years, with a median age of 35 years and a mean age of 38.1 years. This age distribution means that a majority of the women were college-age (17–22) during the height of the women's movement (1967–76). Moreover, most of the women had activist backgrounds. Over three-fourths (78.2 percent) of the informants either belonged to or had previously been involved in women's organizations. Women overwhelmingly (83.2 percent) self-identified as "Chicana feminist."

Nearly three-fourths of the women said they were either "very familiar" or "somewhat familiar" with literature on the American women's movement. Over half also indicated they were either "very familiar" or "somewhat familiar" with feminist theoretical writings.[31]

This group of Chicanas does not represent all women of Mexican descent in the United States. They are academicians or highly educated women who inform the public discourse on feminism and women's issues. Moreover, as educated Chicanas they constitute one end of the continuum that forms the Chicana experience. Their perceptions, therefore, offer an excellent way to build knowledge on Chicanas and American feminism.

The Chicana Movement

Slightly over one-half of the women posit the existence of a Chicana movement that is qualitatively distinct from the American women's movement and the Chicano movement through a praxis based on the multifaceted dimension of Chicanas' experiences. That is, the Chicana movement exposes class, racial/ethnic, and cultural contradictions that distinguish the Chicana movement from the women's movement. For example:

> The Chicana movement was a separatist movement which emerged out of the contradictions Chicanas found in white women's organizations and groups in practice and theory. It added the dimension of race and class. This movement was also largely working-class inspired while the WM [women's movement] was largely middle class.
>
> —Graduate student, age 30

This perception, widely held among the informants and grounded in the relevant literature, argues that women's movement activists are predominantly middle-class white women who do not appreciate the nature of working-class and racial/ethnic oppression.

Some of the women emphasized that the Chicana movement emerged in response to racism within the American women's movement:

> It has become clear that racism which has inhibited white women from sharing power with women of color has led to a distinct Chicana movement, however weak.
>
> —Graduate student, no age given

Chicanas also described the Chicana movement as grounded in the unique cultural heritage of the Chicano/Mexicano people. They argued, moreover, that Chicanas are members of a colonized minority group with a cultural standard distinct from that of the white majority. Proponents of this viewpoint charged that white feminists are largely insensitive to Chicano culture and thereby exclude Chicana concerns from the women's movement.

When asked to describe the Chicana movement vis-à-vis the Chicano movement, women overwhelmingly proclaimed that the Chicana movement parted company with the Chicano movement by challenging patriarchy. They attribute the political dissent that led to the development of a distinct Chicana feminist movement to the patriarchal relations within the Chicano movement, the Chicano community, and the family:

> The contemporary Chicana movement has its origins in the Chicano movement and arose as a collective response to the *machismo* which surfaced among our compañeros to make menudo [tripe soup] while men talked strategy. In fact, I believe that one of the factors which precipitated the decline of the Chicano movement was machismo.
>
> —Faculty member, age 33

Despite Chicanas' antagonism toward male domination within the Chicano movement they still identify with the collective Chicano struggle:

> Chicanos y [and] Chicanas share many of the same dreams and I feel that the Chicana movement has a greater affinity with the Chicano movement than with the women's movement.

> —Faculty member, age 33

Tension between Chicanas' need for racial/ethnic solidarity and their struggle for gender equality reverberates throughout the responses. Women who advocate a feminist agenda report being asked to prove their loyalty to *la causa* [the cause] by agreeing to defer the struggle against gender oppression until racial/ethnic domination is abolished. This "loyalty test" stems from the nationalist character of the Chicano movement which identified race/ethnicity as the "primary contradiction," thereby producing an antagonistic climate for Chicana feminists. Within the Chicano movement, labels were often used as mechanisms of social control to discredit Chicanas who articulated a feminist political agenda:

> Overall the Chicano movement was great! But too many men (Chicano) became uptight when Chicanas began asking for and later demanding equality within the movement. Many of us were labeled as *agabachadas* [white-identified] or worse. Chicanas were seen more as a hindrance or decoration than as equal participants.

> —Faculty member, age 44

While all informants deplored sexism in the Chicano movement, some acquiesced to a "we need to stay within the fold" perspective to maintain unity within the movement:

> It [Chicana movement] has been distinct from the Chicano movement because they did not deal with women's issues or even family issues. We could not split the movement—we had to sacrifice ourselves for the movement.

> —Graduate student, no age given

The informants explained the development of a Chicana movement as irrevocably bound to Chicano cultural nationalism. This sentiment harkens back to the politics of the late 1960s and early 1970s wherein gender concerns were subsumed under the "larger struggle" against racial/ class oppression.

The perception of the MALCS survey respondents regarding the unique quality of the Chicana movement in relation to the American women's movement and the Chicano movement mirrors the sentiments of Chicana activists of the late 1960s and early 1970s. Like Chicana feminists of that period, MALCS survey informants reaffirmed that class, race/ethnicity, and cultural differences distinguish the Chicana movement from the American women's movement. The women argue that patriarchal relations within the Chicano movement served as the primary catalyst for the emergence of a Chicana movement.

Forty women who responded to the survey did not believe that a unique Chicana movement exists. They indicated that although Chicanas shared social and political interests separate from those of other women and Chicano men, they had not coalesced on these issues either ideologically or organizationally. Instead, they claim Chicanas' struggle for equality is waged within small, dispersed groups.

Chicana Feminism

Nearly all of the informants (83.2 percent) self-identified as Chicana feminists while seventeen eschew this label. Sixty-four discussed the meaning of Chicana feminism.[32]

Based on content analysis of the responses, three internally coherent and distinct voices emerged which depict different facets of Chicana feminism. To create a typology of Chicana feminism, we established three categories: *Chicana Liberal Feminism* (n=28), *Chicana Insurgent Feminism* (n=23), and *cultural nationalist feminism* (n=13). Each category expresses a collectivist orientation and is grounded in the material condition of the Chicana/o people. Women in each category articulate a commitment to improve the socioeconomic condition of Chicanas. Key differences emerge, however, with respect to the interpretation of social inequality and the preferred strategies to resist and redress Chicana subordination. Our typology captures a sense of the tension among liberal reformist, revolutionary, and nationalistic ideological positions.

Chicana Liberal Feminism centers on women's desire to enhance the well-being of the Chicano community, with a special emphasis on improving the status of women. Undergraduate students and staff were the most likely to articulate these views (80 percent). Almost one-third of Chicana faculty and graduate students also favored a liberal-reformist tradition (28.6 percent and 30 percent, respectively). Chicana empowerment—economic, social, and cultural—is a key theme in this category.

Chicana [feminism means] living my personal and professional life in line with certain principles: equality, shared power, mutually reinforcing and empowering relationships among women and with men (when that is possible).

—Faculty member, age 37

Women described several strategies to empower Chicanas, ranging from a personal approach (e.g., "support" other Chicanas) to a social reformist stance (e.g., "develop policy to meet Chicanas' needs").

Only when we are able to improve our socio-economic level will we be able to determine policy in this country and gain access to the upper echelons of decision-making processes. We can't wait for THEM (males or white females) to liberate us—no one will adequately address our issues except us.

—Faculty member, age 51

In general, respondents argued that Chicanas' lack of power emanates from at least two systems of stratification (race/ethnicity and gender) that are intertwined and that must be addressed simultaneously. They believe, however, that Chicana subordination can be redressed through institutional reforms that improve Chicanas' access to education, employment, and opportunity. They emphasize bringing Chicanas into the political and social mainstream.

[The] term "Chicana" in itself represents a certain degree of feminism. She strives to understand the political, social, and economic state her people are in and actively seeks to make changes that will advance her raza [people].

—Graduate student, age 26

Women in this category advocate change within a liberal tradition similar to that of the women's rights branch of the American women's movement. This perspective reaffirms Chicanas' desires to develop a personal awareness of women's needs within the context of the social and economic situation of the Chicano community at large. Although critical of the low socioeconomic conditions of the Chicano people, the Chicana liberal feminist perspective adopts a political strategy that falls short of the more radical critique articulated by Chicanas who form the category identified as insurgent feminism.

361

Chicana Insurgent Feminism draws on a tradition of radical thought and political insurgency. Slightly over half of the graduate students (52.2 percent) and 42.9 percent of Chicana faculty expressed views consistent with these traditions. Women in this category were also slightly younger (33.1 years) than the average.

Chicana Insurgent Feminism emphasizes how Chicana inequality results from three interrelated forms of stratification—race/ethnicity, class, and gender:

> Chicana feminism means the struggle to obtain self-determination for all Chicanas, in particular that Chicanas can choose their own life course without contending with the pressure of racism, sexism and poverty. It means working to overcome oppression, institutional and individual. Chicana feminism is much more than the slogan: "the personal is political"; it represents a collective effort for dignity and respect.
>
> —Faculty member, age 33

This perspective locates the source of Chicana oppression within the cultural expressions and social institutions of a hierarchically stratified society. In a tone reminiscent of Chicano cultural nationalism, the informant cited above calls for Chicana self-determination which encompasses a struggle against both personal and institutional manifestations of racial discrimination, patriarchy, and class exploitation. She expands the "personal is political" position of the American women's movement beyond the individual woman to embrace the community of Chicana women, and the Chicano community at large. This informant did not call for revolutionary change, but it is implicit within her formulation of Chicana self-determination.

The intensity of Chicanas' articulations of insurgent feminism varies. Some call for revolutionary change to end all forms of oppression:

> I believe that the impact of sexism, racism and elitism, when combined result in more intensely exploitive, oppressive and controlling situations than when these conditions exist independently of one another. The status and quality of life of the Chicano community as a whole can only improve/change when that of women within that community changes/improves. Any revolutionary change must include a change in relationships between men and women.
>
> —Faculty member, age 50

This woman argues that the cumulative effects of oppression are particularly pronounced for Chicanas. Like the previous informant, she connects the liberation of Chicanas to the overall struggle of the Chicano community. Her words, however, impart a more strident and uncompromising exposition of feminism that ties the liberation of the Chicano community to the struggle against patriarchy. Politically, she espouses a radical praxis advocating revolutionary change.

Other respondents extend insurgent feminism to include a critique of homophobia and solidarity with other oppressed peoples:

> It means that I am active and critical with respect to political, social and cultural manifestations of sexism, racism, Hispanophobia, heterosexism, and class oppression, and committed to working with others to create a more just society. It also means that I am moved by a sense of ethnic solidarity with Chicano, Mexican and other Latino people.

—Faculty member, age 40

This woman views political activism as a critical component of Chicana feminism. Like the other informants, she deplores the social subordination of Chicanas by race, class, and gender. She and a small but vocal group of women call for the recognition of oppression on the basis of sexual orientation within Chicana feminism. This is one dimension of the Chicana experience that has not been systematically incorporated into the agenda for Chicana liberation.

Chicana Insurgent Feminism advances what one woman referred to as "oppositional discourse," which challenges analytic frameworks that dichotomize the multiple sources of Chicana oppression while positing alternative frameworks grounded in their concrete experiences. Those in this category argue for theoretical-intellectual work that is not reactive but created from a Chicana-centered position, taking into account the multiple sources of Chicana subjectivity. This includes an internal critique of Chicano/Mexicano culture to revitalize and empower the community. The more strident voices within Chicana Insurgent Feminism may reflect, in part, greater involvement with the feminist groups and higher levels of political activism within these groups vis-à-vis Chicana liberal feminists or Chicana nationalist feminists. For example, three-fourths of Chicanas in this category report either past or present membership in feminist groups, compared with 61 percent of liberal feminists and 54 percent of nationalist feminists. When we presented respondents with six types of political activities (march, demonstration, sit-in, letter writing campaign, conference, and other), those women in the Chicana Insurgent Feminism category reported the highest levels of participation in the various activities (2.4 activities on average).[33]

In general, Chicana Insurgent Feminism engages in a critique that calls for the radical restructuring of society. Chicanas voice commitment to developing alternative theories, empowerment through political insurgency, and social action to realize Chicana self-determination.

Finally, Chicana Cultural Nationalist Feminism includes a small group of women who identify as feminists but who are committed to a cultural nationalist ideology that emphasizes maintaining traditional cultural values. According to this view, a Chicana feminist politic must uphold Chicano/Mexicano culture:

> I want for myself and for other women the opportunities to grow and develop in any area I choose. I want to do this while upholding the values (cultural, moral) that come from my being a part of the great family of Chicanos.

> —Graduate student, age 41

Reminiscent of the notion popularized within the Chicano movement (that all Chicanos are members of the same family—*la gran familia de la raza*), Chicana Cultural Nationalist Feminism articulates a feminist vision within the ideological rubric of la familia and advocates struggle for justice and gender equality while adhering to Chicano cultural traditions, forms, and ideologies:

> It involves the recognition that we must continue the struggle for women's rights and responsibilities within a cultural context.

> —Faculty member, age 43

Chicana Cultural Nationalist Feminism overlooks the possibility that Chicano/Mexicano cultural traditions often uphold patriarchy. Caught between the need to reverse the historical subordination of Chicanas without challenging the patriarchal underpinnings of a cultural nationalist politic, Chicana nationalist feminists rarely articulate concrete strategies to realize their dual goals. Instead, they offer brief philosophical statements that reaffirm cultural values. This speaks to the difficulty of reconciling a critique of gender relations within the Chicano community while calling for the preservation of Chicano culture.

Conclusion

The Chicana movement and Chicana feminist discourse emerged from the dialectical relationship between the ideology and politics of the Chicano movement and the American women's movement of the late 1960s and early 1970s. They developed from Chicanas' desires to move beyond what they perceived as indifference to their racial/ethnic, cultural, and class interests on the part of the American women's movement and the feminism it advocated. They also felt compelled to counter the antipathy of the Chicano movement toward a critique of gender relations and patriarchy in the Chicano community. Chicanas argued for an alternative discourse—one that would integrate the eradication of patriarchy in the Chicano community within a struggle against racial/class domination.

Despite their criticism of American feminism, study informants overwhelmingly self-identified as Chicana feminists. However, the fact that more women identified as Chicana feminists (n=84) than affirmed the existence of a distinct Chicana movement (n=54) suggests that the two phenomena are related to one another but are not mutually dependent. Informants may not be aware of sustained organizational activities that embrace a Chicana feminist political agenda. Or, women may interpret the meaning of a distinct Chicana movement in different ways. That is, women recognize the existence of small dispersed groups that advocate for Chicana rights but do not believe this constitutes a distinct Chicana movement. Conversely, other women interpret Chicana feminist activities as comprising a distinct Chicana movement.

Based on informants' descriptions of Chicana feminism we developed the following typology: Chicana Liberal Feminism, Chicana Insurgent Feminism, and Chicana Cultural Nationalist Feminism. Chicana Liberal Feminism centers on the conviction that Chicanas' life chances can be improved by modifying the existing structures of opportunity through both personal and political efforts. Chicana Insurgent Feminism vociferously critiques inequality by race/ethnicity, class, gender, and sexual orientation and calls for a sustained political struggle to restructure society. Cultural nationalist feminism conveys the sentiment that women's interests must be expressed within a cultural maintenance framework.

Our discussion of the various perspectives of Chicana feminist voices poses critical questions for the future of Chicana feminism. While a concern with redressing the historical condition of Chicanas cuts across all three categories, the groups vary with respect to the centrality of gender oppression, the critique of Chicano culture, and the preferred political form of struggle. One question that comes to mind is whether or not differences among the perspectives portend a prominent role for ideological struggles in the future development of Chicana feminism. The relatively small number of Chicanas adopting a cultural nationalist ideology attests to its general decline in the Chicana/o community. The inherent contradictions within Chicana nationalist feminism and the lack of coherent political strategies make it unlikely that the sentiments articulated within this perspective will play a major role in the future of Chicana feminism.

On the other hand, future political agendas and preferred strategies may divide along liberal-reformist and more revolutionary lines. Women in both categories espoused distinct perspectives and strategies to realize Chicana liberation. Chicana Liberal Feminism accepts the premise that the life chances of Chicanas can be enhanced through programs aimed at incorporating them into all facets of existing social institutions while fostering changes through established political processes. Although women in this category advocate gender, and racial equality, they are not as likely to emphasize the struggle against all forms of patriarchy as women in the Chicana Insurgent Feminism category. Chicana Insurgent Feminism provides the most sweeping analysis of domination based on class, race/ethnicity, and sex/gender. Those who fall into this category question the value of social integration by offering a vision of society that requires a revolutionary transformation, placing gender liberation as a prerequisite to human liberation.

Another possibility is unity based on a commitment to Chicana liberation within the context of the overall liberation of the Chicana/o people. This goal could attenuate political differences and lead to a common praxis to redress class, racial/ethnic, and gender oppression. Our analysis points to the viability of this scenario inasmuch as Chicana feminist discourse across all three categories affirms the significance of the Chicana struggle to the social and political struggles of the Chicano/Mexicano population.

Notes

Authors' names are listed randomly. We thank Linda Facio, Sarah Fenstermaker, Adaljiza Sosa Riddell, Judith Stacey, and the anonymous reviewers of *Aztlán* for their helpful comments on earlier drafts of this article. The authors are responsible for any errors or inconsistencies.

1. Several ethnic labels are used in this article. First, people of Color refers to Chicanos/ Mexican Americans, Puerto Ricans, Native Americans, Asian Americans, and African Americans, all of whom are native or colonized minorities. See A. Hurtado, "Relating to Privilege: Seduction and Rejection in the Subordination of White Women and Women of Color," *Signs: Journal of Women in Culture and Society* 14, no. 4 (1989): 833. We find Hurtado's capitalization of the word "Color" appropriate since it refers to specific racial/ethnic minority groups. Second, "women of Color" refers to women within each racial-ethnic minority group.

2. B. Thornton Dill, "Race, Class, and Gender: Prospects for an All-Inclusive Sisterhood," *Feminist Studies* 9 (1983): 131–50; M. Baca Zinn, L. Weber Cannon, E. Higginbotham, and B. Thornton Dill, "The Costs of Exclusionary Practices in Women's Studies," *Signs: Journal of Women in Culture and Society* 11 (1986): 290–303; Gloria Hull, Patricia Bell Scott, and Barbara Smith, *All Men Are Black, All Women Are White, but Some of Us Are Brave* (Old Westbury N.Y.: Feminist Press, 1982); N. Alarcon, "Chicana Feminist Literature: A Re-vision Through Malintzin/ or Malintzin: Putting Flesh Back on the Object," in Cherríe Moraga and Gloria Anzaldúa, eds., *This Bridge Called My Back: Writings by Radical Women of Color* (Watertown, Mass.: Persephone, 1981); A. E. Quintana, "Chicana Motifs: Challenge and Counter-Challenge," in *Intersections: Studies in Ethnicity, Gender, and Inequality* (Pullman: Washington State University Press, 1988), 197–217.

3. In social science literature, "Chicana" and "Chicano" typically refer respectively to women and men of Mexican descent residing in the United States. See M. Tienda, "The Mexican American Population," in A. H. Hawley and S. M. Mazie, eds., *Non-Metropolitan America in Transition* (Chapel Hill: University of North Carolina Press, 1981), 502–48. "Chicano" is also a broad term that includes both males and females who claim Mexican heritage (i.e., the Chicano community). These labels offer an alternative to the more common ethnic identifiers "Mexican" and "Mexican American"; see J. A. Garcia, "'Yo Soy Mexicano': Self-Identity and Socio-Demographic Correlates," *Social Science Quarterly* 62 (March 1981): 88–98. These labels were popularized during the Chicano movement to affix a political orientation—one that affirmed the need to struggle against the historical oppression of people of Mexican descent in the United States—to an ethnic identifier. See Rodolfo Acuña, *Occupied America: A History of Chicanos*, 2d ed. (New York: Harper & Row, 1981) and A. Gutiérrez and H. Hirsch, "The Militant Challenge to the American Ethos: 'Chicanos' and 'Mexican Americans'," *Social Science Quarterly* 53 (March 1973): 830–45. See also F. Peñalosa, "Toward an Operational Definition of the Mexican American," *Aztlán: Chicano Journal of the Social Sciences and the Arts* 1 (1970): 112. In recent years (post-1980s), the political dimension within the terms "Chicana" and "Chicano" has declined even as usage of the label "Hispanic" has grown. To maintain the integrity of the political and ethnic identification of this study's informants, we refer to the original political meaning of both "Chicana" and "Chicano."

4. Acuña, *Occupied America*; C. Muñoz and M. Barrera, "La Raza Unida Party and the Chicano Student Movement in California," *Social Science Journal* 19 (April 1982): 101–19.

5. This section summarizes the emergence of the "second wave" of the

American women's movement that relates to our analysis of the emergence of the Chicana movement and Chicana feminist discourse. For a more complete treatment of the women's movement, see Judith Hole and Ellen Levine, eds., *Rebirth of Feminism* (New York: Quadrangle Books, 1971) and J. Freeman, "The Women's Liberation Movement: Its Origins, Structure, Activities, and Ideas," in *Women: A Feminist Perspective*, 3d ed. (Palo Alto: Mayfield Publishing Co., 1984): 543–56.

6. Freeman, *Women*; Alison M. Jagger, *Feminist Politics and Human Nature* (Totowa, N.J.: Rowman and Allanheld, 1983).

7. Margaret L. Andersen, *Thinking About Women: Sociological Perspectives on Sex and Gender*, 2d ed. (New York: Macmillan, 1988); Jagger, *Feminist Politics*.

8. Angela Y. Davis, *Women, Race and Class* (New York: Vintage Books, 1981); Bell Hooks, *Feminist Theory: From Margin to Center* (Boston: South End Press, 1984) and Bell Hooks, *Ain't I a Woman: Black Women and Feminism* (Boston: South End Press, 1981); Hull, Scott, and Smith, *All Men Are Black*; Moraga and Anzaldúa, *This Bridge Called My Back*.

9. C. Nieto, "Chicanas and the Women's Rights Movements," *Civil Rights Digest* 6 (spring 1974): 36–42; A. Nieto-Gómez, "Chicana Feminism," *Caracol* 2, no. 5 (1976): 3–5. A. Sosa–Riddell, "Chicanas and El Movimiento," *Aztlán: Chicano Journal of the Social Sciences and the Arts* 5 (spring/fall 1974): 155–65.

10. Adelaida del Castillo, "La Visión Chicana." *Encuentro Femenil* 2 (1974): 46–8, esp. 46.

11. Del Castillo, "La Visión Chicana"; Nieto-Gómez, "La Feminista"; E. Martínez, "La Chicana," in *Third World Women* (San Francisco: Third World Communications, 1972): 130–2; Francisca Flores, "Equality," *Regeneración* 2 (1973): 4–5.

12. This section, which reviews key facets of the Chicano movement and Chicano cultural nationalism to contextualize the growth of Chicana feminism, is intended to be useful both to Chicano studies scholars as well as to readers wishing to gain more understanding of the topic.

13. Acuña, *Occupied America*; T. Almaguer, "Toward the Study of Chicano Colonialism," *Aztlán: Chicano Journal of the Social Sciences and the Arts* 2 (1971): 7–22; M. Barrera, C. Muñoz, and C. Ornelas, "The Barrio as an Internal Colony," in *People and Politics in Urban Society*, Urban Affairs Annual Review, vol. 6, ed. Harlan H. Hahn (Beverly Hills, Calif.: Sage Publications, 1972): 465–99; Robert Blauner, *Racial Oppression in America* (New York: Harper and Row, 1972).

14. Blauner, *Racial Oppression*; Ronald T. Takaki, *Iron Cages: Race and Culture in Nineteenth-Century America* (New York: Albert A. Knopf, 1979); David Montejano, *Anglos and Mexicans in the Making of Texas, 1836–1986* (Austin: University of Texas Press, 1987).

15. Alfredo Mirande, *The Chicano Experience: An Alternative Perspective* (Notre Dame Ind.: University of Notre Dame Press, 1985); J. R. Macias, "Nuestros Antepasados y el Movimiento," *Aztlán: Chicano Journal of the Social Sciences and the Arts* 5 (spring/fall 1974): 143–53.

16. A. Navarro, "The Evolution of Chicano Politics," *Aztlán: Chicano Journal of the Social Sciences and the Arts* 5 (spring/fall 1974): 57–84; Barrera, Muñoz,

and Ornelas, "The Barrio"; R. Santillan, "The Politics of Cultural Nationalism: El Partido De La Raza Unida in Southern California, 1969–1978" (Ph.D. diss., Claremont College, 1978).

17. Chicano Coordinating Committee on Higher Education, *El Plan de Santa Barbara: A Chicano Plan for Higher Education* (Santa Barbara, Calif.: La Causa Publications, 1969); R. Alvarez, "The Unique Psychohistorical Experience of the Mexican American," *Social Science Quarterly* 52 (1971): 15–29.

18. T. Almaguer, "Historical Notes on Chicano Oppression: The Dialectics of Racial and Class Domination in North America," *Aztlán: Chicano Journal of the Social Sciences and the Arts* 5 (spring/fall 1974): 27–56; and T. Almaguer, "Class, Race and Chicano Oppression," *Socialist Revolution* 5 (1975); Mario Barrera, *Race and Class in the Southwest: A Theory of Racial Inequality* (Notre Dame, Ind.: University of Notre Dame Press, 1979).

19. M. Baca Zinn, "Mexican-American Women in the Social Sciences," *Signs: Journal of Women in Culture and Society* 8 (1982): 259–72; D. A. Segura, "Chicanas and Triple Oppression in the Labor Force," in *Chicana Voices: Intersections of Class, Race and Gender*, ed. Teresa Córdova et al. (Austin: Center for Mexican American Studies, University of Texas at Austin, 1986), 47–76; A. M. García, "The Development of Chicana Feminist Discourse, 1970–1980," *Gender and Society* 3 (June 1989): 217–38.

20. Martha P. Cotera, *The Chicana Feminist* (Austin: Information Systems Development, 1977), 31.

21. E. Longeaux y Vásquez, "The Mexican-American Woman," in *Sisterhood Is Powerful*, ed. Robin Morgan (New York: Vintage, 1970), 379.

22. M. Vidal, *Women: New Voice of La Raza* (New York: Pathfinder Press, 1971).

23. Anna Macias, *Against All Odds* (Westport, Conn.: Greenwood Press, 1982).

24. Macias, *Against All Odds*.

25. Nieto-Gómez, "Chicana Feminism," 5.

26. Ibid., 3-5.

27. F. Flores, "Conference of Mexican Women: Un Remolino," *Regeneración* 1 (1971): 1–4.

28. García, "Chicana Feminist Discourse."

29. Ibid.

30. Adaljiza Sosa Riddell, ed., *Mujeres Activas en Letras y Cambio Social, Noticiera de M.A.L.C.S.* (Davis: University of California, Chicano Studies Program, 1983).

31. While both of these answers cannot be standardized (e.g., one woman's sense of being "very familiar" with literature on the American women's movement may differ substantially from that of another woman), we are confident that informants gave fairly accurate self-assessments. We base this evaluation on a content analysis of the different ways women describe the major agendas of the American women's movement and the relative ease with which they refer to various types of feminist theories (e.g., socialist feminism). Accordingly, women who indicated they were "very familiar" with either the American women's movement or feminist

theoretical writing gave far more detailed and knowledgeable descriptions than women who indicated they were "slightly familiar" or "not familiar" with these writings.

32. Thirteen women provided nonspecific answers with no discernable pattern and seven women did not elaborate on the meaning of Chicana feminism.

33. Women who articulated Chicano liberal feminism reported an average of 1.8 activities and Chicano nationalist feminists reported 2.1 activities. Between one-half and two-thirds of Chicano insurgent feminists had participated in marches and demonstrations compared with one-third of nationalist feminists and liberal feminists.

Chicana Identity Matters

Deena J. González

What is involved in the taking of a name, suggests the Chicana lesbian feminist theoretician Gloria Anzaldúa (1987), unites our search for a Chicano/a identity in this century. Some searches defy categorization. Disunited in our self-labeling—"Hi"-spanic, Latino, Mexican American, even Chicano American—our ruminations constantly project a homecoming that eludes us. This also unifies our condition in this century and is instructive. "They caught us before we had a chance to figure it all out," Chicana/o activists protest. Our laments are ongoing proclamations, as enduring as José Vasconcelos's concept of "La Raza Cósmica," which he espoused in the 1920s. His concept of an enduring race was one thing, our self-identification is another. The word Chicana has always been difficult to use, especially if applied to women living in the previous centuries. Illusory even today, many Spanish-surnamed, Mexican-origin women refuse the term Chicana.

Still, we Chicana historians make an effort to apply the concept. Why? Our contemporary conditions are as illustrative as our histories, particularly the histories of the unnamed, of women. For women who have no name, Anzaldúa suggests this: "She has this fear that she has no names, that she has many names, that she doesn't know her names; She has this fear that she's an image that comes and goes clearing and darkening" (43). For women who remain faceless despite their consistent presence in documents, this business of acquiring identity is the basis for living and for life, is the basis of the struggle for selfhood—in our (Chicana) present but also in "their" (Aztec/Native or mestizo) pasts (Hernández 1993).

We find tremendous consolation in tracing the sources of our empowerment—the struggle for identity and for recognition is one, but only one, struggle in a long history of finding or locating identity. Lending identity, as historians do, is another important task, but it is often undiscussed although it lies on the flip side of the identity coin. Identity is both assumed and given; some people have "more" identity, some less. Every day, historians lift out of the records, or find in the records, or situate persons in records—our fundamental task is to organize this information in selective categories, and this is not easy. Who is denigrated in one century is reified in the next.

Malinche (of Mexico, translator to the Spanish conqueror Hernán Cortés) and Doña Gertrudis Barceló (of New Mexico, nineteenth-century businesswoman) are examples. For mainstream historians, ignoring a group—say women of Mexican descent, as many have done—is part of a selection process; not naming women constitutes including them by omission. For the most part, in mainstream history texts and in the works of Chicano historians, Chicanas are absent. It is in these omitting spaces that Chicanas have found a place in the debates raging through the historical profession, and there, we occupy a pivotal if uncomfortable role because we resurrect images and real persons from the past. Our task as Chicana historians is twofold—to resurrect and to delineate/revise. How do we do justice to both, and then translate our findings into languages that majority or dominant societies understand? Do we even want to do that? Our choices are neither simple nor clear. Here are examples from our very ordinary existences as historians and as self-identified Chicanas.

To the new generation of western American historians—the revisionist brigade, as they have been called—the "West" is a place, a region, a state of mind, a culture; wide-ranging, long, far, distant, pockmarked by the dynamics of contest and conflict, consensus, and contradiction. Not an easy place to reside, in other words. But to Chicana/o historians, the West is really the Mexican North.[1] The concepts we use and the configurations we bring to our work, whether of class (upper and working) or of the sexualized, gendered, racialized systems (in matrices traced like virgin, martyr, witch, or whore; or Native, mestiza, or Chicana) are different.[2] Never has the sun-bonneted helpmate, sturdy homesteader, or ruddy miner or rancher been less useful to our projects. For us, teaching a class in the history of the American West, then, makes no sense. We ask, why not call it a history of the Mexican North? Why not call it a history of many names, of places termed by Native historians as far back as they can remember the Dancing Ground of the Sun, or by Chicano/a historians, Aztlán? You see our dilemmas and the new directions we are plotting. Add to this that few historians, except the most recent professionally trained, were schooled in Chicano/a history. We are self-trained. Where do we begin, what do we name our undertaking, what organizes our chronology? The questions link our investigations with the preoccupations of other historians.

These issues reflect my themes for this article: Chicana is a contemporary term, but can be applied to Spanish-speaking and Mexican-origin women in any area presently considered territory of the United States. Historians may well be bothered by the renaming, although established courtesies indicate that people should be known by their preferred terms. In 1980, the U.S. government ignored the protocol and lumped us together under the generic "Hispanic," rewriting history, so to speak, by suggesting that the tie to Spain was greater than the tie to our indigenous heritage. This may have suited other Latino groups living in the United States, but it caused a new wave of dissension among Chicano/as. As Luis Valdez (1994) postulated, "Why be an adjective, and not a noun? Why Hispanic? It doesn't compute. Why not Germanic, a Germanic?"

For Chicanas, one dilemma in self-identification set in not because we do not know who we are or are misguided in applying labels, but because like many other terms, Chicana has always been problematized as an identity in waiting, as an incomplete act. Philosophically, spiritually, or politically, Chicanas do not all look at the world in the same way, or even in ways Euro-Americans might understand. It is not true that we do not know who we are. If anything, we should suffer the accusation that we know too much who we are, have too much identity.

Add to this the internal, embattling ideological wars dominating our newly created spaces in the academy. Chicanas most agree on the name we have selected for ourselves; problematized, discussed, and assessed, it provided the point of departure, but everything since then has spun away from an assumed "core" of understanding. The fractures are rampant and also hidden from the mainstream. (Unless you have followed the recent Chicano studies debates at University of California at Santa Barbara, where at least one conclusion can be drawn—Chicanas and Chicanos do not agree on all issues.) Mainly, we least discuss our differences in favor of presenting a united front in the academic theater that would most often like to get rid of us all. To say fracture is to speak of secrets or to name lies. In our conferences of the past years, we have begun to witness that a resurgent Chicano/a nationalist student movement contradicts Chicano/a faculty agendas. Among Chicanas, lesbian feminist pedagogies and scholarship parted ways with other types of Chicana (feminist) practices long ago. The majority of Chicana lesbian feminist scholars do not feel comfortable operating within the confines and structures of the overwhelmingly male-identified, even "minority," organizations that exist within the academy. The majority of Chicana lesbian academics are not out, and many fear being outed. At one

Ford Foundation fellows gathering, gay/lesbian Chicano, African American, and Native American academics discussed the policies of revelation, with one group decidedly arguing for secrecy, while those of us with tenure urged our colleagues to consider the fact that in most departments, very little is truly secret—least of all who pairs up with whom.

Continuing with the practices and politics of identifying, of self-identification, and the constructions of identity, mixed-race Chicana and Native/Chicana women decry the implicit racism that parades a Native/Othered guest lecturer before a Chicana conference not much interested in exploring this old division, but that would rather project a falsely unified consciousness by listing the speakers as "foremothers." These are also examples from our daily lives as Chicana academics.[3]

Probing such politics and policies of identity and location, contemporarily as I have just done, or historically as I intend next, is difficult because self-designation is a twentieth-century exercise full of self-consciousness. Locating the identity of subjects long since dead, in the case of my work on nineteenth-century Nuevo Mexicanas, is equally problematic because the people I write about exist in the cultural and collective memories of the Chicano/Hispano families of Santa Fe. Ancestry remains exceedingly important in the lives of northern Nuevo Mexicanos. The twin processes of naming and revealing engender further responsibilities and prerogatives and have been contextualized for that reason in these opening passages.[4]

Some might want to search the past for clues about how we came to our contemporary ideological impasses over the significance of our identities. Identity today, our autobiographical anecdotes reveal and the documents detailing the lives of nineteenth-century Spanish-Mexican women suggest, is not the same as identity once was. Nineteenth-century Spanish speakers named themselves as village residents first, as members of particular families second, then as (Catholic) parishioners, and, continuously, as non-Indians. Without Native people—*against* whom they would identify—the Spanish-speaking, mestizo and nonmestizo might not have chosen specific identities at all, adopting instead a more colonialist attitude that rendered indigenous residents nonexistent.

As we know today, identity formulations have as much to do with what one carries inside as with what one encounters outside. Indigenous people thus existed as opposites to the Spanish, and then, in the case of the majority mestizo population (that is, after the first twenty-five years of conquest and colonization by the Spanish), their ongoing presence delineated a clearing space within which a small but tenacious conquistador class could continue to roam, relocate, and define itself, if uneasily. Physical appearance—or phenotype as geneticists might say—by itself helped identity concerns hardly at all, as we see in the present when we must piece together color, speech, dress, and many other "markers" to situate or locate one (an-other's) identity.

Mexico and the Southwest witnessed various color representations. After the first phases of conquest between Natives and Europeans, "Indian" actually began signifying non-Spanish-speaking, not non-Spanish, as very few Spanish-speaking residents of the northern frontiers could label themselves pure-blooded Spanish, even if they were of the criollo class (that is, were descendents of people self-designated as Spanish but born in the New World), even if color supported their sense of superiority. In the early part of the nineteenth century, in the midst of creating and adopting a *criolloized* existence, many used their labels not simply to delineate an ethnic identity, but to designate their classes primarily. This fragile existence as frontiers people transcended other ponderings over and beyond their quests for specific, regional identities, as Santa Feans, as Tucsonenses, as Tejanos. The migrations northward of mixed-race peoples, some studies suggest, signaled among the migrants an improved class status. Resettlement, they imply, hastened social and economic mobility, but was best considered locale by locale. The resulting identity formations were lodged in a hodge-podge system that was best understood by residents of a region, by insiders, and only loosely by those living throughout the distant territories of the former Spanish Empire (Morner 1967).

Categorization primarily on the basis of any single identifying characteristic—that is, skin color, language skill, religious devotion, or birthplace—would be a mistake. Finally, on the question of the origins of the identity models I am asserting here, or on the origins of Chicana identity, it is important to bear in mind that insider/outsider concerns operated on a multi-tiered and in a multidirectional social system; a conquistador class may have sought to assert its power through identity manipulations. Wannabes—those seeking upper-class status or non-lowest-class status—in Tucson, Santa Fe, San Antonio, determined that harkening back to a conquistador heritage was better than claiming mestizo or indigenous ethnicity. The state, or Empire in this case, supported the denials readily enough: identity cards were common, and rules and regulations from both church and state dictated marriage choices, to name only two examples of how race or ethnicity were also determined or ordained.

From the beginning of Spanish contact, then, the search for identity hinged on questions of status, and social location, as well as on the relationship to the state or empire, which is to say pro-Crown, or later, pro-Spain or pro-Mexico, or later still, pro-revolution.

In New Mexico, whose Spanish-Mexican women I speak about next, the hyphenations and terms were equally complex. "Spanish-Mexican" appeared as early as the colonial period (Castañeda 1990). It was used interchangeably with "gente de habla español," at times to connote a criollo heritage, and otherwise to signify Spanish-Catholic background and Spanish linguistic dominance.[5] By 1820, a new sense of Mexicanness pervaded, with even criollos picking up the label "Mexican." Thus, Mexican still was recognized for the indigenous, Aztec word that it was (Me-shi-can), but it was hispanicized sufficiently (Me-ji-cano/a) that it also came to be recognized as the basis for an evolving national identity. Mexico (the country) would not name itself until later, but already politicians, officials, criollos, mestizos, and Natives used the word and applied Mexican, if infrequently, to themselves. In the independence movements, adaptation of an indigenous word, of course, marked the severed bonds to Spain, and Mexico and Mexicanos continue to this day to glorify and uphold the concept of an indigenous, mixed-race inheritance. Unfortunately for us Mexican/Chicano residents of the southwestern United States, the federal government is abysmally ignorant of this rich heritage about naming and identity formations.

An added ingredient in the rumblings about Spanish versus Mexican, Indian versus non-Indian, criollo versus mestizo in the nineteenth century was the steady reality of continuous race and cultural mixture. We might even say that non-Indian did not deny Indianness, but was also a realistic statement about Spanish-language dominance. In places like northern Mexico and in the upper Rio Grande valleys that later constituted New Mexico and Colorado, few original settlers maintained "pure" Spanish blood. For one, immigration from the interior of Mexico was a constant phenomenon throughout the nineteenth century. Mestizos from central Mexico and mixed-race migrants with Spanish linguistic skills from such northern states as Sonora and Chihuahua moved north into New Mexico and Texas. This continued even after the U.S. invasions of the 1820s, 1830s, and 1840s.

Additionally, religion ordered other considerations: few Catholics married non-Catholics. In New Mexico, *genízaros*, or detribalized Catholic converts of Indian descent, married Spanish-Mexicans. The hyphenated term "Spanish-Mexican" captures readily the forged racial/ethnic, religious, and political minglings on the northern Mexican frontier and seems extremely appropriate in its application to the nineteenth century, but again, only if listeners recognize that Spanish-Mexican reflects *mestizaje*.

For Chicanas living after 1820, the changing political and economic configurations, as Mexico declared its independence and the United States its interest in Mexico's northern territories, mirrored other problems—not more choices, but different ones. Change, in fact, caught up to the frontiers people. Soon, Missouri traders and merchants began pushing into the economic centers of the frontier, especially toward Santa Fe, with wagons loaded with manufactured items. The wagons creaked and groaned into this most populated Mexican community west of the Mississippi River, a town of over 4,000 persons that by frontier standards qualified as a full-fledged city. The hardy perseverance of the wagons, the survival of goods on the pathways from the distant states along the Mississippi/Missouri corridor, and the knowledgeable drivers became images to be carefully considered by the locals. The long and short of it was that the Mexican frontier of the north had been neglected by the interior governing departments as they fought for or against independence instead, and this predisposed to a certain extent Santa Fe's residents toward embracing the North American articles, if not their purveyors.

Economic desires could not mask for long, however, lingering racial, cultural, and sexual tensions. Their appearance was aided by the underlying values and ideologies of impudent merchants from the United States. The trader/trapper generation arriving in Santa Fe, men like James Ohio Pattie or William Messervy, despised the town's adobe structures and exhibited an unabashed disdain for local customs. Their comments conveyed far more than the typical anti-Mexican sentiment we know guided the travel literature of this period. Josiah Gregg, in a famous volume published some time later, preached a stereotypic notion of social stasis: "The arrival of the caravan at Santa Fe changes the aspect of the place at once. Instead of idleness and stagnation which its streets exhibited before, one now sees everywhere the bustle, noise, and activity of a lively market town." A physician by training, Gregg reported that nothing was wrong with Santa Fe and New Mexicans that a bit of merchandising could not cure.

No single character better symbolizes the way in which identity questions and issues were on the one hand central and important, or on the other, nearly ignored by historians, than Doña Gertrudis Barceló. Owner of Santa Fe's largest gambling saloon and bar, expert monte card dealer, and a fascinating businesswoman, she received the highest praise and worst criticism of every Euro-American in town. Matt Field depicted the saloon as a place "where her calm seriousness was alone discernible.... Again and again the long fingers of Señora Toulous swept off the pile of gold, and again were they replaced by the unsteady fingers of her opponent." In her, these restless wanderers recognized their own hungry search for profit, but they disparaged her for it. Josiah Gregg called Mexicans "lazy and indolent." James Josiah Webb determined that all Mexicans did was "literally dance from the cradle to the grave." In the *Congressional Record* of the period, speeches and statements equated brown skin color with promiscuity, immorality, and decay. Albert Pike in New Mexico in 1831 called the area around Santa Fe "bleak, black, and barren." New Mexicans, he said, were "peculiarly blessed with ugliness." Frank Edwards, on a military expedition—illegal at that—called Mexicans "debased in all moral sense," and they amounted to little more than "swarthy thieves and liars." Francis Parkman, historian of the West, would argue a decade later that people in this part of the country could be "separated into three divisions, arranged in order of their merits: white men, Indians, and Mexicans; to the latter of whom the honorable title of 'whites' is by no means conceded." When the United States conquered Mexico, the boundary commissioner declared that the "darker colored" races were inevitably "inferior and syphilitic."

Literally thousands of other references mirrored the racist values and conquering ideologies of the United States, heightening the fervor over destiny and superiority, gloating over, as a *Harper's* reporter stated, "an ignorant, priest-ridden peasantry."[6]

The racial idiom of these nineteenth-century illegal immigrants from the United States up until 1848, and subsequently when the territories were snatched from Mexico, suggests that sometime in this period identity matters came to be shaped by anti-Mexican fervor as much as by proud ownership of the term Mexican. For women of the former Mexican north, the sexual idiom of the time, of the sort that denigrated the famous La Tules but also others who labored for the newcomer class, is equally important to understand. Women were made active agents in a town that Gregg said bustled with activity, including sexual activity, or so they said. Prostitution in the period before conquest was illegal and its punishment was banishment from the town. Illicit sexual liaisons, partner exchange, and all the rest were recorded in the court records, so sexual expression outside the confines of marriage was clearly evident; to read the newcomers' accounts, however, would suggest that all Spanish-Mexican women did, when not dancing, was have sex with the Euro-American men. For that reason, I have sought in previous work to portray some of the harsher realities, to expose the ways in which women most often worked at several jobs, such as household management, laundress, seamstress, and domestic; many operated carts on the plaza, and once a new wage, tax, and economic system was in place, these aspects of frontier life became even more necessary in explaining women's survival. Many students of history would like to make the case that La Tules operated a brothel and was doing her own share of exploitation, but there is no evidence to support the fantasy, and left unframed by the racial and sexual degradations colonization imposes, the conclusion encapsulates historically a form of misogyny.

What becomes clearer about the last decades of the nineteenth century is that until then, Spanish-speaking or Spanish-surnamed women enjoyed some degree of mobility between towns and within extended family networks. That becomes much less the case in the twentieth century, and possibly until World War II, especially in the defense industries, because of wage work based in the factories, where Chicanas were locked into the lowest-paying and most depreciated jobs of all. Thus, our contemporary moves into urban centers followed in two stages. The first occurred between the Great Depression and roughly 1940, as rural-to-urban migration soared and urban wage economies as well as migration from Mexico increasingly drew Mexicana and Chicana workers into the larger cities of Texas, New Mexico, Arizona, and California, and to a lesser extent toward selected states of the Midwest and the East. A second followed after World War II when the war machine actually drew them in, but only to position them in war industry work or service occupations.

Identity formulations in those urban spaces, where bilingual skill was necessary for negotiating daily living, was still oppositional, but this time it resembled "a pulling away from" rural identity, small-town identity, or extended or localized family. City migrants were often the first generation to leave their villages or small towns, often the first generation to travel such long distances (in that way, they resembled some colonial ancestors), often the first generation to speak English fluently, or to combine English and Spanish. Truly, what we see in this grouping, then, is a Chicana generation, if we understand Chicana as a twentieth-century phenomenon characterized by bilingualism, biculturalism, and shifting economic status—not necessarily better, but different (steady wage work as opposed to erratic wages, weekly paychecks as opposed to haphazard payments or payment by the piece or job). Also, a degree of independence, that is, a movement away from traditional racial, sexual, and religious governance, seems to prevail in the depictions by the few scholars who have begun to examine Chicanas in this era. I hesitate to argue too strongly that this is definitively the first generation of self-identifying Chicanas—that comes later in the 1960s, and I hesitate to mark it in the history books, to hail these women as "true" Chicanas, because if we have learned anything about authenticity and the power of authenticating, such differentiations proceed along contrary lines historically and contemporarily. Who is a real Chicana feminist is unanswerable in general terms and, so, who can be designated as the first discernible Chicana generation is equally ungeneralizable.

The search for home or homeland, another marker along the identity road, interestingly would be left to the next generation of urban Chicanas, and it is here that lesbian feminist theoreticians like Gloria Anzaldúa (1987), Cherríe Moraga (1983, 1993), Emma Pérez (1991, 1995), Alicia Gaspar de Alba (1989, 1993) and others take up the search for identities in the multiples; it is among this most recent generation of self-identified Chicanas that more fluid identities can be located. What may be important about each may be the linkage between identity and homeland. Each author reflects a working-class heritage (or, for Gaspar de Alba, a strict Mexican, "untainted" ancestry/class, that is, non-*pocho*), a bilingual understanding of the world, and a centering of mother, grandmothers, or sisters. Each longs for a space or site of reunification, and one can envision some generation of psychoanalysts, deconstructionists, and social historians engaging with these longings as a search for womb, mother, or homeland. The linkages could be dehistoricized, but I would like to resurrect the historical again to "read" this literature differently.

The political self-consciousness pervading the works of the Chicana lesbian feminist writers just named is one more marker along the path of their identities; another, I have suggested, is their nod to history and location, to family pasts and memory: In her novel *Gulf Dreams* (1995), Pérez recalls "the sound of the hammer reflected his love for us, pound for pound," as she gathers up memories of her father's upholstery shop located in front of their small-town, Texas home; in Moraga's autobiographical essay, "There was something I knew at that eight-year-old moment that I vowed never to forget—the smell of a woman who is life and home to me at once"; in Gaspar de Alba's autobiographical statement when she names herself "the first Chicana fruit of the family."

Moraga (1993) claimed her mother's race, her brother claimed their (white) father's. Chicana, to this way of thinking, is racialized as blood (genetic) and not ethnicity or identity, something less true in Anzaldúa (1987) and Pérez (1991) who both have Mexican parents and see Chicana as embracing mestiza pasts, more blurring rather than less. In Gaspar de Alba's poetry and reflections (1989, 1993), Chicana becomes an identity assumed around linguistic borders because "English was forbidden at home and Spanish was forbidden" in her Catholic girls' school. Moraga privileges the color/blood connection, casting her choice in the direction of Chicana, whereas Anzaldúa, Pérez, and Gaspar de Alba search for and construct an ethnicity of the borderlands, the Rio Grande, and ultimately, Mexico. For Anzaldúa and Pérez regional identity and ethnic identity or nationality derive from a rural tejana experience, for Gaspar de Alba from a Mexican border zone. Their Chicana identities are lodged in *lo mexicano* whereas Moraga's (1983), at least in the earlier volume, stems from a differently assumed identity based on something chosen—either/or white or Chicana (the latter being the metaphorical land of her mother).

The bifurcations evident in Moraga's work reveal a personal journey that mirrors more than motherland or homeland searches. It is a search to be duplicated by many. Young Chicana lesbians coming to their twin identities first as Chicanas and then as lesbians revere Moraga as guru, understandably given the different stages of consciousness woven into her autobiographical ruminations. As Gaspar de Alba (1993) notices in "Tortillerismo," a review of some of these texts, Anzaldúa's mestiza consciousness is far more difficult to grasp for those whose racial and ethnic consciousness is absent, or de-historicized, or regarded as something that can be everchangingly shed or adopted at will.[7] I suggest that Anzaldúa's and Pérez's Chicana lesbian identities seem more "fixed" precisely because both hail from villages in Texas, and Gaspar de Alba's because she is a *fronteriza* who traversed with agility the U.S.-Mexican border as she did the public/private, English/Spanish one. Moraga grew up in Los Angeles in a household with different borders, but decidedly not with sustained geographic proximity to Mexico. It could also be argued that in her case, familiarity with Los Angeles is familiarity with the world. Her coming into a Chicana consciousness after 1980, a moment of consciousness explained by Gloria Anzaldúa who met her at a conference and posed the inevitable "Who/what are you?" is more than anecdote because the moment marks consciousness of the most intimate and powerful kind, the seconds of declaration, "I am" or "I think I am." Each of the writers listed here explains a similar process of identity-situating and each politicizes that moment radically by disavowal, rejection, or embrace. The moment configures itself distinctively and becomes not only a space for empowerment, but a space for departure, a signal of difference.

The question that emerges from the revelatory texts or writings of Chicana lesbian feminists is not who or what is to be made more of or less of, or who is more Chicana (those closest to Mexico?), or who less (those not?), but rather, as I am suggesting, how *much* to be Chicana and in what circles or locations to situate that identity, or have it situated for one (as reflected in the question "Who/what are you?"). Self-constructed, the lesbian memoirs of Anzaldúa and Pérez—more than Moraga's—locate their identity formulations across several centuries, Gaspar de Alba across two countries; theirs, I would argue, is in keeping with historical memory, even in their rejection of the masculinist aspects of that history. Their work exhibits the tendency to assert a "we," of family, community, or ethnicity, to speak of an historical "us"; far less evident is the focused "I," a tone detectable in many of Moraga's pieces.[8] Moraga's work, then, might well be of the future because it patterns outward, from a dominant urban, First World existence (as she says in *Loving in the War Years*, a "passing," male-centric yet fatherless household/family, and importantly, an English-dominant domain). Anzaldúa, Pérez, and Gaspar de Alba did not share the life of post–World War II Los Angeles. Such childhoods emerged *not* from the gringo/Chicana parental racial dyad, or even cultural one. Thus, they stand apart from many contemporary movements that seek the move toward that next level of mestiza consciousness stretching beyond Spanish/ Indigenous and embracing many other multiple ethnicities and identities; in a set of words, the transnational, transmigratory, First World cultural polyglot of the next century, in a name, Los Angeles. On that plain, then, Moraga's experiences meet up with Anzaldúa's, Pérez's, and Gaspar de Alba's to complete a cycle.[9] The pattern is not lost on historians or cultural anthropologists of the Southwest who recall Aztlán as the spiritual homeland of the Aztecs who, in humble beginnings southward, lived in a rattlesnake-infested swamp and eventually dominated Tenochtitlán and beyond. I am intrigued about future projections for this type of work and scholarship; perhaps the artist Gronk's forecast is on the mark and we historians can paraphrase, "L.A. is [indeed] everywhere." In a self-stylized or highly conscious urban form, one can imagine, for example, a Chicana/ Native/Euro-American, or Third World Other/Transgendered person reinvoking Anzaldúa's mestiza consciousness and reinscribing it with new meanings. Similarly, a new generation of middle-class, university-educated Chicanas may lay claim to a different mestizaje-ized identity altogether that revolves primarily around, or is lodged across, the spaces of sexuality, class, ethnicity, physical abilities. The step in that direction constitutes one Chicana (postmodern) condition; the contradictions and differences among even this small group of active writers and academics suggest the need for fuller interrogations or readings of their work.

Such problematizing of our histories also needs to take into account another departure, that is, the movement of these writers and other women of color like them into the academic theatre. Setting aside for a moment the trivialized pursuit of multiculturalism in education (what such scholars as Gayatri Spivak call "ethnomania" unleashed in the academy or in the public schools), let me say that these writers must also be understood as a first generation of self-identified lesbians *and* first-generation creative writers or scholar/activists. These linkages do denote some radical historical disjuncturing because, on the one hand, we have in them, in ourselves, a movement into Western European–patterned, formal educational systems, of the research type, *and* that move has come at a moment when the environments new to us are reorienting themselves in the very directions we argued for outside *their* walls. Although this means that, for the most part, we are ignored (the statistics on faculty hiring and on graduate student recruitment are appalling on the question of diversity), and our work is still most often ignored or disdained, we occupy, as a first generation, yet another *sitio*, to use Emma Pérez's term, a new site of, or for, identity; Anzaldúa's "she has this fear," with which I opened, can be understood if contextualized against our invisibility or absence in the academy, but is less understandable if layered over the extremely rich pronouncements, creative, historical, and artistic expressions of our poets, storytellers, and scholars. We are engaged by their debates and praxis in the academy and their work allows our minds to linger in the spaces outside of it as well. The undertaking will have an impact because, as we know in U.S. society, and in Latin America, race and ethnicity matter.

Notes

Reprinted from *Culture and Difference: Critical Perspectives on the Bicultural Experience in the United States*, ed. Antonia Darder (Westport, Conn.: Bergin and Garvey, 1995.)

1. For examples of the newer, revisionary work, see Milner 1996.

2. For a review of this literature, see Castañeda 1992.

3. The example comes from a MALCS conference in 1993, and was made by observers and participants at the gathering. MALCS (Mujeres Activas en Letras Y Cambio Social) is one of the only national Chicana academic organizations in the country.

4. For a more complete review of the historical practice of revelations, see also González, forthcoming.

5. On another label, see Miranda 1988.

6. For citations and a review of this literature, see González 1993.

7. See Gaspar de Alba 1993b.

8. The clearest example is evident in Moraga's *The Last Generation* (1993); see the chapter opening on post-Sandinista society.

9. See Stanford critic Yvonne Yarbro-Bejarano's rereading of Moraga's creative work, forthcoming from the University of Texas Press.

Works Cited

Anzaldúa, G. 1987. *Borderlands/La Frontera: The New Mestiza*. San Francisco: Spinsters/Aunt Lute Press.

Castañeda, A. 1992. "Women of Color and the Rewriting of Western History: The Discourse, Politics, and Decolonization of History." *Pacific Historical Review* 11 (November): 501–533.

———. 1990. "Gender, Race, and Culture: Spanish-Mexican Women in the Historiography of Frontier California." *Frontiers* 11: 8–20.

Gaspar de Alba, A. 1993a. *The Mystery of Survival and Other Stories*. Tempe, Ariz.: Bilingual Review Press.

———. 1993b. "Tortillerismo: Work by Chicana Lesbians." *Signs: Journal of Women in Culture and Society* 18, no. 4 (summer): 956-63.

———. 1989. *Three Times a Woman*. Tempe, Ariz.: Bilingual Review Press.

González, D. Forthcoming. *Refusing the Favor: The Spanish-Mexican Women of Santa Fe, 1820–1880*. New York: Oxford University Press.

———. 1993. "La Tules of Image and Reality." In *Building with Our Hands: New Directions in Chicana Studies*, ed. Beatriz Pesquera and Adela de la Torre. Berkeley: University of California Press.

Hernández, I. 1993. "In Praise of Insubordination, or What Makes a Good Woman Go Bad?" In *Transforming a Rape Culture*, ed. E. Buchwald, P.R. Fletcher, and M. Roth, 376–92. Minneapolis: Milkweed Editions.

———. 1992. "Open Letter to Chicanas: On the Power and Politics of Origin." In *Without Discovery: A Native Response to Columbus*, ed. R. González. Seattle: Broken Moon.

Milner, C. III, ed. 1996. *The Re-Significance of the American West*. New York: Oxford University Press.

Miranda, Gloria. 1988. "Racial and Cultural Dimensions of *Gente de Razón* Status in Spanish and Mexican California." *Southern California Quarterly* 70: 265–78.

Moraga, C. 1993. *The Last Generation*. Boston: South End Press.

———. 1983. *Loving in the War Years: Lo que nunca pasó por sus labios*. Boston: South End Press.

Morner, M. 1967. *Race Mixture in the History of Latin America*. Boston: Little Brown.

Pérez, E. 1995. *Gulf Dreams*. Berkeley, Calif.: Third Woman Press.

———. 1991. "Sexuality and Discourse." In *Chicana Lesbians: The Girls Our Mothers Warned Us About*, ed. C. Trujillo. Berkeley, Calif.: Third Woman Press.

Valdez, L. 1994. "The Hemispheric American." Lecture delivered at Claremont McKenna College, Claremont, California.

Latino Performance and Identity

David Román

AUTHOR'S NOTE: *I wrote this essay in 1997, at the invitation of Aztlán's new editor Chon Noriega, to publicize the new work of Latino performers and playwrights to an audience that would have everything to gain from learning about these artists. I also wanted to argue for the centrality of theater and performance studies to the field of Chicano and Latino studies, especially as the latter were being reconstituted in Aztlán. This essay is therefore introductory by design. Since the publication of my essay, two important books on the topic have appeared: Alberto Sandoval-Sánchez's* José, Can You See? Latinos On and Off Broadway *and Alicia Arrizón's* Latina Performance: Traversing the Stage. *I also edited a special issue on Latino performance for* Theatre Journal, *which appeared in March 2000. Together, these three publications amplify the work of the growing list of Chicano and Latino theater and performance artists, many of whom I was unable to discuss in this short essay. Readers should keep in mind, then, that the artists discussed in the essay are but a few of the many people who have invigorated and enriched the field. Please keep in mind, too, that there are many other folks who work behind the scenes: directors, designers, composers, dramaturges, and technicians whose contributions to the theater are indispensable. Many of these people, of course, are also Chicano and Latino. Their collaborative efforts combine to create Chicano and Latino theater. Keep in mind, finally, that Chicano and Latino theater assumes an audience and that this audience is you.*

Within the world of academia, the idea that performance shapes social identity has been argued by various scholars who work in postmodern, queer, and critical race studies; so much so that this concept is now nearly axiomatic. Within the world of performance, the boom in identity-based work, especially autobiographical performances by artists from socially and culturally marginalized groups, has led many people to assume that most contemporary performance will be about the performer's own identity. Theatre and performance studies, the field where these two worlds often overlap, has sought to define the link between performance and identity, calling for scholarship that attends to both the function of performance in the public sphere and the contested site of the embodied subject. Latino

From *Aztlán: A Journal of Chicano Studies* 1, no. 1 (1970): 1–12.

and Chicano performers and scholars have consistently participated in these projects, but the force of these endeavors has yet to impact the field of Chicano and Latino studies. In this essay, I want to call attention to some recent work by Chicano and Latino artists centering issues of performance and identity. Before discussing specific artists, I will rehearse the key terms that define the fields of Latino studies and performance studies.

As Chicano and Latino scholars and activists have argued, the term "Latino" itself encompasses so many different nationalities, ethnicities, and cultural backgrounds that to rely on the term as an organizing label of social identity veils the fact that such terms, used to fashion private and public identities, are sites of struggle and historical negotiation. Chicana and Latina feminists, for example, have demonstrated that the terms Latino and Chicano, as well as the political movements from which these terms derive, often require the bracketing of other factors of identity (gender and sexuality, for example) in order to secure the mission under which these terms have historically been deployed. Nonetheless, it has been politically efficacious for people from quite distinct cultural backgrounds and ideological positions to meet and organize under the label of Latina/o and Chicana/o in order to register an oppositional stance to majoritarian institutions. The issue of identity, or how we define ourselves to ourselves and to others, has thus been among the defining political concerns of Chicana/os and Latina/os, and has produced an impressive amount of discussion and debate.

"Performance" also, in its own way, has been subject to a similar process of scrutiny and debate. Scholars in theatre and performance studies have long addressed the distinctions between theatre and performance; recently these debates have focused on the question of performance not only within theatrical production, but also within the larger social arena. Scholars of Chicano and Latino performance have also had to grapple with a set of distinct issues, including, as Diana Taylor explains, that there is no equivalent word for performance in Spanish. The term *performance*, in its most generous employment, suggests not only conventional theatre but any number of cultural occasions and social processes that involve ritual, movement, sound, and/or voice on the one hand, and the various individual and communal roles that socialized subjects embody in the world, on the other. In this sense, the term performance calls into question the ideological systems associated with theatre, systems that connote not only already established aesthetic conventions, but the political biases associated with these criteria. Not all performance sets out to achieve artistic notoriety or institutional legitimization. Our assessment of performance should therefore not rely simply on questions of aesthetics, a problematic enterprise to begin with, but on the role of performance in the public sphere. Performance studies begins with the premise that performance—in all its possibility, from theatre to ritual and from public to private—is a cultural practice fundamental to cultural formations of individual subjectivity and social negotiations of communal identity and that sets as its project an investigation of this process.

Latino performance—from its earliest manifestations in the religious and secular cultural rituals of the indigenous people of the Southwest to the incorporation of many of these rituals into the nascent theatre conventions of the mid-nineteenth century—has primarily functioned to rehearse and enact various Latino cultural beliefs and customs. In this sense, Latino performance has historically been by, for, and about Latinos. From the itinerant Mexican players who performed for the communities around the early California missions in the coastal cities of San Diego, Los Angeles, and San Francisco, to the pan-Hispanic vaudeville houses of early immigrants in New York, Florida, California, and the Southwest, Latino performance can be understood as, in the words of theatre historian Nicolás Kanellos, "protecting the home culture and language in exile, educating the youth in the traditional customs and mores, providing the ideological and spiritual leadership that was needed to fend off the threat of assimilation to Anglo-American culture." From this perspective, performance functioned to preserve a cultural identity threatened by centuries of immigration and exile. But, from another perspective, Latino performance also provided Latinos a space within the public sphere to negotiate and rehearse shifting social mores and internal conflicts. For these reasons, Latino performance continues to be, in Jorge Huerta's apt phrase, "a necessary theatre." Huerta was describing the Chicano theatre movement, which grew out of farm-worker struggles in the 1960s, and the role that theatre and performance played in organizing an oppressed and exploited people politically. Identity was central to these occasions and, as Yolanda Broyles-González points out, was itself a question of considerable concern and debate among participants. And yet, despite these internal tensions, it was through these community-based performances of the 1960s (such as those of California's Teatro Campesino) that Chicanos were able to claim an agency that reformulated their sense of identity from one of oppression and victimization to one of resistance and survival. As in California, theatre and performance provided a means for Latinos to explore questions of identity in areas throughout the United States. In New York City, for example, the production of *La*

Carreta (The Oxcart), a 1954 play written by René Marqués and directed by Roberto Rodríguez, two Puerto Ricans, proved so successful that Rodríguez and Miriam Colón launched El Circulo Dramatico, the first Latino theatre group to have its own theatre in 1956. The sixty-seat theatre, located in Times Square, opened with a Cuban play and closed its doors two years later. In 1967, Colón founded the Puerto Rican Traveling Theatre, a company that remains active to this day.

Contemporary Latino theatre and performance is indebted to these earlier traditions and motivations. In fact, many recent performers and playwrights explicitly invoke traditional Latino performance styles, cultural practices, and theatre scripts. In this way, contemporary Latino performance draws upon and helps to construct a Latino theatre history. This new generation of artists builds upon the significant cultural work of earlier generations of performers even as they critique it. Consider, for example, Cherríe Moraga, whose influential writing on gender, class, sexuality, and nationalism has long been recognized within Chicano and Latino studies but whose important theatre work has been less fully acknowledged. In *Heroes and Saints* (1992), the third play of her recently published trilogy, Moraga addresses the effects of environmental racism on a Chicano farmworker community. The play pays tribute to the history of Chicano theatre by revisiting *The Shrunken Head of Pancho Villa*, Luis Valdez's foundational play from the 1960s, a play that addressed the struggles of farmworker families. Moraga utilizes and revitalizes the traditions of Chicano theatre by animating her theatre with a decidedly inclusive feminist poetics and politics.

In *Heroes and Saints*, questions of identity—political, sexual, spiritual—are negotiated through kinship and community. The play, as Yvonne Yarbro-Bejarano writes, "rather than presenting 'positive images' of the Chicano family, explores the ways we are both constrained *and* empowered by our culture." If identity in Valdez's play was primarily organized by the political urgency of Chicano nationalism, which prioritized ethnic and cultural alliance over all other factors, Moraga's play demonstrates how Chicano politics benefits from a more dynamic conception of identity that attends to gender, sexuality, and spirituality. *Heroes and Saints* critiques the heteronormativity and masculinization of traditional Chicano politics (and, by extension, theatre) while providing a new model from which to socially organize. The intertextual relationship between Moraga and Valdez's plays invites audiences to locate and identify shared political concerns in two distinct moments of Chicano history and the shared forms of address,

Irma St. Paule and Sarah Erde in a scene from Migdalia Cruz's play, Another Part of the House. *Directed by David Esbjornson at Classic Stage Company in New York City, March 1997.*
Photo credit: *T. Charles Erickson*

beginning with the theatre itself, that enable cultural change. Audiences are also asked to consider the plays' various points of departure, a reminder that political change is a continuous process not without its own internal conflicts and contrasting points of view. Furthermore, Moraga's play—like most of contemporary Chicano and Latino culture—insists upon its location within a specific Latino cultural tradition and legacy. I cite Moraga here as a specific case of a larger cultural process and not as its exception.

Other playwrights have also been inspired by previous traditions and texts and have focused their work accordingly. Puerto Rican playwright Migdalia Cruz's new play *Another Part of the House* (1997), for example, revises Federico García Lorca's Spanish classic *The House of Bernarda Alba* (1936)—a realist drama set in 1930s Spain about the tyrannical widow who sentences her five daughters to remain isolated in the house for an eight-year mourning period—in part by moving it from Spain to prerevolutionary Cuba. "I was interested in how the old world of Spain still influences our new world," Cruz explains. Cruz's play comments upon the legacy of Spanish colonialism and upon the tragic lives of women who uphold, or attempt to resist, oppressive political and cultural regimes. Two of the rebellious women seeking freedom from this world—Bernarda's mother and her youngest daughter—die by the end, casualties both of Bernarda's tyrannical rule and the larger cultural forces that condition Latina lives. *Another Part of the House*, like *Heroes and Saints*, begs the question: What are the possible subject formations and political alliances available to Latinos amidst social turmoil, political oppression, and human suffering? In José Rivera's new play *The Street of the Sun* (1997), this question haunts the Latino characters who attempt to survive the urban chaos of contemporary Los Angeles. In one scene, two of these characters—Jorge Cienfuegos, the aspiring Puerto Rican writer who is the play's protagonist, and Bianca, a Cuban playwright from New York City and friend of Jorge's who has relocated to Los Angeles to break into Hollywood—discuss the need for Latinos to support one another despite their differences.

Rivera, a Puerto Rican playwright whose plays are often described as examples of contemporary magical realism, appropriates the narrative conventions of Latin American novelists such as Gabriel García Márquez in order to begin to answer these questions of cultural identity and collective survival. *The Street of the Sun* combines elements of magical realism, ancient indigenous mythology, and popular Latino *telenovelas* to demonstrate the various means used to resist and respond to the stereotypes of Latinos produced by Hollywood and reinforced by the dominant cultural imaginary.

391

The play stages Latinos in a multiracial world, a world where Latinos from various cultural backgrounds must interact not only with each other, but with others who struggle to survive as well. The play's vast spectrum of geographic, racial, and class differences provides the Latino characters a context from which to explore questions of identity, and underscores how this process affects (and is affected by) the larger social world in which they live.

Moraga, Cruz, and Rivera are among the most important contemporary Latino playwrights at work in the theatre today. Their plays address concerns central to Chicanos and Latinos, which resonate deeply within the field of Chicano and Latino studies. These issues include the exploration of Chicano and Latino cultural legacies, antecedents, and traditions; the political implications (such as nationalism and essentialism) that often accompany such projects; the various historical formations of politicized Chicano and Latino subjects and the ramifications of such subject formations in the public world; and the demarcation of new areas—both material and imagined—of Chicano and Latino sociality, including the theatre.

Latino playwrights exploring identity intervene primarily through their dramaturgy and circulate their work in the conventional space of the theatre. Latino performance artists are less constrained by traditional dramatic conventions, including venue, and often work in nontheatrical settings. Most performers tour extensively, adapting their work to accommodate different performance venues, including schools and universities, nightclubs, and community centers. Latino performers address identity in any number of ways; the diversity of performance styles within Latino performance says as much about the different subject positions of Latino performers as it does about the diversity and flexibility of the medium. Latino performers also invoke earlier theatrical and performative modes, often bringing into representation little known or undocumented Latino performances from earlier historical periods. Culture Clash, the popular male Latino performance trio, bears the influence of early Chicano theatre and the belief that performance should remain oppositional to the exploitative practices of the dominant Anglo culture. While Culture Clash exposes popular Latino stereotypes and satirizes Latino icons, they also humorously address any number of topical Latino issues ranging from immigration and deportation to English-only movements and overpopulation. But like the earlier Chicano theatre of the 1960s and 1970s from which they depart, Culture Clash reinforces a type of cultural nationalism that collapses all Latino experience into a unified (heterosexual male) subject. In short,

Culture Clash, the popular Latino-Chicano comedy troupe, includes (l-r) Ric Salinas, Herbert Siguenza, and Richard Montoya.
Photo credit: *Aldo Panzieri*

by failing to account for the differences among Latinos, Culture Clash inadvertently performs the very limits of the identity politics they practice.

Culture Clash's more recent work, however, demonstrates a marked shift in the subject and style of performance. In *Radio Mambo* (1994), the three performers interviewed over seventy-five people from different ethnic, racial, socioeconomic, and religious backgrounds in order to recreate these people through performance, playing all the parts themselves. The subject under scrutiny was Miami, a city with a rich and complicated history of Latino immigration. This mode of performance, most immediately associated with Anna Deavere Smith's award-winning project *On the Road: A Search for American Character*, allowed Culture Clash to perform identities other than their own. In this work, and in their new commission *Radio: Bordertown*, an ethnographic performance of San Diego, Culture Clash performs multiple subjects marked by race, gender, class, and region. Rather than obscuring difference, a critique often lodged against their earlier work, Culture Clash now sets out to foreground it. By calling attention to the racial and ethnic formation of their real-life characters, they also begin to call attention to how they themselves—as three Latino men—are racialized and gendered subjects. In other words, they too embody identities performed on stage and off.

Most solo Latino performers have gone to great lengths to address this issue of the embodied Latino subject. From Guillermo Gómez Peña's insistence on locating himself as a border subject in a transglobal economy to Carmelita Tropicana's campy efforts to explore the serious effects of Cuban exile, to Luis Alfaro's lyrical meditations on sexual and class oppression in Los Angeles, Latino performers have consistently explored the idea of the embodied Latino subject in both local and global geopolitical contexts. These performers investigate the racial and ethnic formation of the Latino subject, and use their own bodies as the sites of cultural reference and contestation. Gómez Peña and Coco Fusco's famous collaboration, *Two Undiscovered Amerindians Visit* (1992), where the two performers displayed themselves for three days in a cage as authentic indigenous people recently discovered, demonstrates this self-conscious effort to reference the Latino body within already existing perceptions in the popular imaginary. Latino identity, Gómez Peña and Fusco suggest, is formulated through and against these stereotypes. In order to foreground this point, Gómez Peña and Fusco need to perform it. Performance becomes the means to render visible the racist and colonial gaze; once visible it can be demystified and exposed. The exchange between performer and spectator puts pressure on the latter to locate and perform their own positionality.

A similar dynamic between performer and spectator is put into motion in *Stuff* (1996), a recent collaboration between Coco Fusco and Nao Bustamante. The two performers exaggerate various iconic roles for Latina women in a series of humorous skits. Fusco and Bustamante serve their spectators food, offer sex tips and erotic advice, teach exotic dances, and generally go to great effort to entertain their audiences. In doing so, they ask the audience to consider its complicity in perpetuating sexist and exoticizing practices. By dressing and undressing on stage as they shift from role to role, the performers deliberately provoke the spectator's eroticizing gaze in order to trouble it. For Fusco and Bustamante, Latina identity involves a series of negotiations around both these dominant images and problematic scripts—the "stuff" referenced in the title—and the various cultural networks that produce them. In performing the very roles projected onto Latinas, Fusco and Bustamante call into question the signifying referents of the Latina body. They ask: How does one perform Latina? For whom and to what end? Because their collaborative work also involves audience participation, and because the composition of that audience varies from performance to performance, the question is never completely answered by any single performance. *Stuff* happens, but like the dynamics of identity itself, its meaning and effect depend on the immediate context in which it unfolds.

Solo performers may also address Latino identity through autobiography. In *Downtown* (1990), Luis Alfaro, a Chicano playwright, performer, and community activist, narrates his upbringing in the Pico-Union district, the heavily populated and impoverished Latino neighborhood in downtown Los Angeles. *Downtown* also tracks Alfaro's gay identity, and demonstrates how sexual identity and ethnic identity are politically interrelated. Throughout the performance, spectators witness Alfaro's identity formations as he maneuvers through the social landscape of Los Angeles. Alfaro performs not only himself but also the various characters who have populated his world. As he embodies these various characters—gang members, undocumented garment workers, homosexual partners—he pays tribute to their neglected lives and the role they have played in his own. As *Downtown* makes clear, autobiography entails the telling of other people's stories as well as one's own.

Sometimes autobiography even entails creating a completely fictionalized character in order to tell one's own story. Alina Troyano, the Cuban performer and playwright, created the character Carmelita Tropicana, as a

Luis Alfaro performing Downtown.
Photo credit: *Courtesy of Luis Alfaro*

counterpersona. Troyano, a fixture of New York City's downtown performance world for over a decade, has appeared as Carmelita in over a dozen
plays, often in collaboration with her sister Ela Troyano, the filmmaker.
But it is only in her most recent work, *Milk of Amnesia/Leche de Amnesia*
(1994), that Alina Troyano attempts to untangle the multiple forces that
led to Carmelita's creation in the first place. *Milk of Amnesia* eloquently

396

Carmelita Tropicana in a scene from Milk of Amnesia, *directed by Ela Troyano.*
Photo Credit: *Dona McAdams*

and humorously sets out to explore the loss of a coherent sense of identity within the context of exile; it tells the story of Carmelita's amnesia and a return trip to Cuba in order to reclaim her memory and sense of self. *Milk of Amnesia*, as José Muñoz persuasively puts it, "meditates on the centrality of memory to the lived reality—the lifeworlds—of Cuban Americans."

This theme of memory and its link to identity is also evident in Marga Gomez's *Memory Tricks* (1993) and *A Line Around the Block* (1995). For Gomez, identity involves the exploration of her parents' lives. The daughter of a Cuban vaudeville impresario and a Puerto Rican dancer, Gomez grew up in Harlem in the midst of this Latino performance world. In her work, Gomez pays tribute to her parents by recycling both their public performances and private anecdotes. In doing so, Gomez records the legendary, if largely undocumented, Latino entertainment scene in New York City in the 1950s and 1960s. The individual memories that compose Gomez's stories are thus recirculated as the collective reenactment of a lived cultural heritage. The point here, as it is with much Latino solo performance, is that memory is not merely a nostalgic longing for a previous moment of cultural stability. Rather, memory is a means to investigate the individual and collective meanings of identity. The reenactment of memory in Latino autobiographical performance, like the citational referencing of Latino

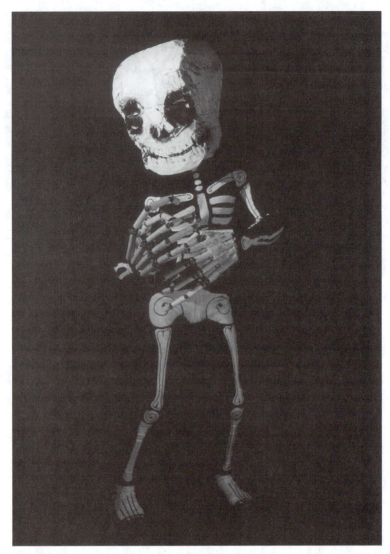

Paul Timothy Diaz dancing Día de los vivos, *1996.*
Photo Credit: *Ian Nies, courtesy of the Archive of movement coalition for AIDS awareness.*

conventions in contemporary Latino theatre, is a symbolic intervention into the under-represented worlds of Latino cultural history.

Latino performance considers the lost worlds of Latino cultural history and sets out to embody them. Paul Timothy Diaz, a Bay Area Latino performer, references this process in his dance *Día de los vivos*, a piece that both references and revises traditional Day of the Dead rituals held in honor of the ghosts of past worlds. Unlike other solo performers who rely on narrative to convey identity and cultural memory, Diaz relies exclusively on movement and dance. In one section, Diaz begins to dance with the frame of a *Día de los muertos* skeletal figure, the iconic image of death. Eventually, Diaz steps inside the frame and rather than dancing *with* the skeleton he now dances *as* the skeleton. Diaz appropriates the myths associated with Day of the Dead to call attention to his own body's embattled history and, specifically, to his battle with AIDS, and to honor other people who are also living with AIDS. Diaz was inspired to create the dance during a period of debilitating illness in 1995 and premiered the piece in 1996, at a time when he was unsure of his own ability to perform it. *Día de los vivos*, although created by Diaz as a dance of death, now references his body's revitalization through new drugs and treatment options for people with HIV. The revival of Diaz's dance stands, then, as a revival of his life. In *Día de los vivos*, identity is located in (and through) an embattled body, a body that is marked racially and culturally—as Latino—and marked also by disease. Diaz moves through multiple sites of memory and culture, and in doing so, locates his own identity within a larger history of Latino performance, gay culture, and AIDS activism.

The performers I have discussed in this essay construct a variety of Latino identities through performance. Their work summons a Latino world at once material and mythic, real and imagined, embodied and remembered. These performers insist on the visibility and coherence of Latino identity even as they refuse to stabilize that identity as any one image, role, stereotype, or convention. Like the very terms "Chicano" and "Latino," contemporary Latino theatre and performance shapes—and reshapes—the terms of identity in the act of performing them. These performances extend beyond the stage and continue to reverberate in the public world, where Latinos enact their everyday lives. Scholars in Chicano and Latino studies would thus benefit from a more engaged response to the important work in Latino theatre and performance. Put simply, Latino culture cannot fully be understood without factoring in the social and political significance of Latino performance.

Notes

I would like to thank Jorge Huerta, Richard Meyer, and Chon Noriega for their helpful comments and suggestions.

1. The indispensable foundational work of Chicano and Latino theatre historians such as Nicolás Kanellos and Jorge Huerta is rarely cited or reprinted in Latino scholarship, nor is the work of feminist scholars of Latina/o and Chicana/o theatre such as Yvonne Yarbro-Bejarano and Yolanda Broyles-González. Such neglect suggests that the marginalization of theatre and performance studies within the academy operates within Chicano and Latino studies as well. Overall, Chicano and Latino theatre scholarship has made more of an impact in theatre and performance studies.

2. See, for example, the most important journals in the field: *Theatre Journal* and *TDR: A Journal of Performance Studies*. These journals publish regularly on the question of, and debate on, what defines the field. Marvin Carlson's *Performance: A Critical Introduction* (New York: Routledge, 1996) provides an excellent survey of the issues involved in theatre and performance studies.

3. Diana Taylor, "Opening Remarks," in *Negotiating Performance: Gender, Sexuality, and Theatricality in Latin/o America*, ed. Diana Taylor and Juan Villegas (Durham: Duke University Press, 1994), 1–16. Taylor provides an enormously helpful introduction to these issues, including a discussion of the vexed issue of identity-based terms such as "Hispanic," "Latino," and "Chicano."

4. Nicolás Kanellos, *A History of Hispanic Theatre in the United States: Origins to 1940* (Austin: University of Texas Press, 1990), 199–200.

5. Jorge Huerta, *Necessary Theatre: Six Plays About the Chicano Experience* (Houston: Arte Público Press, 1989), 5.

6. Yolanda Broyles-González, *El Teatro Campesino: Theatre in the Chicano Movement* (Austin: University of Texas Press, 1994).

7. See Joanne Pottlitzer, *Hispanic Theatre in the United States and Puerto Rico* (New York: Ford Foundation Publications, 1988), and especially Elisa de la Roche, *Teatro Hispano! Three Major New York Companies* (New York: Garland Publishing, 1995). De la Roche traces the development of the Puerto Rican Traveling Theatre, INTAR, and El Repertorio Español from their origins in the 1960s.

8. Yvonne Yarbro-Bejarano has written extensively on Moraga's theatre. See her essays "Cherríe Moraga's *Shadow of a Man*: Touching the Wound in Order to Heal," in *Acting Out: Feminist Performances*, ed. Lynda Hart and Peggy Phelan (Ann Arbor: University of Michigan Press, 1993), 85–104; and "The Female Subject in Chicano Theatre: Sexuality, 'Race', and Class," in *Performing Feminisms: Feminist Critical Theory and Theatre*, ed. Sue-Ellen Case (Baltimore: Johns Hopkins University Press, 1990), 131–49. These essays will be published along with others in her forthcoming book, *The Right to Passion: Collected Essays on Cherríe Moraga* (Austin: University of Texas Press, forthcoming). See also Jorge Huerta's "Moraga's *Heroes and Saints*: Chicano Theatre for the '90s," *Theatre Forum* 1, no. 1 (1992): 49–53.

9. Cherríe Moraga, *Heroes and Saints and Other Plays* (Albuquerque: West End Press, 1994). The other two plays also in this anthology are *Giving Up the*

Ghost and *Shadow of a Man*.

10. Yvonne Yarbro-Bejarano, *The Right to Passion* (forthcoming).

11. Migdalia Cruz, "Program Notes for *Another Part of the House*" (New York, Classic Stage Company, 1997).

12. Although even here there are discrepancies. Very few Latino playwrights are produced by mainstream theatres. Of the three playwrights I've discussed only José Rivera's work has been staged regularly at major regional theatres such as the Mark Taper Forum in Los Angeles, which produced *The Street of the Sun*. On this issue of access, see Jorge Huerta, "Looking for the Magic: Chicanos in the Mainstream," in Taylor and Villegas, *Negotiating Performance*, 37–48. While Huerta's discussion centers on Chicano theatre, his ideas resonate for all Latino playwrights. Also, I should point out that these playwrights also intervene by writing roles for Latino actors and by providing opportunities for other Latino theatre workers.

13. The founding members of Culture Clash included two women, Marga Gomez and Monica Palacios, both now important solo performers. José Antonio Burciaga, also a founding member who left the group, has written on the internal conflicts within Culture Clash in *Spilling the Beans* (Santa Barbara, Calif.: Joshua Odell Editions, 1995). I discuss Marga Gomez in this essay; for a discussion of Monica Palacios, see Yvonne Yarbro-Bejarano, "The Lesbian Body in Latina Cultural Production," in *Entiendes? Queer Readings, Hispanic Writings*, ed. Emilie Bergmann and Paul Julian Smith (Durham: Duke University Press, 1995), 181–97.

14. On Anna Deavere Smith's work, see Sandra L. Richards, "Caught in the Act of Social Definition: On the Road with Anna Deavere Smith," in *Acting Out: Feminist Performances*, ed. Lynda Hart and Peggy Phelan (Ann Arbor: University of Michigan Press, 1993), 35–54; and Tania Modleski, "Doing Justice to the Subjects: Mimetic Art in a Multicultural Society," in *Female Subjects in Black and White: Race, Psychoanalysis, Feminism*, ed. Elizabeth Abel, Barbara Christian, and Helene Morgan (Berkeley: University of California Press, 1997), 57–76.

15. See Coco Fusco, "The Other History of Intercultural Performance," *Drama Review* 38, no. 1 (1994): 143–67.

16. I discuss Luis Alfaro's work in detail in a chapter of my book, *Acts of Intervention: Performance, Gay Culture, and AIDS* (Bloomington: Indiana University Press, 1998).

17. José Muñoz, "No es Fácil: Notes on the Negotiation of Cubanidad and Exilic Memory in Carmelita Tropicana's *Milk of Amnesia*," *Drama Review* 39, no. 3 (1997): 77. This issue also includes my interview with Carmelita Tropicana, "Carmelita Tropicana Unplugged," and the full script of *Milk of Amnesia*.

IV.
Remapping the World

Remapping the World
Introduction

Rafael Pérez-Torres

While critically questioning notions of self and place and identity, Chicano studies has also been concerned with trying to establish new worlds of order and meaning. The desire to remap what has been made unfamiliar has remained a strong trend within Chicano criticism and theory. This desire results in a consideration of what it means not only to work in a Chicano vein, but to intervene in already established critical and scholarly fields. These fields—sociology, literary study, sociolinguistics, history, anthropology—get reclaimed and reconfigured by a desire to forge a new intellectual geography.

Strikingly different in tone and topic, the essays in this section seek to intervene in the process by which knowledge and meaning are shaped. As a result, they often deploy the very methodologies of social science, Marxist criticism, or cultural studies that they interrogate. Each of these essays, from a variety of perspectives, considers how Chicano studies redraws the boundaries of traditional scholarship. In this sense, the essays reflect how subaltern studies—including Chicano scholarship—serves to undo and remake intellectual projects, simultaneously questioning and participating in the worlds of academic inquiry.

A persistent concern in Chicano studies has been its position and role within institutionalized systems of knowledge. The foundational "Plan de Santa Barbara" sought ways to incorporate Chicano studies as a component of the university while retaining the most democratic and participatory elements of the Chicano movement. The plan, adopted by a statewide student conference held at the University of California at Santa Barbara in 1969, outlined programs based on ideals of independence and self-determination within institutions of higher education. It led to the establishment of Chicano studies programs guided by the belief that Chicano students, faculty, administrators, employees, and the community should be the central and decisive designers and administrators of those programs. This emphasis upon community involvement and shared governance forms a powerful concern as Chicano studies becomes a discipline.

Within an increasingly stratified and specialized educational environment, Chicano studies questioned how this relationship would be understood. The essays in "Remapping the World" address this issue in at least two ways: they consider the role of Chicano studies within a larger community of scholars and critics, and they extend the idea of community to incorporate the variability and difference inherent in the idea of community itself. Chicano scholarship over the past thirty years has explored the experiences of sexualized and gendered constituencies, individuals self-identified as multiethnic and multiracial, the role that professionalization and education have played in the development of Chicano identities, and other elements in the varied histories of Mexican-descent people in the United States. The more scholars stake a claim in the subjectivities that the term "Chicana/o" may signify, the more complexly the category of community gets redrawn and reshaped.

The interrogation of privileged categories such as community and identity provides one critical element of Chicano scholarship. This questioning leads to the type of institutional repositioning these essays explicitly or implicitly address. The critical examination of ontological and epistemological categories on the part of Chicano/a scholars resonates with much productive scholarship undertaken in a number of disciplines and fields since the 1960s. As these essays demonstrate, scholars of Chicano studies seek to create more than a dialogue with the pressing intellectual concerns of their moment—they seek to intervene in them. This dialogue transforms the intellectual terrain of both Chicano studies and more traditional academic disciplines and, as these essays amply illustrate, it reconsiders the relationship between Chicano/a scholarship and other institutionalized forms of knowledge.

A strength of Chicano studies has been its ability to employ the analytical categories of traditionally recognized critical projects while at the same time sustaining and engaging often discredited forms of knowledge. The scholarship has preserved and critiqued tradition and heritage, ethics and wisdom. It has also questioned how these issues construct notions of self in dialectical relationship to community and other social relationships that imply continuity. Chicano studies seeks to find new and dynamic functions within and without institutional settings in order to develop what one might call a migratory consciousness, one capable of negotiating a complex and often troubling intellectual, cultural, political, and social landscape. These essays in their own ways engage with the development of that consciousness.

Maxine Baca Zinn looks at the failure of social science to adequately explain changes in Chicano families and their gender roles as a result of the Chicano movement. She argues that these changes are due neither to modernization nor to acculturation, as several sociological studies assume. Rather, it is the family's participation in the movement itself that has led to two types of transformation. Integration occurs as families and communities fight together to resist the effects of racial discrimination; and the creation of new linkages and associations between men and women leads to an alteration in traditional sex-role relationships.

Baca Zinn draws on the controversial framework of internal colonialism to explain some of the pressures leading to the transformation of the Chicano family. She bases her argument on the idea that Mexican and Chicano populations in the United States experience types of oppression and domination characteristic of classic colonialist systems. The idea of internal colonialism has by and large been dismissed or discredited by many in the Chicano scholarly community, though it had at the time Baca Zinn wrote her article a good deal of currency. She argues that the Chicano movement is not reformist. Rather, it is revolutionary in nature because it seeks to remake the colonial situation by forging fundamental institutional changes and politicizing masses of Chicanos. The weight of her argument rests on the premise that the revolutionary force of the movement transforms not just the structures of dominant society but also the sociocultural traditions of Chicano people.

The underlying concern of Baca Zinn's essay is to understand social transformation within a Chicano political context. The forms that political struggles take engender more dynamic conditions than those traditionally ascribed to Chicano communities by social science studies. Her essay thus situates machismo and male domination within the larger forces of colonization. In so doing, it seeks to consider Chicano attitudes toward machismo in ways other than those favored by typical sociological assessments of male dominance. This may lead to understanding machismo not as a pathology, but as a calculated response to hostility, exclusion, and racial domination in a colonized society.

As this conclusion illustrates, Baca Zinn's argument is very provocative. It reflects a type of resistant scholarship placing Chicano concerns at the center and not the periphery of academic inquiry. The inversion implied in this move opens the essay to a number of critiques, including that it dissociates Chicano studies from other more traditional and institutionalized intellectual work. Angie Chabram takes up this problem head-on by tracing the interrelationship between Chicano cultural criticism and the institutional and intellectual conditions inflecting its production.

In "Chicano Critical Discourse: An Emerging Cultural Practice," Chabram maps the critical—primarily literary—terrain of Chicano academic discourse as it develops from the 1960s to the 1980s. Her extensive—and extensively researched—essay identifies general trends within contemporary Chicano criticism as a type of emergent subaltern practice. Her essay thus responds to the move within dominant cultural and literary studies toward extensively theoretical and elite concerns in the 1980s. The stratification between the cosmopolitan world of cultural criticism and the peripheral world of cultural production creates, Chabram argues, a false dichotomy between the hegemonic center and the subaltern marginal. With this essay, she seeks to position Chicano cultural discourse in relation to larger critical practices. The discussion asserts that as theory and practice are inextricably bound together, so too are centrality and marginality.

The essay sketches out three areas of investigation. It maps important alterations in the production and consumption of Chicano criticism, it broadens the scope of existent critical studies in order to account for links between emergent and established critical traditions, and it highlights alternative theoretical frameworks that may better understand Chicano critical discourse. Each of these areas focuses on the changing terrain in the production and consumption of critical discourse. They locate the change in theoretical and cultural interests within the material and historical conditions of Chicano intellectual development. Thus the growth of the Chicana/o critical enterprise—including the movement away from nationalist (primarily masculinist) paradigms, the creation of new forms of metacritical inquiry, and the growing professionalization of Chicano critics and writers—prove all to be interrelated events.

The tendency for Chicano critics to cluster into circles or groups, for example, is due less to a desire for critical coherence than as a part of the complex development Chicano scholars experience in negotiating specific institutional and intellectual trends. At the same time, the fragmentation and asymmetrical distribution of critical and cultural products is due to the configuration of both established cultural institutions and alternative practices. Drawing on the critical work of Edward Said and Terry Eagleton as well as on personal interviews with many Chicano and Chicana critics and scholars, the essay attempts to demarcate the shifting boundaries of Chicano critical studies as part of and apart from entrenched critical practices.

The intellectual borders that Chicano scholars have sought to traverse become, in Rosaura Sánchez's essay "Mapping the Spanish Language along a Multiethnic and Multilingual Border," a quite literal geopolitical entity. Her essay focuses on how the border fosters conditions of possibility for ways in which future social transformation may be enacted. She makes the observation that, given the continuing large-scale immigration from Mexico, Mexico could be said to be reterritorializing the Southwest. Of course, the border represents a barrier to this immigration, a social space of concrete social practices preserving clearly demarcated political boundaries. While these boundaries are defended, the very concept of the nation-state proves increasingly irrelevant under multinational and transnational capitalism. Within this latest form of capitalism, Sánchez argues, change will come not at the level of nation-states but at the level of relations of production. Here, collectives defined by ethnicity, nation, and language can have new and important roles to play in the social dynamic.

The border region forms a multiethnic, multilingual, multiracial, and multicultural space. Language, Sánchez argues, may very well prove to be one of the elements key in fostering collective social action and group identity. This is especially true given the heterogeneous nature of Latino populations in the border states of the Southwest. Even more critical may be the role that ethnicism (as opposed to nationalism) plays under the supranational framework of advanced global capitalism. Given the number of Mexican immigrants and their historical ties and kinship to residents of the Southwest, Spanish will continue to be a viable and important language, one that may help to draw together diverse constituencies seeking to enact social change. Along with English, Japanese, and Chinese, concludes Sánchez, Spanish will become one of the world languages of the Pacific Rim. Ultimately, language, ethnicity, and class are all variables that will affect political and collective action against social conditions that create and foster unemployment, poverty, homelessness, and violence.

Looking not to the future of social configurations in the Southwest as Sánchez does, Eric Avila examines the way civic institutions have underpinned the construction of suburban racial identity. "The Folklore of the Freeway: Space, Culture, and Identity in Postwar Los Angeles" explores the role freeways have played in establishing and maintaining social and class divisions in the largest city of the Southwest. Avila's essay considers how diverse peoples of Los Angeles have understood and assigned meaning to the freeway and its impact on the spatial and economic development of the metropolis.

Specifically, Avila looks at the folklore that has developed around the freeway. In official civic culture, he notes, it is seen as a symbol of progress and modernity, making possible the promise of a technologically advanced future. Throughout the history of American popular culture, progress has been defined as part and parcel of the national identity. Thus, in the 1950s, Walt Disney celebrates in his newly opened theme park (connected to the rest of Los Angeles, appropriately, by the Santa Ana Freeway) the coming of the freeways with the ride Autopia. For those who suffered the imposition of the freeway upon their neighborhoods, however, it represented a type of disruption and symbolized a civic powerlessness recorded in a variety of cultural forms. Through murals, novels, and poetry, Chicano and Chicana artists have transformed the significance of the freeway by revealing its divisive and destructive effects.

Chicano culture thus highlights the countervalent forces of modernity. The freeway created a new spatial experience of the city, redefining what metropolitan life could be like, while simultaneously catalyzing the disintegration of older and more familiar patterns of life. Ultimately, Avila observes, the contradictions and complexities that emerged from the history of the L.A. freeway system reflect the complex and contradictory ways Chicano communities and individuals have at once opposed and participated in the modernization of their city.

Undertaking an analysis of the past and its effects on the present configuration of knowledge, KarenMary Davalos in "Chicana/o Studies and Anthropology: The Dialogue that Never Was" revisits a conversation Chicano scholars initiated with Anglo anthropologists in 1967. Her essay asserts that Chicana and Chicano scholars have for thirty years tried to foster a decolonized social science. It in effect re-examines the role and function of Chicano studies in relation to traditional disciplinary boundaries. The work of Chicana feminists especially has formed a critique of such ideas as community, patriarchy, and heterosexism. This critique grew from conditions of inequality within established academic institutions as well as from experiences of organized resistance to racial, gender, and class discrimination outside the academic environment.

Davalos traces the development of Chicano studies in anthropology and sociology, locating its birth in the struggle for social change embodied

410

by the Chicano movement. Scholars engaged with these fields—influenced as much by Marxist thought as by models of internal colonialism—emphasized that culture is materially based and that academic representations of Chicano experiences have been constrained and deformed by inadequate methodologies. Chicana scholars take up this critique, Davalos notes, by forging an analysis that challenged both traditional forms of knowledge and knowledge produced by Chicano and Mexican scholars. These feminist scholars thus engage in a dialogue that articulates how multiple experiences of race, class, gender, and sexuality can conflict with ideals about community, family, and culture.

Her essay underscores the fact that representations of Chicano and Chicana experiences are constantly being developed. Chicano scholars have questioned how traditional studies portray and understand concerns relevant to Chicana/o communities. The work of these scholars addresses issues of misrepresentation, the suppression of voice, the validity of ethnographic authority, objectivity, and the politics of research. They raise questions about their own position inside and outside the academy. Davalos's essay thus provides an informative metacommentary, a self-reflection raising the very questions that have from the first characterized Chicano scholarship.

The essays of this section illustrate how the academic and intellectual missions of Chicano studies can be understood not principally in terms of ethnic or racial representation, but through a multiplicity of experiences, identities, and concerns. The essays undo the ontological category of singular ethnic otherness that the term "Chicano" sometimes represents. They assume a critical position interrogating the relation between knowledge and power, between self and other, between margin and center. They contest the conditions that have allowed certain forms of knowledge to appear natural while others seem relegated to the realm of the exotic. Finally, they seek to redraw the boundaries that set up divisions between knowledge, action, and being. They are concerned not just with remapping the world, but with locating new and changing historical subjects who not only live in the world, but change it.

Political Familism
Toward Sex-Role Equality in Chicano Families

Maxine Baca Zinn

AUTHOR'S NOTE: *"Political Familism" is very much a product of its era. Written in the early 1970s, it should be read today for what it offers epistemologically as well as conceptually. I wrote this essay during the last year of my doctoral studies; when the Chicano population was marginalized in the field of sociology. I drew on the emerging tools of Chicano Studies to challenge family theories that erased people of color. Using an "insiders perspective," I took issue with common portrayals of our families as deviant, deficient, and the chief cause of Mexican subordination in the United States. By refuting cultural caricatures and highlighting the social situations and contexts shaping Mexican orgin families, I made the case that Chicano families were not cultural relics. I argued that across the country, our families were being reconfigured by social activism. Instead of criticizing minority families for failing to follow a uniform pattern of family development and change, a Chicano perspective offered a location from which to see aspects of family life that were obscure from other, more privileged vantage points.*

Over the past three decades, this essay has held up surprisingly well as part of a larger body of revisionist scholarship on racial-ethnic families and women of color. In fact, my discussion contained many seeds that would sprout into a new framework. It would join the critiques of feminists and other people of color. Eventually, our work would recast the family field. The following threads, which appear in "Political Familism," are now distinguishing features of a structural diversity model of family life: (a) attention to families' location in relation to the political and economic institutions that distribute resources and opportunities, (b) families as settings of resistance to external forms of oppression (race and class) as well as settings of patriarchal oppression, and (c) families as they are constructed through the interplay of social structure and human agency.

Chicano Studies and family sociology have produced an explosion of scholarship that would refine and advance the essay if I were writing about the impact of Chicano social activism on family life today. Because this analysis was done before we used the concept of gender, my "sex roles" approach to male dominance and women's struggles for equality is dated. Today's analysis would require a more complex treatment of the family as a gendered institution. Nevertheless, the issues raised in this piece were vital in laying the groundwork for the development of multiracial feminism.

From Aztlan: A Journal of Chicano Studies 1, no. 1 (1970): 1–12.

The essay was written when the Chicano movement had made important strides and was expanding possibilities in many social arenas. It reflects the optimism of the times. The critical edge we brought to our work as partisan intellectuals served us well in challenging sacred cows and earning legitimacy for our work. Despite the extraordinary changes that have occurred in society and scholarship since this piece was written, it retains valuable lessons for thinking about race, gender, and family life.

The Chicano family has been described by social scientists against a backdrop of inflexible tradition. Recent studies, however, reveal changes in Chicano families. This paper analyzes family and sex-role transformations. I refute the notion that changes in the family result simply from the modernization or acculturation of an ethnic group. Chicano family structure and sex-role relationships are indeed undergoing some far-reaching changes. But I propose that many of these changes are generated by conditions unique to the Chicano experience—conditions that produce responses to structural domination in U.S. society.

Participation of total family units in the Chicano movement has on one level an integrating function, and on another level a role-equalizing function. On the one hand it pulls the family, the community, La Raza, together to fight racial discrimination. On the other hand it requires an alteration of traditional sex-role relationships and the creation of new associations and linkages between men and women.

Acculturation and Family Structure

Social science has assumed that the process of acculturation changes traditional relationships in "ethnic" families. The assumption has been that there is a general movement in acculturating groups toward family egalitarianism. Ethnic or subordinate group family transformations are seen in an evolutionary perspective of world-changing family patterns. Overall shifts occur from extended kinship units with rigid sex-role divisions to nuclear, autonomous, egalitarian family units.[1] With industrialization, urbanization, and modernization, the family as an institution is expected to move gradually from an extended structure to a nuclear structure. This modernization is said to give rise to a new "modern" orientation among women and to bring about a trend toward greater equality between the sexes.

Concern with acculturation of the Chicano family is reflected in earlier studies of this institution.[2] Recent investigations of the Chicano family indicate that it is moving in the direction of the ideal-typical nuclear family

413

with its emphasis on sex-role equality. A 1967 study by Manual Ramirez on the identification of Chicano family values revealed that Chicanos identified with traditional Mexican family values of conformity, strict child rearing, and authoritarian submission. However, he found that Chicanos exhibited signs of "Americanization" in the form of decreasing identification with traditional patterns of male authority and separation of the sexes.[3]

In examining changes in marriage roles that accompany the acculturation of Chicanas, Tharp and his colleagues found that the more acculturated the wife, the greater the marriage role resembled an egalitarian-companionate pattern.[4]

In *The Mexican American People*, the family is presented as an institution that has undergone significant departure from the traditional pattern. Shifts in the structure of the family are explained in terms of movement of substantial sections of the population into the urban middle class. According to the study, familism and patriarchy, two characteristic features of traditional Chicano families, no longer define family structure.[5]

Ellwyn Stoddard in his book *Mexican Americans* gives considerable attention to changing family patterns. He concludes that the traditional family is giving way to a modern family lifestyle characterized by greater rates of exogamy and increased geographical, social, and occupational mobility. This trend, he continues, is much like trends that have occurred in other immigrants who have been assimilated into the dominant society.[6]

Each of these works interprets changes in the structure of the Chicano family as inevitable changes that accompany modernization and acculturation of ethnic groups. They view changes in sex-role relationships in developmental terms, as the results of Americanization and gradual assimilation to the dominant society. However, interpretations of Chicano social institutions that rely exclusively on assimilationist analytic frameworks result in neglect of certain sociological realities. Thus they must be considered incomplete, erroneous, or both.

Racism, Resistance, and Family

An alternative framework must be adopted. It is necessary to steer analysis away from assimilation and toward a perspective that includes the concepts of oppression, opposition, and change. The internal colonialism framework best incorporates these notions. This framework, based on similarities between classic colonialism and oppression of racial groups in the United States, posits that the subordination of Chicanos is the result of oppression by a dominant Anglo minority.[7] It also posits inevitable opposition by those groups subject to racial subordination. In this resistance and opposition to colonial status we find conditions specifically relevant to changing familial patterns occurring among Chicanos.

Social and political activism of Chicanos must be seen in light of attempts by racially oppressed groups, both within and outside of the United States, to alter those conditions that render them powerless. Although nationalist liberation movements in the Third World and El Movimiento have developed out of structurally different sociopolitical conditions, both are responses to common processes of social oppression. As diverse and expansive as the Chicano movement is, it is nevertheless a response to the pervasive structural control that Anglo society maintains over Chicanos. Broadly conceived, El Movimiento is a decolonization movement. Of course, questions arise concerning the revolutionary versus reformist orientations of organizations and activities that constitute El Movimiento. Obviously, it is impossible to characterize the entire Chicano movement as either reformist or revolutionary. However, insofar as Chicano movement activities seek to make fundamental changes in institutions of the dominant society that control the lives of Chicanos, the movement is revolutionary. Insofar as masses of Chicanos are politicized in an intensive manner and imbued with the idea of creating a new order of things, the movement is revolutionary.[8] What is more immediately relevant to this discussion is that regardless of how it is categorized, the Chicano movement aims to decolonize Anglo-Chicano relationships.

Decolonization struggles occur at many different levels and exhibit many ranges of activity. They involve conscious, continuous development and modification of political strategies and traditional behavior patterns. The Chicano movement has had an impact not only on structures of the dominant society that have served to maintain racial subordination, but also on sociocultural traditions of Chicano people.

A guiding principle of the Chicano movement that cuts across specific organizational goals and tactics is the preservation and maintenance of family loyalty. Ideologically, this principle is expressed by two concepts: *la familia de la Raza* and *carnalismo*. La familia de la Raza unites Chicanos to struggle as a family tied together by carnalismo, the spirit of brotherhood. Organizationally, these concepts take the form of total family participation in ongoing struggles for racial justice.

This fusing of cultural and political resistance may be referred to as political familism. It is a process of cultural and political activism that

415

involves the participation of total family units in the movement for liberation. Political familism is a phenomenon in which the continuity of family groups and the adherence to family ideology provide the basis for struggle. El Movimiento has gone into the Chicano home. It has become a family affair that demands total involvement from all family members.[9] While this phenomenon has not yet been empirically documented, there is evidence that points to the profound importance of the *familia* in the Chicano movement.

César Chávez's early successes in the farmworker movement may be partly attributed to the fact that he converted the *huelga* into a strike of families by basing the union structure on the strong family structure.[10] The triumphant Chicano revolt against the Crystal City, Texas, school district in 1969 (an event that helped precipitate the formation of La Raza Unida Party in that state) drew its organizational support from the Chicano family.[11] José Angel Gutiérrez, the leading figure in the formation of La Raza Unida Party in Texas, expresses the political significance of total family participation:

> You know, civil rights are not just for those under 21. They're for everybody—for grandma, for daddy and mamma, and los chamaquitos and primos and sisters and so on. We've all got to work together. That means that all of us have to pitch in…. You see, La familia mexicana está organizada.[12]

At the first Chicano Youth Liberation Conference held in Denver in 1969, a position paper entitled "El Plan Espiritual de Aztlán" expressed commitment to a family-based movement of Chicanos:

> Our cultural values of home and family will serve as powerful weapons to defeat the gringo dollar system and encourage the process of love and brotherhood.[13]

The Denver-centered Crusade for Justice operates on a family principle: a system of family ties extending beyond the immediate family to a family of all Chicanos. At its weekly meetings, both young and old participate in what amounts to a family gathering, a strictly non-Anglo phenomenon.[14]

Family activism, a defining feature of the contemporary Chicano movement, is not restricted to the political arena. Cultural and schooling programs also utilize the familia as a basic organizing principle. Describing Chicano pursuits at the University of California at Davis, Jesús Leyba explains:

The easiest way to understand the organizational structure under MECHA (Movimiento Estudiantil Chicano de Aztlán) is to compare it to the extended family.... If you think of MECHA as the core family unit, then the other activities would be carried out by members of the extended family units: this insures that everyone has a voice in and understands what every subunit is doing.[15]

Project Consejo at the University of New Mexico aims to secure college admission for the "high risk" students and to assist them to use their talents, skills, and cultural values to successfully complete a university education. Project Consejo's unique approach to counseling students is based on the familia concept:

This stresses the close family ties in Chicano families starting with the children and working its way up the family ladder to the grandparents. It is based on a spirit of cooperation and unity.[16]

The key to unity for La Raza has been found in the various manifestations of Chicano nationalism. According to movement leader and philosopher Rodolfo "Corky" González Chicano nationalism arises from La Familia Chicana:

What are the common denominators that unite the people? The key common denominator is nationalism ... nationalism becomes La familia. Nationalism comes first out of the family, then into tribalism and then into alliances that are necessary to lift the burden of all suppressed humanity.[17]

Making the traditional family the basis of a decolonization movement is not unique to the Chicano movement. Tanzania, under the leadership of Julius Nyerere, assumed ideological unity with the concept "ujamaa" or familyhood. After Tanzania's independence from Britain, the process of decolonization was carried forth by adherence to family ties, symbolized by the traditional African family and was based on "practices and attitudes which together meant basic equality, freedom and unity."[18] This is not to suggest that African socialism and Chicano nationalism are altogether parallel. However, the use of the family, a basic traditional social institution, in these two anticolonial movements may indicate something about resistance by racially oppressed groups.

In the process of becoming independent or maintaining separation from the dominant society, oppressed peoples take those cultural patterns that have fostered their survival in the face of oppression and use them as

417

political guides for resistance and revolution. Cultural revitalization phenomena become important in anticolonial movements.[19] In many respects, El Movimiento's emphasis on family unity and family participation is an expression of cultural revitalization. It is important to ask why the familia has emerged as a basis for the collective movement. Very likely the familia's present cultural and political significance is not simply a return to, or a rejuvenation of, Mexican cultural tradition. Rather, the present significance of the familia has strong roots in the historical function that the Chicano family has performed in protecting individuals from the hostilities of Anglo white society. Melford E. Spiro, writing about "ethnic" groups in the United States, notes that family traditionalism serves to reduce the stress of culture contact by offering solidarity support.[20] Chicanos, unlike European ethnic groups, have remained subject to control by institutions of the dominant society. They have thus required the protection that the family affords long after the initial period of contact with the dominant society. Robert Staples's historical analysis of the Chicano family treats the institution as one that has undergone various adaptations in order to meet the changing requirements of society. The extended traditional family, being an essential cultural component, has functioned as a protective device against the larger society.[21] The Chicano kinship system, based on intensity and primacy of the familia, has functioned as a source of trust, refuge, and protection in a society that systematically exploits and oppresses Mexicans.

The first and most characteristic cultural resistance to colonialism is the maintenance of values and ways of life in the face of modernization.[22] The Chicano family has operated as a mechanism of cultural resistance during periods when political resistance was not possible. Adherence to strong family ties and to a pattern of familial organization with distinct sex-role differentiation has not indicated a mere passive acceptance of tradition. This adherence has afforded protection, security, and comfort in the face of the adversities of oppression: it has expressed Chicano cultural identity in a society that destroys cultural distinctions.

The political significance of the family has its roots in the history of Chicano political organization. Miguel Tirado's analysis of organizational behavior since 1910 points to involvement of families as a contributing factor to the longevity and vitality of political organizations. [23]

Contemporary political familism has significant consequences both in terms of its impact on the Chicano movement and in terms of those changes that it has brought about in the Chicano family. Family involvement in political activities has made possible the retention of special bonds between family members at a time when the trends toward urbanization and atomization of family life move to eliminate extended family ties. Although the structure of family life among urban Chicanos may be described as nuclear, familism has not been abandoned. Rather, its focus has been shifted to another institutional setting—the social movement for racial justice. As the familia concept has taken on a new meaning, it has created new organizational and ideological bonds between Chicanos who are politically united as a familia in La Causa.

Political familism has wrought considerable changes in Chicano families. Organizational commitment to total family involvement in the Chicano movement results in new patterns of behavior as women take part in movement activities. Political activism places Chicanas in situations requiring modification of both male and female traditional roles. The dynamics of political familism both enable Chicanos to maintain familial ties and provide conditions for the transformation of traditional sex roles.

Revolution, Family Structure, and Women's Roles

El Movimiento's demands for Chicano activism are not incongruent with men's traditional sex-role expectations; however, they do place new role expectations on women. As Chicanas have become involved in movement activities that seek to change patterns of racial equality, many aspects of their subordination as women have come to the surface. By involving themselves in activities of El Movimiento, women have found that they have had to confront not only an externally imposed system of racial domination, but also a system of sexual domination within their own cultural setting.

The history of women's involvement in revolutionary struggles is one in which women have encountered opposition as they become involved in activities that challenge traditional male dominance. Sheila Rowbatham's book *Women, Resistance and Revolution* identifies a relationship between social revolution and feminism. She has found that while the specific conditions of revolution remain distinct, women's experience in revolutionary movements is repeated. Political activity challenges women's and men's traditional positions; it changes women's relationship to the family, and it generates conditions for the emergence of women's consciousness.[24]

Recognition of the common structural position of women in revolutionary movements should not obscure the unique historical conditions of Chicanas or their unique struggles in El Movimiento. Adaljiza Sosa Riddell provides an insightful historical analysis of the experiences of women in Mexico. She discusses the conquest by Spaniards, and the subsequent experiences of women who became Chicanas either as a result of the conquest of Mexico by the United States, or by migration to this country. Both these incidents of colonization imposed two forms of domination on Mexican women: racial and sexual. Reflecting the views of the Catholic church on women, the Spanish conquerors regarded the native women as heathens in need of redemption, and as loose women who could be exploited without fear of punishment. Chicanas experienced similar treatment in the United States. They entered the U.S. economic and political system at the lowest stratum. Again they were sexually and economically exploited, this time by Anglo white colonizers.[25]

The history of the revolutionary emergence of women in colonized societies accentuates women's unconventional modes of cooperation in political revolt. Departures from traditional sex-role behaviors made necessary by revolution lead women in nationalist liberation movements to discover their own powers, strengths, and talents—to demand changes in the system of power relationships based on sex. Such departures also bring about efforts by men to defend their established positions of dominance. As far as the position of women is concerned, the Chicano movement echoes previous nationalist revolutionary movements. Conditions for a sex-role revolution within a political revolution have been generated. Attempts to equalize the Chicano movement in sexual terms have resulted in unique activities and expressions of Chicana consciousness.

Social science literature abounds with descriptions of Chicano sex-role relationships in which males are aggressive, tough, and dominating, while females are submissive, suffering, dependent, and passive. It is necessary to refute stereotypes that describe Chicanos as passive reactors to traditional values. Although most sex-role descriptions are static, one-dimensional, and in need of refutation, the inescapable truth remains that sex-role relationships in Chicano sociocultural systems are characterized by patterns of male dominance.

Political familism has provided the conditions for changes in patriarchal patterns of Chicano relationships. Participation of total Chicano family units in political and quasi-political activities has placed women in situations that require new forms of behavior, thus restructuring their relationships with Chicano men. By saying that assertiveness and independence are required of women as well as of men who are challenging the dominant system and demanding a better life for their people and their children, I do not mean that Chicanas have not been active, assertive, or strong women in the past. I believe that they have always possessed these traits, and that historical research will uncover the importance of women's activities in the Chicano experience. I am suggesting that the call for total family participation in the Chicano struggle has resulted in necessary changes in relationships between men and women. Women's involvement in El Movimiento has begun to transform patterns of male exclusiveness as women participate in meetings and strikes, as they seek and acquire meaningful schooling and employment, and as they forge new directions for achieving the collective goals of La Raza.

The Chicano movement calls for changes not only in conditions that are externally imposed by the dominant society, but also in Chicano behaviors. Movement rhetoric makes much of the creation of "La Raza Nueva." This emphasis undoubtedly provides opportunities for Chicanas to act autonomously as new expectations are placed on them. Nevertheless, Chicanas often find themselves in the ambiguous position of consciously striving to alter traditional subordinate roles while at the same time having to defend Chicano cultural conditions.

Chicanas are increasingly articulating the conviction that cultural integrity and the elimination of their traditional subordination are not incompatible. Elena Garcia makes this point about Chicana consciousness:

> Chicana consciousness is an integral part of the new breed, the Chicano movement, Chicanismo. Chicana consciousness defined is not a white women's liberation movement being that we are working within a cultural context, a Chicana context.... Chicana consciousness can thus be defined as working within the cultural context, yet not upon limitations of the self, the new Chicana self. As Chicanas we respect our men. We respect the home, the familia. This is all dealing within the cultural context. Yet times are changing. You are coping with a new Chicana, a Chicana working within the college system. A Chicana who is seeing that her place need not only be in the home. She is sensing her ability beyond that, yet not excluding it.[26]

Enriqueta Longeaux y Vásquez's writings on the Chicana, which have appeared in many publications, also emphasize change within a cultural context. Consider the following passages from the essay "Soy Chicana Primero":

> The Chicana is needed by her people for part of the equality of Raza is cultural survival.... In working for her own people a Raza woman becomes more capable and gains confidence, pride and strength. This strength is

both personal and as a people. She gains independence, security and more human strength because she is working in a familiar area, one in which she puts her corazón and love.... This is the kind of spirit and strength that builds and holds firm La Familia de La Raza.[27]

Chicanas are consciously creating for themselves new role models that differentiate them from other types. In a pamphlet written for Chicanas, Gloria Guardiola and Yolanda Garza Birdwell deal with the following concepts: Chicano culture, the traditional woman, the middle-class woman, the professional woman, and "the Chicana." The Chicana stands out as the ideal, the aim, the type of woman Chicanas should aspire to become because of her active political and social participation. The authors urge Chicanas to work toward a new social order that guarantees the equal involvement of the whole Chicano family.[28]

Political familism has jarred the Chicano family at one level because total family participation results in changes in the relative position of men and women. Such changes have hurled Chicanas out of their traditional subordinate roles. It would be inaccurate to conclude that male dominance has disappeared, but political activism of the women of La Raza has weakened the patriarchal patterns. Political familism has disrupted the sex-role stability of Chicano families. Ideologically, Chicanos may support the virtues of total family involvement, but for individual men and women, this involvement may present difficulties as they attempt to adjust to the changes that political familism demands.

Machismo

The male-dominated Chicano family is frequently discussed in terms of the machismo cult. The importance that the notion of machismo has acquired in social science literature and in El Movimiento prompts the following discussion.

In social science literature, machismo is most often associated with irresponsibility, inferiority, and ineptitude.[29] This culture trait as well as the adoption of a tough pose in family relationships has been attributed to Mexican and Chicano males and is said to be a compensation for feelings of inadequacy and worthlessness. Both machismo and female submissiveness are said to reinforce one another to impede productive, instrumental achievement-oriented behavior.

Analysis of colonization often fosters misuse of the macho concept. This misuse takes the form of identifying a system of economic, political, and psychological colonization. Where objective conditions of oppression and subordination exist, inferiority is said to be internalized by members of the colonized group who develop psychological mechanisms to compensate for their subordination. Rowbatham, in her discussion of colonized women, notes the presence of psychological colonization:

> The man's reaction is partly the age-old response of the male oppressor, but it is also something else. The White imperialists not only colonize economically, but psychologically. They usurped the men from their "manhood"; they took over from the colonized men control of their women.[30]

The widely accepted interpretation of machismo is that it is an attempt by men to compensate for their inferiority. This interpretation (whether one locates the cause of oppression in the social structure or in psychological characteristics of the oppressed) attributes machismo and its corresponding pattern of female submissiveness to pathological characteristics of the oppressed. In effect this interpretation finds Chicanos themselves responsible for their own subordination due to their dysfunctional cultural responses.

The validity of this prevailing social science interpretation of machismo is open to serious question.[31] This is not to say that the concept itself must be abandoned. However, if the concept is to be more than a cultural stereotype, it must be used in a discriminative manner. One viable approach is to examine the way in which machismo is perceived and defined by Chicanos themselves, rather than relying exclusively on social science categories for definition. Such an investigation would undoubtedly yield some indication of the positive dimensions of machismo. This approach may enable us to ask questions that would lead to an understanding of male dominance and aggression of the oppressed as a calculated response to hostility, exclusion, and racial domination in a colonized society. It is possible that aggressive behavior of Chicano males has been both an affirmation of Mexican cultural identity and an expression of their conscious rejection of the dominant society's definition of Mexicans as passive, lazy, and indifferent.[32]

The machismo issue has become central to questions concerning women's roles in the Chicano movement. Machismo is seen by many Chicanas as an obstacle to revolutionary struggle. Jennie Chávez's description of the dilemmas she faced as a woman in a university Chicano organization has a familiar ring to many Chicanas:

> As soon as I started expounding my own ideas the men who ran the
> organization would either ignore my statement, or make a wisecrack about
> it and continue their own discussion. This continued for two years until
> I finally broke away because of being unable to handle the situation.[33]

Lionela López Saenz denounces machismo, stating that the machismo
syndrome advocates absolute power and authority, thus subordinating
Chicanas.[34] Mirta Vidal claims that the awakening of Chicano consciousness has been promoted by the machismo that women encounter in the
movement. Furthermore, this behavior, "typical of Chicano men," is a
serious obstacle to women anxious to play a role in the struggle for Chicano
liberation.[35] Such calls for an end to male domination have caused dissent
within the Chicano movement, but they have not gone unheeded.

The Black Berets of Albuquerque have redefined machismo in terms
of revolutionary struggle:

> We want equality for women. Machismo must be revolutionary ... not
> oppressive. Under this system our women have been oppressed both by
> the system and our own men. The doctrine of machismo has been used
> by our men to take out their frustrations on their wives, sisters, mothers
> and children. We must support our women in their struggle for economic
> and social equality and recognize that our women are equals within our
> struggle for liberation. Forward hermanas in the struggle.[36]

Armando Rendón has attempted to move machismo beyond its negative
sex-role connotations and to link it with the Chicano movement in a
political sense:

> The essence of machismo, of being macho, is as much a symbolic
> principle of the Chicano revolt as it is a guideline for the conduct of
> family life, female relationships, and personal self-esteem. To be macho
> in fact is an underlying drive of the gathering identification of Mexican
> Americans which goes beyond a recognition of common troubles. The
> Chicano revolt is a manifestation of Mexican Americans exerting
> their manhood and womanhood against the anglo society. Macho, in
> other words, can no longer relate merely to manhood, but must relate
> to nationhood as well.[37]

Whether a redefinition of machismo as a political concept can be rec-
onciled with women's full and equal participation in revolutionary struggle
remains to be seen. Chicanas' censure of machismo is important in that such
demands for sexual equality stem not from the adoption of Anglo patterns
of sex-role relationships, but rather from Chicanas' experiences, which

have shown how patterns of traditional male dominance have inhibited the active participation of women in Chicano liberation struggles.

As social and political involvement of Chicanas flourishes, so does their consciousness as women take shape. The question of the role of women in society, of Chicanas in El Movimiento, is a much debated issue. Because male dominance has been a major pillar of Chicano life, the issue has become a highly emotional one. Never before have Chicanos, both men and women, discussed so openly and intensely questions relating to sex roles in the Chicano community. An ongoing dialogue continues between men and women, between young Chicanas and their mothers, between those who claim to be "brown" feminists and those who resist any affiliation with feminism. In spite of these differences, it has become clear that a new mode of liberation is evolving out of Chicano liberation.

Conclusion

Changes in the structure of Chicano families cannot be attributed solely to acculturation or modernization. While sex roles are moving in the direction of equalization, this movement should not be taken to signal the assimilation of Chicanos.

The Chicano movement has fostered a situation in which nationalism and feminism are both important components. They are in some ways contradictory, yet as political familism has taken on real meaning, men and women have come to need and depend on each other in new ways. Political familism itself does not transcend sex-role subordination. But within the varied expressions and manifestations of El Movimiento are changes in sex-role relationships and family structure, as well as the seeds of new roles for the women and men of La Raza.

Notes

1. William J. Goode, *World Revolutions and Family Patterns* (London: The Free Press of Glencoe, 1963): 1–26.

2. See for example Alice B. Culp, *A Case Study of 35 Mexican Families* (1921; reprinted, San Francisco: R and E Research Associates, 1971); Ruth Tuck, *Not with the Fist* (New York: Harcourt Brace and Co., 1946); and Norman D. Humphrey, "The Changing Structure of the Detroit Mexican Family," *American Sociological*

Review 9 (December 1944): 622–6.

3. Manuel Ramirez, "Identification with Mexican Family Values and Authoritarianism in Mexican Americans," *Journal of Social Psychology* 73 (1967): 3–11.

4. Roland G. Tharp, Arnold Meadow, Susan G. Lennhoff, and Donna Satterfield, "Changes in Marriage Roles Accompanying the Acculturation of the Mexican American Wife," *Journal of Marriage and the Family* 30 (August 1968): 404–12.

5. Leo Grebler, Joan Moore, and Ralph Guzmán, *The Mexican American People* (New York: The Free Press, 1970), 350–70.

6. Ellwyn Stoddard, *Mexican Americans* (New York: Random House, 1973), 103–4.

7. See Tomás Almaguer, "Toward the Study of Chicano Colonialism," *Aztlán* 2, no. 1 (spring 1971); Rodolfo Acuña, *Occupied America* (New York: Canfield Press, 1972); Joan W. Moore, "Colonialism: The Case of the Mexican American," *Social Problems* 17, no. 4 (spring 1970); Mario Barrera, Carlos Muñoz, and Charles Ornelas, "The Barrio as an Internal Colony," in *People and Politics in an Urban Society*, ed. Harlan Hahn, Urban Affairs Annual Reviews, vol.. 6 (Beverly Hills, Calif.: Sage Publications, 1972).

8. Ron E. Roberts and Robert Marsh Kloss argue that the differentiating factor between revolution and reform lies in the degree of mobilization of the masses of people: "Many successful reforms have been effected without great commitment by the masses. The case is different with a successful revolution. In this case, the masses must be mobilized to overturn elites and to make basic institutional changes." *Social Movements: Between the Balcony and the Barricade* (St. Louis: C. V. Mosby Company, 1974), 38.

9. Abelardo Delgado, *The Chicano Movement: Some Not Too Objective Observations* (Denver: Totinem Publications, 1971), 3.

10. Carey McWilliams, introduction to *North from Mexico* (New York: Greenwood Press, 1968).

11. Armando G. Gutiérrez, "Institutional Completeness and La Raza Unida Party," in *Chicanos and Native Americans*, ed. Rudolph O. de la Garza, Z. Anthony Kruszewski, and Tomás A. Arciniega (Englewood Cliffs, N.J.: Prentice Hall, 1973), 113–23.

12. Excerpts from a speech by José Ange Gutiérrez in *Viva La Raza*, ed. Julian Nava (New York: D. Van Nostrand Co., 1973), 145.

13. "El Plan Espiritual de Aztlán" (paper presented at the Chicano Youth Liberation Conference, Denver, Colo., March 1969).

14. Armando B. Rendón, *Chicano Manifesto* (New York: Macmillan, 1971), 169.

15. "A Sense of Togetherness," *La Luz* 3, no. 3 (June 1974): 40.

16. Lobo (University of New Mexico), 14 November 1973.

17. Rodolfo "Corky" González, "What Political Road for the Chicano Movement?" *The Militant*, 30 March 1970. Reprinted in *A Documentary History of the Mexican Americans*, ed. Wayne Moquin and Charles Van Doren. (New York: Praeger, 1971), 488.

18. Julius K. Nyerere, *Freedom and Unity* (London: Oxford University Press, 1967), 10.

19. Robert Blauner, *Racial Oppression in America* (New York: Harper & Row, 1972), 95.

20. Melford E. Spiro, "The Acculturation of American Ethnic Groups," *American Anthropologist* 57 (1955): 1247.

21. Robert Staples, "The Mexican American Family: Its Modification Over Time and Space," *Phylon* 32, no. 2 (1971): 179–92.

22. Blauner, *Racial Oppression*, 116.

23. Miguel David Tirado, "Mexican American Community Political Organization: The Key to Chicano Political Power," *Aztlán* 1, no. 1 (spring 1970): 53–78.

24. Sheila Rowbatham, *Women, Resistance, and Revolution* (New York: Vintage Books, 1971).

25. Adaljiza Sosa Riddell, "Chicanas and El Movimiento," *Aztlán* 5, no. 1 and 2 (spring/fall 1974): 155–65.

26. Elena Garcia, "Chicana Consciousness: A New Perspective, A New Hope," in *La Mujer en Pie de Lucha*, ed. Dorinda Moreno (San Francisco: Espina del Norte Publications, 1973), 4.

27. Enriqueta Longeaux y Vásquez, "Soy Chicana Primero," *El Cuaderno* 1, no. 1 (1970): 17–22.

28. Gloria Guardiola and Yolanda Garza Birdwell, "The Woman: Destruction of Myths, Formation and Practice of Free Thinking" (n. p., 1971).

29. Miguel Montiel, "The Chicano Family: A Review of Research," *Social Work* 18, no. 2: 22–31.

30. Rowbatham, *Women, Resistance, and Revolution*, 205.

31. For a critique of uncritical use of the machismo concept, see Miguel Montiel, "The Social Science Myth of the Mexican American Family," *El Grito* 3, no. 4 (summer 1970).

32. For a discussion of characterizations of the oppressed as a rejection of the oppressors' stereotype, see Stephen R. Warner, David T. Wellman, and Leonore J. Weitzman, "The Hero, The Sambo, and The Operator: Three Characterizations of the Oppressed," *Urban Life and Culture* 2, no. 1 (1973).

33. Jennie V. Chavez, "An Opinion: Women of the Mexican American Movement," *Mademoiselle* 74 (April 1972): 82.

34. Lionela López Saenz, "Machismo, No! Igualdad, Si!" *La Luz* 1, no. 2 (May 1972): 19.

35. Mirta Vidal, "New Voices of La Raza: Chicanas Speak Out," *National Socialist Review*, October 1971.

36. From *Venceremos!*, July 1971. Reprinted in Stoddard, *Mexican Americans*, 105.

37. Rendón, *Chicano Manifesto*, 104.

Chicano Critical Discourse
An Emerging Cultural Practice

Angie Chabram-Dernersesian

To the critics of Chicano literature:

"But I am saying that we should look not for the components of a product but for the conditions of a practice."

Raymond Williams, *Problems in Materialism and Culture*

"Literary theory, in the forms in which we know it, is a child of the social and political convulsions of the sixties."

Terry Eagleton, *The Function of Criticism*

In "Literary Criticism: The State of the Art," Walter Kendrick laments: "It is no longer so easy as it was even ten years ago for a critical book to rely on empiricism, common sense, or flashes of insights; now for good or ill, critics of whatever persuasion are obliged to declare a methodology, to locate themselves somewhere in relation to the brilliant, often bewildering constellation formed by structuralism, semiotics, deconstruction, and the other schools of thought which have transformed the reading of texts."[1] In *American Literary Criticism* Arnold L. Goldsmith concurs, adding: "So much criticism of criticism has been written in America, with abstract theory, piled on theory, that it seems at times as though only the most erudite initiates can scale the verbal mountains and breathe their rarified air."[2] In the preface to *Literary Theory* (1983), Terry Eagleton alerts his readers that in the past few decades "the very meaning of 'literature,' 'reading' and 'criticism' has undergone deep alteration."[3]

From *Aztlan: A Journal of Chicano Studies* 1, no. 1 (1970): 1–12.

Introductory remarks of this nature have become so commonplace within general (meta)critical studies that it is scarcely possible to read an account of contemporary literary theory or criticism that does not make reference to the altered nature, increasing difficulty, and sophistication of contemporary critical discourse. Perhaps the most dramatic effects of the so-called "theoretical revolution" on criticism can be witnessed in the massive appearance of a wide range of monographs, interviews, and guides, designed to introduce the uninformed (and the casually informed) reader to the works of major critical figures, schools, and debates, as well as to a number of theoretical reflections surrounding the "crisis" of criticism, the "function" of criticism, the "institution" of criticism and yes, even the "failure" of criticism. As Edward Said correctly ascertained in his now classic "Reflections on American 'Left' Literary Criticism," "Never before in the history of American literary culture has there been such widespread and such serious, sometimes technical and frequently contentious discussions in literary criticism. Every critic or teacher is affected by the discussion."[4]

The growing significance of criticism as a widely accepted, highly sought, increasingly specialized domain of intellectual activity has already given way to a new "confident comprehensiveness" within recent critical studies, particularly among popularizing guides that propose to settle its frequently changing frontiers.[5] A striking example of this current can be witnessed in W. J. T. Mitchell's "The Golden Age of Criticism," in which the author institutes a division of the world into "critical" (metropolitan) centers of empire (Europe and the United States) and "literary" (colonial) peripheries of empire (South America, South Africa, Australia, and the Middle East) in an attempt to reconcile criticism's expansiveness and seeming concentration within specific realms of literary production.[6]

Were it not for the selective criteria at work in the designation of national (domestic) literary cultures, one could easily point an accusing finger at Mitchell for his faulty suggestion that the "Golden Age" of criticism has not traversed the oppositional polarities that he activates upon reordering the world of culture according to the designs of a newly discovered, yet no less potent, First World critical imperialism. Though strikingly "confident," his narrative of twentieth-century criticism draws attention because of its lack of "comprehensiveness." Are we really to believe that Latin Americans, South Africans, Australians, and inhabitants of the Middle East do not produce critics of notable stature? That they do not count with texts of significant critical import?

Closer to home, we might well ask whether the critical production of historically marginalized groups (Chicanos, Blacks, Asians, Native Americans, etc.) has remained immune from so much theorizing and such widespread classroom talk, whether their emergent critical discourses aren't deserving of a space within Mitchell's conflated elliptical survey.[7] From a general theoretical perspective, we might even be prompted to question whether it is true that criticism is the privileged terrain of particular races, nationalities, classes, geographical zones, and forms of political and social organization.

I draw attention to these elements, not so much to underscore the types of social and political considerations that inform Mitchell's critical boundaries (though they are very instructive), as to highlight the types of gaps that may accompany any number of recent "comprehensive" efforts to organize a canon of American criticism. Though generally less favorable than Mitchell in their appreciation of alternative literary traditions, mainstream critics of American literature have tended toward a similar type of "confidence" while activating comparable domestic oppositions between the critical situations of established and alternative emergent literary cultures.

The unspoken assumptions that have historically provided the justification for these types of boundaries are, first, that all has been said and done once the brilliant constellation of master critical works within advanced literary cultures has been examined, and second, that peripheral critical discourses have nothing or little to contribute to ongoing critical debates. These assumptions are predicated upon the mistaken belief that criticism is a unified, homogeneous discourse, the value of which can be measured in direct proportion to its representation within widely recognized authoritative works, circulation within specific text milieus, and formal relationship to a stable, universally accepted body of literary texts. Such commonly held beliefs would not, of course, be quite so harmful if they weren't accented by parallel assumptions at the levels of class, race, and gender, or if they weren't so firmly anchored in educational institutions, where, as Raymond Williams reminds us, admission and incorporation into the "selective" tradition take place.

The degree to which these values and practices have functioned to subvert "difference" within prominent literary circles would appear to signal a growing disparity between the practice of criticism and its theory, for this subversion is being effected within the very same literary institutions where deconstruction has already reached its heyday, where the limits of critical discourse have been expanded to incorporate adjacent domains of knowledge on an unprecedented scale. Even more instructive is the fact that these trends are so prevalent in a period of critical history in which the object of (literary) critical discourse is increasingly being called into question, wrestled from its stable location, and situated within a wide range of "cultural" or "signifying" practices.[8]

If it is true, as Eagleton has suggested, that (literary) critical discourse is a "kind of talk" about literature that envelops "a whole field of meanings, objects, and practices," then it follows that critical discourses of all types should provide ample ground for examining a broad range of social, cultural, as well as strictly literary-critical experiences, independent of the place that these discourses may occupy in relation to a fixed canon of works. It only stands to reason that those frequently disqualified sectors, which foregrounded the relations between criticism and society by the very conditions of their emergence and deployment of theory in practice, should be included as contributors and not passive receptors of the critical problematics of our time.

Though highly promising, such an organic approach to the study of criticism remains difficult at this point in history. Plagued by faulty assumptions and uncertain as to how the links between different critical spheres might be formulated, critics of Anglo American literature threaten to set into motion the types of dynamics that initially separated emergent literatures from their more established literary counterparts. Already a severe imbalance can be detected in the production and consumption of critical studies associated with these domains; thus while monographs that examine the critical problematics associated with established sectors now abound in record numbers, such is not the case with those associated with alternative sectors (Black, Chicano, feminist, to cite a few). Not only are these critical traditions notably underrepresented in contemporary histories and surveys of criticism, but it is not unusual that they are also beyond the immediate reach of students of Anglo American literature who are frequently as perplexed as are their instructors when asked to identify critical figures, debates, and chronologies associated with the alternative sector.

As is true in the highly competitive arena of university life, ignorance has its price. What might elicit a reluctant "I don't know" in relation to one critical sector (the established one), in relation to another (the alternative, emergent) elicits a statement of disbelief: "It must not exist," or a condemnatory valuation: "It must not be very good." In cases such as the latter, the master text ultimately surfaces as the authoritative work, conferring legitimacy or illegitimacy on the critical tradition at hand. This occurs despite the fact that the master text may be fraught with absences and silences (cultural lacunae) that radically call into question its "authoritative" stature.

That the negative repercussions of the underrepresentation of emergent traditions extend to the greater critical sector becomes readily apparent upon reviewing the notable contributions of these traditions to recent critical history. Aside from reconstructing the forms, the values, and the lineages of "alternative" literary cultures, they effected significant alterations in the existing modes and structures of general literary production, bringing to the forefront criticism's tacit complicity with specific ideological formations. In recent years, emergent critical traditions have also made valuable theoretical contributions in works such as *Black Feminist Criticism; Figures in Black; Black Literature and Literary Theory; "Race," Writing, and Difference; Feminist Literary Theory; Feminist Literary Criticism; Modern Chicano Writers; Contemporary Chicano Fiction;* and *Making a Difference.*

Future attempts to assess the importance of these traditions for general histories of criticism, if they are to be truly productive, should include inquires into the respective histories of each of these traditions. Only through this type of critical specificity can the full impact of their social, ideological, and artistic functions be measured.

This essay does not propose to chart the significant roads traveled by alternative, emergent critical formations since their bold appearance onto the critical landscape. However, it does examine some of the recent developments that have surfaced in Chicano critical discourse—that body of writing that emerged in response to the artistic practices generated by the Chicano movement in select cultural institutions. Rather than providing a metacommentary on individual critical works in the fashion of its predecessors, this essay sets out to identify general trends within contemporary Chicano criticism, and to examine some of the problems that have arisen in its conceptualization.

This deviation from the norm is conscious; it is intended to draw attention to the fact that Chicano criticism, as it exists today, is a dynamic, ever-changing field, which requires much careful scrutiny and a wide-ranging, integrated approach, capable of responding to its multifaceted existence within various forms and spheres of critical activity. Toward this end "Chicano Critical Situations" maps out important alterations in the production and consumption of Chicano criticism; "Chicano Critical Studies" and "Exploring the Horizons" examine the possibilities of broadening the scope of existing critical studies to account for the links between emergent and general critical traditions; and "Reconceptualizing Chicano Critical Discourse" and "Taking the Word" point to alternative theoretical frameworks for examining Chicano critical discourse. Guided by Raymond Williams's insistence "that we should look not for the components of a work but for the conditions of a practice," subsequent divisions address the conditions that surround the production of Chicano critical discourse.

Chicano Critical Situations

Since its inception in the 1960s, Chicano criticism has undergone profound transformations that are readily evident in its ever increasing sophistication and its now substantial volume. Nonetheless, relative to its significant maturation in recent years, its scholarship has lagged notably behind. To date, there are no extensive histories, encyclopedias, or monograph-length theoretical accounts dedicated to its appraisal. Among those Chicano metacritical works that have appeared over the last twelve years, Joseph Sommers's "From the Critical Premise to the Product: Critical Modes and Their Application to a Chicano Literary Text" is undoubtedly the most comprehensive study that has appeared on the topic.[9] With this essay, which stands as a benchmark in the development of Chicano critical thought, Joseph Sommers further established Chicano criticism as an important domain of scholarly investigation. He not only shed light on many of the basic critical assumptions that underlie Chicano critical modalities (the historical-dialectical, the culturalist, and the formalist), but he inspired a succession of writers to recognize the important developments in Chicano criticism, thus setting the stage for the expansion of the Chicano critical essay into yet other forms of metacritical activity.

Since the appearance of Joseph Sommers's essay, a number of critical monographs on Chicano literature have appeared. A cursory survey of the most significant monographs produced within the last decade or so would certainly include *Aztlán y México: Perfiles literarios e históricos; Five Poets of Aztlán; Contemporary Chicana Poetry; Chicano Poetry: A Response to Chaos; Chicano Poetry: A Critical Introduction; Introduction to the Chicano Novel; Contemporary Chicano Fiction; La novela chicana escrita en español; Narrativa chicana contemporánea; Chicano Theatre; Mexican American Theatre; Chicano Literature; A Decade of Chicano Literature; Modern Chicano Writers; The Identification and Analysis of Chicano Literature; Beyond Stereotypes; Chicano*

Literature: A Reference Guide; Acerca de la literatura: Diálogos con tres autores chicanos; Partial Autobiographies; Chicano Authors; International Studies in Honor of Tomás Rivera; The Rolando Hinojosa Reader; Chicana Creativity and Criticism: Charting New Frontiers in American Literature; and *La literatura chicana a través de sus autores.* To this list, several issues of literary journals dedicated solely to Chicano criticism can be added, along with a significant body of dissertations on Chicano literature.[10]

This proliferation of Chicano critical texts has been accompanied by a steady growth of international attention to Chicano literature and criticism in countries such as France, Germany, Spain, and Mexico. Several prominent foreign-based publishing outlets have also begun to carry the works of Chicano critics. Among the most notable examples in recent years are Mexico's Siglo XXI, *Texto Crítico, Plural,* and Fondo de Cultura Económica.[11] Furthermore, with greater frequency than ever, European and Latin American critics are circulating their critical essays on Chicano literature within prominent national literary institutions.

Significant trends in publication can also be discerned within the United States, where a good number of critical monographs have been published by prestigious university presses and regular mainstream publication outlets. Chicano critical essays have also made sporadic appearances in mainstream journals such as *Modern Language Notes, Diacritics, Ideologies and Literature, The Denver Quarterly, Hispania, Latin American Literary Review, Latin American Theatre Review,* and *Cultural Critique,* although the bulk of these essays is still concentrated in ethnic or Chicano journals. Outside this sphere, Chicana critical works have begun to surface with regularity in feminist journals such as *Third Woman, Feminist Studies, Frontiers,* and *Signs,* primarily as a result of the growing number of Chicana critics (including Sylvia Lizárraga, Marta Sánchez, Rosaura Sánchez, María Herrera-Sobek, Rosa Linda Fregoso, Yolanda Broyles-González, Soñia Saldivar-Hull, Norma Alarcón, Cordelia Candelaria, Alvina Quintana, Clara Lomas, and Yvonne Yarbro-Bejarano) who are examining women's writings and the images of the Chicana in literature and, in the process, rewriting Chicano criticism. Norma Alarcón, editor of *Third Woman* and *The Sexuality of Latinas,* comments on some of the motivations that have spurred waves of recent Chicana critical production while discussing her own critical ventures:

> I was aware from the very beginning that the establishing of a Chicano intellectual tradition was very male dominated—endocentric, if you will. It was often the case that women were only being included in this tradition if their point of view fit under the cultural nationalist banner.

By then, it was already clear to me that we had to nurture our women writers in such a way that they weren't censored even if what they had to say wasn't acceptable to the entire community. That's why I decided to publish Chicanas and Latinas. ... For the journal, I chose the title *Third Woman* as a way of pointing to the connections between Chicanas and other Third World women, especially Latinas.

In my own work, I'm interested in translating our experience, no matter how painful. My essay in *This Bridge Called My Back* (1983), which was later translated under the title *Esta puente, mi espalda* (1998), was kind of a breakthrough in this sense. Because I was claiming my own voice at the same time that I was recuperating a female historical space, and establishing a discursive formation within which to ground that tradition.[12]

Norma Alarcón's work forms part of an unprecedented and culturally significant *Chicana* critical enterprise that rivals cultural nationalism as a motivating social and political force in Chicano letters. At present, Chicana critics are not only altering categories of received criticism, bringing their own cultural and literary innovation to bear on preexistent literary, critical categories, but they are also painstakingly unearthing the Chicana literary voice in newspapers, periodicals, oral histories, chronicles, memoirs, autobiographies, theatrical performances, Mexican revolutionary writings, and wherever Chicana literary productions are found.

It would not be an exaggeration to suggest that we are rapidly moving into an age of Chicano/a criticism. Not only has this critical production fared considerably well in relation to the total volume of literature produced within the same time period, but recent trends defy previous years when literary anthologies prevailed over critical monographs by substantial margins.[13]

Signs of this critical passage can also be detected in the progressive movement toward more academic forms of critical discourse and in the proliferation of modern literary theories and perspectives (especially Marxist, formalist, mythic, feminist, poststructuralist, semiotic, and phenomenological) throughout recent Chicano critical endeavors. The growing number of works dedicated to Chicano critical reflection and evaluation is also reflective of the burgeoning of Chicano criticism. As Terry Eagleton has suggested elsewhere: "The moment when a material or intellectual practice begins to 'think itself,' to take itself as an object of intellectual inquiry, is clearly of dominant significance in the development of that practice; it will certainly never be the same again."[14]

The significance of these developments can only be fully appreciated when considering that they have taken place within an emergent critical discourse, whose existence (in the present form) only dates back a few decades and which, for all practical purposes, has experienced the theoretical revolution in literary studies from the very periphery of the dominant critical culture and its supportive institutions. If this were not enough, passage to "critical self-consciousness" has meant movement away from nationalistic paradigms and the creation of new forms of metacritical inquiry for "thinking" this intellectual watershed.

Any discussion of the transformations that have swept Chicano criticism that does not mention the plight of the critic is incomplete, for it is the critic who initially generates the critical text and places it in the literary circuit, thus contributing to its multiple affiliations with other textual practices, critics, and institutional sectors. The critic does not, however, escape the influences of the specific context in which s/he operates. As Edward Said explains: "Critics are not merely the alchemical translators of texts into circumstantial reality or worldliness; for they too are subject to and producers of circumstances, which are felt regardless of whatever objectivity the critic's method proposes."[15]

One area where these mutually confirming forces come together is in the altered professional circumstance of the critic. In contrast to the early years, which saw an onslaught of "popular" (uncertified) critics who worked in nonspecialized informal cultural sectors, the majority of critics of Chicano literature are now members of national literary academies—generally at the assistant and associate professor level. Increasingly their critical production is oriented toward the completion of professional obligations when this is possible.[16] This formation has undoubtedly contributed to the growing professionalization of Chicano critical discourse, and to the proliferation of book-length monographs.

In addition to the growing professionalization of Chicano critical discourse, there has also been a notable shift in the position of the Chicana scholar-critic. Chicana critics currently occupy more varied critical roles, functioning as editors and reviewers for literary journals and anthologies and as authors of books, journal articles, and the like. This portrait would appear to offer a stark contrast to the early years—to the first phase of Chicano criticism—where the term "critic of Chicano literature" was almost always synonymous with male, although even at that point in time Chicana critics were actively practicing criticism and inaugurating a mode of self-reflective Chicano metacritical discourse that would for the most part exclude them as subjects of metacritical history. The Chicana scholar-critic has had a significant impact on literary and critical history since much of what is known about Chicana writers and critics can, in fact, be attributed to the Chicana critics themselves, who have promoted these writers and critics in daily institutional (academic) life.

Another development that is rarely mentioned, but nonetheless significant for understanding the types of alterations experienced by Chicano criticism in recent years, is the ongoing tendency of critics of Chicano literature to cluster into individual "circles" or "schools" of criticism. Thus, it is now possible to speak candidly, though modestly, about the existence of a Yale circle of Chicano critics, an Austin circle, a Santa Barbara circle, and last but not least, a La Jolla circle. These institutional affiliations do not signify that the circles of Chicano critical thought alluded to are homogeneous or that they necessarily replicate the predominant theoretical perspectives associated with specific educational settings. However, these affiliations do illustrate the literary-institutional forces that are impacting the conceptual development of this emerging critical discourse.

The Chicano presence at Yale offers an interesting case in this regard. Several prominent critics of Chicano literature, including Juan Bruce-Novoa, Ramón Saldívar, José David Saldívar, and Héctor Calderón, have all had important affiliations there, as professors, graduate students, or undergraduates. In a series of interviews that I conducted with each of these critics, they acknowledged that this professional affiliation with the "Yale critics" and "Yale deconstructionist movement" did have a significant impact on their critical work—though the nature of this impact varied tremendously with each individual critic.

Ramón Saldívar, for instance, in recalling the culture shock that he experienced upon moving from Edinberg, Texas, to New Haven, Connecticut, cites "Paul de Man as the single most important intellectual influence" on him during the course of his study at Yale. Saldívar's professional biography exemplifies the manners in which diverse critical traditions and professional experiences have converged to produce new theoretical directions in Chicano criticism. As a graduate student at Yale he produced a dissertation on narrative theory, later published as *Figural Language in the Novel* (1984), under the direction of J. Hillis Miller and Paul de Man, while teaching courses on Chicano literature and culture. Upon arriving at the University of Texas at Austin as a professor, his interest in narrative theory was directed toward Chicano literature, and he wrote the much cited "A Dialectic of Difference: Toward a Theory of the Chicano Novel."[17] Saldívar charted the process that led him to adapt certain aspects of poststructuralist theory to the Chicano literary experience:

I had already evolved from my original work in literary theory on Jacques Derrida and the whole structuralist and poststructuralist debate to the notion of "difference." It struck me that in the case of the Mexican American you had precisely a concrete historical example of what Derrida was talking about in abstract, philosophical terms. It seemed like a fitting parallel, especially to what he was saying in his essay "Difference." Juan Bruce-Novoa was making a similar kind of argument, though not from Derrida's point of view ... he [Juan] was moving in another direction and exploring some of the possibilities of thinking theoretically and abstractly and in a non–Anglo American critical tradition, about Chicano literature. So his notion of Mexican American existing in the space between Mexican and American was something which I sympathized with very much ... [18]

A very different trajectory can be followed in the case of Juan Bruce-Novoa, author of *Chicano Poetry* (1982), *Chicano Authors* (1980), various translations, and scores of critical essays, who joined the faculty of the Spanish department at Yale in 1974 (after completing a dissertation on Juan García Ponce at the University of Colorado) and soon thereafter published his highly polemical "The Space of Chicano Literature." Here Bruce-Novoa downplayed the influence of poststructuralism on his intellectual formation, reformulating as well the phenomenological orientation that distinguishes his view of Chicano literature from Ramón Saldívar's:

When I came to Yale, I had a strong theoretical background, but it wasn't the type prevalent in the English Department. ... Most of my readings were oriented through Mexican essays from the generation of Juan García Ponce. ... They ... took me to Bataille and Blanchot ... Derrida was not one of my principal readings but through García Ponce, I read the people who influenced Derrida. ... I always rejected the binary oppositions of French linguistic theory. ... I saw that binaries are anti-Chicano; as soon as we adopt binaries we're in trouble. In the first essay. ... I talk about the Chicano as an inter-space; that is, neither one of the poles.

It's really the synthesis. ... Ramón [Saldívar] says there's no synthesis, but synthesis does not mean end ... it's a constant dialectic that can never be achieved until death. ... I really do believe in this other space ... where it [the literary object] has its own subject.[19]

Yet another perspective on the Chicano experience at Yale is recorded by Héctor Calderón, former professor and graduate student of Spanish literature at Yale, who completed a dissertation on language and consciousness in the novel under the direction of Emir Rodríguez Monegal and Roberto González Echevarría "in an attempt to bring historical depth to post-structuralism." Subsequently, Calderón published *Conciencia y lenguaje en la novela* (1988) along with various critical essays that examine Chicano narrative genres from the perspective of "the ideology of literary form."[20] In this excerpt he chronicles his initial impressions of Yale:

> You have to understand what it was like when I came to Yale. ... The tremendous excitement. ... It was the period from '75 to '77 ... everything was in the formative stages, a very exciting time to be in literature. So then maybe my third or fourth week at Yale, I walked into an auditorium to hear Derrida speak, and I remember having people point out Geoffrey Hartman and Paul de Man, J. Hillis Miller. And the atmosphere was sort of: "Here is the word." The final answer was about to be given, and these critics were gathered to hear it.
>
> Another thing that bothered me about Yale, offended me even, was this notion that history does not exist. You know ... that you can't write history anymore. That even the subject doesn't exist. Again, that seemed to exclude a whole group of people who were very much involved with history. ... The Chicano movement itself was not only making history at that moment, but it was a process in history, and there did not seem to be a space for thinking about that within a framework that says: "There's no subject, there's no history. ..."[21]

José David Saldívar, himself a former student at Yale, professor of literature at the University of California at Berkeley, editor of *The Rolando Hinojosa Reader,* and author of critical essays that locate the emergence of a Chicano-Chicana subject in narrative,[22] concurs, elaborating:

> It seems a bit ironic that just when all of these [mainstream] critics are talking about the end of the subject ... that we should have Chicanos, peoples of color, and feminists, finally beginning to see themselves as subjects, as capable of action instead of just being acted upon. ... It may not be a coincidence that mainstream critics are talking about the end of the subject just when those people who've been cut off from power become aware of their potential role—as subjects—within the historical moment.[23]

These excerpts are of interest, not only because they allow us to speculate on the impact that intellectual formation exerts on a critic's work, but because they furnish an example of how the Chicano critical tradition and the Chicano movement itself mediated the professional experiences and literary perspectives of these critics at Yale. This type of mediation, aside from producing a substantially different set of cultural problematics from those initially registered by Martin, Arac, and Godzich in their account of *The Yale Critics,*[24] also explains the types of adaptations that are produced in contemporary literary theory by Chicano critical discourse. It would, however, be erroneous to universalize the professional affiliations described above to other circles or to assume that Chicano critical activity is limited to the institutional settings mentioned in this essay—the range of possibilities is as varied as are the individual critical histories that, together, make up the Chicano critical experience. What is indisputable, however, is the decisive role that Chicano writers and critics have played in fomenting Chicano critical expression in their capacity as mentors. Though space does not permit acknowledgment of all the deserving, the most visible include: Norma Alarcón, Américo Paredes, Rosaura Sánchez, Gustavo Segade, Bernice Zamora, Arturo Madrid, Sergio Elizondo, Jorge Huerta, Arturo Islas, Sylvia Gonzales, Luís Dávila, Sylvia Lizárraga, Phillip Ortega, Juan Bruce-Novoa, Juan Rodríguez, Nicolás Kanellos, Tomás Ybarra-Frausto, Erlinda Gonzales-Berry, Rolando Hinojosa, María Herrera-Sobek, Gloria Anzaldúa, Alejandro Morales, Cherríe Moraga, and Tomás Rivera. Hispanists such as Yvonne Yarbro-Bejarano, Luis Leal, Joseph Sommers, Carlos Blanco-Aguinaga, and Justo Alarcón have also done their part in training future critics of Chicano literature.

The most influential circles of Chicano criticism have also made contributions worthy of note: the Santa Barbara circle has contributed to the development of a tradition of historical scholarship that has unearthed many early Chicano literary texts; the San Diego circle, to a budding Marxist tradition that dialogues with the works of Eagleton, Jameson, and Sánchez Vásquez; the Yale circle, to the consolidation of various poststructuralist and phenomenological trends; and the Austin circle, to the writing of literary histories that draw from folklore and a cultural studies methodology.

An idea of the diverse elements that have converged to produce influential Chicano critical perspectives or networks can be derived from examining the Texas circle, which surfaces largely as a result of the appearance of seminal literary histories inspired by Américo Paredes's *With His Pistol in His Hand,* a text which itself prefigures the Chicano critical tradition in its contemporary renditions. The now classic "The Evolution of Chicano Literature," for example, was written by Raymund Paredes, who not only studied with Américo Paredes at the University of Texas at Austin, but co-authored one of the early anthologies of Chicano writers with his mentor.[25] After producing a dissertation on the Mexican image in American literature, which sought to "rewrite Cecil Robinson's *With the Ears of Strangers* from a Chicano point of view," Raymund Paredes wrote several essays that identify the origin of anti-Mexican sentiment in the United States and examine the folk base of Chicano literature. In this passage, he discusses the significance of Américo Paredes's work for contemporary literary scholarship:

> Yes. There is definitely a group of students trained at UT Austin heavily influenced by Américo Paredes's work. It is important that Paredes is both a literary scholar and an anthropologist; many people tend to forget his training as a literary critic. But up until about fifteen years ago, when he began attracting graduate students whose emphasis was in Chicano studies, he taught conventional American literature courses. ... You know, they talk about Paredes, and the obvious influence he's had on a generation of critics. ... But you can see why the response has been so overwhelmingly positive. If you go back and reread his criticism, it continuously holds up ... He makes it clear how important it is to establish the cultural landscape in which Chicano writers are composing their works.[26]

This type of "generational" distribution among critics of Chicano literature, with a range of two and often three tiers, is a relatively new phenomenon. So, too, is the appearance of the literary critic, reared and saturated in the field of Chicano literary studies. While doing fieldwork for a study, "Conversations with Chicano Critics," I was taken aback by the overwhelming number of prominent critical figures who had no formal instruction in this area of study. More often than not, they had actually gained access to the discipline through individual study and the teaching of Chicano literature and culture courses in prominent literary institutions. The experience of one of my respondents is not atypical. When asked if he had ever taken a course in Chicano literature, he answered, "No, there were no courses. I taught the first course myself ... I wasn't exactly assigned, more like recruited."

The institutional challenges that these critics encountered—and continue to encounter—within national literary institutions are exemplified in the case of a pioneer Chicano critic who narrates his stormy entrance:

> I went there as a Chicano professor, and I was very conscious of being a Chicano professor ... I became involved with the students ... the first week I was there, my picture appeared in the paper ... The Chicano students and I went to ask for funds and it got violent ... I was called into the Chair's office and he said: "If your picture appears in the paper again, you won't have a job with this university."[27]

Not only were these critics faced with negotiating the place of Chicano literature within established literary circles less than sympathetic to their objectives, but they were also faced with the arduous task of laying the foundation for studying a literary tradition in the absence of readily available reference works. As Juan Rodríguez, editor of *Las crónicas diabólicas de Jorge Ulica*, responded when asked about the critical figures who had influenced him:

> There were no critics of Chicano literature, as far as I knew ... so I was working on the basis of my own perception of the world ... But there were two things I was trying to do ... One was to make sense of what was before me in terms of Chicano literature, to put it into some type of context. And the other thing was to make it legitimate ... So I was conscious of defending Chicano literature.[28]

The experiences of these as well as many other critics of Chicano literature— their valuable service activity, formidable intellectual strides, unyielding persistence in the face of minimal professional compensation—form an important chapter in Chicano critical history. Their contributions also deserve a place among—or at least alongside of—monographs like *The Yale Critics*, *Twentieth-Century Literary Criticism*, *American Critics at Work*, *Contemporary Literary Critics*, and *American Literary Criticism*, as evidence of the "other" literary revolution, which has yet to fully occupy libraries, bookstores, and graduate seminars.

Together with the previously mentioned developments, the experiences of these critics offer valuable insights into the processes and forces that are currently shaping the contours of an emergent critical practice as it passes into a qualitatively new phase of its existence, simultaneously charting terrain that is familiar and unfamiliar to general critical sectors. Much groundwork will have to be laid to do justice to the breadth and depth of this critical passage. Present lacunae in the field point to the need for additional metacritical studies that could explore the historical trajectory of Chicano criticism—its early origins, critical influences and associations—and update Joseph Sommers's classificatory schema to reflect the new approaches to Chicano literature that have surfaced since the publication of his seminal work. Recent developments also need to be reviewed in light of new conceptual frameworks that assess and evaluate the altered nature of Chicano critical discourse, its linkages with other emergent discourses, its appropriation of contemporary literary theory, and its relationship to greater critical traditions. This promises to be one of the most challenging and exciting of present metacritical endeavors, for it entails bringing together traditions that have been linked by contradictory relations of rupture and continuity, as well as operating within a mode of intellectual inquiry whose parameters have yet to be defined in a manner that could respond effectively to such a formidable historical challenge. Charting this new critical terrain will require much reflection and evaluation, not only of future possibilities of broadening the scope of existing metacritical studies, but of past metacritical studies—their priorities, limitations, and lacunae—for it is "in history" (to quote Jameson) that criticism is practiced.

What follows is my own reflection on the state of metacritical studies pertaining to Chicano criticism; though tentative, it identifies some of the problems that have surfaced in the conceptualization of Chicano critical discourse, while proposing areas of critical research that could permit a redefinition of its current parameters. More attention to the particular concerns it raises is essential if this critical discourse is to shed its marginal status within the history of contemporary critical problematics. It is in this spirit that critical trends are examined, beginning with those that concern Chicano critical studies.

Chicano Metacritical Studies: Expanding the Parameters

In many respects, Chicano critical studies have thrived in recent years. In addition to their notable proliferation, they have increasingly grown into specialized domains of critical inquiry. The upshot of this is the appearance of several Chicano critical essays that evaluate critical approaches to Chicano literature, offer lengthy commentaries on the works of individual critics, and reflect on the problems involved in classifying Chicano literature or criticism.[29] Nonetheless, these studies have only succeeded in offering a partial description of the significant developments that have transpired in Chicano criticism, ignoring for the most part the complex processes that have generated these developments. The criticism of Chicano criticism has tended toward summational inventories of literary perspectives, which, while illuminating basic critical assumptions in textual analysis, have fallen short in accounting for the noteworthy historical trajectory of Chicano criticism and its participation in multiple sectors of literary production.

Furthermore, studies of this nature generally fail to articulate their assumptions regarding Chicano critical discourse and to consider the ways in which general critical works, which ponder the nature and function of criticism itself, might be incorporated into a theoretical rendition of Chicano criticism as an emergent critical practice. In this particular respect, Chicano metacritical studies have fallen well behind much of the vanguard of Chicano literary criticism itself, a domain that is increasingly conscious of the theoretical presuppositions that inform its reading of any number of texts and its dialogue with any number of literary traditions.

The gap between these two domains of literary scholarship must be eradicated if the potential of Chicano critical theory is to be fully realized and if the breadth of its diverse fields of material and symbolic production are to be properly accounted for. But the negative repercussions of this hermetical tendency in Chicano critical studies assume even more widespread proportions when one considers that the function of metacriticism of this nature is to discern questions of vital significance for the discipline at large.

Further development and refinement of the scope of Chicano metacritical studies are particularly important at this point in history, especially in light of the fact that Chicano criticism is undergoing, on a reduced yet accelerated scale, many of the developments experienced within the Anglo American and European literary contexts since the early 1970s. The appearance of new theoretical perspectives, forms of analysis, and terms of critical discourse in Chicano criticism are symptomatic of other, more sweeping critical transformations such as the radical reformulation of the accepted notions of Chicano literary genres, the nature and lineages of the Chicano literary tradition, and the boundaries of Chicano critical discourse itself.[30]

While documenting the extent of this transformation is essential if we are to gain an understanding of the significant roads traveled by Chicano criticism within the past decade or so, it is also essential that this transformation be contextualized in terms of a new critical movement, which has altered not only the types of theoretical frameworks deployed in the analysis of Chicano literature, but also current notions of Chicano criticism and its function in society. No longer can this function be considered in isolation from the problematics of general critical problematics, as was true in the early years. The heightened development of Chicano criticism, together with our growing awareness of its linkages with other critical sectors, requires that this function be dialectically articulated from within the very critical traditions and institutional contexts that are mediating its symbolic readings or interpretations of reality under the impact of determinate social and historical conditions.

Likewise, examination of the types of literary perspectives that inhabit Chicano critical discourse should ideally include attention to the manner in which Chicano critical theory travels from one institutional environment to another and to the manner in which this movement gives way to a dynamic process of appropriation and adaptation, where critical theories are constituted and reconstituted—often completely transformed—by virtue of their accommodation to the exigencies of new and distinct textual and cultural milieus.[31]

This is not to suggest, as Henry Louis Gates Jr. does, that the circulation of ideas necessarily involves a unidirectional movement from the mainstream to the alternative sector, where "non-Western," "non-canonical" critics appropriate the most sophisticated theories in order to reappropriate and "legitimize" their own literary discourses.[32] Clearly, alternative sectors are not static repositories of critical problematics; they, too, generate them and, I might add, not "outside" the Western conventions of literary and critical receptivity. As one of the participants in my survey remarked when asked to comment on the problems involved in classifying Chicano narrative genres:

> It is a very difficult issue, and it's a problem of applying the notion of genre to Chicano literature, which is, after all, a very specific literature. It's not "Western" literature in the conventional sense, yet it has grown both from within the tradition of Western literature, and in response to the pressures from the periphery of Western culture. If you think in terms of where we're educated, the universities we attend, the institutional framework which transmits a European, in some cases a very British, tradition, and then you examine the cultural bonds with Mexican or Latin American tradition—this dual formation, First World and Third World, is going to come through. ... A Chicano writer has a certain social formation that may run counter to the Western tradition at the same time that he or she has an ideological formation that is Western. It's there, we can't deny either aspect.[33]

Not all the distinctive features of emergent critical discourses can be traced to ethnic content, intellectual formation, and specific ideological frameworks or cultural experiences. Irregular conditions of literary (and therefore, critical) production have also negatively affected the way in which emergent discourses relate to other critical spheres and movements, often functioning to limit the scope of their influence and capability of promoting emergent literatures within the extant primary and secondary literary institutions.[34] It is the disparate nature of these conditions of production that has largely nurtured the illusion that alternative emergent discourses exist "outside" general critical practice.

These conditions of production are well illustrated in the case of Chicano literary criticism. Not only is this criticism practiced within multiple channels of literary production, but these channels coexist within varying relations of homology, conflict, and disjuncture, and they potentially differ insofar as their intended objectives, perceptions of Chicano literature, and reading publics are concerned.

The most prevalent channels of Chicano literary (and critical) production are alternative ones. These include both specialized channels for the diffusion of literary works (namely, Chicano literary journals, conferences or associations, or book distributors that deal strictly with literature) and nonspecialized channels such as Chicano studies programs, reference libraries, and interdisciplinary journals such as *Aztlán*. Chicano literary criticism also participates in specialized established literary channels (when incorporated into regular literature departments, mainstream publication outlets, bookstores, and libraries) as well as in nonspecialized channels for the diffusion of general cultural activity.

These channels (the established and the alternative) do not, however, exist with complete independence of one another. Nowhere is the overlap more vividly illustrated than in the not-so-uncommon professor of Chicano literature, who teaches in a Spanish or English department and a Chicano studies program, who publishes critical essays in both mainstream and alternative literary journals, and whose critical work is then listed in bibliographic indexes such as the *Modern Language Association Bibliography* and the *Chicano Periodical Index*. Also of significance in this regard is the frequency with which the alternative channels serve as catalysts for the reception of Chicano literary texts in college libraries, language departments, and bookstores.

The channels of production and consumption of Chicano literature and criticism are thus both interactive as well as semiautonomous from one another. Together they form a complex, asymmetrical totality of structures that do not duplicate one another's functions, and that are not uniformly incorporated into the various national cultural institutions in the patterns described here. While differing in the manner and extent to which they promote Chicano literary activity, they remain bound to the predominant structures of literary production by contradictory and unequal relations of subordination and marginalization. Viewed from this perspective, all Chicano critical activity (including that which inhabits the established sector) can be seen as participating in an "alternative" production insofar as this production seeks to promote a body of writings that continues to exist on the periphery of the greater literary world.

To be sure, these conditions of production have left their imprint on Chicano critical discourse: they have contributed to the uneven and fragmentary nature of its articulation, they have retarded its organization in the manner typical of more established critical traditions; and they have functioned to distance it from the mainstream of critical activity. Future studies would do well to detail the manner in which these conditions of production have affected Chicano critical expression—both materially as well as ideologically—throughout its most salient periods of historical development.

Another subject that merits further attention by Chicano metacritical studies is the impact that class, race, and educational opportunities have had upon the constitution and subsequent development of Chicano critical practice. Already Elizabeth Bruss (*Beautiful Theories*) and Terry Eagleton (*The Function of Criticism*) have argued from a general, critical perspective that "the problem of a new heterogeneity of ethnic heritage and race and class erupting into what had been the small and traditionally restricted world of higher education" formed an integral part of the transformations that shook national literary institutions in the period from the late 1960s onward.[35]

Indications are that these elements would prove to be central in the case of Chicano criticism. It is no secret to anyone that prior to the Chicano movement it was virtually impossible to speak of a Chicano critical tradition in the sense that we know and recognize it today. That the modern origins of Chicano critical history coincide with the Chicano movement is not accidental: the social, political, and economic struggles associated with this movement set into motion the educational reforms that permitted the entrance into prominent literary institutions of a good number of those individuals who would later dedicate themselves to the study of Chicano literature.

That race was a partial determinant of the constitution of Chicano critical discourse can be evidenced by the fact that the majority of its producers were—and continue to be—Chicanos, although members of other ethnic groups have intermittently engaged in this production. To date, there are no studies that examine the individual social formation of Chicano critics in relation to their professional experience and development. Nonetheless, the autobiographical accounts of some of the best known point to the significance of Bruss's assertion regarding the types of class interests that mediated the literary institutional reforms of the 1960s. When asked about their backgrounds, they variously answered:

> On my father's side we come from a long line of mule drivers, my granddad and my great granddad, and his father too, as far as I know. My own father was always a farmworker. ... Generally from the Valley up into Arkansas.

... Like Malcolm X says, it was from "can't see in the morning to can't see at night." I remember having a bloated stomach ... I know what it's like to cry, to hurt of hunger ... dying of hunger. ...

My parents are working-class people. ... My father worked as a crew member and eventually as a foreman in ... the shrimp industry. ... I worked in the plants myself.

On my father's side they were railroad workers. In fact I'm the first one not to work on the railroad.

For a long time he [my dad] ran my grandfather's bakery. ... He delivered candy, notions, cigarettes, things like that to stores.

My father was a semi-skilled laborer. He worked for the Texas highway department. ... My mother ... she was a cotton picker and she also worked in a moccasin factory.

Their parents' educational backgrounds are also revealing. Of the eight critics interviewed, none had parents who had enjoyed the privilege of a university education, although the majority of their parents had received some level of elementary school instruction, and a few were self-taught. The experiences of the critics themselves in elementary and high school are equally instructive. Most make reference to the problematic integration of Mexicans into local schools, and to the strained race relations that this provoked. As one respondent explained:

Externally, many of the schools ... appeared to be more or less integrated. Internally they were quite segregated, and this was accomplished by means of tracking. It was ABCDEF sections. ... I was quickly made aware of what the F level was and who it designated. Completely Mexicano.

Another respondent identified a similar experience from a slightly different perspective when describing high school:

So in high school, there would be maybe three or four Chicanos and one or two Blacks in each of your classes; you'd go into a classroom and look for your friends, you always knew to look in the back right-hand corner ... it was kind of weird to be there with all of these Anglos that you'd never had contact with before in your life ... So it was kind of a segregated-integrated situation.[36]

Many of the individuals who would go on to institutionalize Chicano literature and criticism were among the very first in their families to attend college. While their experiences varied tremendously, most launched their careers in Chicano literary studies from adjacent, established disciplines, generally without a great deal of institutional support, and later joined the workforce in educational settings where they were among a handful of minority professors.

At this time one can only speculate on the impact that the social, economic, and institutional experiences of these individuals has had upon their critical practice. If it is true, as Eagleton has suggested, that all literary responses are deeply imbricated with the kind of historical individuals we are, then it is not difficult to imagine that these formative experiences should mediate the Chicano critical experience in a decisive fashion. Much remains to be done in documenting this mediation, particularly in terms of its significance for the various ideological formations that have interlaced Chicano critical discourse at the moment of aesthetic interpretation and evaluation.

Exploring the Horizons: General Critical Studies

Along with these elements, an assessment of the nature of the representation of Chicano criticism within the broader sphere of general critical studies is desirable if the extent and domains of its activity are to be properly charted in future (meta)critical endeavors. Here as well we encounter problems, but of a substantially different nature. While the most politically and historically engaged accounts of criticism have already tacitly acknowledged the existence of emergent critical formations, even calling for a reappraisal of their importance for recent critical history, this reception has been less than satisfactory. It is generally the case that when a passing allusion is made to the alternative critical sector, it is as a means of documenting the "crisis" in the institution of criticism, or it is in the service of applauding the consolidation of "oppositional" literary perspectives. While such allusions potentially lack depth and acumen, nowhere is the lack of rigor more evident than in the pervasive tendency of mainstream critics to include emergent critical formations under homogeneous categories of "ethnic" or "countercultural" criticism with little or no regard for their concrete particularities, unique historical trajectories, and internal dynamics. Contemporary poststructuralist readings of modern critical history provide a recent example of this problematic tendency within recent literary scholarship. Upon identifying emergent critical formations in terms of a basic "differential" relation to general critical discourse, they generally nullify or flatten the distinctive features that set these critical traditions apart.

Some of the problems that arise when their particularities are not addressed become evident upon considering the manner in which they interact with mainstream literary institutions. Though generally marginalized, emergent critical formations do not experience this condition uniformly. The irregularities that are characteristic of their representation within the greater literary culture can be readily noted upon comparing the growing reception of feminist criticism to the scant reception of Black criticism, and to the almost nil reception of Chicano criticism, which has suffered from the exclusionary practices of both the Anglo American and the Spanish-speaking literary worlds.[37]

Another domain where the lack of consensus between emergent critical formations can be witnessed is at the level of ideology. Until only very recently it was believed that these formations, by virtue of their critique of the marginalization of the artistic practices of specific racial, gender, and cultural groups, had delivered a uniform response to mainstream practices and literary assumptions. Nonetheless, studies have begun to unearth their heterogeneous—and oftentimes contradictory—critical responses.

The culturalist movement, which virtually dominated the early phase of Chicano criticism, serves as a case in point. Although this movement successfully combated the stereotypical representations of Chicanos within the greater literary culture, it frequently drew from idealist mainstream literary and philosophical perspectives that postulated a basic separation between literature and social life. The extremes to which it was possible to arrive with the partnership between certain variants of phenomenological criticism and cultural nationalism made it possible to castigate the mainstream for its omission of Chicano cultural products, while at the same time offering philosophical configurations (nonhyphenated spatial metaphors, ethereal or racial essences) of Chicano culture which posited its virtual absence as a form of material production.

Insufficient attention has been paid to examining the manner in which this "counter-discourse" appropriated and modified existing literary perspectives in the early phase of its existence, although this topic promises to yield much in the way of broadening current understanding of its conceptual development. What is clear thus far is that early Chicano critical works—like their Black counterparts—generally avoided inserting themselves directly into mainstream critical traditions, though they were adamant about demarcating the boundaries of the Chicano literary tradition. In fact, many of the debates that were being waged within the greater literary culture surrounding literary production appeared in an often concealed, often inconspicuous fashion in Chicano critical discourse, almost, but not quite, overshadowed by the desire to use critical practice as a domain for cultural affirmation. In his preface to *Literary Theory*, Eagleton has suggested that "hostility to theory usually means an opposition to other people's theories and an oblivion to one's own."[38] While a measure of both of these elements contributed to the markedly antitheoretical flavor of much of early Chicano criticism, this attitude cannot be properly understood without accounting for the particular objectives that marked its inception.

Along with the general movements of the 1960s that challenged the social, cultural, and political practices of the dominant social formation by proposing other modes of social development, the eruption of the Chicano movement gave birth to a criticism wedded to alternative literary values and committed to bringing about significant transformations in the existent structures, values, and boundaries of literary production and consumption. If the dominant literary culture had responded with censure or neglect to Chicano literature, classifying it as nonexistent, scant, or unworthy of incorporation, then this emergent criticism would exalt Chicano literature's merits, outline its significant historical and geographical lineages, and reiterate the innovation transmitted through popular flavor. If dominant notions of traditional academic mainstream criticism—transmitted throughout mainstream literary institutions—had functioned as real material constraints for the diffusion of Chicano literature and criticism, then it was necessary to create new critical perspectives, new alternative literary institutions, and new reading publics. If the legacy of literary marginality had condemned Chicano literature to relative obscurity and/or isolation, then it was necessary to rethink the relations of literary production, and to substitute the peripheral location of Chicano literary forms on the literary map for a central one.

While this reorganization, reevaluation, and reaffirmation of Chicano literary and critical perspectives signified a break with the idea of a "singular" national literary tradition free of rupture, conflict, and contradiction, it did not refashion alternative values in a literary ideological vacuum. Those critical strategies borrowed from existing conventions, approaches, and traditions, nourishing them with the conventions embedded in alternative as well as established literary institutions of cultural production. In the final instance, the articulation of Chicano critical discourse involved a unique conjuncture between the general ideological formations of the larger social order, the particular ideological formations of the group (particularly of those associated with the Chicano movement), and their foregrounding in aesthetic categories derived from various literary sectors (the Anglo American, Latin American, and Spanish).

From this particular conjuncture, a wide array of (Chicano) critical perspectives—mythic, culturalist, existentialist, formalist, historical, and phenomenological—flourished under a metacommentary whose referent was generally cast as the "Chicano experience," though this experience was not always well served by such definition. This practice was especially common among the culturalist variants, which even in their most sophisticated renditions of immanent and formalist criticism, would succeed in organizing their principles around a discourse of culture whose loyalty was directed toward the "authenticity" of the Chicano, almost never toward the literary theories and traditions that they also spoke and disseminated.

This privileging of the ideological formations associated with the group, combined with the objective fact that Chicano criticism developed with a certain degree of autonomy from mainstream literary institutions, did produce interesting innovations in the critical format, innovations that continue to appear in more sophisticated renditions. Unlike most conventional academic literary criticism which had already passed through years of professionalization, altogether subordinating popular forms of criticism to more scholarly endeavors (such as the critical essay, the monograph, and the literary article), Chicano literary criticism—aside from including these forms—drew widely from the literary manifesto, newsletter, chapbooks, and journalistic criticism, generally flaunting this usage in the most academic of professional settings. Such a practice was intentional, as Juan Rodríguez describes when speaking about his literary newsletter *La carta abierta*:

> On the other hand, I wanted that informal tone. As a matter of fact I'd played with the idea of calling it *Chismes*. Because I believed at the time and believe to this day that if we start doing everything just like the Academy does it—it means essentially sterilizing our communication. And when that happens, we've lost the battle. ... You don't have to use nineteenth-century Spanish to say something that's legitimately critical. This I think is especially true when you're dealing with a literature that grows so immediately out of a popular background. ... You can even use Chicano slang, and there can still be a critical judgment.[39]

These types of critical objectives did affect the type of expression utilized in the early period. Chicano critical discourse incorporated any number of (popular or standard) variants of Spanish or English, frequently code-switching from one language to another, mimicking the popular lingo of university students and community activists, and promoting new critical vocabularies. It also encoded as its audience a greater "Chicano" community through the use of the collective voice in literary analysis, generally as a means of fostering the political and social concerns associated with the Chicano movement. These trends offer a marked contrast to the contemporary period where Chicano critical endeavors are tending toward more conventional forms of expression and appealing to a general literary audience, not explicitly differentiated on the basis of ethnicity, culture, or class. The long-range effects of this growing critical professionalization require much scrutiny, particularly if the collective spirit of the early years is to be safeguarded alongside the growing theoretical impulse in Chicano critical endeavors.

Reconceptualizing Chicano Critical Discourse: Global Perspectives

This brief overview of some of the features of early Chicano critical discourse highlights some of the interesting dynamics that emergent critical formations have brought to general critical practice. Though rarely credited for doing so, they have enriched twentieth-century critical history by virtue of their popular thrust, decentering of the dominant literary tradition, and broad interdisciplinary perspectives. While these elements may have initially placed emergent critical discourses at odds with the "organic" sensibility of mainstream critics of previous decades, new and exciting possibilities now exist for examining these discourses within a larger theoretical context, particularly now with the growing intersection between literary theory and cultural studies, and the rising dissatisfaction within the institution of literary criticism.

Nevertheless, any "serious" attempt to recontextualize the mapping of critical alternatives to account for their linkages to general critical history would have to begin by examining the chain of events that have for so long muted the voice of budding critical discourses within the greater literary culture. It is not by accident, for example, that the "Chicano renaissance" of the 1960s was inaugurated with literary journals, publishing houses, and anthologies that carried the headings *Chicano Voices*, Grito de Aztlán, and *El Grito*. As the editors of the anthology titled *El Espejo* made clear in the opening pages, the idea was to authorize the work to "speak for itself" and "for the people" that it represented. The discursive character intentionally assigned to this cultural production was a means of gaining control over a collective destiny through the reappropriation of language. Bakhtin describes the significance of such a process in his *Discourse in the Novel:*

> Language, for the individual consciousness, lies on the borderline between oneself and the other. The word in language is half someone else's. It becomes "one's own" only when the speaker populates it with his intention, his own accent, when he appropriates the word, adapting it to his own semantic and expressive intention. Prior to this moment of appropriation, the word does not exist in a neutral and impersonal language (it is not, after all, out of a dictionary that a speaker gets his words!), but rather it exists in other people's mouths, in other people's contexts, serving other people's intentions: it is from there that one must take the word, and make it one's own.[40]

"Taking the word" in the 1960s translated into writing Chicano literary histories and critical essays that counteracted the pejorative images and values associated with the cultural production of the Mexican population in the United States. "Taking the word" in the 1980s translates into rewriting not only histories of Chicano literature and criticism, but also the histories of the greater tradition, from the perspective of these and other formerly excluded or partially incorporated sectors. As a prominent Chicano critic remarked when asked about his preference for Edward Said's *Orientalism:*

> Another thing I like about Said's book is the way he recognizes that you cannot talk about minority cultures without a considerable amount of reference to the majority culture ... you have to take the majority culture into account. This is a process already familiar to us from studies of American slavery, whether in the United States or Latin America. The slave has to know the master better than the master knows the slave. It seems to me that Chicano writers have always understood American culture very well. They have responded to it with a sensitivity that a lot of Chicano critics haven't noticed.[41]

Populating critical histories with the intention of the newly discov-ered sensibilities and expressive modes of national minorities, women, and working-class sectors involves more than just refurbishing linkages obfuscated under the weight of deliberate cultural suppression and/or benign neglect. It also involves exploring how one's word has populated the discourse of others, and discovering to what ends it has done so. Viewed from this standpoint, the problematic reception of alternative emergent formations—their omission or qualification as "anthropological" (not "critical") ventures, designated to illuminate "local" (not "national") literary cultures—provides ample ground for examining the formal, institutional, and textual strategies, and the ideological perspectives that have gone into shaping the greater critical tradition. In this light, recent trends in general critical studies would appear to confirm Edward Said's observation that the significant alterations that have swept literary institutions since the decline of New Criticism haven't substantially curbed "the prevailing ideology of even advanced literary criticism," which continues to be pronouncedly ethnocentric and "indifferent to everything but the political-social status quo."[42]

Notwithstanding the fact that criticism has been inordinately slow in recognizing and documenting the links between the critical "boom" (the proliferation of European theory in the United States) and the eruption of alternative emergent critical formations, parallels can and should be drawn between them. Both of these movements were symptomatic of the decentering of the Anglo American literary tradition, insofar as this tradition drew from a moral and spiritual ideal of the English classics; both signified a departure from the orthodoxy and parochialism of New Criticism; and both unwillingly elicited nationalistic responses from mainstream elements, which identified these movements as "foreign" and warned against their adverse effects upon the then-consecrated language of mainstream academic criticism.

What distinguished these movements—aside from their most immediate critical influences, perspectives, readership, and geographical affiliations—was the nature of their reception within prominent literary institutions. The transplantation of European critical theory shook the center of the professional critical world, impacting at every level of its language, and creating a new set of "star critics" whose work would formulate the new literary canon, ultimately constituting what has been termed a "New New Criticism."

Although the eruption of national alternative critical formations such as Chicano critical discourse also produced noteworthy critical thinkers and literary perspectives, their influence has remained largely peripheral to greater critical developments—no doubt as a result of a history of cultural suppression and the type of small-scale artistic infrastructure associated with these writings. However, the fact remains that, along with other critical formations of the period, Chicano critical discourse took part in the social thrust, cosmopolitanism, proliferation of new critical journals, renovation of critical discourse, comparative studies, critique of liberal humanism, and speculative spirit—elements that Elizabeth Bruss links to an "Age of Theory" dating back to the late 1960s.

Only a broad-based theoretical perspective, which accommodates the multifarious, competing expressions of critical discourse in its diverse cultural and textual milieus, can do justice to the complex dynamics that have historically engaged emergent critical discourses with larger movements such as the one described above. Only a perception of Chicano critical enterprise as an extensive, dynamic field of symbolic and material practices that unite diverse intellectual and cultural spheres into historically variable forces and relations of literary production can begin to unravel the complexities of its existence as a partially incorporated emergent critical formation.

Already the most provocative metacritical works have begun to outline the merits of such "global" or "systemic" visions of criticism, suggesting that these perspectives could, in fact, signal the way toward the return of criticism to its rightful and original public mandate, where it served as purveyor and commentator of a larger social dynamic. Not so long ago, Edward Said, in *The World, the Text, and the Critic*, crystallized this notion upon identifying a fifth form of "secular" criticism which he envisaged would function as a new "critical consciousness" and a "bold interventionary movement," engaging in the political questions of power and authority that involve men and women in contemporary society.[43]

Taking the Word

Chicano criticism, with its particular manner of configuring varied cultural and linguistic traditions, its participation in an expansive constellation of "alternative" and "established" literary institutions, and its dual critical dialogue with the Spanish and English literary worlds, provides a viable starting point for laying one of the foundations of such a global cultural vision. Certainly, the popular origins of this criticism, together with its vital links with an informal public sphere and its engagement with such realities as class oppression, sexism, and political domination, confirm its involvement with a "worldly circumstance," as surely as does its recent incorporation of any number of readings or interpretations of social reality communicated through modern literary theories and practices.

With reference to the latter, I might add that the indissoluble bonds that link Chicano critical discourse to a greater critical dynamic are not to be limited to the contemporary period, which has seen a narrowing of the intellectual horizons that inform established and alternative critical spheres. Ever since its emergence, the fate of Chicano criticism—its initial consolidation as a counter-discourse, its erratic development, and its limited incorporation into prominent literary institutions—has been sealed to the modes and patterns of development of the greater literary world. It could, in fact, be argued that the tardy appearance and progressive marginalization of Chicano critical discourse played a central role in the successful constitution of the dominant literary Anglo American canon and modes of production as we know them today. This becomes clear when considering that criticism plays an important role in defining social perceptions of what constitutes literature insofar as it "selects," "processes," and "rewrites literary texts," reconstituting the writings of a people into an object as well as a subject of academic inquiry.[44] Without the benefit of a supportive institutionalized body of criticism to promote them in the early years of their existence, it is not surprising that alternative traditions (such as Chicano literature) were systematically excluded from this type of literary definition, leaving the way open for culturally homogeneous literary conceptions.

As we rapidly move into what proves to be a rich and productive phase in the development of Chicano critical discourse, we will be faced with the substantial challenge of defining the parameters and objectives of this discourse in ways that would no doubt seem inconceivable to that early generation of Chicano critics, who boldly inaugurated it with their admirable struggles within the institution of literary criticism. Our success in responding to this challenge will depend largely upon our ability to circumvent those strategies of containment that would sever Chicano critical discourse from its multiple determinants and expressions, and upon our ability to reconceptualize it within the various domains of its influence, directing it toward the values, practices, and social realities that engendered it. Though formidable, this slanting of criticism toward questions of pedagogy, education, and social and cultural practice[45] promises much in the way of contributing to a second theoretical revolution, where criticism ceases to be a self-contained field or the privileged discourse of an enlightened and culturally dominant few.

457

Notes

I would like to express my sincere gratitude to those Chicano/a critics whose voices are recorded in this essay.

1. Walter Kendrick, "Literary Criticism: The State of the Art," *Thought* 59, no. 235 (1984): 514–26.

2. Arnold L. Goldsmith, preface to *American Literary Criticism: 1905–1965*, Twayne's United States Authors Series, vol. 3 (Boston: Twayne, 1979).

3. Terry Eagleton, preface to *Literary Theory: An Introduction* (Minneapolis: University of Minnesota Press, 1983), vii.

4. Edward Said, "Reflections on American 'Left' Literary Criticism," in *The World, the Text and the Critic* (Cambridge: Harvard University Press, 1983), 158.

5. As Walter Kendrick proposes: "Ever since the earliest days of American structuralism, in the 1960s, popularizing guides have been common, but the most recent books of this kind exhibit a confident comprehensiveness missing from older efforts. It seems that, after almost two decades of confusion and intramural wrangling, literary theory has settled down sufficiently for a coherent map of it to be drawn." "Literary Criticism," 514–15.

6. W. J. T. Mitchell, "The Golden Age of Criticism: Seven Theses and a Commentary," *London Review of Books* 9, no. 12 (1987): 16–17.

7. A similar question could be posed in relation to the critical traditions of the Spanish-speaking literary worlds. Rarely, if ever, are the names of critics such as Adolfo Sánchez Vásquez, François Pérus, Octavio Paz, Noé Jitrik, and Roberto Fernández Retamar found in "comprehensive" accounts of criticism that appeal to an "international" critical domain.

8. Accordingly, critical discourse is dislodged from its traditional location. Eagleton explains: "The [critical] discourse itself has no definite signified, which is not to say that it embodies no assumptions: it is rather a network of signifiers ... Certain pieces of writing are selected as being more amenable to this discourse than others, and these are what is known as literature or the 'literary canon.' The fact that this canon is usually regarded as fairly fixed, even at times as eternal and immutable, is in a sense ironic, because since literary critical discourse has no definite signified it can, if it wants to, turn its attention to more or less any kind of writing. Some of those hottest in their defence of the canon have from time to time demonstrated how the discourse can be made to operate on non-'literary' writing ... For though I have said that critical discourse has no determinate signified, there are certainly a great many ways of talking about literature which it excludes, and a great many discursive moves and strategies which it disqualifies as invalid, illicit, non-critical, nonsense. Its apparent generosity at the level of the signified is matched only by its sectarian intolerance at the level of the signifier." *Literary Theory*, 201–203.

9. Joseph Sommers, "From the Critical Premise to the Product: Critical Modes and Their Application to a Chicano Literary Text," *New Scholar* 6 (1977): 34–50.

10. See, for example, Evangelina Enríquez's "Toward a Definition of, and Critical Approaches to, Chicano(a) Literature" (Ph.D. diss., University of California, Riverside, 1981).

11. A few of the essays that have been published in *Plural* are: Dieter Hermes, "La literatura chicana y la teoría de las dos culturas," 22, no. 158 (November 1984): 33–39; Yvonne Yarbro and Tomás Ybarra-Frausto, "Zoot-Suit y el movimiento chicano," 9, no. 103 (April 1980): 49–56, and Armando Miguélez, "La frontera como espacio literario," 12–16, no. 138 (March 1983): 19–23.

12. Norma Alarcón, interview by Angie Chabram, July 1988.

13. For an account of some of the recent trends in the publication of Chicano literature and criticism, see Robert Trujillo et al., "An Essay on Collection Development and Bibliography of Chicano Literature Published 1980–1984." *Lector* 3, no. 1 (July–August 1984): 20–28. Chicano criticism has proliferated despite its lack of representation within mainstream criticism.

14. Terry Eagleton, *Criticism and Ideology: A Study in Marxist Literary Theory* (London: Verso, 1976), 17.

15. Said, *The World*, 35.

16. In describing critics of Chicano literature Charles Tatum effects an unfortunate division between "young relatively inexperienced academics who are searching for their own critical approach" and "critics well established in their fields" who are applying their own well-defined approaches. Suffice it to say that youth does not exclude the possibility of expertise in a field or of having a well-defined critical method. Perhaps most serious is Tatum's disregard of the fact that one of the most pressing concerns of critics in recent years has been to formulate adequate theoretical approaches for the study of Chicano literature. For an account of Tatum's position on this topic, see *Chicano Literature*, Twayne's United States Authors Series, vol. 433 (Boston: Twayne, 1982), 193.

17. Ramón Saldívar, "A Dialectic of Difference: Toward a Theory of the Chicano Novel," in *Contemporary Chicano Fiction*, ed. Vernon E. Lattin (New York: Bilingual Press, 1986), 13.

18. Ramón Saldívar, interview by Angie Chabram, January 1986.

19. Juan Bruce-Novoa, interview by Angie Chabram, August 1988.

20. Héctor Calderón, "Rudolfo A. Anaya's *Bless Me, Ultima:* A Chicano Romance of the Southwest," *Crítica* 1, no. 3 (fall 1986): 21–47.

21. Hector Calderón, interview by Angie Chabram, May 1988.

22. José David Saldívar, "Towards a Chicano Poetics: The Making of the Chicano-Chicana Subject," *Confluencia* 1, no. 2 (spring 1986): 10–17.

23. José David Saldívar, interview by Angie Chabram, May 1986.

24. Their account responds to the gap between Anglo American and Continental criticism. For a more complete discussion of this thematic, see Arac, Godzich, and Martin, eds., *The Yale Critics: Deconstruction in America*, vol. 6 of *Theory and History of Literature* (Minneapolis: University of Minnesota Press, 1983).

25. Raymund A. Paredes and Américo Paredes, eds., *Mexican-American Authors* (Boston: Houghton Mifflin, 1972). See also Raymund A. Paredes, "The Evolution of Chicano Literature," *MELUS* 5 (summer 1978): 71–110.

26. Raymund A. Paredes, interview by Angie Chabram, June 1988.

27. Juan Rodríguez, interview by Angie Chabram, May 1986.

28. Juan Rodríguez, interview.

29. Examples of the first group include: Carmen Salazar Parr, "Current Trends in Chicano Literary Criticism," *Latin American Literary Review* 5, no. 10 (spring–summer 1977): 8–15 and "Literary Criticism," in *A Decade of Chicano Literature (1970–1979): Critical Essays and Bibliography*, ed. Luis Leal et al. (Santa Barbara: Editorial La Causa, 1982), 65–72; Justo Alarcón, "Consideraciones sobre la literatura y crítica chicanas," *La Palabra* 1, no. 1 (spring 1979): 3–21; Angie Chabram, "Corrientes en la crítica literaria chicana," *La Opinión*, February 1986, 4–5; and Juan Armando Epple, "Literatura chicana y crítica literaria," *Ideologies and Literature* 4, no. 16 (1983): 149–71. Examples of the second include: Sylvia Lizárraga, "Observaciones acerca de la crítica literaria chicana," *Revista Chicano-Riqueña* 10, no. 4 (fall 1982): 55–64; Francisco Lomelí, "Crítica y literatura chicanas: maduración y reto," *Confluencia* 1, no. 2 (April 1987): 1–3; Juan Bruce-Novoa, "La crítica chicana de Luis Leal," *La Palabra* 4, nos. 1 and 2, (spring–fall 1982–1983): 25–40; Salvador Gilereña and Raquel Quiroz González, eds., *Luis Leal: A Bibliography with Interpretative and Critical Essays* (Berkeley: Chicano Studies Library, 1988); and Lauro Flores, "En torno a la teoría de las dos culturas y su aplicación a la literatura chicana," in *In Times of Challenge: Chicanos and Chicanas in American Society*, ed. John García, Mexican American Monograph Series, no. 6 (Houston: University of Houston, 1988): 25–31. Examples of the third include Lauro Flores, "Notas básicas para la literatura chicana," *La Palabra* 3, no. 1 (spring 1981); no. 2 (fall 1981): 21–29; and Luis Leal, "Literary Criticism and Minority Literatures: The Case of the Chicano Writer," *Confluencia* 1, no. 2 (April 1987): 4–10.

30. For recent perspectives on Chicano narrative, see Rosaura Sánchez, "From Heterogeneity to Contradiction: Hinojosa's Novel," in *The Rolando Hinojosa Reader*, ed. José David Saldívar (Houston: Arte Público Press, 1984), 76–100, and "Voces, códigos y cronotopos en la literatura chicana," *Revista Chicano-Riqueña* 13 (spring 1985): 54–63; Héctor Calderón, "Rudolfo A. Anaya's *Bless Me, Ultima*"; and Ramón Saldívar, "A Dialectic of Difference." The criticism of Chicana literature has also grown considerably, altering earlier perceptions of the Chicano literary tradition. Recent examples of this budding criticism include: *Beyond Stereotypes: The Critical Analysis of Chicana Literature*, ed. María Herrera-Sobek (New York: Bilingual Review Press, 1985); Yolanda Julia Broyles González, "Women in El Teatro Campesino: Zápoco estaba molacha la Virgen de Guadalupe?," in *Chicana Voices: Intersections of Class, Race, and Gender*, ed. Ricardo Romo (Austin: CMAS Publications, 1986), 162–88; Ramón Saldívar, "The Dialectics of the Chicano Novel: Gender and Difference," in *Mexico and the United States: Intercultural Relations in the Humanities*, ed. Juanita Luna Lawhn et al. (San Antonio: San Antonio College, 1984), 151–60; María Herrera-Sobek and Helena María Viramontes, eds., *Chicana Creativity and Criticism: Charting New Frontiers in American Literature* (Houston: Arte Público Press, 1988); Yvonne Yarbro, "Teatropoesía by Chicanas in the Bay Area: Tongues of Fire," *Revista Chicano-Riqueña* 11 (1983): 78–94; Sylvia Lizárraga, "Images of Women in Chicano Literature by Men," *Feminist Issues* 5, no. 2 (fall 1985): 69–88; Norma Alarcón, "La literatura feminista de la chicana: una revisión a través de Malintzín," in *Esta puente, mi espalda*, ed. Cherríe Moraga and Ana Castillo (San Francisco: Ism Press, 1988), 321–43; and Marta Ester Sánchez, *Chicana Poetry* (Berkeley: University of California Press, 1985).

31. As Edward Said explains: "Cultural and intellectual life are usually nourished and often sustained by this circulation of ideas, and whether it takes the form of acknowledged or unconscious influence, creative borrowing, or wholesale appropriation, the movement of ideas and theories from one place to another is both a fact of life and a usefully enabling condition of intellectual activity. Having said that, however, one should go on to specify the kinds of movement that are possible, in order to ask whether by virtue of having moved from one place and time to another an idea or a theory gains or loses in strength, and whether a theory in one historical period and national culture becomes altogether different for another period or situation." *The World*, 226.

32. Gates originally suggests: "For non-Western, so-called noncanonical critics, getting the 'man off your eyeball' means using the most sophisticated critical theories and methods available or to reappropriate and to define our own 'colonial' discourses. We must use these theories and methods insofar as they are relevant to the study of our own literatures." Henry Louis Gates Jr., ed., *"Race," Writing, and Difference* (Chicago: University of Chicago Press, 1985), 14.

33. Calderón, interview.

34. In "Categories for a Materialist Criticism" Terry Eagleton situates literary production within the cultural ideological apparatus: "That apparatus includes the distribution (publishing houses, bookshops, libraries and so on), but it also encompasses a range of *'secondary supportive' institutions* [emphasis mine] whose function is more directly ideological, concerned with the definition and dissemination of literary standards and assumptions. Among these are the literary academies, societies and bookclubs, associations of literary producers, distributors and consumers, censoring bodies, and literary journals and reviews." *Criticism and Ideology*, 56.

35. Terry Eagleton, *The Function of Criticism* (London: Verso, 1984), 88.

36. All citations are taken from my "Conversations with Chicano Critics: Portrait of a Counter-Discourse." (Unpublished).

37. This trend is well illustrated in "Literary Criticism: The State of the Art," where Walter Kendrick states: "Of all our contemporary critical modes, *feminist* [emphasis mine] criticism remains the most tendentious and the most liable to wholesale dismissal," 515. From another perspective, Grant Webster includes feminist and Black criticism but does not include mention of any Chicano literary criticism ("American Literary Criticism: A Bibliographic Essay," *American Studies International* 20, 1 [Autumn 1981]:20).

38. Eagleton, *Literary Theory*, viii.

39. Rodríguez, interview.

40. Mikhail Bahktin, *Discourse in the Novel*, quoted in Gates, *"Race," Writing, and Difference*, 1.

41. Paredes, interview.

42. Edward W. Said, "Roads Taken and Not Taken in Contemporary Criticism," in *Directions for Criticism*, ed. Murray Krieger and L. S. Dembo (Madison: University of Wisconsin Press, 1977), 33.

43. Said describes the "realities" that should be taken into account by the "critical consciousness": "The realities of power and authority—as well as the resistances offered by men, women, and social movements to institutions, authorities

and orthodoxies—are the realities that make texts possible, that deliver them to their readers, that solicit the attention of critics." *The World,* 5.

44. Eagleton elaborates: "All literary works, in other words, are 'rewritten' if only unconsciously, by the societies which read them; indeed there is no reading of a work which is not also a 're-writing.' No work, and no current evaluation of it, can simply be extended to new groups of people without being changed, perhaps almost unrecognizably, in the process; and this is one reason why what counts as literature is a notably unstable affair." *Literary Theory,* 12. Later on, quoting from Roland Barthes, Eagleton summarizes: "Literature ... is what gets taught" (197).

45. See William E. Cain, *The Crisis in Criticism* (Baltimore: Johns Hopkins University Press, 1984), 249.

Bibliography

Alarcón, Justo S. "Consideraciones sobre la literatura y crítica chicanas." *La Palabra* 1, no. 1 (spring 1979): 3–21.

Alarcón, Norma. "La literatura feminista de la chicana: una revisión a través de Malintzín." In *Esta puente, mi espalda,* edited by Cherríe Moraga and Ana Castillo, 321-43. San Francisco: ISM Press, 1988.

Arac, Jonathan, Wlad Godzich, and Wallace Martin, eds. *The Yale Critics: Deconstruction in America,* vol. 6 of *Theory and History of Literature.* Minneapolis: University of Minnesota Press, 1983.

Broyles-González, Yolanda Julia. "Women in El Teatro Campesino: Zípoco estaba molacha la Virgen de Guadalupe?" In *Chicana Voices: Intersections of Class, Race, and Gender,* edited by Ricardo Romo, 162–88. Austin: CMAS Publications, 1986.

Bruce-Novoa, Juan. "La crítica chicana de Luis Leal," *La Palabra* 4, no. 1-2 (spring-fall 1982- 1983): 25–40.

———. *Chicano Poetry: A Response to Chaos.* Austin: University of Texas Press, 1982.

———. "The Space of Chicano Literature." *De Colores* 1, no. 4 (1975): 22–41

Bruss, Elizabeth. *Beautiful Theories: The Spectacle of Discourse in Contemporary Criticism.* Baltimore and London: Johns Hopkins University Press, 1984.

Cain, William E. *The Crisis in Criticism: Theory, Literature and Reform in English Studies.* Baltimore and London: Johns Hopkins University Press, 1984.

Calderón, Héctor. "Rudolfo A. Anaya's Bless Me Ultima: A Chicano Romance of the Southwest." *Critica* 1, no. 3 (fall 1986): 21–47.

Chabram, Angie. "Conversations with Chicano Critics. Portrait of a Counter Discourse." Unpublished manuscript. University of California, Davis, 1986.

———. "Corrientes en la crítica literaria chicana." *La Opinión,* February 1981, 43.

Culler, Jonathan. *The Pursuit of Signs.* Ithaca: Cornell University Press, 1981.

Eagleton, Terry. *The Function of Criticism: From the Spectator to Post-Structuralism.* London: Verso, 1984.

_____. *Literary Theory: An Introduction*. Minneapolis: University of Minnesota Press, 1983.

_____. *Criticism and Ideology: A Study in Marxist Literary Theory*. London: Verso, 1976.

Enríquez, Evangelina. "Toward a Definition of, and Critical Approaches to, Chicano(a) Literature." Ph.D. diss., University of California, Riverside, 1982.

Epple, Juan Armando. "Literatura chicana y crítica literaria." *Ideologies and Literature* 4, no. 16 (1983): 149–71.

Flores, Lauro. "En torno a la teoría de las dos culturas y su aplicación a la literatura chicana." In *Times of Challenge: Chicanos and Chicanas in American Society*, edited by J. García. Mexican American Monograph Series, no. 6. Houston: University of Houston, 1988.

_____. "Notas básicas para la literatura chicana." *La Palabra* 3, nos. 1 and 2 (spring-fall 1981): 21–29.

Gates, Henry Louis, Jr., ed. *"Race," Writing, and Difference*. Chicago: University of Chicago Press, 1986.

_____. *Black Literature and Literary Theory*. London: Methuen., 1984.

Gilereña, Salvador, and Raquel Quiroz González, eds. *Luis Leal: A Bibliography with Interpretative and Critical Essays*. Berkeley: Chicano Studies Library, 1988.

Goldsmith, Arnold L. Preface to *American Literary Criticism: 1905–1965*. Twayne's United States Authors Series, vol. 3. Boston: Twayne, 1979.

Hermes, Dieter. "La literatura chicana y la teoría de las dos culturas." *Plural* 22, no. 158 (November 1984): 33–39.

Herrera-Sobek, María, ed. *Beyond Stereotypes: The Critical Analysis of Chicana Literature*. New York: Bilingual Review Press, 1985.

Herrera-Sobek, María, and Helena Maria Viramontes, eds. *Chicana Creativity and Criticism: Charting New Frontiers in American Literature*. Houston: Arte Público Press, 1988.

Hohendahl, Peter Uwe. *The Institution of Criticism*. Ithaca and London: Cornell University Press, 1982.

Kendrick, Walter. "Literary Criticism: The State of the Art." *Thought* 59, no. 235 (1984): 514–26.

Leal, Luis. "Literary Criticism and Minority Literatures: The Case of the Chicano Writer." *Confluencia* 1, no. 2 (April 1987): 4–10.

Lizárraga, Sylvia. "Images of Women in Chicano Literature by Men." *Feminist Issues* 5, no. 2 (fall 1985): 69–88.

_____. "Observaciones acerca de la crítica literaria chicana." *Revista Chicano-Riqueña* 10, no. 4 (fall 1982): 55–64.

Lomelí, Francisco A. "Crítica y literatura chicanas: maduración y reto." *Confluencia* 1, no. 2 (April 1987): 1–3.

Miguélez, Armando. "La frontera como espacio literario." *Plural* 12–16, 138 (March 1983): 19–23.

Mitchell, W. J. T. "The Golden Age of Criticism: Seven Theses and a Commentary." *London Review of Books* 9, no. 12 (1987): 16–17.

Moraga, Cherríe, and Gloria Anzaldúa, eds. *This Bridge Called My Back*. New York: Kitchen Table Press, 1983.

Paredes, Raymund A. "The Evolution of Chicano Literature." *MELUS* 5 (summer 1978): 71–110.

Paredes, Raymund A., and Américo Paredes, eds. *Mexican American Authors*. Boston: Houghton Mifflin, 1972.

Said, Edward W. *The World, the Text, and the Critic*. Cambridge: Harvard University Press, 1983.

———. "Roads Taken and Not Taken in Contemporary Criticism." In *Directions for Criticism*, edited by Murray Krieger and L. S. Dembo, 33–54. Madison: University of Wisconsin Press, 1977.

Salazar Parr, Carmen. "Towards a Chicano Poetics: The Making of the Chicano-Chicana Subject." *Confluencia* 1, no. 2 (Spring 1986):10–17.

———. "Literary Criticism." In *A Decade of Chicano Literature (1970–1979): Critical Essays and Bibliography*, edited by Luis Leal, Fernando de Necochea, Francisco Lomelí, and Robert G. Trujillo, 65–72. Santa Barbara: Editorial La Causa, 1982.

———. "Current Trends in Chicano Literary Criticism." *Latin American Literary Review* 5, no. 10 (spring-summer 1977): 8–15.

Saldivar, Ramón. "A Dialectic of Difference: Toward a Theory of the Chicano Novel." In *Contemporary Chicano Fiction*, edited by Vernon E. Lattin, 13–31. New York: Bilingual Press, 1986.

———. "The Dialectics of the Chicano Novel: Gender and Difference." In *Mexico and the United States: Intercultural Relations in the Humanities*, edited by Juanita Luna Lawhn et al., 151–160. San Antonio: San Antonio College, 1984.

Sánchez, Marta Ester. *Chicana Poetry*. Berkeley: University of California Press, 1985.

Sánchez, Rosaura. "From Heterogeneity to Contradiction: Hinojosa's Novel." In *The Rolando Hinojosa Reader*, edited by José David Saldívar, 76–100. Houston: Arte Público Press, 1984.

———. "Voces, códigos y cronotopos en la literatura chicana." *Revista Chicano-Riqueña* 13 (spring 1985): 54–63.

Sommers, Joseph. "From the Critical Premise to the Product: Critical Modes and Their Application to a Chicano Literary Text." *New Scholar* 6 (1977): 34–50.

Tatum, Charles. *Chicano Literature*. Twayne's United States Authors Series, vol. 433. Boston: Twayne, 1982.

Trujillo, Robert, Andrés Rodríguez, and Richard Kiy. "An Essay on Collection Development and Bibliography of Chicano Literature Published 1980–1984." *Lector* 3, no. 1 (July-August 1984): 20–28.

Webster, Grant. "American Literary Criticism: A Bibliographic Essay." *American Studies International* 20, no. 1 (autumn 1981) 3–45.

Williams, Raymond. *Problems in Materialism and Culture: Selected Essays*. London: Verso, 1980.

Yarbro-Bejarano, Yvonne. "Teatropoesía by Chicanas in the Bay Area: Tongues of Fire." *Revista Chicano-Riqueña* 11, no. 1 (1983): 78–94.

Yarbro-Bejarano, Yvonne, and Tomás Ybarra-Frausto. "Zoot-Suit y el movimiento chicano." *Plural* 9, no. 103 (April 1980): 49–56.

Mapping the Spanish Language along a Multiethnic and Multilingual Border

Rosaura Sánchez

Amidst a new wave of nativism and increased hostility against immigrants not only in the United States but throughout Europe—as evident in xenophobic firebombings in Germany, "ethnic cleansing" in the former Yugoslavia, new French intentions to restrict immigration (Weiner 1993, sec. 4-1) and proposed U.S. congressional bills for immigration reform—it is impossible to focus on the language of Latinos in the southwestern U.S. border states without considering it within the context of (a) a world-wide phenomenon of ethnic intolerance and (b) a marked trend toward demographic diversity in the United States, increasingly multiethnic and multilingual. "Control of the borders" is the repeated cry of the political right, echoed in published attacks against multiculturalism and calls for preserving a national identity based on northern European culture, all direct outgrowths of concern over the growing ethnic minority populations and periodic economic crises with their varying rates of unemployment, both naively attributed by nativists to the growing presence of immigrants.

The U.S. Census Bureau estimates in a 1982 report that by the year 2000 the U.S. population will include 9 million immigrants who entered the country after 1986, including their descendants; by 2030, the Bureau further predicts that there will be 32 million post 1986 immigrants and their descendants (Bureau of the Census 1982, 1). These statistics on undocumented immigrants (Miller and Ostrow 1993, A22) and detailed press accounts of the hundreds of "foreign" languages spoken in this country today frighten anti-immigration nativists, despite assurances by those who downplay any potential political threat from the largest of the immigrant groups, Latinos, by pointing to their political fragmentation (Shorris 1992, 26). Statistics can, no doubt, be variously interpreted. What cannot be denied, however, is the growing multilingual and multiethnic diversity of the country and especially of the U.S. Southwest, underscored by the multiplicity of languages spoken. Spanish, Chinese, Tagalog, Vietnamese, Korean, German, Japanese, French, Italian, Portuguese, Farsi, Armenian, Cambodian, Laotian, Polish, Arabic, Hebrew, Russian, the languages of North India, Pakistan, and Bangladesh, as well as other languages of Europe, southwestern Asia, and India are some of the major languages spoken in this country today by thousands, by millions in some cases, and in the case of Spanish—the top non-English language—by over seventeen million speakers (see tables 1 and 2) (Quintanilla 1993, E2). In view of this multilingualism, the states along the U.S.-Mexican border (see table 9) can no longer be seen simply as bilingual and bicultural, as language statistics for California clearly reveal (see table 2). For very concrete historical reasons, the border states are increasingly and preeminently multilingual, multiethnic, multi-racial, and multicultural. And while one-third of undocumented immigrants to the United States come from Europe and Asia, a full two-thirds are estimated to arrive from Mexico and other parts of Latin America.

The 1,933-mile border separating Mexico and the United States is a national boundary established, for the most part, in 1848 to separate two countries, nation-states that, in turn, epitomize the polarization of the world into center and periphery nations. Like any political boundary, the "border" between Mexico and the United States is a historical and contingent demarcation, the result of hegemonic practices and in no way a necessary, God-given, or "natural" partition. Spanish cartographers already in the early sixteenth century would map the southern part of the United States, from Florida to Louisiana, Texas, and New Mexico, and claim it for the Spanish Crown; after explorations had led Cortés to Baja California, Coronado would travel to Arizona and up the Colorado River, extending Spanish territory as far north as the southern boundary of Nebraska. During the same century Juan Rodríguez Cabrillo explored the Pacific, sailing from Natividad (Colima) to San Diego and as far north as Monterey Bay and beyond (Cleland 1947, 1–15). Before then, of course, regional maps were configured orally and multilingually by the many hundreds of native tribes, who often tied their spatial configurations to mythic interpretations of the landscape (Vallejo 1875, I: 13–14). For close to three hundred years the Southwest was considered the northernmost frontier of

New Spain and geological markers, like rivers, deserts, mountain chains, gulfs, and oceans, which today serve to divide and designate boundaries, were mere geographical features of the colonized territory.

Demography and geography do not, however, tell the entire story. The political story of Spanish colonialism would keep the Indian population either in a servile position to Spanish and later Mexican settlers, despite their growing linguistic and cultural assimilation, or in a hostile position, resisting the incursions of the colonists and the devastation of their way of life. Geopolitics would, however, play a key role in this northernmost Spanish area, for domination required occupation, but distance and inaccessibility, except by ship or arduous trekking on foot or by horse, would provide for only small Spanish and later Mexican settlements; sparse settlement and isolation would facilitate the region's eventual invasion by U.S. settlers and troops.

In the decade of the 1840s the map of the Southwest would be redrawn as an outcome of the U.S. policy of expansionism ("Manifest Destiny"). Spain's failure to develop its colony's economy before Mexican independence in 1821 and the political chaos during the 1830s and 1840s would leave Mexico weak and unable to resist the U.S. invasion of its territory and capital. By the 1870s the *californio* Mariano Guadalupe Vallejo could only look back and lament their loss of land, their loss of political and economic power as a conquered population, their proletarianization, and their linguistic oppression (1875, vol. 5).

Linguistic Cartography

Political maps, however, do not coincide nor are they synonymous with linguistic maps. They too do not account for the entire story. In fact, Mexico's weak nineteenth-century military, economic, and political power and its twentieth-century economic dependence have, perhaps ironically, furthered the expansion of its geolinguistic power, for today, given the large-scale immigration north, it could be said that Mexico is demographically and linguistically reterritorializing the Southwest. The Latino population is fast becoming the largest minority population of the United States, as well as being the population with the lowest income and the highest rate of poverty (Bureau of the Census 1991c, 7–8). Latinos are expected to surpass the African American minority in size early in the twenty-first century (see table 15) and to become the majority population in the state of California by the year 2040 if not earlier (Miller and Ostrow 1993, A22). Today, the

467

Latino population resides not only in the Southwest but throughout the United States; yet its marked concentration (about 63 percent) in the southwestern part of the United States has led—particularly for Latinos of Mexican origin who recall their historical roots in the region—to the discursive construction of the "border" states as "homeland" (see table 14).

The more recent reconfiguration of the linguistic and demographic map of the United States has to be seen, then, as part of a broader historical phenomenon: a product not only of nineteenth-century imperialism and the mass migration of Mexicans, but also of postwar (1945–1970) globalization of labor (Amin 1992, 9) and post-1950 critical social, economic, and political conflicts that triggered the migration of Asian, Caribbean, and Latin American immigrants. The restructuring brought on by the globalization of capital, which has led to the exportation of labor-intensive work and technology from industrialized nations to developing nations, has not, however, improved economic conditions in developing areas. Thus, despite the relocation of industries to the Third World, reports indicate that as a result of labor-saving technological advancements that increase productivity with a smaller work force, Latin American and African unemployment rates have also risen and led, in turn, to increased international migration to industrialized centers [Havemann and Kempster 1993, 1,4].

The phenomenon of domestic and international migration is worldwide. The United Nations Population Fund estimates that there are now 100 million foreign immigrants throughout the world and millions moving within particular nations from rural to urban areas. This geographical and occupational migration relocates migrants in Western Europe, the United States, Japan, and the large urban centers of the Third World. Major cities of both industrial and developing nations, such as São Paulo, Calcutta, Bombay, Beijing, Shanghai, Tokyo, Los Angeles, and Mexico City, thus continue to expand at what can only be termed mind-boggling rates. The case of Mexico is a clear example. The United Nations Fund for Population Activities reports that Mexico now exports about 10 percent of its labor force to the United States. Domestic migration within Mexico has also led to a concentration of its population in urban areas. Mexico City is now listed by the U.N. Population Fund as the largest metropolitan area in the world, with 20.2 million; in the year 2000 it is expected to continue as the largest urban center in the world with a population of 25.6 million (Meisler 1993, A4).

Often the situation of immigrant workers is neither quickly nor vastly improved by migrating, since unemployment rates are often high as well in the industrialized countries, as is evident, for example, in the 7.4 percent average unemployment rate for the United States in 1992 and a corresponding 10 percent figure for Western Europe in 1993 (Havemann and Kempster 1993, 1). Yet for these immigrants, whether documented or undocumented, even low-wage employment in service industries, agriculture, and secondary industries in the core countries is considerably better than their situation of unmitigated poverty back home. It is for this reason that these international immigrants are estimated to send back a highly significant $66 billion in remittances to their home countries every year, "a total that makes these remittances second in value only to oil in world trade," according to the United Nations (Meisler 1993, A4). As the trend toward low-wage employment and unemployment increases in the United States, given restructuring, and as social and health services for the unemployed are diminished, a worsening scenario looms ahead, characterized by increased homelessness, crime, especially drug addiction and dealing, and both generalized and state (police) violence in the ghettos and barrios of large urban areas where many ethnic/lingual minorities and recent immigrants are forced by economic circumstances to reside.

The growing polarization of U.S. society, with the wealthy getting wealthier and the poor poorer, along with a markedly reduced middle class, has catalyzed hostility against newcomers who serve as scapegoats for conditions produced by multinational capitalism. The aggression displayed of late by neo-Nazis in their violence against Turkish and North African immigrants in Germany and elsewhere in Europe is evident as well in the United States in increased racist violence against African Americans, Asians, and Latinos, especially recent Mexican immigrants. This racist nativist hostility is of course not new in a country that has had a long "tradition" of racism against Chinese immigrants, Blacks and Latinos. In the twentieth century, for example, we need only recall the cyclical media blitzkriegs against Mexican immigrants, beginning with the repatriation of Mexican immigrants in 1930–1931 and continuing with media reports promoting violence against the "zoot suiters" of the 1940s, the deportation of "wetbacks" in the 1950s, and the raids and border violence against "Mexican illegals" throughout the 1970s, 1980s, and 1990s. Specifically, neonativists fomenting anti-immigrant hysteria periodically argue that immigrants are responsible for unemployment, rising crime statistics, a stagnant economy, and the devaluation of the "American way of life." To halt what they allege is the immigrant drain on county and state resources, neonativists have gone so far as to propose that access to basic human services be denied to immigrants, as was the case with Proposition 187 in California (Cornelius 1993, B7). This hostility is evident as well in Congress, where one House member (Representative Mazzoli, Democrat of Kentucky and co-author of the 1986 immigration bill), proposed a constitutional amendment that would "revoke the sacrosanct right to citizenship for anyone born on American soil whose parents are here illegally" (Miller and Ostrow 1993, A1). Immigration has been termed "the problem of the decade" by Attorney General Reno as well, while Senator Simpson (Republican of Wyoming), the other co-author of the 1986 immigration bill, has advocated more stringent measures to determine the credibility of claims of political persecution and called for an identification card for all those seeking work. Even moderates like California Senator Feinstein have felt compelled to advocate for tougher measures against undocumented workers (A1, A22–23), including the strengthening of the Border Patrol with monies raised by levying a $1 toll on persons entering the country (Skelton 1993, A3) and repatriation of prisoners who are foreign nationals (Bunting and Miller 1993, A18). News of the discovery of boatloads of undocumented Chinese and Haitian immigrants, as well as the increased focus on Middle Eastern immigrants after the bombing of the World Trade Center in New York have further fueled anti-immigrant sentiment in this country.

Immigration issues continue to divide the heterogeneous Latino community as well, with some native and resident Latinos also pointing a finger of blame at undocumented workers for high unemployment rates and the lack of public services in their communities, even as others perceive the underlying racism behind this anti-immigrant sentiment (Navarrete 1992, M6; Bunting and Miller 1993, A18). What especially divided the Latino community in California was Proposition 187, approved by voters in 1994, an initiative to deny nonemergency medical care, public assistance, social services, and education to undocumented residents. Of course, positions on immigrant labor in the United States have always been controversial, and often contradictory, with the strongest advocates of deportations of undocumented workers and denial of social services to undocumented residents also, not surprisingly, supporting proposals for the immigration of skilled and professional immigrants (Skelton 1993, A3). The reasons are of course clear. Foreign computer programmers, for example, are paid much less than local workers. Media emphasis on the social cost of undocumented workers in this country often fails to recognize the billions ($29 billion in 1990) paid by Latinos in taxes (Bunting and Miller 1993, A18), as well as the contributions of this labor force to the economy despite (or more precisely because of) their extreme exploitation and oppression. Undocumented workers in rural areas, forced to live in huts, makeshift encampments, canyons and excavated holes in ravines, arroyos, and hills (McDonnell 1987, 1), often alongside high-tech business parks or upscale suburban centers, have become a dispossessed and dehumanized labor force, as is the case for agricultural workers in North San Diego County. It is only when undocumented workers become "visible" that suburbanites become incensed and begin demanding their "removal." These workers are only the latest wave of immigrants along the border. They represent the most recent migratory wave and are the Latino newcomers who in days to come will inevitably settle here and assimilate to the regional culture.[1]

Unlike earlier immigrant streams from Mexico that brought hundreds and sometimes thousands of men to work in the fields, on the railroad, and on the ranches of the Southwest, recent immigrant flows to the United States from Latin America, especially from Central America and Mexico, have included a good number of women. This too is a worldwide phenomenon; according to the U.N. Fund for Population Activities report on global migration, nearly half of all the world's migrants are women, often relocating on their own. The report further indicates that these women migrants end up in the lowest-paying jobs, become trapped in immigrant communities, and are vulnerable to abuse. Interestingly, they are also said to be more likely to send money home ("Migration Across Borders" 1993, A24). This phenomenon is linguistically as well as socially significant, for in the past, not only has the immigrant been gendered male but men have also dominated petitions for legalization of status (Passel 1992, 21). From here on out, the newly arrived immigrant is as likely to be a woman as a man; linguistically the shift will be particularly relevant in terms of language maintenance, for it is women who determine the mother tongue of their children. Immigrant men, marrying or fathering children with women born in or long-term residents of this country, are not generally the principal caretakers of children and consequently do not often determine the home language. In the case of Latino women, especially young undocumented immigrant women, there is the additional likelihood of their working as nannies in other Latino or Anglo homes. Given the growing percentage of Latino women who work (now 51.4 percent), there is a high probability that the caretaker of young Latino children is a monolingual Spanish-speaking woman, probably of Mexican or Central American origin. The Spanish-speaking "nanny" will thus help establish a grounding in Spanish in homes that, whether Latino or Anglo, might otherwise be marked as English-dominant.

Beyond Push and Pull

Uneven development and economic imbalances produced by multinational corporations in the periphery are not of course the sole stimulus for emigration. Economists have long noted that for every centrifugal "push" there is also a centripetal "pull" factor, that is, an attraction or draw of the immigrant labor force by industries of the highly developed nations, as has been, in fact, the case in the United States since the nineteenth century. But, in addition to these economic immigrants, who account for the majority of the cases of migration and include middle-class professional immigrants, there are also a significant number of political refugees requesting asylum in this and other countries. The flow of political immigrants to the United States is closely correlated to the numerous military interventions by this country, both covertly and overtly, during the nineteenth and twentieth centuries (Mexico, the Philippines, Korea, Vietnam, Cambodia, Laos, Chile, Grenada, Panama, for example), and to military coups carried out by U.S. allies in Latin America (Nicaragua, Uruguay, Argentina, Chile, Guatemala, Honduras, El Salvador, to name a few). In recent history, both political and economic refugees have come to the United States from Cuba, Haiti, other parts of Latin America, various parts of Asia and Africa, as well as Eastern Europe, bringing with them their respective languages. Legislative proposals by Simpson, Helms and others have sought to reduce the number of cases for asylum by an on-the-spot "expedited" inspection of arriving immigrants, in what would result in the denegation of a number of legitimate applications for asylum. Proposals such as this represent one more barrier set up to limit the number of undocumented immigrants—political and economic—from entering the United States (Miller and Ostrow 1993, A23), estimated by the United Nations to have been 7.4 million in the decade of the 1980s (Meisler 1993, A4).

As a consequence of sequential migratory flows, the United States continues to be a land of immigrants; but, increasingly, in recent years these immigrants are of Third World origin. There are now, for example, thought to be about 7 million Asians and Pacific Islanders in this country. The complex and highly heterogeneous population of Asians, Pacific Islanders, and American Indians is projected to triple by the year 2040 (U.S. Bureau of the Census 1982, 1). African Americans, now 28 million, are expected to increase by 50 percent by the year 2030 (1) The number of Latinos, a group that includes Mexicans, Puerto Ricans, Cubans, Central and South Americans as well as Spaniards, is more difficult to fix given

472

the large number of undocumented immigrants, but 1990 Census Bureau reports gave the figure of 22,354,059 Latinos (U.S. Bureau of the Census 1991c, 2). If to this statistic we add a conservative estimate of three million or more undocumented workers, clearly by the middle of the 1990s there were already over 25 million Latinos in the United States. In the year 2000 there are now some 32 million Latinos, a population expected to double by the year 2030, when, given the latest increase, it will exceed the projected 50 million (see table 15), due not only to immigration but to a high fertility rate. Taken together, Latinos, African Americans, and Asians may well constitute over half the population of the United States long before the year 2080, as had been earlier predicted. In the long run, demography and geography alone will not be the decisive factors, but they will undoubtedly provide the grounding for more immediate social and economic struggles; these changing geopolitical variables will in turn shape people's identification and contribute to the intensification of particular political contradictions, tensions, and organized struggles impacting property relations in the United States and specifically the Southwest region.

The Fixed/Fluid Border

The "border" has recently become a trendy term. Within literary and cultural studies the construct has been used with a good deal of laxity to refer to any number of boundaries within disparate semantic fields. Some critics tend to exalt and fetishize the U.S.-Mexican border or "the borderlands," while others deny the very existence of a border between the two countries. The border is not of course some "twilight zone" or idealized space; it is a social and political space used at one level to demarcate a political boundary and hegemonic power; at other levels, however, political and geographical national boundaries do not delimit or curtail the impact of U.S. economic and political power, which extends as far south as Tierra del Fuego and beyond. Global economic and political penetration in turn gives rise to a questioning of the sovereignty of nation-states under multinational and transnational capitalism (Miyoshi 1993, 744). Critics suggest that with the replacement of a national bourgeoisie by transnational capitalists, nation-states as traditionally conceived have become increasingly irrelevant, as their primary reason for being, to protect a national economy, is now circumscribed or even defunct (743). If, however, these national formations are taken as illusions, how then is the phenomenon of increased nationalism in evidence in Eastern Europe to be explained? The phenomenon could, as Hobsbawm indicates, simply be residual, that is, "unfinished business" (1992, 165), or analyzable, along with other world ethnic and religious antagonisms, as "neoethnicism" (Miyoshi 1993, 744). In any event, it is important in all these discussions to distinguish between nation and state, for while nation-states might become increasingly permeable and weak, the idea of national communities could, on the other hand, continue to be powerfully imagined under the illusion of communal boundaries. In fact, far from being in decline at the end of the twentieth century, ethnicism and identity based on factors other than nationality have undergone a global revival along with xenophobia and what might be termed neoracism (Miyoshi 1993, 744; Balibar 1991, 21).

The much-heralded demise of the nation-state may, however, be grossly exaggerated. The case of Mexico provides a striking example, especially if we consider the degree to which the North American Free Trade Agreement (NAFTA) of 1994 has further intensified the transnationalization of the Mexican economy. Mexican state sovereignty could thus be said to be on the decline, particularly if one considers the success with which transnational corporations and global finance capital have imposed structural adjustment policies on the Mexican economy, traditionally the domain of state policy-making. On the other hand, even in those areas dominated by global entities (IMF, World Bank, and multinational corporations) the state still plays a key management role, organizing market and property relations for global capital, and maintaining its repressive and ideological functions. The state's survival ensures that national cohesion is maintained; the state's role is to elicit and organize consensus, while exercising its power as well through coercion and violence, if need be, as has been obvious in the Mexican government's actions in Chiapas.

The relation of globalization to linguistic mapping becomes clearer if one considers that one direct result of NAFTA and the impact of transnational capital has been the dislocation of workers from defunct national industries unable to compete with U.S. industries and products. This increased unemployment together with Mexican economic crises during the 1990s made crossing the border to the north all the more urgent, if not inevitable, for large numbers of Mexicans. Far from suggesting a future "borderless" transnational world, physical reality points to a reinforced and even militarized border. The line between the two nation-states persists because the political boundary is real, material; it can prove to be both violent and deadly, as those attempting to cross without authorization to this "side," *el otro lado,* by crossing the "line"—the fence, desert, or river—have found. In these discussions it is useful to make use of Lefebvre's notion of the border as both a *field of action* (an area marked by particular political and social relations) and a *basis for action* (the produced space within which state power enables these relations) (Lefebvre 1991, 191). We need as well to recall that the U.S.-Mexico border is the edge of the periphery, marked by a string of over 135,000 transnational *maquila* industries (assembly plants) relocated on Mexican soil from Tijuana to Matamoros in order to make use of and exploit cheap Mexican labor. Migration to work in border maquilas is often the first stop before crossing the border to the U.S. side, where, as previously indicated, there is extensive use of cheap undocumented Mexican labor in every sector. This contradictory configuration of the border as a volatile and strategic area is directly linked to and revealing of the state's power, on the one hand, to make commercial concessions that benefit capitalist interests, and, on the other, to exert its coercive force and function.

In many ways the situation on any border, but especially a border between a superpower and a modernizing nation-state, is paradoxical, for in organizing and regulating space in a particular way, states simultaneously create a fuzzy and complex site, an ambiguous ideological field, capable of generating contact, conflict, divergence, and opposition, explaining in this regard why borders are reconfigurable.

Geographically, the U.S. border region has been viewed in its greater extension as the border states or even as the former Mexican Southwest. Locally, the border is more specifically a space limited to a radius of ten to twenty miles around the nation-state boundary. It is the site of crossing, often a mere transitional area, as in the case of San Diego, in view of the fact that most immigrants are headed for points north. In Texas the local border, especially the Valley, is already an area of Mexican concentration where Chicanos/Mexicanos often represent over 90 percent of the county and city population (see tables 10 and 11). But new immigrants generally move beyond this poverty-stricken area and head for Houston, San Antonio, Dallas or Chicago, metropolitan areas where employment beckons. Thus, as the population of Mexican origin in the U.S. increases and extends throughout the country, with a growing number of sites of Mexican immigrant population concentration, one sense of the "borderlands" could be figuratively viewed as extending all the way to the Canadian border.

As previously argued, the U.S. border states are demographically heterogeneous social spaces, not simply bilingual and bicultural but multiethnic, multiracial, and multilingual. A similar cultural heterogeneity, however, can be found along the border area within Mexico, for in addition to its various native and more recently arrived indigenous populations from Oaxaca, it has, in the last thirty years especially, attracted mass migration of displaced workers from Mexico's interior. This is evident in the demographic explosion of border towns and cities such as Tijuana, whose population now numbers over two million people, far outnumbering San Diego (see table 10). In addition to the domestic Mexican migration to the area, there is also a history of German, Russian, and Chinese immigrants during the nineteenth and twentieth centuries, as well as the migration of Spanish political refugees during the 1930s and scattered Anglo and Jewish immigrants, all residing among its largely Mexican mestizo population. While the area is diverse, ethnic heterogeneity is however greater in the United States, as previously noted. The following statistics bear this out: in the Los Angeles Unified School District eighty languages other than English are spoken by 44 percent of the 641,000 students, with Spanish, Armenian, Korean, Cantonese, Tagalog, Vietnamese, Russian, Farsi, Cambodian, and Hebrew as the most widely spoken (see tables 2 and 3) (Quintanilla 1993, E2).

Multilingual diversity within this border area does not of course preclude the dominance, in particular enclaves, of particular classes and ethnic groups and a particular language. Clearly the dominance of English on the U.S. side of the border is subject to socio-spatial contingencies. Thus, within particular U.S. urban areas, Spanish, Korean, or Chinese, for example, may be the dominant language, especially in communities and areas of large immigrant concentration such as the Texas Valley, the Imperial Valley of California, and cities such as San Antonio, Los Angeles, or San Francisco.[2] Los Angeles County, for example, claims the largest Mexican, Armenian, Korean, Filipino, Salvadoran, and Guatemalan communities outside the respective home nations and the largest Japanese, Iranian, and Cambodian populations in the United States (see table 3) (E2). For this reason, in given ethnic zones oral and written communication can occur primarily in the minority language. Quintanilla reports that in Los Angeles there are broadcasts in seventeen foreign languages on KCSI-TV, not including Spanish, and that fifty foreign-language newspapers are published in the county as well (E2). In the greater Los Angeles area as well, there are three Spanish-language television stations, several Spanish-language newspapers, many Spanish-language bookstores, video rental stores, record/tape/compact disc shops, and movie theaters, as well as numerous other commercial establishments in which Spanish is the dominant or only language spoken, to the point that Spanish-language radio is the highest ranked in terms of listeners. Other ethnic communities have some of these same services available in languages other than English throughout the United States.

What was once termed a situation of diglossia or bilingualism is clearly now a situation of heteroglossia, with a multiplicity of languages occupying the same space. Thus on Alvarado Street in Los Angeles between Echo Park and MacArthur Park, and often within the same block, one can find commercial establishments catering to several ethnic populations and advertising their wares in Spanish, Korean, Chinese, and English. Some ethnic restaurants or small grocery stores may draw a diversity of customers, but the same cannot be said for other establishments (El Million Dollar theater in downtown L.A., for example), which cater to a particular ethnic clientele (in this case a distinctly Latino, primarily Spanish-speaking, audience). Thus behind the surface of heteroglossia lies a layering of cultural and lingual monotopias, monolingual sites that are often spatially contained within segregated social sites, but more often fragmented and scattered within larger spatial confines.

The cultural and linguistic diversity evident along the border zone has led to estimates terming California the first Third World state in the United States, with the Latino population expected to be the majority population in the State by or before the year 2040 (Miller and Ostrow 1993, A22). Current statistics indicating over 17 million speakers of Spanish in the United States place almost a third of them in California (see tables 1 and 2). The state as a whole, with a population of 29.7 million in 1993 and 32.2 million in 1998 has more than 8.6 million non-English speakers who speak 230 non-English tongues (Quintanilla 1993, E2).[3] More important, the state's multiethnic diversity attests to its status as a border state not only in relation to Mexico but to the entire Pacific Rim (see tables 2 and 9), as evidenced in its large Asian immigrant population. In a way, the cycle of immigration from Asia to the Americas that began over 25,000 years ago continues today across the Pacific. In a sense, too, their descendants, the mestizos and Indians of Latin America, are reversing the direction and moving north rather than south.

Language in a Multilingual Space

The crucial question at stake in these discussions is: What role can language use play in this social space of multi-diversity? Language itself can be viewed abstractly, as an ideal grammar, or sociolinguistically and sociospatially, as a network of discourses that function to construct our public and private lives. Along the border there are clearly several networks in operation, not all equally powerful, not all hegemonic, not all dominant within particular social spaces, not all equal in social and cultural exchanges. Because these networks are socially produced and the product of particular social relations clustering within given social spaces, they operate hierarchically at the intersection of a multiplicity of political, economic, and cultural relations. Each discourse can thus be described in terms of layered social relations. A network of contradictions, disparities, conflicts, and particular socio-spatial configurations are the underpinnings for particular discourses and for the dominance or subordination of particular communal networks. It is these collectively produced discourses that interpellate individuals, serve to construct identities, and—importantly—condition language choice and use.

A common language has always played a role in what Hobsbawm calls proto-nationalist movements and has been crucial in identifying speakers as members of a supra-local language community. For Hobsbawm, who sees nationalism as a product of the modern state, proto-nationalist movements arise prior to the formation of a state, although states are also capable of mobilizing already existing ethnic, lingual, or religious attachments (1992, 46). Language in fact can serve to link individuals with a particular state (47), especially if it is a "print" language (Anderson 1987) or the language of mass media, by constructing the notion of community and creating an identity in relation to a collectivity or "imagined community." Identity is thus not a given, not an essence determined by biology or heredity, but a discursively constructed identification. This construction is generated by an ensemble of relations, all discursively articulated in varying over-determined patterns within particular social spaces, and in this formation language has a key role.

Of course often the print languages that serve to generate a sense of "community" or "nation" are minority or elite languages, as was the case, for example, in Peru after independence, since the majority of the population spoke indigenous languages and not Spanish. Colonialism and the political domination of criollos ensured that Spanish would become the official language, and not until much later, in the latter half of the twentieth century, did modernization and the need for a skilled labor force lead to the implementation of bilingual education and a recognition of the utility of indigenous languages as teaching tools for *castellanización*, that is, the Spanish-language assimilation and literacy of indigenous populations throughout Latin America. Language loyalty or monolingualism is thus not a necessary ingredient for the formation of a state, although it is undoubtedly an important ingredient in the formation of a nation. By the same token, the multiplicity of languages within Mexico, for example, obviously did not impede the creation of a Mexican state, nor did the wide use of Quechua hinder the establishment of a Peruvian state. The same could be said of Guatemala or Ecuador or any number of multilingual states across the globe. As Hobsbawm indicates, "languages multiply with states, not the other way around" (1992, 63).

The Case of Ireland: Commonalities and Differences

Linguistic diversity is often perceived as a problem by nativists, whose notion of a strong nation-state rests on the exclusion of all cultural difference. Historically, however, as previously noted, the language policy of a particular nation-state does not necessarily reflect the linguistic makeup of the majority of the population; the "national" language may in fact be a minority language, even the language of the colonizer, as was often the case in African nations after independence. Yet it cannot be denied that minority language loyalty, in opposition to the hegemonic language, may serve as a rallying strategy and prove to be useful to a nationalist movement, as in the case of Ireland; the fact that in this case the construct of language loyalty was merely strategically significant becomes evident afterwards, when state policy and efforts supporting the use of the Irish language were unable to overturn a century-old switch to the language of the hegemonic power in the region, English. Language loss of Irish had been initiated long before, perhaps as early as 1851 (Macnamara 1975, 65). Thus despite language revival movements of the nineteenth century, and the creation of the Gaelic League in 1893 to "de-Anglicize Ireland," even nationalist writings were not expressed in Irish but in English (67–66). The Irish language revivalist movement did, however, play a part in fomenting political awareness; in fact the leaders of the revolutionary movement to gain Irish independence were all members of the Gaelic League (68). Language, however, was also seen as a divisive element, contributing to the civil war with Northern Ireland since the northern Presbyterians' ancestors had never spoken Irish (68–69). With the establishment of the Irish Free State in 1922, Irish and English were both declared official languages of Ireland and efforts were made to promote the Irish language in schools and colleges. Yet despite all these efforts, especially supported by the Irish middle class, by 1971 only 3 percent of the population spoke Irish (65, 87), although 76 percent of the population, as indicated in a national survey in 1964, did favor the teaching of Irish as a second language (83). The case of Ireland is especially interesting to the discussion at hand because here clearly identity was not linked exclusively to language use but rather to a series of elements including language, territory, religion, literature, a history of struggle against British colonialism, and later, the creation of a nation-state. The loss or undermining of one element, language, thus did not weaken the overall sense of an "imagined community." Interest in promoting a "national" language may in the long run be set aside after independence by leaders of nationalist movements driven by goals of modernization of the newly formed state through use of the formerly imposed colonial language; the choice is of course always strategic and political. Fragmentation within linguistic groups is common, in fact the norm, and has never determined national allegiances, with speakers of a shared language often preferring to secede from a territory, as was the case of Uruguay, a Southern Cone region manipulated by the British to separate from Argentina.

The Irish example is both relevant and interesting for the variety of elements that come into play, including territory, religion, language, history, and economics. Clearly, Irish economic dependence has determined language choice, despite nationalism. The choice, however, as previously indicated, was a long process and affected three and a half million people, not including the Irish abroad and in Northern Ireland. In the specific case of the Latino population in the United States, the scope of the issue expands markedly, for Spanish is the home language of over 17 million in the United States and, more importantly, is a language spoken by over 352 million people worldwide.

Unlike the Irish, however, Latinos in the United States are overwhelmingly immigrants or the descendants of immigrants to the United States, although in some areas of the Southwest, such as the Texas Valley or the northern part of New Mexico, there are still descendants of Spanish colonists who arrived in the eighteenth century.[4] The transnational migration of Latinos to the United States is, in that sense, similar to the diaspora brought on by conquest, migration, and colonization of many national minorities throughout the world (Gilroy 1987, 155). But unlike the movement of other diasporic populations, Latino immigration to the United States has been ongoing for 150 years, and is not the result of one catastrophic event; moreover, migration has been in large part to an area to which there are historical claims as Mexican territory. Given the multiethnic, multilingual configuration of the border today and the diversity of "imagined communities," Spanish will not play a role comparable to that of Gaelic, at least not until Latinos are the majority population. The Latino population is, it bears recalling, heterogeneous and includes Mexicans, Central Americans, South Americans, Cubans, Puerto Ricans and Spaniards. Latino concentrations in the United States, given ethnic and racial segregation, have enabled the construction of a new Latino identity (see tables 9 and 12), an identification in progress that has not yet solidified, precisely because of the population's fragmentation on the basis of national origin, generation, and class.

The Latino community in the United States is (as the Census Bureau makes abundantly clear with its listings of "non-hispanic white" and "non-hispanic black") multinational and multiracial; it is a population that includes mestizos, indigenous people (Native Americans), blacks, mulattos, criollos (whites), and Asians (see table 9). But Latinos are not a synthesis of races; they are no mystical "raza cósmica," nor can they be defined essentialistically under any one rubric. Latinos are a heterogeneous population, politically fragmented and culturally diverse, yet united in part by a history of Spanish conquest and colonialism, a history of proletarianization and disempowerment in the United States, and, to a large extent, by a common language, Spanish. Ethnic identity for the Latino population is thus for the most part a matter of national origin or descent and language, rather than a matter of race or *mestizaje*. As Hobsbawm again acutely observes, "the crucial base of an ethnic group as a form of social organization is cultural rather than biological"(1992, 63). This diversity has not however eliminated intra-Latino racism, with light-skinned Latinos, for example, often disdainful or condescending toward dark-skinned Latinos, nor has it led to eliminating class distinctions; but it has, on the other hand, enabled the construction of an identity that transcends these differences, if only momentarily, as for example when Sammy Sosa hits a home run.

Identification as a Latino today in the United States persists nevertheless, despite differences. Consciousness of a greater Spanish-speaking collectivity gives rise to a contingent identity that emerges as much from separation from other countrymen as from increased contact with other Latinos. In some cases identification with the larger Latino community, that is, the willingness to transcend national identity, comes after a generation of residence in the United States. The first generation is more likely to identify on the basis of national or regional origin, and in the case of Mexicans, often on the basis of attachment to a particular Mexican state, city, or town. Identity as "Mexican" rather than "Latino" has been the norm for the majority Latino population, given their superiority in numbers and concentration as the sole Latino minority in some areas of the

Southwest. That situation is, however, undergoing a marked shift in some areas, as Mexicans, Salvadorans, Nicaraguans, Guatemalans, Hondurans, and other Latinos begin to share the same residential spaces. In areas where a diversity of Latin Americans reside, the umbrella term "Latino" is and has been the preferred identity of all, as is evident in the California Bay area or in Chicago; in some cases it is a supplementary identity, after that of national origin, deployed strategically when a supranational notion of collectivity is sought.

Spanish language use is today the key cultural difference that identifies Latinos. If, however, Spanish were no longer the language of over half of the Latino population, Latino identity would not necessarily disappear. In the particular case of Chicanos, the loss of the Spanish language has not obliterated identity on the basis of national origin, at least for first- and second-generation persons of Mexican origin, who for the most part continue to identify ethnically as Chicanos, Mexicanos, or Mexican Americans, even after becoming English-dominant or even English monolinguals. An overall language shift appears highly unlikely, however. Given the large percentage of first-generation Latinos in this country, Spanish will not fade from the linguistic map any time soon, at least not in the twenty-first century. For this reason, Spanish will continue to figure as a key element within the ensemble of factors and relations determining the cultural and political identity of the Latino population in the Southwest.

Identification is, however, a two-way process. One identifies and is identified. Dominant society, through the Census Bureau and the media, has, for example, chosen to call this group "Hispanics," a term viewed as Eurocentric and rejected by many Latinos for stressing white colonialist roots over an indigenous or mestizo background. The preferred term, "Latino," its eurocentricity notwithstanding, is viewed as linking Spanish-speaking residents in the United States with Latin America. Whether as "Hispanics" or "Latinos," the state and media have succeeded in constructing this diverse population as one collectivity, in the process facilitating ethnic awareness and affirming the notion of Latinos as a single "imagined" community (Anderson 1987). Clearly the sheer number of Latinos in the United States—some 32 million in the year 2000—is also having an impact and gaining a visibility for the population. This demographic growth has not gone unnoticed, especially by marketing experts who are fully aware of the aggregate Latino household income which has increased significantly since 1982, and in 1990, according to 1990 Census Bureau reports, totaled some $173 billion. Although this income represents only about 5 percent of the U.S. total income figure of $3.5 trillion, it is still a sizable market share (U.S. Bureau of the Census 1991c, 5), not often taken into account when immigrants are accused of costing the border states a considerable amount in educational, medical and correctional services (Bunting and Miller 1993, A18). It is as consumers of commodities and services that the collectivity has been linguistically and culturally addressed by advertisers, and in so doing these companies have—perhaps unwittingly—strengthened an identification of ethnicity, even if one has to acknowledge that being "ethnic" in the United States has been in good measure depoliticized, and relegated to the level of marketing niches.

If, however, as Hobsbawm indicates, in the future it will be ethnicism rather than nationalism that will flourish within a supranational frame-work (1992, 191), perhaps it is time to begin to speculate on the role that ethnicism will play within civil society and the degree to which it can be manipulated by the state for its own supranational policies, particularly those affecting the Pacific Rim, that is, Asia and Latin America, and benefiting transnational corporations. The multilingual diversity of the U.S. population may give rise to a society on the model of Hong Kong, with its multiethnic technocrats and managers, but given the class and racist structure of U.S. society, it is more likely that the greater part of the multiethnic population will not form part of this elite. The role to be played by ethnicism and minority languages in a stratified society is yet unclear: they could simply be additional "chips" to be played by the state and global capital, or they could be politicized by Latinos themselves and serve as a strategy for organizing along international ethnic/race and class lines. In view of the number of Latino soldiers, military advisers, and drug (DEA) officers that have been sent to Latin America, odds are that the state is way ahead of us in the identification and use of its diverse multicultural human "resources."

As in the case of Ireland, more immediate economic and political factors will undoubtedly write the story of language choice for the Latino minority, at least for the time being. But what will happen during the twenty-first century when Latinos are the majority population in particu-lar regions and states and over half of this Latino population is first or second generation and still in great measure Spanish-dominant? Even if third- and fourth-generation Latinos are by then English-dominant—or, most probably, English monolinguals, especially in the case of middle-class families—the space of large segregated urban barrios and ghettoes that are expected to burgeon (over 90 percent of the Latino population now reside in metropolitan areas according to census figures) will still be predominantly Spanish-speaking.[5] It will be the socio-spatial configuration of about sixty million Latinos in the United States before the year 2060 and their economic and political power that will determine the survival of Spanish and even its status as the first or second language of the Southwest region (see table 15).

Language loyalty or linguistic identity, like culture in general or even ethnicity, may ultimately be politically irrelevant, but for now it is an obvious factor that can be tapped for political identification and organization; in fact language, culture, and ethnicity/race are strategic factors for struggle because they are precisely the tools used by hegemonic forces to oppress, exploit, and divide populations. As Chatterjee points out, ethnicity is often the basis for exclusion even in the realm of cultural production and education (1985, 15). The relation between ethnicity/national origin and language was legally recognized during the U.S. civil rights movement. In court cases for the rights of language minority students, one significant outcome was the 1974 Supreme Court *Lau v. Nichols* decision (Keller and Van Hooft 1982; Avila and Godoy 1979) indicating that discrimination on the basis of language was in fact discrimination on the basis of national origin. More recent cases of workers charging racial and linguistic discrimination at the workplace have argued that English-only policies in the workplace are forbidden by federal law, as Reginal Welch, communication director for the Equal Employment Opportunity Commission in Washington, D.C., explains: "An individual's first language is part of his national heritage and forbidding him to speak that language is discrimination based on national origin" (O'Donnell 1993, B3).

Language oppression is nothing other than racism, for as Balibar indicates, the new racism is a *differentialist racism* based on cultural differences, that is, on language, descent, and tradition as well as on race (1991, 21, 61). This neoracism often disguises itself and focuses not on race or ethnicity but on maintaining social boundaries and differences by insisting on "the harmfulness of abolishing frontiers, the incompatibility of life-styles and traditions" (21). These are segregationist tactics manipulated by dominant races or groups to establish barriers and exclude particular ethnic/racial populations. What is equally clear is that the group suffering racist policies often retaliates by deploying difference itself—often a culturalist essentialism—as a basis for political struggle. As political scientists and theorists such as E. San Juan, Cornel West, and Mario Barrera have noted, in the United States race and class must be necessarily considered jointly in any analysis of working-class minority populations, particularly in view of the institutional racialization (Balibar 1991, 210) common to particular occupational sectors within which the majority of ethnic minority workers can be found,[6] all lower-paying occupations, offering less stability and with implications at the level of housing segregation and educational attainment. It is, ironically, this racialization of low-wage occupations that has also contributed to the maintenance of Spanish within these particular employment domains, just as low income and high poverty levels maintain Latinos within barrios, for often it is only in these inner-city communities that low-income housing is available. Thus difference, especially linguistic difference, is maintained through the construction of barriers and creation of closures that guarantee exclusion; yet it is in turn that very enforced structural difference that can serve as a basis for identification and concomitantly political struggle.

A more blatant expression of intolerance for ethnic/racial and linguistic differences is evident in the English-only movement pushed by the organization U.S. English. The leaders of this organization—which has long advocated making English the national language and eliminating bilingual education, bilingual ballots, and other multilingual services for non-English-speaking residents—have also been prominent in FAIR (Federation for American Immigration Reform), a racist anti-immigration organization (Trombley 1986). The group's success in making English the official state language in several states in the union provides a good indication of the country's intolerance for minority culture (Trombley 1986), despite the recent efforts of academics to promote multiculturalism and the business sector's embrace of "diversity" marketing.

In the face of linguistic oppression and intolerance for minority languages, speakers of these languages often respond in one of two ways: (a) submit to the proposal that English should be the only public language and accept the proposition that bilingualism creates divisiveness while assimilation and English monolingualism increase the possibility of socioeconomic success, or (b) reject any Anglocentric attempt to impose an official language and a Eurocentric notion of culture, and resist language loss (even while advocating the acquisition of English), by supporting the use of minority languages and strengthening the development of minority student cognitive skills in their native language. In a world where English is the first or second language of over 777 million people, as well as the language of the global market, science, and the strongest economic and military power in the world, acquisition of English is a must, but English proficiency is no guarantee of socioeconomic success, as shown by the number of poor whites and English-speaking minorities suffering unemployment, homelessness, and destitution in the United States. No one can deny that the pressures placed on lingual minority residents to acquire English are tremendous. The long-term maintenance of minority languages is clearly contingent upon a number of social, economic, and political factors, but human agency, that is, collective agency and choice, undoubtedly plays a part as well, as previously suggested.

Language Maintenance and Shift

The Latino community, as we have noted above, includes member who are rural and urban, temporary and permanent residents, documented and undocumented immigrants, employed and unemployed, professionals as well as manual laborers and operatives, metropolitan and suburban residents, young and old, and is characterized not only as being multinational and multiracial but also multigenerational, with a continual presence of first-generation immigrants. All of these traits and differences contribute both to the strengthening of language loyalty and use of the minority language and to language shift and the fragmentation of the Latino population. Whatever strengthens linguistic contact, that is, interaction of Latinos with other Spanish speakers, works toward language maintenance. Thus ethnicity, poverty, low income, and gender are all factors that segregate collectivities, creating minority language enclaves, and as a result reinforce language differences, that is, maintenance of the native immigrant language. By the same token, whatever fragments the Latino community and divides it spatially, diminishing interaction between Latinos, works against language maintenance and in turn facilitates language shift. Freeways and rezoning of residential areas divide communities, but so do class differences. Thus professionals, for the most part, have little to do with nonprofessionals, whether fellow countrymen or other Latinos, unless it is to hire them as maids, gardeners, nannies, and other types of manual workers. Often Latino professionals live in predominantly Anglo areas and have little or no contact with other Latinos. National and regional origin likewise divides the population, with social interaction often being limited to activities with fellow countrymen.

Curiously, generation is a double-edged variable. It is a significant factor determining ethnic and linguistic contact, for incoming immigrants tend to form insular communities by settling close to family, countrymen and friends in particular barrios. A study by Hurtado and others (1992), offers interesting insights into the generational makeup of the Latino population in California. Hurtado estimates that 65 percent of Latinos in California in 1989 were first-generation residents, 23 percent were second-generation and 12 percent were third-generation. A large number of first-generation immigrants clustering in metropolitan communities on the basis of national or regional origin guarantees a strong Spanish-dominant Latino presence. Nationwide, first-generation immigrants are said to represent half of the growth in the Latino population from 1980 (16 million) to 1990 (22.3 million) (U.S. Bureau of the Census, 1). If the generational distribution of one decade is reproduced during the next fifty years as expected and given the rapid pace of growth of the Latino population—expected to be about five times as fast as the rate experienced by the non-Hispanic population—there will continue to be a substantial Spanish-speaking population in the Southwest and in the country as a whole, as marketing experts have recognized and capitalized upon already.

Generational differences, however, can also serve to fragment the Latino population, for often long-time residents or Latinos born in this country who are English-dominant or monolingual have little or no interaction with newcomers. This generational difference is also evident in the schools, where the school population not only divides racially (whites, blacks, and Latinos) but also generationally, with English-speaking Chicanos (second-, third-, or fourth-generation Latinos) and Spanish-speaking Mexicanos (first-generation) often at odds. Along the U.S.-Mexico border upper-class Mexicans crossing the border to attend local high schools clash with working-class Chicanos as well. But the opposite is also evident, with Chicanos disdaining the non-English-speaking recently arrived working-class Mexican immigrants. In the latter case, these tensions are not long-lasting because of the phenomenon that I will term *achicanamiento*, that is, acculturation to the local Chicano culture. Newly immigrated children from Mexico or other parts of Latin America who live in barrios and attend local community schools rapidly adopt the dress, hair style, and ways of the local children and teenagers. They join gangs and other groups. Divisions occur subsequently on the basis of turf and gang allegiances rather than strictly on the basis of generation or national origin. And linguistically, of course, soon young immigrants begin to code-switch, mixing Spanish and English in their speech. The process of code-switching is an international linguistic phenomenon and common among bilingual speakers. By the time first- or second-generation working-class Latino students get to colleges and universities, they are all in a similar linguistic and social situation, as Latino student protests at the University of California at Davis demonstrated from 1989 to 1990. They are now "Chicanos," whether originally from Mexico, El Salvador, Guatemala, Argentina, Colombia, Puerto Rico, or Cuba, because their lived experience in the United States is that of working-class Chicanos. Like their Chicano counterparts, they have had little or no formal training in Spanish. English is their dominant school language, but Spanish is—whatever the variety—their home language.

The political impact of generational and national origin differences among Latinos became strikingly clear after the 1992 Los Angeles uprisings in response to the first court decision in the Rodney King case. Some Chicanos, aware that at least half of the arrested looters were Latinos, tried to distance themselves as third-generation "Mexican Americans" from newly arrived immigrants, declaring, as did Navarrete, that "the ethnic link between the two groups [Central Americans and Chicanos] is thin—no more pronounced than the one joining dark-skinned African-Americans with dark-skinned Haitians denied entry into the United States" (Navarrete 1992, M6). Unlike Navarrete, other ethnic minorities have taken a transnational perspective that enables solidarity across borders.[7] In a post-uprising column published in the *Los Angeles Times*, Navarrete further acknowledges feeling economically and "culturally" threatened by Latinos and suggests with FAIR that "Mexican Americans" are opposed to "excessive immigration" (M6). The Navarrete example serves to show how generation, class, and political orientation can intersect to produce a Chicano/Latino voice that echoes the hysteria of the political right in the United States, as so often has been the case with other Latino columnists, such as Richard Rodríguez, who are then ably manipulated by the mainstream media. Fortunately, for every Navarrete there are many second- and third- generation Chicanos/Latinos who argue against nativist racist proposals to curb immigration selectively and identify with working-class Latinos from Mexico, the Caribbean, and Central and South America.

Linguistic acculturation of ethnic/lingual minorities is thus contingent on a number of social factors. In a revealing study by Portes of 5,000 students who are the children of Cuban, Haitian, Filipino, Mexican, and Vietnamese immigrants, a high percentage of all surveyed students indicated that their knowledge of English was good or very good, but only a high percentage of the Latino children indicated having a good command of their parents' native language (see table 6). About half of the children of Vietnamese immigrants said they prefer English over their parents' language, and in the case of children of Mexican descent, fewer than half (44 percent). This linguistic loyalty and maintenance of the parents' language correlated well with the students' perception of discrimination, that is, their sense of being different and ill-treated because of that difference. Mexican and Haitian children were less willing to kowtow to interviewers by praising the United States as the best country in the world, revealing thereby a sense of identity not entirely determined by hegemonic discourses (see table 6). Although Portes's conclusion is that these immigrant children are "well on their way to being fluent English speakers, even, one could argue, on the way to monolingualism" and that "it is the parents' language, not English, that is endangered" (Sontag 1993, A6), his study also allows for a different reading of the data. Clearly language shift is contingent upon a number of factors and evidently identification with one's nationality, ethnicity, race, or class in the face of discrimination and rejection can counter expectations and play a role in language solidarity, triggering an individual's choice to maintain his/her immigrant parents' language.

Language maintenance and shift has also been affected by bilingual education in schools with large concentrations of limited-English speakers. These programs, established since the 1970s primarily to foster the transition from the minority language to English, have long been the target of the political right, despite the increased educational attainment of students in some of these bilingual programs, as has been made clear in the case of the Calexico School District in California. In a 1993 report issued by the Little Hoover Commission, on the other hand, the California Department of Education was criticized for teaching immigrant children their native language rather than teaching them to speak English (Chávez 1993, A19). This type of misrepresentation of bilingual programs that teach both English and the student's native language, and the virulent attack against them, widespread for three decades, directly led to Californian voters' approval of Proposition 227, an initiative that substantially curtailed the use of bilingual education. Failure of voters and politicians to recognize and address the linguistic and cognitive needs of immigrant children is shortsighted and deplorable, particularly in view of the fact that at the end of the twentieth century one in four California students is an English learner (Rumberger and Gándara 2000, 1). The lack of appropriate educational programs is evident in statistics showing Latinos with the highest dropout rate in the nation; 30 percent of the nation's dropouts are Latinos. The consequences for educational attainment for Latinos are clear. The Census Bureau indicates that only half of Latino adults have completed high school; 22

percent have completed one or more years of college, and one in ten has completed four or more years of college (see table 5) (U.S. Bureau of the Census 1991a, 4).

This low educational attainment explains in part the dwindling numbers of Latino students in colleges and universities. A report issued by the University of California Latino Eligibility Task Force reveals that only 4 percent of Latino high school graduates in this state are fully "eligible" for admission to the university. In a state where Latino students numbered 1,200,000 in 1985 and were expected to reach 3,100,000 by 2005 (Latino Eligibility Task Force 1993, 8), enrollment of Latino students at the University of California has dropped drastically since the adoption in 1995 of Sp-1 and Sp-2, University of California regulations banning affirmative action, and in the wake of Proposition 209 in 1996, the California initiative that overturned affirmative action policies statewide. The decline in the presence of Latinos at UC campuses is also, of course, directly related to the rising cost of a college education, the overall low-income status of Latino students (see tables 7 and 8), and, more importantly, the weak academic preparation provided by barrio and ghetto schools.

In the face of this critical exclusion of significant numbers of Latino and African American students from institutions of higher education, one has to wonder what provisions are being made by the state for placing these young ethnic minorities. It appears that the state has a different kind of institutionalization in mind for us. Statistics indicate that "today's entering Latino kindergartner is as likely to go to jail as meet the admission standards of the state universities" (Acuña 1990, B7). In his review of Campbell's book *Choosing Democracy*, Acuña indicates that by the year 2000 inmates in California prisons may exceed 300,000 and it is likely that 50 percent will be Latino (B7). Davis reports that, in the United States, "32.2 percent of young black men and 12.3 percent of young Latino men between the ages of twenty and twenty-nine are either in prison, in jail, or on probation or parole" (1997, 267). The growth of the prison industry would suggest that the state prefers to spend thousands of dollars to incarcerate minority youth rather than spend the money to educate and employ them. Persistent unemployment and poverty have been shown to contribute to teenagers' gang affiliation, drug abuse, and drug dealing, often the easiest way to make money in our barrios and ghettoes. The problem of violence in Latino communities is now at a critical level. As the population increases it will continue to face many problems, especially the need to gain control of its own urban spaces and improve its educational attainment level, if it is not to end up being the poor, laboring, and lumpen *majority* ruled by a white minority, as previously was the case in South Africa (see tables 10, 11, and 12). Here too Spanish could possibly play a strategic role in organizing the Spanish-speaking population and preparing it for employment, school/college, and wide-ranging political struggle.

Any proposal for the use of Spanish as a strategic language for politicization requires that we have more detailed information on the actual use of Spanish, since usage tends to vary according to generation, age, residence, occupation, and education. Although linguistic trends are set at the community level, most studies on Spanish language use depend on anecdotal data and interview-surveys of individuals that provide attitudinal information and self-assessment of language use and maintenance (see Portes study, cited in Sontag 1993). These studies have not allowed for indications of the actual proficiency of the surveyed population in one or both languages, nor of actual language use within different communities and in a variety of domains. More attention clearly needs to be centered on functions within particular social spaces and in relation to socio-spatial practices and power relations. It is the ensemble of social relations and situational factors such as audience, speech acts, social functions, domain, as well as generation, age, class, national origin, even mood, that determine language choice and language variety or register. Thus, given the various possible combinations of these factors, within any given social site intimate/familial, informal, and formal varieties of language may intersect. That is to say, no social site is limited to one language variety, nor do divisions of social space in terms of private and public hold as determining categories since the private and public always overlap. Likewise formal, informal, intimate, and familial spaces also intersect, giving rise to continuous shifting between varieties and sometimes between languages.

As a result, there is no set pattern of language use that can be established to describe the current diversity of Latino families. All that can be said, following Lewis, is that there is a great deal of dynamic bilingualism in the border states and beyond. This dynamic or changing bilingualism is triggered by occupational and/or geographical mobility and often signals a beginning shift in language function from one language to another (Lewis 1972; Sánchez 1983). Once the overlapping is widespread, with both languages competing for particular functions within particular social sites (a case of transitional bilingualism), then, inevitably, one of the languages will come to dominate and displace the other. A more stable bilingualism would call this model of language shift into question, although historically a balanced bilingualism is more often policy than reality, as in the case, for example, of Belgium, where regional monolingualism (French or Flemish) is the norm. In the United States, predictions of language shift for second- and third-generation Spanish speakers are generally based on the assumption that Spanish will continue to be a minority language. What will transpire when Latinos become the majority in the state of California and in particular regions of the Southwest is another matter; given two supranational languages (English and Spanish), the choice will likely be as much political as economic and cultural.

Language and Culture

Language and culture are not of course synonymous. In fact, language is sometimes said to be the carrier or vector of culture, although clearly more than one culture can share the same language, as is evident in comparing a former colonial power, for example Spain, and a former colony, any one of the Latin American countries. Culture is of course not nation- or language-specific, as there are generally a variety of cultures within any one country, and one can point to marked differences between cultural practices in nations speaking the same language (for example, Mexico and Spain). Aspects of one culture may be shared by more than one language as well, as is evident in the internationalization of particular aspects of U.S. culture shared by the bourgeoisie of the Western world, whether English, French, German, Dutch, Spanish, Swedish, Danish, or Portuguese. The same is true for Latin America, as indicated, for example, by Carlos Monsiváis, who has written on the Northamericanization of bourgeois culture in Mexico City. The increasing "USAmericanization" of the entertainment industry worldwide likewise has important implications that often transcend class, culture, and language.

Culture, we know, is both material and discursive. It is the sum of the cultural production and cultural (i.e., economic, social, political) practices of a community, including a collectivity's way of life on the basis of structural positioning and its patterns of housing, dress, eating, work, and leisure; but culture is also a construct, a discursive formulation of the history, social practices, traditions, and identity of a collectivity. This cognitive mapping is especially evident in cultural production, be it in literature, music, film, or other signifying practices through which a collectivity makes sense of its social space (Jameson 1991, 51). The fact that culture is an ideological construction allows as well for cultural "inventions" or the retrieval of residual culture, often made necessary by particular histories of language suppression, cultural oppression, or proto-nationalism. Smith, for example, in discussing "invented traditions" notes that the Scots invented the tradition of tartan and kilt in the mid-eighteenth century (1991, 177). Deane, on the other hand, makes the point that when late-nineteenth century England, seeking to revive its national identity, determined to supplement the national character with the Celtic element, it gave the Irish the opportunity to modify the Celt into Gael and to use this identity as the basis for constructing their radical difference and a movement for liberation. In this fashion, their very Celtic nationalism was, in part, produced by the colonial power that suppressed it (Deane 1990, 11–13). Culture and descent thus appear to be stressed and highlighted in areas on the verge of losing their language in order to heighten ethnic or national identity. These two examples are striking for their similarities to U.S. Southwest experiences. Here attempts to bolster national identity through a multiethnic supplementarity have recently called for a recognition of multinational and multiethnic roots, evident in a series of televised programs on early Jewish, Italian, and Chinese immigrants, African slavery and forced migration, the Mafia, the westward movement of white and black settlers, and Japanese displacement to relocation camps during World War II. To a degree, this media recognition is meant to disarm and channel ethnicism through appropriation and selective rendering of ethnic experiences. The Latino experience, on the other hand, has not been as visible on television, although this also is changing. But in schools in the Southwest, inclusion of units on a historical Spanish and Mexican past have served to affirm Chicano/Latino ties to the territory and to mark historical changes. As a result, students whose parents were deprived of knowledge of their past are today being made aware, at least minimally, of ethnic roots and imperialist policies that led to U.S. expansionism and the appropriation of half of the Mexican territory in 1846–1847, even as Latino history is integrated into the U.S. national narrative.

The relation between language and culture is thus intimate but one does not imply the other. Nationalism or ethnicism may in fact call for stressing one or the other or both. In the U.S. Southwest, however, there is no "Spanish" culture, only a diversity of Latino cultures, but the Spanish language has been linked to these cultures at every level, especially within cultural production. Despite what writers like Rodríguez (1981) have said—in ignorance or perhaps because he himself never developed a network of Spanish discourses for multiple functions in both private and public spheres—Spanish has been, since the sixteenth century in some cases and since the eighteenth in others, both a private and a public language in the Southwest. Before 1846 (1836 in Texas) Spanish was of course the official and dominant language of the Spanish and later Mexican Northwest. After the U.S. invasion, Spanish continued to be the language of the conquered population and the language of most of their oral and written cultural production, including music, poetry, narrative, and theater. The testimonials of the californios interviewed by Hubert H. Bancroft for his historiographic project, for example, are all narrated in Spanish. The early literature (poetry and romantic novels) produced in New Mexico after 1846 is also in Spanish (Leal 1985). Kanellos and Miguélez have traced the history of Spanish and Mexican theater in the Southwest from the sixteenth century to the twentieth century and documented the various Mexican troupes and special theaters constructed for various Spanish-language traveling theater companies.

In the nineteenth century, as in the twentieth, Spanish as a "print" language was most in evidence in the regional Spanish-language newspapers, such as San Antonio's *El Bejareño*, San Francisco's *La Gaceta, La Crónica*, and *El Nuevo Mundo*, Brownsville's *El Cronista del Valle*, Las Vegas, New Mexico's *El Hispano Americano*, Santa Barbara, California's *La Gaceta* or Laredo's *El Correo de Laredo*, all of which attest to the formal and public function of the Spanish language in the Southwest even after invasion (Tatum 1981, 58; Rodríguez 1983, 208). By the twentieth century each major city of the Southwest had at least one Spanish-language newspaper. Chief among them would be *La Prensa* (San Antonio), *La Opinión* (Los Angeles), *El Tucsonense* (Tucson), *La Crónica* and *El Demócrata Fronterizo* (Laredo). In areas where there was no separate Spanish-language publication, separate Spanish-language columns would often be included on a regular basis as part of English-language newspapers. Border cities have also had access to Mexican newspapers. Tatum estimates that between 1848 and 1958 about 400 Spanish-language newspapers appeared (58). More recently, as might be expected, the circulation of Spanish language newspapers has increased notably; in 1987, for example, Los Angeles had three daily newspapers: *La Opinión*, with a circulation of about 72,000, *Noticias del Mundo*, between 35,000 and 50,000 readers; and *El Diario*, with a circulation of 40,000 (Rosenstiel 1987). The three newspapers combined offered advertisers over 150,000 readers each day.

Spanish has had a long-standing place as the language of radio as well. The decade of the 1930s would bring the creation of two powerful Mexican radio stations, XEQ and XEW, whose transmission could be picked up throughout the U.S. Southwest, allowing the population of Mexican origin at least an evening (when reception of the airwaves was more likely) of Spanish-language music, newscasts, comedy hours, mysteries, romantic radio dramas and variety shows (Ybarra-Frausto 1983). During this same period the production of the Mexican film industry featuring Mexico's most famous screen stars (Pedro Infante, Jorge Negrete, Gloria Marín, Pedro Armendáriz, María Félix, Emilio Tuero, Dolores del Río, Carlos López Moctezuma, and many others), reached Latino movie houses in the Southwest, where a faithful clientele lined up every weekend to see these Spanish-language films. Now, of course, these and hundreds of other films produced since that golden era are available at local video stores in the Southwest and beyond, specializing in Spanish-language music (cassettes and compact discs) and Latin American and Spanish videos, along with a wide range of more current video fare.

The advent of television and the availability of VCRs have led to the closing of many Spanish-language movie houses, except in the larger cities where theaters like El Million Dollar in Los Angeles have served as much for film showings as for live musical variety shows. It is, however, Spanish-language television, available locally and via cable, that has best served to create an "imagined" national Latino community, to an extent that Spanish-language theater, newspapers, magazines, or radio never did, for these stations have created a nationwide network of viewers heretofore unimaginable. It is now possible to transmit the same message in Spanish to millions of viewers in New York, Seattle, Chicago, Miami, El Paso, San Benito, San Francisco, and San Diego, and furthermore, for this programming to be shared by viewers in Guadalajara, Caracas, and Madrid. Likewise, Spanish-language radio, with its steady stream of popular Latin American hits, rivals the outreach capacity of television, but only in a limited sense, for radio stations do not generally transmit beyond a few hundred miles. Radio stations based along the Mexican border, although transmitting from the United States, have the capacity of reaching the entire Southwest, Northwest, and the western part of Mexico. Night radio programs often serve for the transmission of messages from Mexican nationals in the United States to family members in various parts of the Mexican republic; other times family members in Mexico resort to the use of these same airwaves to search for and contact their relatives in the United States especially during times of family crisis.

Local radio stations, on the other hand, serve as an important network uniting immediate communities and barrios. These Spanish-language stations did not exist in the 1920s and 1930s, for then only limited blocks of time sold to brokers were made available for Spanish programming. In 1979, Gutiérrez and Schement estimated a total of 41 Spanish-language radio stations in the Southwest. By 1980 there were 67 Spanish-language radio stations in the United States and in the year 2000 there are at least 559, with new stations opening up in small midwest towns as well as in larger cities across the country (Tobar 2000, A18). Already in 1973 there were over 250 radio stations airing some segments of Spanish-language programming in the United States and by 1978 there were over 600, with 100 of these stations broadcasting almost entirely in Spanish (Gutiérrez and Schement, 1979, 5). The increase in Spanish-language radio stations and partial programming in the 1990s is undeniably directly linked to the demographic growth. In Los Angeles, with seven Spanish stations in 1991 (Puig 1991, 9), it is, as previously indicated, a Spanish-language station, KLAX-FM, that has the largest audience of all radio stations in the city (Quintanilla 1993, E2). Local Spanish-language stations in the United States serve an important function beyond advertising goods and services; they too create a sense of community and belonging in the process of transmitting not only news broadcasts, popular music and radio soaps, but also public service announcements and calls for assistance, for example to aid earthquake or hurricane victims in Latin America (Puig 1991, 89), and more importantly, for political action, as in the call in 1994 for support of what was a massive Latino demonstration against Proposition 187. Because these Spanish-language stations cater primarily to the largest Latino group, the Chicanos/Mexicanos (9), they not only provide an "imagined" interlocutor to Latinos suffering from isolation, but they acculturate other Latinos to the regional Mexican culture. Latinos residing in border towns have of course had Mexican radio stations available for a longer period of time. With an increase in Spanish-language radio stations throughout the country—and often in even the smallest of communities such as Liberal, Kansas, population 17,000 (Tobar 2000, A1), where stations can be found changing from an English format to Mexican *ranchera* music, for example— the "border" creeps ever further north.

These Spanish-language radio stations of course appeal primarily to new immigrants and older Latino adults, since Latino teenagers and young adults are more likely to listen to English-language stations. In fact, popular dance music and "oldie goldie" stations in Los Angeles have a large Latino audience (Puig 1991, 89). For this reason, in an effort to appeal to the eighteen-to-thirty-four-year-old Latino listener, some stations, such as

KLVE-FM in Los Angeles, offer selections by more contemporary artists, rock in Spanish, and the music of well-known U.S. stars who record in both Spanish and English. Far from fearing total acculturation of the young and language loss, managers of these Spanish-language stations indicate that as teenagers mature and become aware of their ethnicity, they tend to return to the radio stations favored by their parents. These monolingual Spanish stations also predict a growing bilingual media (with bilingual deejays who code-switch, as is common in Texas radio stations, for example), and even Spanish-language talk radio, as already exists in Miami (90) and Los Angeles.

The power of Spanish-language media has of course been recognized by marketing experts and there is ample proof of massive Spanish-language advertising of products previously advertised only in English. This advertising is not of course limited to television, radio, and newspaper ads, for there are now billboards and busboards in Spanish throughout Latino communities, as well as Spanish-language newspaper inserts and flyers, and increasingly, ads on the Internet. More importantly, the products, the commodities themselves, now often offer bilingual, and since NAFTA, trilingual, instructions on use or preparation. Public spaces, such as bus and train stations, airports, and post offices also offer instructions in Spanish, as do numerous business and public centers, telephone operators, and signs, particularly public and traffic signs. Utility bills are often bilingual as well. The proliferation of printed Spanish has undoubtedly changed dramatically in the last twenty years. Even the California state lottery offers Spanish-language oral and printed instructions at every computerized Lotto stand. The impact of the Latino community on the market goes beyond language, as is evident in the availability of consumer goods targeted for this group but now consumed by the general public. Fruits and vegetables previously only available in Latino stores, frozen Mexican food (burritos, tacos, tamales, enchiladas, etc.), canned *menudo*, salsa, canned refried beans, corn leaves and cornmeal dough (masa) for the making of tamales, corn and flour tortillas, Mexican sweet bread, religious candles, and piñatas are now available in most mainstream supermarkets of the Southwest. Even Planters Peanuts has come out with a spicy peanut assortment previously only found in Mexican and Chinese stores. Consumerism, like tourism, has finally allowed the market to discover a Mexican past and present. Thus all cultural spaces can be appropriated by the market, commodified and emptied of political potential. The "border" itself, as a cultural configuration, has been converted into an accessible artifact (as in the TV ad "Run for the border"), at the same time that, for undocumented workers, it is a barrier, always potentially deadly, to surmount.

Despite the proliferation of the printed word in Spanish advertising, publishing of Latino research and creative works in Spanish continues to be less widespread. The few token apertures in mainstream presses have been, for the most part, in English, although there is now some evidence of bilingual marketing—particularly of Latina works by mainstream presses—as in the case of Cisneros's fiction. The same is true for filmmaking, with limited exceptions. Minority publishers are also moving toward English-language publication, almost exclusively. For example, a fast screening of the 1993 catalog of Arte Público Press, the most influential Latino press in this country today, would reveal that out of about 176 titles, only twenty are works in Spanish. Professional and educated Latinos, especially those who are not first-generation scholars or writers, are writing primarily in English. In this regard, it is important to recall that only about 10 percent of Latinos complete four or more years of college, as compared to 22.3 percent of the non-Latino population (U.S. Bureau of the Census 1991a, 3; 1991c, 2). The educational attainment rates differ substantially by Latino origin, however, with only 6.2 percent of those of Mexican origin completing four years of college or more, as compared to 18.5 percent of those of Cuban origin (see table 5). What is clear, however, is that the English-writing intellectual Latino elite often has little to communicate to the incoming Spanish-speaking Latino/a immigrants or to the working-class Latinos/ as in the barrios and ghettos of metropolitan areas. These academics are producing for mainstream English-speaking America and for other college and educated/assimilated Latinos. Tapping the 22 percent of Latinos who move beyond high school and the 51.3 percent who graduate from high school (1991a, 3) as potential readers or viewers would, on the other hand, enable writers to bridge the gaps now opening up between Latino culture producers and the general Latino population. Spanish-language publications could target the majority of Latinos in the United States today, but this market is being served by Mexican rather than U.S. Latino publishers.

Conclusion

Latinos in the United States, as we have sought to underscore, are a diverse population, multinational in origin, and multiracial. The Spanish presently being spoken in the border states reflects this multinational diversity. Today the entire linguistic map of Latin America and Spain, all the posited dialectal zones (Canfield 1981; Cárdenas 1970) can be found in the U.S. Southwest, where on the basis of intonation, morphology, pronunciation, and vocabulary one can place peninsular, Chilean, Argentinean, Cuban, Puerto Rican, Salvadoran, Guatemalan, Peruvian, Ecuadorian, Colombian, Mexican, and Chicano varieties in schools, supermarkets, colleges, and universities, on city buses and trains, at workplaces, beauty salons, department stores, and large retail stores (see tables 12 and 13). The multiple varieties spoken within each nation-state have migrated north, producing a linguistic state of flux; only time will reveal which elements from which varieties survive and predominate in the Southwest. Undoubtedly, given the number of Mexican immigrants and their historical and kinship ties to long-time residents of the Southwest (see tables 4, 13, and 14), it will in all likelihood be Mexican Spanish varieties that will dominate the U.S. linguistic map.

The relation of Spanish to English is clear for the present. Spanish is a minority language, subordinate to the dominant language and in danger of being displaced as the home and community language of second- and third-generation Latinos. Its future is not as clear given the rapid demographic, economic and political changes already evident today and in gestation for the next century (see tables 4, 9, and 15). Will economic interests prevail, as in the case of Ireland, and lead to mass language shift or will mass immigration and a growing Latino population shift the balance in the direction of Spanish? Will the United States become a predominantly Spanish-speaking country? Will the decline of nation-states and the creation of supranational entities lead to an Anglicization of the entire continent? Surely Nicolás Guillén's worst nightmare ("el mundo todo yanqui, todo Faubus/ ... Pensad por un momento, imaginadlo un solo instante") cannot lie ahead. The scenario of a Spanish-speaking Latino population at the service of transnational corporations in the management of the Latin American continent is no more comforting. Perhaps multilingualism and cultural diversity in the United States and especially in the Southwest will be maintained. The recent success of striking janitors in Southern California, who despite their diverse racial and ethnic composition came together as a class in their labor struggles, is an indication of transracial, transethnic, and translingual alliances. Class, then, can become a modality for the affirmation and acceptance of other types of differences. In fact, ethnicism and language loyalty could have a new role to play in the social dynamic of an international work force. Already labor organizers working with Mexicanos/Chicanos displaced in California by industries relocating to Mexico, like Navarro of the Watsonville Teamster Local 912, for example, have begun contacting and attempting to organize Mexican workers in relocated Green Giant industries in Irapuato, Mexico (Cockburn 1993, B7).

History teaches us that seven hundred years of Moorish domination of the Spanish peninsula did not eradicate the Latin languages introduced a thousand years before A.D. 711 by the Roman invaders. But the earlier Iberian languages did all disappear after the Roman invasion, leaving only a trace of their presence in the names of rivers, mountains, and towns, except of course in the case of the Basque language Euskera. This language, the origin of which is unknown, survived for one simple reason: Euskera speakers' unwillingness to acculturate and isolation in their mountainous area where they could preserve their language and culture for centuries, until industrialization brought mass migration of workers into the Basque region. At that point Euskera was on the verge of disappearing. Nationalist interests, however, and the death of the fascist dictator Franco have allowed for a revitalization of the language and its introduction into the educational system. This language policy faces an uphill battle, for as in the case of Ireland, there are relatively few speakers of Euskera left.

By contrast, the invasion of the Southwest by English speakers took place only 150 years ago and now the mass migration into the region of millions of speakers of the Spanish language is opening the doors to an ethnic and language revival. Will a stable bilingualism ensue, or will the Southwest's millions of Latinos come to speak English and only English? The dynamic bilingualism now in operation forecasts language shift, but its direction is not as evident as a decade ago. Linguistic assessments are, however, contingent and prognostications are risky. In the end, language choice will more than likely be a political as well as an economic decision. Language loyalty may in fact turn out to be the strategy needed to overcome the Latino collectivity's fragmentation. Language, ethnicity, and class are all variables that will need to be deployed for political action if the multiethnic population of the U.S. border states is, in the twenty-first century, to effectively address and change those social conditions that create and foster an unjust class structure, state violence, racism, unemployment, poverty, homelessness, drug abuse, and intra/ intergroup violence.

Appendix

Table 1. Use of Language Other Than English at Home by Origin
(in the United States in 1990 by residents 5 years old and older)

Spanish	17,345,064
French	1,930,404
German	1,547,987
Chinese	1,319,462
Italian	1,308,648
Tagalog	843,251
Polish	723,483
Korean	626,478
Vietnamese	507,069
Portuguese	430,610
Indo-European*	578,076
Indic**	555,126
Total	25,975,658

  * Indo-European languages include several European, southwest Asian, and Indian languages.
**Indic languages include languages of North India, Pakistan, and Bangladesh.
Source: U.S. Census Bureau data, cited in Quintanilla (1993).

Table 2. Use of Language Other Than English at Home by Origin
(in California in 1990 by residents 5 years old and older)

Spanish	5,478,712
Chinese	575,447
Tagalog	464,644
Vietnamese	233,074
Korean	215,845
German	165,962
Japanese	147,451
French	132,657
Italian	111,133
Portuguese	78,232
Indo-European*	231,654
Indic**	119,318

**Indo-European languages include several European, southwest Asian, and Indian languages.
**Indic languages include languages of North India, Pakistan, and Bangladesh.
Source: U.S. Census Bureau data, cited in Quintanilla (1993).

Table 3. Use of Language Other Than English at Home by Origin
(in Los Angeles County in 1990 by residents 5 years old and older)

Spanish	2,564,775
Chinese	209,107
Tagalog	155,996
Korean	124,290
Japanese	63,921
Vietnamese	51.313
French	40,921
German	39,849
Arabic	29,039
Italian	28,454

Source: U.S. Census Bureau, data cited in Quintanilla (1993).

Table 4. Latino Population of the United States by Origin

Year	Total	Mexican (%)	Puerto Rican (%)	Cuban (%)	Central & South Am. (%)	Other Latino (%)
1985	16,940,000	60.6	15.1	6.1	10.2	8.0
1987	18,790,000	63.0	12.0	5.0	11.0	8.0
1991	21,400,000*	62.6	11.1	4.9	13.8	7.6

*The 1990 Census recorded 22,354,059 "Hispanic persons."
Sources: U.S. Bureau of the Census 1985, 1987, 1991c.

Table 5. Educational Attainment Rates of Latinos by Origin
(in the United States in 1991 by percentage of population
25 years and over)

Origin	Less than five years of school	Four years of high school or more	Four years of college or more
Total Latino	1.6	51.3	9.7
Total Non-Latino	12.5	80.5	22.3
Mexican	15.9	43.6	6.2
Puerto Rican	8.4	58.0	10.1
Cuban	7.7	61.0	18.5
Central & South American	8.9	60.4	15.1
Other Latino	5.6	71.1	16.2

Source: U.S. Bureau of the Census 1991a.

Table 6. Self-Assessment with Respect to Language Choice, Discrimination, and Assessment of the United States
(5,000 eighth- and ninth-grade students of immigrant parentage in Miami and San Diego)

Student Origin	Say knowledge of English good or very good (%)	Say knowledge of parents' non-Eng. Language good or very good (%)	Prefer English over parents' native language	Experience discrimination	Consider U.S. best country in the world (%)
Cuban-American	99%	89%	94%	29%	80%
Haitian-American	95	31	87	66	35
Filipino-American	97	29	88	63	62
Mexican-American	85	80	44	65	54
Vietnamese-American	81	42	51	65	67

Source: Data from a study directed by Alejandro Portes at Johns Hopkins University, and reviewed in Sontag (1993).

Table 7. Employment and Unemployment Rates of Latinos by Origin and Sex
(in the United States in 1991 by percentage of population 16 years and over)

Total Latinos in civilian labor force		64.7 %
Latino Males in civilian labor force		78.2
Mexican	80	
Puerto Rican	66	
Cuban	73	
Central & South American	84	
Other Latino	74	
Latino Females in civilian labor force		51.4
Mexican	51	
Puerto Rican	42	
Cuban	55	
Central & South American	58	
Other Latino	56	
Latino males in the civilian labor force who are unemployed	10.6	
Latino females in the civilian labor force who are unemployed	9.2	
Total Latinos in the civilian labor force who are unemployed	10.0	

Source: U.S. Bureau of the Census 1991c.

Table 8. Poverty Rates among Latinos by Origin
(in the United States in 1990 by percentage of population 18 years of age and over)

Total Latino		38
Mexican	36	
Puerto Rican	57	
Cuban	31	
Central & South American	35	
Other Latino	36	
Total non-Latino		18

Source: U.S. Bureau of the Census 1991c.

Table 9. Latino Population in Border States, 1990

	All persons	Total Latino	Non-Lat. White	Non-Lat. Asian	Non-Lat. Black	Non-Lat. Native Am.
California	29,760,021	7,687,938	17,029,126	2,710,353	2,092,446	184,065
Texas	16,986,510	4,339,905	10,291,680	303,825	1,976,360	52,803
Arizona	3,665,228	688,338	2,626,185	51,530	104,809	190,091
New Mexico	1,515,069	579,224	764,164	12,587	27,642	128,068

Note: Latino population includes people of all races.
Sources: U.S. Bureau of the Census 1992b, 1992c, 1992d, 1992e.

Table 10. Latino Population Distribution in Border States and Selected Border Counties, 1990

	Total population	Total Latino population	Percentage of population that is Latino
California	29,760,021	7,687,938	25.8
Texas	16,986,510	4,339,905	25.5
Arizona	3,665,228	688,338	18.8
New Mexico	1,515,069	579,224	38.2
California counties			
Los Angeles	8,863,164	3,351,242	
San Diego	2,498,016	510,781	
Orange	2,410,556	564,828	
Santa Clara	1,497,577	314,564	
San Bernardino	1,418,380	378,582	
Alameda	1,279,182	181,805	
Riverside	1,170,413	307,514	
Sacramento	1,041,219	121,544	
Fresno	667,490	236,634	
Kern	543,477	151,995	
Imperial	109,303	71,935	
Texas counties			
Harris	2,818,199	644,935	
Dallas	1,852,810	315,630	
Bexar	1,185,394	589,180	
El Paso	591,610	411,619	

Hidalgo	383,545	326,972	
Cameron	260,120	212,995	
Midland	106,611	22,780	
San Patricio	58,749	29,809	
Starr	40,518	39,390	
Maverick	36,378	34,024	
Willacy	17,705	14,937	
Dimmit	10,443	8,688	
Zapata	9,279	7,519	
Sutton	4,135	1,866	
Arizona counties			
Maricopa	2,122,101	345,498	
Pima	666,880	163,262	
Yuma	106,895	43,388	
Santa Cruz	29,676	23,221	
New Mexico counties			
Bernalillo	480,577	178,310	
Doña Ana	135,550	76,448	
Santa Fe	98,928	48,939	
Valencia	45,235	22,733	
Río Arriba	36,365	24,953	
Los Alamos	18,115	2,008	

Sources: U.S. Bureau of the Census 1992b, 1992c, 1992d, 1992e.

Table 11. Latino Population Distribution in Border States and Selected Border Cities, 1990

	Total population	Total Latino population
Texas cities		
El Paso	515,342	355,669
Laredo	122,899	115,360
Brownsville	98,962	89,206
McAllen	84,021	64,672
Harlingen	48,735	34,613
Del Rio	30,705	23,698
Edinburg City	29,885	25,668
Eagle Pass	20,651	19,678
Kingsville	25,276	15,765
New Mexico cities		
Albuquerque	384,736	132,706
Las Cruces	62,126	29,124

Sources: U.S. Bureau of the Census 1992d, 1992e.

Table 12. Latino Population Distribution in Border States by Origin, 1990

	Total Latino	Mexican	Puerto Rican	Cuban	Other Latino
California	7,687,938	6,118,996	126,417	71,977	1,370,548
Texas	4,339,905	3,890,820	42,981	18,195	387,909
Arizona	688,338	616,195	8,256	2,079	61,808
New Mexico	579,224	328,836	2,635	903	246,850

Sources: U.S. Bureau of the Census 1992b, 1992c, 1992d, 1992e.

Table 13. California Latino Population by Origin, 1989
(in percent)

Mexican	85
Salvadoran	7
Guatemalan	4
Other	4

Source: Hurtado 1992, cited in Latino Eligibility Task Force 1993.

Table 14. Geographic Distribution of the U.S. Latino Population, 1989
(in percent)

California	34
Texas	21
Arizona, Colorado, New Mexico	8
New York	10
New Jersey	3
Florida	8
Illinois	4
Remainder of U.S.	12

Source: U.S. Bureau of the Census 1989a.

Table 15. Population Projections by Race and Spanish Origin, 1982-2080
(numbers in millions)

	Total	Latino	White Non-Latino	Black	Other races
1982	232.1	15.8	183.5	27.7	5.9
1985	238.6	17.3	186.8	29.1	6.4
1990*	249.7	19.9	192.0	31.4	7.5
1995	259.6	22.6	196.2	33.7	8.5
2000	268.0	25.2	198.9	35.8	9.5
2010	283.2	30.8	202.6	40.0	11.7
2020	296.6	36.5	204,5	44.2	13.7
2030	304.8	41.9	202.4	47.6	15.6
2040	308.6	46.7	197.2	50.3	17.3
2050	309.5	50.8	190.8	52.3	18.9
2060	309.7	54.2	184.8	53.7	20.4

| 2070 | 310.4 | 57.2 | 180.0 | 54.9 | 21.9 |
| 2080 | 310.8 | 59.6 | 176.0 | 55.7 | 23.4 |

Note: Data for middle series projections. Numbers do not add up to total because people of Spanish origin may be of any race.

* Projected figures in 1982 for 1990 (19.9 million Latinos) in fact proved inaccurate. The 1990 Census Bureau figures predict a Latino population of 22,354,059 Latinos, a statistic that corresponds to the projected figures for 1995. An addition of an estimated two million undocumented Latinos would place the actual population in 1990 near the projected population for the year 2000 ten years later.

Source: U.S. Bureau of the Census 1982, table P.

Notes

This article has undergone revision since its initial publication. My thanks to Beatrice Pita for all her helpful comments and to Angie Chabram-Dernersesian for the opportunity to revise this essay.

1. Responding to this demographic reality (albeit recently) the AFL-CIO is calling for amnesty for six million undocumented immigrants and repeal of the federal sanctions against employers who hire them (*Los Angeles Times* 18 February 2000, A15).

2. In fact the town of El Cenizo, Texas, where 80 percent of the 7,800 residents speak only Spanish, recently made Spanish the official language of the town (USA Today 17 December 1999, 21A).

3. Unfortunately most of the Native American languages spoken in California before 1846 are now for the most part extinct; only thirty of some one hundred native languages previously used in the area are still spoken, and only by a handful of American Indians (Feldman 1993, A3).

4. Although the first permanent Spanish settlement at Santa Fe dates from 1610, most of the Spanish settlement in New Mexico took place during the 1700s.

5. To counter this density, there are already plans to relocate and disperse this population; in the future, according to Henry G. Cisneros, former secretary of Housing and Urban Development, the push will be to move minorities out from the inner cities to the suburbs through the construction of public housing outside the metropolitan area (DeParle 1993, A8).

6. Latino men, for example, are more likely to be employed in operator, fabricator and laborer occupations (29 percent) and in service occupations (54 percent) than non-Latino men (U.S. Bureau of the Census 1989a, 4). Latino women, on the other hand, are more likely to be employed in service industries (26 percent), in technical, sales, and administrative support (40 percent) and in positions as operators, fabricators, and laborers (14 percent) than non-Latino women (U.S. Bureau of the Census 1991c, 3).

7. Black leaders such as Jesse Jackson and other human rights activists who have protested the U.S. government's policy of forcible return of Haitians fleeing their country recognize the many faces of racism and have joined forces to counter it.

References

Acuña, Rodolfo. 1990. "California Commentary: Life Behind Bars Is No Way to Build Character." *Los Angeles Times*, 12 February, B7.

Amin, Samir. 1992. *Empire of Chaos*. New York: Monthly Review Press.

Anderson, Benedict. 1987. *Imagined Communities*. London: Verso.

Avila, Joaquín Guadalupe, and Ramona Godoy. 1979. "Bilingual/Bicultural Education and the Law." In *Language Development in a Bilingual Setting*, ed. Eugen J. Briere, 15–33. Los Angeles: National Dissemination and Assessment Center.

Balibar, Etienne. 1991. "Racism and Nationalism." In *Race, Nation, Class: Ambiguous Identities*, edited by Etienne Balibar and Immanuel Wallerstein. London: Verso.

Barrera, Mario. 1979. *Race and Class in the Southwest: A Theory of Racial Inequality*. Notre Dame, Ind.: University of Notre Dame Press.

Bunting, Glenn F., and Alan C. Miller. 1993. "Feinstein Raises Immigration Profile." *Los Angeles Times*, 18 July, A3, A18.

Canfield, D. Lincoln. 1981. *Spanish Pronunciation in the Americas*. Chicago: University of Chicago Press.

Cárdenas, Daniel. 1970. *Dominant Spanish Dialects Spoken in the United States*. Arlington, Va.: Center for Applied Linguistics.

Chatterjee, Partha. 1985. *Nationalist Thought and the Colonial World: A Derivative Discourse*. London: Zed.

Chávez, Stephanie. 1993. "Panel Assails State's Bilingual Education." *Los Angeles Times*, 10 July, A19.

Cleland, Robert Glass. 1947. *From Wilderness to Empire: A History of California, 1542–1900*. New York: Alfred A. Knopf.

Cockburn, Alexander. 1993. "When Jobs Go South — A True Parable." *Los Angeles Times*, 27 July, B7.

Cornelius, Wayne A. 1993. "Neo-nativists Feed on Myopic Fears." *Los Angeles Times*, 12 July, B7.

Davis, Angela. 1997. "Race and Criminalization." In *The House that Race Built*, edited by Wahneema Lubiano, 264–79. New York: Pantheon Books.

Deane, Seamus. 1990. Introduction to *Nationalism, Colonialism and Literature*. Minneapolis: University of Minnesota Press.

DeParle, Jason. 1993. "Housing Secretary Carves out Role as a Lonely Clarion Against Racism." *New York Times*, 8 July, A8.

Feldman, Paul. 1993. "Breathing New Life into Dying Languages." *Los Angeles Times*, 12 July, A3, A20–1.

Foucault, Michel. 1986. "Of Other Spaces." *Diacritics* 16, no. 1: 22–7.

Gilroy, Paul. 1987. *"There Ain't No Black in the Union Jack."* London: Hutchinson.

Guillén, Nicolás. 1958. "Little Rock." In *La paloma de vuelo popular*. Buenos Aires: Editorial Losada.

Gutiérrez, Felix F., and Jorge Reina Schement. 1979. *Spanish-Language Radio in the Southwestern United States*. Mexican American Studies Monograph no. 5. Austin: University of Texas.

Havemann, Joel, and Norman Kempster. 1993. "The Case of the Disappearing Worker: What's Gone Wrong?" *Los Angeles Times*, 6 July, 1,4.

Hobsbawm, E. J. 1992. *Nations and Nationalism since 1780*. Cambridge: Cambridge University Press.

Hurtado, Aída, David E. Hayes-Bautista, R. Burciaga Valdez, and Anthony C. R. Hernández. 1992. *Redefining California: Latino Social Engagement in a Multicultural Society*. Los Angeles: University of California Chicano Studies Research Center.

Jameson, Fredric. 1991. *Postmodernism or The Cultural Logic of Late Capitalism*. Durham: Duke University Press.

Kanellos, Nicolás. 1983. "Two Centuries of Hispanic Theatre in the Southwest." In *Mexican American Theatre*, ed. Nicolás Kanellos. Houston: Arte Público Press.

Keller, Gary D., and Karen S. Van Hooft. 1982. "A Chronology of Bilingualism and Bilingual Education in the U.S." In *Bilingual Education for Hispanic Students in the United States*, ed. Joshua Fishman and Gary D. Keller, 13–19. New York: Teachers College Press.

Latino Eligibility Task Force. 1993. *Latino Student Eligibility and Participation in the University of California*. Santa Cruz: University of California.

Leal, Luis. 1985. *Aztlán y México: Perfiles literarios e históricos*. Binghamton, N.Y.: Bilingual Review Press.

Lefebvre, Henri. 1991. *The Production of Space*. Cambridge: Blackwell.

Lewis, E. Glyn. 1972. *Multilingualism in the Soviet Union*. The Hague: Mouton.

López, Ronald W., and Darryl D. Enos. 1973. "Spanish Language Only Television in Los Angeles County." *Aztlán* 4, no. 2: 283–313.

Macnamara, John. 1975. "Success and Failures in the Movement for the Restoration of Irish." In *Can Language Be Planned?* ed. Joan Rubin and Bjorn H. H. Jernudd. Honolulu: University of Hawaii Press.

McDonnell, Patrick. 1987. "North County's Farm Worker Camps: Third World Squalor Amid Affluence." *Los Angeles Times*, 17 August, sec. 2, 1–3.

Meisler, Stanley. 1993. "Migration Viewed as 'Human Crisis.'" *Los Angeles Times*, 7 July, A4.

"Migration Across Borders, to Cities Nears Crisis, U. N. Says." 1993. *Washington Post*, 7 July, A1, A24.

Miguélez, Armando. 1983. "El Teatro Carmen (1915–1923): Centro del Arte Escénico Hispano en Tucson." In *Mexican American Theatre*, edited by Nicolás Kanellos, 52–67. Houston: Arte Público Press.

Miller, Alan C., and Ronald J. Ostrow. 1993. "Immigration Policy Failures Invite Overhaul." *Los Angeles Times*, 11 July, A1, A22–3.

Miller, Greg. 1993. "Border Conference to Urge Projects by Private Industry." *Los Angeles Times*, 15 July, A5.

Miyoshi, Masao. 1993. "A Borderless World? From Colonialism to Transnationalism and the Decline of the Nation-State." *Critical Inquiry* 19 (summer 1993): 726–51.

Monsiváis, Carlos. 1984. "Cultura Urbana y Creación Intelectual." In *Cultura y creación intelectual en América Latina*, edited by Pablo González Casanova, 25–41. Mexico: Siglo XXI.

Navarrete, Rubén. 1992. "Should Latinos Support Curbs on Immigration?" *Los Angeles Times*, 5 July, M1, M6.

O'Donnell, Santiago. 1993. "2 D.C. Officers Say Speaking Spanish Got Them Reprimanded." *Washington Post*, 11 June, B3.

Passel, Jeffrey S. 1992. "Demographic Profile." *NACLA* 26, no. 2 (September): 21.

Puig, Claudia. 1991. "Off the Charts." *Los Angeles Times*, 7 April, 9, 89, 90.

Quintanilla, Michael. 1993. "They Don't Understand." *Los Angeles Times*, 5 July, E1–2.

Rodríguez, Juan. 1983. "Notas sobre la evolución de la prosa de ficción." In *A través de la frontera*, 207–13. Mexico: Instituto de Investigaciones UNAM.

Rodríguez, Richard. 1986. "SIN Is In." *California*, April, 78–80,102–4, 107–9.

———. 1981. *Hunger of Memory*. Boston: David R. Godine.

Rosenstiel, Thomas B. 1987. "Los Angeles Papers Speak a New Language." *Los Angeles Times*, 9 November, A1, A19.

Rumberger, Russell, and Patricia Gándara. 2000. "Crucial Issues in California Education 2000: The Schooling of English Learners." *Newsletter* (University of California Linguistic Minority Report) 9, no. 3 (spring): 1–2.

Sánchez, Rosaura. 1983. *Chicano Discourse: socio-historic perspectives*. Rowley, Mass.: Newbury House Publishers.

San Juan, E. 1989. "Problems in the Marxist Project of Theorizing Race." *Rethinking Marxism* 2, no. 2: 58–80.

Shorris, Earl. 1992. "Latinos: The Complexity of Identity." *NACLA* 26, no. 2 (September): 19–26.

Skelton, George. 1993. "Feinstein Takes Immigration Out of Closet." *Los Angeles Times*, 12 July, A3.

Smith, Anthony D. 1991. *The Ethnic Origins of Nations*. Cambridge: Blackwell.

Sontag, Deborah. 1993. "A Fervent 'No' to Assimilation in New America." *New York Times*, 29 June, A6.

Tatum, Charles. 1981. "Some Examples of Chicano Prose Fiction of the Nineteenth and Early Twentieth Centuries." *Revista Chicano-Riqueña* 9, no. 1: 58–67.

Tobar, Hector. 2000. "Heartland Tuning In to Spanish." *Los Angeles Times*, 23 June, A1, A18.

Trombley, William. 1986. "Prop. 63 Roots Traced to Small Michigan City." *Los Angeles Times*, 20 October, sec. 1, 3, 20–1.

U.S. Bureau of the Census. 1992a. *1990 Census of Population. General Population Characteristics. Metropolitan Areas.* CP-1-1B. Washington, D.C.

———. 1992b. *1990 Census of Population. General Population Characteristics. Arizona.* CP-1-4. Washington, D.C.

———. 1992c. *1990 Census of Population. General Population Characteristics. California.* CP-1-6. Washington, D.C.

———. 1992d. *1990 Census of Population. General Population Characteristics. New Mexico.* CP-1-33. Washington, D.C.

———. 1992e. *1990 Census of Population. General Population Characteristics. Texas.* CP-1-45. Section 1 of 2. Washington, D.C.

————. 1991a. *Educational Attainment in the United States: March 1991 and 1990*. Prepared by Robert Kominski and Andrea Adams. Current Population Reports: Population Characteristics. Series P-20, no. 462. Washington, D.C.

————. 1991b. *The Asian and Pacific Islander Population in the United States: March 1991 and 1990*. Prepared by Claudette E. Bennett. Current Population Reports: Population Characteristics. Series P-20, no. 459. Washington, D.C.

————. 1991c. *The Hispanic Population in the United States: March 1991*. Prepared by Jesús M. García and Patricia A. Montgomery. Current Population Reports: Population Characteristics. Series P-20, no. 455. Washington, D.C.

————. 1989a. *The Hispanic Population in the United States: March 1989*. Prepared by Jorge H. del Pinal and Carmen DeNavas. Current Population Reports: Population Characteristics. Series P-20, no. 444. Washington, D.C.

————. 1989b. *Population Estimates by Race and Hispanic Origin for States, Metropolitan Areas, and Selected Counties: 1980 to 1985*. Prepared by David L. Word. Current Population Reports: Population Estimates and Projections. Series P-25, no.1040-RD-1. Washington, D.C.

————. 1987. *Persons of Spanish Origin: March 1987*. Current Population Reports: Population Characteristics. Washington, D.C.

————. 1985. *Persons of Spanish Origin: March 1985*. Current Population Reports: Population Characteristics. Washington, D.C.

————. 1982. *Projections of the Population of the United States, by Age, Sex and Race: 1988 to 2080*. Prepared by Gregory Spencer. Current Population Reports: Population Estimates and Projections. Series P-25, no. 1018. Washington, D.C.

————. 1981. *Projection of the Hispanic Population: 1982 to 2080*. Current Population Reports: Population Estimates and Projections. Series P-25, no. 995. Washington, D.C.

Vallejo, Mariano Guadalupe. 1875. "Recuerdos Históricos y Personales Tocantes a la Alta California." Vols. 1 and 5. Manuscript, Bancroft Library, University of California at Berkeley.

Weiner, Tim. 1993. "On these Shores, Immigrants Find a New Wave of Hostility." *New York Times* 13 June, sec. 4, l.

West, Cornel. 1988. "Marxist Theory and the Specificity of Afro-American Oppression." In *Marxism and the Interpretation of Culture*, ed. Cary Nelson and Lawrence Grossberg, 17–29. Chicago: University of Illinois Press.

Ybarra-Frausto, Tomás. 1983. "La Chata Noloesca: Figura del Donaire." In *Mexican American Theatre*, ed. Nicolás Kanellos, 41–51. Houston: Arte Público Press.

The Folklore of the Freeway
Space, Culture, and Identity in Postwar Los Angeles

Eric Avila

Modern environments and experiences cut across all boundaries of geography and ethnicity, of class and nationality, of religion and ideology: in this sense, modernity can be said to unite all mankind. But it is a paradoxical unity, a unity of disunity: it pours us all into a maelstrom of perpetual disintegration and renewal, of struggle and contradiction, of ambiguity and anguish. To be modern is to be part of a universe in which, as Marx said, "all that is solid melts into air."

—Marshall Berman, *All That Is Solid Melts into Air: The Experience of Modernity*

Man loves to create roads, that is beyond dispute. But may it not be ... that he is instinctively afraid of attaining his goal and completing the edifice he is constructing? How do you know, perhaps he only likes that edifice from a distance and not at all at close range, perhaps he only likes to build it, and does not want to live in it.

—Fyodor Dostoyevsky, *Notes from the Underground*

Los Angeles in the age of the freeway saw a profound transformation in the shape of the city and the color of its inhabitants. It fulfilled its destiny by becoming the ultimate "fragmented metropolis."[1] The acceleration of suburbanization, coupled with the dramatic expansion of the city's nonwhite population (African Americans and Chicanos in particular), created a regional geography splintered into isolated pockets of race and class. As the historic ethnic diversity of communities like Boyle Heights and Watts gave way to expanding brown barrios and black ghettos, new communities

512

sprouted on the urban fringe, insulated from the racialized masses of the inner city. This was not an accident of poor planning. It was, in fact, the outcome intended by homeowners, realtors, developers, and government officials who sought to preserve southern California's legacy of building separate and unequal communities.[2]

Various civic institutions of postwar Los Angeles underpinned the construction of suburban whiteness. Central to that process was the freeway, which furthered the production of white space within the larger urban region. The freeway did not cause white flight, but it did sharpen the contrast between white space and nonwhite space in the postwar urban region by creating a conduit for capital flight away from downtown and by wreaking havoc upon the inner-city communities of East and South Central Los Angeles. Although many urban historians have traced the evolution of the freeway system and its impact upon the spatial and economic development of the metropolis, very few have considered how diverse peoples of Los Angeles have understood and assigned meaning to that complex process.[3]

As the freeway took shape, a folklore developed in the regional culture that reflected the very different ways in which people experienced the freeway and its construction.[4] The folklore of the freeway surfaced in such diverse cultural productions as public ceremonies, theme parks, novels, murals, and poems, and reflected a cultural response to modernization in the postwar, postindustrial American city. Such cultural productions revealed a deep ambivalence about the introduction of the freeway. On the one hand, the freeway emerged in official civic culture as a symbol of progress and modernity, a harbinger of a better tomorrow. On the other hand, Chicanos and Chicanas, who suffered the imposition of the freeway upon their neighborhoods, questioned the good it brought to their city and drew upon cultural forms to record that experience. Chicanos and Chicanas are but one social group that came to terms with the Los Angeles freeway, but their interpretation of the freeway illuminates the larger cultural response to the structural transformation of urban life in postwar, postindustrial America.

Sixteen Freeways in Search of a Suburb

Central to that process was the freeway. It did not initiate residential and industrial development in suburban southern California, but it facilitated such development by paving access to undeveloped land. Under the landmark Collier Burns Act of 1947, Los Angeles County received millions of state dollars for freeway construction. Although the bill was aimed at developing the state highway system as a whole, it clearly favored the construction of freeways in the state's metropolitan areas. Thus Los Angeles County received a larger piece of the pie.[5] The construction of metropolitan freeways directed the movement of people and their money toward the suburbs and away from the inner city, promoting what some scholars call the "Lakewoodization" of suburban southern California—the process by which independent municipalities "seceded" from city and county government to form exclusive and homogeneous suburban communities.[6]

The emerging pattern of freeway construction ensured the vitality of suburban society in the Southland: a radial pattern extending outward from downtown like spokes, and a concentric pattern encircling the downtown in a series of rings. The concentric pattern of development undermined both the spatial and symbolic importance of downtown. The arc of the 405 Freeway is a good example of this kind of development because it bears no relation to the historic center of the city. It emerged during the late 1950s and early 1960s as a corridor through the affluent Westside, connecting the postwar centers of suburban whiteness in Orange County and the San Fernando Valley. Development like the 405 Freeway assisted the popular perception that Los Angeles was a centerless city, despite the thousands of people who actually lived in that center. Unlike systems of mass transportation in other American cities, which were developed to serve the downtown area, the Los Angeles freeways bolstered decentralized development and vitiated downtown.

Early on, public officials in East Los Angeles identified the economic hardship the freeway brought to their communities. Recalling J. B. Priestly's famous description of turn-of-the-century Los Angeles as "sixteen suburbs in search of a city," Ninth District Assembly Member Edward F. Elliot modified the maxim in 1961, describing postwar Los Angeles as "sixteen freeways in search of a suburb."[7] Elliot deplored the decline of downtown as an economic center of the region, pointing to the severe loss of downtown retail sales. In 1950, 75 percent of all retail sales in the city of Los Angeles occurred in the downtown district. By 1960, with the completion of suburban shopping malls and regional shopping centers, that number had dwindled to a mere 18 percent. In response to such figures, Elliot concluded that "the suburbs have taken the rest of the business." Although a complex of factors is to be held accountable for this development, the assembly member pointed to the freeways, arguing that they had become "speedways to carry the buying public through instead of into the central business area."

Elliot also decried the way in which downtown "had become encircled, cut up and glutted by freeways," recognizing that the impact of the freeways upon the Eastside was not only economic, but also physical. Certainly, the construction process itself unleashed massive destruction and chaos upon the inner-city communities of East and South Central Los Angeles. Because property values in those areas were disproportionately lower than in the suburbs, East and South Central Los Angeles became prime locations for massive interchanges consuming vast amounts of property. In Boyle Heights alone, the freeways displaced one-tenth of the local population, an especially devastating statistic in light of the vast influx of new residents to the Eastside and the desperate shortage of housing in the area.[8]

Of course, the state was aware that people were not going to welcome freeway construction in their backyards. Throughout the 1950s and 1960s, an official publicity campaign emphasized the importance of the freeways to Los Angeles and claimed overwhelming public support for freeway construction. Even those who were displaced by the freeway, according to the state, gladly abandoned their homes and communities to make way for its construction. In the process of building the Harbor Freeway through a neighborhood of East and South Central Los Angeles, for example, the California Division of Highways lauded the people of that community:

> Southerly of Exposition Boulevard, the freeway location is through an area of older houses that some of the occupants have owned for thirty years or more. Some of the occupants are older people who expected to live in their homes for the rest of their lives. It would be assumed, in approaching owners of this type that one would meet with tears, hesitation, reluctance and perhaps outright defiance when asked to move. This is not the case. The older folks seemed to have resigned themselves to the fact that they should not stand in the way of progress and gladly cooperate. This is the rule rather than the exception. We have met wholehearted cooperation and support many times where least expected.[9]

Through such allegations, the state justified the building of freeways in older, downtown neighborhoods. (Sources from those neighborhoods tell much different stories, as I shall address later.)

The Popular Culture of Progress

In the best tradition of world's fairs, expositions, and Wild West shows, which glossed over the horrors of nineteenth-century industrialization and expansion, the dark side of freeway construction was sublimated by an affirmative regional popular culture. Walt Disney, for example, went to great lengths to celebrate the construction of the freeway in Southern California. Disney not only shared the popular faith in the promise of unrestricted automobility, but also realized that the freeways, the Santa Ana Freeway in particular, were crucial to the success of his enterprise, Disneyland. Following the advice of the Stanford Research Institute, Disney strategically situated his theme park alongside the proposed route of the Santa Ana Freeway and built a parking lot twice the size of the park—the largest in the nation in the mid-1950s. In fact, Disney built a miniature road system inside his theme park and called it a "ride." The Autopia Ride was a mile-long "freeway" upon which one could safely drive miniature gasoline-powered cars. That the line for the Autopia Ride in Disneyland today is among the shortest in the park is not surprising, given the technological savvy of American audiences at the end of the twentieth century. Nonetheless, the inclusion of the Autopia Ride among the thirteen original attractions in 1955 suggests that as few as forty years ago it was possible to imagine the Los Angeles freeways as a ride—an attraction for popular fun and amusement. Indeed, freeways were attractive to Disney's suburban audiences, who readily accepted his representation of the freeway as a symbol of American progress and modernity. Along with a rocket-ship ride and a simulated lunar expedition, the freeway in 1955 seemed at home in Tomorrowland, that section of the theme park dedicated to postwar idealizations of a bright American future.

Autopia was not the earliest attempt to link the freeway to the course of American progress from sea to shining sea. In 1941, various civic officials gathered to dedicate the Pasadena Freeway, the first to open in Los Angeles. As in earlier celebrations of progress in American history, this one was explicitly racialized. Present at the ceremony, along with the mayor of Los Angeles, the governor of California, and the reigning queen of the 1941 Tournament of Roses Parade was a man described by local newspapers as "Chief Tahachwee." The so-called chief (photographs of the event suggest he was white) was dressed in a costume that resembled not the modest apparel of Southern California's indigenous populations but, rather, the wildly elaborate costume of an Indian in a Hollywood western. As if the massive feathered bonnet and excessive costume jewelry were not enough to convey authentic "Indianness," a photograph in a state publication reveals the Indian seated "Indian-style" with the state director of public works. Together, the Indian and the bureaucrat smoke a peace pipe. By 1941, stereotypical images of the "White Man's Indian" were all too familiar. The presence of a "primitive" or "savage" Indian at the opening ceremony of a freeway, however, makes clear that it belonged to an unambiguously Anglo American progress, much like its predecessor—the railroad. The presence of the friendly Indian may also have signaled the final surrender of Native Americans to the encroachment of Anglo American civilization. Indeed, official coverage of the ceremony smugly declared, "To the beating of tribal drums, Chief Tahachwee relinquished the rights of his people in the Arroyo and formally transferred the property to the State." [10]

The symbolic exploitation of Native Americans in the opening ceremony of the Pasadena Freeway is appropriate, given the fate of southern California's indigenous populations. The freeway, after all, materialized the Anglo American worldview, which saw history as a highway—an unbroken path of linear progress toward distant horizons. Such a worldview clashed with that of the Indians, who viewed the cosmos as cyclical and lived according to a principle of regenerative growth. Ultimately, that clash proved fatal for the Indian, who was unable to survive not only the degenerative forces of guns, disease, and alcohol but also the linear conception of progress in which history pushed relentlessly forward, often over the peoples who stood in its path. "Thrown onto the highway of history," Indians could not withstand the force of Anglo American progress, symbolized in the freeway.[11] Long after their conquest in Southern California, Indians could safely return as figments of the Anglo American imagination to commemorate such civic works as the freeway.

Throughout the history of American popular culture, progress has been defined as "American" in contrast to the "un-Americanness" of the Other. Often, that contrast is racialized. The opening ceremony of the Pasadena Freeway demonstrates the way public space is implicated in the contrast of white and nonwhite, using Indians as the racialized Other. Such popular signifiers of progress legitimized the physical and economic destruction wrought upon the inner-city communities of Blacks and Latinos. Although the process hardly needed legitimization—the freeway would have punctured those communities in any case—official Los Angeles (vested in such political authorities as the mayor of Los Angeles and the governor of California, and in such cultural authorities as Walt Disney) took great measures to gild the freeway with the cultural legacy of Anglo American progress in Southern California. Beneath the optimistic gloss, however, the experience of destruction and dislocation informed the cultural production of other social groups in Los Angeles during the age of the freeway.

517

The Hegemony of the Freeway

The Autopia Ride of Disneyland and the opening ceremony of the Pasadena Freeway underscore a hegemonic interpretation of the freeway, in which oppression and domination are legitimized through the production of culture. Hegemony, however, often says more about the dominator than the dominated. To end the story here would be disingenuous. More important, it would ignore those historical actors whose words and deeds complicate a facile understanding of the freeway as an incontestably hegemonic or oppressive device. Citizens of East Los Angeles (predominantly Chicano), for example, registered formal protests against the construction of the freeway throughout the 1950s. They packed public hearings with the California Division of Highways to voice their opposition; they met in neighbors' homes to organize community opposition; and they formed several community groups to fight the onslaught of the freeway, such as the Eastside Citizens' Committee Against the Freeway and the Freeway Fighters. They also wrote to local papers, which routinely published the letters of an angry community. One such letter poignantly asked the question, "Five freeways now slash through Boyle Heights, namely the San Bernardino, the Santa Ana, the Golden State and now the Pomona. Question is, how do you stop the freeways from continuing to butcher our town?"[12]

Chicanos and Chicanas took action against the freeway through other means besides the institutional networks of committee hearings, community activism, and letters to the editor. Folklore, after all, is as complex and contradictory as the people who create it. Sometimes folklore underscores the dominant perceptions of a society; other times it is a venue for alternative ones. While theme park attractions and manufactured Indians represent popular understandings of the freeway in the 1940s and 1950s, they are but one aspect of the folklore of the freeway. Chicanos and Chicanas of Los Angeles enriched that folklore by drawing upon traditional and nontraditional cultural forms to record their experience of the freeway and its construction. Such cultural productions do not summarize the perceptions of Chicanos and Chicanas in Los Angeles, but they do enlarge our understanding of the complex cultural responses to modernization in the age of the freeway.

In the Tujunga Wash of the Los Angeles River, Judith Baca's mural *The Great Wall of Los Angeles* depicts the struggle of freeway construction during the 1950s. In that section of the mural entitled "Division of the Barrios," a Chicano family is divided—mother and son on one side, father and daughter on the other. In between, the freeway writhes, imposing a wide gulf between them. Baca's image plays on the word itself, taking the "free" out of "freeway." In her image, the freeway is instead an oppressive monolith dividing and constricting instead of unifying and mobilizing. The *muralista* personifies the freeway as a serpentine, parasitic force, preying upon Chicano families and asphyxiating the old Los Angeles barrios.

Nostalgia, even melancholy, marks other Chicano and Chicana recollections of life before the freeway. For many who grew up in the cities of southern California, the freeway plowed over backyards, churches, and schoolhouses—now just debris in the path of progress. In the poem "The Journey," by Patricia Preciado Martin, the narrator walks with her grandmother through the old barrio where she grew up. Little is left from the days of her youth, however, save the sparse geraniums that grow in the cracks of the pavement. At the heart of the old barrio, the freeway stands, indifferent to childhood memories of family and community. Walking through a much-changed barrio, the grandmother recalls a river that ran through the town. The freeway, however,

> had cut the river from the people.
> The freeway blocks the sunshine
> The drone of traffic buzzes like a giant sleeping bee
> A new music in the barrio.[13]

The "new music" of the barrio also resonates in the poetry of Lorna Dee Cervantes. In her poem *Beneath the Shadow of the Freeway*, Cervantes implicates the freeway in the gendered oppression of Chicana women by men—Anglo and Chicano alike. The narrator of the poem remembers life with her "woman family"—her mother and grandmother, as well as the fleeting men. Wayward men are in stark contrast to the sanctuary of her grandmother's home, "the house she built with her own hands," a central image of the poem. More striking, however, is the contrast between the home and the freeway, the "blind worm wrapping up the valley from Los Altos to Sal si Puedes." The freeway fills the author with dread: "Every day at dusk as Grandma watered geraniums the shadow of the freeway lengthened." The "cocky disheveled carpentry" of her grandmother's home is juxtaposed against the inhuman symmetry of the freeway monolith. The freeway, the poet suggests, was built by men—men infatuated with movement, mobility, and most of all, escape. Two central oppositions gird *Beneath the Shadow of the Freeway*—men's movement versus women's anchoring, and the freeway's movement versus the house's stability. Wrapped in such

519

contradictions, the narrator concludes, "In time, I plant geraniums, I tie my hair in braids, and trust only what I have built with my own hands."[14]

The freeway has invoked a complex range of emotions among Chicana poets and artists—defiance, nostalgia, suspicion, and dread. Some Chicano writers even bring the freeway into their fantastic and surreal imagination. In *The Road to Tamazunchale*, by Ron Arias, the freeway frames the fantasies of Don Fausto, a very old man on the verge of death who lived in the barrio of Los Angeles. The freeway is such a prominent part of his daily environment that he invokes the freeway in one of his many fantasies—a Peruvian shepherd leading his herd of alpacas onto the Los Angeles freeway. The scene is loaded with Bunuelian illusions and ambiguities:

> "What's that?" Mario said, jumping up.
> Fausto hurried to the sidewalk. "Vente, don't be afraid," he told Mario, then stepped off the curb into the mass of bobbing, furry heads. The shepherd, lagging behind, seemed confused by the traffic lights and horns. At the intersection leading to the freeway on-ramp the frightened alpacas blocked a row of funeral cars, headlights on. Fausto, shouting and waving his hoe, stumbled up the ramp and tried to turn the herd from disaster. Mario ran after him, catching a glimpse of the motorcycle escort, racing to the head of the funeral procession.[15]

Drawing upon the imagery of García Márquez, Mario Vargas Llosa, and Alejo Carpentier, Arias makes the freeway a link between the Los Angeles barrio and Latin American cultural expression. Although Arias wrote *The Road to Tamazunchale* in 1987, long after the freeway hacked its way through the barrio, his reference to it demonstrates another way Chicanos derived meaning from that process: by immersing the freeway in the cultural currents of Mexico and South America. The author skillfully defamiliarizes an ordinary, yet prominent, structure of the barrio landscape, rendering it part of the make-believe world of Don Fausto. Although the freeway is not of the barrio, Arias shows how it is woven into the fabric of his community. He does not accept the freeway for what it is, but strips it of its functionalism and uses it as a magical stage for dream and fantasy.

While theme parks and public ceremonies affirmed the dominant perception of the freeway, Chicanos and Chicanas contradicted such official paeans to progress through a counterfolklore that assigned a very different meaning to the freeway. Their endeavors, however, were more than a Pavlovian response to oppression. The work of Baca, Martin, Cervantes, and Arias demonstrates the ways in which Chicano artists and writers have exploited the freeway as a source of creative inspiration, and, in that process, imparted their own identity to the public spaces of the city. Chicanos and Chicanas could not change the course of the freeway, but they could change its meaning. Such a contrast between the dominant meaning of the freeway and the Chicano meaning of the freeway illuminates the larger cultural conversation between the intentions of cultural producers and the uses of cultural consumers. Chicanos and Chicanas used the freeway to construct a discourse of resistance to its imposition upon their world, and in doing so, defied the intended meanings of city engineers, public officials, and cultural impresarios.

A more contemporary example of this dialogue around the built environment recalls another cultural practice that thrives in the Los Angeles barrio. During the late 1970s and early 1980s, a graffiti-writing explosion hit the Bronx in New York. There, most of the work was painted on the sides of subway cars. With no subways to "bomb," however, Los Angeles taggers aimed for the freeways. In the words of one local tagger, "Everybody takes the freeways. Everybody, everybody and their mother sees this. This is like the subways in New York, except that you move past it instead of having it move past you."[16] The tagger has named a very important cultural practice, that of taking public space and using it as a means of self-expression. Graffiti is a good example of what anthropologist James Scott calls "hidden transcripts"—jokes, songs, folklore, graffiti, and other cultural expressions that manifest a dissident political culture.[17]

On the freeway, however, such transcripts are not so hidden. True, freeways eliminate the kind of cultural encounters that were routine in the "democratic" spaces of older American cities (Olmsted's Central Park is perhaps the most celebrated example). High above (and sometimes below) the landscape of human activity, the freeway removes the driver from social contact. For many, the freeway is a safe passage through the ghetto or the barrio that (by design, many would argue) maintains the social distance between separate and unequal worlds. Even so, graffiti works against the "out of sight, out of mind" principle of urban design. It is a highly visible reminder of the Other—inner-city Chicano and Black youth. While the city spends $150 million a year in its war on graffiti, and while homeowners and public officials rail against graffiti as "visual pollution,"[18] such well-funded efforts are unable to stop the expressions of power sprayed onto the wall, which articulate presence, convey identity, and personalize the impersonal universe of the sprawling metropolis. Despite the trend toward the privatization of public life in the postindustrial metropolis, graffiti on the freeway is a reminder that "they" are still here. Cultural dialogues

521

are still at work in the spaces of the city, even in a "city of quartz" like Los Angeles. While urban scholars and theorists rightly disparage the "destruction of public space," "the militarization of city life," and the "South Africanization of Los Angeles,"[19] such criticisms often obscure the counternarratives, counterstrategies, and counterexpressions that assert and maintain humanity, even in a space as inhuman and alienating as the Los Angeles freeway.

Beyond the Barrio

The use of the freeway as an urban canvas for the expression of diverse Chicano identities compels a more balanced perspective on the relationship between the Los Angeles freeway and the Chicano community. To say that that relationship can be characterized by conflict, defiance, and resistance *only* would be specious, as other aspects of the Chicano experience shed a more ambiguous light upon the freeway. The folklore of the freeway, for example, is complicated by the work of Gil Cuadros, another Chicano writer who understands the inner contradictions of the Los Angeles freeway. In his novel *City of God*, Cuadros reminisces about his childhood in the barrio and his adult life as a gay man searching for sex in the boozy discos of West Hollywood, "Rage, Revolver, Motherlode and Mickey's." West Hollywood is far from his home in City Terrace, where he grew up with a homophobic father and an abusive mother, but it is the place where he can momentarily forget the whispers and dirty looks of his old neighborhood. Not that he is "at home" in West Hollywood—the author recounts the racism and condescension of the "West Hollywood bar types—blond hair, blue eyes," who crave "hot Latin, brown-skinned, warm, exotic, dark, dark, dark" men. His identity is as fractured and fragmented as Los Angeles itself, a "hot Latin" in one world, a "faggot" in the other. The freeway is his link between these imperfect worlds. It is the space in between his two selves—his West Hollywood incarnation and his Chicano roots in the barrio. "Driving the San Bernardino is the closest I get to Mecca," Cuadros muses as he passes over the landmarks of his youth. "I was born below this freeway, in a house with a picket fence now plowed under." But there is no sweet sorrow here:

> I imagine the house still intact, buried under the dirt and asphalt, dust and neglect. Hidden under a modern city, this is my Aztlan, a glimpse of my ancient home, my family. All it takes is a well-chosen phrase to cave-in. Mom, why did you burn my hands with the iron and say it was

an accident? Tattoo my arms with the car's cigarette lighter? Make me wish your wish, that I was never born? Make me admit they are all lies. I starved and refused your breast, lavished me instead with gifts and I would destroy them … dolls without eyes, legs, heads. Like the house, these words spiral in on themselves, stab into the moist earth and rot; the angry lords eat their own. Ivy grows over this hell hole. The sprinklers kick on. The traffic roars. [20]

Cuadros reviles both the privilege of a happy childhood and the nostalgia that infused others' memories of life before the freeway. Even before the freeway smashed the barrio into dust, the pain and misery had grown unbearable for some. For Cuadros and others like him, once trapped in the small world of the barrio, the freeway is both a way out and a way in—an escape from intolerance and a path to passion, love, even death. Cuadros's memories light the spatial paradox of the freeway—it is both savior and destroyer.

The Chicano folklore of the freeway shelters a variety of ways in which Chicanos and Chicanas have represented (and represented themselves upon) the Los Angeles freeway. And yet, such musings about how Chicanos and Chicanas have imagined the freeway speak little to how they use the freeway in ways like everyone else. While Chicanos and other Latinos were concentrated in East Los Angeles during the postwar period, there is no longer a monolithic barrio of which we can speak. Since the 1960s (and even before), the Chicano community has dispersed throughout the metropolis and to such far-reaching suburbs as Whittier, Norwalk, Alhambra, Montebello, and Pico Rivera. The socioeconomic gains of Chicanos and Chicanas in recent decades have accelerated their dispersal throughout the region. Central to that process is, also, the freeway, which bestows upon suburban Chicanos the same opportunities of access and mobility as it bestowed upon an earlier generation of white suburbanites.[21] The barrio, like other working-class immigrant and ethnic neighborhoods, is inspired by the great modern dream of mobility. To live well is to move up socially; and to move up socially is often, but not always, to move out physically. "Sal si Puedes" is more than a local joke in southwestern barrios, it is a moral imperative—an imperative that breaks down the old barrios from within, even as the freeways break them up from without. And more often than not, due to the peculiar circumstances of life in Los Angeles, the freeway is the key to realizing that imperative. It is the most accessible, most immediate means of securing the American dream of movement and mobility. Now our only complaint is that for many the dream is unfulfilled and people are not moving about fast enough or freely enough.

Conclusion: Modernity and Its Discontents

The history of freeway construction in metropolitan Los Angeles transcends the particularities of space and time. The history of any freeway recalls the triumphs and tragedies of millions who found themselves overpowered by progress in various spatial and temporal contexts—Haussmann's Paris, Moses's New York, and Porfirian Mexico City. Even in a city as postmodern as Los Angeles, the recent history of freeway construction demonstrates that the energy of modernization has yet to cease and that the experience of modernity permeates both historical and contemporary consciousness. But, as Marshall Berman reminds us, that experience is one of contradiction and paradox. The freeway, as a comprehensive system of mass transit imagined and implemented by a technocratic cadre of planners and engineers, is a quintessentially modern space. Even in its totality, however, the freeway cannot mask the seething tensions within postwar Los Angeles. Alas, it created new ones.

The history of freeway construction in postwar Los Angeles illuminates the countervalent forces of modernity. While the freeway gave rise to a new experience of the city, it simultaneously catalyzed the disintegration of older, familiar patterns of life in the "little worlds" of localized communities. This contradiction points to what Theodor Adorno and Max Horkheimer identified as the "Dialectic of Enlightenment"—in which the Enlightenment gave rise to new systems of domination and oppression. Every aspect of Western progress has not been without its dark twin: expansion/conquest, industrialization/enslavement, construction/destruction. Such dualities define the experience of modernity and inform the history of Los Angeles in the age of the freeway, a world of "disintegration and renewal, of struggle and contradiction, of ambiguity and anguish."[22]

Chicanos and Chicanas, a people born of the globalized forces of modernity, bore the brunt of freeway construction as they endured displacement and dislocation. Somehow, their voices have been absent from historical accounts of freeway construction in postwar Los Angeles. This is not surprising given that the voices of the oppressed have usually been missing from larger histories of modernity and modernization. Adorno and Horkheimer, like other Marxist cultural critics, overlooked another dialectic within the Dialectic of Enlightenment—that between the oppressor and oppressed. While historians and scholars often focus upon the former, the victims of progress have not been silent in the face of their oppressor—man or machine. Chicanos and Chicanas devised various means to resist the freeway through the organized channels of political protest, as well as through the production of culture. The two should not be viewed separately, but rather as strategies designed to preserve neighborhoods or the memory of them when gone.

Other complexities remain. The history of the Los Angeles barrio in the age of the freeway is more than the simple story of us versus them. The folklore of the freeway, or the cultural response to modernization, is broad enough to encompass both the complexity of metropolitan society in postwar Los Angeles and the diversity of the city's Chicano community. Although Chicanos and Chicanas derived meaning from and assigned meaning to the freeway in ways that defied or subverted official meanings, those meanings were not uniform and were not shared by some Chicanos and Chicanas, namely those who used the freeway to forge new identities and to explore the world beyond the barrio. Chicanos and Chicanas were sometimes at odds with the forces of modernization, and sometimes at odds with each other. Perhaps they understand the complexities and contradictions of the Los Angeles freeway so well because those complexities and contradictions are their own.

Notes

For their help with this article, I would like to thank Lawrence W. Levine, Anthony Macias, Louis Suarez Potts, and the editorial staff of *Aztlán*. This article is taken from chapter 2 of my dissertation, "The Great Wall of Los Angeles: Los Angeles in the Age of the Freeway" (University of California, Berkeley, 1997).

1. Robert Fogelson, *The Fragmented Metropolis: Los Angeles, 1850–1930* (Berkeley: University of California Press, 1993).

2. See Gary Miller, *Cities by Contract: The Politics of Municipal Incorporation* (Cambridge: Massachusetts Institute of Technology Press, 1981); and Douglas Massey and Nancy Denton, *American Apartheid: Segregation and the Making of the Underclass* (Cambridge: Harvard University Press, 1993).

3. A few who have done so include David Brodsly, *L.A. Freeway: An Appreciative Essay* (Berkeley: University of California Press, 1981); and Reyner Banham, *Los Angeles: The Architecture of Four Ecologies* (New York: Penguin, 1973). See also Eric R. Avila, *Reinventing Los Angeles Popular Culture in the Age of White Flight, 1940–1965* (Ph.D. diss., Department of History, University of California, Berkeley, 1997).

4. "Folklore" is defined here as meaning assigned to a particular object or experience by cultural consumers or producers that resonates with wide segments

of the population. Although folklore is often associated with preindustrial societies, popular culture (culture that is widely accessible and widely accessed) is viewed in recent scholarship as "the folklore of industrial society." Thus, my use of it. See Lawrence W. Levine, "The Folklore of Industrial Society: Popular Culture and Its Audiences," in *The Unpredictable Past: Explorations in American Cultural History,* ed. Lawrence Levine (New York: Oxford University Press, 1993).

5. Brodsly, *L.A. Freeway*, 115.

6. Miller, *Cities by Contract*, 85.

7. *Eastside Sun*, 26 January 1961.

8. Carlos Navarro and Rodolfo Acuña, "In Search of Community: A Comparative Essay on Mexicans in Los Angeles and San Antonio," in *20th Century Los Angeles: Power Promotion and Social Conflict*, ed. Norman Klein and Martin Schiesl (Claremont, Calif.: Regina Books, 1990), 203.

9. California Division of Highways, *California Highways and Public Works* 33, nos. 5–6 (May–June 1954): 15.

10. California Division of Highways, *California Highways and Public Works* 32, nos. 3–4 (January 1941): 4–5.

11. Douglas Monroy, *Thrown Among Strangers: The Making of Mexican Culture in Frontier California* (Berkeley: University of California Press, 1990).

12. *Eastside Sun*, 11 November 1957.

13. Patricia Preciado Martin, "The Journey," in *Infinite Divisions: An Anthology of Chicana Literature*, ed. Tey Diana Reboldo and Eliana S. Rivero (Tucson: University of Arizona Press, 1993), 167.

14. Lorna Dee Cervantes, "Beneath the Shadow of the Freeway," in *Emplumada* (Pittsburgh: University of Pittsburgh Press, 1981).

15. Ron Arias, *The Road to Tamazunchale* (Tempe, Ariz.: Bilingual Press/Editorial Bilingue, 1987), 44–45.

16. Ruben Martínez, *The Other Side: Notes From L.A., Mexico City, and Beyond* (New York: Verso Press, 1993), 121.

17. James Scott, *Domination and the Arts of Resistance: Hidden Transcripts* (New Haven: Yale University Press, 1990). See also Robin D. G. Kelley, *Race Rebels: Culture, Politics and the Black Working Class* (New York: The Free Press, 1994).

18. Martínez, *The Other Side*, 118.

19. These quotes are taken from Mike Davis, *City of Quartz* (New York: Verso Press, 1990), perhaps the most influential book on contemporary Los Angeles. Similar perspectives on the "postmodern" city can be found in Michael Sorkin, ed., *Variations on a Theme Park: The New American City and the End of Public Space* (New York: Hill and Wang, 1992).

20. Gil Cuadros, *City of God* (San Francisco: City Lights, 1994), 54–55.

21. W. A. V. Clark and Millan Mueller, "Hispanic Relocation and Spatial Assimilation: A Case Study," *Social Science Quarterly* 69, no. 2 (June 1988): 836.

22. Marshall Berman, *All That Is Solid Melts into Air: The Experience of Modernity* (New York: Simon and Schuster, 1982), 326.

Chicana/o Studies and Anthropology
The Dialogue That Never Was

Karen Mary Davalos

AUTHOR'S NOTE: *There is good news and bad news about the relationship between Chicana/o studies and anthropology. First, the good news—Chicana/o scholars have intervened in cultural anthropology, and for the past decade presenters at the annual meeting of the American Anthropology Association have been addressing decolonial methods, approaches, and research findings. In her 2004 Presidential Address, notably at the association's one-hundredth meeting, Louise Lamphere critically challenged the discipline to recognize the contributions of marginalized anthropologists, women, and ethnic minorities. The bad news is that the journals in cultural anthropology continue to ignore the topic of Chicana/o cultural anthropology. Only two articles on Mexican Americans have been published in the organization's flagship journal and three articles have appeared in* Cultural Anthropology *since 2001, although a couple of comparative works described the lives of Chicanos. The discipline's persistent marginalization of Chicana/o cultural anthropology has not stopped the intellectual productivity of Chicana/o anthropologists, and dozens of books, monographs, and articles have engaged ethnographic research from the decolonial orientation. Indeed, the real victory is that current graduate students in cultural anthropology are expected to have a healthy skepticism about the discipline and its conventions of white privilege. Give it another forty years and the dialogue will be rich, varied, and consistent.*

Since the late 1960s, the majority of anthropologists have ignored three decades of "natives talking back," an ironic move for a discipline based on listening to so-called natives. This neglect made it possible for Paul Rabinow to claim incorrectly that "there has been almost a total silence about the power/ knowledge relations within the discipline in recent years" (1985, 10). By decrying the "strange complicity of silence" (11), Rabinow intended to encourage anthropologists to investigate the "micro-relations

From *Aztlán: A Journal of Chicano Studies* 23, no. 2 (1998): 13–45.

527

among the interpretive community" (11) in order to determine the source and direction of the "new" ethnographic writing. He was not convinced that the new ethnographic writing "emerged directly out of decolonisation or the Vietnam war," and he suggested that scholars turn to "the institutional setting in which it emerged: the American Academy of the late 1970s and early 1980s" (10).

Like the majority of anthropologists, Rabinow was unaware that Chicano scholars like Américo Paredes and Octavio Ignacio Romano-V. had initiated this type of investigation and critique of North American anthropology's colonial-like practices in the late 1960s and early 1970s.[1] This essay revisits a Vietnam-era conversation Chicano scholars initiated with "Anglo" anthropologists in 1967.[2] It traces the growth and development, including the pauses, of this dialogue primarily within the social sciences and the ways in which a new field—Chicana/o Studies—emerged from the invitation to an exchange on social analysis. Though their voices fell on deaf ears and their ideas have subsequently been omitted from the anthropological canon, Chicano and Chicana scholars are fundamental to the current postmodern focus on voice, ethnographic authority, positionality, and the politics of representation.[3] This essay argues that by initiating a critique of the substantive and theoretical (mis)representations of Mexican Americans, Chicana/o scholars anticipated a new anthropology and the problems of an apolitical postmodernism by encouraging a decolonized social science (Harrison 1991a and Arvizu 1978b).[4]

This essay also examines the dialogue offered by Chicana feminists. While still ignored or demonized in some corners of academia, even Chicano Studies (see I. García 1996), the feminist dialogue served as a catalyst for important developments in Chicana/o scholarship and postmodernism and offered significant layers to the Chicana/o palimpsest of representation. Since the mid-1970s, Chicana feminists have challenged the normalization of the Chicano family and gender roles and aimed to retrieve Chicana history, particularly social, cultural, and political contributions. Initially speaking from a cultural nationalists' paradigm, Chicanas later explored feminist perspectives. This dialogue grew into a critique of "the community," patriarchy, and heterosexism; as such, it offered new understanding on authenticity, culture, and authority.

Finally, this essay suggests that these dialogues were initiated because of inequalities within the "American Academy" and the struggles against race, class, and gender inequalities outside of the academy, some of which were directly connected to the Vietnam War. For example, the Chicano

Moratorium, an anti-Vietnam demonstration that focused on the disproportionate Mexican American casualties of the war, galvanized the Chicano
civil rights movement in general. Out of this wide-spread movement, the
performing, visual, and literary arts flourished; Mexican American students
gained access to four-year colleges in record numbers (many through the
G.I. Bill); and public discourse acknowledged the political and economic
presence of Mexican Americans. Even Chicana/o scholars—like me—too
young to have participated in the Vietnam War or the Chicano Movement
are finding that our place within the academy is directly connected to
the legacies of the civil, social, and political movements of the 1960s and
1970s as well as our efforts to "decolonize ourselves" (Anzaldúa 1990, xvii).
Thus, critical attention to the particular context—the moment, space,
and language in which Chicana/o anthropologists opened a dialogue—can
produce a nuanced view of representation and power.

Chicano Scholarship: Crying Out for Justice

In the late 1960s, Octavio I. Romano-V., an anthropologist, and Nick C.
Vaca, a sociologist, founded the Chicano journal *El Grito: A Journal of
Contemporary Mexican-American Thought* and published it through Quinto
Sol Publishing, an independent Chicano-owned press. Dripping with wit
and sarcasm and full of the conviction of self-determination, the editorial page—most likely authored by Romano and/or Vaca—announced
their agenda for *El Grito*: "The exposure of [the] fallacious nature [of the
social sciences] and the development of intellectual alternatives" (1967,
4). They hoped that the journal would create "a forum for Mexican-
American self-definition and expression" (4). Though influenced by the
larger social and political movements in which they participated, which
demanded social justice through self-determination, the crux of their
revisionist agenda lay in their hyperbolic and satirical representation of
"Mexican-Americans" and "social scientists." Allow me to quote at length
from their first editorial:

> Contrary to the general pattern of ethnic minorities in the history of
> the United States, Mexican-Americans have retained their distinct
> identity and have refused to disappear into The Great American Melt-
> ing Pot. Not having the good grace to quietly disappear, we have then
> compounded our guilt in America's eyes by committing the additional
> sin of being glaringly poor in the midst of this affluent, abundant, and
> over-developed society.

> In response to this embarrassing situation, American ingenuity has risen to the occasion and produced an ideological rhetoric that serves to neatly explain away both the oppressive and exploitative factors maintaining Mexican-Americans in their economically impoverished condition, and Mexican-Americans' refusal to enthusiastically embrace The American Way of Life. (4)

The tone of the opening paragraphs suggested that the reader not take the text literally but as poetic imagination. The text proclaimed Romano's and Vaca's own rhetorical strategy and outlined the mythical qualities for the Mexican Americans who resist assimilation. In addition, the text addressed the history and living conditions of Mexican Americans, who did not follow "the general pattern" of immigration and assimilation. As many Chicana/o intellectuals, poets, and leaders have noted, they did not cross the border, the border crossed them.

Having identified the "embarrassing situation" in which Mexican Americans have retained their cultural difference, Romano and Vaca proceeded with their satire of the "ideological rhetoric" that renders Mexican Americans as:

> simple-minded but lovable and colorful children who because of their rustic naïveté, limited mentality, and inferior, backward "traditional culture," choose poverty and isolation instead of assimilating into the American mainstream and accepting its material riches and superior culture. (4)

The phrase "superior culture" was a subtle hint about the foundation of the "ideological rhetoric." Indeed, the following text implied that racism is the source for this representation of Mexican Americans and that it was prevalent and unquestioned among those who engage in cultural analysis and description.

> Formulated and propagated by those intellectual mercenaries of our age, the social scientists, this rhetoric has been professionally certified and institutionally sanctified to the point where today it holds wide public acceptance.... Yet this great rhetorical structure is a grand hoax, a blatant lie—a lie that must be stripped of its esoteric and sanctified verbal garb. (4)

Identified as fiction writers whose words carry power and authority, "social scientists" promote and perpetuate racism. The biting tone also functions to unveil the myth that all concerned with culture are objective, including Chicano scholars.[5] *El Grito*'s founders recognized that representation is mediated by nationalism, capital, political power, and racism. Thus, through tone, Romano and Vaca created an agenda for *El Grito* that is embedded in politics, the assertion of position, and struggle. Furthermore, this agenda reflected *Chicanismo*, as it requires a specific positionality, the creation of a new Chicano subject, and the assertion of a new Chicano author. "Only Mexican-Americans themselves can accomplish the collapse of this and other such rhetorical structures by the ... development of intellectual alternatives" (4). In fact, by 1973 Jose Limón could count at least nine Chicano scholars who "exposed the academically cloaked versions of [racist] stereotypes" used to describe Mexican Americans (1973, 258, 268).

While *El Grito*'s first editorial echoed an essentialist and nationalist agenda, subsequent contributions to the dialogue were devoted less to these ideologies. For example, in his essay, "Minorities, History and Cultural Mystique," Romano deconstructed the "fusion of the Protestant Ethic, cultural Darwinism, with American liberalism (sic)" within social science theory (1967). Using satire and wit, he unmasked the defunct blame-the-victim paradigm of social science, which "repeatedly describes people in the lower rungs of society as underachievers, retarded, fatalistic, tradition bound, emotional, etc., etc., etc." (9). He did not proclaim that Mexican American scholars were exempt from promoting such a model. According to Romano, the culture of poverty theory was popular among every "ethnicity, skin color, group history, tradition, and religious affiliation" (11). All ex-victims, he argued, use this rhetoric to blame present victims. Implicating class interests and other privileges, Romano explained that social scientists perpetuate their "self-interest" through a theoretical model that legitimates their own power and social status (9). Unfortunately, Romano's satirical style and substantive focus make it difficult to determine how contributors to *El Grito* should resist the ideological forces that shape social science and "self-interest." Nevertheless, Romano named social science texts as "tribal rhetoric" and "the fiction" of a culture, and thereby connected ethnographic authority to politics and power (10).

In contrast to Romano's jeremiad tone, Nick Vaca's writing strategy in *El Grito* was even-handed and methodical (1970a, 1970b). His articles, designed as a three- or four-part study of social science research on Mexican Americans, contributed to the dialogue on representation by addressing *why* social scientists apply particular theoretical models. In part 1, addressing the years 1912–1935, he suggested that research before the mid-1930s was influenced by social, political, and economic relations between Mexico and the United States. For example, he argued that conflict, such as the annexation of Texas and slavery, produced "friction" or "cultural difference" between "Mexicans and Anglos" that eventually played out in "social science studies" (1970a, 6). More critically, he linked the restrictive immigration acts of the 1920s to the pseudo-scientific quest for evidence of Nordic racial superiority and the simultaneous argument that "national unity depended upon racial and cultural homogeneity" (8). He found that racial or biological determinism gained support during this time but was challenged by structural-environmental determinism. In short, Vaca developed the dialogue on representation and power by describing the specific ideologies—nationalism and racism—that shaped research questions and findings between 1912 and 1935.

In part 2, addressing the years 1936–1970, Vaca employed another strategy. While his work was not completely absent of satire and metaphor, the tone and style of part 2 was unmistakably academic. For example, Vaca was thorough (reviewing 138 studies published between 1936 and 1970); comprehensive (reviewing work in psychology, sociology, and anthropology); critical (examining the limits of each study); and "objective" (analyzing Mexican, Mexican American, and Anglo American scholars with equal rigor). He did not pretend neutrality, however, as his own interpretation favors the work of George I. Sanchez and the structural-environmental framework.

The bulk of the essay chronologically traced the "etiological frameworks" of the three disciplines (1970b, 18). Vaca noted that the biological model was dominant during the early part of the century, though challenged by the structural-environmental and cultural paradigms. Central to his critique was the increasing authority of cultural determinism in explaining Mexican American underachievement. Vaca demonstrated that by the early 1950s, cultural determinism had complete hegemony in social science research while structural-environmental determinism was granted "leper status" (20). He concluded that the value system attributed to Mexican Americans and the one attributed to Anglos merely served to rationalize "the social ills of the Mexican-American in the United States without indicting Anglo institutions" (45) (fig. 1). Ironically, this work ended with the unanswered question "Is Mexican-American culture really composed of those negative values that have been attributed to it?"(46). Though other scholars continue the dialogue, Vaca never answered this question—the intended topic of the unwritten third piece. Nevertheless, Vaca's most significant contribution to the conversation is his suggestion that the power and politics of racism and nationalism, which in turn can disguise the sources of oppression, mediate research. His work implies that social science is a "handmaiden" of these ideologies, supporting the Vietnam-era charge that anthropology was the handmaiden of colonialism.

Mexican American Value System	Anglo Value System
Subjugation to nature	Mastery over nature
Present oriented	Future oriented
Immediate gratification	Deferred gratification
Complacent	Aggressive
Nonintellectual	Intellectual
Fatalistic	Nonfatalistic
Nongoal oriented	Goal oriented
Nonsuccess oriented	Success oriented
Emotional	Rational
Dependent	Individualistic
Machismo	Effeminacy
Superstitious	Nonsuperstitious
Traditional	Progressive

Figure 1. Mexican-American and Anglo Value Systems (Vaca 1970b, 45).

In several ways, Romano (1968) had already engaged Vaca's question about Mexican American culture. In his second *El Grito* publication, "The Anthropology and Sociology of the Mexican-Americans: The Distortion of Mexican-American History," Romano narrowed his attack to the "rhetoric" of anthropology by challenging the heart of the discipline: its concept of culture. In anthropology, Romano explained, cultures and peoples are imagined as discreet units, unaffected by time and space. This totalizing view of culture, he argued, operates to mystify contemporary social conditions and the unequal distribution of power. Critically engaging each anthropologist whose ethnographies describe Mexican Americans "as virtually stagnant and actionless" (25), Romano attacked Ruth Tuck, Lyle Saunders, Margaret Clark, Munro Edmonson, Arthur Rubel, Celia Heller, William Madsen, Florence Kluckholn, Julian Samora, and others for perpetuating "pernicious, vicious, misleading, degrading, and brainwashing" "opinions" (24).[6] Pointing to Mexican American political struggles, leadership, collective resistance against military action, and labor organizing, Romano demonstrated that Mexican Americans are not only "participants in history" but also "generators of the historical process" (14). As if in answer to Vaca's question, Romano noted that Mexican Americans do not have the "negative values" attributed to them (see also Romano 1969). His essay ended with a rejection of the concept of "traditional culture" (read "negative values") and a call for the representation of "the intellectual history of Mexican-Americans" (1968, 25).

In fact, Romano (1969) approximated such a representation in "The Historical and Intellectual Presence of Mexican-Americans," his third installment in *El Grito*. In this piece, his characterization of culture contributed significantly to the dialogue. While Romano celebrated the "biculturalism" and "Cultural Nationalism" of the Chicano Movement, he did not assume a singular, unified Mexican American community, philosophy, or experience, which is often the premise of the cultural nationalist paradigm as well as cultural determinism, the theoretical model at the center of the Romano-Vaca critique. The bulk of the essay was devoted to descriptions of the various philosophies and ideologies that stem from particular historical experiences, though he did not address feminism or the work of Sor Juana Inés de la Cruz in his analysis of Mexican intellectual thought. Nevertheless, he noted that an oversimplification of Mexican Americans not only resembles the "monolithic" and "ahistorical" representation found in anthropology and sociology, but also renders Mexican Americans as "totally and irrevocably Americanized" (45). His aim was to offer the complexity of Mexican and Mexican American philosophy as a new representation of Chicanos. Thus, Romano admitted that even his own textual representations of Mexican Americans are never neutral but seek to amend the unequal distribution of power.

Material Bases Culture

Though they did not specifically enter into dialogue with North American anthropologists or critique the colonial-like practices of that discipline, several Chicana/o scholars did engage in a dialogue on culture. As if to acknowledge the "indifference, exclusion, and paternalism" (Arvizu 1978a, 12) of "Anglo" anthropologists—the intended but absent interlocutor—Chicana/o scholars engaged each other in conversation and by doing so further developed and constructed a voice, position, and authority.[7] Moreover, by engaging in a dialogue on culture "outside" of anthropology, Chicana/o scholars initiated a challenge that later became more central to their work. That is, by developing a concept of culture, they opened to question anthropology's claim on the subject. Finally, the early dialogue on culture placed less emphasis on an essentialized "Anglo" anthropologist and more on the class, race, education, gender, and linguistic abilities of the social analysts—though not all of these issues were evenly developed.

For example, influenced by the internal colonial model, both Juan

Gómez-Quiñonez (1977) and Diego Vigil (1978) argued that culture is materially based, fluid, and contradictory, a position that challenges cultural determinism.[8] Turning to the structural inequalities generated by capitalism and to a lesser extent racism, they posited that Mexican Americans do not automatically share the same social position, though historically many Mexican Americans have been poor and working-class. According to historical materialists, such as Gómez-Quiñonez and Vigil, the "strain and conflict" of capitalism explained Mexican American unemployment, under-education, crime, and other social problems (Gómez-Quiñonez 1977, 16). In addition, they recognized the diversity of positions within a class and community, acknowledging that it is difficult to achieve unity among Mexican Americans.

Furthermore, historical materialists also questioned the centrality of cultural identity and "tradition" in unifying Chicanos, and Gómez-Quiñonez was one of the more explicit critics of cultural nationalism. "Without class identification and political participation," he stated, "cultural identification and paraphernalia ... [are] often merely decorative" (1977, 18). Indeed, his criticism had the effect of challenging all textual representations of Chicano culture since it does not intrinsically promote political participation or class struggle. Nevertheless, while cultural nationalists and historical materialists such as Gómez-Quiñonez had not come to consensus on the concept and role of culture, they shared a concern for the economic and social inequalities of Chicano experience. Throughout the 1970s, they continued to negotiate strategies for eradicating discrimination. Unfortunately, they also shared a lack of attention to gender and sexual inequalities, a perspective taken up by feminist Chicanas and addressed later in this paper.

Laughing at the Problem of Anthropology

Ten years after Romano and Vaca attempted to enter into a dialogue with North American anthropologists, Américo Paredes (1978) reestablished the critique of the politics of anthropology, a turn that clarified the conversation as he directly engaged issues of objectivity, fieldwork, ethnographic interpretation, and anthropological authority. Effectively rejecting an essentialist model for "Anglo" anthropologists that characterized them as racist or colonial, Paredes asserted that anthropologists are a liberal, even left-of-center bunch who unknowingly perpetuate stereotypes.

> We know that the anthropologist is conditioned to make allowances for his own biases; his training is supposed to discipline him in viewing potential data with the highest degree of objectivity possible. But perhaps the methodological safeguards to compensate for a normal degree of bias are not working very well. Anthropologists may need to re-examine the argument that they can give us substantially true pictures of a culture by following time-honored methods. (2)

According to Paredes, the problem in anthropology was the uncritical application of "time-honored methods," notably fieldwork and the scientific method, in complex societies stratified by race, ethnicity, and class. Specifically, he questioned the length of field trips, "the magic condition known as rapport," the search for "raw anthropological data" or facts, and the assumption that objectivity guarantees neutrality (8).

Advancing a sophisticated deconstruction of anthropology and knowledge, then, Paredes raised epistemological, ethical, and political concerns. Primarily, he confounded the claim that culture (and language) are transparent and as such are readily knowable through fieldwork.

> Closer to the heart of the problem is the matter of language…. [T]he ability to communicate was enough of a goal for the ethnographer who wanted to elicit kinship terms or to work out taxonomies of plants, animals or statuses. It is a different matter when you attempt to interpret people's feelings and attitudes in actual speech situations…. Unwarranted generalizations may be reached on the basis of a misinterpretation of words, especially if a dialect expression is taken in its standard dictionary meaning or a metaphorical expression is taken literally. (3)

Paredes called for a more subtle and thorough comprehension of the field language and repeatedly implied that native Spanish speakers, particularly Chicanos, are better qualified for research among Mexican Americans. Admonishing anthropologists who "lack a real familiarity with the language" (8) and mistake "words" for facts, Paredes suggested that only a Chicano—such as himself—would understand the double meanings, the performance, or figurative style of Mexican American speech events.[9] His reinterpretation of Munro Edmonson's mistranslation of a song is a classic among Chicana/o students. For Edmonson, the song signaled Mexican fatalism as it tells of a man who bows to his destiny to be wounded by *esa tuna* (this prickly pear).[10] Paredes pointed out that the song is not about a prickly pear at all but a woman's favors (fig. 2).

Original Spanish	Edmonson's trans.	Paredes's trans.
Guadalajara en un llano	Guadalajara on a plain	Guadalajara on a plain
Mexico en una laguna	Mexico on a lake	Mexico on a lake
me he de comer esa tuna aunque me espine la mano	I have to eat this *tuna* even if it pricks me	Out of this thorny cactus, danger I will pluck this *tuna*, beauty

Figure 2. Comparison of translations of a Spanish copla song.

Paredes's discussion of the social context of speaking and research offered a more profound critique of anthropology. According to Paredes, the anthropologist's perceptions of Mexican Americans influence how they approach communication. Having a low estimation of Mexican Americans, Paredes explained, anthropologists assume that Mexican Americans are "incapable" of "artistic" expression, and their "underestimation of the in-formant" produces inaccurate interpretations. Simply put, they lack objectivity and neutrality. In an effort to recuperate Mexican American artistic and performative agency, Paredes offered dozens of reinterpretations of the work of Arthur Rubel, William Madsen, Munro Edmonson, and Michael Kearney.

The reinterpretations offer significant commentary on anthropology's mode of authority. Fieldwork is anthropology's singular achievement, as the modern anthropologist, unlike his armchair predecessor, establishes his expertise by "being there." Paredes confounded this assertion by demonstrating that "being there" does not prevent mistranslation, misunderstanding, and misrepresentation. Using gentle humor, the voice of reason, and irony with an edge, Paredes politely called anthropologists ignorant (Rosaldo 1985, 408). These are not merely embarrassments (or to borrow Clifford's phrase, "predicaments") of anthropology—Paredes in effect contested the foundation of anthropological authority itself.

Paredes's work also encouraged us to examine the positionality of the ethnographer. As Paredes noted, misunderstanding is not simply a factor of language and bias. It also occurs because anthropologists ignore how social interactions are conditioned by "[their] very presence" (1978, 28). That is, anthropologists did not account for their position as individuals of a specific race or class—and I would add gender, sexuality, and other cultural differences. Drawing on both his training in folklore and his experience as an ethnic minority, Paredes argued:

> More recognition must be given to the process that takes place when a fieldworker interviews an informant. This should be true of all situations,

but it is crucial when an Anglo fieldworker is working with a minority informant…. Both fieldworker and informant occupy varying roles in the same large[r] society, and they are highly aware of each other's presumed position in that society. (27)

Paredes suggested that anthropologists pay more attention to the ways in which "positions" shape ethnographic encounters and ethnographic texts.

Anticipating the postmodern claim that ethnographies are partial truths since they can only represent the "voice" of the researcher, Paredes noted that unequal social relations also influence ethnographic writing strategies. Turning to Kearney's ethnography of the Zapotecs of Ixtepeji,[11] Paredes observed:

Kearney can give the reader a beautifully complete description of ritual drinking behavior, but he gives us no details on how the legend of "La Llorona" is performed. Even more, *he does not give us a single text of the legend as it is told in Ixtepeji*, where presumably he heard it many times. He works with a summary (a tale-type if you will) published elsewhere by other authors. Yet, he bases some sweeping generalizations about Ixtepejano family and interpersonal relations on this folk narrative. (9, emphasis added)

The suppression of the informant's own voice, Paredes explained, is a strategy to legitimate the anthropologist's scientific authority. He concluded by arguing that anthropologists are obligated to represent the informant's voices with their own, a call that approximates the postmodern concern for multivocality.

Chicana Feminist Voices

It was Chicana feminists, however, who actually took Paredes's argument seriously. As if in reply to his challenge, Chicana feminists offered their own voices to the practice and politics surrounding representation. Indeed, while early Chicano scholarship could contemplate the issues surrounding representation, authority, culture, voice, and power, it did not initially examine the role of patriarchy in shaping curriculum and research, the centrality of gender and sexuality in Chicana/o experience, and the effects of heterosexism and patriarchy on constructing intellectual authority. Following Chabram, "I do not wish to idealize our predecessors" (1990, 241). Therefore, it is essential to acknowledge the limitations of early Chicano scholarship and to analyze the role of Chicana feminists in expanding the parameters of the field. For instance, Paredes's attention to performance and joking among men included an understanding of the social construction of masculinity but it lacked a sensitivity to women. Though Mexican American women are cast as the eternal butt of their jokes, Paredes claimed that the stylized form of banter "rarely causes offense" (1978, 17). Yet he did not report the voices of women. On a larger scale, scholars such as Romano and Gómez-Quiñonez omitted women as agents in Mexican American history, particularly in leading class struggles. Thus, the Chicano critique of anthropology and social analysis may have anticipated postmodern anthropology but it certainly did not foreshadow the contributions of Chicana and lesbian scholars, particularly in the deconstruction of culture, community, and tradition and the reconfiguration of knowledge and power.

In fact, Chicanas have been at work on reformulating what has counted as knowledge and the redistribution of intellectual power since the formative years of the field.[12] By 1971 Chicanas forced the Chicano Committee on Higher Education in California to adopt a resolution to revise *El Plan de Santa Barbara*, the original blueprint for Chicano Studies. They called for the recruitment of Chicana faculty and administrators and the inclusion of Chicana curriculum in all Chicano Studies programs (A. García 1992, 54). Chicanas have also been central in challenging both the "culturalist" and male bias of El Plan (Sosa Riddell 1974; López 1977, 19; Pardo 1984) and in pointing out the subsequent omissions in Chicano Studies research and curriculum (A. García 1986, 1992; Orozco 1986; Pardo 1984, 1980). Some Chicanas have been central in the rearticulation of a Chicana and Chicano Studies as well as a Women's Studies that accounts for race, class, gender, and sexuality (Alarcón 1990; Anzaldúa 1990; Baca Zinn et al. 1986; Cotera 1977; A. García 1992; Moraga and Anzaldúa 1983; Pérez 1993; Sandoval 1990; Trujillo 1993). According to Chabram, the "splitting" of the Chicano subject with "the markers *o/a*, *a/o* announce the end of the nongendered Mexican American subject of cultural and political identity; they reinscribe the Chicana presence, which had been subsumed under the universal ethnic denomination *Chicano*" (1993, 39).

Enabling more than a simple corrective to the sexism and male bias of the field, Chicana feminists forced a dialogue on the limited representation of culture (read also community/family/tradition). In general, they articulate a Chicana subject that is complex, heterogeneous, ambiguous, and liminal—a subject that refuses static boundaries and representations and therefore also expands the boundaries of a Chicano subject. In dialogue with such literary critics, writers, and activists as Norma Alarcón, Ana Nieto Gomez, Cherríe Moraga, and Gloria Anzaldúa, Chicana feminists

539

in the social sciences insisted on the multiple positions of Mexican American women as their lives are shaped by gender, sexuality, class, ethnicity, race, age, language, and other factors. They did not limit their critique to "Anglo" representations of Chicanas but also challenged Mexican and Chicano scholars for stereotyping Chicanas as passive, subservient, and weak. For example, early contributions to the dialogue by Maxine Baca Zinn (1975, 1979) challenged distorted representations of Chicanas. Ironically, while Baca Zinn, Romano, and Vaca assess nearly the same type of sociological literature from very different perspectives, their descriptions of the misrepresentation of Chicanos and Chicanas are strikingly similar. Baca Zinn noted that:

> Chicanas are variously portrayed as exotic objects, manipulated by both Chicano and Anglo men; as long-suffering mothers subject to the brutality of insecure husbands, whose only function is to produce children; and as women who themselves are childlike, simple and completely dependent upon husbands, brothers and fathers. (1975, 20)

Following the work of feminist anthropologist Michele Z. Rosaldo (1974), Baca Zinn documented the informal and unrecognized power of Chicanas in the domestic sphere and thus challenges the view that "machismo (compulsive masculinity) … underlies family structure" (Baca Zinn 1975, 22). She argued that Chicano families deviate from the ideal "patriarchal-authoritarian model" (21) since women are "more central than fathers in Chicano families" (23). She did not suggest that patriarchy is nonexistent or that mother-centered families are egalitarian. Instead, she posited that men and women have responsibility and power in their own spheres. In the following, she summarized M. Rosaldo's model of public-private spheres and applied it to Chicana/o experience.

> Men have traditionally represented their families in matters outside the home. They have been responsible for the family's economic support, and this responsibility has necessitated activity in institutions which are external to the family. On the other hand, women have traditionally been responsible for man-aging the day-to-day affairs of family living…. Like women everywhere, Chicanas' control of household and family matters is the source from which their power is derived. As Chicanas go outside of the domestic sphere and become involved in public sphere activities, they gain additional sources of power. (27)

Though Baca Zinn offers new interpretations of Chicana action and power, she did not problematize Chicana labor outside of the home. Maria

Linda Apodaca (1979) did, though, raising important questions about the historical and material position of women inside and outside the home. In fact, Patricia Zavella clarified Apodaca's call for attention to class relations in shaping Chicana/o experience. Zavella's (1987) research on Chicana cannery workers in California used a feminist perspective that accounts for the conflicting demands of patriarchy and capitalism.

In general, a feminist analysis contributes to the deconstruction of the normalized view of "the Chicana" and her role in "the Chicano family" and supports challenges to male dominance and privilege in the academy and at large. Thus, unwilling to accept that they were *vendidas* to the "community" or "Chicano Studies" and refusing to reduce all human experience to an essentialized masculine and heterosexual subject-identity, Chicana feminists engage in a dialogue on how the conditions and multiple experiences of race, class, gender, and sexuality could conflict with loyalty to community/family/culture/scholarship as it was initially defined. Currently, this dialogue is producing a collective Chicana consciousness that names itself as author(ity) of its own subject-identities.

Therefore, the invention of a Chicana subjectivity overlaps with critical attention to the politics of research. While questioning the normalized gender roles and limits of cultural purity, Chicana feminists also find themselves rethinking the insider/outsider duality that relies on clearly demarcated cultural borders. Baca Zinn challenges Paredes (1978) and others who assert that so-called ethnic insiders can easily gain access to informants and establish rapport because they are sensitive to community norms, issues, and language. My own work among Mexicanas in Chicago taught me to reject the cartography of "outsiders" and "insiders" as women variously told me I was "too dark" for a Mexican, an American, or a Chicano; or that my Spanish was "too perfect" for a pocha or working-class Mexicana (Davalos 1996, 102). Some women incorrectly suspected that I was from Mexico City since my use of Spanish was "too formal."

Zavella (1987, 1993) candidly reflects on her fieldwork among women of Mexican descent who do not share her "privileges as an educated woman," feminist perspective, or ethnic identity (1993, 58). In both her projects among working-class women in California and New Mexico, she realizes that her own assumptions about ethnic affiliation do not guarantee rapport with informants as she negotiated her status in the field. She uses this discovery in the field to challenge the politics of identity within academia, particularly the "rigid construction of ethnic identity" that "muted the internal political and theoretical differences among Chicana

541

(and Chicano) scholars" (69). The following narrative recounts Zavella's experience with ethnic politics:

> On two occasions, I made presentations on our research findings in ways that respected our informants' construction of identity and tried to contextualize their meanings. Yet I was attacked and my integrity questioned when I used the term *Spanish* [to describe New Mexican informants]. Puerto Rican scholars in particular strongly objected to the use of *Spanish*. One colleague claimed—to general agreement—that he had never even heard of any-one using the term *Spanish American* "in the community," so he could not understand how I could use it. They grilled me about my motivations and purposes, questioned my relationships with informants, and demanded to know how I would use the data.... [T]hey implied that I was identifying with the white power structure and would use the data in ways that would harm my informants. (67)

Feeling as if she had "violated the Chicano/Latino academic cultural norms of ethnic identification" (68), Zavella initially retreated but later realized that the contesting principles of feminism and Chicano/Latino academic norms were more than textual dilemmas to be addressed ethnographically. She notes that the conflict echoes the "Chicano movement ideology," which silenced Chicana representations of them as "feminists" (58). Zavella concludes that a Chicana feminist ethnography must respect women's constructions of their identity while also remaining accountable to "Chicano/Latino" academic audiences. She encourages Chicana feminist ethnography that "would present more nuanced, fully contextualized, pluralistic self-identities of women, both as informants and researchers" (72).

In many ways, Chicana feminists, especially those whose work is interdisciplinary, offer the most profound advancements on the overlapping subject/object. For example, Emma Pérez (1993) and Carla Trujillo (1993) convincingly decode the cultural purity/gender/sexuality hierarchies within Chicana experiences and aim to dismantle the hegemony of heterosexuality and patriarchy. Both scholars alternate between a first- and third-person narrative, demonstrating how they play between the subject/object positions. Trujillo's (1991, 1998) anthologies of Chicana and lesbian literature further complicate a Chicana/lesbian position since she literally produces the space and language (Pérez 1993) of this subjectivity/objectivity. In similar fashion, Anzaldúa (1987) celebrates an ambiguous Chicana subject-position, the new mestiza, without pathologizing contradiction and conflict, though she is more attentive to imagining a hemisphere without domination.

The nostalgic and romantic vision of Anzaldúa does not preclude other scholars, particularly Chicana feminists, from building on the palimpsest of Chicana/o representation. Frequently, Chicana feminists anticipate and reconfigure postmodernist concerns by questioning not only representation but also the authority anthropologists claim over the realm of culture. Thus, while the initial dialogue aimed to include a Chicano anthropology or to decolonize anthropology, Chicana feminists and other women of color "challenge the closed borders of that territory" and work to create their own field (Behar 1995, 3). For example, the contributors to *This Bridge Called My Back* and *Making Face, Making Soul* assert that "anthropologists and similar specialists … were no longer the unique purveyors of knowledge about cultural meanings and understandings" (7). As Moraga states in her poem, "For the Color of My Mother," "I am a white girl gone brown to the blood color of my mother/*speaking for her* through the unnamed part of the mouth/the wide-arched muzzle of brown women" (1983, 12, emphasis added). Moraga recognizes the ambiguous status of Native American ethnographer Ella Deloria and African American ethnographer Zora Neale Hurston, who both served as welcomed "native" informants but were excluded as scholars in anthropology (Behar 1993, 85). Even their status as students of Franz Boas, the "father" of American anthropology, did not authorize Hurston's or Deloria's work. Chicana feminists, such as Moraga, do not intend to become native informants; so they speak for themselves.

Indeed, *This Bridge Called My Back* is a dialogue with feminists of color that invites "white" women to listen, but ultimately demands "a new connection …, set of recognitions …, site of accountability …, [and] source of power: US [women of color]" (Bambara 1983, vi). The contributors were no longer willing to serve a "white" women's movement but aimed to create their own agendas, coalitions, and actions in order to establish "freedom even in the most private aspects of our lives" (Moraga 1983, xix). Certainly, the editors interpret their ability "to retrieve control of their book" from Persephone Press, a "white women's press of Watertown, Massachusetts and the original publishers of *Bridge*," and to publish it through Kitchen Table: Women of Color Press (Moraga and Anzaldúa 1983), as an effort to redistribute power and authority in concrete way. Appropriately, they democratize access to writing and representation by including a variety of genres, such as poems, speeches, letters, and stories as well as publishing those "who have been silenced before uttering a word, or, having spoken, have not been heard" (Anzaldúa 1990, xvii). As Romano's corpus of work demonstrates, they refuse to separate creative writing from critical writing, lived experience from social theory. They expand the dialogue initiated by Romano and others because they embrace the variations of race, ethnicity, social privilege, gender, and sexual orientation—not just class and culture. That is, they note hierarchies within Chicano Studies, Women's Studies, and other disciplines and acknowledge that these hierarchies reflect those outside the academy. They offer their work as an interrogation of privileged male and heterosexual discourse, counting it as knowledge and authentic.

Consequently, Chicana feminists find binary oppositions or a singular cause too limiting for the analysis of complex and multifaceted experiences and practices. Thus, they are learning to braid theory into a constellation of models, making "*trenzas* of different analytical and experiential meanings" (González 1998, 85). The ability to shift from one model (i.e., critical race theory or materialism) to another (i.e., male domination or homophobia) produces an interlocking but not rigid theoretical articulation of experiences and practices. The Chicana feminist trenzas often require the reader to change her own position in order to understand the multiple voices and paradigms woven throughout a text. Indeed, Gloria Anzaldúa warns readers that these maneuvers are essential for understanding *Making Face, Making Soul* (Anzaldúa 1990, xvii). This shifting and simultaneity operate as a method for research and a practice for survival as it allows Chicana feminists to proclaim all of their identities, affiliations, and experiences without diminishing, ranking, or erasing any one.

Turning Anthropology Inside Out: A Decolonized Anthropology

The work of Chicana/o social critics, then, raises issues about the politics of representation; but unlike the postmodern concern with textual power and authority, Chicana/o scholars demand a redirection and redistribution of power both inside and outside of the academy. Therefore, their recognition of the politics of representation is not an exclusive focus on ethnographic production (i.e., writing styles and writing strategies). Admittedly, as Renato Rosaldo notes, Chicana/o scholars are concerned with textual representation, asking, "Who decides whether or not an ethnographic report is significant or accurate?" (1985, 412). In effect, Chicana feminists add, "Who decides whether or not the report is inclusive?" I suggest that they are ultimately concerned with the use or misuse of ethnographic texts since Chicana/o scholarship is not simply additive but transformative. They do not recover the history, literature, sociology, folklore, law, and art of Mexican Americans simply to enhance library collections. The work of Chicana/o scholars calls for change. In fact, "giving something back" to the "community" has become a premise of Chicana/o scholarship. The challenge to use cultural analysis and description in the effort to redirect power suggests that Chicana/o scholars aim to decolonize anthropology and the social sciences in general (not just reinvent it after the collapse of modernism). Granted a critique of colonialism emerges from the collapse of the modern, but the decolonizing aspects of Chicano/a scholarship distance it from conventional and postmodern anthropological projects.[13]

The following section describes the ways in which Chicana/o scholars not only anticipated postmodern anthropology but also had the forethought to answer some of the critics of postmodern anthropology by promoting a decolonized practice (Harrison 1991a; Arvizu 1978b).[14]

As Edmund Gordon (1991) illustrates, postmodern anthropologists are largely concerned with epistemological issues, focusing on how the practice of research and writing is a social construction shaped by politics (Clifford and Marcus 1986; Marcus and Fischer 1986). The deconstruction of ethnographic writing has produced so-called experimental ethnographies written in multiple voices, dialogues, and styles. Postmodern anthropologists suggest that these experimental writing strategies confound the author's authority. While postmodern anthropologists scrutinize ethnographic authority, they do not, however, interrogate the politics or culture of anthropology itself, notably the disproportionate rates of unemployment and underemployment among women and ethnic minority anthropologists, infrequent citation of women and ethnic minority anthropologists, and the canonization and promotion of "white" males (see Lutz 1990; Caplan 1988, Behar 1993).

In contrast, Chicana/o scholars engage a critique of ethnographic authority in order to redistribute power both inside and outside the academy. They contest the arbitrary traditions and processes that sustain various types of inequality in the academy and at large. Thus, unlike postmodern anthropologists who restrict their collaborative experiments to textual practices, Chicana/o scholars are designing research projects that emerge from dialogues with specific neighborhoods, groups, and localities; they are writing for nonschooled audiences; and they are publishing with presses that target Mexican American consumers.

The emphasis on "community-based" or applied research and writing has led Chicanas/os to institutionalize collaboration through organizations and programs that bridge the academy and the community and offer a platform on which open dialogue can occur. In fact, dialogic organizations, such as the National Association of Chicana and Chicano Studies and Mujeres Activas en Letras y Cambio Social, are the standard in the Chicana/o intellectual community.[15] Students of Chicana/o Studies are also committed to dialogue as witnessed by the number and variety of programs that bring poor and working-class youth to college campuses, internships that place college students in underprivileged communities, or classes that give college credit for community action. While dialogic organizations and programs tend to favor explicitly applied research, they do link theory with practice through sustained conversation.

In some ways, the call for a connection between theory and practice emerged from the critique of social science. For example, Gómez-Quiñonez (1977) holds the intellectual accountable to "challenging social hegemony" by "wag[ing] an ideological struggle within the political process" (22). He also suggests a decolonized social science by claiming that intellectuals operate as "critics" who "question culture, the past, the present, and the future" (22). Similarly, Chicanas are holding Chicano activists and scholars accountable to the struggle for self-determination by stating that they do not wish to go unrecognized for their contributions to the Movement and by questioning Chicano/Mexican culture and so-called traditional gender roles. In very concrete ways, Renato Rosaldo (1994) has been promoting the dialogue for a politicized intellectual who takes part in the redesign of the Western culture curriculum at Stanford University; who writes about his experience; and who consistently grounds the issues of curriculum, affirmative action, and institutional change in the real demographic changes that have *already* taken place in the classroom and the library stacks. Like many Chicana/o scholars, Rosaldo does not claim neutrality when it comes to cultures of oppression and hate; rather he imagines a place that operates on the "ethic of love" (410). Indeed, the politically motivated and "interested" Chicana/o scholar is often contrasted to the "self-interested" and "disinterested" scholar, though initially these terms were narrowly defined and nearly anyone producing "theoretical," "critical," or "esoteric" work was referred to as a *vendido/a*.

Chicana/o scholars are concerned with the discursive articulation of a Chicana/o subject. Certainly, the initial critique of anthropology called for an "alternative" ethnographic representation of Mexican Americans and it asserted a new Chicano subject. As the editorial pages of *El Grito* and as Chicana activism demand, Chicana/o Studies is producing scholarship that contests the stereotype that Mexican Americans are an oppressed luckless group with no language, no culture, and no motivations. Anthropologists such as José Cuellar, Martha Menchaca, Margarita Melville, Olga

Nájera-Ramírez, Sylvia Rodríguez, J. Diego Vigil, Carlos G. Vélez-Ibañez, and Patricia Zavella want their alternative representations of Mexican Americans to change public policy and opinion as they describe the agency of Mexican Americans. Even scholars that address ideological change, such as Mónica Russel y Rodríguez (1997), aim to transform the way we think about and, eventually, the way we interact with Chicanas/os. On the whole, Chicana/o social scientists are reinventing a formerly nonlegitimate subject and recuperating Mexican American subjectivity (Chabram 1990, 239).

Admittedly, not all Chicana/o anthropologists create alternative ethnographic representations, but even those who do not reject the conventions of anthropology "break with the anthropological tradition of bounded community studies" by examining experience across time and place (Vélez-Ibañez 1997, 11). Currently, most Chicana/o scholars argue that in order to consider the effects of domination, research on the Mexican-descent population must address multiple locations, communities, and time periods. They convincingly use a multisite methodology since it is particularly appropriate for research on communities that have various migration experiences, social and personal connections to a "homeland," or dispersals throughout two nations. Coupled with a theoretical model that accounts for intracultural diversity, this method allows scholars to create dynamic representations of the people they study.

For example, Jose Limón (1994) confounds a convention of anthropology by "studying up" and across and interrogates westernized dualities found within Chicana/o scholarship. His analysis of his intellectual precursors John Gregory Bourke, J. Frank Dobie, Jovita Gonzalez, and Américo Paredes is linked to his ethnographic account of a very specific place, South Texas. This is no community study, as Limón describes the recurrent folk poetics of South Texas as cultural maneuvers of post-modernity, characterized by permanent unemployment, a secondary labor market, urbanization, racial segregation, and the emergence and growth of a Mexican American middle class. This latter observation is part of the ongoing dialogue over class and the simultaneous critique of cultural nationalism. Yet Limón further develops the dialogue by illustrating that domination and subordination are never total or complete, and challenges even Paredes's reading of South Texas without rejecting his work all together. Limón appears to support a Chicana/o palimpsest of representation instead of "white-washing" the historical context of that production.

Finally, Chicana/o scholars position their alternative representations as the foundation for a new discipline: Chicana/o Studies, though initially conceived as Chicano Studies. This emergent field objects to the "selective imposition of intellectual premises, concepts, methods, institutions, and related organizations [on] a subordinate group" (Arce 1978, 77) and aims to produce an alternative vernacular. Working in multiple forms, styles, and genres, Chicana/o scholars 1) write in multiple languages, 2) write with "interestedness," 3) write with humor, wit, and sarcasm, 4) publish for audiences at large, and 5) acknowledge the self as both subject and object. For example, Norma Cantú invents her own genre and refers to her book, *Canícula*, as "fictional autobioethnography" since the work is based on her own childhood but tells a larger story of life *en la frontera* (1995, xi). Renato Rosaldo (1989) writes in a style that refuses simple classification, as his work employs ethnographic description, cultural critique, autobiography, literary analysis, Chicana/o Studies, and anthropology. Thus, in many ways, Chicana/o Studies transcends the disciplinary model and at times is certainly *anti*disciplinary, a turn that shares proximity to the postmodern deconstruction of disciplinary boundaries but nonetheless acknowledges the irony of dispersing the canon at the very moment that Chicanas/os arrive at the doors of the academy.

Conclusion

More than thirty years ago, Chicano scholars tried to convince anthropologists that research on Mexican Americans was lacking in quality and quantity. As Rosaldo (1985) points out in his review of Chicano anthropology, the one-sided conversation between Chicano social scientists and the silent anthropologists began as an angry assault but developed into a nuanced, tongue-in-cheek review. Chicana feminists entered the dialogue shortly thereafter and questioned the quality and quantity of work on women, lesbians, and the family. Their challenge was issued not just to "Anglo" social analysts but to "white" feminists, Mexican, and Chicano scholars and activists. In general, the emergent discipline developed dialogue on (mis)representation, the suppression of the informant's voice, ethnographic authority, objectivity, politics of research, and a rejection of totalizing theory that rendered Mexican Americans as timeless, bounded, fatalistic, and homogeneous. In short, it took on "the enlightenment tradition of rationality, deductive thinking and abstract theory"—the same critical sources for postmodern anthropology (R. García 1992, 10). Yet, the applied and critical emphasis of Chicana/o scholarship sidesteps the limitations of postmodernism by connecting theory and practice, text and power.

In particular, the strategy of positioning the self within the text is more profound than the contemporary modernist practice that exiles the author's acknowledgement of herself to the preface and footnotes and the postmodern use of the first-person narrative throughout the text. Whether by design or default, at each stage of research—from development to publication—Chicana/o scholars open a dialogue about their position and identities inside and outside of the academy. In addition, their positionality is often more than a simple matter of first-person narrative; it is a profound bias to empower the people under investigation. Still, in order to successfully transform what counts as knowledge, Chicana/o scholars need to dialogue—not monologue—about the reduction of their scholarship to descriptions of "difference" or celebrations of "cultural diversity" (see Johnson and Michaelson 1997, 4–5).

After all, in spite of our own attention to voice and authority, we must be heard or I suspect our lives and scholarship will increasingly become the focus of the Reagan-era backlash. Granted, the silence on our work is not simply because Chicana/o scholars have not fully entered the canon. The latest generation of Chicana/o scholars, including myself, studied under the protectorship of tenured Chicana/o faculty in anthropology and other departments. In short, we may have initiated a decolonized social science that questions the academy's tendency to trace all intellectual developments to Europe (Foucault, Barth, Derrida, etc.), but we have yet to pinpoint all sources that have kept us from full citizenship in academia and at large. Unfortunately, the oppressive tactics that stalled our dialogue with anthropologists are recurrent and *changing*. As Limón (1994) acknowledges, the scene has become more subtle than Paredes imagined, and Chicana/o anthropologists are lost and found again and again in the academy as affirmative action swings in and out of favor, moving some of us up and out of working-class to middle-class positions that rely on the un- and underemployment of whole segments of Mexicanos and Latinos.

Notes

I would like to thank Mónica Russel y Rodríguez, Miguel Diaz Barriga, Olga Nájera-Ramírez, Carlos Vélez-Ibañez, Richard Handler, Heather O. Leider, David G. Stanton, and the anonymous reviewers of *Aztlán* for their comments on earlier versions of this paper. I would also like to thank Renato Rosaldo for teaching me to endure life in the belly of the beast. Of course, all errors and conclusions are my own.

1. A critique of colonial relations was certainly central to Chicana/o scholarship. The now defunct internal colonialism model operates as an underlying premise for much of the early scholarship. Romano and Nick Vaca as well as Paredes were fluent in this model, and, as I suggest, their critique of anthropology is in part a rejection of a colonial anthropology. The document, *Grito del Sol*, Special Issue: Decolonizing Anthropology (1978), is an example. The special issue is the only record of a panel organized by Chicana/o anthropologists for the 1975 American Anthropological Association (AAA) Annual Meeting in San Francisco. Though the AAA Program Committee rejected the panel, "A Chicano Perspective on Decolonizing Anthropology," the organizers, including Steven Arvizu, held the panel on the Sunday morning following the close of the annual meeting.

2. This essay is primarily limited to the initial dialogue between Chicano and Anglo anthropologists and among Chicana/o social scientists writing in the 1970s and 1980s. It does briefly address, however, scholarship produced after the 1970s that is concerned with culture, the representation of Mexican Americans, and the role and identity of the Chicana/o intellectual. It is not a comprehensive review of Chicana/o anthropology or the field of Chicana/o Studies. My goal is to demonstrate that Chicano and Chicana scholars have been engaging in a dialogue about voice, representation, the politics of research, and authority prior to the 1980s North American fascination with postmodernism. Feminist anthropologists (see Behar and Gordon 1995) have raised similar arguments, suggesting that a postmodern genealogy begins in the Americas as well as in Europe and among women as well as men. Further research could demonstrate that no one population, group, or intellectual school has en-joyed a monopoly on these issues.

3. Guillermo Gómez-Peña (1986) makes a similar argument about Chicano artists who deconstructed the Eurocentric art world and art market long before "postmodern art" was fashionable.

4. Although Renato Rosaldo's 1985 review of Chicano anthropology appeared in the canon-setting *Annual Review of Anthropology*, the conditions under which he began the review still exist today: namely, we are known only to ourselves. Because anthropology continues to erase Chicana/o research, I quote extensively from several Chicana/o scholars in an attempt to give voice to those so effectively silenced by the discipline. This strategy may prove cumbersome for some, but it allows me to practice a decolonialized social science. Finally, and as a part of such a practice, I acknowledge the work of Angie Chabram (1990), whose close reading of Chicano scholarship and anthropology inspired this paper.

5. Though I agree with Rosaldo's (1985) assessment of Chicano anthropology, I am less certain than he is in distinguishing the Romano-Vaca critique from that of Américo Paredes's. According to Rosaldo, the Romano-Vaca "strident assault" posited that institutional racism in America made it impossible for social scientists to be objective, whereas Paredes's assessment of anthropology, a "more modulated posture[,] showed that the ethnographies of Madsen and Rubel erred less in overt prejudice than in the more subtle (and therefore more pernicious) unconscious perpetuation of stereotypes" (408). Clearly, one can read the Romano-Vaca editorial as "a rude assault" (408), but I also hear hyperbole and satire, literary devices meant to encourage the reader to challenge everything in the text (not to

take it literally) and to alert us to the complexity of the subject. Readers should not forget that Romano was also writing poetry and short stories, some of which employed "brutal cynicism" (see, for example, Eugene Fraire-Aldava 1973).

6. In this essay, Romano clarifies his claim that even Mexican American social scientists are not exempt from "fallacious" analysis since Julian Samora is included in his lineup. It is revealing, however, that Samora's positionality has been largely unexplored.

7. Indeed, as the dialogue expanded, one could not determine a single, homogeneous, or essential voice, position, or authority but multiple, contradictory, ambiguous and contingent voices, positions, and authorities that produced an equally diverse range of representations of Mexican Americans—serving as a blow to cultural determinist and other static models of culture. For an analysis that does not discredit Chicana/o diversity, see Cooper Alarcón (1997).

8. Here, I would add that the materialist perspective of culture develops Romano's (1967) previous claim that all social scientists are influenced by "self-interest" as it locates those interests in class and race relations.

9. Ironically, while Paredes could see the limits of essentializing Anglo anthropologists, he did not question his own essentialist vision of Mexicans. It is as if Paredes wants us to believe that all Chicanos are native Spanish-speakers, share in the same rural experience, and engage similar metaphors and styles of performance. Yet elsewhere, as Limón notes, Paredes is dissatisfied with the pachuco/pocho of South Texas whose urban sensibilities (i.e., using microphones to sing and dancing to polkas) offend what Paredes envisions as authentic folklore and song (1994, 91–94).

10. Paredes points out that not only does Edmonson misinterpret the song, authored in the classic Spanish copla form, but he misidentifies it as one of the "modern tin-pan alley songs of Mexico" composed in "near-nonsense" (Edmonson 1967, 359, as quoted in Parades 1994, 7).

11. Because Paredes's analytical project is Greater Mexico, the geographic region from the southwestern United States to the Yucatan Peninsula, Kearney's ethnography in southern Mexico is included in his critique of anthropology.

12. Alma García's (1997) edited collection reprints over eighty documents that challenge patriarchy, cultural nationalism, sexism, and androcentrism in Chicano scholarship and practice. It is revealing, however, that many of the documents did not gain national or even regional circulation until García's publication.

13. Though I agree with Angie Chabram's assessment of the postmodern project of Chicano scholarship (1990, 241), it is my position that the revisionist agenda of Chicana/o scholarship, grounded in the goals of the Chicano Movement that aimed to achieve social equality in all public institutions, leads to a decolonized anthropology.

14. In concert with Faye V. Harrison and the contributors to *Decolonizing Anthropology*, I am concerned with colonizing practices that extend beyond classic colonial sites. I am particularly interested in those spaces of violent intrusion made in the name of white supremacy and patriarchy. Here I am thinking of neocolonial practices such as the dislocation and concentration of Native Americans in reservations, the deportation of Mexicans and the militarization of the border,

the detainment of Asian Americans during World War II, abortion restrictions, opposition to same-sex marriages, and the entire history of slavery and its legacy.

15. My understanding of dialogic institutions comes from Tchen (1992).

Works Cited

Alarcón, Norma. 1990. "The Theoretical Subject(s) of *This Bridge Called My Back* and Anglo-American Feminism." In *Making Face, Making Soul*, ed. G. Anzaldúa, 356–69. San Francisco: Aunt Lute.

Anzaldúa, Gloria. 1987. *Borderlands/La Frontera: The New Mestiza*. San Francisco: Aunt Lute.

———, ed. 1990. *Making Face, Making Soul/Haciendo caras: Creative and Critical Perspectives by Women of Color*. San Francisco: Aunt Lute Books.

Apodaca, Maria Linda. 1979. "The Chicana Woman: An Historical Materialist Perspective." In *Women in Latin America: An Anthology from Latin American Perspectives*, ed. Eleanor Burke Leacock et al., 81–101. Riverside, CA: Latin American Perspectives.

Arce, Carlos. 1978. "A Case of Academic Colonialism: Chicano Participation in the Academe." *Grito del Sol* 3, no. 1: 75–104.

Arvizu, Steven F. 1978a. "Critical Reflections and Consciousness." *Grito del Sol* 3, no. 1: 119–23.

———, ed. 1978b. "Special Issue: Chicano Perspectives on Decolonizing Anthropology." *Grito del Sol* 3, no. 1.

Baca Zinn, Maxine. 1979. "Chicano Family Research: Conceptual Distortions and Alternative Directions." *Journal of Ethnic Studies* 7, no. 3: 57–71.

———. 1975. "Chicanas: Power and Control in the Domestic Sphere." *De Colores* 2, no. 3: 19–31.

Baca Zinn, Maxine, Lynn Weber Cannon, Elizabeth Higgenbotham, and Bonnie Thornton Dill. 1986. "The Costs of Exclusionary Practices in Women's Studies." *Signs* 11, no. 2: 290–303.

Bambara, Toni Cade. 1983. "Foreword." In *This Bridge Called My Back*, ed. C. Moraga and G. Anzaldúa, vi–viii. New York: Kitchen Table, Women of Color Press.

Behar, Ruth. 1993. "Expanding the Boundaries of Anthropology." *Visual Anthropology Review* 9, no. 2: 83–91.

Behar, Ruth, and Deborah A. Gordon, eds. 1995. *Women Writing Culture*. Berkeley: University of California Press.

Cantú, Norma Elia. 1995. *Canícula: Snapshots of a Girlhood en la Frontera*. Albuquerque: University of New Mexico Press.

Caplan, Pat. 1988. "Engendering Knowledge." *Anthropology Today* 4, no. 5: 8–12.

Chabram, Angie. 1990. "Chicana/o Studies as Oppositional Ethnography." *Cultural Studies: Special Issue on Chicana/o Cultural Representations* 4, no. 3: 228–47.

Chabram Dernersesian, Angie. 1993. "And, Yes … The Earth Did Part: On the Splitting of Chicana/o Subjectivity." In *Building with Our Hands: New Directions in Chicana Studies*, ed. A. de la Torre and B. M. Pesquera, 34–56. Berkeley: University of California.

Clifford, James. 1988. *The Predicament of Culture: Twentieth-Century Ethnography, Literature, and Art*. Cambridge: Harvard University Press.

Clifford, James, and George Marcus, eds. 1986. *Writing Culture: The Poetics and Politics of Ethnography*. Berkeley: University of California Press.

Cooper Alarcón, Daniel. 1997. *The Aztec Palimpsest: Mexico in the Modern Imagination*. Tucson: University of Arizona Press.

Cotera, Martha P. 1977. *The Chicana Feminist*. Austin: Information Systems Development.

Cuellar, José. 1980. "A Model for Chicano Culture for Bilingual Education." In *Ethnoperspectives in Bilingual Education Research*, ed. R. V. Padilla, 179–204. Ypsilanti: Eastern Michigan University.

Davalos, Karen Mary. 1996. "*La Quinceañera*: Making Gender and Ethnic Identities." *Frontiers: A Journal of Women Studies* 16, nos. 2/3: 101–127.

"Editorial." 1967. *El Grito* 1, no. 1: 4.

Fraire-Aldava, Eugene. 1973. "Octavio Romano's 'Goodbye Revolution, Hello Slum': A Study of Ironic Tone and Meaning." *Aztlán* 3, no. 1: 165–70.

García, Alma. 1992. "Chicano Studies and 'La Chicana' Courses: Curriculum Options and Reforms." In *Community Empowerment and Chicano Scholarship*, ed. M. Romero and C. Candelaria, 53–60. Berkeley, Calif.: National Association for Chicano Studies.

———. 1986. "Studying Chicanas: Bringing Women into the Frame of Chicano Studies." In *Chicana Voices: Intersections of Class, Race and Gender*, ed. T. Córdova, N. Cantú, G. Cardenas, J. García, and C. M. Sierra, 19–29. Austin: Center for Mexican American Studies Publications.

García, Alma M., ed. 1997. *Chicana Feminist Thought: The Basic Historical Writings*. New York: Routledge.

García, Igancio M. 1996. "Juncture in the Road: Chicano Studies since 'El Plan de Santa Barbara.'" In *Chicanas/Chicanos at the Crossroads*, ed. D. R. Maciel and I. D. Ortiz, 181–203. Tucson: University of Arizona Press.

García, Richard A. 1992. "Creating Consciousness, Memories and Expectations: The Burden of Octavio Romano." In *Chicano Discourse: Selected Conference Proceedings of the National Association for Chicano Studies*, ed. J. Tatcho Mindiola and E. Zamora, 6–31. Houston: University of Houston, Mexican American Studies Program, NACS Publication.

Gómez-Peña, Guillermo. 1986. "A New Artistic Continent." In *Made in Aztlán*, ed. P. Brookman and G. Gómez-Peña, 86–96. San Diego: Tolteca Publications, El Centro Cultural de la Raza.

Gómez-Quiñones, Juan. 1977. *On Culture*. Popular Series No. 1. Los Angeles: UCLA Chicano Studies Center Publications.

González, Francisca E. 1998. "Formations of *Mexicananess: Trenzas de identidades multiples* / Growing Up *Mexicana*: Braids of Multiple Identities." *Qualitative Studies in Education* 11, no. 1: 81–102.

Gordon, Edmund T. 1991. "Anthropology and Liberation." In *Decolonizing Anthropology: Moving Toward an Anthropology for Liberation*, ed. F. V. Harrison. Washington, D.C.: Association of Black Anthropologists and American Anthropology Association.

Harrison, Faye V. 1991a. "Anthropology as an Agent of Transformation: Introductory Comments and Queries." In *Decolonizing Anthropology Moving toward an Anthropology for Liberation*, ed. F. V. Harrison, 1–14. Washington, D.C.: Association of Black Anthropologists and American Anthropology Association.

———. 1991b. "Ethnography as Politics." In *Decolonizing Anthropology: Moving toward an Anthropology for Liberation*, ed. F. V. Harrison. Washington, D.C.: Association of Black Anthropologists and American Anthropology Association.

Johnson, David E., and Scott Michaelsen. 1997. "Border Secrets: An Introduction." In *Border Theory: The Limits of Cultural Politics*, ed. S. Michaelsen and D. E. Johnson, 1–39. Minneapolis: University of Minnesota Press.

Limón, Jose E. 1994. *Dancing with the Devil: Society and Cultural Poetics in Mexican-American South Texas*. Madison: University of Wisconsin Press.

———. 1973. "Stereotyping and Chicano Resistance: An Historical Dimension." *Aztlán* 4, no. 2: 257–70.

López, Sonia A. 1977. "The Role of the Chicana Within the Student Movement." In *Essays on La Mujer*, ed. R. Sánchez and R. M. Cruz, 16–29. Los Angeles: UCLA Chicano Studies Center Publications.

Lutz, Catherine. 1990. "The Erasure of Women's Writing in Sociocultural Anthropology." *American Ethnologist* 17, no. 4: 611–627.

Marcus, George E., and Michael M. J. Fischer, eds. 1986. *Anthropology as Cultural Critique: An Experimental Moment in the Human Sciences*. Chicago: University of Chicago Press.

Melville, Margarita B. 1978. "Mexican Women Adapt to Migration." *International Migration Review* 12, no. 2: 225–35.

Menchaca, Martha. 1995. *The Mexican Outsiders*. Austin: University of Texas.

———. 1993. "Chicano Indianism: A Historical Account of Racial Repression in the United States." *American Ethnologist* 20, no. 3: 583–603.

Moraga, Cherríe. 1983. "For the Color of My Mother." In *This Bridge Called My Back*, ed. C. Moraga and G. Anzaldúa, 12–13. New York: Kitchen Table, Women of Color Press.

Moraga, Cherríe, and Gloria Anzaldúa, eds. 1983. *This Bridge Called My Back: Writings by Radical Women of Color*. New York: Kitchen Table, Women of Color Press.

Nájera-Ramírez, Olga. 1996. "Media Representations of Charreria: Tradition of Torture?" Paper read at The National Association for Chicana and Chicano Studies XXIII Annual Conference, at Chicago, Illinois.

Orozco, Cynthia. 1986. "Sexism in Chicano Studies and the Community." In *Chicana Voices: Intersections of Class, Race and Gender*, ed. T. Córdova, N. Cantú, G. Cardenas, J. García, and C. M. Sierra, 11–18. Austin: Center for Mexican American Studies Publications.

Pardo, Mary. 1984. "A Selective Evaluation of El Plan de Santa Barbara." *La Gente*: 14–15.

———. 1980. Mexicanas/Chicanas: Forgotten Chapter of History." *El Popo* 14, no. 4: 8.

Paredes, Américo. 1978. "On Ethnographic Work among Minority Groups." In *New Directions in Chicano Scholarship*, ed. R. Romo and R. Paredes, 45–69. La Jolla: Center for Chicano Studies.

Pérez, Emma. 1993. "Sexuality and Discourse: Notes From a Chicana Survivor." In *Chicana Critical Issues*, ed. N. Alarcón et al., 45–69. Berkeley: Third Woman Press.

Rabinow, Paul. 1985. "Discourse and Power: On the Limits of Ethnographic Texts." *Dialectical Anthropology* 10, nos. 1/2: 1–22.

Rodríguez, Sylvia. 1989. "Art, Tourism, and Race Relations in Taos: Toward a Sociology of the Art Colony." *Journal of Anthropological Research* 45, no. 1: 77–99.

Romano-V., Octavio. 1969. "The Historical and Intellectual Presence of Mexican Americans." *El Grito* 2, no. 2: 32–46.

———. 1968. "The Anthropology and Sociology of the Mexican-Americans: The Distortion of Mexican-American History." *El Grito* 2, no. 1: 13–26.

———. 1967. Minorities, History and Cultural Mystique." *El Grito* 1, no. 1: 5–11.

Rosaldo, Michelle Zimbalist. 1974. "Woman, Culture, and Society: A Theoretical Overview." In *Woman, Culture, and Society*, ed. M. Z. Rosaldo and L. Lamphere, 17–42. Stanford, Calif.: Stanford University Press.

Rosaldo, Renato. 1994. "Cultural Citizenship and Educational Democracy." *Cultural Anthropology* 9, no. 3: 402–411.

———. 1989. *Culture and Truth: The Remaking of Social Analysis*. Boston: Beacon Press.

———. 1985. Chicano Studies, 1970-1984." *Annual Review of Anthropology* 14: 405–27.

Russel y Rodríguez, Mónica. 1997. "(En)Countering Domestic Violence, Complicity, and Definitions of Chicana Womanhood." *Voces: A Journal of Chicana/Latina Studies* 1, no. 2: 104–141.

Sandoval, Chela. 1990. "Feminism and Racism: A Report on the 1981 National Women's Studies Association Conference." In *Making Face, Making Soul*, ed. G. Anzaldúa. San Francisco: Aunte Lute.

Sosa Riddell, Adaljiza. 1974. "Chicanas and El Movimiento." *Aztlán* 5, no. 1: 155–165.

Tchen, John Kuo Wei. 1992. "Creating a Dialogic Museum: The Chinatown History Museum Experiment." In *Museums and Communities: The Politics of Public Culture*, ed. I. Karp, C. M. Kreamer, and S. D. Lavine. Washinton, D.C.: Smithsonian Institution Press.

Trujillo, Carla. 1993. "Chicana Lesbians: Fear and Loathing in the Chicano Community." In *Chicana Critical Issues*, ed. N. Alarcón et al., 117–125. Berkeley: Third Woman Press.

———, ed. 1991. *Chicana Lesbians: The Girls Our Mothers Warned Us About*. Berkeley: Third Woman Press.

———, ed. 1998. *Living Chicana Theory*. Berkeley: Third Woman Press.

Vaca, Nick. 1970a. "The Mexican-American in the Social Sciences, Part I: 1912–1935." *El Grito* 3, no. 3: 3–24.

———. 1970b. "The Mexican-American in the Social Sciences, Part II: 1936–1970." *El Grito* 4, no. 1: 17–51.

Vélez-Ibañez, Carlos G. 1997. "Chicano Drivers of Ideas in Anthropology Across Space and Place." Paper read at Conference of Transforming the Social Sciences through Latina/o Studies, Michigan State University.

———. 1996. *Border Vision: Mexican Cultures of the Southwest United States.* Tucson: University of Arizona Press.

Vigil, Diego. 1978. "Marx and Chicano Anthropology." *Grito del Sol* 3, no. 1: 19–36.

Vigil, J. D. 1983. "Chicano Gangs: One Response to Mexican Urban Adaptation in the Los Angeles Area." *Urban Anthropology* 12, no. 1: 45–75.

Zavella, Patricia. 1993. "Feminist Insider Dilemmas: Constructing Ethnic Identity with 'Chicana' Informants." *Frontiers: A Journal of Women Studies* 18, no. 3: 53–76.

———. 1987. *Women's Work and Chicano Families: Cannery Workers of the Santa Clara Valley.* Ithaca: Cornell University Press.

V.
Continuing to Push Boundaries

Continuing to Push Boundaries
Introduction

Chon A. Noriega

In reviewing the articles published in *Aztlán* since 2000, several trends are notable: the strategic use of autobiographical narration within scholarship across several disciplines (see *I Am Aztlán: The Personal Essay in Chicano Studies*), the increased attention to mass media and public culture, and, above all, the exploration of the "intersectionality" of race, sexuality, and citizenship.

This section includes five essays that examine such intersectionality from the perspectives of family history, cultural expression, and social citizenship. Robert Chao Romero's essay, "El destierro de los Chinos: Popular Perspectives on Chinese-Mexican Intermarriage in the Early Twentieth Century," examines Chinese-Mexican intermarriage during the early twentieth century. Romero's study goes beyond presenting a simple historical examination of the "phenomenon of Chinese-Mexican intermarriage" by destabilizing the notion of mestizaje that has been a cornerstone of Chicana/o studies and historiography. Steven Volk and Marian Schlotterbeck's essay, "Gender, Order, and Femicide: Reading the Popular Culture of Murder in Cuidad Juárez," examine three cultural responses to the femicide of women in Ciudad Juárez, Mexico. These include photographs by Julian Cardona, a novel by Carlos Fuentes, and lyrics by Los Tigres del Norte. Volk and Schlotterbeck argue that "even as these artists express a profound sympathy for the victims' plight, their representations, which are based on patriarchal binaries of male dominance and female submissiveness, often act to revictimize the women."

John Alba Cutler's essay, "Prothesis, Surrogation, and Relation in Arturo Islas's *The Rain God*," examines Arturo Islas's 1984 novel *The Rain God* through the intersection of discourses about disability, sexuality, and ethnicity. In particular, Cutler examines the novel's queer bodies in relation to Islas, arguing how the author's "place in Chicano literary history relates to the shifting contours of Chicano ethnicity." Ultimately, Cutler offers an original reading of *The Rain God* that highlights how the novel "envisions bodies coming into relation with each other—a familial love that allows for recognition of difference as something other than abnormality." Jessica E. Jones essay, "Spatializing Sexuality in Jaime Hernandez's *Locas*," examines "the graphic landscape" of Jaime Hernandez's comic, *Locas: The Maggie and Hopey Stories*. Jones argues that *Locas* presents a new vision of sociability, *familia*, and sexuality through its interplay of bodies and space. In the end, this interplay "produces a queer urban Aztlán." Finally, Adelaida R. Del Castillo's essay, "Illegal Status and Social Citizenship: Thoughts on Mexican Immigrants in a Postnational World," provides an insightful and timely exploration of "social citizenship" for Mexican immigrants in a postnational world.

The above essays can be seen in the contexts of the four thematic sections that organized the first edition, with Romero in "Decolonizing the Territory," Volk and Schlotterbeck in "Performing Politics," Cutler and Jones in "Configuring Identities," and Del Castillo in "Remapping the World." Together, these essays complement the earlier essays while bringing new critical issues and approaches to the foreground. As is characteristic of the field of Chicano studies, these authors continue to challenge the boundaries of race, gender, sexuality, citizenship, and, as filmmaker Lourdes Portillo says in her classic documentary *La Ofrenda: The Days of the Dead* (1988), "whatever else needs a little push."

Illegal Status and Social Citizenship
Thoughts on Mexican Immigrants in a Postnational World

Adelaida R. Del Castillo

AUTHOR'S NOTE: *The unauthorized status of undocumented Mexican immigrants in the United States remains a timely subject of concern and continues to pose a challenge to the fixity of the nation-state and its traditional liberal notions of citizenship. That "citizens without consent" practice a kind of citizenship considered by theorists to be of far greater consequence than its political counterpart invites a rethinking of past strategies used for the defense of undocumented immigrant workers in the United States that extends beyond the nation-state. The social construction of unauthorized immigrants as human persons and individual rights-holders invites their protection through a universal human rights discourse both within the political community and before international bodies that challenges the belief that legal citizenship or nationhood is vital to the practice of full rights.*

Importantly, the human rights of undocumented women merit attention. An estimated three million undocumented immigrant woman, most of them impoverished Mexicans, reside in the United States, representing one-third of the unauthorized immigrant population in the country. Lack of access to social services, including housing, employment, healthcare, childcare, and mental health, adversely impacts the quality of their lives. As a labor force they are more likely to be deprived of a living wage and are less likely to solicit help when they are victims of sexual harassment and/or sexual abuse. We don't know how many undocumented immigrant women are victims of sexual assault during migration trajectories nor how many are victims of domestic abuse while residing in the United States. A human rights discourse would argue that by virtue of their humanity, women share equally inalienable and inviolable rights that entitle them to goods, services, and opportunities to be provided by the political community and society in general and as such are not predicated on nationality or territoriality nor based on distinctions of legal or illegal status.

This paper is intended as a preliminary statement on unauthorized immigrant status and the making and practice of social citizenship in the state.[1] I will refer to unauthorized or undocumented Mexicans living

From *Aztlán: A Journal of Chicano Studies* 27, no. 2 (2002): 11–32.

561

in the United States as agents of economic, social, and cultural consequence and as individual rights-holders. This approach reconceptualizes
the undocumented immigrant as a human person and acknowledges the
practice of social citizenship by illegal immigrants through their creation
of community in host countries. That undocumented Mexican immigrants
have for generations created community and practiced citizenship without
consent in the United States questions the fixity of political communities.
The unauthorized enactment of social citizenship by those outside the state
as well as the application of a human rights discourse to the situation of
undocumented Mexican immigrants remove the latter from the parameters
of the state and invite a postnational approach to the challenges posed by
undocumented immigrants.

The remaking of civic identity is perhaps what Hannah Arendt had
in mind when she referred to the global conditions of the past century
as marked by stateless persons, refugees, and those deprived of rights.
Habermas (1992) envisions an emergent world citizenship ushered in by
a greater human democracy. In Europe, notions of a "citizen's Europe" are
being used to create a citizenship that extends beyond the nation-state
to a European Community. Here in San Diego where I live, the constant
presence of Mexican immigrants creates my shared community: I eat their
food, listen to their music, speak their language, watch their media, know
their manners, and hire their labor.

Living on the unitedstatesian side of the border, one is daily reminded
of the marks of privilege—legal status, an overprotected political border,
and the benefit of social entitlements denied illegal immigrants who help
to pay for them through taxes.[2] At times, particularly when the economy is
precarious, to live in San Diego is to live on the badlands of a moral geography (Shapiro 1994) where vigilante nativist groups take measures of their
own to prevent illegal immigration. This fear of and mobilization against
unauthorized immigrants reveals an outside presence within the state that
contests territoriality and disrupts normative procedures of membership
in the nation-state (Brubaker 1989; Soysal 1994, 1996). My interest in
this topic is based on my experience as an observer of transnationalism on
the U.S.-Mexican border, as well as on the growing literature on notions
of citizenship and the more recent anthropological interest in the human
rights of immigrant workers.[3] For more than a decade, theorists have been
turning their attention to the theoretical, practical, and unintended consequences of the movement of immigrant populations to the nation-state.[4]
Of special interest are the meaning and construction of citizenship status

and the possible redundancy of the nation-state to this process (Brubaker 1989; Wallace 1990). Anthropological interest in the human rights of immigrant workers is in part the outcome of a humanitarian concern for these people by social scientists who have lived among them or worked with them, or who are themselves descendents of immigrants from Mexico or other countries. Attention to global interconnectedness and the discourse on borderlands would seem to encourage a global, transnational defense of the undocumented immigrant once perceived as a human person entitled to rights.

In the following presentation, I will argue that unauthorized Mexican immigrants practice a kind of citizenship in the United States that results in an expression of social rights or social citizenship. In doing so these immigrants defy the state's political and judicial prerogatives and challenge fundamental standards of civil society, nationhood, and national borders by operating on a "postnational" or beyond-the-state level (Kearney 1991; Soysal 1994). I will refer to the practice of creating community and the utilization of social rights in the host country as *postnational citizenship*, and argue that it consists mostly of informal, sometimes makeshift, activities at the local level that suggest a civic identity and social citizenship made possible by the benefits and government largess of the welfare state.[5] That is to say, in a liberal democratic society such as ours, where the "citizen" is reproduced through cultural norms, civic education, and cultural resources (Bridges 1994), unauthorized immigrants reproduce cultural and social citizenship primarily through the deployment of *survival strategies* in the host country. These strategies involve the use of established cultural norms, resources, and institutions, but may also involve informal networks of social service and resources. Such is the outcome of lived life by immigrant populations acting out daily-life aspects of global events and demographic changes often caused by the very nation-states to which they immigrate (Sassen-Koob 1982).

Citizenship

Political citizenship in Western liberal democracies could be described as the modem equivalent of the feudal privilege and inherited status that greatly enhanced one's life chances (Carens 1987). But life chances for outsiders may not be the objective of principles of citizenship that traditionally emphasize politico-legal membership in a community based on ascription (place of birth) or line of descent (ethnic identity).[6] Ethnic homogeneity as a basis of citizenship may have an unsure future as societies become more and more diverse through the influx of guest workers, asylum seekers, refugees, and illegal immigrants, as well as the shifting of national boundaries and, in Germany, post-Communist reunification. Some would argue that the development of a West German identity has resulted in the exclusion of long-term foreign residents as well as ethnic Germans from the former German Democratic Republic (Fulbrook 1996). Ascriptive citizenship, too, is perceived as problematic in a democratic society. Schuck and Smith, for example, argue that American ascriptive citizenship is contrary to the democratic exercise of choice: "In its purest form, the principle of ascription holds that one's political membership is entirely and irrevocably determined by some objective circumstance—in this case, birth within a particular sovereign's allegiance or jurisdiction. According to this conception, human preferences do not affect political membership; only the natural, immutable circumstances of one's birth are considered relevant" (1985, 4). These authors contend that American citizenship calls for "consensual citizenship" as more faithful to the spirit of choice that inspired the founding of the incipient United States. Schuck and Smith argue that this country's Founding Fathers intended for individual consent to decide political affiliation based on the free choices of individual citizens. This interpretation, they insist, is more consistent with the country's "commitment to consent" and has implications for how citizenship status should be established if the country's pledge to free individual choice is to be honored. Citizenship status, then, should not be based on birthright (which is imposed without the individual's consent), but rather on a process of mutual consent between the national community and the individual. Lastly, Soysal (1994, 1996) believes that future conceptualizations of citizenship will have to consider more seriously supranational phenomena such as the growth of international migration, the intervention of international organizations, and the moral weight of universal human rights advocacy. Soysal argues, for example, that Turkish guest workers in Europe operate on a postnational level of citizenship rights. My own interpretation of postnational citizenship draws from her work and returns to the question of life chances by addressing the matter of universal human rights for the undocumented immigrant.[7]

Social Citizenship

Half a century ago, T. H. Marshall conceptualized citizenship as evolving from a combination of civil, political, and social elements in the eighteenth, nineteenth, and twentieth centuries. All three elements refer to rights: the political element refers to the right to participate in the exercise of political power; the civil element refers to rights considered indispensable for individual freedom, such as freedom of speech, religion, and thought, physical liberty, and the right to own property; and, lastly, the social element refers to rights associated with the welfare of a people, such as the right to a decent standard of living, leisure, and goods, the right to work, and the right to social services such as education, health care, housing, unemployment insurance, pensions, social security, and so on. Social rights, then, address a minimum expectation of standards, goods, and services to be anticipated from the welfare state, that is, the liberal democratic state organized to provide these (Roche 1992). Social citizenship also assumes that individuals have a duty to work in order to generate tax revenues to pay for the benefit of social rights and the welfare state (Marshall 1950; Roche 1992). Illegal immigrants, I contend, both benefit from the social services of the host country and fulfill the duty of full citizens to create tax revenues through their labor to pay for these services.

Social rights are important to our discussion because they are sensitive to political and economic structural changes, including those caused by industrialization and postindustrialization. I agree with Roche (1992) that the global organization of capitalism has undermined social citizenship for full citizens, as is evident in the changing standards for the quality of life, but I would argue that this same phenomenon presents possibilities for the social rights of noncitizens as well. In less developed countries with uneven economies such as Mexico's, the postindustrial presence of capital has helped to "push" labor out by making it superfluous. In Mexico's case, much of this labor has sought work, albeit illegally, in the healthier economy of its neighbor, the United States. Illegal residence in this country has, in turn, made it possible for immigrants to access the services, resources, and higher standard of living of the welfare state even if procured without consent.

This access to social citizenship by unauthorized immigrants has not escaped the notice of the political right and forms part of its nativist discourses. In 1994, the growing presence of illegal Mexican immigrants in California spurred right-wing groups and their supporters to push for the passage of Proposition 187, denying illegal immigrants access to indispensable social services including education and health care.[8] The measure passed with 59 percent of the vote, reflecting citizens' fears that illegal immigrants are a burden on the state's social service system despite their economic contributions to the state's economy. A study by RAND's National Defense Research Institute found that immigrant labor, both legal and illegal, is responsible for the majority of the state's labor force growth, outpacing the economic growth for the rest of the nation. California's employment growth is directly attributed to the lower cost of immigrant labor when compared to the cost of native labor. The same study found that for the period 1991–1993 there were no significant differences between natives and immigrants in their use of public services (McCarthy and Vernez 1998, 29–45).[9] Refusal by California's electorate to acknowledge these economic benefits to the state denies unauthorized immigrants legal access to their social rights, even though they fulfill the social duties of a full citizen by working and paying taxes. Almost two decades ago specialists warned that Mexican immigrant labor to this country would, in effect, constitute a subsidy to the U.S. economy, representing a transfer of human capital and an expansion of this country's reserve army of labor (Bustamante and Cockcroft 1983). These concerns draw attention to the social and moral dimension of universal human rights to be discussed later.

Illegal Immigrants and Postnational Citizenship

Postnational discussions of the nation-state stress a transnational community's relations to institutional, juridical, and spatial notions rather than to bounded political territories.[10] In the late twentieth century, the nation-state in Europe and the Americas took preliminary steps toward open borders and economies to facilitate economic, commercial, labor, and cultural collaboration between nations.[11] Latin America established a common market community that would also allow for cultural exchanges. The Mercado Comun del Sur (MERCOSUR) was established in 1991 by Argentina, Brazil, Paraguay, and Uruguay; its integration offers social, economic, cultural, and political postnational relations and open borders between its member states.[12] In contrast, the North American Free Trade Agreement (NAFTA) between the United States, Mexico, and Canada has yet to set provisions for the free movement of labor between its member states.[13] Despite this, I believe, through the exercise of social rights in the host country and unauthorized travel across national borders, illegal Mexican immigrants have unintentionally set a precedent of postnational participation and cultural exchange in North America. Though immigrants' survival strategies must be resilient enough to withstand the pressure of their socioeconomic, political, cultural, and moral stigmatization by the broader civic community, postnational citizenship should not be seen as the outcome of premeditated maneuverings by immigrant groups, but rather as the unintended consequence of economic, social, and political phenomena.

This local-level reproduction of citizenship by unauthorized immigrants contributes to a civic identity that does not necessarily assume the equality of the full citizen in the host country, although it does assert the natural freedom of all human persons to pursue and make a living wherever possible. The civilizing cultural practices of undocumented immigrant communities contest civic discourses that privilege only full citizens as special members of society and as free and equal individuals. For the full citizen, this free and equal status is obtained through participation in activities related to the public sphere. For the illegal immigrant, the public sphere is flexible, local, and informal.

Though liberal political theory does not invite conceptualizations of citizenship without a nation-state framework, I believe that ethnographic research among undocumented Mexican immigrants shows the generation of what can be considered *social citizenship* patterns by those who fall outside the parameters of the nation-state. How is this possible? Let us turn to ethnography to better understand these practices. Ethnographies are well suited for capturing the meaning and particulars of lived experience over time because of their use of participant observation and extensive periods of field research. The cultures of groups and individuals in Mexico have been the subject of numerous anthropological studies for well over half a century (Redfield 1930; Lewis 1951, 1961; Cancian 1965; Diaz 1966: Foster 1967; Kearney 1972; Chiñas 1973; Romanucci-Ross 1973; Kemper 1977; Lomnitz 1977; Vélez-Ibáñez 1983; Chant 1985; Behar 1993; Del Castillo 1993; Gutmann 1996). Their immigrant travels to and settlement in the United States have also generated ethnographic studies. For at least a generation, anthropologists have followed the lives, settlement patterns, and survival strategies of undocumented Mexican immigrants in this country (Dinerman 1978; Melville 1981; Chávez 1985, 1988, 1990, 1991; Kearney 1986; Chavira 1988; Chavira-Prado 1992, n.d; O'Connor 1990; Villar 1990; Goodson-Lawes 1993; Hondagneu-Sotelo 1994; Hirsch 1998, 1999; Pessar 1998; Ibarra 2000).[14] Ethnographic studies tell us that Mexican undocumented immigrants enter the country illegally, secure employment, reunite their families or form new ones, establish and sustain households, and look after the needs and interests of their communities. This settlement process is an important aspect of immigrants' self-perception as community members who have adjusted both socially and emotionally (Chávez 1991).

Tarascans in Southern Illinois

Recruited mainly as temporary migrant workers from Cherán, Michoacán, Mexicans came to southern Illinois in the late 1960s to assist in the labor-intensive harvesting of apples and peaches, the region's principal commodity crops. The recruitment of lone male migrants to the area discouraged permanent settlement until wives and other family members began to migrate in the late 1970s. According to Chavira-Prado (1992, n.d.), Tarascan immigrants in southern Illinois are predominantly undocumented, Spanish speaking, and impoverished. The division of labor in migrant camps ranks undocumented immigrant workers below legal migrants and locals and relegates undocumented immigrant women below everyone else. Most often this means that undocumented Tarascan women assume the lowest paid, most physically demanding jobs in the packing houses and double as a reserve army of labor.

As if to duplicate being-in-the-world in forms reminiscent of sender communities, Tarascans in southern Illinois attempt to buffer the troubles and challenges of newcomer families by forming networks of mutual aid and trust (*confianza*) that make possible loyalties and obligations between kin and ritual kin (Chavira 1988; Chavira-Prado 1992, n.d.). The material assistance, access to services and resources, and exposure to knowledge and information that result from these networks of aid speak to the paramount importance of becoming engaged in community as fictive kin, *compadres* (godparents), *ahijados* (godchildren), and friends (n.d.), contributing to one's civic responsibility to community.

Though not full members of the body politic, Tarascans nonetheless appropriate rights and services for their communities and participate as individuals in society. They find work, settle, establish viable cultural communities, comply with the law, pay taxes, send their children to public schools, and make use of public and private resources by taking advantage of church, child care, medical, and welfare services. They are, in effect, practicing social citizenship. Not surprisingly, scholars suggest that social, civic, economic, and even political rights have come to be based on residency and labor, not citizenship status, causing the erosion of distinctions between citizen and alien (Schuck 1989). Adversarial political forces in this country intent on generating anti-immigrant legislation suggest to us that, indeed, denial of legal status does not preclude immigrant access to *the social rights of full citizens*.

Women and the Creation of Community

Studies also describe the impact of gender difference on immigrants' adjustment to the host environment (Hondagneu-Sotelo 1994; Hirsch 1998; Ibarra 2000). For more than a generation, women have represented as much as 52 percent of the undocumented immigrant population in the United States (Simon and DeLey 1986). I have argued elsewhere that gender-appropriate norms, their performance and pretense, allow Mexican women in Mexico an inordinate degree of control over the family (Del Castillo 1993). In this country, Mexican immigrant women make possible access to institutions and agencies that serve the family such as schools, clinics, and religious groups.[15]

Gender difference, for example, is significant to the survival and adaptive strategies of immigrant Tarascan communities in southern Illinois (Chavira 1988; Chavira-Prado 1992). Women assist in the re-creation of community through the use and maintenance of sociocultural patterns of interaction based on the social networks of the sending community (Chavira-Prado n.d.).[16] They also enhance the quality of life for family members by making use of community resources such as health care for U.S.-born children and pregnant women, church charities, school lunch programs, and day care centers. Women broker the goods, services, and opportunities that these programs offer to their families by gathering information about them and testing their quality and usefulness through their social networks (1992, n.d.). By the late 1990s, Tarascan undocumented laborers and their families had established communities in or adjacent to Cobden, Murphysboro, and Carbondale by purchasing homes or plots of land. Cobden public schools now offer bilingual programs and a Migrant Head Start program, churches in all three communities offer at least one service in Spanish, health care literature is bilingual, Mexican food products are sold in some stores, video stores stock films in Spanish, and Cobden's community park serves as a public space for Mexican families to gather on weekend afternoons (n.d.).

The Tarascan data attest to the continued importance of women in a transnational context by showing that: (a) immigrant communities without women lack a sociocultural basis for growth; (b) women integrate themselves into male immigrant communities by providing resources and services not readily available to the men; (c) women make use of subsistence work as well as public and private subsidy resources to compensate for diminished male incomes during low employment periods; and, finally, (d) women act as mediators of sociocultural conflict (Chavira 1988; Chavira-Prado 1992, n.d.).

The U.S. Constitution ensures the rights of citizens and noncitizens alike, and the state is responsible for enforcing these rights within its territory. In this case, then, "citizenship gives rise to no distinctive claim" (Carens 1987).[17] The state is entrusted and expected to enforce the rights that individuals already enjoy by birthright. But human identity is not neutral. The political culture that formally declares human beings as "free and equal" decidedly adheres to a practice of *preferences* that does not encompass everyone. It speaks a moral language that may rank and discriminate according to class, ethnicity, gender (Bridges 1994), and legal status. Excluded from *political citizenship,* illegal immigrant workers have been excluded from a public discourse that, quite frankly, erases the value of their lives and makes possible egregious acts of violence against them. We have only to recall the brutal beating of undocumented immigrants by Riverside and Los Angeles police officers, the forced detention and enslavement of undocumented farmworkers by growers, and the murder of undocumented immigrants by private U.S. citizens. These and related acts represent a gross violation of the human rights of illegal immigrants. Therefore, advocacy on behalf of undocumented immigrant workers for the defense of their human rights before an international authority seems a rational and necessary step.

Universal Human Rights

Since 1945, the international community has recognized and formally sought to establish human rights norms as part of customary international law.[18] These rights are considered a birthright because the human person is perceived to be rational, moral, and inherently endowed with dignity, worth, equality, and freedom. By virtue of their humanity, then, individual persons share equally inalienable and inviolable rights that entitle them to goods, services, and opportunities to be provided by the political community and society in general.[19] The national and international support given human rights groups and their causes attests to the moral force of these arguments.

It is important to recognize that human rights norms privilege the individual rights of the person over those of national membership (Soysal 1996) and over the claims of a sovereign people, since these operate within limits set by individual human rights. Not surprisingly, human rights claims can create tension between the rights of the individual and the will of the people in liberal democracies when the latter violates the human dignity and fundamental freedoms of the human person (Donnelly 2001).

Scholars (Soysal, Weaver) note that the articulation and elaboration of human rights on a global scale has worked to bestow many citizenship rights and privileges on populations not belonging to a national group, such as immigrants. I have argued that undocumented Mexican immigrants in the United States acquire access to the rights and privileges of citizens when they adapt to the host country and create community, even though they do so without consent. Once we place the plight of undocumented immigrants in the context of universal human rights, we constitute them as free and rights-bearing individuals entitled to pursue a life of human dignity through the right of mobility and the right to work in just and favorable conditions (Article 23, Universal Declaration of Human Rights).[20] Already the practice of social citizenship without the benefit of political citizenship places the undocumented Mexican immigrant outside the purview of the state, but a human rights discourse situates the undocumented immigrant within an international community capable of championing his or her rights even though it is the duty of the state to promote, respect, and protect all human rights and freedoms. A human rights discourse helps to redefine the status and expand the rights of undocumented immigrants. Though rights do not in themselves constitute a legal tradition, human rights speak to a particular moral attitude or notions of "right reason" that apply to all human beings (Vincent 1992, 252–53). In this sense, immigrants, even if illegal, are rights-holders.

Not surprisingly, the United Nations–sponsored World Conference Against Racism (WCAR) in 1978 and 1983 included "those who are undocumented" on its list of migrant workers in need of human rights protection (Grange 2001). The 1978 WCAR Programme of Action called for migrant workers "to be given treatment no less favourable than nationals," including "contracts, right to reside, trade union activities, access to tribunals, communication in own language, franchise in local elections, right of family reunion, social security, retirement pensions, health care, educational opportunities, preservation of cultural identity, acquisition of property within and outside country." The 1983 WCAR Programme of Action echoed these requests and also called for migrants to have access to courts and tribunals, remuneration equal to that of nationals, and equal treatment regarding social security and retirement pensions; it further stipulated that children of migrant workers should receive education in their mother tongue and on aspects of their culture. In 1997, however, the U.N. Seminar on Immigration, Racism and Racial Discrimination noted that a 1990 international convention to protect the human rights of migrant workers was a "near failure" because few states had ratified the agreement. The most recent WCAR, in 2001, omitted the term *undocumented* when it listed migrant workers in need of protection (although it did refer to "victims of illegal trafficking").

Still, for more than a generation, nongovernmental organizations have made use of human rights arguments to question intrastate and cross-border violations of people's rights, even though previously (immediately after World War II) these claims had been the exclusive function of the nation-state. While civic or national rights can only be realized by "a people," one need not belong to a nation to benefit from human rights, since these are not predicated on nationality or territoriality nor based on distinctions of legal or illegal status. Consequently, the growing ability of individuals and nonstate agencies to make international claims for the human rights of groups has consequences beyond the state (Jacobson 1996). When immigrant workers and their sympathizers take to the streets to protest violations of their rights and denial of access to social citizenship (as was the intent of California's Proposition 187), they too utilize the urban space of the state as an institutional platform from which to address a broader international and constitutional order. In this way, illegal immigrants and their supporters expand the notion of "the people" and challenge the belief that legal citizenship (or nationhood) is vital to the practice of full rights.

Just how international human rights ethics and institutions are impinging on the nation-state remains a matter of contention. Some scholars believe that, as Jacobson says, "the state is becoming less constituted by 'the people' in the face of human rights codes and agencies" (2). That is, the devaluation of citizenship favors the importance of international human rights. Within the nation-state itself, nationality is more and more often reconceptualized to mean *nationality as a human right* and not as a principle that reinforces state sovereignty. There are those who believe that this suggests the nation-state may no longer adequately frame the labor and social parameters of citizenship status in a globally integrated arena.[21] Some theorists have gone so far as to argue that the nation-state has become historically obsolete.[22] Others prefer to speak of rights and obligations "nested" within distinct political communities that challenge exclusive notions of state sovereignty.[23]

Conclusion

I have argued that undocumented Mexican immigrant communities unintentionally undermine the authority of the state to regulate social citizenship status when these communities strive to adapt to life in the United States. They do so by making use of the resources and benefits offered by the welfare state to which they contribute economically with their labor and taxes, helping to keep state economies such as California's afloat. Importantly, access to the benefits of social citizenship makes the latter of greater use and value to unauthorized immigrant communities than political citizenship, which remains an exclusionary function of the state.

The concept of a weaker role for the state as arbiter of labor and social citizenship challenges notions of the fixed political boundaries of the state; the United States ultimately cannot contain the undocumented immigration of Mexicans in pursuit of a decent wage and standard of living. This quest by undocumented immigrants raises questions concerning universal human rights. Once again, this contests the power of the state as necessarily the final arbiter of the human rights of unauthorized communities within its boundaries.

With the growing acceptance of human rights issues as part of international politics in the past thirty years, we have seen the displacement on several occasions of state power by international agencies acting on behalf of a broader international society and a greater good. The presence of unauthorized Mexican immigrants in the United States and their practice of social citizenship have too often been countered with stark violations of their human rights. I have suggested that the protection of undocumented communities is better undertaken by international organizations, given that human rights have increasing moral and political authority that goes beyond that of the nation-state.[24] That is, the state can be held accountable to an international community with the power (however limited) to redress wrongs.

Finally, I have suggested that state sovereignty in the United States has been disrupted by the unauthorized practice of social citizenship by illegal immigrant Mexicans, forcing a rethinking of social, political, and human rights and nationhood status. This being the case, transnational political entities may in the future have to replace more and more functions of the state in response to the growing number of floating populations who traffic the globe transnationally. The emergent twenty-first century will no doubt see a greater shift from national to transnational institutional standardization and legislation, facilitating the formation of a kind of "world citizenship" to accommodate the rights and dignity of one of the least protected populations—undocumented immigrant workers.

Notes

1. I will use *unauthorized, undocumented,* and *illegal* as interchangeable designations for immigrants without legal status in the host country.

2. Kearney (1991, 55, 71, note 9) has coined this term based on the Spanish usage of *estadounidense* to refer to people of the United States. Mexicans have told me that the term *American* includes all peoples who inhabit the Americas, including Mexicans; therefore, they prefer the more accurate *estadounidense* when referring to citizens of the United States.

3. See, for example, Downing and Kushner 1988; Weaver 1988; Del Castillo 1997; Nagengast and Vélez-Ibáñez 2004; and Vélez-Ibáñez 2004.

4. This literature grew substantially in the 1990s. For some of the literature prior to this period see Schmitter 1979; Schuck and Smith 1985; Turner 1986; Carens 1987; Brubaker 1989.

5. Some theorists argue that membership in the welfare state is far more significant than political membership, which they see as declining in importance. See Schuck 1989.

6. Ethnic identity links a community of people integrated geographically or by shared culture and ethnicity, as in the case of Germany.

7. See Cesarani and Fulbrook 1996.

8. Proposition 187 made illegal aliens ineligible for public services, public health care (unless an emergency), and public education at the elementary, secondary, and postsecondary levels. In March 1998, a federal judge ruled most of Proposition 187 unconstitutional for several reasons, including a prior Supreme Court decision (*Plyler v. Doe,* 1982) that entitles all children under eighteen to public education regardless of their immigration status. The court cited the general principle that immigration law is a federal, not a state-level, issue. The court did uphold the provision of Proposition 187 that makes the manufacture, distribution, sale, or use of false citizenship or residence documents a felony offense. Governor Davis has sent Proposition 187 into mediation. Although no action has taken place so far, it could possibly reach the Supreme Court if the appeals process is not dropped by the state.

9. These services include cash assistance, nutrition, health, and housing programs, with the exception of school lunch and breakfast programs for the children of immigrant parents.

10. Similar notions were anticipated by medieval concepts of civil participation where society is not identical with its political organization. Hegel, too, conceptualized civil society as existing beyond the state (Taylor 1990). In contrast,

Schuck and Smith, in *Citizenship without Consent* (1985), attribute the origins of birthright citizenship to notions of feudal status, sovereignty, and allegiance.

11. For questions of cultural significance and the creation of the European community see Shore and Black 1996.

12. See Ferrer 1996.

13. A discussion of NAFTA's impact on Mexico's economy is offered by Carolyn Wise (1998). For a comparison between the common market economies of North America and Europe, see Gianaris 1998.

14. The recipient of one-third of all immigrants (legal and illegal) to this country, California is an important destination for migrants. Between 1990 and 1995, 1.5 million immigrants entered the state, bringing California's immigrant population to a total of 8 million in 1995. Of the 5 million illegal immigrant residents in this country, an estimated 2 million reside in California. For the past forty years, the influx of Mexican immigrants has represented the single largest immigrant group in California, peaking in the 1980s. Presently, 50 percent of all immigrants to California are Mexican and Mexico is the primary source of illegal immigration to the United States. See McCarthy and Vernez 1997, 1998.

15. In California, K-12 school enrollment increased by one-third in 1996, with much of this increase attributed to the entry of immigrant children and children born in the United States to immigrant parents. See McCarthy and Vernez 1998.

16. In his study of social networks, *Rituals of Marginality*, Carlos Vélez-Ibáñez (1983) documents the importance of these activities in a Mexican context.

17. This is not to deny the body politic where citizenship means political membership or where sovereign people are the source of the supreme authority of the nation in a liberal democracy.

18. In 1945 the Covenant of the League of Nations expressed concern for human rights. International human rights instruments adopted by the United Nations include the Universal Declaration of Human Rights adopted by the U.N. General Assembly in 1948, the International Covenant on Economic, Social, and Cultural Rights (1976), the International Covenant on Civil and Political Rights (1976), the Optional Protocol to the International Covenant on Civil and Political Rights (1976), the Second Optional Protocol to the International Covenant on Civil and Political Rights (1991), the Vienna Declaration and Programme of Action (1993), and the human rights provisions of the Helsinki Final Act (1975).

19. The International Bill of Human Rights opens with: "All human beings are born free and equal in dignity and rights. They are endowed with reason and conscience and should act towards one another in a spirit of brotherhood." The Universal Declaration of Human Rights presents the "inherent dignity and ... equal and inalienable rights of all members of the human family" as the basis of "freedom, justice and peace in the world."

20. Other human rights relevant to undocumented Mexican immigrants include the rights to self-determination; life; freedom of movement and choice of residence; protection of the family unit: equal access to courts and tribunals; presumption of innocence until proven guilty; equal protection under the law: freedom from torture and cruel, inhumane, or degrading treatment or punishment; freedom from slavery or servitude; liberty and security of person. In addition, there

are rights to one's own culture, to leave any country and enter one's own, etc. See Weaver 1988.

21. This would not apply to declarations of war and hostility by the state toward terrorist groups perceived as a threat to its national security and, by consequence (unintended or not), the persecution of immigrant groups with which terrorists are identified. Such now appears to be the case for Arab Muslims in the United States, thousands of whom are being held without due process since the destruction of the World Trade Center on September 11, 2001.

22. For discussion of the transnational movement of labor in a postnational context, see Soysal 1994; Cesarani and Fulbrook 1996; Jacobson 1996. For a discussion of the nation-state as moribund see Wallace 1990.

23. See Donnelly 2001.

24. See Donnelly 2001, 140-42.

Works Cited

Behar, Ruth. 1993. *Translated Woman: Crossing the Border with Esperanza's Story*. Boston: Beacon Press.

Bridges, Thomas. 1994. *The Culture of Citizenship: Inventing Postmodern Civic Culture*. Albany: State University of New York Press.

Brubaker, William R., ed. 1989. *Immigration and the Politics of Citizenship in Europe and North America*. Lanham, MD: University Press of America.

Bustamante, Jorge A., and James D. Cockcroft. 1983. "Unequal Exchange in the Binational Relationship: The Case of Immigrant Labor." In *Mexican-U.S. Relations: Conflict and Convergence*, ed. Carlos Vasquez and Manuel Garcia y Griego, 309–23. Los Angeles: UCLA Chicano Studies Research Center and Latin American Center.

Cancian, Frank. 1965. *Economics and Prestige in a Maya Community: The Religious Cargo System in Zinacantán*. Stanford, CA: Stanford University Press.

Carens, Joseph H. 1987. "Aliens and Citizens: The Case for Open Borders." *The Review of Politics* 49, no. 2: 251–73.

———. 1989. "Membership and Morality: Admission to Citizenship in Liberal Democratic States." In *Immigration and the Politics of Citizenship in Europe and North America*, ed. William R. Brubaker, 31–49. Lanham, MD: University Press of America.

Cesarani, David, and Mary Fulbrook. 1996. *Citizenship, Nationality and Migration in Europe*. New York and London: Routledge.

Chant, Sylvia. 1985. "Family Formation and Female Roles in Queretaro, Mexico." *Bulletin of Latin American Research* 4, no. 1: 17–32.

Chávez, Leo R. 1985. "Household, Migration, and Labor Market Participation: The Adaptation of Mexicans to Life in the United States." *Urban Anthropology* 14, no. 4: 301–46.

———. 1988. "Settlers and Sojourners: The Case of Mexicans in California." *Human Organization* 47, no. 2: 95–108.

———. 1990. "Coresidence and Residence: Strategies for Survival Among Undocumented Mexicans and Central Americans in the United States." *Urban Anthropology* 19, nos. 1-2: 31–62.

———. 1991. "Outside the Imagined Community: Undocumented Settlers and Experiences of Incorporation." *American Ethnologist* 18: 257–78.

Chavira, Alicia. 1988. " 'Tienes que ser valiente!': Mexicana Migrants in a Midwestern Farm Labor Camp." In *Mexicanas at Work in the United States,* ed. M. B. Melville, 64–74. Houston: University of Texas, Mexican American Studies Program.

Chavira-Prado, Alicia. 1992. "Work, Health, and the Family: Gender Structure and Women's Status in an Undocumented Migrant Population." *Human Organization* 51, no. l: 53–64.

———. n.d. "Gender Difference and Marginalized Immigrants: Tarascan Women as Household Providers and Settlers." Unpublished manuscript.

Chiñas, Beverly. 1973. *The Isthmus Zapotecs: Women's Roles in Cultural Context.* New York: Holt, Rinehart and Winston.

Del Castillo, Adelaida R. 1993. "Covert Cultural Norms and Sex/Gender Meaning: A Mexico City Case." *Urban Anthropology* 22, nos. 3–4: 237–58.

———. 1997. "Postnational Citizenship in Los Angeles." Paper presented at conference titled Women and Migration in Latin America and the Caribbean: New Theoretical and Historical Perspectives, Princeton University.

Diaz, May N. 1966. *Tonala: Conservatism, Responsibility, and Authority in a Mexican Town.* Berkeley: University of California Press.

Dinerman, Ina R. 1978. "Patterns of Adaptation among Households of U.S.-Bound Migrants from Michoacán, Mexico." *International Migration Review* 12, no. 4: 485–501.

Donnelly, Jack. 2001."Ethics and International Human Rights." In *Ethics and International Affairs: Extent and Limits,* ed. Jean-Marc Coicaud and Daniel Warner, 128–60.Tokyo: United Nations University Press.

Downing, Theodore E., and Gilbert Kushner, eds. 1988. *Human Rights and Anthropology.* Cambridge, MA: Cultural Survival, Inc.

Ferrer, Aldo. 1996."Mercosur: Trayectoria, situación actual y perspectivas." *Desarrollo Económico* 35, no. 140.

Foster, George. 1967. *Tzintzuntzan: Mexican Peasants in a Changing World.* Boston: Little, Brown.

Fulbrook, Mary. 1996."Germany for the Germans? Citizenship and Nationality in a Divided Nation." In *Citizenship, Nationality, and Migration in Europe,* ed. David Cesarani and Mary Fulbrook, 88–105. New York and London: Routledge.

Gianaris, Nicholas V. 1998. *The North American Free Trade Agreement and the European Union.* Westport, CT: Praeger.

Goodson-Lawes, J. 1993."Feminine Authority and Migration: The Case of One Family from Mexico." *Urban Anthropology* 22, no. 3–4: 277–97.

Grange, Mariette. 2001."Elements for a Draft Declaration and Programme of Action for the World Conference versus the 1978 and 1983 World Conferences: Final Documents." Retrieved March 3, 2002, from www.december18. net/declarations2.htm.

Gutmann, Matthew. 1996.*The Meanings of Macho: Being a Man in Mexico City.* Berkeley and Los Angeles: University of California Press.

Habermas, Jurgen. 1992."Citizenship and National Identity: Some Reflections on the Future of Europe." *Praxis International* 12, no. 1: 16.

Hirsch, Jennifer. 1998. "Migration, Modernity, and Mexican Marriage: A Comparative Study of Gender, Sexuality, and Reproductive Health in a Transnational Community." PhD diss., Johns Hopkins University, Baltimore, MD.

———. 1999. "En el norte la mujer manda: Gender, Generation and Geography in a Mexican Transnational Community." *American Behavioral Scientist* 42, no. 9: 1332–49.

Hondagneu-Sotelo, Pierrette. 1994. *Gendered Transitions: Mexican Experiences of Immigration.* Berkeley and Los Angeles: University of California Press.

Ibarra, Maria de la Luz. 2000. "Mexican Immigrant Women and the New Domestic Labor." *Human Organization* 59, no. 4: 452–64.

Jacobson, David. 1996. *Rights across Borders: Immigration and the Decline of Citizenship.* Baltimore: Johns Hopkins University Press.

Kearney, Michael. 1972. *The Winds of Ixtepeji: World View and Society in a Zapotec Town.* New York: Holt, Rinehart and Winston.

———. 1986. "From Invisible Hand to Visible Feet: Anthropological Studies of Migration and Development." *Annual Review of Anthropology* 15: 331–61.

———. 1991. "Borders and Boundaries of State and Self at the End of Empire." *Journal of Historical Sociology* 4, no. 1: 52–74.

Kemper, Robert V. 1977. *Migration and Adaptation: Tzintzuntzan Peasants in Mexico City.* Beverly Hills, CA: Sage.

Lewis, Oscar. 1951. *Life in a Mexican Village: Tepoztlán Restudied.* Urbana: University of Illinois Press.

———. 1961. *The Children of Sanchez: Autobiography of a Mexican Family.* New York: Random House.

Lomnitz, Larissa A. 1977. *Networks and Marginality: Life in a Mexican Shantytown.* New York: Academic Press.

Marshall, T. H. 1950. *Citizenship and Social Class and Other Essays.* Cambridge: Cambridge University Press.

McCarthy, Kevin, and Georges Vernez. 1997. *Immigration in a Changing Economy: California's Experience.* Santa Monica, Calif.: RAND.

———. 1998. *Immigration in a Changing Economy: California's Experience—Questions and Answers.* Santa Monica, CA: RAND.

Melville, Margarita B. 1981. "Mexican Women Adapt to Migration." In *Mexican Immigrant Workers in the United States,* ed. Antonio Rios Bustamante, 119–24. Los Angeles: UCLA Chicano Studies Research Center Press.

Nagengast, Carol, and Carlos G. Vélez-Ibáñez, eds. 2004. *Human Rights, Power, and Difference: The Scholar as Activist.* Oklahoma City: Society for Applied Anthropology.

O'Connor, Mary I. 1990. "Women's Networks and the Social Needs of Mexican Immigrants." *Urban Anthropology* 19, nos. 1–2: 81–98.

Pessar, Patricia. 1998. "The Role of Gender, Household, and Social Networks in the Migration Process: A Review and Appraisal." In *Becoming American/America Becoming,* ed. Josh DeWind, Charles Hirschman, and Philip Kasinitz. New York: Russell Sage Foundation.

Redfield, Robert. 1930. *Tepoztlan, A Mexican Village: A Study of Folk Life*. Chicago: University of Chicago Press.

Roche, Maurice. 1992. *Rethinking Citizenship: Welfare, Ideology, and Change in Modern Society*. Cambridge, U.K.: Polity Press.

Romanucci-Ross, Lola. 1973. *Conflict, Violence, and Morality in a Mexican Village*. Chicago: University of Chicago Press.

Sassen-Koob, Saskia. 1982. "Recomposition and Peripheralization at the Core." In *The New Nomads,* ed. Marlene Dixon and Susanne Jonas, 88–100. San Francisco: Synthesis Publications.

Schmitter, Barbara. 1979. "Immigration and Citizenship in West Germany and Switzerland." Ph.D. diss., University of Chicago.

Schuck, Peter H. 1989. "Membership in the Liberal Polity: The Devaluation of American Citizenship." In *Immigration and the Politics of Citizenship in Europe and North America,* ed. William R. Brubaker, 51–65. Lanham, MD: University Press of America.

Schuck, Peter H., and Rogers M. Smith. 1985. *Citizenship without Consent: Illegal Aliens in the American Polity*. New Haven: Yale University Press.

Shapiro, Michael. 1994. "Moral Geographies and the Ethics of Post-Sovereignty." *Public Culture* 3: 479–502.

Shore, Cris, and Annabel Black. 1996. "Citizens' Europe and the Construction of European Identity." In *The Anthropology of Europe: Identities and Boundaries in Conflict,* ed. Victoria A Goddard, Josep R. Liobera, and Cris Shore, 275–98. Oxford: Berg.

Simon, Rita J., and Margo C. DeLey. 1986. "Undocumented Mexican Women: Their Work and Personal Experiences." In *International Migration: The Female Experience,* ed. Rita J. Simon and Caroline B. Brettel, 113–32. Totowa, NJ: Rowman and Allenheld.

Smith, Anthony D. 1990. "Towards a Global Culture?" *Theory, Culture and Society* 7, no. 2–3: 171–92.

Soysal, Yasemin Nuhoglu. 1994. *Limits of Citizenship: Migrants and Postnational Membership in Europe*. Chicago: University of Chicago Press.

———. 1996. "Changing Citizenship in Europe: Remarks on Postnational Membership and the National State." In *Citizenship, Nationality, and Migration in Europe,* ed. David Cesarani and Mary Fulbrook, 17–29. New York and London: Routledge.

Taylor, Charles. 1990. "Modes of Civil Society." *Public Culture* 1: 95–118.

Turner, Bryan S. 1986."Personhood and Citizenship." *Theory, Culture, and Society* 3, no. 1: 1–16.

Twine, Fred. 1994. *Citizenship and Social Rights: The Interdependence of Self and Society*. London: Sage Publications.

Vélez-Ibáñez, Carlos G. 1983. *Rituals of Marginality: Politics, Process, and Culture Change in Central Urban Mexico, 1969–1974.* Berkeley: University of California Press.

———. 2004. "The Human Rights Issues of the Commoditization and Devalorization of the Mexican Population of the Southwest United States." In *Human Rights, Power, and Difference: The Scholar as Activist*, ed. Carol Nagengast and Carlos G. Vélez-Ibáñez. Oklahoma City: Society for Applied Anthropology.

Villar, Maria de Lourdes. 1990. "Rethinking Settlement Process Among Mexican Migrants in Chicago." *Urban Anthropology* 19, no. 1–2: 63–79.

Vincent, R. J. 1992. "The Idea of Right in International Ethics." In *Traditions of International Ethics*, ed. Terry Nardin and David Mapel, 250–69. Cambridge: Cambridge University Press.

Wallace, William. 1990. *The Transformation of Western Europe.* London: Pinter.

Weaver, Thomas. 1988. "The Human Rights of Undocumented Workers in the United States–Mexico Border Region." In *Human Rights and Anthropology*, ed. Theodore E. Downing and Gilbert Kushner, 73–90. Cambridge, MA: Cultural Survival, Inc.

Wise, Carolyn, ed. 1998. *The Post-NAFTA Political Economy: Mexico and the Western Hemisphere.* University Park: Pennsylvania State University Press.

Gender, Order, and Femicide
Reading the Popular Culture of Murder in Ciudad Juárez

Steven S. Volk and Marian E. Schlotterbeck

AUTHOR'S NOTE: *It takes a considerable quantity of truly awful news to push a story of the mass murder of women in one city out of the news. But that is just what has happened with coverage of the "femicides" of Ciudad Juárez. In an effort to crack down on the drug cartels, Mexican President Felipe Calderón, shortly after his election in 2006, deployed more than 40,000 soldiers and federal police agents throughout the country. Some 7,000 soldiers and 2,000 federal police occupied Juárez. The result has been an unprecedented hurricane of violence, with Juárez at its tumultuous center. The city was buffeted by more than 2,640 murders in 2009 and is on a pace to break that record in 2010. A whopping 97% of those polled in November 2009 said they felt unsafe in their city, and a majority expressed their distrust of the authorities.*

In the face of the spreading carnage, non-drug related murders of the women of Juárez continue but merge into the daily announcements of the discovery of another "narcograve" or the murder of yet another pair of fifteen-year olds. Ascertaining the exact number of femicides in Juárez has proven to be so difficult that, in mid-2009, a Chihuahua state legislator proposed a resolution to the state legislature requiring a count be made. The Chihuahua state attorney general's office (PGJE) contends that there were 447 women murdered between 1993 and the end of 2008, but the media regularly references more than 600 deaths. Based on an application by the Inter-American Commission on Human Rights, the Inter-American Court of Human Rights (IACHR) directly addressed whether Mexico failed to protect three of the victims of these crimes in a trial which concluded in late 2009. In a mixed finding, the Court required the State to fully investigate the murders from a "gender perspective," as well as punishing the officials accused of irregularities (El Paso Times, Oct. 14, 2009; Frontera NorteSur, May 5, 2009). As Judge Diego Garcia-Sayán wrote, "Without doubt, [violence against women] is one of most extended and persistent expressions of discrimination throughout the world, and it is reflected in conduct ranging from subtle and veiled manifestations to inhuman and abusive situations" (Inter-American Court of Human Rights, Case of González et al. ["Cotton Field"] v. Mexico, judgment of November 16, 2009, p. 152). And yet, for all of this, Mexican authorities have convicted only one man of a single murder, and even this case is highly suspect.

From *Aztlán: A Journal of Chicano Studies* 32, no. 1 (2007): 53–86.

Much as we observed when the article was first published, in the absence of any reasonable or responsible state response and, in fact, in the face of irrefutable evidence that local and regional officials were willfully preventing the arrest and trial of likely suspects, the cultural world has continued to draw attention to the cases and offer its own "solutions" to the crisis. Films (Bordertown, dir. Gregory Nava, 2006; Juárez, dir. Alex Flores, 2007; El Traspatio, dir. Carlos Carrera, 2009), songs (by Tori Amos, At the Drive In, Bugs Salcido), and books on the subject continue to appear; perhaps the most famous is the posthumous publication of Chilean writer, Roberto Bolaño, whose 2666 is partially set in Ciudad Juárez (disguised as "Santa Teresa"). While the femicide victims have now been buried under even more corpses, they have not been forgotten.

Ya se nos quitó lo macho o nos falta dignidad.

—Los Tigres del Norte, "Las mujeres de Juárez"

Lilia Alejandra Garcia Andrade was last seen at 7:30 p.m. on February 14, 2001, by her co-workers as she walked toward an abandoned lot next to the maquiladora where she worked in Ciudad Juárez, Mexico. The seventeen-year-old mother of two crossed this unlit empty field every day to catch a bus home after work. That night she never arrived, and her mother reported her missing the next day. Her physically and sexually assaulted body was found in the lot one week later; she had been strangled to death. Those responsible for Lilia's death have not been arrested (Kahn 2003; Washington Valdez 2005, 200–4).

The story of Lilia Alejandra is all too familiar in Juárez, Mexico's fourth-largest city, sprawled across the border from El Paso, Texas. In the last thirteen years, between 400 and 500 young girls and women have been murdered in or near the city (Washington Valdez 2005, 320).[1] Some suspects have been arrested, including Abdel Latif Sharif Sharif ("the Egyptian"), members of the Rebels gang, Edgar Alvarez Cruz, and a few bus drivers. But the bodies continue to appear in vacant lots throughout the city and on the town's outskirts, scattered like plastic bags blown by the desert wind. Juárez has become a city of femicide.

Diana Washington Valdez and other journalists have identified a number of likely suspects, but, she maintains, "not one of the true murderers [involved in] this long decade of serial sexual crimes has been jailed" (2005, 237). As the murders continue unabated, not only have they generated a demand that the state act to end the killings (Ravelo Blancas 2004), but they have also triggered a dynamic cultural response. Videographers and filmmakers, novelists, poets, photojournalists, songwriters, and rock bands are but a few of the artists who have addressed the crisis facing Juárez's women. The broadening significance of this cultural response is evident in two new Hollywood films on the subject: *Bordertown*, directed by Gregory Nava, with Jennifer Lopez as a journalist investigating the murders, and *The Virgin of Juárez*, featuring Minnie Driver. Indeed, it is precisely because the state has failed so abjectly in stopping these murders that "fictional" narratives have become both the site where victims are mourned and the means by which justice can be restored. Cultural producers have filled the vacuum left by state officials who continue either to shun their responsibilities or to conceal the guilty.

This is not a novelty in historical terms. Unsolved murders, particularly those on a large scale and those targeting women, generate considerable social anxiety which artists address—and sometimes exploit (Caputi 1987). At the same time, these are works of the imagination, and even those authors most steeped in the forensic literature of the murders "solve" their cases only by leveraging what is known to arrive at well-informed speculations (Bard 2004; Gaspar de Alba 2005; Murillo 2002). Significantly, we argue, what they disclose is often the very hypostasis of their social anxiety, and what is revealed is who, or what, at the most essential level, is responsible for a situation in which women continue to be killed with impunity.

Culture, Stuart Hall reminds us, is "concerned with the production and the exchange of meanings" (1997, 2). The meanings being produced about the murders are often about Juárez itself and thus are fundamentally rooted in its location as both "border" and "borderland," as the frontier that unites and separates two nation-states, and as a contested zone in which identities, in this case gender identities, are rearticulated. To read about the Juárez femicides therefore requires that we unpack the explicit geography of this particular "transitional" setting (Rosaldo 1993, 207–8) and that we specify the anxieties that women's location in this geography have created for the artists whose work we will examine here.

Our article examines three responses to Juárez and the murders: the photojournalism of Julián Cardona, a novel by Carlos Fuentes, and a song by Los Tigres del Norte. We conclude that even as these artists express a profound sympathy for the victims' plight, their representations, which are based on patriarchal binaries of male dominance and female submissiveness, often act to revictimize the women. As many cultural producers locate women's active incorporation into the wage labor force as the engine that generated Juárez's "disorder," then it follows that "order" can only be restored when female passivity is reasserted. We also explore how the work of feminist critics, specifically Alicia Gaspar de Alba, challenges this approach by highlighting female/subaltern resistance and addressing the victims' basic rights while raising vital questions about gender identity on a highly militarized border.

Borders, Borderlands, Juárez

Gloria Anzaldúa's foundational discussions introduced the border/border-lands as a doubled space, a physical zone where "two or more cultures edge each other," as well as a form of consciousness (mestiza) that promoted intimacy between cultures as it challenged the binary thinking central to Western, masculinist thought (1987, preface, 79–80). Anzaldúa posits the border as a metaphorical construct of great potential, yet she never forgets that the "U.S.-Mexican border *es una herida abierta* where the Third World grates against the first and bleeds" (3). While Anzaldúa had a profound impact on how writers later theorized the borderlands space (Anzaldúa 1990; Calderón and Saldívar 1991; Castillo and Tabuenca Córdoba 2002; Fox 1999; Michaelsen and Johnson 1997; Mignolo 2000; J. Saldívar 1997), many scholars have begun to deemphasize the physical reality of the border space, deterritorializing the border in favor of a reading that highlights its metaphorical possibilities as a nonspecific site of ethnic, racial, and gen-dered interactions (Hicks 1991, xxiii–xxxi). Performance artist Guillermo Gómez-Peña, for example, maintains that geopolitical borders have "faded away," that Manhattan, as well as Mexico City, looks like "downtown Tijuana on a Saturday night" (1992, 60).

We resist that perspective. If border theory has presumed to "erode the hegemony of the privileged center by denationalizing and deterritorializing the nation/state" (Lugo 1997, 45), the concrete reality of the U.S.-Mexico border reminds us of this move's limitations by providing a dramatic display of state power that reinforces territorial integrity and nationalism. The U.S.-Mexico border is today one of the more militarized zones on earth. It is populated on the U.S. side by 11,000 Border Patrol agents as well as thousands of officials from the U.S. immigration and customs services, the Drug Enforcement Agency, the Federal Bureau of Investigation, and the U.S. military, along with state troopers and local police, not to mention a growing population of civilian vigilantes (the Minutemen and others). Their counterparts on the Mexican side include federal soldiers and state judicial police (*judiciales*), all the way down to a virtual army of private security guards at local assembly plants (Dunn 1996; Andreas and Biersteker

2003; Andreas 2000). The massive military presence on the border reflects a U.S. concern with immigration and drugs, but it is also directly linked to the integration of the U.S. and Mexican economies, particularly after the implementation of NAFTA in 1994. This connection goes back even further in the case of Juárez, which has operated as the primary center of export-based assembly plants, called "maquiladoras" or "maquilas," since 1965. It is this combination of state and private force alongside the machinery of late-capitalist, globalized production that suggests that the border on which the femicides are occurring exists both as a space where a new consciousness has generated challenges to traditional identities and as a very real territory of power and violence.

In their insightful study, Debra Castillo and María Socorro Tabuenca Córdoba argue that the extent to which borderlands theorists emphasize the physicality of the border/borderlands space often tracks with the writer's own location. U.S. (Chicana/o) perspectives, they observe, often privilege the notion of the border as metaphor, thereby "eras[ing] geographical boundaries" between the United States and Mexico. Central Mexican perspectives, in contrast, will more often ignore theoretical issues (as well as women's literary production) while insisting on the importance of the geopolitical divide between the two countries. If these views circulate with greater (U.S. Chicana/o) or lesser (central Mexico) success, the authors continue, the views and voices of border writers themselves are rarely heard. Rosario Sanmiguel, Norma Cantú, Sheila Ortiz Taylor, and Rosinda Conde are little known by readers who may be quite conversant with the work of Carlos Monsiváis, Carlos Fuentes, Laura Esquivel, or Guillermo Gómez-Peña (Castillo and Tabuenca Córdoba 2002, 5–7). For Ciudad Juárez–El Paso writer Rosario Sanmiguel, for example, personal and political borders shape her life and inflect her writing. The border "strikes at you from every angle," she observed in a conversation with Castillo and Tabuenca Córdoba (2002, 8). "The fact is that the United States is right next to us and the Migra is constantly watching. . . . The border is the way in which we dwell and walk through all its spaces."

Our analysis takes from this perspective, insisting on both the physical and the theoretical aspects of the border/borderlands. To begin, we locate Juárez, the scene of the murders, as a site-specific locale with an explicit history, political economy, and geography. At the same time, because our three primary examples of cultural responses to the femicides situate Juárez as a complex zone where gender roles and gender consciousness are formed and challenged, we also interrogate the city as a metaphorical space of identity transformation inherent in Anzaldúa's doubled notion of the borderlands. In this sense, Alejandro Lugo has suggested, we cannot separate border zones as "sites of creative cultural production" from border zones as "sites of lucrative manufacturing production" in the globalization of capital (1997, 57).

To explore cultural responses to the Juárez crisis, we have chosen works that originate in each of Castillo and Tabuenca Córdoba's three sites of border literature. Los Tigres del Norte is a Chicano band from California; Carlos Fuentes is a novelist from central Mexico; and Julián Cardona is a photojournalist from Juárez. It should be noted that the work of the central Mexican writer, Fuentes, circulates immeasurably more widely than that of Los Tigres, which is, nevertheless, a highly popular band. Cardona's photographic work is the least well known of the three, mostly appearing in Juárez publications, although his photographs lately have gained visibility in wider artistic and political circuits. While the three cultural producers have different access to public opinion, they do share important analytic roots, all developing their arguments about the Juárez murders from within the parameters of patriarchal discourse. Thus they are led to similar conclusions as to why the murders are happening and what needs to be done to restore "order" in the region.

Indeed, "order" and "disorder" occupy a critical terrain at the heart of the works of Los Tigres, Fuentes, and Cardona when they invoke the Juárez murders. Most bourgeois notions of order from Émile Durkheim onward have been constructed around a fear of "social disintegration" and "mob" rule. As Jane Flax has argued, "Western philosophers created an illusory appearance of unity and stability by reducing the flux and heterogeneity of the human and physical worlds into binary and supposedly natural oppositions. Order is imposed and maintained by displacing chaos into the lesser of each binary pair" (quoted in Torres 2005, 197). Explicitly or implicitly, these artists locate the root cause of Juárez's "disorder" (femicide) in a political economy that upended traditional "order" by placing women in men's roles as it generated the city's "subordinated modernity" (Méndez B. 2004, 8). Even as they express a profound sympathy for the victims, these cultural producers, to differing degrees, narratively revictimize Juárez's women by representing them within a framework of male dominance and female submissiveness, ultimately suggesting that it was women's substantial integration into the wage economy (and the changes this brought to the local sexual economy) that challenged order in Juárez and placed them in harm's way. If, for these cultural producers, female praxis generated "disorder," then "order" will only be restored when female passivity is reasserted.

At the same time, not all the cultural responses to Juárez's femicides are organized within patriarchal binaries. A number of feminist writers, film-makers, singers, and other artists have addressed the murders in important creative endeavors. Lourdes Portillo, one of the earliest and most keenly sensitive feminist critics, interrogated the femicides in her documentary, *Señorita extraviada* (2001); her work has been reviewed in these pages and elsewhere (González 2003; Portillo 2003; Enríquez 2004). Here, as a counterpoise to the three primary examples, we discuss Alicia Gaspar de Alba's *Desert Blood* (2005), one example of an emerging literature that not only deplores the murders but also highlights female/subaltern resistance, addresses the victims' basic rights, and raises vital questions about the responsibility of the state itself.

Locating Juárez: Gender and Labor on the Global Assembly Line

Juárez sits uncomfortably at the fractured intersection of late capitalism's globalized political economy and a sexual economy that remains stubbornly patriarchal. While historically the northern border was not of economic interest to the Mexican state, by the late 1950s politicians in Mexico City sought to incorporate it more fully into the national economy through the Programa Nacional Fronterizo (PRONAF) and the Programa de Industrialización Fronteriza, or Border Industrialization Program (BIP) (Martínez 1978, 115–16, 152). PRONAF, dating from 1961, was the state's response to stigmatized images of Mexican border towns as dens of vice servicing males from across the border (Sklair 1993, 30). In 1965 it was overshadowed by the more explicitly development-centered BIP, which ushered in the rapid growth of the maquiladora industry throughout the border region (Martínez 1978). Implemented the year after the termination of the binational bracero program, the BIP was designed to resolve the problem of unemployment along the border as the United States tightened its immigration regulations. The problem was particularly acute in Juárez, where Mayor Felix Alfonso Lugo worried that the unemployed migrants who remained had "become a social and economic burden" (Martínez 1978, 198 n. 52).

After the first maquiladoras opened in Juárez, the quiet border town saw its population explode as migrants from central and southern Mexico flooded north in search of employment, pushing the city far out into the harsh Chihuahuan desert. For the Mexican government, the maquilas' arrival was seen as the first step in a development plan that would spread capitalist modernization not just to the border but to all of Mexico (Baerresen 1971; Fernández-Kelly 1983; Iglesias Prieto 1997; D. Peña 1997; Sklair 1993). Value added by maquiladoras increased from 1 million pesos in 1974 to 38 billion pesos in 2004. But instead of development, the maquiladoras generated what Luís H. Méndez (2004, 8) termed "subordinated modernity" by vaulting over the historic project of industrialization in favor of late capitalism's model of globalized production (see also García Canclini 2001, 49–65).

Maquila employment in Juárez rose from 3,135 in 1970 to 249,509 by 2000, but the population of the city itself increased nearly threefold, to 1.2 million (Sklair 1993, 35, 99; INEGI 2005). Thus, while demand for wage labor grew dramatically, the BIP never significantly lowered Juárez's unemployment rate. Further, and contrary to assumptions that returning migrant men would find work on the newly industrialized frontera, maquiladora managers turned to young Mexican women as their primary labor force. Indeed, maquila-based growth was predicated on a highly gendered economic formula that cast women both as producers charged with bringing modernity to Mexico through their labor on the global assembly line, and as consumers in the modern markets that would inevitably accompany development. But the replacement of male with female workers challenged existing patriarchal structures and generated a deep well of male resentment and female vulnerability. In fact, maquiladora industrialization ultimately created a gendered and racialized political economy and shaped the city's geography in ways that facilitated, absorbed, and, perhaps, promoted femicide.

For employers, the ideal maquila worker was "docile, undemanding, nimble-fingered, nonunion and unmilitant" (Sklair 1993, 172). These traits were seen as critical to maintaining a low-wage regime, the essential ingredient of the assembly plants' competitiveness in world markets, and they were read as "female" characteristics. Still, while women accounted for nearly 80 percent of Juárez's maquiladora workers through the early 1980s, by 2004 they were just over one-half of the maquila workforce (INEGI 1991, 6; 2005). Scholars have suggested a number of reasons for this change, including industry restructuring and the fact that women in many plants began organizing to improve their conditions and pay (Bacon 2005; Fernández-Kelly 1983, 144–50; Iglesias Prieto 1997, 81–97). Tamar Diana Wilson (2002, 34) argues that economic stringencies forced men to become the "docile, nimble-fingered" (i.e., feminine) workers coveted by employers; thus regendered, men began to be hired into jobs previously filled only by women (Salzinger 2004, 54–55; Sklair 1993, 173).

Wilson's argument is cogent, but it downplays the fact that women's labor and women's bodies are observed, managed, and threatened in ways that men's are not. Key here, of course, are issues of reproduction, manipulation of the sexualized body, and susceptibility to sexual attack. Maquiladoras are inordinately intrusive work sites for women; supervisors monitor female reproductive power from the moment of first hiring (pregnant women are denied jobs) and throughout their employment. In most plants, women must show supervisors their bloody tampons monthly to remain employed (Arriola 2000; Fernández-Kelly 1983, 1997; Iglesias Prieto 1997; Sanmiguel 1994). At the same time that the plants continually monitor women's fertility, their sexualized bodies are literally paraded around in a steady cycle of employer-sponsored "beauty pageants" (Iglesias Prieto 1997, 75). Not surprisingly, male supervisors frequently demand sexual favors from female workers in return for (promises of) advancement, demands to which some accede. As María Patricia Fernández-Kelly put it, "women often find themselves in situations where they have to resort to their sexuality to gain a sense of precarious power in the labor market" (1983, 141). In the end, while the ratio of female to male maquila workers has tended toward parity, it is women who remain exceptionally vulnerable inside and outside the plants.

The Geography of Danger

If Juárez's political and sexual economies meet within the maquiladoras, to what extent are the murders about the border assembly plants? Julia Monárrez (2000, 2003), of the Colegio de la Frontera Norte in Tijuana, estimates that only 20 percent of the murdered women worked in the maquilas. In that sense, the exploitation of gendered bodies cannot adequately explain the murder of gendered bodies (Fregoso 2003, 7; Washington Valdez 2005, 57). Nevertheless, the murders cannot be understood without recognizing the specific ways that maquila development shaped both the political and the sexual economy of the border (Lugo 1995). Gaspar de Alba (2003, 106–8) makes the point exquisitely in her "Kyrie Eleison for La Llorona," particularly in the startling enjambement between the third and fourth lines noted by Suzanne Chávez-Silverman (2003, 225):

> You've gone the way of the alligators
> in San Jacinto Plaza.

You've traded your midnight cry for the graveyard

shift and a paycheck at the maquila.
That mushroom cloud hovering
over mount Cristo Rey

is your shadow.[2]

The nature of maquiladora development increased the danger to *all* Juarense women whose subaltern status placed them in harm's way. This is evident in a number of examples. In the first place, high levels of female employment, by challenging pervasive notions of the male as primary wage earner, added to a reservoir of male resentment against all women. For women, entrance into the paid labor force often meant acquisition of greater independence, increased status within the family, and freedom to socialize outside the home (Kopinak 1995, 31), leading to a need for complex negotiations regarding how these changes would be understood and implemented in the local context. An early promotional tract boosting maquiladora industrialization spotlighted the ways in which patriarchy would see the challenge of a female workforce:

> Now, it is often the daughter, working in an industrial plant, who becomes the main source of family income. . . . When the father does work, it happens not infrequently that the daughter earns more. Certainly male egos, of fathers and would-be boyfriends, must suffer some deflation from this dramatic change in the economic influence of these young women. (Baerresen 1971, 34)

Hints of later tropes that would locate Juárez's social "problem" in its female workforce appeared as early as the 1970s, when maquilas were still expanding vigorously. Writing in the *New York Times,* John Crewdson (1979) detected a "dimming" of the maquiladoras' promise because "the plants employ few men . . . for almost every woman who is lucky enough to find such jobs, there is a husband or a brother or a son who is likely to remain out of work." In another *New York Times* article five years later, Juárez's mayor attributed the "social disequilibrium" plaguing the city to all the men who found themselves "with nothing to do while their wives [go] to work." With women making up 80 percent of total assembly-line employment in 1982, Juárez, according to the Maquiladora Association's president, had "become a matriarchy" (March 19, 1984). The latter characterization stretches reality beyond recognition but offers a central image informing masculinist cultural production surrounding the Juárez murders.

To the extent, then, that the failure of maquiladora development began to be written in terms of men's absence from the maquilas, women workers were cast as a problem rather than as another exploited group within Mexico's struggling development plans, and all women became a target for male resentment.

Second, the rapid and speculative nature of maquila expansion created an urban geography of marginality that ultimately affects all women who have no choice but to negotiate specific neighborhoods, a situation particularly acute for female maquila workers (Méndez 2004; S. Peña 2005, 289; Staudt 1986, 115). While Juárez's two main industrial parks are located south and east of the historic city center, most maquila workers live in *colonias*, poorly served shantytowns that sprang up in the desert and hills southwest of Juárez (Lloyd 1986, 48). Many women begin or end their long commutes in darkness, walking through the poorly lit sprawl of the *colonias*, rendering them highly vulnerable to attack; they may also board maquila-supplied or city buses, some of whose drivers have been implicated in sexual assaults (Washington Valdez 2005, 154–58). At the same time, maquila-led development generated a downtown geography that is dangerous to all women who cannot afford to cross it in a private vehicle (Braine 2004, 32). The face of urban Juárez is pockmarked by empty lots (*lotes baldíos*) generated by the feverish land speculation that accompanied the first plants. Large parcels of urban space that never reached development stage were simply left vacant. In their movement through the city, poor women on foot traverse these lotes baldíos, spaces in which the bodies of murdered women are frequently found. As one journalist observed, "To walk through downtown Juárez is to know and deeply regret that you are a young woman" (Balli 2003, 112).

Third, maquiladoras are highly dependent on continual flows of migrant women from the center and south of Mexico. Migration north in search of (often illusive) assembly work severs the women's traditional communal ties and social networks; indeed, many of the murder victims are *anónimas*, recent arrivals who have no kin in the city. Esther Chávez Cano, director of Casa Amiga, the only women's shelter in Juárez, noted that women "have been taught to work. But they haven't been taught to live in a violent city with problems like this one. They come here very trusting, because in rural areas customs are much different" (quoted in Quinones 2001, 146). Not only are women prey to the systematic misogyny of Juárez's patriarchal society, including the state, but their lack of kinship ties on the border means that their killers have little to fear from family retribution.

591

Finally, as a significant group of wage earners, women have become important consumers of urban entertainment (bars, discotheques, dance halls, restaurants, *cervecerías*) and are no longer present in these places solely as workers (prostitutes, waitresses) (Fernández-Kelly 1983, 133–44; González Montes et al. 1995; Woods 2002). The nightlife in the city's old downtown has reoriented from male-centered forms of entertainment to cabarets catering specifically to Juárez's new wage earners: young women with cash incomes. On weekends, women workers out for an evening of relaxation pack Juárez's clubs. Wondering how anyone who had spent a grueling forty-eight-hour week on a factory floor could look forward to a night of dancing, Fernández-Kelly asked a maquila worker and was told: "If you don't go out and have fun, you will come to the end of your days having done nothing but sleep, eat, and work" (1997, 535). And yet, as women workers began to socialize outside the home and spend their own wages, they were quickly depicted by the patriarchal society as *maquilocas*, sexually provocative and promiscuous women. While a number of ethnographers have pointed to the highly "precarious" path that women must walk when using sexuality as a means of advancement in the plants (Fernández-Kelly 1983, 133–44; 1987; Iglesias Prieto 1997, 74–80; Salzinger 2003), what is striking about the maquiloca image is how maquila labor and sexuality are so often fused, ultimately making their way into explanations of the Juárez murders. When Debbie Nathan writes of "maquila sexuality [that] spills out of the plants during time off" (1999, 27), and Charles Bowden connects the exploitable aspects of the female body by arguing that "the only cheap thing in Mexico is flesh, human bodies you can fornicate with or work to death" (1996, 48), they come unwittingly close to reproducing the logic of Mexican officials who attempt to explain the disappearances of young women within Juárez. City officials have often asserted that the disappeared were leading *doble vidas*, double lives: as one said, "Many of the murdered women worked in factories during the week and as prostitutes during the weekend in order to make more money" (quoted in Fregoso 2000, 138). Portraying the victims as women who deceived their families by becoming prostitutes, Mexican authorities both dismissed their deaths and made them responsible for their own murders (Fregoso 2000). In 1999, the Chihuahuan state attorney general darkly implied that "it is impossible not to get wet when you go outside in the rain; it is also impossible for a woman not to get killed when she goes out alone at night" (quoted in Woods 2002, 143).

If these factors alone were not enough to place Juárez's poor and working-class women in danger, the shift of maquila manufacturing to other low-wage producers, particularly China, has intensified the city's chaos. Just since 2001 over 50,000 maquila workers have lost their jobs in Juárez (INEGI 2005), throwing the city's economy into a tailspin. Economically depressed and downwardly mobile cities are dangerous places for everyone, but in Juárez the generalized economic downturn has particularly increased women's vulnerability. To the extent that patriarchal society blamed women for occupying "male" positions in the wage economy, it also (ironically) looked to them as a fundamental part of Juárez's dream of modernization. When that project began to collapse in the face of Chinese competition, women became the scapegoats for its failure.

The Juárez femicides, then, represent a very specific "disorder" within a city already marked by a series of other convulsions. What is at stake when writers, photographers, singers, and other cultural producers take these murders on board, ultimately, is not just how they address the specifics of a gruesome history that stretches back more than a decade, but how (and whether) they locate the murders within the broader set of circumstances that produced them. Their consideration of the Juárez murders reveals a diagnosis of the proper framework of "order" itself. In considering the work of Julián Cardona, Carlos Fuentes, and Los Tigres del Norte, we argue that while decrying and lamenting the deaths, they fix the cultural territory of the murders within a familiar set of masculinist binaries. While the deployment of these binaries produces different results for each—orienting the photographic work of Cardona, dominating the novelistic work of Fuentes, and producing the female noncitizen in the musical work of Los Tigres—it indicates that for an important set of cultural producers whose work circulates widely, "order" will only return to Juárez when the "proper" (patriarchal) relations between men and women are reestablished.

Photographing the Maquiladoras: Julián Cardona's "Morir despacio"

Julián Cardona, a writer and photographer based in Ciudad Juárez, is one of the city's keenest observers. His photography, which appears frequently in Juárez, has also been featured in influential articles about the femicides that have reached audiences beyond the borderlands (Bowden 1996, 1998, 2000, 27–33). In his masterful photo essay from 2000, "Morir despacio: Una mirada al interior de las maquiladoras en la frontera E.U./México" (Dying Slowly: A Look Inside the Maquiladoras on the U.S.-Mexico Border), Cardona pointedly juxtaposes scenes of well-ordered assembly plants with a text that foregrounds the structural violence of the maquiladoras. His images and text pose the argument that maquila women are "dying slowly" but just as steadily as the murder victims whose bodies appear in the desert. "On the assembly lines in Ciudad Juárez," Cardona writes, "one sees the faces of . . . 13, 14-year-old girls who for five dollars a day give their lives to produce *world class product*."[3] Cardona not only satirically links assembly work and drug trafficking—the italicized words appear in English in the original—but also discloses the allusive link between maquilas and murder: factory workers "give their lives" in the plant itself.

Cardona's photographs document the ways in which maquila industrialization shapes the lives of those on the assembly lines. His visual language is strongly informed by classical tropes that circulate widely in Hispanic Catholic society. The essay's opening image, *A Young Girl at Work*, reveals a child-woman at her machine, her face and eyes lifted upward (fig. 1). Behind her, two male supervisors confer. If the viewer first reacts to her youth, it is the Christian imagery informing the photograph that will be most striking to a borderlands audience. Indeed, the photo is a remarkable contemporary take on a classic compositional theme, the "education of the Virgin," which portrays Mary as a young girl, either with her mother or alone; it was popular among seventeenth-century Spanish painters, particularly Francisco de Zurbarán and Bartolomé Esteban Murillo (fig. 2).[4] "Education," in this sense, implies upbringing, not formal instruction, and in Cardona's update the two supervisors have taken over the young woman's tutelage from her mother. Significantly, these images provide a central representation of Christian womanhood as one of chastity, submissiveness, and acquiescence to divine commandment.

Cardona returns to this theme at the close of the series. In *A Young Girl and Her Future*, we see an even younger girl in the maquiladora (fig. 3). The pig-tailed *niña*, hands clasped tentatively behind her back, contemplates a satellite dish, likely assembled in the plant. An empty chair dominates the central space of the photograph. Cardona's intricate composition captures both *the* future (instantaneous mass communications) and *her* future—we can envision the girl perched on the no-longer-empty chair, tirelessly assembling products she will never own. Unlike the first image in the series, in which the subject's personality is so richly displayed, the final image stuns us by its evacuation of the subject's identity; it is the only photograph in the series in which all we see of a worker is her back. Cardona's portrayal is of an assembly process that drains the very life from its workers, again linking real deaths in the desert to the "slow deaths" of maquila workers.

Figure 1. Julián Cardona, A Young Girl at Work, 1998. Reproduced by permission of the photographer.

Figure 2. Francisco de Zurbarán, The Childhood of the Virgin, c. 1660. The State Hermitage Museum, St. Petersburg.

Figure 3. Julián Cardona, A Young Girl and Her Future, 1998. Reproduced by permission of the photographer.

Between the opening and closing photographs of present and future workers, both suffused with visual markers of purity and innocence, Cardona elaborates maquila culture with a series of photographs featuring women and men at work as well as images suggesting the ways in which supervisors use the plants to showcase their female workers' sexuality. In one photograph, two women workers walk down a corridor lined with photographs of beauty pageant contest winners. They are followed, and by all appearances, watched, by two male managers. A second photograph is labeled in Spanish: "Trabajadoras se visten y maquillan para participar en el concurso de belleza Señorita RCA . . ." The English translation that is provided ("Maquila workers getting ready for Miss RCA beauty contest . . .") misses one of Cardona's central ironies. In Spanish, *maquillar* is to put on makeup. Yet, to the extent that Cardona's essay is about the "maquilas," it hard to avoid his subtle argument that while female workers are assembling "world class product," they are themselves being made up, reassembled (fig. 4).

Plant managers regularly hold beauty contests to reaffirm "traditional standards of feminine beauty and behavior" and to impress upon women workers that the plants care about their "physical and emotional well-being" (Iglesias Prieto 1997, 75). Cardona's photograph displays a number

Figure 4. Julián Cardona, Maquila Girls Getting Ready for Their Plant's Annual Miss RCA Contest, *1999. Reproduced by permission of the photographer.*

of women preparing for the pageant. Most are dressed in formal gowns, while the worker in the foreground, who is being "assembled" (made up) by another worker, wears a traditional Mexican costume. Iglesias Prieto argues that the maquilas' promotion of beauty pageants is intended to "reaffirm women's subordination by promoting mildness, submission, and passivity" (75). But, as the dress indicates, they also work to instill a sense of tradition (nationalism) and unity—the notion that "We are all one big family," as a poster in one plant reminds its workers (80).

How are we to read Cardona's essay? "Morir despacio" begins and ends with images of virginal immaculacy, of innocent girls whose lives are draining away on the assembly line. In its interior photographs, we are reminded that sexuality is also assembled and displayed on the lines. The iconography of sexuality in Latin America has long been dominated by a framework that centers on the binary of purity and carnality, the so-called *virgen-puta*, or virgin-whore, continuum (Alarcón 1989; Zavella 1997). While the text of "maquila workers getting ready" suggests the ways in which maquiladoras continuously manage their female workers' bodies, it also reiterates this traditional cultural framework for representing women and sexuality. Cardona's essay avoids the innuendo generated by authorities who link female sexuality to rape and murder. But in his mapping of the ontogeny of the female maquila worker, Cardona portrays purity in binary opposition to sexuality. He handles his subjects with dignity; indeed, he elevates one to the level of the mother of God. But his photographs are grounded in the iconography of female passivity that, ironically, recapitulates the female "docility" that was at the heart of the maquiladora project.

In this way, Cardona's photographs, which provide a valuable look behind the closed doors of maquiladoras, continue to work not just within a Christian imaginary but within a specific Mexican-Catholic binary elaborated by Octavio Paz and others. By dividing Mexican womanhood between la Virgen de Guadalupe and la Chingada (the "violated mother" or the "fucked one"), Paz not only plotted the virgin-whore binary but also marked *both* sides by their submissiveness. "Guadalupe is pure receptivity," Paz wrote, but "the Chingada is even more passive" (1985, 85). Paz's approach informs Cardona's work which, in its portrayal of Juárez's crisis, trades on the patriarchal binary. But it is Carlos Fuentes who drives this reading toward its ultimate conclusions.

The Center Reassembles the Border: Carlos Fuentes's *Crystal Frontier*

If Cardona's representation of Juárez speaks to the persistence of masculinist binaries among the cultural producers closest to it and most sympathetic to the plight of the city's women, these traditional binaries can even more stridently define the work of writers who do not know the city as well and who have never (unlike Cardona) walked on a *rastreo*, the search for bodies that private organizations conduct in the lands surrounding the city. When Carlos Fuentes addresses the border, not only does he deploy Paz's traditional binaries, but his distance from the subject and more resolutely patriarchal stance help shape a work that ultimately locates the roots of the femicides in an economic project that replaced men with women and locals with southern migrants.

Fuentes's work circulates considerably more widely than Cardona's. Indeed, Fuentes is typically seen as Mexico's preeminent writer, a status even more exaggerated outside Mexico, where he serves as "translator" of (central) Mexico's culture and history to English-speaking, predominantly U.S. audiences. And it is the difficult relationship between Mexico and the United States that is on display in *The Crystal Frontier: A Novel in Nine Stories* (1995), which highlights the reflective, distortive border that joins and separates the two countries.

Leonardo Barroso is the wealthy, business-savvy Mexican protagonist of the novel. Much like the earlier Fuentes character Artemio Cruz, he personifies the vast corruptions of contemporary capitalism in Mexico as generated by a mix of U.S. imperialism and homegrown greed. A maquila owner himself, Barroso cynically describes the factories as the solution to Mexico's quest for modernity. "The progress of the nation can be measured by the progress of the maquiladoras" (127), Barroso proclaims grandly to his U.S. backers. Through Barroso, Fuentes showcases maquiladoras as symbolic of the ills of Mexican society, a theme that he explores in "Malintzin of the Maquilas," one of the nine stories, which narrates the lives of women maquiladora workers in Juárez. These women's histories are familiar. They have migrated from central and southern Mexico to Juárez to take up tedious assembly jobs, thereby becoming their families' primary breadwinners. They suffer the sexual harassment of male supervisors who continually observe them from panoptic vantage points. And they are sustained by female camaraderie that sweeps them outside the shop floor and into Juárez's vibrant cabarets and bars.

While Barroso is much more interested in accumulating wealth than in promoting Mexico's economic development, he is quite happy to advertise the maquiladoras as highways of progress for the nation and for Mexican women in particular. The maquiladoras

> liberated women from farming, prostitution, even from machismo itself . . . because working women soon became the breadwinners of the family, and the female head of the family gained a dignity and a strength that set her free, made her independent, made her a modern woman. And that, too, was democracy—didn't his partners from Texas agree? (127)

Barroso's argument foregrounds a metonymy that has been a familiar trope of maquila boosters and that has a well-worn colonial history: "civilization" ultimately rests on the liberation of women from the oppression of "traditional" society. Even as Mexican capitalists and U.S. managers clearly understand the quotidian reality of Juárez's female workers—the U.S. partner at one point skeptically wonders "how many times [Barroso has] staged" his "little act" (134)—they still seek refuge in a narrative in which maquila industrialization stands as a signifier of progress for women and democracy for the nation.

Fuentes has been a vocal critic of NAFTA and of Mexico's historic acquiescence to the interests of U.S. capital. Even the one-dimensional Barroso accepts that Mexico has been pulverized by globalization: "We dreamed we were in the first world and woke to find ourselves back in the third" (174). Yet despite Fuentes's critical reading of globalization's impact on Mexico, his presentation of its repercussions on the female workforce is freighted with traditional conceptions of a "proper" gendered order. The elemental social politics at play in "Malintzin of the Maquilas" is revealed one night when four maquila women head to the Malibú, their habitual rendezvous. The club, packed with working women, is a chaos of rock-and-roll dancing, theatric ceremonies in which naked, dark-skinned Mexican women are "married" to gringos, and roving Chippendale men in bow ties, boots, and jock straps. As Fuentes enters the Malibú, he engages the imagery of the maquiloca, the "hypersexual" maquila worker targeted by authorities as the real cause of Juárez's problems. On this night, as one hunk dances toward the group of maquila friends, "the girls elbow one another. In my bed, just imagine. In yours. If only he'd take me, I'm ready. If he'd only kidnap me, I'm kidnappable" (*kidnapeable*) (136).

Perhaps one can overlook Fuentes's transposition of kidnapping fantasies from male murderers to female clubbers, for his novel was published just as the Juárez femicides emerged. But the tragedy he fashions in his story suggests that death is the legitimate price paid by women who threaten patriarchal society. While the maquila friends are enjoying themselves, one of them, a single mother named Dinorah, receives word that her young son whom she left tied to a table in her shack has strangled himself on the cord. In the scene of grief that follows in the *colonia*, an older male neighbor wonders, his voice heavy with nostalgia,

> if they were right in coming to work in Juárez, where a woman had to leave a child alone, tied like an animal to a table leg. The poor innocent kid, how could he not hurt himself? The old people pointed out that such a thing wouldn't happen in the country—families there always had someone to look after the kids, you didn't have to tie them up, ropes were for dogs and hogs. (140)

For Fuentes, while maquilas are the visible sign of Mexico's dual failure to confront U.S. corporate interests and design an economy capable of sustaining its population, the tragedy of the maquiladora project, symbolized here by the death of a male child, is rooted in women's economic and sexual displacement of men. Both the new political economy (where women have become heads of households) and the new sexual economy (where *women* now stuff money into the *men's* g-strings) remove women from the home and challenge nostalgic visions of the extended and imagined (Mexican) community. As Dinorah's friends wrestle with how to console her, a gray-bearded voice of tradition observes, "My father used to tell me . . . that we should stay peacefully in our homes, in one place. He would stand just the way I am now, half in and half out, and say, 'Outside this door, the world ends'" (140–41). Fuentes fails to recognize that, with the man standing in the doorway, it is the woman who remains trapped inside, the woman for whom the world begins outside the door.

Fuentes's portrayal of the Malibú reproduces the club as a familiar exotic location quite common in colonializing discourses (Castillo and Tabuenca Córdoba 2002, 68). Even though he populates it with working Mexican women and barely dressed men, Fuentes only reverses, without unpacking, the traditional trope of the border as a magnet for U.S. men searching out scantily clad Mexican women. In the hands of writers more familiar with Juárez and less beholden to male fantasy, the club scene on the border is more fully realized. This is clear both in ethnographic (Fernández-Kelly 1983, 1997) and literary accounts. When Rosario Sanmiguel takes her male protagonist into the Mona Lisa club in the title story of *Callejón sucre y otros relatos*, we enter a location that reflects the long history of Juárez and allows for introspection, revelation, and reality, not just the parading of fantasized stereotypes (Castillo and Tabuenca Córdoba 2002, 59–68; Sanmiguel 1994). Similarly, when Alicia Gaspar de Alba's protagonist, Ivon, enters the bars on La Mariscal or Calle Ugarte in *Desert Blood*, she desensationalizes them by locating them within their own specific histories ("Mariscal" arises not from a famous general but from the smell of *mariscos*, or seafood, that wafted out of the brothels) and establishing them as sites where women act as more than sexual commodities. Ivon is searching for her kidnapped sister; as she leaves a bar called the Red Canary, she slaps the American boy demanding the attention of the *puta* tending the bar (2005, 185, 199–206).

Fuentes's deployment of maquiloca imagery inside the Malibú ("hair flying, breasts bouncing, asses shaking freely," 135), particularly when coupled with the innocent's death that occurs while all this shaking is going on, reveals his narrative as occupying the traditional masculinist iconography of a Mexico populated by saints and sluts. Fuentes discloses his organizing binary in the chapter's seemingly curious title, "Malintzin of the Maquilas." Marina is one of the four women who go clubbing and work together assembling TVs. Her parents named her after "their desire to see the ocean," *el mar* (114), yet Fuentes relocates her historically and ideologically. Marina was the Spanish-Christian name Cortés bestowed on his indigenous translator-mistress. The Aztecs had called her Malinche, but her original name was Malintzin.

Fuentes has covered this territory previously, most suggestively in *Todos los gatos son pardos*, where multiple naming evoked fractured identities.

> Three were your names, woman. . . . Malintzin, your parents said: witch, goddess of bad luck and of the blood feud. . . . Marina, your man said, remembering the ocean by which he came to these lands. . . . Malinche, your people said: traitor, mouthpiece and guide for the white man. (1997, 13–14, our translation)

If "Malinche" in *Todos los gatos* is a clever strategist who turns against Moctezuma's tyranny only to discover that both he and Cortés were "simple trinkets of two empires" (168), and "Marina" is located in the promise of movement that the sea provides, then of all the nominative possibilities, "Malintzin" is the most troubling. Malintzin is *una diosa*, a goddess, yes, but a dark one (14). Many of the witch-like characters who populate Fuentes's novels are drawn from his interpretation of the Aztec goddess Coatlicue; she possesses both life-giving and life-taking characteristics (Carbonell 1999), as evidenced by Teódula Moctezuma in *Where the Air Is Clean* (Durán 1980). In *Todos los gatos*, however, Malintzin is one-dimensional, an offshoot of Paz's Chingada, whose "taint is [seen to be] constitutional and resides in her sex" (Paz 1985, 85–86).

Of course, the representation of Coatlicue is deeply contested and occupies a certain foundational space within both Chicana/o and borderland studies (del Castillo 1974; Anzaldúa 1987; Blackwell 2003). Coatlicue, "Serpent Skirt," was a creator goddess in pre-Columbian Mesoamerica. Anzaldúa and others have argued that as male-dominated forces came to control Azteca-Mexica culture, they ruptured the dualistic Coatlicue (1987, 27–51). One aspect of Coatlicue hived off was "Tonantsi," who became the "good mother" and, after the conquest, was absorbed into the "Guadalupe/ Coatlapopeuh" identity where she was desexualized, ultimately giving rise to the virgin-whore dichotomy. For Anzaldúa, Coatlicue "represents duality in life, a synthesis of duality, and a third perspective," and Anzaldúa's call for the creation of a new mestiza consciousness rests on "unlearning" the virgen-puta dichotomy (1987, 46, 84). Fuentes, of course, insists on this binary in "Malintzin of the Maquilas," narrating the provocative and destructive Dinorah against a naïve and trusting Marina.

It is certain, as Lanin Gyurko has pointed out, that Fuentes sees the Malinche figure as the consciousness of the Mexican nation, not as a traitor (Cypess 1991, 121; Gyurko 1977, 257). By contrast, Paz insists that "the Mexican people have not forgiven [her] for her betrayal" (1985, 86). It is highly significant, then, that in *The Crystal Frontier*, Fuentes has chosen to title his tale of maquila women "Malintzin of the Maquilas," for Malintzin is the witch, bringer of bad luck, sower of chaos. For Fuentes, maquila women are not traitors (an interpretation of Fuentes that Nathan [1999, 28] puts forward), for they are incapable of Malinche's dramatic action. They are "Malintzins," signifiers of disorder. The tragedies to which they bear witness are calamities that they have brought upon themselves. Goddesses of the blood feud, they have trespassed the boundaries of tradition and therefore share responsibility for the disaster that has befallen them, Juárez, and Mexico.

A View from the North: Los Tigres del Norte and "Las mujeres de Juárez"

Murders and maquilas have been recurrent themes in corridos and *norteño* music since the late 1990s, as well as becoming a part of U.S. and Latina/o folk and Mexican *rockera* music.[5] The cultural valence of this message is important not just because the singers draw large audiences, but because these songs are composed by critics of the maquiladoras' globalization project and staunch defenders of the rights of women and workers. The work of the popular conjunto band Los Tigres del Norte is characteristic of this, as it narrates explicit themes of resistance and reordering in its response to the femicides.

Los Tigres del Norte formed in the late 1960s around Jorge Hernández, the accordionist and main singer, together with his brothers and their cousin Oscar Lara. Originally from Sinaloa, Mexico, they crossed into California as undocumented workers in 1968 and settled in San Jose. Fama Records offered them their first contract in the early 1970s and, having contemporized their sound by adding electric instrumentation, Los Tigres soon achieved crossover success. Their identification as a progressive border band was solidified with the release of "Contrabando y traición" (Contraband and Betrayal) in the mid-1970s, a hugely popular song that created the subgenre of the *narcocorrido*. In 1987, Los Tigres won a Grammy award for "Gracias, América sin fronteras." The band has attained a significant critical standing within Chicana/o culture. Anzaldúa begins her paradigm-setting work, *Borderlands: La Frontera = The New Mestiza* (1987), with an epigraph drawn from Los Tigres; José David Saldívar defines them as "mass cultural intellectuals" whose work deserves serious theoretical evaluation (1997, 1–4).

In 2004, when the images of Juárez that circulated most widely were of young women's brutalized bodies, Los Tigres del Norte released "Las mujeres de Juárez" (The Women of Juárez) on their *Pacto de sangre* album. The song, written by Paulino Vargas, sparked a controversy when it was banned from radio play in Juárez because, local officials argued, it damaged the city's reputation. Band member Luís Hernández maintains that Los Tigres "always wanted to sing about this problem. But we didn't want to get too political. We wanted to . . . tell the [Mexican] government to do something, that we want a solution" (*Chicago Sun Times*, April 4, 2004). Jorge Hernández sings "Las mujeres de Juárez" in classic conjunto style, marked by a strong polka backbeat played on the accordion. But the driving, upbeat tempo takes nothing away from the gravity of the theme. "The subject is serious," Luís insists, "so we tried to make that point by the way [Jorge] sings the song."

The song opens by arguing that the state's inability to solve the murders of Juárez's women is both suspicious—the lyrics speak of its "untouchable impunity"—and humiliating. As with much other cultural work on Juárez, it links the murders to the city's maquiladoras, describing the victims as "mujeres trabajadoras basto de maquiladoras / cumplidoras y eficientes, mano de obra sin igual" (homespun women maquila workers / reliable and efficient, hired hands without equal).[6] While satirizing the corporate voice, the verse carries a second meaning: the victims are humble working women, not maquilocas. The song delivers its principal message in the third stanza by revealing the "shame" and "humiliation" that "we" have come to feel in Mexico: "Ya se nos quitó lo macho o nos falta dignidad" (either we have already lost our manhood or we lack dignity). It is hard to read the imagined "we" and "our" as other than male referents, given the prominence of "lo macho" in the text, and this is critical to the band's interpretation. The murder of Juárez's women is to be read as a sign of Mexico's squandered masculinity.

The precise nature of this attack on "lo macho" is elaborated in subsequent verses which, spoken rather than sung, are delivered with two inflections. The first part of the verse, pronounced in a direct reportorial voice, stages the murder victims within the iconic space of motherhood:

> Woman is a blessing and a miracle of faith, the fount of creation
> She gave birth to the Czar and she gave birth to the King and even
> Jesus Christ Himself was born of a woman.

By this move Los Tigres removes the women of Juárez from their critical position within the city's political economy and relocates them as reproducers, their import solely within a sexual economy. María Herrera-Sobek has characterized the corrido as a "male-dominated genre" featuring male authors, "masculine-oriented themes," and a "strongly patriarchal ideology" (1990, xviii). And Ramón Saldívar argues that one of the reasons for the decline of the corrido "as a viable resistance form" in the 1930s was its inability to break from Mexican patriarchal discourse (2006, 177). In that sense, "Las mujeres de Juárez" remains firmly within traditional patterns of corrido representation, where women most often (but not always) appear as archetypal mother figures. What is notable in this song, however, is that the representation of women as mothers stands in unresolved tension with the view of the victims as "homespun maquila workers." If Cardona and Fuentes work within the virgen-puta binary, Los Tigres offers a contrast between reproduction and production.

The speaker's tone becomes more urgent and challenging as the song continues, rallying his listeners to action. Because the state itself is implicated in the murders, "It is the moment, citizens, to live up to our responsibility / If the law does not resolve this, we must / Punishing the cowards who abuse women." It is possible that by calling on "citizens" to take the law into their own hands, Los Tigres exhorts both men and women to act. Yet, in light of the band's representation of women primarily as mothers and victims, it seems hard to avoid the conclusion that both "citizens" and "we" refer only to the men of Juárez. Chandra Mohanty's question, raised in a different context, is equally valid here: "Who are the insiders and outsiders in this community? What notions of legitimacy and gendered and racialized citizenship are being actively constructed within this community?" (2003, 188–89).

As the corrido resumes its conjunto-polka rhythm, the responsibility of "lo macho" is juxtaposed to, indeed generated by, the "tears, laments, and prayers . . . / of the agonized mothers [who] cry on heaven to have pity / that the bodies be given to them so that they can be buried properly." Many of the victims' bodies have never been found and thus these women enter into the painful narratives of the disappeared. The psychological burdens of mourning a disappeared loved one have been well documented in the literature on the "dirty wars" of South and Central America (Hollander 1997, 117). While the lack of bodies and formal accountability have presented women's organizations in Argentina and elsewhere with an excruciating set of choices regarding the demands they bring to the state (Bouvard 1994), Los Tigres has removed the women and their organizations from these decisions. Only the men ("citizens") make the demands, appealing to the state to heed the tears of grieving mothers by producing the victims' bodies. The victims and their mothers are conflated, equally incapable of action.

The approach of Los Tigres found an unusual echo in the rockera band El TRI, which recorded a song of the same title in 2004. The rock band, one of Mexico's most popular, not only emphasized female passivity but also issued a traditional call for justice to be meted out in the next world: "Biblical justice" they argue, will punish the killers even if the police won't.

By setting the responsible male in apposition to the sorrowful female, Los Tigres redresses the crime of femicide with an appeal to traditional gender roles. The force of the corrido comes from its demand that men take matters into their own hands and "punish the cowards who abuse [our] women." Accordingly, the band would resolve these crimes by reasserting female passivity (victims, sufferers) and male vigilantism. After all, it is better to be *chingones* than *chingadas*.

Unlearning Dichotomy, Foregrounding Resistance: Gaspar de Alba's *Desert Blood*

Representations that present Juárez as a "matriarchy," the femicides as punishment for challenging patriarchy, and the solution to the crisis as the reassertion of male vigilantism and female submissiveness have attracted sizeable audiences, but they are not the only cultural responses to the murders. Among the many artists who have disputed masculinist readings of the Juárez femicides are novelists (Gaspar de Alba), documentary filmmakers (Portillo, Ursula Biemann, Alejandra Sánchez Orozco), songwriters and singers (Lila Downs, Tori Amos, Los Jaguares), visual artists (Tania Acosta Ayala, Claudia Bernal), poets (Juan Ríos Cantú, Emma Rueda), and others. While space does not allow for a full examination of these resistant and contestatory narratives, one example will provide a sense of their challenge to patriarchal readings of the crisis.

Alicia Gaspar de Alba, who grew up on the El Paso–Juárez border, is a professor of Chicana/o studies and English at the University of California, Los Angeles, where in 2003 she organized a major international conference on the Juárez femicides. Her work includes poetry, historical novels, art criticism, short stories, and essays. Her first work of detective fiction, *Desert Blood: The Juárez Murders* (2005), employs traditional (if noirish) strategies of the genre to address the murders.

Gaspar de Alba's semi-autobiographical main character, Ivon Villa, adumbrates Anzaldúa's mestiza consciousness; she is a citizen of a borderlands nation. The progeny of strong, stubborn women, she is perhaps even the great-great-granddaughter of Pancho Villa, adding to the sense that a new imagined community is being narrated. Ivon—who changed her name from "Yvonne" after she came out—leaves her El Paso–Juárez home to pursue her studies. She ends up in Los Angeles, finishing her dissertation and teaching women's studies. Returning to El Paso in order to adopt a baby from Juárez, Ivon finds herself drawn into the city's maelstrom when the still-pregnant mother of her soon-to-be-adopted child is kidnapped and brutally murdered, an act quickly followed by the kidnapping of Ivon's own sixteen-year-old sister.

Desert Blood follows the standard lines of contemporary noir detective fiction: the state apparatuses charged with solving crimes are themselves actively complicit in them. In the face of this, Ivon becomes the detective, and her (fictional) investigations reproduce elements of actual inquiries carried out by journalists and local organizations as she draws the reader's attention to narcotraffickers, the local power elite (the "Juniors"), snuff-movie producers, and maquila owners.

Desert Blood parts company with the other narratives we have examined in a number of ways, not least of which is its authorship by a lesbian feminist. While consistent with the demands of detective fiction to produce a culprit— Ivon ultimately reveals a vast web of depraved private and state agents—the novel ultimately concludes, "What did it matter *who* killed them? This wasn't a case of 'whodunit,' but rather who was allowing these crimes to happen?" (333). This question orients her approach as she probes the relationship between sex and profit. *Desert Blood* reminds us that "not all the girls who have died were *maquiladora* workers" (251), yet the social and economic realities created by the assembly plants provide the underlying dialectic for the murders. As Father Francis, a sympathetic Catholic priest who works on the border, observes, "The women are being sacrificed to redeem the men for their inability to provide for their families, their social emasculation, if you will, at the hands of the American corporations" (252). Ivon's judgment when she comes upon a mutilated body in the desert is even more bitter: "The irony of it: an assembly worker disassembled in the desert" (255). Thus, Gaspar de Alba's critique of the Juárez murders is much more systemic than that of Patrick Bard, another novelist who engaged the Juárez murders through detective fiction (2004). Bard's journalist-detective uncovers a vast conspiracy at work without eluci- dating the basic economic and social forces that provide the oxygen for this murderous conflagration. It is Gaspar de Alba's Ivon who becomes a detective in the original sense of the word, not only discovering what has been "artfully concealed," but exposing it to the light of day.

607

Perhaps the most important manner in which *Desert Blood* departs from other texts we have examined is that in narrating a history of women who are victims, the author populates her novel with strong and resistant women. Juárez may be far from a matriarchy, but in *Desert Blood* Gaspar de Alba has created her own gynocentric community inhabited by borderlands women who have "unlearn[ed] the *puta/virgen* dichotomy" (Anzaldúa 1987, 84). As with many noir tropes, the novel's "heroes" (including Ivon and her sister) are capable of acts that are exasperating, foolish, and dangerous to themselves and others, yet they call on their internal strength and intelligence to survive. But, unlike the characters in traditional detective fiction, Gaspar de Alba's characters only survive because they are supported by a (largely but not exclusively) female community built around extended family, friends, and lovers. Significantly, this community stretches beyond fictional characters to include a very real cultural and political community. Tori Amos's song "Black Dove" (1998) provides Irene, Ivon's kidnapped sister, with a bridge to sanity and strength during her ordeal. Amos wrote that the nightmarish images of the song arose from her own sexual abuse as a child (*Die Zeit*, November 11, 1999), and her own gloss on the murders appeared the following year in "Juárez" (1999), a song written in the voice of the desert itself, which is about survival and truth even though "no angel came" to save the murdered women.

Conclusion: Citizens and Rights

At its most basic level, as Mohanty has suggested, what is at stake in the Juárez femicides is nothing less than the gendered and racialized boundaries of citizenship (2003, 188–89). The masculinist virgin-whore binary, which underlies the photographic work of Cardona and dominates the novelistic work of Fuentes, ultimately produces the female noncitizen in the musical work of Los Tigres del Norte. That Los Tigres argues forcefully for redressing the murders of *las mujeres de Juárez* does not change the fact that their protection is a beneficence, not a right, and therefore depends on the generosity of (male) citizens. Gaspar de Alba, Portillo, and others whose cultural treatment of the Juárez femicides is grounded in feminism ultimately root their critiques of this approach not just in the metaphorical territory of identity, but in the modernist concept of rights—the rights of women, of the living, and of the dead; the right to live peacefully and to be treated with dignity in death. Toward the end of Ursula Biemann's video *Performing the Border*, journalist Isabel Velásquez poignantly remarks, "It's not very difficult if you're watching the evening news to see the corpse of a girl right there. Even if she's dead, she has rights. Her image is her right, even if she's not here" (1999). In the same way, Chicana singer Lila Downs's beautifully rendered "La niña" (The Girl) compels the listener to pay attention to the forces that have shattered the rights of her *niña*, Rosa María, a sad-faced maquila worker whose job is "finishing her off" and whose patron saint "is on vacation every day" (2001).

In the end, we understand, rights are only won and held through action. "To be silent is to acquiesce" (Portillo 2001). By rejecting the deployment of patriarchy as a solution to the Juárez femicides, these resistant works push their audiences to think more deeply both about metaphorical borders and about the forces that have produced the very real border that has become a nightmare for poor and working-class women. By doing so, these counternarratives ultimately return dignity and agency to the women of Juárez, both living and dead.

Notes

The authors gratefully acknowledge the help and advice of Anuradha Needham and Pablo Mitchell of Oberlin College and, in particular, the insightful critiques and suggestions of the three anonymous readers. The final product and its conclusions remain, of course, the sole responsibility of the authors.

1. According to the most authoritative account, there were 440 femicides in Juárez between 1993 and 2004 and an additional 74–260 unexplained disappearances of women and girls (see Washington Valdez 2005, 299–320). The latest suspect in the cases, Edgar Alvarez Cruz, was arrested in Denver in August 2006.

2. Excerpt from "Kyrie Eleison for La Llorona" copyright © Alicia Gaspar de Alba; reproduced with the permission of Alicia Gaspar de Alba and Arte Público Press.

3. Our translation. The Spanish text that accompanies the photo essay on the Almargen website (Cardona 2000) has varied over time.

4. The authors thank William Hood, Mildred C. Jay Professor of Art at Oberlin College, for his insightful observations on these points.

5. These include Tori Amos, "Juárez"; Lila Downs, "La niña"; El TRI, "Las mujeres de Juárez"; Mujeres en Fuga, "El boulevard de los sueños destrozados" and "Una más en Juárez"; Ana Gabriel, "Tiempo de actuar"; Mónica Vidal, "Ni una más, sin su mirar"; and Alejandro Lerner, "De mariposa a cruz."

6. Excerpt from "Las mujeres de Juárez" reproduced with permission of Univision Music Publishing.

Works Cited

Alarcón, Norma. 1989. "Traddutora, Traditora: A Paradigmatic Figure of Chicana Feminism." *Cultural Critique* 13: 57–97.

Andreas, Peter. 2000. *Border Games: Policing the U.S.-Mexico Divide.* Ithaca, NY: Cornell University Press.

Andreas, Peter, and Thomas J. Biersteker, eds. 2003. *The Rebordering of North America: Integration and Exclusion in a New Security Context.* New York: Routledge.

Anzaldúa, Gloria. 1987. *Borderlands: The New Mestiza = La Frontera.* San Francisco: Spinsters/Aunt Lute.

———, ed. 1990. *Making Face, Making Soul / Haciendo Caras: Creative and Critical Perspectives by Feminists of Color.* San Francisco: Aunt Lute.

Arriola, Elvia. 2000. "Voices from the Barbed Wires of Despair: Women in the Maquiladoras, Latina Critical Legal Theory, and Gender at the U.S.-Mexico Border." *DePaul Law Review* 49: 1–69.

Bacon, David. 2005. "Stories from the Borderlands." *NACLA Report on the Americas* 39, no. 1: 25–30.

Baerresen, Donald W. 1971. *The Border Industrialization Program of Mexico.* Lexington, MA: Lexington Books.

Balli, Cecilia. 2003. "Ciudad de la muerte." *Texas Monthly,* June, 108–17, 170–73.

Bard, Patrick. 2004. *La frontera: Una novela de denuncia sobre las muertes de Juárez.* Mexico City: Grijalbo Intriga.

Biemann, Ursula. 1999. *Performing the Border.* New York: Women Make Movies.

Blackwell, Maylei. 2003. "Contested Histories: *Las Hijas de Cuauhtémoc,* Chicana Feminisms, and Print Culture in the Chicano Movement, 1968–1973." In *Chicana Feminisms: A Critical Reader,* ed. Gabriela F. Arredondo, Aída Hurtado, Norma Klahn, Olga Nájera-Ramírez, and Patricia Zavella, 59–89. Durham, NC: Duke University Press.

Bouvard, Marguerite Guzman. 1994. *Revolutionizing Motherhood: The Mothers of the Plaza de Mayo.* Wilmington, DE: Scholarly Resources.

Bowden, Charles. 1996. "While You Were Sleeping: In Juárez, Mexico, Photographers Expose the Violent Realities of Free Trade." *Harpers,* December, 44–52.

———. 1998. *Juárez: The Laboratory of Our Future.* New York: Aperture.

———. 2000. "Camera of Dirt: Juárez Photographer Takes Forbidden Images in Foreign-Owned Factories." *Aperture* 159 (Spring): 27–33.

Braine, Theresa. 2004. "Murder in the Desert." *Business Mexico,* January, 32.

Calderón, Hector, and José David Saldívar, eds. 1991. *Criticism in the Borderlands: Studies in Chicano Literature, Culture, and Ideology.* Durham, NC: Duke University Press.

Caputi, Jane. 1987. *The Age of Sex Crime.* Bowling Green, OH: Bowling Green State University Popular Press.

Carbonell, Ana Maria. 1999. "From Llorona to Gritona: Coatlicue in Feminist Tales by Viramontes and Cisneros." *MELUS* 24, no. 2: 53–74.

Cardona, Julián. 2000. "Morir despacio: Una mirada al interior de las maquiladoras en la frontera E.U./México." *Almargen* (Ciudad Juárez). http://www.almargen .com.mx/#.

Castillo, Debra, and Maria Socorro Tabuenca Córdoba. 2002. *Border Women: Writing from La Frontera*. Minneapolis: University of Minnesota Press.

Chávez-Silverman, Suzanne. 2003. "Gendered Bodies and Borders in Contemporary Chican@ Performance and Literature." In *Velvet Barrios: Popular Culture & Chicana/o Sexualities*, ed. Alicia Gaspar de Alba, 215–27. New York: Palgrave Macmillan.

Crewdson, John. 1979. "U.S. Industry in Mexico's Border Cities: A Promise Dims." *New York Times*, February 22.

Cypess, Sandra Messenger. 1991. *La Malinche in Mexican Literature: From History to Myth*. Austin: University of Texas Press.

del Castillo, Adelaida R. 1974. "Malintzin Tenepal: A Preliminary Look into a New Perspective." *Encuentro Femenil* 1, no. 2: 58–78.

Dunn, Timothy. 1996. *The Militarization of the U.S.-Mexico Border, 1978–1992: Low-Intensity Conflict Doctrine Comes Home*. Austin: University of Texas Press.

Durán, Gloria B. 1980. *The Archetypes of Carlos Fuentes: From Witch to Androgyne*. Hamden, CT: Archon Books.

Enríquez, Alejandro. 2004. "Lourdes Portillo's 'Señorita Extraviada': The Poetics and Politics of Femicide." *Studies in Latin American Popular Culture* 23: 123–36.

Fernández-Kelly, María Patricia. 1983. *For We Are Sold, I and My People: Women and Industry in Mexico's Frontier*. Albany: State University of New York Press.

———. 1997. "Maquiladoras: The View from the Inside." In *Gender in Cross-Cultural Perspective*, ed. Caroline B. Brettell and Carolyn F. Sargent, 525–37. Upper Saddle River, NJ: Prentice Hall.

Fox, Claire F. 1999. *The Fence and the River: Culture and Politics at the U.S.-Mexico Border*. Minneapolis: University of Minnesota Press.

Fregoso, Rosa Linda. 2000. "Voices Without Echo: The Global Gendered Apartheid." *Emergences: Journal for the Study of Media & Composite Cultures* 10, no. 1: 137–55.

———. 2003. *MeXicana Encounters: The Making of Social Identities on the Borderlands*. Berkeley: University of California Press.

Fuentes, Carlos. 1977. *Todos los gatos son pardos*. 7th ed. Mexico City: Siglo Veintiuno.

———. 1995. *The Crystal Frontier: A Novel in Nine Stories*. Trans. Alfred Mac Adam. New York: Farrar, Straus and Giroux.

García Canclini, Néstor. 2001. *Consumers and Citizens: Globalization and Multicultural Conflicts*. Trans. George Yúdice. Minneapolis: University of Minnesota Press.

Gaspar de Alba, Alicia. 2003. *La Llorona on the Longfellow Bridge: Poetry y otras movidas*. Houston: Arte Público.

———. 2005. *Desert Blood: The Juárez Murders*. Houston: Arte Público.

Gómez-Peña, Guillermo. 1992. "The New World (B)order." *High Performance* 15, nos. 58–59: 58–65.

611

González Montes, Soledad, Olivia Ruíz, Laura Velasco, and Ofelia Woo, eds. 1995. *Mujeres, migración y maquila en la frontera norte*. Mexico City: Colegio de México.

González, Rita. 2003. "The Said and the Unsaid: Lourdes Portillo Tracks Down Ghosts in *Señorita Extraviada*." *Aztlán: A Journal of Chicano Studies* 28, no. 2: 235–40.

Gyurko, Lanin. 1977. "The Vindication of La Malinche in Fuentes' 'Todos los gatos son pardos.'" *Ibero-Amerikanisches Archiv*, n.s., 3, no. 3: 233–66.

Hall, Stuart. 1997. *Representation: Cultural Representations and Signifying Practices*. Thousand Oaks, CA: Sage.

Herrera-Sobek, María. 1990. *The Mexican Corrido: A Feminist Analysis*. Bloomington: Indiana University Press.

Hicks, D. Emily. 1991. *Border Writing: The Multidimensional Text*. Minneapolis: University of Minnesota Press.

Hollander, Nancy Caro. 1997. *Love in a Time of Hate: Liberation Psychology in Latin America*. New Brunswick, NJ: Rutgers University Press.

Iglesias Prieto, Norma. 1997. *Beautiful Flowers of the Maquiladora: Life Histories of Women Workers in Tijuana*. Trans. Michael Stone with Gabrielle Winkler. Institute of Latin American Studies (ILAS) Translations from Latin America Series. Austin: University of Texas Press.

INEGI (Instituto Nacional de Estadística Geográfica e Informática). 1991. *Estadística de la Industria Maquiladora de Exportación, 1974–1982*. Mexico City.

———. 2005. *Industria Maquiladora de Exportación*. Mexico City. http://www.inegi. gob.mx/est/contenidos/espanol/rutinas/ept.asp?t=emp75&c=1811.

Kahn, Irene. 2003. *México: Muertes Intolerables: Diez años de desapariciones y asesinatos de mujeres en Ciudad Juárez y Chihuahua*. AMR 41/027/2003. Mexico City: Amnistía Internacional Sección Mexicana. Summary at http://www.amnistia .org.mx/modules.php?name=News&file=article&sid=78.

Kopinak, Kathryn. 1995. "Gender as a Vehicle for the Subordination of Women Maquiladora Workers in Mexico." *Latin American Perspectives* 21, no. 1: 30–48.

Lloyd, William J. 1986. "Land Use Structure and the Availability of Services in Ciudad Juárez." In *Social Ecology and Economic Development of Ciudad Juárez*, ed. Gay Young, 47–64. Boulder, CO: Westview.

Lugo, Alejandro. 1995. "Fragmented Lives, Assembled Goods: A Study in Maquilas, Culture and History at the Mexican Borderlands." PhD diss., Stanford University.

———. 1997. "Reflections on Border Theory, Culture, and the Nation." In Michaelsen and Johnson, *Border Theory*, 43–67.

Martínez, Oscar J. 1978. *Border Boom Town: Ciudad Juárez since 1848*. Austin: University of Texas Press.

Méndez B., Luís H. 2004. "Violencia simbólica en el territorio maquiladora fronterizo." *El Cotidiano* 125 (May–June): 7–20.

Michaelsen, Scott, and David E. Johnson, eds. 1997. *Border Theory: The Limits of Cultural Politics*. Minneapolis: University of Minnesota Press.

Mignolo, Walter D. 2000. *Local Histories / Global Designs: Coloniality, Subaltern Knowledges, and Border Thinking*. Princeton, NJ: Princeton University Press.

Mohanty, Chandra Talpade. 2003. *Feminism Without Borders: Decolonizing Theory, Practicing Solidarity*. Durham, NC: Duke University Press.

Monárrez, Julia Estela. 2000. "La cultura del feminicidio en Ciudad Juárez, 1993–1999." *Frontera Norte* 12, no. 23: 87–117.

——. 2003. "Serial Sexual Femicide in Ciudad Juárez, 1993–2001." *Aztlán: A Journal of Chicano Studies* 28, no. 2: 153–78.

Murillo, Enrique. 2002. *Las muertas de Juárez*. Granada Hills, CA: Condor Pictures.

Nathan, Debbie. 1999. "Work, Sex and Danger in Ciudad Juárez." *NACLA Report on the Americas* 33, no. 3: 24–30.

Paz, Octavio. 1985. *The Labyrinth of Solitude*. New York: Grove Press. Orig. pub. 1947.

Peña, Devon G. 1997. *The Terror of the Machine: Technology, Work, Gender, and Ecology on the U.S.-Mexico Border*. Austin: University of Texas, Center for Mexican American Studies.

Peña, Sergio. 2005. "Recent Developments in Urban Marginality along Mexico's Northern Border." *Habitat International* 29, no. 2: 285–301.

Portillo, Lourdes. 2001. *Señorita Extraviada*. San Francisco: Xochitl Films.

——. 2003. "Filming *Señorita Extraviada*: The New Killing Fields." *Aztlán: A Journal of Chicano Studies* 28, no. 2: 228–34.

Quinones, Sam. 2001. *True Tales from Another Mexico: The Lynch Mob, the Popsicle Kings, Chalino, and the Bronx*. Albuquerque: University of New Mexico Press.

Ravelo Blancas, Patricia. 2004. "Entre las protestas callejeras y las acciones internacionales: Diez años de activismo por la justicia social en Ciudad Juárez." *El Cotidiano* 125: 21–32.

Rosaldo, Renato. 1993. *Culture and Truth: The Remaking of Social Analysis*. Boston: Beacon.

Saldívar, José David. 1997. *Border Matters: Remapping American Cultural Studies*. Berkeley: University of California Press.

Saldívar, Ramón. 2006. *The Borderlands of Culture: Américo Paredes and the Transnational Imaginary*. Durham, NC: Duke University Press.

Salzinger, Leslie. 2003. *Genders in Production: Making Workers in Mexico's Global Factories*. Berkeley: University of California Press.

——. 2004. "From Gender as Object to Gender as Verb: Rethinking How Global Restructuring Happens." *Critical Sociology* 30, no. 1: 43–62.

Sanmiguel, Rosario. 1994. *Callejón Sucre y otros relatos*. Chihuahua, Mexico: Ediciones del Azar.

Sklair, Leslie. 1993. *Assembling for Development: The Maquila Industry in Mexico and the United States*. San Diego: University of California, Center for U.S.-Mexican Studies.

Staudt, Kathleen A. 1986. "Economic Change and Ideological Lag in Households of Maquila Workers in Ciudad Juárez." In *Social Ecology and Economic Development of Ciudad Juárez*, ed. Gay Young, 97–120. Boulder, CO: Westview.

Torres, Mónica. 2005. "'Doing Mestizaje': When Epistemology Becomes Ethics." In *EntreMundos/Among Worlds: New Perspectives on Gloria E. Anzaldúa*, ed. AnaLouise Keating, 195–203. New York: Palgrave Macmillan.

Washington Valdez, Diana. 2005. *Cosecha de mujeres: Safari en el desierto mexicano.* Mexico City: Océano.

Wilson, Tamar Diana. 2002. "The Masculinization of the Mexican Maquiladoras." *Review of Radical Political Economics* 34, no. 1: 3–17.

Woods, Tyron P. 2002. "Globalizing Social Violence: Race, Gender and the Spatial Politics of Crisis." *American Studies* 43, no. 1: 127–53.

Zavella, Patricia. 1997. "'Playing with Fire': The Gendered Construction of Chicana/Mexicana Sexuality." In *The Gender/Sexuality Reader: Culture, History, Political Economy*, ed. Roger N. Lancaster and Micaela di Leonardo, 402–18. New York: Routledge.

Sound Recordings

Amos, Tori. "Black Dove." *From the Choirgirl Hotel.* Atlantic/Wea, 1998.

———. "Juárez." *To Venus and Back.* Atlantic/Wea, 1999.

Downs, Lila. "La niña." *Border / La Linea.* Narada World, 2001.

Gabriel, Ana. "Tiempo de actuar." Unpublished, performed in 2004.

Lerner, Alejandro. "De mariposa a cruz." *"De mariposa a cruz": Juárez, Stages of Fear.* Fonovisa, 2005.

Mujeres en Fuga. "El boulevard de los sueños destrozados." *Brujas.* Ediciones Pentagrama, 2005.

———. "Una más en Juárez." *Brujas.* Ediciones Pentagrama, 2005.

Los Tigres del Norte. "Contrabando y traición." *16 Super Exitos.* Fonovisa, 1991.

———. *Gracias América sin fronteras.* Fonovisa, 1994.

———. "Las mujeres de Juárez." *Pacto de sangre.* Fonovisa, 2004.

El TRI. "Las mujeres de Juárez." *El TRI. 35 Años.* WeaRock, 2004.

Vidal, Mónica. "Ni una más, sin su mirar." Unpublished, performed in 2002.

"El destierro de los Chinos"
Popular Perspectives on Chinese-Mexican Intermarriage in the Early Twentieth Century

Robert Chao Romero

Since its inception in the early 1970s, the academic discipline of Chicana/o studies has largely embraced a racial model of "mestizaje," emphasizing the dual cultural contributions of the Spanish and the indigenous peoples of Mexico. Drawing on the Mexican postrevolutionary writings of José Vasconcelos, Manuel Gamio, and Alfonso Caso, most existing Chicana/o studies scholarship describes Mexico as a mestizo society resulting from the collision of Spanish and indigenous cultural elements. Emblematic of this dominant view, El Plan Espiritual de Aztlán, an important manifesto of the Chicano movement, states: "With our heart in our hands and our hands in the soil, we declare the independence of our *mestizo* nation. We are a bronze people with a bronze culture. Before the world, before all of North America, before all our brothers in the bronze continent, we are a nation, we are a union of free pueblos, we are *Aztlán*."[1]

In recent years, this traditional model of mestizaje has drawn criticism from Chicana/o scholars such as Maria Josefina Saldana-Portillo, Gloria Anzaldúa, Ana Maria Alonso, and Alexandra Minna Stern, based upon its limited view of race and gender.[2] One important race-based critique relates to the model's subtle racism toward the indigenous population of Mexico. Saldana-Portillo, for example, argues that mestizaje, with its parallel ideology of *indigenismo*, "fetishizes" a residual Indian identity while effectively excluding contemporary Indians (2001, 403). A further criticism of mestizaje stems from its myopic focus upon the Spanish and indigenous contributions to Mexican culture and its exclusion of other ethnic groups such as Africans, Arabs, and Asians. A growing body of scholarship seeks to uncover the forgotten history of Mexico's African population, or *raíz olvidada*, and to highlight the important contributions made by Africans to the development of Mexican culture.[3] This literature asserts that the African heritage of Mexico was deliberately erased from historical memory in the context of efforts by the postrevolutionary Mexican government to create a unified mestizo national identity.

Notwithstanding these critiques of the mestizaje theory vis-à-vis Mexico's blacks, few scholars have examined the role of Asians in the development of Chicano/Latino culture and identity. Despite the historic and contemporary presence of millions of ethnic Asians in Latin America and the growing "Asian-Latino" population of the United States—which numbers more than 300,000, according to the 2000 national census—the fields of Chicano and Latino studies have been slow to incorporate Asians within their discussions of racial theory. Chicana/o studies in particular have been reluctant to address the role of the Chinese and Japanese in the formulation of Mexican and Chicano mestizaje. Although the Chinese historical presence in Mexico dates back 400 years, and Mexico's Chinese population once numbered in the tens of thousands, the Chicana/o studies literature on this topic is virtually nonexistent.

Through an examination of the phenomenon of Chinese-Mexican intermarriage in early-twentieth-century Mexico and the U.S. Southwest, this essay explores some of the historical factors that account for the exclusion of the Chinese from traditional models of mestizaje. It focuses on popular attitudes toward Chinese-Mexican intermarriage through the lens of popular culture—comedy sketches, cartoons, poetry, and musical recordings. Building on this historical base, this article argues for the revision of traditional models of mestizaje and the incorporation of Chinese and other Asian groups into the racial theorization of Chicano/Latino studies. It calls for the creation of a new intellectual space within the field—what might be called "Asian-Latino" or "Chino-Chicano" studies—in which scholars can explore the historical and contemporary interactions between Asians and Latinos in Latin America and the United States.

Pablo Chee and Chinese Immigration to Mexico, 1882–1940

The case study of Pablo Chee exemplifies the important historical phenomena of Chinese immigration to Mexico and Chinese-Mexican intermarriage during the early twentieth century. Pablo Chee immigrated to Chiapas, Mexico, from the Nam Hoy district of Guangdong, China,

Figure 1. Pablo Chee with his wife Adelina and son Manuel in 1914. Arrival Investigation Case Files, Box 866, Folder 13976/7–3, Record Group 85, Immigration and Naturalization Service, National Archives and Records Administration, Pacific Region, San Bruno, CA.

in November 1901. Eight years later he married Adelina Palomegus in Tapachula, Chiapas, and on January 10, 1910, Chee's Mexican bride gave birth to a son, Manuel Jesus Chee. Together with Adelina and Manuel, Pablo traveled to China in 1914 (fig. 1).

In 1915, however, Pablo returned to Mexico, leaving his Mexican wife and child in China in his home village of Kow Kong. As the first-born son of a successful overseas merchant, young Manuel attended a British school in Guangdong. Following his return to Mexico, Pablo Chee increased his fortune as a successful businessman engaged in a wide variety of endeavors, serving as a merchant of groceries and general merchandise and investing in several thousand acres of ranchland along with a hotel and a saloon. Capitalizing upon his extensive commercial successes, Chee eventually also gained the right of legal domicile in the United States under the Section 6 merchant exemption of the Chinese Exclusion Act. In 1924 Chee applied for permission from the U.S. Immigration and Naturalization Service to bring his wife and child from China to live in the United States (Pablo Chee case file).

Pablo Chee's immigration to Mexico coincided with the migration of tens of thousands of Chinese to Mexico during the late nineteenth and early twentieth centuries.[4] Following the passage of the Chinese Exclusion Act of 1882, which barred the legal immigration of Chinese male laborers to the United States, Chinese immigrants flocked to Mexico, hoping to use it as a back door into the United States. They sought also to take advantage of the commercial opportunities created by the economic modernization plan of Porfirio Díaz, and many became successful entrepreneurs.[5] Although the Chinese community of Mexico numbered only 1,023 in 1895, by 1926 it had grown to 24,218, and the Chinese became the second-largest foreign ethnic community in Mexico, after Spaniards. Present in every state of Mexico except Tlaxcala, the Chinese were especially numerous in the northern borderland states and territories, where they monopolized small-scale trade. In 1926, 1,037 Chinese resided in the state of Chihuahua, 3,758 in Sonora, and 5,889 in the territory of Baja California (Ministerio de Fomento 1895; Secretaria de la Economía Nacional 1930, 38–39).

Although the vast majority of Chinese immigrants to Mexico were male, the Chinese community of Mexico was far from a bachelor society. Significant numbers of Chinese men in Mexico were married to Chinese women who lived in their home villages in China, and a few of the most privileged brought Chinese wives to live with them in Mexico. In addition, Chinese men, like Pablo Chee, also intermarried with Mexican women at relatively high rates. In a sample of 80 married Chinese males residing in the city of Chihuahua, Chihuahua, in 1930, 28 were married to Mexican women. In Hermosillo, the state capital of Sonora, 14 of 119 Chinese immigrant marriages were to local Hispanic women. Of 82 married Chinese immigrant males residing in the Sonoran border city of Nogales in 1930, 12 reported interracial marriages with Mexican women. In addition to civil and ecclesiastical marital unions, significant numbers of Chinese male immigrants engaged in extramarital free unions with Mexican women. Municipal census records for 1930 show 11 free unions between Chinese men and Mexican women in Chihuahua, 9 in Hermosillo, and 7 in Nogales.[6]

Chinese male immigrants in Mexico sired many offspring in their marital and extramarital unions with Mexican women. The Chihuahua census records of 1930 registered 90 children of Chinese men and their Mexican wives and 18 children born of extramarital free unions with Mexican women. The Hermosillo sampling records 48 children born to Chinese fathers and Mexican wives, as well as 8 children conceived within free unions. In Nogales, census takers registered 26 Chinese-Mexican children born of interracial marriages and 7 born of free unions.

Popular Mexican Perspectives: Comedy, Cartoons, Poetry, and Corridos

Beyond quantitative data on Chinese-Mexican intermarriage, one finds frequent references to such cross-cultural unions throughout popular Mexican culture.[7] Spoken-word comedy recordings, cartoons, poetry, and corridos of these years comment upon a wide range of themes and topics pertaining to Chinese-Mexican unions, including courtship, marriage, cross-cultural children, abandonment, and even family relocation to China. As will be discussed in detail later in this essay, much of this commentary was couched within the broader nationalistic ideology of the Mexican Revolution.

MOCKING CHINESE COURTSHIP STRATEGIES

According to popular perception, wealthy Chinese immigrant merchants lured naïve Mexican women into marriage by promising them lives of material comfort and prosperity. This courtship strategy is playfully depicted in a spoken dialogue recording titled "El Chino," which was commercially released by the Brunswick Record Corporation in 1937 (Rodríguez and Rodríguez 1937).[8] The comedic dialogue, set in Texas, parodies a conversation between a prosperous Chinese businessman named Ching Choman and a young Mexican woman named María. In the conversation, Ching aggressively courts the favor of María, who is already engaged to be married. As part of his strategy, Ching tells María that he is very rich and promises to buy her whatever she wants in exchange for a marriage commitment. In addition, Ching tells María that her Mexican boyfriend is no good and useless, and he criticizes the boyfriend and other Tejanos for being lazy and depending upon their wives to support them. Despite Ching's persistent pleas in broken and heavily accented Spanish, María ultimately rejects him, insisting that she is an honorable woman.

> CHING: María, yo mañana subiendo gloria y queriendo llevar una virgencita.
>
> MARÍA: Sí, pero esta virgencita ya tiene su novio. Además ¿tú quien eres? Yo ni te conozco ni sé como te llamas.
>
> CHING: Me llamo Ching Choman.
>
> MARÍA: ¿Ching que? Mira pues, si éste ya no me la rayó.

CHING: No te enojes María. Yo quiero decirle que tu novio no sirve, no sirve.

MARÍA: ¿Cómo que no sirve?

CHING: Tejano nunca trabaja, siempre la pobrecita mujer trabaja para mantenerlo. . . . Muchacha bonito como tú siempre queriendo bueno vestido, mucho zapato. Y este chinito está muy rico y bueno para marido. El que tú tienes no sirve.

MARÍA: No le hace, con tal de que me quiera me conformo.

CHING: Mariá, yo te juro amor eterno. Tú serás la reina de mi casa y te compro todo lo que quieras. Con tal de que me des tu . . . corazoncito de divina mujer encantadora.

MARÍA: Oye, oye que ya te estás atascando y si sigues así te doy una cachetada.

CHING: Tú dame lo que quieras con tal de que me des algo.

MARÍA: Oye tú, que yo soy una señorita muy honrada.

(CHING: María, tomorrow I am going to give praise [go to church] and I want to take a nice virgin.

MARÍA: Great, but this virgin already has a boyfriend. Besides, who are you? I don't know you. I don't even know your name.

CHING: My name is Ching Choman.

MARÍA: Ching what? Well, what do you know, this guy just cussed at me. ["Ching" sounds like the first word of a very offensive Spanish phrase, "chinga tu madre," which translates as "screw your mother."]

CHING: Don't get angry, María. I want to tell you that your boyfriend is no good, no good.

MARÍA: What do you mean, no good?

CHING: A Texan never works. The poor woman always works to support him. . . . A pretty girl like you always wants nice dresses, many pairs of shoes. And this Chinese guy is very rich and will make a good husband. The one you have is useless.

MARÍA: So what.

CHING: María, I promise you eternal love. You will be the queen of my house, and I will buy you whatever you desire. As long as you give me

. . . the heart of a divine and charming woman.

MARÍA: Hey, hey, you're going too far. If you keep it up, I'll give you a slap on the cheek.

CHING: Give me whatever you want as long as you give me something.

MARÍA: Listen, you, I am an honorable young lady.)

CONDEMNING INTERRACIAL MARRIAGE

Even though popular Mexican culture sometimes found humor in the courtship antics of Chinese male immigrants, Mexican women who married Chinese suitors were shunned and scolded as "dirty," "lazy," "unpatriotic," and "shameless." Chinese-Mexican marital unions were condemned as marriages of convenience in which lazy Mexican women avoided work thanks to financial support from their Chinese husbands. Such cross-cultural relationships, moreover, were said to threaten the ruin of Mexican womanhood and to defile the Mexican nation. A number of cartoon sketches, poems, and corridos exemplify these popular critical attitudes.

The cartoon in figure 2 unsympathetically portrays a Mexican woman suffering the consequences of an interracial marriage of convenience.[9] The caption reads:

Ah infeliz! . . . Creíste disfrutar de una vida barata al entregarte a un chino y eres una esclava y el fruto de tu error es un escupitajo de la naturaleza.

(Oh wretched woman! . . . You thought you would enjoy a cheap life by giving yourself to a Chinese man, but instead you are a slave and the fruit of your mistake is a freak of nature.)

According to the cartoonist, the woman entered into an interracial marriage hoping to secure for herself an easy life, free from financial worry. Instead, she has become a slave to her Chinese husband and the reluctant mother of a subhuman, alienlike offspring that she now seeks to abandon.

An anonymous poem from around 1910 titled "El destierro de los Chinos" (Exile of the Chinese) expressed similar condemnation of Mexican women who chose to marry or become romantically involved with Chinese immigrant men. The poem reads in part:

Ningún descubrimiento han hecho

¡Ah infeliz!.... Creíste disfrutar de una vida barata al entregarte a un chino y eres una esclava y el fruto de tu error es un escupitajo de la naturaleza....

Figure 2. Cartoon showing imprisoned Mexican wife and unwanted interracial offspring. From Espinoza (2003, 77, 36).

Pagando con dinero chino
Tan solo han venido a arruinar
Al genero femenino . . .

Pero debemos fijarnos
A tolerar la imprudencia
Que las de la grande culpa
Son las mujeres malvadas

Que no conocen vergüenza
Que se ponen a llorar
De lo a gusto que han vivido
Y el tronido que han de dar

Esas hembras desdichadas
Jamás conocen vergüenza
De lo que si están tapadas
Es de pura conveniencia

Y les digo la verdad
Sin temores de arranquera
Que la que con chino vive
Es pura convenenciera

No les gusta trabajar
Y mujer desvergonzada

Quiere que el chino la asista
Se que la traiga planchada

Y les gusta presumir
Sin tener inteligencia
Lo que habían de conseguir
Es un poco de vergüenza

Al gobierno le encargamos
Aunque me crean imprudente
Que deberían de expulsarlos
A estas tres clases de gente

Las primeras que sean las viejas
Que hacen con chinos unión
Y no conocen vergüenza
Porque manchan su nación

Y hay que darles su propina
A la carrera y al trote
De quemarlas con aceite
Con leña y con chapopote[10]

(They haven't made a discovery
Paying with Chinese money
They've only come to ruin
The female kind . . .

But we must make an effort
To tolerate imprudence
The ones who are to blame
Are the wicked women

They know no shame
They begin to cry
About how comfortably they have lived
And their eventual decline

Those wretched females
Know no shame
What's in it for them
Is pure convenience

I tell you the truth
Without fear of public outrage
That she who lives with a Chinese man
Is a woman of pure convenience

They don't like to work
This shameless woman
She wants the Chinaman to support her
And keep her well dressed

And they like to boast
Without any brains
What they need
Is a little bit of shame

We hold the government responsible
Even though you may think me unwise
They should exile
These three types of people [Chinese, Mexican women who marry them,
and Arabs]

The first should be the women
Who make unions with Chinese men
They know no shame
Because they are staining the nation

And we should give them their due
Right quick
Burn them with hot oil
With firewood and tar)

In harsh and inflammatory language, this poem excoriates Chinese immigrant men for bringing about the downfall of Mexican women, who are said to be bought off with "Chinese money." Mexican women who reciprocate the affections of Chinese men are chastised as wicked, shameless, and pitiful, and deserving of being burned with hot oil. Similar to the cartoon in figure 2, this poem asserts that Chinese-Mexican interracial unions are simply arrangements of convenience by which lazy Mexican women avoid work by relying upon their Chinese lovers for financial support. Inserting a twist of revolutionary nationalism, the anonymous author of this poem also condemns such women as unpatriotic individuals who "stain" the Mexican nation.

Similar themes are expressed in a song titled "Los Chinos" (The Chinese). Released by Columbia Records in 1913, just three years after the onset of the Mexican Revolution, the song echoes the sinophobic sentiment of the cartoon and poem. Composed by Eduardo Tavo in the traditional ballad style of a Mexican corrido and performed by artist Gómez-Acosta, this song scolds Mexican women who date or marry Chinese men, calling them dirty and shameless women who marry for the love of money. It makes specific reference to the anti-Chinese agitation in Sinaloa during this period.

Por ahí va la bola
Pongan atención
Sabrá Dios lo que suceda
Que ahí viene el cometa
Ya no sabré
Ya no habrá trajes de seda

Lo digo por muchas muchachas
Muchachas de Mazatlán
Que vayan buscando barcas
Que ya no habrá para pescar

Aquí comenzó por algunos chinos
Que sus tiendas han cerrado
Y las mexicanas que le comerciaban
Toda la noche han llorado

Y muchos dicen que miento
Porque digo la verdad
Que a un mexicano quieren
Solo por casualidad

Muchas mexicanas quieren a los chinos
Porque no tienen vergüenza
Y no les da pena hacerse el molote
Los dos componen la trenza

Y luego se van al espejo
Todas con su chino al lado
Y uno al otro se pregunta
Quien tiene el mejor peinado

Toda mexicana que quiere algún chino
Ha de ser muy descarada
Y sin miramientos por toda la raza
Debe de ser despreciada

Lo digo por muchas muchachas
De México tan cochinas
Que por amor al dinero
Se hacen menos que las chinas

Yo ya me voy, yo ya me despido

Porque yo no soy de aquí
Y cuando te encuentren besando un chino
Hagan recuerdos de mi

Y digan que ya se fue a la tierra
Te echaremos al olvido
Pídele a Dios que no vuelva
Para que no cante el corrido

Si alguna mujer que oiga estos versos
Con un chino está casada
No debe sentirse
Porque lo que digo es la purito pelada

Que soy un hombre grosero
De seguro lo dirán
Pero más groseras son
Las chicas de Mazatlán

(There goes the angry mob
So pay close attention
Only God knows what will happen
Here comes the big news
I don't know what will happen
But there will be no more silk outfits [in reference to the clothing of the Chinese]

I am saying this in reference to many young women
Young women of Mazatlán
Go look for your way out [by marrying a Chinese man]
Because soon there will be none left

It started with a few Chinese
That had their stores closed down
And all of the women who did business with them
Cried all night

Many say that I am lying
Because I am telling the truth
They will fall in love with a Mexican
Only on rare occasions

Many Mexican women love the Chinese
Because they have no shame
And they aren't ashamed to make a Chinese bun in their hair
They both make the braid together

Then they go to the mirror

With their Chinese at their side
And one asks the other
Who did a better job fixing their hair

All Mexican women that love a Chinese man
Should be ashamed
And without hesitation
Should be shunned by all the people of Mexico

I say this because many women of Mexico
Dirty women
For the love of money
They make themselves less than a woman of China

I am leaving now, I am saying farewell
I am not from this area
But when they find you kissing a Chinese man
You will remember me

You can say that I disappeared
And you can forget about me
Just pray to God that I don't return
To sing this corrido again

If a woman who hears these verses
Is married to a Chinese
She should not feel so proud
Because what I say is the truth

You will surely say
That I am a rude man
But worse still
Are the women of Mazatlán)

This corrido situates sinophobic anti-miscegenation sentiment within the specific historical events of the Mexican Revolution. In addition to its explicit condemnation of intermarriage between Chinese men and Mexican women, this song recalls the violence perpetrated against the Chinese community of Mazatlán during the revolutionary years. In 1911–13, revolutionary activists of Sinaloa organized public protests against the Chinese and sought to compel the Chinese to flee the city of Mazatlán under threat of mob violence (GRDS 1911–13). In this corrido, Tavo paints an ominous picture of the anti-Chinese agitation: "There goes the angry mob. . . . Only God knows what will happen. . . . Soon there will be none left" (referring to the Chinese community of Mazatlán). The song mentions the forced closure of Chinese shops that occurred in Sinaloa during this period: "It started here with a few Chinese that had their stores closed down, and all of the women who did business with them cried all night."

It is against this historical backdrop of revolutionary mob violence perpetrated against the Chinese that Tavo presents his harsh critique of Chinese-Mexican intermarriage. Similar to the plaint of the previous poem and cartoon, he complains that Mexican women who pursue cross-cultural relationships with Chinese men do so "for the love of money" and as a dishonorable means of finding a "way out" of economic hardship. In addition, he derides such women as "shameful" and "dirty" and asserts that they "should be shunned by all the people of Mexico." As a unique criticism not addressed in the previous two sources, moreover, the author chides the Mexican wives of Chinese husbands for their adoption of Chinese cultural norms. Specifically, he pokes fun at their selection of an Asian hairstyle: "And they aren't ashamed to make a Chinese bun in their hair. They both make the braid together. Then they go to the mirror with their Chinese at their side and one asks the other who did a better job fixing their hair."[11]

Defending Mexican Manhood

On a deeper level, this corrido and the previous sources suggest that Mexican men felt their manhood threatened by Chinese males who wielded greater economic—and presumably sexual—power. Thus in the comedy sketch "El Chino," Ching tells María that her Mexican boyfriend is "no good" because "a Texan never works. The poor woman always works to support him." Ching goes on to boast of his wealth and ability to buy her nice things. Revealing similar gendered insecurities, the anonymous, presumably male author of the poem "El destierro de los Chinos" also alludes to Chinese economic power: "She who lives with a Chinese man is a woman of pure convenience. They don't like to work. . . . She wants a Chinaman to support her and keep her well dressed." In an effort to offset the Chinese male advantage, the corrido attempts to feminize Chinese men through critical reference to the long queue that Chinese immigrant males wore, which the song sarcastically compares to the woman's own hairstyle: "They both braid the hair together."

Defense of the sexual and economic honor of the Mexican male population of northern Mexico became a central goal of the anti-Chinese movement.[12] It was a driving force in the attacks against Chinese merchants that took place in Sinaloa between 1911 and 1913 as part of the organized anti-Chinese campaigns. The perception of a Chinese sexual and economic threat was exacerbated by severe reductions in the Mexican male population of Sonora in the early twentieth century. Reacting to the Sonoran "man shortage" and to the perceived Chinese male advantage, a small group of Mexican shopkeepers and entrepreneurs formed the Commercial Association of Businessmen in Magdalena, Sonora, in 1916. This group stated as its explicit goal the elimination of the Asian merchants through all available legal means. The organized anti-Chinese campaigns culminated in the eventual expulsion of virtually the entire Chinese population from the state of Sonora in 1931.

CRITICIZING ABUSE, POLYGAMY, AND SPOUSAL REPATRIATION TO CHINA

While asserting that Mexican women were lured into interracial relationships by promises of wealth and an easy life, popular Mexican culture simultaneously characterized Chinese-Mexican intermarriages as relationships of abuse and slavery. The contrast between women's expectations of a luxurious life and the harsh reality of abusive marriages is reflected in the caption of the cartoon in figure 2: "Oh wretched woman! . . . You thought you would enjoy a cheap life by giving yourself to a Chinese man, but instead you are a slave."

Other cartoons articulate this imagery of slavery and neglect even more clearly. In figure 3, two Mexican wives or concubines are depicted as the slaves of their polygamous Chinese husband, who is whipping them and

MUJER MEXICANA:—Si la locura o la ignorancia te hace esposa o manceba de un chino y éste te quiere llevar a su patria, antes que resolverte a seguirlo apura una dósis de veneno o clávate un puñal en el corazón......

Figure 3. Cartoon showing relocated Mexican concubines in China. From Espinoza (2003, 77).

using them as animals to plow his field in China. The harshness of their experience is underscored by their attire and facial expressions: the two women are barefoot, clothed in tattered rags, and groaning from exhaustion and overwork. The abusive treatment of these Mexican women, moreover, is set in stark contrast to the serene Orientalist backdrop featuring snow-capped mountains and pagodas. Through their toil in the fields, it appears that the two Mexican concubines are slaving to support the opulent lifestyle of their Asian master, who makes his home in one of the extravagant pagodas nestled in the mountain valley.

The accompanying caption further highlights these themes:

> MUJER MEXICANA—Si la locura o la ignorancia te hace esposa o manceba de un chino y éste te quiere llevar a su patria, antes que resolverte a seguirlo apura una dosis de veneno o clávate un puñal en el corazón . . .

> (MEXICAN WOMAN—If insanity or ignorance has led you to become the wife or concubine of a Chinese man and he wants to take you to his homeland, before you decide to follow him, take a dose of poison or drive a dagger into your heart . . .)

According to the cartoonist, therefore, the physical abuse and neglect in an interracial marriage with a Chinese man is so intolerable that suicide by poison or stabbing would be preferable.

In addition to this primary theme of slavery, this cartoon also highlights secondary themes of concubinage and polygamy. The cartoonist explicitly raises this issue through his caption, which refers to a *manceba* (concubine or mistress). However exaggerated, this caption provides limited qualitative evidence that some Mexican women served as concubines to Chinese immigrant men. This notion is supported by the quantitative data drawn from Sonora and Chihuahua census records that show the occurrence of free unions between Chinese men and Mexican women. Although the census records do not elaborate upon the nature of the free unions, it may be that some of the Chinese men who engaged in these unions with Mexican women remained married to Chinese women left behind in China. The cartoon allows room for such an interpretation: although the setting is rural southern China, there is a conspicuous absence of any Chinese women in the picture. It may be implied that these two Mexican women are wives or concubines of secondary status who are laboring to support not only their Chinese husband but also the household of his preferred Chinese wife. This secondary concubine status of Mexican women is also conveyed by the lyrics of "Los Chinos," which suggest that the Mexican wives hold a status below that of their Chinese counterparts: "I say this because many women of Mexico, dirty women, for the love of money *they make themselves less than a woman of China*" (italics added).

Finally, this cartoon also raises the interesting historical issue of spousal relocation to China. As happened in the case of Pablo Chee, some Mexican wives did return to China to live in the home villages of their Chinese husbands and raise their cross-cultural offspring. Although Pablo Chee's narrative is neutral as to the experience of Adelina Palomegus in Guangdong, figure 3 vividly depicts the supposedly harsh life of Mexican women who chose to follow their Asian spouses to China. The caption issues a stern warning to those who might be considering such a move: "Before you decide to follow him, take a dose of poison or drive a dagger into your heart." Unfortunately, according to the historical record, this depressing depiction of life in China for Mexican women was sometimes a reality. In the 1930s, during the presidency of Lázaro Cárdenas, many Mexican women in China petitioned the government of Mexico for permission to return to their homeland because of their unhappiness in China. Such permission was granted, and significant numbers of Mexican women returned to Mexico.[13]

A different but equally negative outcome is suggested by the cartoon in figure 4. In this illustration, the Chinese male character, dressed in merchant's garb, is shown with his back turned and hand waving in a gesture

Figure 4. Mexican bride and Chinese husband on their wedding night and five years later. From Espinoza (2003, 36).

631

of dismissal. He is uttering an incomprehensible statement in Chinese, perhaps announcing his imminent departure. Through this combination of body language, speech, and nonverbal communication, it appears that the Chinese man is abandoning his Mexican wife and children after a short marriage of five years. This cartoon, therefore, may be viewed as representing a strong social critique against Chinese immigrant men who were thought to abandon their Mexican wives and cross-cultural progeny after brief stints of marriage.

Like figure 3, this cartoon depicts marriages between Chinese men and Mexican women as relationships of abuse and neglect. It shows a before-and-after depiction of a Mexican woman and her Chinese husband on their wedding night and five years into the marriage. In the first image we see a lustful, Mongoloid-looking Chinese male literally salivating over his beautiful, buxom Mexican bride. She is depicted as naïve and eager, stylishly adorned and clothed in fine raiment in an elegant bedroom with an expensive standing mirror and exotic Asian privacy partition. Five years later, the erstwhile Mexican maiden appears emaciated and disheveled, clothed in tattered rags and a servant's apron and bereft of the fine accoutrements bestowed upon her as gifts on her wedding night. The message of the cartoon is clear: Lured into marriage by false promises of material prosperity, this Mexican woman has become the forsaken servant of a disinterested and abusive Chinese immigrant husband who married her for base sexual pleasure. Abandonment is her ultimate fate.

In addition, this cartoon offers a strong commentary on the issue of multiracial children. It depicts the progeny of the Chinese-Mexican union as gangly, degenerate Mongoloids. Though of both Chinese and Mexican ancestry, the cartoon children do not share any phenotypical characteristics with their Mexican mother and instead are drawn as miniature reflections of their Asian father. One implication of this portrayal is that the cartoonist (and the broader Mexican population) did not consider the offspring of Chinese-Mexican interracial unions to be legitimately Mexican. This popular perspective finds partial official legitimization in the Mexican municipal census of 1930. In these records, Mexican census takers categorized the offspring of Chinese male nationals and Mexican women as ethnically Chinese. If the Chinese fathers were nationalized Mexican citizens, the children were designated Mexican nationals for purposes of the census. But despite this legal classification, they were not treated as Mexican by the society.

Racial Formation and the Mexican Revolution

Such critical portrayals of Chinese-Mexican children as racially degenerate were based upon the view that the Chinese represented a threat to Mexican mestizaje and the development of a unified national racial identity. In the years following the revolution, mestizaje became the dominant paradigm of national and racial formation, and the mestizo was established as the unifying symbol of Mexican national identity (Renique 2000; 2003, 218). Although there existed competing conceptions of mestizaje, and especially differing views about the proper means of incorporating the indigenous population into the Mexican mainstream, all versions of mestizaje excluded the Chinese. Even José Vasconcelos, the most well-known proponent of the theory of mestizaje, argued for the exclusion of the Chinese from membership in the Mexican racial community: "If we reject the Chinese, it is because man, as he progresses, multiplies less, and feels the horror of numbers, for the same reason that he has begun to value quality" (1997, 20). From the standpoint of the "ideal mestizaje," the Chinese represented a "step backward in the anthropological search for the prototypical [Mexican] man" and a threat to the "purity of Aztec blood" (Renique 2003, 223–24). Based upon the perceived Chinese threat to Mexican national ethnic identity formation, Chinese-Mexican interracial marriages were deemed particularly offensive because they resulted in the production of mixed offspring who departed from the ideal mestizaje of Spanish and indigenous. These critical attitudes are reflected in the cartoons that depict Chinese-Mexican children as misshapen, subhuman, degenerate Mongoloids.

Chinese-Mexican interracial marriages were deemed especially offensive to regional models of *blanco-criollo* racial formation in northern Mexico. Postrevolutionary racial theorists divided Mexico geographically into a "Creole north," an "indigenous south," and a "central region" characterized as mestizo. In Sonora, the birthplace of the organized anti-Chinese campaigns and the center of Mexican sinophobia, a male blanco-criollo identity predominated. The prototypical Sonoran was depicted in Mexican popular culture as a "white" male of Spanish ancestry with a racial identity distinct from that of the indigenous and mestizo majority populations of central and southern Mexico. Important mestizaje theorists such as Manuel Gamio, moreover, lauded the blanco-criollo racial characteristics of northern Mexico as a model for the future development of Mexican mestizaje. From the standpoint of the patriarchal blanco-criollo elite of Sonora, therefore, Chinese-Mexican intermarriages threatened to bring about the racial degeneration of the Sonoran people. The Sonoran elite condemned the offspring of Chinese-Mexican unions as a "new racial type still more degenerated than [Mexico's] naturally abject indigenous castes." They harshly depicted Chinese Mexicans as "the product of filthy unions" who embodied the worst "vices and degeneration" of both Chinese immigrants and the Mexican lower classes (Renique 2003, 215–18).

These elite regional attitudes toward Chinese-Mexican unions are reflected in the cartoon in figure 4. Consistent with the blanco-criollo racial identity of northern Mexico, the young woman in the cartoon is portrayed as fair-skinned, phenotypically white, and culturally Westernized. In contrast, her Chinese husband is drawn as an unattractive, stereotypical Asian male with exaggerated Mongoloid features. Their children, of Chinese-Mexican ancestry, do not resemble their blanco-criollo mother but instead show the undesirable racial characteristics of their Asian father. The message of the cartoon is clear and consistent with localized Sonoran ideals of racial formation: Chinese-Mexican interracial unions threatened a racial degeneration of northern Mexico because they produced an inferior, nonwhite Asian racial type.

Popular critiques of Chinese-Mexican intermarriage were also bound up in larger discourses of economic nationalism. Revolutionary activists associated Chinese merchants with U.S. and European capitalist interests that they blamed for the downturn of the national economy and the commercial exploitation of the Mexican populace. Within this framework of economic nationalism, Chinese immigrants were portrayed as foreign exploiters of the Mexican people who, through intermarriage and numerical proliferation, promoted the ruin of the Mexican nation and Mexican womanhood. This perspective is clearly articulated in the poem, spoken-word dialogue, and corrido examined earlier in this essay. Tying the Chinese economic threat to the dangers of Chinese-Mexican intermarriage, the anonymous author of the poem "El destierro de los Chinos" warns:

> Que si el Gobierno la deja
> Hunde a nuestra nación . . .
> Porque es mucho interés
> Que tomen esa precaución
> Que ya de árabes y chinos
> No abunden en nuestra nación.
> Es preciso preguntarles
> Señores, hasta en sus casas
> Que cuales son sus productos
> de esas dos clases de razas.

Ningún descubrimiento han hecho
Pagando con dinero chino,
Tan solo han venido a arruinar
Al genero femenino.
Eso es lo mejor que han hecho,
Los chinos caras de perro
Y por eso les pedimos
Para los chinos el destierro.
Es fuerza que haya quien se fije
Con cuidado y atención
Que esos chinos desdichados
No engendren en nuestra nación.
Que hacen con chinos unión
Y no conocen vergüenza,
Porque manchan su nación . . .
Pídanle a Dios chinos maulas,
Con todo su Corazón
No que vengan a lincharlos
Si llega la revolución.

(If the government lets them,
They will swamp our nation . . .
It is urgent to take steps
So that Arabs and Chinese
Don't overrun our country . . .
Gentlemen, in your own homes,
Which of your household products come
From these two races?
They haven't made a discovery
Paying with Chinese money.
They've only come to ruin
The female kind.
That is the best thing they have done,
The dog-faced Chinese.
And that's why we ask
For the exile of the Chinese.
It is necessary that somebody takes notice
With care and attention
So that those wretched Chinese
Don't breed in our nation . . .
The women that make a union with the Chinese . . .
Know no shame
Because they are staining the nation . . .
Pray to God, man from China,
With all your heart

That they don't come and lynch you
If the revolution comes.)

In the language and opinion of the author, the Chinese threatened to swamp or sink the Mexican nation through economic exploitation, racial intermarriage, and numerical reproduction. Though owing their livelihoods to the sale of their products to Mexican consumers, Chinese (and Arab) merchants were viewed as not contributing to national development—"They haven't made a discovery paying with Chinese money." Instead, implies the poet, Chinese merchants used their ill-gotten profits to entice Mexican women into marriage. Such unions engendered the "ruin of the female kind," and Mexican women who participated in them were said to "stain" the Mexican nation. As a final violent expression of revolutionary nationalism, moreover, the author warned Chinese immigrant males who engaged in cross-cultural marriages of potential death by lynching.

In contrast to the acerbic tone of "El destierro de los Chinos," the spoken-word recording "El Chino" demonstrates this connection between revolutionary nationalism and opposition to Chinese-Mexican intermarriage in a light-hearted way. In an interesting twist, the author of this comedy sketch accomplishes this through dialogue spoken by Ching, the Chinese antagonist of the skit. In halting Spanish, Ching proclaims to the Mexican maiden María:

> México muy bueno para los extranjeros. Los americanos tener pozos de petróleo. Los ingleses, ellos dueños de muchas minas, grandes terrenos. Los alemanes tener ferreterías. Los españoles, dueños de cantinas y tiendas de abarrotes y panaderías. Chinitos tener muchos restaurantes y lavanderías. En fin, todos los extranjeros hacer dinero. Oye, y los mexicanos que hacen? Nada, pues que no ves que ellos son los revolucionarios? Unos son las camisas verdes, otros las rojas y otros las doradas. Unos gritan, "Que viva el asilillo! Otros, "Que muera la Calles!" Otros, "Que viva la Cárdenas!" Y todos con la carabina "pun-pun" aquí, "pun-pun" allá, pero no más.

> (Mexico is good for foreigners. The Americans have oil wells. The English own large mines, large tracts of land. The Germans have hardware stores. The Spanish are owners of bars, markets, and bakeries. The Chinese own many restaurants and laundries. In conclusion, all the foreigners are making money. So what are the Mexicans doing? Nothing, because don't you see they are revolutionaries? Some wear green shirts, some red shirts and others gold shirts. Some yell out, "Long live Zedillo." Others yell, "Death to Calles!" and still others, "Long live Cárdenas!" All of them with their carbines doing "bang bang" here and "bang bang" there, that's all.)

Consistent with the nationalistic perspective expressed in "El destierro de los Chinos," Ching affirms that Chinese merchants, like their European and American counterparts, have profited greatly from their commercial relations with the Mexican people. Trivializing the aims of the Mexican Revolution, Ching jests that native Mexicans have been excluded from this financial bonanza because of their violent and misguided preoccupation with armed struggle.

This comedy sketch further emphasizes the economic theme when it portrays Ching as seeking to lure María into marriage through his wealth earned as a foreign businessman:

CHING: Muchacha bonita como tú siempre queriendo bueno vestido, mucho zapato. Y este chinito está muy rico. . . . Te compro todo lo que quieras.

MARÍA: Y de que vivías allá?

CHING: Era propietario del Clan de Tonali cabaret y retiro.

MARÍA: Ese famoso retiro que anuncian por el radio?

CHING: El mismo, el mismo . . .

(Ching: A pretty girl like you always wants nice dresses, many pairs of shoes. And this Chinese guy is very rich. . . . I will buy you whatever you desire . . .

María: And how did you earn a living?

Ching: I was the owner of the Clan de Tonali, cabaret and resort.

María: The famous resort they advertise on the radio?

Ching: The same one, the same one . . .)

The author of "El Chino" therefore threads together the twin themes of economic nationalism and Chinese-Mexican interracial marriage. Like the anonymous composer of "El destierro de los Chinos," he depicts the Chinese as foreign capitalists who have become rich at the expense of the Mexican populace. With their wealth earned as leeches on the Mexican economy, moreover, they seduce "honorable" Mexican women into cross-cultural relationships through extravagant promises of financial security and material wealth. This comedic dialogue and poem clearly demonstrate that popular critiques of Chinese-Mexican unions were often couched within broader discussions of revolutionary economic nationalism. As previously discussed in the analysis of the corrido "Los Chinos," moreover, such popular criticism unfortunately also sometimes expressed itself in sinophobic violence.

Law 31 and Legal Prohibitions against Chinese-Mexican Intermarriage

Sinophobic popular sentiment and opposition to Chinese-Mexican interracial marriage found official government sanction in anti-miscegenation laws passed by the Sonoran state legislature on December 13, 1923. "Law 31" prohibited marriage between Mexican women and Chinese males under penalty of a 100- to 500-peso fine to be enforced by local municipal authorities. The text reads:

LEY NUMERO 31

ALEJO BAY, Gobernador Constitucional del Estado Libre y Soberano de Sonora, a sus habitantes sabed:

Que el H. Congreso del Estado, me ha dirigido la siguiente Ley Num. 31
QUE PROHIBE EL MATRIMONIO DE MEXICANAS CON INDIVIDUOS CHINOS.

ARTICULO PRIMERO—Se prohíbe el matrimonio de mujeres mexicanas con individuos de raza china, aunque obtengan carta de naturalización mexicana.

ARTICULO SEGUNDO—La vida marital o unión ilícita entre chinos y mexicanas será castigada con multa de $100.00 a $500.00, previa justificación del hecho, por los medios que establece el derecho común y será aplicada por las autoridades municipales del lugar donde se cometa la infracción. (Espinoza 1932, 35)

(LAW NUMBER 31

ALEJO BAY, Constitutional Governor of the Free and Sovereign State of Sonora, to its inhabitants, lets it be known:

That the H. State Congress has sent to me the following Law No. 31
WHICH PROHIBITS THE MARRIAGE OF MEXICAN WOMEN TO CHINESE PERSONS.

FIRST ARTICLE—Prohibits the marriage of Mexican women with persons of the Chinese race, even if they obtain a Mexican naturalization card.

SECOND ARTICLE—Marital life or illicit union between Chinese men and Mexican women will be punished with a fine of 100 to 500 pesos, subject to justification of the act, according to the means established by common law and will be applied by the municipal authorities in the place where the infraction is committed.)

As anti-miscegenation legislation, Law 31 embodied and articulated the popular perspectives expressed in the spoken-word comedic recording, cartoons, poetry, and corrido previously examined. Known as one of the "nationalistic laws" of the organized anti-Chinese campaigns, it sanctioned the racist and revolutionary attitudes of the Mexican populace by officially punishing Chinese-Mexican intermarriages. In a virulent expression of revolutionary nationalism, article one of the law barred intermarriage even with Chinese men who had become naturalized Mexican citizens. Article two extended the law's reach beyond the official institution of civil and ecclesiastical marriage to enforce strictures upon Chinese men and Mexican women engaged in extramarital free unions.

Although an ostensible victory for revolutionary opponents of Chinese-Mexican interracial marriage, Law 31 was not widely or consistently enforced by Sonoran state and local officials. According to José Angel Espinoza, a prominent leader of the organized anti-Chinese campaigns, official application of these laws was limited because of the systematic bribery of magistrates, judges, and government officials by Chinese community organizations known as "tongs." In addition, Chinese community groups hired high-class Mexican lawyers (derisively labeled "chineros") who successfully defended the right of Chinese men to marry freely with Mexican women (Arana 1918). Commenting upon the success of Chinese immigrants in resisting the application of the anti-miscegenation laws, Espinoza lamented, "The rich Chinese tongs gathered money, paid attorneys, bribed magistrates and judges, and laughed, with the cunning and cynical laughter of a stubborn and calculating coolie" (1932, 37–38).

Although in most instances Chinese immigrants managed to evade enforcement of Law 31, the case of Francisco Hing represents an interesting legal anomaly and counterexample. In violation of Law 31, Hing, a Chinese immigrant, married a Mexican woman in the state of Sonora. Although he was a naturalized Mexican citizen, his marriage was deemed invalid by Sonoran officials in accordance with article one of the anti-miscegenation statute. Taking his claim all the way to the highest court of the land, Hing challenged the constitutionality of Law 31 in an effort to secure official legal recognition of his marriage. In September 1930, however, the Mexican Supreme Court rejected Hing's legal claim and affirmed the constitutionality of Sonora's anti-miscegenation laws by an overwhelming majority ("Intervenciones de los diputados" 1988, 95–97).

Conclusion: Revisioning Mestizaje and "Chino-Chicano" Studies

An analysis of popular commentary on Chinese-Mexican interracial marriage can contribute to the emerging body of Chicana/o scholarship that reexamines traditional notions of mestizaje. Chicana/o scholars such as Alexandra Minna Stern, María Josefina Saldana-Portillo, and Ana Maria Alonzo have recently published important works challenging the traditional view of mestizaje popularized by José Vasconcelos. While scholars such as Saldana-Portillo focus upon an analysis of the relationship between Indianism and Chicanismo, an analysis of the Chinese and Asian components of mestizaje adds a new racial dimension to the discussion.

As this essay has endeavored to show, the Chinese were a familiar presence in Mexico during the early twentieth century. They made up the second-largest foreign ethnic community in the country and monopolized small-scale trade in northern Mexico, where they eventually became targets of organized anti-Chinese campaigns. Marital and free unions between Chinese men and Mexican women produced significant numbers of interracial offspring. The exclusion of these Asian Mexicans from traditional models of mestizaje flows from specific historical efforts of the Mexican postrevolutionary government to create a unified national mestizo identity. In this context, the Chinese served as a convenient scapegoat and ethnic "other" that the larger mestizo population could rally around and against.

Anti-Chinese discourses of the early twentieth century extended beyond the geographic boundaries of Mexico into the Chicano communities of the southwestern United States. Though it had its roots on the Mexican side of the borderlands, in Sonora, anti-Chinese ideology spread rapidly to Chicano communities in Texas, Arizona, and California. The transnational nature of Mexican anti-Chinese sentiment is evident in the comedic recording "El Chino," which is an imagined dialogue (in Spanish) between a Chinese merchant and a Mexican woman in Texas. Indeed, both recordings analyzed by this article are drawn not from Latin American music archives but from the UCLA Chicano Studies Research Center's own Frontera Collection. Both recordings were also produced by North American record companies (Columbia Records and the Brunswick

Record Corporation). Thus, the intermarriage patterns and anti-Chinese sentiment analyzed in this article reflect transnational experiences and attitudes present in both the United States and Mexico during the early twentieth century.

The cross-cultural marriages described in the recordings and cartoons took place in Chicano communities of the Southwest as well as in Mexico. Many Chinese borderland merchants lived transnational lives, moving between Mexico and U.S. Chicano communities. Like Pablo Chee, they typically first resided in Mexico, where they married Mexican women and became Mexican citizens, and later came to live their lives as merchants in U.S. border towns like Nogales, Arizona, and Calexico, California.

These connections provide important historical background for understanding the contemporary Asian-Latino community of the United States, Asian-Latino relations, and Asian-Latino coalition building. The 2000 U.S. census recorded the presence of more than 300,000 individuals of Asian-Latino ancestry. These individuals fell into two categories: (1) Latino persons of full Asian ancestry, presumably ethnic Asians who immigrated from Mexico and other parts of Latin America to the United States, and (2) persons of mixed Latino and Asian ancestry. There is scant research on this huge community of Asian Latinos, and the discipline of Chicano/Latino studies needs to wrestle with how to incorporate these individuals within the existing racial theory of the field. This essay on Chinese-Mexican inter-racial patterns provides important historical context for understanding this contemporary phenomenon. Indeed, many Asian Latinos in the United States can trace their ancestry to Chinese immigrants who first settled and intermarried in Mexico during the early twentieth century (fig. 5).

In addition to the secondary migration of large numbers of Asians from Latin America to the United States, "Chino-Chicano" communities are rapidly developing in Los Angeles. Within the past twenty years, cities of the San Gabriel Valley such as Alhambra, Monterey Park, Hacienda Heights, Rosemead, and El Monte have been transformed into Asian-Latino communities in which Chinese-ancestry and Mexican-ancestry populations make up the majority. With the development of these interra-cial communities have come Chinese-Mexican racial tensions and conflict in the educational and political arenas. Although few may realize it, these racial tensions are not new and have deep historical roots: the two groups have met before. Fortunately, in addition to the conflict that has resulted from the recent development of Chino-Chicano communities, efforts have also begun to build Asian-Latino coalitions.[14]

Figure 5. The author (center) with Rosita Chiu (left) and a friend in Restaurante Beijing in Mexico City, 2005. Rosita is the daughter of a Mexican mother and a Chinese father who immigrated to Mexico in the 1920s.

Finally, this study also suggests the need to create a new intellectual space within the disciplines of Latin American, Latino, and Chicano studies that explores the historical and contemporary interactions between Asians and Latinos in both Latin America and the United States. Such an intellectual program might be termed "Asian-Latino studies" or, more playfully, "Chino-Chicano studies," and would fuse the research agendas of Latin American studies, Chicano/Latino studies, and Asian American studies. This new field of research would examine the historical trajectory of Latino-Asian and Chino-Chicano relations in the United States, Mexico, and Latin America from the sixteenth century to the present. In addition, it would uncover and analyze the often-overlooked Asian contributions to Latin American and Chicano/Latino culture and identity.

As a further topic of inquiry, Chino-Chicano studies would examine the historical and sociological experiences of Chicanos/Latinos of Chinese, Asian, and partial Asian ancestry living in the United States.[15] As specific topics of research, it would analyze their experiences of cultural adaptation in the United States as well as the variations of ethnic/cultural identity possessed by this unique segment of the Chicano/Latino community. An analysis of

Chinese-Mexican intermarriage during the early twentieth century, as part of a social history of the Chinese of Mexico, can provide the historical context for understanding contemporary Chino-Chicano identity and cultural relations. It thus represents a small but important step toward the development of the new field of Asian-Latino, or Chino-Chicano, studies.

Notes

Since the original publication of this article, the author has completed a book-length social history of the Chinese in Mexico. See Robert Chao Romero, *The Chinese in Mexico, 1882-1940* (Tucson: The University of Arizona Press, 2010).

This article is based on a paper presented at the Faculty Research Exchange organized by the UCLA Chicano Studies Research Center in April 2004. The author thanks the UCLA Chicano Studies Research Center for their support during the 2003–4 and 2004–5 academic terms, and the university President's Office for the postdoctoral fellowship funding that made the initial research and writing of this article possible. The author extends special thanks to his home department, the UCLA Department of Chicana and Chicano Studies, for the generous research funding that allowed completion of this article. The author is especially grateful to the two anonymous readers for their insightful comments that greatly strengthened this article. Finally, the author thanks Leonardo Melchor for his assistance in transcription and translation of recordings from the UCLA Frontera Collection and the poem analyzed in this article. Other translations are the author's.

1. El Plan Espiritual de Aztlan was adopted by the First National Chicano Liberation Youth Conference in Denver, Colorado, in March 1969.

2. See especially Saldana-Portillo (2001).

3. For example, see Bennett (2003) and Cuevas (2004).

4. For general readings on Chinese immigration to Mexico, see Hu-DeHart (1980) and Romero (2003).

5. For an examination of Chinese immigrant smuggling to the United States from Mexico during this period, see Lee (2002, 2003) and Romero (2004/2005).

6. All references in this essay to Mexican municipal census records are records of the Dirección General de Estadística from 1930: "Censo de población del municipio de Chihuahua, Chihuahua, 1930"; "Censo de población del municipio de Hermosillo, Sonora"; and "Censo de población del municipio de Nogales, Sonora." The records were microfilmed by the Genealogical Society of Utah, Salt Lake City.

7. For an interesting comparison with Mexican-Punjabi marriages in the Imperial Valley of California, see Leonard (1992).

8. This recording and the corrido titled "Los Chinos" were identified and researched using the UCLA Frontera Digital Archive. This archive and audio clips of these two recordings can be accessed online at http://digital.library.ucla.edu/frontera/. For more on the Frontera Digital Archive, see Romero (2005).

9. This cartoon and those in figures 3 and 4 are from José Angel Espinoza's *El ejemplo de Sonora* (1932). In prose and cartoon, *El ejemplo de Sonora* chronicles the organized anti-Chinese movement in the state of Sonora during the early twentieth century.

10. Excerpt from "El destierro de los Chinos: Que se pongan a llorar de lo a gusto que han vivido y el tronido que han de dar," broadside (xfPQ7260 C6 no. 376), reproduced with permission of The Bancroft Library, University of California, Berkeley.

11. This "braid" worn by Chinese immigrant males refers to the queue that all Chinese men were required to grow in order to distinguish them from Manchurians of the ruling Ching Dynasty. After the collapse of the Ching Dynasty in 1919, the queue fell out of use.

12. For further reading on the fusion between masculinity and postrevolutionary nationalism, see Alonso (1995), Irwin (2003), and O'Malley (1986).

13. Little is known or published about this repatriation of Mexican women during the Cárdenas regime, so it is difficult to speculate on the exact number that returned or the precise reasons for their return. It may be that Mexican wives found their experiences in China to be socially and culturally isolating. The historical record is unclear as to whether the harsh cartoon depictions examined in this article were accurate.

14. For more on Asian-Latino coalition building from the perspective of Asian American studies, see Park and Park (1999) and Ropp (2000).

15. For writings on Asian-Latino multiethnic cultural identity and historical interactions in the United States, see Delgado (2000) and Guevarra (2003a, 2003b).

Works Cited

Alonso, Ana Maria. 1995. *Thread of Blood: Colonialism, Revolution, and Gender on Mexico's Northern Frontier.* Tucson: University of Arizona Press.

Bennett, Herman L. 2003. *Africans in Colonial Mexico: Absolutism, Christianity, and Afro-Creole Consciousness, 1570–1640.* Bloomington: Indiana University Press.

Cuevas, Marco Polo Hernandez. 2004. *African Mexicans and the Discourse on Modern Nation.* Dallas: University Press of America.

Delgado, Grace. 2000. "In the Age of Exclusion: Race, Region, and Chinese Identity in the Making of the Arizona-Sonora Borderlands, 1863–1943." PhD diss., University of California, Los Angeles.

Espinoza, José Angel. 1932. *El ejemplo de Sonora.* Mexico City: n.p.

Guevarra, Rudy P., Jr. 2003a. "Burritos and Bagoong: Mexipinos and Multiethnic Identity in San Diego, California." In *Crossing Lines: Race and Mixed Race across the Geohistorical Divide,* ed. Marc Coronado, Rudy P. Guevarra, Jeffrey Moniz, and Laura Furlan Szanto. Santa Barbara: University of California, Multiethnic Student Outreach.

————. 2003b. "Clueless." In *Crossing Lines: Race and Mixed Race across the Geohistorical Divide*, ed. Marc Coronado, Rudy P. Guevarra, Jeffrey Moniz, and Laura Furlan Szanto. Santa Barbara: University of California, Multiethnic Student Outreach.

Hu-DeHart, Evelyn. 1980. "Immigrants to a Developing Society: The Chinese in Northern Mexico, 1875–1932." *Journal of Arizona History* (Fall): 275–312.

"Intervenciones de los diputados Walterio Pesqueira, Juan de Dios Batiz, Francisco Trejo y Julio Bustillos, Cámara de Diputados. Martes 30 de septiembre de 1930." 1988. In *Chinos y Antichinos en México: Documentos para su estudio*, ed. Humberto Monteon Gonzales and José Luis Trueba Lara. Guadalajara, Jalisco, Mexico: Gobierno de Jalisco, Secretaria General, Unidad Editorial.

Irwin, Robert McKee. 2003. *Mexican Masculinities*. Minneapolis: University of Minnesota Press.

Lee, Erika. 2002. "Enforcing the Borders: Chinese Exclusion along the U.S. Borders with Canada and Mexico, 1882–1924." *Journal of American History* 89, no. 1: 54–86.

————. 2003. *At America's Gates: Chinese Immigration during the Exclusion Era, 1882–1940*. Chapel Hill: University of North Carolina Press.

Leonard, Karen. 1992. *Making Ethnic Choices: California's Punjabi Mexican Americans*. Philadelphia: Temple University Press.

Ministerio de Fomento. 1895. *Censo general de la Republica Mexicana verificado el 20 de octubre de 1895, resumen del censo de la Republica*. Mexico City: Dirección General de Estadística.

O'Malley, Ilene. 1986. *The Myth of the Revolution: Hero Cults and the Institutionalization of the Mexican State, 1920–1940*. New York: Greenwood Press.

Park, Edward J. W., and John S. W. Park. 1999. "A New American Dilemma? Asian Americans and Latinos in Race Theorizing." *Journal of Asian American Studies* 2, no. 3: 289–309.

Renique, Gerardo. 2000. "Anti-Chinese Racism, Nationalism and State Formation in Post-Revolutionary Mexico, 1920s–1930s." *Political Power and Social Theory* 14: 91–140.

————. 2003. "Race, Region, and Nation: Sonora's Anti-Chinese Racism and Mexico's Postrevolutionary Nationalism, 1920s–1930s." In *Race and Nation in Modern Latin America*, ed. Nancy Appelbaum, Anne S. MacPherson, and Karin Alejandra Rosemblatt, 211–36. Chapel Hill: University of North Carolina Press.

Romero, Robert Chao. 2003. "The Dragon in Big Lusong: Chinese Immigration and Settlement in Mexico, 1882–1940." PhD diss., University of California, Los Angeles.

————. 2004/2005. "Transnational Chinese Immigrant Smuggling to the United States via Mexico and Cuba, 1882–1916." *Amerasia Journal* 30, no. 3: 1–16.

————. 2005. "Música de la Frontera: Research Note on the UCLA Frontera Digital Archive." *Aztlán: A Journal of Chicano Studies* 30, no. 1: 233–37.

Ropp, Steven Masami. 2000. "Secondary Migration and the Politics of Identity for Asian Latinos in Los Angeles." *Journal of Asian American Studies* 3, no. 2: 219–29.

Saldana-Portillo, Maria Josefina. 2001. "Who Is the Indian in Aztlan? Re-Writing Mestizaje, Indianism, and Chicanismo from the Lacandon." In *The Latin American Subaltern Studies Reader*, ed. Ileana Rodriguez, 402–23. Durham, NC: Duke University Press.

Vasconcelos, José. 1997. *La raza cósmica*. Trans. Didier T. Jaen. Baltimore: Johns Hopkins University Press.

Archival Sources

Arana, José María. "Al margen del informe del C. Gobernador del Estado Dr. Cesareo G. Soriano." Magdalena, Mexico, April 4, 1918. José María Arana Papers, University of Arizona Library Special Collections, Tucson.

"El destierro de los Chinos: Que se pongan a llorar de lo a gusto que han vivido y el tronido que han de har." Undated broadside. Item xfPQ7260 C6, no. 376. Bancroft Library, University of California, Berkeley.

GRDS (General Records of the Department of State). [U.S. consular agent] Wilson to Secretary of State, Mexico City, November 2, 1911; Wilson telegram, Mazatlán, March 16, 1912; Wilson telegram, Mazatlán, no. 115, October 21, 1912. U.S. consul William Alger to Secretary of State, Mazatlán, Sinaloa, March 17, 1912; Alger to Secretary of State, San Diego, CA, December 10, 1913. Hamm to Secretary of State, Durango, Mexico, September 18, 1913. In microfilm roll, "Chinese Question in Mexico, 1910–1930," Record Group 59, Decimal File 312.93, 1910–29, 1930–39; 704.9312, 1910–29, 1930–39, University of Arizona Main Library, Tucson.

"Pablo Chee, Chinese Exclusion Act Case File 2295/7." National Archives, Pacific Region, Laguna Niguel, CA.

Rodríguez, Netty, and Jesus Rodríguez. "El Chino." Vocalion, Brunswick Record Corporation, 1937. UCLA Frontera Digital Archive. http://digital.library.ucla.edu/frontera/.

Secretaria de la Economía Nacional. 1930. *El Servicio de Migración en México por Landa y Pina Jefe del Departamento de Migración*. Mexico City: Talleres Gráficos de la Nación. Bancroft Library, University of California, Berkeley.

Tavo, Eduardo. "Los Chinos." Columbia, 1913. UCLA Frontera Digital Archive. http://digital.library.ucla.edu/frontera/.

Prosthesis, Surrogation, and Relation in Arturo Islas's *The Rain God*

John Alba Cutler

> Because the person in pain is ordinarily so bereft of the resources of speech, it is not surprising that the language for pain should sometimes be brought into being by those who are not themselves in pain but who speak on behalf of those who are. . . . Thus there come to be avenues by which this most radically private of experiences begins to enter the realm of public discourse.
>
> —Elaine Scarry, *The Body in Pain*

> The notion of a writer who speaks for the realities, myths, legends, hopes, dreams, and frustrations of an entire people suggests a kind of prophet or super priest. And this kind of writer is always a danger or an asset according to the dominant party line.
>
> —Arturo Islas, "Writing from a Dual Perspective"

The discourses of ethnicity, sexuality, and disability all confront similar questions of how to reconcile the materiality of bodies with their social construction, and Chicano author Arturo Islas wrestled with these questions throughout his life and in his fiction. After a childhood bout with polio left him with a limp and ulcerative colitis left him permanently dependent on a colostomy bag, Islas experienced acutely the way that physical differentiation complicates social relationships, including relationships already complicated by his ethnicity and gay sexuality. In a journal entry dated March 25, 1978, Islas lamented,

> Why can't I regard sex casually? Why can't I see it for what it is? It has to do with my *physical condition*, with feeling rejected & humiliated because of my limp & my bag, though *in fact*, no one has rejected me for those

reasons. Still, I feel the constant specter of rejection there everywhere, always worrying about the moment of explanation when I'm finally, completely naked. (Arturo Islas Papers, box 54, folder 3)[1]

Islas intimately connected his physical impairment with his self-perceived inability to fully express his sexuality, even though "*in fact*" others may not have made the connection so explicitly.[2] His understanding of his own body recalls Rosemarie Garland Thompson's distinction of disability as "not so much a property of bodies as a product of cultural rules about what bodies should be or do" (1997, 6).

Miguel Chico, the protagonist of Islas's landmark 1984 novel *The Rain God*, is a vehicle for Islas's artistic exploration of these same challenges. Just as Islas did in life, Miguel Chico battles polio and undergoes surgery that leaves him dependent on an appliance for life. But Miguel Chico does not worry about how his body signifies visually; rather, his anxiety is tactile. "He had forgotten what it was like to be able hold someone, naked, without having a plastic device between them" (Islas 1991, 25). Miguel Chico's appliance ensures his survival while impeding his own self-perceived capacity for genuine physical (here sexual) relation. This is the impasse of prosthesis, extending and maintaining the body, artificially replacing its functions while simultaneously marking its difference from other bodies. David T. Mitchell and Sharon L. Snyder describe the role that prosthetic devices play: "If disability falls too far from an acceptable norm, a prosthetic intervention seeks to accomplish an erasure of difference all together; yet, failing that, as is always the case with prosthesis, the minimal goal is to return one to an acceptable degree of difference" (2000, 7). Yet even that "acceptable degree" of difference interacts in complicated ways with other forms of difference that Miguel Chico experiences, most obviously his sexuality. Similarly, Islas felt that his disability and attendant form of prosthesis always carried with it the "specter of rejection" in his erotic life.

Not surprisingly, considering disability studies' relatively late entry into literary criticism, critical interpretations of *The Rain God* have for the most part deferred broaching the problem of disability. As exceptions to this pattern, Frederick Luis Aldama's recent publications on Islas suggest that a reconsideration of *The Rain God* is timely. My essay seeks both to intervene in critical discussions about the novel as well as to suggest the potential for synthesizing discourses heretofore deployed in disparate conversations about disability, sexuality, and ethnicity. Writing as compensation for a perceived disability is not an unfamiliar cultural narrative, but *The Rain God* complicates that narrative in significant ways.[3] The "acceptable degree of difference" that the prosthesis seeks to achieve bodily for Miguel Chico never obtains because of Miguel Chico's preexisting ethnic and sexual difference. And this essay will address how the work of several commentators curiously maps the compensation-through-authorship narrative from Miguel Chico onto Islas's own body, despite the novel's carefully refined fictiveness. Discussions of Islas in relation to the novel tend not only to conflate the two but even to reimpose Miguel Chico's narrative onto Islas in a strange case of looping. Because Miguel Chico's narrative is already familiar *as narrative*, he becomes the character through which Islas's own vexingly ambiguous life story is made readable.

I begin with the premise that as social categories, ethnicity, sexuality, and disability describe bodies in relation to one another—rather than providing totalizing descriptions of "the body" as such—and in *The Rain God*, the most basic social relation is familiar. For *The Rain God* is first and foremost a family narrative, though as Antonio Márquez observes, "Islas has circumvented the conventional plotting of the family saga" (1994, 4). Just as Miguel Chico in the act of forgetting always remembers what it is like to hold another person, so in the act of exorcising his family demons does he continually reify them as inescapable, discovering that escape may not even lead to fulfillment. The novel insists on the materiality of bodies, but always as bodies *in relation* to one another. It does not move to recuperate "the family" in any banal way, reinscribing traditional hierarchies, but rather to reenvision, to reshape the possibilities of *la familia*, to demand new forms of ethical relation within the networks of filial relation that transfix Chicana/o life. This reading takes seriously Ralph E. Rodriguez's recent invitation to reimagine "family as a fruitful site of politically powerful group relations" (2005, 43).[4]

In what follows, I first demonstrate how the discourses of race, sexuality, and disability in the novel pose critical questions about the nature of bodies in relation. These questions are relevant not only to the novel but also to Islas's lived experience and our own relationship to him as readers and critics. Second, I trace a short history of Islas criticism, paying special attention to the way the author's body becomes imbricated with that of his protagonist, suggesting a problematic politics of surrogation. My purpose in tracing this critical history is to indicate how Islas's place in Chicano literary history relates to the shifting contours of Chicano ethnicity. Finally, I return to the novel to offer an alternative reading that can help us appreciate more fully how it envisions bodies coming into relation with one another—a familial love that allows for recognition of difference as something other than abnormality.

Bodies in Relation

Islas narrates *The Rain God* through the lens of Miguel Chico, a third-generation Mexican American and a member of the Angel family now living in San Francisco, who revisits his memories of the family like an "analyst, interested in the past for psychological, not historical reasons" (1991, 28). The narrative begins with Miguel Chico's own near-death due to a mysterious intestinal disease, an event that forces him to undergo surgery and wear an appliance (presumably a colostomy bag) at his side for the rest of his life. From his home in San Francisco, Miguel Chico remembers his childhood and adolescence, and while the novel is narrated in the third person, this introductory event suggests that Miguel Chico is more than the narrative focalizer—he is the narrator. Empowered by both his education and his self-imposed separation from his family, Miguel Chico revisits his memories, including the suicide of a cousin, his father's affair with his mother's best friend, his uncle's brutal murder, and the decline and death of his grandmother, the family matriarch Mama Chona.

The novel's opening immediately presents sexuality as a mode of relation complicated by disability. Reflecting on the family's "sinners," Miguel Chico remembers standing at his grandmother's deathbed when she reached for his hand and whispered only "la familia" (5). His grandmother's ominous words remind him of "that lost, uneasy feeling he had whenever any of his younger cousins asked him why he had not married. Self-consciously, he would say, 'Well, I had this operation,' stop there, and let them guess at the rest" (5). Disability becomes a convenient mask for Miguel Chico's sexuality, which is never made explicit in the novel.[5] As Juan Bruce-Novoa explains, this coyness serves an important narrative function: "[It] is an allusion to a topic yet unexplained. . . . It is through the metonymic string of references linking Felix and Miguel Chico that the question assumes significance of an allusion to homosexuality, placing in doubt the sincerity of his response" (1986, 75). Bruce-Novoa's observation of how the novel links Miguel Chico to his Uncle Felix, a closet homosexual, suggests that Miguel Chico's sexuality signifies often through the process of surrogation, which I will discuss later. In addition, the fact that Miguel Chico pairs this memory in his mind with his grandmother's deathbed invocation of *la familia* indicates how his sexuality at first seems to proscribe his full participation in the Angel family saga.

But all of this tension and focus on Miguel Chico's sexuality only comes inasmuch as the novel calls attention to his disabled body. The narrative moves immediately from this short memory back to the hospital bed and the operation, showing how Miguel Chico's body can be painfully apparent:

> All of his needs were being taken care of by plastic devices and he was nothing but eyes and ears and a constant, vague pain that connected him to his flesh. Without this pain, he would have possessed for the first time in his life that consciousness his grandmother and the Catholic church he had renounced had taught him was the highest form of existence: pure, bodiless intellect. . . . "Mee-gwell," sang the nurse, "wake up, Mee-gwell." "It's Miguel," he wanted to tell her pointedly, angrily, "it's Miguel," but he was unable to speak. He was a child again. (Islas 1991, 8)

The passage captures vividly what Drew Leder theorizes as the "dys-appearing body," a way of describing how our bodies are not apparent to us except when they are in a state of "dys," or physical or conceptual discomfort (1990, 97). The passage in fact illustrates several layers of "dys" through Miguel Chico's ironic relationship to family and religious ideologies, as well as through the differences it points out between bodily pain and ethnic marginalization. If Miguel Chico's "vague pain" is what connects him to his body, it doesn't allow him to achieve any heightened awareness of that body, and in fact he associates that pain with his body's horrific and alienating medicalization. Physically, he is made of "tubes" and "plastic devices." In Leder's words, "The disruption and constriction of one's habitual world thus correlates with a new relation to one's body. . . . The painful body is often experienced as foreign to the self" (76). Because of this alienation, Miguel Chico feels a compelling attraction to the doctrine of disembodiment, which he has always rejected before as a deleterious symptom of his grandmother's hypocritical piety. Miguel Chico's awareness of his body thus comes at great cost.

Miguel Chico's bodily pain also dominates his experience of ethnicity. While he is annoyed, even angry, at the nurse's inability to pronounce his name, his frustrated voicelessness is characterized as simply another symptom of the disability that reduces him temporarily to a state of childish dependence. In this way the ethnic body signifies as primarily social and conceptual: he's nothing but "eyes and ears," the communicative, social organs through which he interacts with the nurse. Again paradoxically, that social interaction heightens the inescapable materiality of the body when "another voice inside his head [keeps] saying, 'You cannot escape from your body, you cannot escape from your body'" (Islas 1991, 7). In other words, that the ethnic body is social does not reduce its reality as a signifier, but the text demonstrates this only through the moment of bodily pain, through Miguel Chico's entrance into disability, that most permeable of social categories.[6] These early pages of the book thus characterize the body as bearing a triple burden in terms of sexuality, ethnicity, and disability, but they do so by placing the onus of that burden on disability. Miguel Chico displaces his discomfort with his sexuality onto his disability, and he experiences bodily pain as not simply paralleling but actually expressing the inescapability of ethnicity.

Understanding *The Rain God* is largely a question of seeing these critical questions reconfigured as bodies come into relation with one another. The novel is less concerned with advancing a narrative than it is with making a variation on a theme. Thus it reconfigures questions about bodies in different ways across its six narrative sections. Later in "Judgment Day," for example, as Miguel Chico reminisces about Mama Chona, he asks himself, "What . . . did she see when she looked in the mirror? As much as she protected herself from it, the sun still darkened her complexion and no surgery could efface the Indian cheekbones, those small very dark eyes and aquiline nose" (27). Just as Miguel Chico finds his body in pain to be inescapable, Mama Chona cannot escape the visible racial signifiers inscribed on her body, though she rejects them socially. Even Mama Chona's full name, Encarnación Olmeca Angel, symbolizes her ironic disavowal of the racial signifiers her body obviously expresses, showing her alternately to be the "incarnation" of Indianness—as indexed by the name "Olmeca," an allusion to the pre-Cortesian Olmec peoples indigenous to Mexico—or, in the paradoxically juxtaposed Catholic and Indian signifiers, to be the consummate embodiment of a *mestizaje* that defies illusions of racial purity.

Mama Chona experiences her own kind of redemption in the closing pages, but the impasse between sociality and materiality never resolves itself. In the section called "Ants," Miguel Chico's cousin JoEl, Felix's psychologically traumatized only son, puzzles over his grandmother's peculiar habits regarding her skin, intuitively relating them to his Tia Cuca's taboo relationship with a white man:

> JoEl asked why she needed the umbrella, since rain fell only six or seven times a year. . . . "I don't want to burn my skin," she said. "It's dark enough already." JoEl looked closely at her very dark, leathery skin but asked no more questions. It was a mystery, like her wearing even on the hottest days the black woolen dress that reached almost to the ground. The mystery was enhanced by the atmosphere of sin that surrounded Tia Cuca's relationship with Mr. Davis. (144)

Again, the rejection of Indianness comes only by attempting to reject the body, which remains inescapable. Significantly, Mama Chona's mysterious motives in relation to her own body are here associated with her sister's mysterious and rebellious sexuality, again linking the two discourses of ethnicity and sexuality. This is especially apparent in the loaded word "mystery," which seems at once to refer to the fact of Mama Chona's "dark, leathery skin"—as if it were a mystery how it came to be so dark and leathery—as well as to her conservative widow's mourning dress, and to the catechism and mysteries of the Church. The word intimates that transgression lies beneath her black dress's multitudinous folds. In this case, race and sexuality together pose the problem of the body, ironically suggesting that the body is all biology, as opposed to Mama Chona's insistence on intellect.

Uncle Felix's body also poses dilemmas, especially inasmuch as we accept Bruce-Novoa's characterization of its metonymic relationship with Miguel Chico's own. While maintaining a secure position in local society as a husband, father, and factory manager, Felix also seeks out secret homosexual encounters with young soldiers from the nearby army base. He attempts to pick up one of these soldiers at a bar, only to be brutally beaten to death in his own car by the young man. His murder redefines the marginalized ethnic and sexual body as always mediated by horrific trauma. Underscoring this notion, the first time the narrative presents Felix's character, he is already a corpse. To Miguel Chico's father, Miguel Grande, "It was unrecognizable. There was no face, and what looked like a tooth was sticking out behind the left ear. Dried blood and pieces of gravel stuck to the skin. The eyes were swollen shut, bulbous, and insectlike. The back of the head was mushy. The rest of the body was purple, bloated, and caved in at odd places. One of the testicles was missing" (81). The double valence of "unrecognizable" in this context is telling: Miguel Grande, who is the first to arrive at the police station, cannot decipher this mass of flesh, this "it," even as a body, let alone as his brother. The description of the eyes as "insectlike" suggests a Kafkaesque bodily metamorphosis. Not surprisingly, identity and sexuality become the primary sites of that transformation-through-obliteration, so that face and testicle are not simply disfigured, they are forcibly removed.

Only later in the novel do we find that Felix's body unites racial and sexual difference as well as complicates both, just as Miguel Chico's does. Marta E. Sánchez argues that "Felix's unconscious shame and guilt about his ethnicity and race become entangled with his insecurities as a homosexual" (1990, 291). This argument is useful in the way that it sees these bodily discourses as inextricable from Felix's character. But rather than shame, guilt, and insecurity about race and sexuality, Felix's character may actually demonstrate, through his sympathetic lust for life, how received categories of race and sexuality are often locally inadequate. We learn, for example, that Felix "would have no part of" his mother's perverse disavowal of the family's indigenous roots (Islas 1991, 142), and despite her objections, he marries Angie, whom his sister decries as "belong[ing] to that loathsome group of Indians who were herded through the system, taught to add at least since they refused to learn any language properly, and then let loose among decent people who must put up with their ignorance" (128). The classic U.S. black-white dichotomy proves inept for understanding the vagaries of Mexican American racism, which parallels U.S. disdain for dark skin but also inherits Spanish Creole prejudices based on class and especially language.

Similarly, classifying Felix as a "homosexual," or even a "closet homosexual," as I did earlier in this essay, fails to describe adequately the sexual status of Mexican American men (especially of a pre-assimilationist generation) who engage in homoerotic sex. As Tomás Almaguer has documented and Octavio Paz pointed out a generation ago, what counts more in terms of Mexican sexuality is sexual position, so that the so-called active partner may continue to identify as a normal husband and father, even while engaging in only nominally covert, homosexual sex.[7] This explains why the family might be ashamed of Felix yet never question his status as a father or even think of him as a homosexual. It also explains why Felix always takes the role of seducer in his romantic adventures, and why he maintains a traditional position of dominance in his home. If he is a victim of violence, he is also unarguably *machista*, taking advantage of his power as father and employer. In other words, where Miguel Chico's situation at the beginning of the novel calls into question how registers of difference—ethnicity, sexuality, disability—get equated with each other, Felix calls into question the very categories—black, white, Indian, gay—by which we understand those registers of difference.

Sacred Violence and Surrogation

We can trace the challenge that Felix poses to conceptual categories of the body to our initial encounter with his body; whatever else it is, his body is always already horrifically traumatized, even monstrous. If Felix forces us to reevaluate the categories by which bodies relate to one another, his murder and reappearance as the Rain God best exemplify how the novel works to construct new modes of relation through the process of surrogation. Surrogation, a term I borrow from performance critic Joseph Roach, describes a process of substitution in which communities attempt to fill "actual or perceived vacancies [that] occur in the network of relations that constitute the social fabric" (Roach 1996, 2). Roach theorizes that "in the life of a community, the process of surrogation does not begin or end. . . . Into the cavities created by loss through death or other forms of departure . . . survivors attempt to fit satisfactory alternates" (2). In the case of *The Rain God*, I argue that surrogation happens both diegetically and historically, both within Islas's fictional world and in the novel's evolving critical reception and canonization.

In terms of the narrative, Felix's body works as a surrogate for Miguel Chico's own queer, diseased body, inflecting Mama Chona's second iteration of *la familia*. In the first scene of the novel, as Miguel Chico thinks back on his grandmother, he interprets her dying words ("la familia") as a challenge to his sexuality that "attempt[s] to bring him back into the fold" (Islas 1991, 5). In the last scene, however, which situates Mama Chona's death after Felix's murder, *la familia* resonates differently, as unconditional love and acceptance coincident with Felix's reappearance as the Rain God: "'La familia,' she said. Felix walked toward her out of the shadows. . . . He took her in his arms. He smelled like the desert after a rainstorm" (180). According to Bruce-Novoa, Mama Chona confuses Miguel Chico's physical body with Felix's now metaphysical body. The substitution of ideas—*la familia* as capacious rather than narrowly bounded—accompanies the bodily substitution. This movement works paradoxically against the fact that in the novel's fictional world no time has passed between the two framing scenes. They are the same moment, separated only by narrative. The circular structure of the narrative again prevents us from zeroing in on exactly what the body is, underscoring the idea that writing acts as prosthesis for Miguel Chico, since Miguel Chico's growth or release must arise out of narration itself and not out of any specific experiences between two temporal points.

Narratively, Felix's body is thus consummately sacred, acting as a kind of ritual sacrifice to subsume all the potential violence in the community, here the extended Angel family. As René Girard observes about sacrifice, "Because the victim is sacred, it is criminal to kill him—but the victim is sacred only because he is to be killed" (1977, 1). Certainly the same logic operates in Islas's text, so that Felix's body becomes sacred precisely through the scene of unspeakable horror and violence. Even the poetic language used to describe his murder serves to heighten the ritual quality of the violence: "The sound of walking on stones puzzled him because he was surrounded by water. Its reflection and the luster of the boots flashed before him in an irregular, rhythmic motion. . . . The desert exhaled as he sank into water" (Islas 1991, 138). The moment cements Felix's entering into his new identity as the Rain God, a healer of communal wounds. The references to stone and rhythm connote premodern ritual and resonate with the novel's explicit allusion to Netzahualcoyotl, the Aztec poet-king. This is human sacrifice. If the desert landscape in the novel stands in as death and waste, then through ritual violence Felix's body enables life and healing. And since he is linked closely to Miguel Chico, another sexual sinner, surrogation is critical for the latter's own use of narrative as prosthesis.

Not that the characters of the novel explicitly view Felix's murder as a ritual sacrifice; the logic of sacrifice works on a different level. It appears, for example, in the implicit authoritarian approval given to Felix's murder—done "in self-defense and understandably"—by both state and familial agents (87). It also works against the determination of Felix's daughter, Lena, to seek justice: "*In her ignorance* she decided that [Miguel Grande's] love for her father was without conviction" (88, my italics). The story itself insists on some transcendent truth—the solidity of cultural barriers against Mexicans and homosexuals, or the idea that Miguel Grande might both love and be ashamed of his brother simultaneously—that Lena cannot understand until she matures. The effect of that truth, though, is akin to the effects of ritual sacrifice. As characters submit to the state's and culture's determination to look the other way, they submit to the idea that Felix's death is justified, that it somehow stems communal aggression and prevents it from overflowing.

The first critical interpretations of Islas's novel focused largely on the sense of the sacred I have just described. Juan Bruce-Novoa's work, as we have seen, notes the metonymic association of Felix and Miguel Chico as crucial to the novel's exploration of Chicano homosexuality. In her review of the novel for *Bilingual Review*, Erlinda Gonzales-Berry argues that the nightmare Miguel Chico has about a monster late in the novel represents what Girard would call a "monstrous double": it symbolizes "both his illness and his cure, for upon awakening from the nightmare, only Miguel Chico survives; the monster vanishes into the abyss, taking Miguel's fear with him" (Gonzales-Berry 1985, 260). This narrative moment mimics on a smaller level the stemming of violence that Felix's murder provides, and as Gonzales-Berry points out, that threat of violence is both social and physical for Miguel Chico, coming from both his family and his own body. Similarly, in his review for *Revista Chicana-Riqueña*, Héctor Calderón argues that "Islas comes closer than any Chicano writer in producing a tragedy, for the book is really about the sin of pride, hubris, despite the necessity of humility and love" (1985, 69). According to this vision, Felix's murder is the violent act that produces a catharsis, though one might productively wonder whose hubris precipitates the tragedy.

As critical discussions of the novel have become more complex, they have often overshadowed this textualized, thematized substitutive movement with cultural surrogation, where the roles are filled not by fictional characters but by Islas's literary and physical bodies. This has happened in two ways: first, Islas was often used in the early 1990s as an example of how Chicano authors can reshape the American literary canon; and second, scholars since the mid-1990s have emphasized the idea of fictional autobiography in the parallel between Islas's life experiences and those of Miguel Chico. In both cases, the process of surrogation finds in Islas an important originary role within the Chicana/o critical community.

Examples of the first kind of surrogation include studies done by José David Saldívar, Antonio Márquez, and Marta E. Sánchez. In each of these studies, *The Rain God* serves to reshape the American and Chicano literary canons. Saldívar and Márquez, for instance, both note the palpable influence of icons like William Faulkner and Henry James on Islas's work. Saldívar writes that Islas's "interest in such a character [as Miguel Chico] clearly extends beyond his structural use, for, like Henry James before him, he sees the 'large lucid reflector' as no less than 'the most polished of possible mirrors of the subject.' As a consequence of this method, the novelist seems to withdraw from the action, allowing his intense perceiver to discover the subject for himself and in the process reveal it to the reader" (1991, 114). In the context of his chapter, Saldívar uses this analogy to James to explain why publishers initially rejected *The Rain God* as too complex and demanding for a piece of mere "ethnic" literature; the chapter thus effects (successfully) a comparative methodological approach to the novel. Saldívar's description also traces a process in which Miguel Chico's perceptions are substituted for Islas's own, a subtle yet powerful method for revealing to the reader the "subject." Whether "subject" in Saldívar's analysis means the "subject" of the novel or the subjectivity of either the novelist or the protagonist remains intriguingly ambiguous.

The comparative methodology typified by the Henry James analogy points to the type of surrogation operating in Saldívar's article and, even more so, in Márquez and Sánchez's interpretations. Each posits Islas, by virtue of his technical skill and/or artistic vision, as a surrogate for a Chicana/o literary community experiencing some sort of lack. In Saldívar's narrative, Islas specifically fills the place of earlier novelists such as Tomás Rivera and Rolando Hinojosa as a Chicano crafting work of great literary value, only to have publishers dismiss him as merely an ethnic writer. For Márquez and Sánchez, Islas substitutes for a larger lack, locating Chicana/o literature at the same level as acknowledged literary greats in the Anglo and Latin American traditions. Márquez thus asserts that "the difference between Islas's novels and other Chicano historical narratives is his innovative historical imagination. . . . The modernist influences on Islas's fiction can be gleaned from his essays, letters, and more important, from analogues and ironic parallels in *The Rain God* and *Migrant Souls*" (1994, 5–6). In this way, Islas originates a Chicano Literature, capital *L*, and also allows Chicano academics to lay claim to an attractive and established tradition with which we may already be familiar. The formal contextualization of Saldívar's comparative methodology largely disappears: writing may serve as a kind of prosthesis for the disabled body, but here Islas's corpus of work serves as a prosthesis for Chicano literature, the heretofore absent modernist limb.

The second mode of surrogation we find in the critical literature is even more tenuous than this. This mode maps Miguel Chico's fictive body onto Islas's lived body by reading the novel as primarily autobiographical. For example, in similar language, José Muñoz refers to Miguel Chico as Islas's "thinly disguised authorial surrogate" (1999, 32), while Aldama in his biography alludes to the "fictional character Miguelito (a thinly veiled Islas)" (2005, 92). There is obviously a high degree of coincidence between the experiences that the novel describes Miguel Chico as having and Islas's own lived experiences. I would not go so far as to argue that the socio-historical conditions of the novel's production, including Islas's experiences, are irrelevant to its interpretation. But Islas criticism often goes beyond a justifiable impulse to historicize the novel. Calling a text such as *The Rain God* a "thin veil" imbues that text with a degree of immediacy that seems untenable for so highly refined and self-consciously fictive a text. To read the novel as transparently autobiographical is ironically to make the same demand that publishers initially did in their rejections, as Saldívar has shown—that it fully embody a particular notion of oppositional experience, ethnic or gay. This logic allows Miguel Chico to become Islas's surrogate, and then Islas to become a surrogate for a gay Chicano community, but both cases of surrogation oversimplify their subjects, reducing them in an effort to make Islas's work politically legible under the terms of identity politics.

Aldama's work provides an example of how this surrogation can happen even when the critic attempts to attend carefully to Islas's unique complexity: "[This introduction] seeks to recover a complex gay Chicano author who spent a lifetime engaged in physical and textual acts of recovering and discovering in order to clear a space for the articulation of a complex Chicano/a identity and literature and thereby make healthy a contemporary American literary and social corpus" (2003, xxxvii). Here Aldama makes the project of surrogation explicit, positing Islas as a banner-bearing "gay Chicano" with the potential to "make healthy" a diseased American literary body. The logic of prosthesis also returns again, as Aldama claims Islas's identity "clears a space" to fill, which then will make the entire body functional. In addition, by conjoining the two identitarian terms "gay" and "Chicano," Aldama represents Islas's self-understanding as wholly oppositional, with the token modifier "complex" doing little to allow for the tensions between the two terms that would have obtained in the 1980s. Islas, of all people, would have questioned what it meant to be a "gay Chicano" at the height of the AIDS hysteria.[8]

I don't mean here simply to criticize these critical appraisals; Aldama's work especially is a significant contribution to Chicana/o letters. His impressive critical biography of Islas alone represents an important step forward in understanding a complex literary-historical figure. Indeed, Aldama is careful in his biography to note that Islas is "irreducible to a unified self" (2005, xiv). But identifying these sites of surrogation is critical. As Roach puts it, "Because collective memory works selectively, imaginatively, and often perversely, surrogation rarely if ever succeeds. . . . The fit cannot be exact. The intended substitute either cannot fulfill expectations, creating a deficit, or actually exceeds them, creating a surplus" (1996, 2). What Roach identifies about surrogation, what we could call cultural sacred violence, is that it doesn't work, at least not exactly. We see this clearly in *The Rain God*. Felix's death does *not* stem the tide of violence. Far from it, the narrative almost spirals out of control, so that rather than delimiting the family's suffering, the sacred violence unleashes more in kind, triggering JoEl's psychological breakdown and further dissolution of the Angel family.

Nor can surrogation work culturally in this case. What is at stake for the Chicano critical community: Can we find our own gay writer? This perhaps crassly overstates the identity politics involved, but I maintain that we should question the extent to which this particular mode of surrogation reduces both the complexity of Islas's work and the complexity of his significance as a literary historical figure. (Nor does the project of queering Chicana/o literature depend on such a reductionist idea of identity.) We might also question whether this surrogation is problematically enabled by Islas's death in 1991 due to complications from AIDS. Roland Barthes famously proclaimed the author symbolically "dead" in 1968 in an attempt to remove the primacy of authorial intentionality from literary interpretation.[9] But Barthes's "death of the author" is a call to move literary interpretation toward a model of intertextuality that presages the post-structural critique of essentialist identity models. Ironically, Islas's literal death in this case enables his candidacy for a surrogation that potentially reinstates essentialist models, replicating in a troubling way the logic of sacred violence, the body that takes the fall on behalf of the community. I sympathize with the desire to characterize Islas as a radical human rights crusader engaged in a "struggle to guarantee equal rights for all Chicanos, African Americans, American Indians, and Asian Americans" (Aldama 2005, 141). But in fact, the ways in which Islas's own life and career were profoundly indecipherable and often conservative—his self-described literary genealogy from Stegner and Cather; his attraction only to white men; his storied career at Stanford; his shifting relationship to his own body and sexuality—suggest that he only awkwardly fits into such a narrative.

In another vein, this nascent surrogation suggests the changing contours of Chicano ethnicity since the initial publication and review of *The Rain God* in 1984. If it is the case, as Werner Sollors has argued, that boundary construction is constitutive of ethnicity,[10] then we might see the expanding boundaries of Chicano identity—reflected in the desire to embrace a writer like Islas within the canon of Chicano literature—as a sign of encouraging progress. Although Islas self-identified as Chicano and always sympathized with the cause of Chicano empowerment, it's also true that he neither understood that commitment in an unconflicted way nor was ever fully comfortable reconciling his sexual and ethnic identities. In his correspondence with a friend in Spain in 1976, for example, Islas noted of his ethnic identity, "I am not, as you know, a nationalist. Chicano does not conjure up rifles and slogan shouting and sentimentality about 'The People' for me. It is, however, the term which identifies us and under which we have labored, like it or not" (Arturo Islas Papers, box 39, folder 5). While it is unclear whether the "like it or not" is for Islas or for his correspondent, the passage nevertheless reflects Islas's negotiation of what some might consider a paradoxical middle-class Chicano identity. Moreover, while Chicana lesbian feminists such as Gloria Anzaldúa and Cherríe Moraga upset the masculine privilege of Chicano literature in the early 1980s, there was still no substantive male homosexual influence in Chicano literature.[11] Thus, in a journal entry written May 25, 1987, during a Chicana/o studies conference at Stanford, Islas reflected, "I feel fearful/guilty. The connection between my sexuality, which is private, and my tenuous (?) involvement with the Chicano community. I expect them to destroy me, at least to harm me in some way. I do not feel 'them' to be a source of emotional support" (box 55, folder 1). Even this late in his life, almost a decade after coming out to his family and three years after publishing *The Rain God*, Islas continued to feel that his ethnic identity was at odds with his sexuality. Any attempt to understand Islas's fiction within Chicana/o literary history needs to deal fully with these anxieties as integral to evolving conceptions of Chicana/o identity. The veil is thick, indeed.

The Ethics of the Touch

This essay has attempted to articulate one of the most acute problems that *The Rain God* poses: the conflicted condition of bodies in relation. After all, what *is* Islas's body, post-surgery? Is it a social construction, a result of "sexual preference and racial identity"? Or is it a physiological reality, the "sutured anus" a perpetual reminder of its ineluctable materiality? A little unpacking shows these three discourses—about disability, sexuality, and ethnicity—to be as multiply fraught as they are coeval. They beg the question of exactly when Islas's body crosses the line of acceptable difference: whether he still would be unacceptable if Mexican and queer only, or whether disability becomes the final straw, the material register of social fictions with all too real consequences. To use Mitchell and Snyder's words (2000, 3), does disability here become "the master trope of human disqualification . . . a sign of inferior life itself"?

In his introduction to Islas's previously unpublished works, for example, Aldama describes Islas's experience as follows:

> With his so called "shit-bag" at his side that would fill up with feces of its own accord and a sutured anus, his sense of himself as a monster—already ostracized as a result of his sexual preference and racial identity—was magnified ten-fold. Islas's attempts at recovery were physical and psychological. His writing often proved to be the venue for him to work out and recover—at least momentarily—from such traumatic events. (2003, xv)

This description combines several discourses. We see the aspiration toward normality, implied in the term "recovery." We see as well as the perpetual deferral of normality in the case of writing about disability, since that recovery can only be momentary. The colostomy bag filling "of its own accord" with feces also recalls the problem of how disability can become overdetermining; the appliance has its own reckless agency, independent of Islas's body,[12] and Islas's sense of being a monster is "magnified ten-fold."[13]

Positing Islas as a surrogate shows an attempt to navigate the cruces created by the lived experience of ethnic, sexual, and disabled bodies. (If we can just understand who he was!) But *The Rain God* itself envisions another strategy for bodily relation, ending in a surprising twist, with a monstrous birth. Awakened from a nightmare, Miguel Chico reimagines the circumstances of his grandmother's death. Those circumstances powerfully recall the premodern myth of prodigious birth—the belief that what a woman thought about at the moment of conception could influence the physical appearance of the child.[14] We first learn, along with Miguel Chico, important details about the Angel children: "From Mema he had learned that the first Miguel Angel, Mama Chona's only child born of the love she had felt for her husband, was killed while walking down the streets of San Miguel de Allende" (Islas 1991, 162). If the first Miguel Angel is the only child born properly of marital love, then the other Angel children, per the logic of prodigious birth, are monsters. Mama Chona even concludes as much on her deathbed as she reflects: "Mary, children aren't worth the trouble. Sweet and loving as babies, they turn into monsters who cast you aside and compete with one another to see which of them can cause you the most pain" (178). Mama Chona describes her children as monstrous for causing her pain, which as we have already seen has a double alienating effect: it alienates the subject from the bodily self and also from other people.

Mama Chona's monstrous birth is not of a child, however, but rather of her prolapsed uterus, which causes her death: "The monster between her legs was almost out and Mama Chona was glad that it showed no signs of life" (177). But if not life, what does this prodigy signify? According to Lorraine Daston and Katherine Park, in premodern narratives "the monster itself was a paradoxical product of God's mercy, an alert and a warning issued to allow sinners one last chance to reform themselves. . . . Because such catastrophes were communal, Christians usually interpreted monsters as signaling not individual but collective sin" (1998, 181). The idea of collective sin here is apt, if ironized. The book is, after all, Miguel Chico's reflection on the "sinners" that comprise his family (Islas 1991, 4). At first this seems like an indictment of the way the family has ostracized its sexual deviants. But because of the monster that Mama Chona births, the entire family gathers together again over her dying body, so that the novel seems to have expanded beyond this initial, simple parochialism. We could even say that the expansion is an attempt to plead for a different kind of mercy than Daston and Park describe. Instead of averting a divine catastrophe, the mercy that the novel offers is that of ethical relation despite the fact of ethnic, sexual, and bodily pain. At the end of novel, we see not only individuals who are related to one another, but also a *familia* that chooses to relate.

Perhaps nothing represents this new mode of relation more than the way images of monstrosity revolve around, and are defused by, acts of physical touching, returning us to the question of disability and the body. Touching in the novel rises again and again to represent a mode of genuine relation. The novel opens by describing a photograph of Miguel Chico and his grandmother, Mama Chona. The photograph juxtaposes the two bodies around which the novel's action largely revolves, noting that "because of the look on his face, the child seems as old as the woman" (4). The scene is interesting also for what it does *not* say, substituting for physical description of the two characters a description of their clothes: "Mama Chona is wearing a black ankle-length dress with a white lace collar and he is in a short-sleeved light-colored summer suit with short pants" (3). While this tells us nothing about what the two characters look like, it tells us much about how the novel characterizes their initial feelings about their bodies. Mama Chona covers hers almost entirely, denies it, while Miguel Chico, if not outright reveling in his, seems at least to feel no shame by it. Nevertheless, despite these significant differences, the two Angels touch; holding hands, they are frozen in a position of ineradicable connection.[15]

When Miguel Chico lies on the operating table, he hears the doctors' voices and is "impressed by the way they touched him, as if he were a person in pain" (6). The passage resonates with the epigraph to this essay, where Elaine Scarry suggests a need for a relational ethics of pain in the search for "avenues by which this most radically private of experiences [might begin] to enter the realm of public discourse" (1985, 6). However, *The Rain God* imagines an alternative to merely "speaking for" the person in pain. It describes a response *to* pain, or at least the perception of pain in the other, since the doctors speak to him "as if" he were in pain. It functions through the irony that Miguel Chico *is*, through and through, pained. Yet the tenderness that Miguel Chico feels toward the doctors arises when they attempt to minister to him physically, rather than speak for or analyze him. Another example comes after the death of Miguel Chico's cousin. The father, Ernesto, finds comfort in his sister-in-law's touch: "At that moment, he was the loneliest creature she had ever seen. He took her hand and slowly, guided by her, began to feel his loss" (48). As with Miguel Chico before, the moment of relation depends not on an elusive sympathy, not on attempting to articulate the other's pain, but on something more literally tangible, tactile.

In contrast, where *la familia* becomes injurious through patriarchal or machista ideology and homophobia, such as the scene when Nina and Juanita's abusive father (Miguel Chico's maternal grandfather) dies, the text narrates rejection of physical contact: "'Daughters,' he said. 'Behave yourselves.' He reached for their hands, recoiled from the contact, and died with his mouth and eyes open" (44). The moment is shocking for resisting a consummately clichéd physical contact; surely only the most hardened of persons recoils from holding hands on his deathbed. It's also instructive to note that Miguel Grande refuses genuine physical relation in his parenting: "Their physical contact had been limited to a slap in the face or a bone-crushing hug that lacked affection and had been his father's way of showing that at middle-age he was still physically fit" (96). If the tender touch represents for Miguel Chico a genuine mode of relation, nothing could be more opposite than the faked hug, or physical violence, as Felix's murder surely demonstrates.

For most of the novel, Mama Chona also refuses to touch other people because it "remind[s] her of her own body" (164). The irony is poignant. Mama Chona's rejection of the body is always and obviously, if not explicitly, a rejection of relation. She doesn't want to be reminded of the necessary filial relationship her body has produced in childbearing, of her own relationship to indigenous races inscribed on her body. This is the ideology that Miguel Chico attempts to escape, moving away from his "grandmother and the Catholic church he had renounced" to perform liberal academic monasticism and queer sexuality in San Francisco's more liberating space. But as we've seen, Miguel Chico's extreme physical pain, which handicaps his ability to engage in romantic relationships hereafter, forces him to acknowledge that there's something attractive after all in the doctrine.

This realization is not the end point, however, but the beginning. The novel *begins* with Miguel Chico's violently enforced relation to his grandmother, with the observation that physicality is ineluctable, as is suffering. Miguel Chico reflects back on his childhood nurse, now dead: "He felt Maria's hand on his face, her hair smelling of desert sage and lightly *touching* the back of his neck as she whispered in his ear. Every moment is

Judgment Day and to those who live on earth, humility is a given and not a virtue" (29, my italics). It was Maria who initiated him obliquely into the worlds of sexuality and religion. Her touch reminds him of the beauty of that earlier time, and it is the culmination of his decision to accept and even to embrace both his disability and his place within *la familia*. If these things have changed him, then as a result his body is "like a plant onto which has been grafted an altogether different strain of which the smelly rose at his side, that tip of gut that would always require his care and attention, was only a symbol" (28). The image transforms the alienation of the prosthetic into a striking organic signifier.

The narrative thus begins with this spiritual injunction to Miguel Chico to accept his own bodily pain, and it ends with the sacred invitation to filial relation:

> Miguel Chico felt the Rain God come into the room.
>
> —Let go of my hand, Mama Chona. I don't want to die.
>
> "*La familia*," she said. . . .
>
> To Felix, she said, "Where have you been, *malcriado?*" He took her in his arms. He smelled like the desert after a rainstorm. (179–80)

Miguel Chico's interior desperation here, begging Mama Chona to let go of him, does not represent a rejection of the family, as some critics have asserted. Ironically, the scene reverses subject positions. Where Miguel Chico originally rejects Mama Chona's doctrine of bodiless intellect, in the end it is *she* who takes *him* by the hand in love, and she refuses to let go. Felix's reappearance also has an irreducible physicality about it. Just as Miguel Chico embraces his monster in the nightmare, Felix takes Mama Chona in his arms. And since Mama Chona is already holding Miguel Chico's hand, the three must all be touching one another. The changing relationships between family members parallel Miguel Chico's changed relationship to his body.

In each case what begins as a seeming unfortunate, frustrating accident of nature—illness, family—ends as an opportunity to reenvision bodies in relation. Nothing changes. There is no attempt to fix the body or to reorganize the family through surrogation. Nor is it a coincidence that the resolutions of disability and *la familia* parallel each other. This is how the novel sees the disabled, sexual, ethnic body, embracing both its own materiality and also the potential that arises from social interaction.

What, then, of Islas's disabled, sexual, and ethnic body, and of our relation to it? Of course we have no access to that body; we can no longer touch
him. Nor do we have a surrogate in the persona of Miguel Chico. What we
do have in Islas's fictions are touchstones, points of textual reference with
their own materiality and occupying their own social contexts—more clues
than mirrors. We should thus be wary of attempts to fix Islas's body, or his
corpus of work. For example, while Aldama characterizes Islas as "exist[ing]
within different public and personal spaces" and as expressing multiple
"fundamental selves" (2005, xiv), the general trajectory of his biography
nevertheless favors Islas as the transgressor, as boldly "challenging the
many boundaries that threatened to enclose him within restrictive roles—
intellectual, filial, sexual, and racial" (103). But the challenges of *The Rain
God* are very different from the challenges of, for example, Islas's second
novel, *Migrant Souls*. Indeed, rather than reading them both under that
broad rubric, we might productively wonder how the success of *The Rain
God* encouraged Islas to break beyond the constricting boundaries of the
publishing industry to construct more explicit "challenges" to traditional
roles in *Migrant Souls*, which abandons any coyness in relation to Miguel
Chico's sexual identity and more boldly explores the Angels' relation to
their own Indianness. In any case, the difference between the two novels
suggests an important shift in Islas's relation to and refinement of a range of
ideas about the body. And in *The Rain God*, problematizing some configurations of power is not necessarily the same as challenging them.

Near the end of the novel Miguel Chico dreams of a formless monster,
in fact the monster "that had killed [Mama Chona]," that "put[s] its velvet
paw against his gut right below the appliance at his side" (Islas 1991, 159).
Gonzales-Berry writes of this scene that there is "a sense of possession by
[Miguel Chico's] double. His monstrous double could well represent a
symbolic metamorphosis of his appliance, reminder of his illness and his
own impending death, which is at once alien and a part of him" (1985,
260). The reading recalls the idea of prosthesis, a part of the body that
is simultaneously *not* a part of the body. Because the monster doubles
his appliance *and* Mama Chona's monstrous birth, it brings together the
material and the social, the intersection of which was an earlier crux of
this essay. In other words, the monster reminds Miguel Chico again of the
ineluctability of his own monstrous body both as disabled and as part of *la
familia*, the most basic of relational units.

Rather than having Miguel Chico reject the monster, though, the
novel characterizes him as making a crucial choice: "Miguel Chico felt

loathing and disgust for the beast. He turned to face it. Its eyes were swollen with tenderness. . . . He clasped the monster to him—it did not struggle or complain—and threw both of them backward over the railing and into the fog" (Islas 1991, 160). It is the embrace in this passage that I find significant, a moment of physical contact spurred by sudden and surprising "tenderness," which Miguel Chico sees only after he faces the monster. Rosaura Sánchez argues of *The Rain God* that "resentment is the major ideological strategy in the novel. . . . The principal resentment is thus against the patriarchy as constituted in traditional Western society, with its gender roles, power relations, and values" (1991, 120). Roberto Cantú similarly asserts that "the ideological framework of *The Rain God* includes an embedded critique of gender, patriarchy, and traditional views on homosexuality" (1992, 150). Sánchez and Cantú do an impressive job mapping the novel out, but this resentment seems too schematic to describe the moment of tenderness Miguel Chico experiences, and the sweeping generalities of "the family," "traditional Western society," "gender," and "patriarchy" seem too abstract to deal with the intimacy of these bodies.

While less sweeping, however, the novel's work is not therefore less powerful. It is in fact an alternative to natural, comprehensible, even rational resentment. If the body in pain expresses the differences of sexuality and ethnicity problematically, at least the novel defers any overreaching attempt to finally reify those differences. In this sense, we do not even get a full critique of "traditional views of homosexuality," at least not in the sense that the Angels somehow learn to *accept* Felix's and/or Miguel Chico's homosexuality.[16] With its bleak irony, in fact, we can read the novel as critiquing Miguel Chico's solipsism as much as the rest of the family's insularity. This is not finally a novel about *being* different, but rather about connecting. The novel ultimately supersedes phenomenology—the struggle to define what the body *is*, or how subjectivity is experienced in the body—for ethics: a portrait of bodies learning to *act* in relation to one another.[17] As it does so, it walks a fine line, showing a family that learns to love despite physical, racial, and ethnic differentiation, despite past conflict. In these intimate concerns the novel thus paradoxically moves beyond the topical. What we see in *The Rain God* is a glimmer of possibility: a *familia* that learns to love its sinners after all, and a sinner that learns to love his *familia* in return. Difference no longer removes bodies from the norm; instead, it becomes the very grounds of relation. We may not understand much better than before what the body *is*, but we do catch a glimpse of what the body can *do*: touch and be touched.

667

Notes

Special thanks to Rafael Pérez-Torres and Helen Deutsch for guidance in the writing and revision of this paper, and to Brian R. Roberts for his productive criticisms. I would also like to thank Roberto Trujillo and the accommodating staff of the Special Collections at Stanford University Library for their support in supplemental research for this article.

1. The Arturo Islas Papers are housed in the Stanford University Library Special Collections. Because the papers have been slightly reorganized following the dated release of sensitive materials, some citations in this essay may not correspond exactly to those in Frederick Luis Aldama's recent biography of Islas, *Dancing with Ghosts* (2005).

2. In addition to this emotional insufficiency, Islas was also inhibited physically from sexual expression. His sutured anus kept him from taking the passive role in sexual encounters, and after his emotionally devastating breakup with Jay Spears in 1976, he often wondered if his inability to be penetrated frustrated Jay. In his journal for December 14, 1976, Islas described his anxiety as follows: "I have it wired up that a man is only a man if he penetrates another (anal, vagina, the mouth seems only a fair substitute); I can't be penetrated by Jay, so I feel I'm depriving him of his manhood" (Arturo Islas Papers, box 54, folder 1).

3. Historical examples of this narrative from the growing canon of disability studies might include works by the British poet Alexander Pope, American activist and educator Helen Keller, and British essayist and theorist Randolph Bourne. Always in contention, of course, is whether the writer or the reader perceives (and in so doing, constructs) physical difference as disability, and whether he or she reads the subsequent cultural production as "compensation." Wallace Stegner's *Angle of Repose* (1971) is especially relevant as a literary example of this disability narrative. In the novel, the narrator—Lyman Ward, who is confined to a wheelchair due to a crippling bone disease—explicitly views the history he is writing as compensating for his physical disability. Stegner was Islas's dissertation adviser at Stanford University, and José David Saldívar and Aldama, among others, have noted his influence on Islas's work.

4. Rodriguez's reading of Michael Nava's detective fiction in his recent book *Brown Gumshoes: Detective Fiction and the Search for Chicana/o Identity* provides an insightful model of reimagining the family as something other than "an inherently oppressive and conservative structure" (2005, 43). Rodriguez proposes "not a making of *familia* from scratch, but a scratching of *familia*. I suggest that we place the term under erasure, in a Derridean sense. . . . I advocate not for the singular, heteronormative definition of family that dominates mainstream representations, but for the creation of new sets of relations and new lines of personal connection that offer us a language and practice of possibilities for constructing family" (42–43).

5. *Migrant Souls* (1990), Islas's sequel to *The Rain God*, is more explicit about Miguel Chico's sexual identity. Though I refer to *Migrant Souls* as a touchstone text at points in the essay, I have chosen for the sake of space to restrict my close reading primarily to *The Rain God*. *Migrant Souls* follows a more traditional, linear

novelistic narrative trajectory than its predecessor and thus realizes its themes very differently.

6. While race and sexuality are for the most part nonnegotiable as permanent categories of identity—at least from a dominant perspective governed by the binary logic of "self" and "other"—disability is unique for its permeability. Anyone at any time can, by accident of nature, become disabled. By the same token, the possibility of a "cure" promises to correct many forms of disability, though of course the medical language of remediation only exacerbates the deleterious social signification of disability.

7. Almaguer notes that "although stigma accompanies homosexual practices in Latin culture, it does not equally adhere to both partners. It is primarily the anal-passive individual (the *cochón* or *pasivo*) who is stigmatized for playing the subservient, feminine role" (1991, 78). However, while "gay" identity runs along very different lines in Latin American/Mexican culture, this is not a premodern conception of same-sex relations, a Foucauldian evolution from behavior to identity. This distinction is important, since I also describe in the essay a premodern conception of monstrous bodies.

8. Manuel de Jesús Vega makes a similar discursive move in his article "Chicano, Gay, and Doomed: AIDS in Arturo Islas's *The Rain God*" (1996), which argues that Miguel Chico is really suffering from complications of AIDS and that the novel thus serves as an important text for the gay Chicano community. Though Vega doesn't discuss Islas's 1991 death from complications of AIDS, the fact that the text says nothing about the disease suggests that he reads Islas's own illness back (and backwards) onto the novel, though Islas wasn't diagnosed with HIV until 1988, four years after the novel's initial publication.

9. Barthes characterizes writing as "that neutral, composite, oblique space where our subject slips away, the negative where all identity is lost, starting with the very identity of the body writing" (1977, 142). This assertion is an extreme reaction against the kind of hagiographical criticism of the mid-twentieth century that inevitably disguised a conservative political project of identifying the "great" (invariably white) authors of the era. Although we might productively wonder to what extent the body writing slips away—especially in this case, where the material signification of that body as disabled features so intimately in the production of the text—I think that Barthes's basic insight about the importance of resisting the hagiographic impulse in interpretation still holds.

10. Sollors's assertions about ethnicization, as he calls it, also speak to *The Rain God's* narrative aesthetics: "If modern ethnicization is a form of symbolic boundary-constructing which increases cultural vitality, and if ethnic writers have displayed much interest in modern forms of communication, then the literary forms of ethnic writing can hardly be expected to be exclusively traditional. Indeed, the affinities to new forms as adequate expressions of rebirth experiences are strong" (1986, 247).

11. I do not include John Rechy when making this statement, since his work was not read as Chicano literature until later, beginning with Juan Bruce-Novoa's article in 1986.

12. Indeed, in his poem "Scat Bag," Islas described the appliance as demonstrating exactly this kind of recklessness: "I wake from dreams of flying to

find / That, filled with gas, the bag has balloon-like / Tugged at the belly towards the ceiling. / We don't belong there" (2003, 141). Here the scat bag not only operates independent of the body but also seems to aspire to a higher life that the body somehow resists, as if it is a prosthetic for spiritual yearning as much as for physical necessity.

13. The language of monstrosity has special resonance within disability studies as a historical marker of physical differentiation. In Rosemarie Garland Thomspon's words, "The ubiquitous icon of physical anomaly, the monster, exemplifies culture's preoccupation with the threat of a different body. . . . Like the monsters who are their fantastic cousins, disabled characters with power virtually always represent a dangerous force unleashed on the social order" (1977, 22). In *The Rain God*, the language of monstrosity is powerfully subverted as it is redirected at the "normal" members of the Angel family.

14. For more on the phenomenon of prodigious birth, see Lorraine Daston and Katherine Park's study *Wonders and the Order of Nature* (1998).

15. This image, which is based on a photograph included in Aldama's Islas biography (2005, illustrations following 74), also suggests the stickiness of surrogation. While the description in the novel is certainly accurate on many counts when compared with the photograph, it's also clear that the novel has refined the image for thematic relevancy. Thus, we have no sure way of telling that the young Islas in the photograph looks as old as the woman because of his facial expression. Nor can we confidently assert, as does the novel, that in the photograph the two look as if they are "in flight from this world to the next" (Islas 1991, 4). Indeed, we have no way of knowing whether *Islas* looked at this photograph often when he wrote, or whether he invents the scene for Miguel Chico, even if the latter *is* his "thinly disguised surrogate." The photographic image gives a touchstone for understanding the production of the text, but it is a mistake to let it overdetermine the interpretation.

16. Again, this stands in contrast to *Migrant Souls*, where Josie and other family members defend Miguel Chico's gay lifestyle and where the final scene depicts Gabriel, Miguel Chico's brother, praying that "joy [may] enter my brother Miguel Chico's life and may the Church accept people like him with love" (Islas 1990, 246). Although one might argue that such statements could productively suggest interpretive strategies for *The Rain God*, which is the earlier text, one could also assert that it is precisely *The Rain God*'s ambiguity on points such as these, where *Migrant Souls* is so explicit, that makes it a richer text.

17. We might say, in Jeffrey T. Nealon's words, that the novel imagines identity itself "as a hazardous performative *act*—a verb rather than a noun, a multiple becoming rather than an assured process of mourning . . . a subjection that calls for(th) response rather than the revelation of an assured lack of wholeness" (1998, 12).

Works Cited

Aldama, Frederick Luis. 2003. Introduction to *Arturo Islas: The Uncollected Works*, by Arturo Islas, ed. Frederick Luis Aldama. Houston: Arte Público.

———. 2005. *Dancing with Ghosts: A Critical Biography of Arturo Islas*. Berkeley: University of California Press.

Almaguer, Tomás. 1991. "Chicano Men: A Cartography of Homosexual Identity and Behavior." *Differences: A Journal of Feminist Cultural Studies* 3, no. 2: 75–100.

Arturo Islas Papers. Special Collections Library, Stanford University, Stanford, CA.

Barthes, Roland. 1977. *Image-Music-Text*. Trans. Stephen Heath. New York: Hill and Wang.

Bruce-Novoa, Juan. 1986. "Homosexuality and the Chicano Novel." *Confluencia* 2, no. 1: 69–77.

Calderón, Héctor. 1985. Review of *The Rain God: A Desert Tale*. *Revista Chicana-Riqueña* 13, no. 2: 68–70.

Cantú, Roberto. 1992. "Arturo Islas." *Dictionary of Literary Biography*. Vol. 122, *Chicano Writers, Second Series*, ed. Francisco A. Lomeli and Carl R. Shirley, 146–54. Detroit: Gale Research.

Daston, Lorraine, and Katherine Park. 1998. *Wonders and the Order of Nature*. New York: Zone Books.

Girard, René. 1977. *Violence and the Sacred*. Trans. Patrick Gregory. Baltimore: Johns Hopkins University Press.

Gonzales-Berry, Erlinda. 1985. "Sensuality, Repression, and Death in Arturo Islas's *The Rain God*." *Bilingual Review/La Revista Bilingüe* 12, no. 3: 258–61.

Islas, Arturo. 1990. *Migrant Souls*. New York: Avon.

———. 1991. *The Rain God*. New York: Avon.

———. 2003. *Arturo Islas: The Uncollected Works*. Ed. Frederick Luis Aldama. Houston: Arte Público.

Leder, Drew. 1990. *The Absent Body*. Chicago: University of Chicago Press.

Márquez, Antonio C. 1994. "The Historical Imagination in Arturo Islas's *The Rain God* and *Migrant Souls*." *Melus* 19, no. 2: 3–16.

Mitchell, David T., and Sharon L. Snyder. 2000. *Narrative Prosthesis: Disability and the Dependencies of Discourse*. Ann Arbor: University of Michigan Press.

Muñoz, José Esteban. 1999. *Disidentifications: Queers of Color and the Performance of Politics*. Minneapolis: University of Minnesota Press.

Nealon, Jeffrey T. 1998. *Alterity Politics: Ethics and Performative Subjectivity*. Durham, NC: Duke University Press.

Roach, Joseph. 1996. *Cities of the Dead: Circum-Atlantic Performance*. New York: Columbia University Press.

Rodriguez, Ralph E. 2005. *Brown Gumshoes: Detective Fiction and the Search for Chicana/o Identity*. Austin: University of Texas Press.

Saldívar, José David. 1991. *The Dialectics of Our America*. Durham, NC: Duke University Press.

Sánchez, Marta E. 1990. "Arturo Islas's *The Rain God*: An Alternative Tradition." *American Literature* 62: 284–304.

Sánchez, Rosaura. 1991. "Ideological Discourses in *The Rain God*." In *Criticism in the Borderlands*, ed. Héctor Calderón and José David Saldívar, 114–26. Durham, NC: Duke University Press.

Scarry, Elaine. 1985. *The Body in Pain: The Making and Unmaking of the World*. New York: Oxford University Press.

Sollors, Werner. 1986. *Beyond Ethnicity: Consent and Descent in American Culture*. New York: Oxford University Press.

Stegner, Wallace. 1971. *Angle of Repose*. Garden City, NY: Doubleday.

Thompson, Rosemarie Garland. 1997. *Extraordinary Bodies: Figuring Physical Disability in American Culture and Literature*. New York: Columbia University Press.

Vega, Manuel de Jesús. 1996. "Chicano, Gay, and Doomed: AIDS in Arturo Islas's *The Rain God*." *Confluencia: Revista hispánica de cultura y literatura* 11, no. 2: 112–18.

Spatializing Sexuality in Jaime Hernandez's *Locas*

Jessica E. Jones

Maggie "Maggot" Chascarrillo slides down a wall in Jaime Hernandez's fictional graphic barrio of Hoppers 13, and an etching in the sidewalk brings her back to an early escapade with her friend Esperanza "Hopey" Glass (fig. 1, panels 1 and 2). In this flashback the duo has just stolen cigarettes from a local liquor store and runs in fear of the police (panel 3). It is the beginning of their relationship, whose evolution is the focus of *Locas: The Maggie and Hopey Stories* (2004), a compilation of Hernandez's contributions to the *Love and Rockets* comic series. *Locas* shows the girls at punk shows, writing graffiti on barrio walls, coming of age, and entering adulthood on the streets of this predominantly Latino neighborhood just outside Los Angeles.[1]

The girls' rebellious lifestyle isn't all that is policed in the barrio. Their gender, punk aesthetic, socioeconomic status, and ambiguous sexuality situate them in the margins of a space structured by heterosexual, patriarchal norms that the residents of the neighborhood monitor vigilantly. Yet Hopey writes their relationship into the physical space of the barrio in spite of these norms, leaving it to dry in the wet concrete, where it is discovered by Maggie years later. While the barrio polices their bodies, attempting to write them into its margins, their bodies also work like Hopey's declaration of love to remap the spaces around them. They productively spoil, or "queer," the heterosexist, patriarchal codes that govern the barrio to enable alternative forms of sociability.[2]

Just as Hopey writes her relationship with Maggie in the concrete, *Locas* writes a queer Chicana sexuality that is absent from the pages of mainstream comic books and—as Chicana feminists like Cherríe Moraga and Gloria Anzaldúa have pointed out—unrecognized in the space of Aztlán constructed by the Chicano movement, especially at the time the

Figure 1. From Locas: The Maggie and Hopey Stories, 273. *Reproduced by permission of Jaime Hernandez and Fantagraphics.*

comic was first published in 1982.[3] Furthermore, by spatializing the pro-duction of sexuality, this understudied comic writes these queer Chicana bodies into existence on their "own" terms.[4] By situating characters in space, the comic is able to write queer bodies into public, yet at the same time it refuses to reify them as "gay" or "straight." It conveys a particular, localized experience to a crossover audience, depicting queer bodies of color in an intelligible way, without relying on stereotypical representa-tions of *latinidad* prevalent in mainstream publishing.[5] Writing a previously subordinated Chicana identity into the public spaces of the barrio and also the world of mainstream comic book publishing, *Locas* stakes a powerful claim to what Renato Rosaldo and others term "cultural citizenship."[6] In this way, it offers an important terrain for theorizing how an attention to space can help overcome a critical divide in which the body tends to be understood either as material or as socially constructed, as an entity that needs political representation yet cannot be reduced to the fixed identity that representation often requires.[7]

To understand how the body flows within the spatial terrain of the comic, I first provide a brief overview of how space and sexed bodies work to write and rewrite each other and why space has historically been so important in the writing of a Chicana sexuality. I then examine the comic form itself, considering how formal conventions such as gutters make it a rich site for theorizing space and sexuality. Finally, I offer a close reading of *Locas*, providing a brief overview of the barrio as heteronormative space and then showing how Hopey's and Maggie's bodies queer the spaces and panels around them to produce what Lauren Berlant and Michael Warner might call a "queer world": "a space of entrances, exits, unsystematized lines of acquaintance, projected horizons, typifying examples, alternate routes, blockages, incommensurate geographies" (2002, 198). Out of this world making emerge new understandings of Chicana sexuality as well as a reimagining of Chicano familial relations that corrects for a tendency in queer theory to fail to consider their productive potential.

Queer Aztlán: Space and Chicana Sexuality

Space, postmodern geographers argue, is no neutral terrain or "substance-less void" but is actively produced and shaped by ideology (Soja 1989, 17). Writes Henri Lefebvre, "To speak of 'producing space' sounds bizarre, so great is the sway still held by the idea that empty space is prior to whatever ends up filling it" (1991, 15). Yet, although capitalism works hard to obscure its exploitative logic, geographers have successfully shown how the forces of postmodern capital and urban development produce bodies inside the spaces they manipulate in order to maximize profits and maintain existing power relations. For example, Edward Soja argues that underlying the sprawl of Los Angeles, a city seemingly "fragmented and filled with whimsy," are the "hard edges" of a "capitalist, racist and patriarchal landscape" that organizes bodies into a "contingently ordered spatial division of labour and power" (1989, 246, 244). In *Barrio-Logos*, Raúl Villa shows how the Chicano population in Los Angeles is literally placed in "a material and symbolic geography of dominance drawn by the visible hand of urbanizing, mostly Anglo-controlled capital." He calls this process "barrioization"—the physical, social, and ideological control of Chicano bodies through urban renewal projects, freeway construction, police patrols, and "educational and informational apparatuses" (2000, 4).

Working in conjunction with Anglo-controlled capital to produce bodies and regulate spaces are dominant notions of gender and sexuality. National spaces are constructed according to what Jacqueline Stevens calls "the most fundamental structures of the modern state—the rules regulating marriage and immigration" that privilege heterosexual coupling; moreover, everyday spaces are also coded according to sexual norms (1999, xv). In their essay "Sex in Public," Berlant and Warner argue that sex is mediated by a hegemonic national public (everyone from citizens to senators to talk show hosts) who favor the heterosexual couple and the familial mode of societal organization, naturalizing and reinforcing heteronormativity as the "fundamental motor of social organization in the United States" (2002, 205). This ideology tacitly controls behaviors outside of what would ordinarily be thought of as sexual culture: habits such as paying taxes, visiting loved ones, or celebrating a holiday. According to Berlant and Warner, a "whole field of social relations becomes intelligible as heterosexuality, and this privatized sexual culture bestows on its sexual practices a tacit sense of rightness and normalcy" (194). Heteronormative expectation is mapped onto physical spaces—bedrooms, boardrooms, sex shops, and urban streets—where certain types of behavior are condoned and others condemned. Behaviors that fall outside of the heteronorm of reproductive sex tend to be pathologized, forbidden from entering into the public sphere. A same-sex couple kissing or holding hands in public often draws looks of disgust, while mixed-sex couples engaged in the same practices are "invisibly ordinary, even applauded" (Warner 2002, 24). Forms of queer cultural connection like sadomasochism, homoeroticism, or promiscuous sex are also stripped of the intimacy reserved for heterosexual sex. Forms of sociability that fall outside of heteronorms are rezoned, pushed into the closet, coded as private secrets cloaked in shame.

The rezoning of public and private spaces along racial and sexual lines has implications for access to citizenship, as Mary Pat Brady argues through her reading of Terri de la Peña's novel *Margins*. Here Brady shows "how the construction of regulatory arenas such as cities, universities, convents, and cemeteries work in tandem with public discourse to force Chicana lesbians to feel like interlopers" (2002, 87). She further describes how, in the history of modern urban planning, planners saw homosexuality as a dangerous disease harbored by the city and designed open spaces like parks and glass buildings as "anathemas to homosexuals who would then be unable to run for cover" (88–89). In this way, "controlling the category of citizen involves not only governing access to public spaces, including streets and parks, but also controlling how those spaces may be structured and produced" (90).[8] As Renato Rosaldo notes upon observing public spaces, not everyone has equal rights to first-class citizenship or the public sphere because categories such as race and gender "are visibly inscribed on the body" (1997, 29). An attention to the production of public spaces reveals that citizens are not disembodied, universal subjects but rather bodies given unequal access to the public realm on the basis of race, gender, or sexuality.

Chicana feminists are particularly attuned to the spatial dynamics of citizenship, given the importance of reclaiming Aztlán for the Chicano movement. They voice their displacement within this movement and a larger Anglo-dominated society using spatial rhetoric. Brady describes a "sense of spatial urgency" in Chicana literature, arguing that this literature "has, from its inception, contested the terms of capitalist spatial formation, including the attempts to regulate the meanings and uses of spaces, especially the use of space to naturalize violent racial, gender, sexual, and class ideologies" (2002, 7, 6). Norma Alarcón points to the construction of the U.S.-Mexico border to show how "displacement and dislocation are at the core of the invention of the Americas" (1995, 151). Meanwhile, speaking of the importance of territory as "the material basis of every nationalist movement" (1993, 170), Cherríe Moraga argues that

> land is more than the rocks and trees, the animal and plant life that make up the territory of Aztlán or Navajo Nation or Maya Mesoamerica. For immigrant and native alike, land is also the factories where we work, the water our children drink, and the housing project where we live. For women, lesbians, and gay men, land is that physical mass called our bodies. Throughout las Américas, all these "lands" remain under occupation by an Anglo-centric, patriarchal, imperialist United States. (173)

As Moraga suggests when she extends the category of land past the physical space of Aztlán, not only is all space contested, but queer Chicana bodies struggle against at least a triple displacement: outside the norms of mainstream culture, outside the white middle-class feminist and gay and lesbian movements, and also outside the "safe" spaces of Chicano culture and a movement that was supposed to protect them.

Speaking against heterosexual norms and patriarchal assumptions of the Chicano movement, Moraga invokes the house and the closet to register the spatial displacement of queer Chicana sexuality, ordinarily naturalized through the culturally "pure" familial space upon which the movement is based. From its early articulations by Chicana/o activists to its manifestation in cultural productions from the 1990s into the present, *familia*—"the one institution over which [Chicanos] exercised control"—took on both cultural and political significance within the Chicano movement (Fregoso 2003, 73). As Rosa Linda Fregoso shows, it became an "indispensable support system" that articulated an extended brotherhood "capable not only of meeting the needs of its members but also of sheltering them from the violence, exploitation, racism, and abuse perpetrated in the external, public sphere of the Anglo capitalist world" (2003, 73). Preserving family was necessary to ensure success for *la raza* and the Chicano people. Yet Fregoso goes on to show how within this discourse, women paradoxically serve central yet marginalized roles. For example, the mother figure in Gregory Nava's film *My Family* (1995) is positioned at the center of the familia but at the same time lacks narrative agency and seems frozen "within the biologically inscribed role of motherhood" (78). Defining family in such terms replicates oppressive norms of the dominant culture it sets out to critique and also ignores "the diversity of actual familia life in most Chicano/a households" (72). As Moraga argues, Chicano households often closeted issues such as "female sexuality generally and male homosexuality and lesbianism specifically . . . all of which are still relevant between the sheets and within the walls of many Chicano families" (1993, 158). Within the patriarchal space of Aztlán, women could be virgins ("Guadalupe . . . the Mexican ideal of 'la madre sufrida,' the long-suffering desexualized Indian mother") or whores ("Malinche . . . 'la chingada,' sexually stigmatized . . . invoked to keep Movimiento women silent, sexually passive, and 'Indian' in the colonial sense of the word") (157). This left few options for Chicanas who were openly assertive, sexual, or queer. Chicana women who could not fit into the traditional roles of faithful mother, devoted wife, or loyal daughter were cast outside of the household entirely, as whores.

Yet, as Moraga suggests when she claims that "for women, lesbians, and gay men, land is that physical mass called our bodies," spaces can be reclaimed by the bodies that inhabit them. As space shapes sociality, so sociality shapes space. Villa argues that even in the face of extreme poverty and segregation brought about by urban redevelopment, the barrio can also offer residents a positive sense of identity by giving them a sense of "place-consciousness" and shared feeling of *comunidad* (2000, 5). He also charts how residents of Los Angeles barrios resist subordination in an "Anglo city" by laying "claim to cultural and civic space" through the formation of social and institutional networks, while Spanish-language journalists defend the barrio social space through their discursive production (16). Echoing Soja and Doreen Massey, and writing specifically about Chicana sexuality, Brady argues that space is "lived, embodied," not simply "the abstract space of capitalism," but rather participatory, "performative [and] . . . processual, it changes, goes extinct" (2002, 5). She continues, "The production of space involves not simply buildings, transportation and communications networks, as well as social and cultural groups and institutions . . . it also involves the processes that shape how these places are understood, envisioned, defined, and variously experienced" (7). While spaces produce behavior by naturalizing ideological forces, bodies can also push back.

Berlant and Warner argue for queer world making as a strategy for reclaiming space against dominant heteronorms. Pointing out that "urban space is always a host space" and that "the right to the city extends to those who use the city" (2002, 205), they call for the construction of an "architecture of queer space in a homophobic environment" in which queer social practices "try to unsettle . . . garbled but powerful" heteronorms (191, 187–88). To make a queer world is not just to destigmatize homosexual relations but to imagine new forms of sociability, "nonnormative logics and organizations of community, sexual identity, embodiment, and activity" (Halberstam 2005, 6). A queer world is a place in which intimacy is decoupled from heterosexual private life, "domestic space . . . kinship . . . the couple form . . . property, or . . . the nation" and new forms of "nonnormative, or explicit public sexual cultures are created" (Berlant and Warner 2002, 199, 193).

Chicana feminists have argued for a queering of the spatial terrain of the Chicano movement. Reflecting upon the "limitations of 'Queer Nation,' whose leather-jacketed, shaved-headed white radicals and accompanying anglo-centricity were an 'alien-nation' to most lesbians and gay men of color," Moraga imagines a Queer Aztlán, a "Chicano homeland that could embrace *all* its people, including its jotería" (1993, 147, emphasis in original). Similarly, writing in the early 1980s, Anzaldúa imagined a "third country" (1987, 25) described by Frederick Luis Aldama as an "imaginatively recontoured Aztlán, [where] women were no longer imprisoned within patriarchally inscribed cultural spaces (brown and white), nor were queer individuals cast from the Chicano/a fold" (Aldama 2005, 22). Anzaldúa describes the inhabitants of this queer world: "*Los atravesados* live here: the squint-eyed, the perverse, the queer, the troublesome, the mongrel, the mulato, the half-breed, the half dead; in short, those who cross over, pass over, or go through the confines of the 'normal' " (1987, 25). A liminal space of contradiction and fluidity, Anzaldúa's borderland is a place where unnatural geopolitical, sexual, and racial boundaries deconstruct. Like the queer world, it is a place to celebrate the possibilities that emerge from this undoing.

Comic as Borderland: Frames, Gutters, and the Production of Bodies across Space

Through formal conventions such as frames and gutters, comics dramatize the production of bodies in space, making them ripe sites to illuminate dominant discourses of race, gender, and sexuality that strive to naturalize and obscure their spatial logic. In a comic, each frame—its scenes and backdrops—plays a fundamental role in constructing the narrative. The panels of a comic become what Nicholas Mirzoeff (1995) calls "bodyscapes," a "complex of signs"—context, framing, and style—that the artist uses to limit the "range of metaphorical meanings" the represented body could

679

possibly convey (3). For example, panels can highlight character emotion (a dark cloud in the background can be used to show the character's
anger), or they can frame conversation by foregrounding one character over
another or by producing another conversation in the background. Space
also becomes a way to understand time in a comic, the spatial organization
of the bodies within the frame often dictating the order in which the words
and images are read by the reader, or the way events unfold.

By situating the body in the surrounding space, the panels of the
comic allow us to appreciate the body's materiality without reducing it
to an essence or a type. On the one hand, the language of comics is one
of icons, abstracted symbols that almost necessarily rely on stereotypes
to communicate. Explains comic book artist Scott McCloud, "When we
abstract an image through cartooning, we're not so much eliminating
details as we are focusing on specific details. By stripping down an image
to its essential 'meaning,' an artist can amplify that meaning in a way that
realistic art can't" (1993, 30). In the language of comics, then, the surface
of the body is supposed to represent some sort of essence, making it difficult
to inscribe the body without essentializing it. On the other hand, bodies
written into a frame are constantly rewritten through their juxtaposition
with a myriad of objects and words that unfold in the surrounding space:
other bodies, physical structures, and—in the case of *Locas*—bubbles of
dialogue in English and Spanish. Like all socially produced spaces and
the bodies within them, the panels of the comic contain subtexts, double
meanings, and symbols that can be read in a variety of ways by different
audiences, infusing each panel and the bodies within it with layered and
nuanced meaning. Just as the body is material, then, it is also surface, the
product of surrounding discourse that places many intersecting and often
contradictory identities upon it.

In a comic, unlike in a painting, these bodyscapes are connected.
Because a series of panels is placed on the same page, the reader's eyes can
move forward and backward in time, one frame spilling into the next to
create an overall graphic image. The space between each panel is crucial
for this effect. Writes McCloud,

> See that space between the panels? That's what comics aficionados
> have named "the gutter.". . . Here in the limbo of the gutter, human
> imagination takes two separate images and transforms them into a single
> idea. Nothing is seen between the two panels, but experience tells you
> something must be there. (1993, 66–67)

As panels spill into other panels, seemingly distinct spaces of separate panels mingle and come together, infusing with new meaning the spaces and the bodies enclosed within them. Describing the moment in Anzaldúa's *Borderlands* (1987) poem, "Interface," when the narrator can only "'see' her lover 'at the edges of things . . . / Where before there'd only been empty space,'" Brady argues that the contemplation of the "space between . . . and then falling into that space, opens whole new arenas for desire, pleasure, and transformation" (2002, 84, 85). The gutter of the comic works like the interface, a borderlands that not only punctuates the spaces between panels but also reconnects them to produce new meanings. As the characters' narratives intertwine through juxtaposed frames, new forms of relationality and world making unfold.

The gutter of the comic explodes the tension between the materiality of the body and the fluidity of identity as it collects the often contradictory identities of a body that appears differently in panels on the same page. José Quiroga describes how, in Frances Negrón-Mutaner's video *Brincando el charco* (1994), the main character's identity shifts as her body moves into different spaces. A queerness invisible in her family home becomes visible in the disco; she is "white" and then suddenly racialized after she speaks Spanish on the streets of Philadelphia. Quiroga argues that there is "constant tension between the different zones that the body may inhabit" (2000, 194). Identity exceeds the spaces that construct it: "The spaces themselves do not trace the boundaries from one thought to another, but rather allow some of us to see continuities where others see divisions" (193).[9] On the pages of *Locas*, panels locate the body in a variety of spaces and at different moments in time. As a space of transition between these various moments and identities, the gutter is the place where these variously constructed identities bleed into one another. Says Quiroga, "Sometimes categories (sexual and ethnic) deserve to bleed onto each other like an inkspot that leaves a messy residue from one scrap of paper onto another. The stain, the spot that disseminates, is more interesting than the clear configuration of bounded spaces" (193). Located between the border of each frame, the gutter is a place where the often contradictory identities of one character can explode through their collision.

The Maggie and Hopey Stories: Toward a Theory of Space and Sexuality

To understand how these dynamics play out in the graphic world of *Locas*, I will provide a brief overview of the spatial terrain of Hoppers 13, then look more carefully at how Maggie and Hopey's queer bodies fit within the community, helping to reimagine the barrio as a queer world.

SETTING THE SCENE: WELCOME TO HOPPERS 13

Although *Locas* never gives us a complete panorama of life in Hoppers 13, it does provide snapshots of the interiors and exteriors of people's homes and apartments along with businesses, benches, restaurants, parks, highways, and backyards, to create a comprehensive sense of its terrain. The barrio is seen from different perspectives—through the eyes of insiders, the characters who narrate the action, or from the perspective of the reader, an outsider who is alternately confronted by different characters and given extra guidance to understand barrio life. In one panel Hopey glares at the reader and gruffly asks, "What the fuck are you looking at?" (Hernandez 2004, 177). Yet the Spanish slang is consistently translated, providing outsiders with a key to barrio life. The landscape of Hoppers 13 is often in what Charles Hatfield (1997, 7), borrowing from film theory, calls "deep focus": even if there is action in the foreground, the background is also in focus, serving to indicate the complexity of barrio life and the fact that the characters are part of a larger social world, connected to and framed by the spaces that surround them.

Located just outside Los Angeles and believed to be modeled after the Hernandez brothers' hometown of Oxnard, California, Hoppers 13 is also reminiscent of the Mexican barrios of East Los Angeles that Villa describes in *Barrio-Logos* (2000). The barrio is marked as urban, lower-class, and predominately Latino through an iconography of shop and restaurant signs in English and Spanish (auto repair shops, liquor stores, a "Mexican food" stand), densely packed boxy one-story houses, tall apartment complexes, graffitied walls, and low-riding cars, some of which can be seen in figures 2 and 3. Humble one-story abodes with lawns reflect the barrio's sprawling nature, while distant highways suggest the social and physical isolation of its residents who appear to be cut off from access to employment, transportation, and educational opportunities that will take them outside the barrio. Hoppers 13 has its share of urban problems such as unemployment, alcoholism, violence, drugs, and gang warfare. Police patrol the streets, but they are represented more as social

Figure 2. From Locas: The Maggie and Hopey Stories, *297. Reproduced by permission of Jaime Hernandez and Fantagraphics.*

monitors than as agents of law and order as they stop parties and crack down on loitering and graffiti; they are generally avoided by the characters.

The landscape of Hoppers 13 can be read as governed by heterosexist, patriarchal norms, naturalized in the construction of the barrio space. One of the more constant backdrops in the comic—as well as the source of employment for most of the barrio women—is Bumper's Strip Club, its exterior decorated by an icon of a shapely woman, silhouetted and objectified. Bumper's is usually pictured with at least one overly enthusiastic man (sweating, drooling, boggle-eyed) walking toward or away from the club, ostensibly pleased with the performance he has just seen or is about to see. The fact that Bumper's and the sexual economy it signifies has been legally zoned into the neighborhood and that the public display of an objectified woman goes unquestioned suggests the power of dominant heterosexual norms to produce the barrio space. Furthermore, the neighborhood is named after the hydraulics that cholos, male gang members who cruise the streets, put "in their lowrider cars to make them hop" (252), suggesting that the streets of the barrio belong primarily to these men. As Brady argues, landscape is more than "a simplistic description of scenery but rather the conscious construction of a perspective, a way of seeing the region that, in concert with policies, laws, and institutions, physically *makes* the land, produces the landscape materially and sustains it ideologically" (2002, 17 emphasis in original). If buildings like Bumper's produce the landscape materially according to dominant heterosexist norms, the barrio's name helps to discursively cement the ideology that sustains these norms.

The constant reinforcement of the heterosexist and patriarchal ideologies that are built into the barrio is dramatized in the panels of figure 3, which show the interaction between Maggie, Hopey, and various members

Figure 3. From Locas: The Maggie and Hopey Stories, *181. Reproduced by permission of Jaime Hernandez and Fantagraphics.*

of the community. In these panels and throughout the comic, community members offer their perspectives, often voicing their opinions in exchanges with other characters on the barrio streets, all the while framing the bodies within each panel.

As the girls walk the barrio streets, they encounter a group of old men on a front stoop. Hopey is clad in her punk gear, and Maggie, usually dressed in similar apparel, is wearing a skirt because a recent weight gain ruined her last pair of good jeans. In the second panel of the sequence, the men approve of Maggie's skirt because they suggest it will help her find a husband, reinforcing patriarchal and heterosexist ideals according to which women have little value without men. The men, especially Chucho, are a permanent fixture on the street and a regular source of social commentary in the comic. In the allegorical language of the comic book medium, the fact that they speak Spanish and are of an older generation suggests that their voices represent a traditional Chicano culture invested in the heteronormative values of the family structure. The men map Maggie's body according to the dominant norms they represent, rendering other parts of her identity—suggested by the fact that she is with Hopey, for example—invisible. This occlusion of Maggie's queerness is reinforced by the second panel of the scene. The girls' conversation with the men is pushed to the background and their bodies are framed by the image of a slightly overweight woman passing by, her hair neatly curled and groceries in hand, evoking "Guadalupe . . . the Mexican ideal of 'la madre sufrida'" (Moraga 1993, 157) and posing a stark contrast to Hopey and Maggie.

A similar social policing occurs in figure 4, when Hopey puts up fliers to advertise her band and her brother Joey asks about her relationship to Maggie. Joey insists that Hopey and Maggie are lesbian lovers and that Hopey is "spoiling Maggie's chance to be with a real man"; he thus illustrates a continuing public insistence on heteronormativity, even among younger generations (Hernandez 2004, 48). Hopey refuses to be categorized, hoping instead that someday Joey will "see things my way" and accept "things for what they are." But as we see in the last panel of the figure, Joey is stubborn (47).

Joey, like Chucho in figure 3, could be a member of Berlant and Warner's hegemonic public; both men's comments serve as an attempt to police the girls within the public barrio space. While Chucho attempts to contain the girls within a heteronormative framework, Joey tries to explain their actions in terms of what Hopey points to as an equally confining homosexual paradigm when she argues that "just 'cause me and Maggie live together and sleep in the same bed doesn't mean anything." Quiroga, evoking Michel Foucault, notes that power operates by "articulat[ing] the visibility and nam[ing] it as something that it believe[s] to be *other*" (2000, 13, emphasis in original). Just as Joey attempts to categorize Hopey as a "fag," an identity he then can reject as undesirable, Chucho can dismisses Hopey as "lonely and rejected" because of her failure to conform to traditional gender roles. The girls' access to public spaces of the barrio is

Figure 4. From Locas: The Maggie and Hopey Stories, 47. *Reproduced by permission of Jaime Hernandez and Fantagraphics.*

constantly mediated, their bodies produced by heterosexist and patriarchal norms that attempt to categorize and contain them, diminishing the threat their relationship represents by depicting them as abnormal and unhappy.

That the girls' queerness situates them in the margins of barrio culture is further registered spatially by the fact that neither has a permanent home. Although Maggie and Hopey—both under twenty-one when the series begins—are still young enough to live at home and have siblings who do so, neither character lives in her childhood home. They are estranged from their families, who live somewhere outside of Hoppers 13. For example, Maggie's mother appears suddenly in one panel, in town for the confirmation of a relative. Maggie and her mother are shocked to see one another ("Mom! Look at you! What are you doing in town?"/"I never see you!"). But rather than embrace and talk, they exchange only a few words in which the mother criticizes the daughter's physical appearance as sloppy and "getting heavy" (257).

The girls can't afford their own place. For most of the series they live with various friends and relatives, sometimes sleeping separately (as when Maggie lives with her Aunt Vicki and Hopey lives with her ex-girlfriend Terry) and sometimes together on a pull-out couch in the house of a friend. The fact that they can't buy or rent their own place maps their double displacement, spatially constructing them outside the Chicano home and also illustrating the socioeconomic and sexist barriers that face the women living in Hoppers 13. Maggie struggles against becoming the "whore" that rebellious women are made out to be. Although she is trained as a mechanic and does find work in the beginning of the series, traveling to faraway places to repair rockets, she quits because she doubts her abilities as a woman to do the job. She turns instead to flipping burgers, then to assisting her aunt in the women's wrestling ring, and finally to stripping and prostitution. When she tries to get a job again as a mechanic, she waits in long lines, only to receive the implicit message that she shouldn't apply because of her gender. The socioeconomic reality of the spaces that surround the women of Hoppers 13 contains them, paradoxically writing them into more stereotypical female roles.

QUEER WORLD MAKING IN HOPPERS 13

Although it is impossible to deny the production of bodies in Hoppers 13 according to heterosexual and patriarchal norms, it would be a mistake to say that the streets are entirely governed by these norms, just as it would be incorrect to claim that the residents of Hoppers 13 are entirely contained by the forces of Anglo-controlled capital and the urban redevelopment projects that Villa (2000) documents. Space is performative, and just as the neighborhood produces its residents, so do the residents—not all of whom necessarily subscribe to dominant heterosexist ideologies—produce the neighborhood. The residents of Hoppers 13 are a diverse group, multigenerational and multiethnic. There are gang-banging cholos with baggy chinos, sleeveless t-shirts, and slicked-back hair, but there are also female gangsters such as the Widows, women so powerful that being related to one of the group's leaders permanently protects Maggie from men and women alike. There are joggers, men playing soccer in parks, mothers and daughters carrying groceries, children who roam in search of the next adventure, migrant workers, and new immigrants from Mexico. Lone men stand in the alleyways between buildings, old men and women sit on their front stoops, old ladies peek out of convenience store windows. There are also queer punk-rocker women like Maggie and Hopey, with short spiky hair, punk "boy" clothes, and a devotion to the carefree rebellious lifestyle these aesthetics represent.

The girls' bodies are not so easily interpellated; the way they move and behave helps begin to rewrite the spaces around them. For example, in the panel where the girls encountered the old men on the front stoop (see fig. 3), we notice that in contrast to Maggie's more "feminine" appearance, Hopey is skinny and flat-chested, wearing a large overcoat and short hair that make her look like a boy. She's loud and rebellious as she speaks to the men, an attitude also on display in the last panel of the sequence. Here Hopey prepares to throw a bottle at a policeman, Sergeant Sado, who constantly tries to prohibit her from writing graffiti on the barrio walls. Her action shows blatant contempt of a law that condones the display of semi-naked women on the street in front of Bumper's while it prohibits tagging of the same public spaces. Meanwhile, Maggie, even in her skirt, is hardly the image of Latina femininity Chucho probably has in mind. Her body is cloaked in a loose-fitting and open button-down shirt and she wears open-fingered gloves. Her hair, like Hopey's, is in a short, punk style. And her arm is linked to Hopey's.

Moreover, although Hopey and Maggie's bodies are framed, the perspective in these scenes and throughout the text also shifts to capture the girls' own point of view. Their exchanges and commentaries reframe the other characters of the comic and remap the street spaces. In the first series of panels in figure 3, for example, the girls seem relatively unfazed by Chucho's and Joey's comments and address the men directly, challenging their assumptions and the norms they represent. Hopey disregards Chucho's conservative opinions by calling him an "old shit eating" drunk and an "old pathetic heap" (181). Similarly, in figure 4, she refuses to definitively answer her brother's line of questioning, instead deferring and dismissing his efforts to label and control her by firing staples at him. Through this constant exchange and shift in perspectives, the streets of Hoppers 13 evoke Juan Bruce-Novoa's description of the urban Chicano novel as "a progressive space of dialogue, an appropriate space in and through which a more androgenous and humane Chicano identity may be forged" (1988, 105). Just as Rosaldo finds a "classic act of cultural citizenship" (1997, 36) in the reterritorialization of a conservative Anglo-controlled San Jose museum space through the unveiling of a statue of Quetzalcóatl and the presence of Chicano activists in the audience, he might suggest that a similar remapping of space occurs through the writing of Hopey and Maggie's queer bodies in the public streets of the comic. Moreover, by depicting the girl's bodies and offering their perspective, the comic writes the girls' queer bodies into visibility, allowing them to claim rights to the public space of the barrio while also deferring categorization that would reduce the complexity of the identities being represented. Bodies are written into the spaces around them, then constantly rewritten through the interplay of objects and actions, their spatially constructed identities material yet fluid.

Hopey's evasion of sexual categories in figure 4 applies to the rest of the text as well. For example, later on, when Danita asks Maggie if she is a "fag," Maggie responds not that she loves women but that she loves Hopey (268). Maggie and Hopey are seen with men as well as women, and their relationship is understood to be an open one in which they both have sex and are intimate with other people. Similarly, while Maggie and Hopey are often featured naked and in bed together, often these moments are filled with banal conversation about the men in Maggie's life. In a comic full of naked women and ostensibly built around the relationship between two women ("the Maggie and Hopey stories"), Hopey and Maggie rarely kiss or have sex. Sex for Hopey and Maggie, while important, is just one way of strengthening an already strong bond; as Foucault (1990) might argue, it is a transitive act and not the foundation of their identity. While it might be tempting to call the girls "bisexual," to do so would miss the much more radical political work the comic is doing in providing us with bodies that do not fit neatly into such a label, and it would replicate the system of classification that queer studies is positioned to critique. Instead, it seems more fruitful to view the girls' enigmatic relationship as paradigmatic of Berlant and Warner's queer world–making culture, redefining intimacy outside of heterosexual, monogamous coupling. Their bodies are queer not just because they look like "boys" or because they are homosexual, but because of the way they challenge heterosexual norms.

By making the pair visible on their "own" terms, Hopey's and Maggie's queer bodies and the forms of sociability they represent denaturalize heteronorms and render them problematic. The girls reflect an already nonnormative barrio, constituted by nonnormative citizenry: single parents, female-headed households, nonmonogamous couples, children born outside state-sanctioned marriage or "raised in blended familias, among multiple, nonbiological parents, with extended kin, between several households" (Fregoso 2003, 73). Viewed from the girls' perspective, the root of their conflicts with the other characters is not in their own pathologies but with those around them who are trying to render legible these unruly bodies. Once we see things from Hopey's and Maggie's perspective, the fragility of heteronorms in Hoppers 13 begins to register. The streets of the barrio take on a nuanced texture—what Alicia Gaspar de Alba might call a "black velvet" feel, a "working-class, highly layered, textured, and metaphoric sensibility," akin to a "*rasquache* aesthetic that underlies so much of Chicana/o popular culture" (2003, xxiv; see also Ybarra-Frausto 1989). For example, the so-called traditional Chicano family that Chucho seems to yearn for in figure 3 doesn't seem to exist either within or outside the barrio. Maggie's own family, however stereotypically large and religious it might be, is split in two. Her Catholic parents divorced, and her father left the family when she was a child to marry a younger woman. Her mother, said to have gone crazy from the burden of raising so many children alone, left Maggie to be raised by her aunt. The ideal of heterosexual monogamous coupling is further disrupted by the presence of Bumper's, the strip club whose patrons include married men. A scene in which Maggie witnesses a "straight" migrant worker, with a wife and kids in Mexico, having sex with a man further complicates definitions of heterosexuality in this cross-cultural barrio (Hernandez 2004, 624).

When we learn to read a queer subtext in the layers of each panel we see how the writing of both the seemingly static bodies and the spaces that surround them is at the same moment potentially being rewritten and queered. In figure 5, Hopey gets her hair shaved at Leo's barbershop while Maggie watches. In the iconic language of the comic, as a barbershop and not a beauty salon, Leo's could be coded as patriarchal and heteronormative, a place where men get their hair cut by straight male barbers. Barbershops are also places of male sociability, where men talk about sports or politics as they get their hair cut. The large window and the "open/closed" sign in English and Spanish suggest this shop's connection to the community. The barber himself, presumably Leo, is a conservatively dressed older man with shiny shoes, neatly trimmed hair, collared shirt, and loose black pants.

Figure 5. From Locas: The Maggie and Hopey Stories, *183. Reproduced by permission of Jaime Hernandez and Fantagraphics.*

The wrinkles on his face age and dignify him, visually connecting him to traditional Chicano culture.

Yet this seemingly heternormative space takes on a velvet texture when we begin to appreciate the interplay between the bodies and the objects that surround them. Invoking Massey, Brady reminds us that "places are not frozen in time; rather 'places are processes too'" (2002, 112). The romanticized image of the barber shop as a "static sign" of heritage and a timeless bastion of tradition is disrupted with the recognition that space is lived, embodied, and produced. In figure 5, not only are Hopey and Maggie in a male-dominated space, but Hopey is getting a haircut that makes her look like a man. This echoes her "boyish" street performances such as bottle throwing, running, yelling, and electric guitar playing (some of which are featured in the scenes surrounding the barber shop panel on the opposing page of the comic, not included here) and therefore challenges stereotypical gender roles. Heterosexuality is also being questioned. The girls talk not to the barber but to each other, registering the different form of sociability that they also represent through their conversation about living together. As the girls' bodies remap the space, the space rewrites their bodies. Gay pornography magazines clearly visible on the table in the left-hand corner of the scene register its queer subtext and write the girls' anomalous bodies into the space. According to this logic, the barber who looks like an exemplar of traditional values queers Hopey's body, shaving her hair and making her look like a boy. That the barber shop could have always already been queer disrupts a reader's perception of what a heteronormative space might be. Meanwhile, the fact that the symbolism of the magazines is untranslatable to anyone who wouldn't recognize them as gay pornography suggests that queerness is written into visibility yet masked at the same time.

Queering the heteronormative codes that govern the barrio spaces enables alternative forms of sociability. In figures 6 and 7, Maggie (a.k.a. Perla) tells her sister Esther about her time working at Bumper's, with the scene sequence framed as a flashback. Esther's claim that at least she "wasn't no stripper at no place called Bumper's," delivered in a drooping word bubble, reinforces the club's coding as a heteronormative, male-dominated space, populated by men whose eyes boggle at the topless women dancing on the stage before them. The women who dance there, Esther implies, are worthless hypersexualized objects of desire. Panels showing the interior of the club seem to reinforce this notion. There are men receiving lap dances and staring at naked women on the stage. Many of the men are seated and the women are serving them.

Yet Maggie's response to her sister frames her experience working at Bumper's in less stigmatizing terms. Every "punk girl in Hoppers at least knew about Bumper's if they didn't work there waitressing, or . . . yes, stripping!" she declares. The implication is that they did so out of economic necessity and they weren't necessarily tainted by the experience; it was just a job. Without male money there would be no strip club to reclaim, yet Maggie's narrative puts these women in control of the space, remapping the

Figure 6. From Locas: The Maggie and Hopey Stories, *631. Reproduced by permission of Jaime Hernandez and Fantagraphics.*

scene and shifting the way the women's topless bodies are viewed. As she reveals a few pages later, like Terry (the thin woman who dances in the left top panel of figure 7), "every dancer at Bumper's was lesbian or bi" (635). The women's topless bodies, while certainly still feasible objects of male desire, complicate notions of heterosexual desire by queering the forms of heterosexual attraction upon which the men's sex drive is based. The men are unknowingly lusting after unattainable objects of desire.

Figure 7. From Locas: The Maggie and Hopey Stories, *632. Reproduced by permission of Jaime Hernandez and Fantagraphics.*

Significantly, the women are performing not for the men but for each other. Maggie states that Monica only wanted her to be a stripper so "she could check me out herself" (635). The women's queerness could be seen to pertain less to the fact that they are lesbians and more to the queer forms of sociability between them. Figures 6 and 7 show the women's performances in the public space of the strip club but also the private spaces of the women's dressing rooms, where their wigs come off and they speak to one another as people, supporting each other as they get ready to go on stage. Connected by the gutter of the comic, these forms of sociability—the interconnectedness between the women—extend past the private dressing rooms and into the performance area itself, the second set of panels reshaping how the women in the first set are viewed. For example, although the women in the first panel are topless and working (one is waitressing and the other is giving a lap dance), they are also talking to each other. Their conversation connects them and brings them into focus, not as hypersexualized objects of desire but as speaking agents in control of the scene. The women's command of the space is further suggested when Maggie claims that Mr. Bumper had to fire them because of rumors that they were all "gonna murder" him "and turn the place into a full on dyke operation" (635). The women then have built a queer world into the architecture of the strip club.

Yet, as suggested by the lower left-hand panel in figure 7, although the queer world imagined in the text is outside a heteronormative paradigm, the women's relationships in this and other scenes are not configured entirely outside the family structure that naturalizes heteronormativity. The concept of family is not overlooked entirely, as queer theorists such as Berlant and Warner suggest it should be. Paradigmatically, they lament the "nostalgic family-values covenant of contemporary American politics" and argue that the deployment of the family not only reproduces patriarchal and heteronormative ideologies of dominance but it also privatizes citizenship, separating "the aspirations of national belonging from the critical culture of the public sphere and from political citizenship" (Berlant and Warner 2002, 189).[10] In the comic, although intimacy is queered, the world that it produces is not necessarily decoupled from private life, "domestic space . . . kinship . . . the couple form . . . property, or . . . the nation" (199). Instead, *Locas* rewrites family, as do Chicana feminists such as Moraga, who describes her own queer motherhood in *Waiting in the Wings* (1993), or the Chicana Brown Berets, who imagined an extended family of nonbiological sisters (Fregoso 2003, 85).[11] Although they are not biologically related, the women in *Locas* watch out for and support one another as family members might; they are sisters, as the title of the scene sequence, "Butt Sisters," suggests. In figure 6, the entire flashback is framed as Maggie and Esther, blood sisters, wait for the train that will bring Maggie's friend Danita, whom she treats as a "sister" from Hoppers 13, who needs a place to stay.

The overarching "Butt Sister" frame for the narrative also applies to the other scenes in the sequence, especially the queer domestic panels that are juxtaposed across the gutter with scenes from the strip club. For example, in figure 7, scenes from the dressing rooms of the strip club are juxtaposed with a scene from a living room in which Maggie's friends—Izzy, Hopey, and Daffy—express concern about what has become of her in her new job as a stripper. As they huddle around the TV watching cartoons and worrying about their lost "sister," the women's relationships seem to extend beyond friendship to suggest a new, queer form of family. The portrait of "Daddy" on the wall in the lower-left panel of figure 7 highlights the absence of the father figure in this matriarchal restructuring of the family, while the women's nakedness (Hopey is dressed only in a bra and shorts, and when Izzy turns around in the next panel, her open robe reveals her naked frame) further queers the reterritorialized family scene. Similarly, on the facing page of the comic book not illustrated here, a series of panels that show Maggie and Hopey in bed—Maggie confiding her distress at the prospect of working at Bumper's, and Hopey listening to and counseling her—approximates a domestic bedroom scene (633). As Hopey encourages Maggie to believe in herself and go back to working as a mechanic, the comic represents domestic space not as a retreat from the public realm but as a place that better prepares Maggie to navigate this realm on her "own" terms.

Queering the traditional domestic and familial spaces of Chicano culture through the interconnecting gutters of the comic allows for the emergence of a much more accepting, fluid form of familia. It suggests agreement with Ralph E. Rodríguez, who says that while "*familia* needs to have its connections broken from the overdetermined relations of patriarchy that have prevailed in the Chicana/o community . . . summarily dismissing 'family' fails to take seriously the importance of reimagining family as a fruitful site of politically powerful group relations" (2003, 76). Forms of sociability that fall outside a heterosexist paradigm don't necessarily need to fall outside the family structure, which can be used as an important political and social tool in Chicano culture; rather, they can help reimagine them.

Conclusion

Out of the contested spatial terrain of Hoppers 13 and the different performances within its streets, a queer world unfolds in which queer bodies remap spaces by challenging heterosexist and patriarchal norms. The architecture of the queer world is no permanent structure. Like the urban landscape upon which it is constructed, it is a contested space, with bubbles of discourse that challenge patriarchy and heternormativity, fluid social networks, and queer cultural practices that redefine intimacy outside the heterosexual couple. To argue that *Locas* offers us a form of queer world making by helping remap the spatial terrain of Hoppers 13 is not to suggest that the barbershop or the strip club or the streets of Hoppers 13 are becoming homosexual. Instead, queering these spaces gives the barrio streets a different, more nuanced texture—a black velvet feel. In queer urban velvet Aztlán, the body engages with the spaces around it, shifting the way the spaces frame their occupants to enable other forms of sociability and new understandings of familia and Chicana sexuality.

Notes

I wish to thank the following people for their contributions to this essay: Pia Deas, Scott Herring, Kelly Innes, Jane Juffer, Ralph E. Rodríguez, and Joan and Patrick Jones.

   1. First released by independent publisher Fantagraphics Books in 1982 and still in production today, *Love and Rockets* features storylines by two brothers. Gilbert Hernandez's tales tell of community life in the fictional south-of-the-border barrio of Palomar, and Jaime Hernandez depicts Hoppers 13, a multiethnic but mostly Mexican barrio just outside Los Angeles. *Love and Rockets* as a whole has been hailed in mainstream and alternative comic book circles for its innovative form and cinematic style; *Locas* in particular offers a nuanced look at Chicana/o culture through its character development and its portrayal of working-class life and Los Angeles subculture, and especially through its candid depiction of race and sexuality.

   2. I use *queer* as a verb that means to productively spoil or disrupt dominant notions of gender relations and sexuality, or as an adjective that means nonnormative. My usage is in line with that of David Eng, Judith Halberstam, and José Muñoz, who argue for a "queer epistemology" that aims for the "continuous deconstruction of the tenets of positivism at the heart of identity politics" (2005, 3). See also Juana María Rodríguez's *Queer Latinidad*, where she argues that the "breaking down of categories, questioning definitions and giving them new meaning, moving through spaces of understanding and dissension, working through the critical practice of 'refusing explication' is precisely what queerness entails" (2003, 24).

   3. Released when the comic book world was, in the words of Jaime Hernandez, "almost zero Latin . . . almost all white people" (quoted in Benfer 2001, 4), *Love and Rockets* has enjoyed some mainstream success. The Hernandez brothers have been called pioneering figures in the independent comics movement and "perhaps the most influential and revered comic book artists of the '80s and '90s" (1). They have received accolades from *Time* magazine and *Comics Journal* alike.

   4. While comic book scholars Joseph Witek (1996) and Charles Hatfield (1997) have written about the innovative form and style of *Love and Rockets*, little

697

attention has been paid to the comic in the academy in either queer or Chicano studies. William A. Nericcio (2002) offers an exception in his discussion of the comic's engagement with images of Frida Kahlo.

5. While the comic has entered the mainstream, its nuanced representations of Chicana sexuality have resisted stereotyped representations of latinidad—the complex articulation of what might be understood as a Latina/o identity based on any number of factors such as geographic origin, historical circumstances, and language spoken—that are prevalent in the mainstream publishing and comic book worlds. The comic was released at a time when, as Frederick Aldama documents, mainstream publishing houses were responding to the "increased demand for 'ethnic' American culture" by publishing more work by people of color (2005, 90). However, representations in these works tended—and tend—to normalize "brown female bodies (straight and bent) as consumable exotic objects" (94) or reduce them to the "domesticated narrative margins" (95). Writing specifically about mainstream comic books, Dariek Scott notes that "characters of Color . . . were (and on occasion still are) often doubly signified," shaded and dressed distinctively, and associated with ethnic stereotypes (1994, 77). He also describes how the homoerotic overtones of mainstream comics—manifested in young male sidekicks wearing tights—are usually closeted, rarely explicitly displayed or addressed in the same way they are addressed in *Love and Rockets* (80). For more on race and comics, see Scott McCloud's *Reinventing Comics* (2000), especially the chapter on diversity. For more on latinidad, see Juana María Rodríguez's *Queer Latinidad* (2003).

6. Rosaldo defines cultural citizenship as "the right to be different (in terms of race, ethnicity, or native language) with respect to the norms of the dominant national community, without compromising one's right to belong" (1997, 57). He defines a "classic act of cultural citizenship" as "using cultural expression to claim public rights and recognition" for a person or group previously subordinated or treated as a second-class citizen (36). In addition to dramatizing the struggle for public space inherent in the struggle for citizenship, the comic as cultural artifact expands our definition of "'culture' in a narrow sense" and also works to stake a claim to citizenship through the realm of cultural production (36).

7. This critical divide is manifested, for example, in the production of a book such as Judith Butler's *Bodies That Matter* (1993), written—as Butler suggests in the preface to the 1999 edition of *Gender Trouble* (xxiv)—partially in response to critics who accused her theory of performativity, or gender construction, of denying the body's materiality. In *Bodies That Matter*, Butler states that not only do bodies "live and die, eat and sleep; feel pain, [and] pleasure," but their various intersecting identities (however constructed) are often physically marked, making the body more difficult to escape through performance for some than for others (1993, 8). However, insisting too strongly on the materiality of the body brings us into the dangerous territory of claiming that it has some sort of essence that can also then be categorized and controlled. José Quiroga, citing Foucault on the history of sexuality, reminds us that part of the danger of representation is reification: "Power operated . . . in a dual fashion: it articulated the visibility and named it as something that it believed to be *other*"; once the homosexual body was made visible through its location in the homosexual act, homosexuality could not escape classification and

discipline (2000, 13, emphasis in original). For other examples of recent Latina/o studies criticism that engages with versions of this debate, see Juana María Rodríguez's *Queer Latinidad* (2003), especially chapter 2, "Activism and Identity in the Ruins of Representation." See also the introduction to Frederick Aldama's *Brown on Brown* (2005), where he grapples with the construction of the self.

8. For more on space and the production of sexuality, see Judith Halberstam's *In a Queer Time and Place* (2005). She argues that while postmodern geographers such as Edward Soja and David Harvey discuss how space is organized according to the logic of capitalism, they fail to adequately address the role that space plays in naturalizing dominant notions of sexuality. Similarly, in *Times Square Red, Times Square Blue* (1999), Samuel Delany offers a powerful account of how New York City's zoning laws designed to "clean up" Times Square shut down sex shops and pornographic theaters, eliminating the cross-cultural and cross-class sociability occurring within those spaces. While the literature on space and sexuality has tended to focus on "white gay male sexual communities as a highly evolved model that other sexual cultures try to imitate and reproduce" (Halberstam 2005, 12–13), there are increasing studies of sexuality and space that explicitly consider queer bodies of color. For example, see Mary Pat Brady's chapter on Terri de la Peña's *Margins* in *Extinct Lands, Temporal Geographies* (2002); Karen Tongson's "The Light That Never Goes Out" (2007); and Juana María Rodríguez's *Queer Latinidad* (2003).

9. For more on space and the excess of identity, see Juana María Rodríguez (2003). Looking at the discursive construction of the "community forum, the courtroom, the Internet chatroom, the departmental meeting," the author argues that "manifestations of identity can be mapped within specific fields of knowledge, but cannot be contained by them" (8).

10. Although in response to criticism of their antinormativity, Berlant and Warner affirm that "sentimental identifications with family and children are [not] waste or garbage" (2002, 197), their insistence on the need to decouple intimacy from kinship and the domestic suggests that their project lies elsewhere. In *Fear of Queer Planet* (1993), Michael Warner writes, "In a culture dominated by talk of 'family values,' the outlook is grim for any hope that child-rearing institutions of home and state can become less oppressive" (quoted in R. Rodríguez 2003, 76). For other examples of queer theory that critique a familial mode of politics, see Lee Edelman's *No Future* (2004, 2). For more on the relationship between queer theory, Chicana feminism, and familia, see Ralph E. Rodríguez's "A Poverty of Relations" (2003). Rodríguez argues that "we need to disarticulate 'family' from its connections to the belligerent Bush-era family values crusade" and "from the overdetermined relations of patriarchy that have prevailed in the Chicana/o community" and "reterritorialize" it "to enable more productive work such as affirming new notions of community and solidarity" (76). For attempts to reimagine family and kinship within queer theory, see Kath Weston's *Families We Choose* (1991) and Elizabeth Freeman's "Queer Belongings" (2007).

11. In *Waiting in the Wings*, Moraga engages in a discussion of both queer kinship and blood ties by documenting her own "queer story of pregnancy" as well as the nonnormative family that came to sustain her and her son (1997, 22).

Works Cited

Alarcón, Norma. 1995. "Tropology of Hunger: The 'Miseducation' of Richard Rodríguez." In *The Ethnic Canon: Histories, Institutions, and Interventions*, ed. David Palumbo-Liu, 140–52. Minneapolis: University of Minnesota Press.

Aldama, Frederick Luis. 2005. *Brown on Brown: Chicano/a Representations of Gender, Sexuality, and Ethnicity*. Austin: University of Texas Press.

Anzaldúa, Gloria. 1987. *Borderlands/La Frontera: The New Mestiza*. San Francisco: Aunt Lute.

Benfer, Amy. 2001. "Los Bros Hernandez Duet, with Kissing: The Boys Talk about Their Women." Salon.com. www.salon.com/mwt/feature/2001/02/20/kiss_and_tell/.

Berlant, Lauren, and Michael Warner. 2002. "Sex in Public." In Warner 2002, 187–208.

Brady, Mary Pat. 2002. *Extinct Lands, Temporal Geographies: Chicana Literature and the Urgency of Space*. Durham, NC: Duke University Press.

Bruce-Novoa, Juan. 1988. "Homosexuality and the Chicano Novel." In *European Perspectives on Hispanic Literature of the United States*, ed. Genieve Fabre, 98–106. Houston: Arte Público.

Butler, Judith. 1993. *Bodies That Matter: On the Discursive Limits of "Sex."* New York: Routledge.

———. 1999. *Gender Trouble: Feminism and the Subversion of Identity*. New York: Routledge.

Edelman, Lee. 2004. *No Future: Queer Theory and the Death Drive*. Durham, NC: Duke University Press.

Eng, David, Judith Halberstam, and José Muñoz. 2005. "What's Queer about Queer Studies Now?" *Social Text* 23 (Fall/Winter): 1–17.

Delany, Samuel. 1999. *Times Square Red, Times Square Blue*. New York: NYU Press.

Foucault, Michel. 1990. *The History of Sexuality: An Introduction*. Vol. 1. New York: Random House.

Freeman, Elizabeth. 2007. "Queer Belongings: Kinship Theory and Queer Theory." In *A Companion to Lesbian, Gay, Bisexual, Transgender, and Queer Studies*, ed. George Haggerty and Molly McGarry, 295–314. Malden, MA: Blackwell.

Fregoso, Rosa Linda. 2003. *meXicana Encounters: The Making of Social Identities on the Borderlands*. Berkeley: University of California Press.

Gaspar de Alba, Alicia, ed. 2003. *Velvet Barrios: Popular Culture and Chicana/o Sexualities*. New York: Palgrave Macmillan.

Halberstam, Judith. 2005. *In a Queer Time and Place: Transgender Bodies, Subcultural Lives*. New York: NYU Press.

Hatfield, Charles. 1997. "Heartbreak Soup: The Interdependency of Theme and Form." *Inks: Cartoon and Comic Art Studies* 4, no. 2: 2–17.

Hernandez, Jaime. 2004. *Locas: The Maggie and Hopey Stories*. Seattle: Fantagraphics Books.

Lefebvre, Henri. 1991. *The Production of Space*. Malden, MA: Blackwell.

McCloud, Scott. 1993. *Understanding Comics: The Invisible Art*. New York: Kitchen Sink Press.

———. 2000. *Reinventing Comics: How Imagination and Technology Are Revolutionizing an Art Form.* New York: Kitchen Sink Press.

Mirzoeff, Nicholas. 1995. *Bodyscape: Art, Modernity, and the Ideal Figure.* New York: Routledge.

Moraga, Cherríe. 1993. *The Last Generation: Prose and Poetry.* Boston: South End Press.

———. 1997. *Waiting in the Wings: Portrait of a Queer Motherhood.* Chicago: Firebrand.

Negrón-Muntaner, Frances. 1994. *Brincando el charco: Portrait of a Puerto Rican.* Videocassette, 55 min., written and produced by Frances Negrón-Muntaner.

Nericcio, William A. 2002. "A Decidedly 'Mexican' and 'American' Semi[er]otic Transference." In *Latino/a Popular Culture,* ed. Michelle Habell-Pallán and Mary Romero, 190–207. New York: NYU Press.

Quiroga, José. 2000. *Tropics of Desire: Interventions from Queer Latino America.* New York: NYU Press.

Rodríguez, Juana María. 2003. *Queer Latinidad: Identity Practices, Discursive Spaces.* New York: NYU Press.

Rodríguez, Ralph E. 2003. "A Poverty of Relations: On Not 'Making *Familia* from Scratch,' but Scratching *Familia.*" In Gaspar de Alba 2003, 75–88.

Rosaldo, Renato. 1997. "Cultural Citizenship, Inequality, and Multiculturalism." In *Latino Cultural Citizenship: Claiming Identity, Space, and Rights,* ed. William Flores and Rina Benmayor, 27–38. Boston: Beacon.

Scott, Darieck. 1994. "Love, Rockets, Race & Sex." *Americas Review: A Review of Hispanic Literature and Art of the USA* 22, no. 3/4: 73–106.

Soja, Edward. 1989. *Postmodern Geographies: The Reassertion of Space in Critical Social Theory.* New York: Verso.

Stevens, Jacqueline. 1999. *Reproducing the State.* Princeton, NJ: Princeton University Press.

Tongson, Karen. 2007. "The Light That Never Goes Out: Butch Intimacies and Sub-urban Sociabilities in "Lesser Los Angeles." In *A Companion to Lesbian, Gay, Bisexual, Transgender, and Queer Studies,* ed. George E. Haggerty and Molly McGarry, 355–76. Malden, MA: Blackwell.

Villa, Raúl Homero. 2000. *Barrio-Logos: Space and Place in Urban Chicano Literature and Culture.* Austin: University of Texas Press.

Warner, Michael. 2002. *Publics and Counterpublics.* New York: Zone Books.

Weston, Kath. 1991. *Families We Choose.* New York: Columbia University Press.

Witek, Joseph. 1996. "Uncued Closure in *Love and Rockets.*" Paper presented at the Popular Culture Association Conference: Comic Art and Comics, Las Vegas, March 28.

Ybarra-Frausto, Tomás. 1989. "Rasquachismo: A Chicano Sensibility." In *Chicano Aesthetics: Rasquachismo* (exhibition catalog), 5–8. Phoenix: MARS (Movimiento Artístico del Río Salado).

Contributors

ERIC AVILA, associate professor, has taught Chicano studies and history at the University of California, Los Angeles, since 1997. He is the author of *Popular Culture in the Age of White Flight: Fear and Fantasy in Suburban Los Angeles*. During his postdoctoral fellowship at Harvard University's Charles Warren Center for Studies in American History he began research for a second book project: "The Folklore of the Freeway: A Cultural History of Highway Construction." Dr. Avila's research has won various awards and prizes.

MAXINE BACA ZINN, professor of sociology at Michigan State University, received her PhD from the University of Oregon. Her books include: *Women of Color in U.S. Society*, with Bonnie Thornton Dill, and *Gender Through the Prism of Difference*, with Pierrette Hondagneu-Sotelo and Michael Messner. She is the coauthor, with D. Stanley Eitzen, of *Diversity in Families* and *Social Problems*, both of which won the McGuffy Award for excellence over multiple editions from the Text and Academic Authors Association. With D. Stanley Eitzen, she is also the coauthor of *Globalization: The Transformation of Social Worlds* and *In Conflict and Order: Understanding Society*. Dr. Baca Zinn has served as president of the Western Social Science Association. In 2000 she received the American Sociological Association's Jessie Bernard Award for expanding the horizons of sociology to include the study of women.

GILBERTO CÁRDENAS is assistant provost and director of the Institute for Latino Studies at The University of Notre Dame. He holds the Julian Samora Chair in Latino Studies and teaches in the Department of Sociology. Dr. Cárdenas received his BA from California State University, Los Angeles, and his MA and PhD from the University of Notre Dame. His principal research interests are immigration, race and ethnic relations, and visual sociology.

DAVID CARRASCO is the Neil L. Rudenstine Professor of the Study of Latin America at the Harvard Divinity School, with a joint appointment in the Department of Anthropology in the Faculty of Arts and Sciences. Dr. Carrasco descends from several generations of Mexican American schoolteachers on his father's side, while his mother is a celebrated painter of southwestern scenes and indigenous portraits along the U.S.-Mexico border. Dr. Carrasco was the co-producer, along with Albert Camarillo and Jose Cuellar, of the film *Alambrista: The Director's Cut,* which puts a human face on undocumented workers. He was recently awarded the Mexican Order of the Aztec Eagle, the highest recognition the Mexican government gives to a foreign national, for his contributions to the understanding of Mesoamerican religions and the cultures of the U.S.-Mexico borderlands.

ANGIE CHABRAM-DERNERSESIAN is a professor of Chicana/o studies at the University of California, Davis. She is the editor of *The Chicana/o Cultural Studies Reader* and *The Chicana/o Cultural Studies Forum.* She is the coeditor of *Speaking from the Body: Latinas on Health and Culture,* with Adela de la Torre. Her current work concerns cultural representations of health and healing and feminist cultural studies.

JOHN ALBA CUTLER, assistant professor of English at Northwestern University, researches and teaches in the fields of Chicana/o and Latina/o and comparative ethnic American literatures. Other interests include American poetry, cultural studies, and inter-American studies. His current book project argues that the concept of assimilation offers a valuable, if controversial, heuristic for Chicana/o literary history, showing how shifting notions of Mexican American acculturation and structural incorporation mark the evolution of Chicana/o nationalism and gender politics. In addition to his essay on Arturo Islas included here, he has published an article on Chicana/o narratives of the Vietnam War in *American Literature.*

KAREN MARY DAVALOS is chair and associate professor of Chicana/o studies at Loyola Marymount University. Her latest book, *Yolanda M. López,* brings together her research and teaching interests in Chicana feminist scholarship, spirituality, art, exhibition practices, and oral history. Her first book, *Exhibiting Mestizaje: Mexican (American) Museums in the Diaspora,* drew critical praise from a broad audience of reviewers, including *Art Journal* and *American Studies.* She served six years (2003–2009) as the managing editor and lead coeditor of *Chicana/Latina Studies: The Journal of Mujeres Activas en Letras y Cambio Social,* the only interdisciplinary, flagship, peer-review journal of a Latina/o professional organization. Currently she is writing *Chicana/o Art: Improbable Subjects and Political Gestures*, a book informed by sixteen life-history interviews that she conducted with Chicano and Chicana artists, as well as a decade of ethnographic research in southern California.

ADELAIDA R. DEL CASTILLO is an associate professor of Chicana and Chicano studies at San Diego State University. In 2007 she became the first female chair of the forty-year-old department. She is presently editing, with Gibran Guido, an anthology on Chicano gays. She can be contacted at delcast1@mail.sdsu.edu.

SHIFRA M. GOLDMAN is a social art historian who helped pioneer the study of Latin American art. Before retiring, she taught art history in the Los Angeles area for many years and lectured widely on Latin American and modern art. She began the campaign to preserve the 1932 Siqueiros mural in Olvera Street in Los Angeles in 1968, and she was instrumental in the development of the groundbreaking exhibition *Chicano Art: Resistance and Affirmation*, which opened at the University of California, Los Angeles, in 1990. She is the author of *Dimensions of the Americas: Art and Social Change in Latin America and the United State* and *Contemporary Mexican Painting in a Time of Change*. She has contributed to catalogs, encyclopedias, and dictionaries, and her work has appeared in major newspapers and magazines published in the United States and abroad.

JUAN GÓMEZ-QUIÑONES, professor of history at the University of California, Los Angeles, specializes in the fields of political, labor, intellectual, and cultural history. He has published more than thirty writings; among them are *Mexican American Labor 1790–1990*; *Chicano Politics: Reality and Promise, 1940–1990*; and *Sembradores, Ricardo Flores Magon and y el Partido Liberal Mexicano*. He is a past director of the UCLA Chicano Studies Research Center and was a co-founding editor of *Aztlán: A Journal of Chicano Studies*. His current research projects include studies on art and culture, the mobilizations of the 1960s and 1970s, Mexican-African relations, and "Greater Mexican East Los Angeles." Dr. Gómez-Quiñones is active civic affairs, including those addressing civil rights, electoral politics, labor, immigration, legal defense, and youth leadership. He has served as a member of the board for MALDEF, the Latino Museum, The Mexican Cultural Institute, OSIEC, and El Pueblo de Los Angeles Commission.

DEENA J. GONZÁLEZ is the author of *Refusing the Favor: The Spanish-Mexican Women of Santa Fe, 1820–1880* and the coeditor-in-chief of the award-winning *Oxford Encyclopedia of Latinos and Latinas in the U.S.* She publishes regularly in the field of Chicana/o studies, with over thirty articles, book chapters, entries, and reviews to her credit. She is coeditor-in-chief of the forthcoming *Encyclopedia of Latinos and Latinas in Politics, Social Movements, and Law.* She was a cofounder of MALCS (Mujeres Activas en Letras y Cambio Social), the only national Chicana academic organization, and over the past decade she assisted with the development of the organization's flagship journal, *Chicana/Latina Studies*. Dr. González is a professor of Chicana/o studies at Loyola Marymount University, and she has been named an American Council on Education (ACE) Fellow for academic year 2010–11.

RAMÓN A. GUTIÉRREZ is the Preston & Sterling Morton Distinguished Service Professor of History and the College at the University of Chicago, and the director of the Center for the Study of Race, Politics, and Cultures. Between 1980 and 2007 he was the Chancellor's Associates Endowed Chair in Ethnic Studies at the University of California, San Diego, where he founded the Department of Ethnic Studies and the Center for the Study of Race and Ethnicity. He is the author of many works, including *Mexicans in California: Emergent Challenges and Transformations*; *Contested Eden: California before the Gold Rush*; and *When Jesus Came the Corn Mothers Went Away: Marriage, Sexuality and Power in New Mexico, 1500–1848*. He can be contacted at rgutierrez@uchicago.edu.

JORGE A. HUERTA is Chancellor's Associate Professor of Theatre and Dance, Emeritus, at the University of California, San Diego. He is a leading authority on contemporary Chicana/o and U.S. Latina/o theater as well as a professional director. He has published a number of articles, edited three anthologies of plays, and written the landmark books *Chicano Theatre: Themes and Forms* and *Chicano Drama: Performance, Society, and Myth.* Dr. Huerta has directed in theaters across the country, including the San Diego Repertory Theatre, Seattle Group Theatre, Washington D.C.'s Gala Hispanic Theatre, La Compañía de Teatro de Albuquerque, and New York's Puerto Rican Traveling Theatre. Dr. Huerta has lectured and conducted workshops in Chicana/o theater throughout the United States, Latin America, and Western Europe. In 2007 he was honored by the Association for Theatre in Higher Education for "Lifetime Achievement in Educational Theater," and he was awarded the 2008 Distinguished Scholar Award by the American Society for Theatre Research.

JESSICA E. JONES is a PhD candidate in literature at Duke University. She received her BA in urban studies from Brown University and holds an MA in American literature from Pennsylvania State University. Before beginning her PhD she completed a year of independent graduate coursework in Latin American literature at the University of Buenos Aires. She is interested in the cultural production of the Americas.

CHON A. NORIEGA, a professor in the Department of Film, Television, and Digital Media at the University of California, Los Angeles, has been the director of the UCLA Chicano Studies Research Center since 2002 and editor for the CSRC Press since 1996. Dr. Noriega has curated numerous media and visual arts projects and has helped recover and preserve independent films. He was co-curator of *Phantom Sightings: Art after the Chicano Movement*, an exhibition that opened at the Los Angeles County Museum of Art and has traveled to sites in New York, Texas, and Mexico. Dr. Noriega's academic recognitions include the Getty Postdoctoral Fellowship in the History of Art and the Rockefeller Foundation Film/Video/Multimedia Fellowship. He is the author of *Shot in America: Television, the State, and the Rise of Chicano Cinema* and the editor of nine books dealing with Latino media and performance and visual art.

AMÉRICO PAREDES is recognized as one of the foremost Mexican American scholars for his teaching and research on corridos, folkloric ballads, and border stereotypes. He received his doctorate in English and folklore studies from the University of Texas at Austin in 1956, and in 1958 he accepted a position at the university, where he spent the rest of his academic career. He was instrumental in the formation of a center for Mexican American studies in 1970, and he was named its first director. Dr. Paredes was the recipient of a Guggenheim fellowship, the Charles Frankel Prize, and the Order of the Aguila Azteca and the Order of José de Escandón from the Mexican government. Among his writings are *With His Pistol in His Hand: A Border Ballad and its Hero*; *Between Two Worlds*; and *Folklore and Culture on the Texas-Mexican Border*. Dr. Paredes died in 1999.

FERNANDO PEÑALOSA was born and raised in the San Francisco Bay Area, and he spent part of his childhood and youth in Mexico. He was the second Chicano to earn a PhD in sociology. He is the author of more than a hundred articles and a dozen books in a number of fields. Among the latter are *The Mexican Book Industry*; *La selección y adquisición de libros*; *Class Consciousness and Social Mobility in a Mexican American Community*;

707

Chicano Sociolinguistics; Yosemite in the 1930s; El cuento popular maya: Una introduccion; and, most recently, *The Alaka`i: Kaua`i's Unique Wilderness.* He has also translated a number of books dealing with the contemporary Maya of Guatemala from English to Spanish. Dr. Peñalosa retired from California State University, Long Beach, in 1990, and he resides in Rancho Palos Verdes, California. His current research is focused on the classic Yiddish theatre.

RAFAEL PÉREZ-TORRES, a professor of English at UCLA, has published numerous articles on Chicano/a literature and culture, postmodernism, multiculturalism, and contemporary American literature in such journals as *Cultural Critique, American Literary History, Genre, Aztlán,* and *American Literature,* as well as in numerous edited collections. He served as co-curator for the art exhibition *Just Another Poster? Chicano Graphic Arts in California,* and he sits on several editorial boards, including those for *Contemporary Literature* and *American Literature.* He is the author of three books: *Mestizaje: Critical Uses of Race in Chicano Culture; To Alcatraz, Death Row, and Back: Memories of an East L.A. Outlaw,* written with Ernest B. López; and *Movements in Chicano Poetry: Against Myths, Against Margins.* His current work addresses the role of modernity and modernization in the shaping of Chicano culture.

BEATRIZ M. PESQUERA, associate professor emerita of Chicana/o studies at the University of California, Davis, focuses on gender, family, and women's labor. A nationally recognized scholar, she continues her work in Cuba as part of the university's quarter abroad program. She is author, with Denise A. Segura, of "'There Is No Going Back': Chicanas and Feminism," in *Chicana Feminist Issues* (reprinted in *Chicana Feminist Thought*), and editor, with Adela de la Torre, of *Building with Our Own Hands: New Directions in Chicana/o Studies.*

DAVID ROMÁN is a professor of English and American studies and ethnicity at the University of Southern California. His research focuses on theater and performance studies, with an emphasis on contemporary U.S. culture; American studies, with an emphasis on race, sexuality, and the performing arts; Latina/o studies, with an emphasis on popular culture; and queer studies, with an emphasis on archival practices, subcultural histories, and artistic production, primarily in twentieth-century America. Among his publications are *Performance in America: Contemporary U.S. Culture and the Performing Arts* and *O Solo Homo: The New Queer Performance.* His current projects include a book on the racial politics of American theatre in the 1940s; a study of the memoirs of pre-Stonewall gay and lesbian activists; and a historical project on AIDS and cultural production in the 1980s and early 1990s.

ROBERT CHAO ROMERO is an assistant professor in the Department of Chicana/o Studies at the University of California, Los Angeles. He is the author of *The Chinese in Mexico, 1882–1940*. He can be contacted at rcromero@ucla.edu.

ROSAURA SÁNCHEZ is a professor of Latin American and Chicano literature at the University of California, San Diego. Among her publications are *Telling Identities; Conflicts of Interest: The Letters of Maria Amparo Ruiz de Burton*, co-written with Beatrice Pita; *Chicano Discourse: A Socio-Historic Perspective; Entró y se sentó and Other Stories*; and *Lunar Braceros: 2125–2148*, co-written with Beatrice Pita. Dr. Sánchez's research interests include critical theory, cultural studies, and gender studies.

CHELA SANDOVAL teaches courses on de-colonial feminism, power and truth, liberation philosophy, and radical semiotics at the University of California, Santa Barbara. An associate professor, she received her PhD in the history of consciousness from the University of California, Santa Cruz. Dr. Sandoval is the author of *Methodology of the Oppressed* and a variety of articles and chapters on social movement, third space feminism, and critical media theory. Her current book project is on story-wor(l)d-art-performance as activism (SWAPA) and the shaman-nahual/witness ceremony. She is also working on a co-edited anthology on Xican Latina/o indigenous performance. Dr. Sandoval is interested in questions of spirituality, the art of love, and the history of consciousness.

ALEX M. SARAGOZA is an associate professor of Chicano/Latino studies at the University of California, Berkeley. Among his many publications are *The Monterrey Elite and the Mexican State, 1880–1940* and "Golfing in the Desert: Los Cabos and Post-PRI Tourism in Mexico," in *Holiday in Mexico: Critical Reflections on Tourism and Tourist Encounters*. His "Cultural Representation of Mexican Immigration" will be included in the forthcoming *Beyond the Border: The History of Mexican-U.S. Migration*. Dr. Saragoza is currently researching tourism and the national imaginary of Mexico and Cuba in the neoliberal era, and Reaganism and its repercussions for Mexicans in the United States.

Marian E. Schlotterbeck is a doctoral candidate in Latin American history at Yale University. Her dissertation, "Everyday Revolution: Grassroots Movements and the Making of Socialism in Chile, 1960–1973," charts the struggles of anonymous activists in the southern industrial province of Concepción to build a more democratic society. She graduated from Oberlin College in 2005 with highest honors in history for her thesis on popular representations of women and maquiladoras in Ciudad Juárez. She has worked as a research associate at the National Security Archive, and her work has also appeared in *The Nation*.

Denise A. Segura, professor of sociology and affiliated professor in the Departments of Chicana/o Studies and Feminist Studies at the University of California, Santa Barbara, publishes on Chicana feminisms, education, and employment. With Patricia Zavella, she coedited *Women and Migration in the U.S.-Mexico Borderlands: An Anthology*. She is the recipient of the 2008 American Association of Hispanics in Higher Education (AAHHE) Outstanding Latino/a Faculty in Higher Education (Research Institutions) award and the 2007 Lifetime Distinguished Contributions to Research, Teaching, and Service award from the American Sociological Association, Latina/o Sociology Section. Currently she serves as the president of Sociologists for Women in Society and vice president elect of the Pacific Sociological Association.

Adaljiza Sosa-Riddell is a professor emerita and the former director of Chicana/o studies at the University of California, Davis. An esteemed activist, writer, and scholar of Chicana feminism, she was instrumental in founding of Mujeres Activas en Letras y Cambio Social (MALCS) an organization of Chicanas/Latinas/Indigenas working within academia and communities to promote and support work on Chicana, Latina, and Indigena women's issues. She has been published in the proceedings of the National Association for Chicana/o Studies, and she is a published poet whose work has focused on Chicana themes.

Kay Turner holds a Ph.D. in folklore and anthropology from the University of Texas at Austin. Her areas of specialization are in women's performed folklore (especially in the arenas of oral narrative, folk religion, and material culture) and feminist and lesbian/gay/queer interpretations of folklore and popular culture. Her publications include *Beautiful Necessity: The Art and Meaning of Women's Altars*, based on her dissertation on Mexican-American women's home altars, and *Baby Precious Always Shines*, an edited selection of love notes between Gertrude Stein and Alice B. Toklas. She recently published "September 11th and the Burden of the Ephemeral" in *Western Folklore*. With Pauline Greenhill, she is currently editing a new book, *Transgressive Tales: Rethinking the Grimms' Fairy Tales*. Dr. Turner is adjunct professor in the Performance Studies Graduate Program at New York University, where she teaches courses on oral narrative theory, time, and performance, and the performance of gender. She also holds the position of director of folk arts at the Brooklyn Arts Council, where she researches and presents the diverse folk arts and artists of Brooklyn, New York. Her latest project there is *Black Brooklyn Renaissance, 1960–2010*, a yearlong celebration of the contribution of Black artists to Brooklyn and the world.

STEVEN S. VOLK, professor of history at Oberlin College, also chairs Latin American studies and directs the Center for Teaching Innovation and Excellence. He is completing a book on the historical memory in the United States of the overthrow of Chilean president Salvador Allende on September 11, 1973. He can be contacted at steven.volk@oberlin.edu.

Index

academic careers, 108
acculturation, 350, 487–88; family life and, 415–16; language and, 501–2
achicanamiento, 489
Acosta Ayala, Tania, 606
activism, 200–201; Chicano, 317–19, 417
actos, 182, 238
Acuña, Rodolfo, 111–12, 115
Adorno, Theodor, 526
advertising, Spanish-language, 498–99
advocacy, art of, 259
aesthetic/aesthetics: of altars, 299–300, 309; and politics, 323, 387; punk, 673, 688; *rasquache*, 690
aesthetic discourse, 170–71, 173–75
affirmative action, 9
African Americans, 109, 475, 492
African socialism, 419
agabachadas, 356, 361
agricultural labor, 24, 77, 89–92, 98, 136, 418
Aguilar, Linda, 333–34
AIDS activism, 401
Alarçon, Daniel, 199, 212
Alarcón, Norma, 436–37
Alcoff, Linda, 147
Aldama, Frederick Luis, 648, 658–59, 661, 666
Alessio Robles, Vito, 39, 43, 57
Alfaro, Luis, 396, 397, 398
Alonso, Ana Maria, 615
Almaguer, Tomás, 654
Alta California, 59, 339
altars, 231, 299–312; *altarcitos*, 300; bricoleurs, 308
Alurista, 205–9, 272
Alvarez, Rodolfo, 53
American culture, 14, 20, 126–29, 224; assimilation into, 211, 388; contributions to, 297; impact of, 134, 138, 143; understanding of, 454
Americanization, 416
American Literary Criticism (Goldsmith), 430
Americanos, 342

American popular culture, 517–18
Amos, Tori, 606, 608
Anaya, Rudolfo A., 232, 287–88
ancestry, 345–46, 376
Anglos, derogatory terms for, 344
Anglos and Mexicans in the Making of Texas (Montejano), 144–45
Another Part of the House (Cruz), 392, 393
anthropology: 412–13, 529–551
anti-Chinese movement, 625, 627–29, 633
anti-Mexican sentiments, 380
anti-miscegenation, 627, 638–40
Anzaldúa, Gloria, 214–16, 323, 373, 382–85, 421–424, 544–45, 585, 603, 604, 680, 682
Apodaca, Maria Linda, 542
archival collections, 63–64
Argentina, 605
Arias, Ron, 522
Armstrong, Robert Plant, 302
art/artists: freeways and, 411–12; insight and, 260; and politics, 225; religion and, 283; role of, 257–58; semiotics of, 301; social responsibility of, 223, 227–28
Asians, 430, 469; and Mexican culture, 615–16, 641–42; in U.S. population, 472–73, 481, 616
assimilation, 23, 130, 211, 384, 530; of Chicano community/families, 30, 388, 414–15; historical, 60, 62, 118; linguistic, 467, 478, 485; of Mexicans, 336
assimilationist perspective, 114, 130, 180, 224, 336
asylum, 472
autobiography, 124, 146–47, 374, 434; fictional, 657, 658; as performance, 386, 395–97
Avila, Eric R., 409–10, 484
Aztecs, 198, 203, 208, 210, 259–60, 346, 376; mythology of, 602, 656. *See also* Aztlán

Aztlán: as borderland, 214–15; diaspora and, 210; feminist, 677–79; as homeland, 14, 197, 215, 382, 522; notion of, 14, 149, 197–99, 201, 209–10, 212, 382, 673; queer, 676–79; realm/nation of, 205–7; significances of, 204, 207–8, 211, 216; theater and, 226–27, 233. See also Plan Espiritual de Aztlán
Aztlán: A Journal of Chicano Studies, 1, 3, 5

Baca, Judith, 518–19, 520
Baca Zinn, Maxine, 407, 540–41
Bard, Patrick, 607
Bakhtin, Mikhail, 454
Bancroft, Hubert H., 38, 43, 47, 494
Bannon, John Francis, 39–40
Barceló, Doña Gertrudis, 372
Barcena, José M. Roa, 43
Barker, Eugene C., 43
Barreiro, Antonia, 42
Barrera, Mario, 52, 110, 139, 199, 484
barrio/barrios, 23, 61, 77, 95, 101, 328; in comics, 682; film and, 170–189; freeways and, 512, 518–23; language and, 483, 485, 487, 495, 498; political awareness in, 111; as queer world, 682; racism and, 122–23, 127
Barrio-Logos (Villa), 675, 682
Bartlett, John Russell, 46
Barthes, Roland, 660
Bateson, Gregory, 310
Beautiful Theories (Bruss), 447
Belkin, Arnold, 266
Beneath the Shadow of the Freeway (Cervantes), 519
Berlant, Lauren, 674, 675–76, 678, 685, 689, 695
Berman, Marshall, 524
Bernal, Claudia, 606
Berni, Antonio, 268
bibliographies, 34, 36, 107, 234, 446
biculturalism, 379, 534
Biemann, Ursula, 606, 608
bilingualism, 354, 379, 477, 485, 491–92
Billington, Ray A., 43
biography, 44, 48, 50–51, 53, 659–60
Black Berets of Albuquerque, 424
"Black Dove" (Amos), 608
blacks, 14, 18, 338–39, 140, 342, 347, 645; demographics of, 97–100, 133, 481, 490; films portraying, 177; history of, 109–110, 260, 493; in inner city, 517, 521; literary criticism and, 432, 450

Bless Me, Ultima (Anaya), 230, 276–80, 285–94
body/bodies: 285; colonization of, 216; as cultural/racial signifier, 394–95, 399, 597, 648, 649–54; gendered, 589; and identity, 394; queer, 560, 685, 692; relational, 661, 664, 665; sexed/sexualized, 589, 592, 653, 667, 674; and space, 680, 681, 697; as surrogate, 655–60; symbolic, 285, 305–6
bodyscapes, 679–70, 680
Bolle, K. W., 303–4
Bolton, Herbert E., 38–39, 234
border/borders: in film, 182; language and, 515–560; in literature, 598; meaning of, 135, 475; multilingualism and, 321, 381, 409, 454, 465–66, 476–98; open, 566; as political boundary, 474–76
border conflict/control, 47, 56, 197, 465–70, 585
border culture, 116, 117, 583
Border Industrialization Program (BIP), 587
borderlands, 199, 229–230, 473; comics as, 679, 681; history of, 587–88; identity in, 213, 231–232, 321, 394, 409, 583; literature, 39–40, 214, 602, 608, 679; meaning of, 211–12, 214, 475; and transnationalism, 562–63, 641, 681
Borderlands: La Frontera = The New Mestiza (Anzaldúa), 603, 681
border literature, 584, 586, 598–602, 606–7
border states, 468, 483, 500; demographics of, 501–6, 618
border studies, 226–28, 584–86, 593
Bordertown (Nava), 583
Born in East L.A., 13, 175, 176, 181–82
Bosch García, Carlos, 44, 45
bourgeois culture, 473, 492, 586
Bowyer, Edith M., 46
braceros, 84–85, 136–37
Brady, Mary Pat, 676, 678
Brincando el charco (Negrón-Mutaner), 681
Brinkley, Alan, 146
Brockett, Oscar G., 234
Brown, Joseph Epes, 282
Brown Berets, 695
Broyles-González, Yolanda, 388
Bruce-Novoa, Juan, 440, 650, 653, 655, 656, 689
Brunswick Record Corporation, 619
Bruss, Elizabeth, 447, 455
Bustamante, Nao, 395

Calderón, Hector, 437–39, 656–57
calidad, 338–39
California: barrios in, 13; demographics
    of, 83, 92, 96, 197, 467, 487, 504–7;
    employment in, 330–31; exclusion/
    segregation in, 513–15; history/histories
    of, 38–39, 118; immigrant labor in, 566,
    573; Mexican/Spanish communities in,
    23–25, 119, 146, 518–19; migration to,
    379, 565, 603; multilingalism in, 466,
    476–77, 501;
California Division of Highways, 515, 518
Californios, 47, 119, 318, 338, 343, 494
"Call of Prophethood, The" (Watt), 283
Camarena, Jorge González, 266
Camarillo, Albert, 109, 110, 116, 118
Campa, Arthur L., 344
Canícula (Cantú), 548
Cánovas, Agustin Cue, 57
Cantú, Juan Ríos, 606
Cantú, Norma, 548
Cantú, Roberto, 667
capitalism, 125, 678; in Mexico, 119,
    122, 599; racism and, 145–47, 535;
    transnational, 409, 469, 473; value of,
    565
Cardenás, Gilberto, 12
Cardona, Julián, 583, 586, 593–98
carnalismo, 415
Carranza, Venustiano, 266
Carrasco, David, 224–26, 230–31
Carreta, La (Marqués), 389
Carter, Thomas P., 54
cartography, linguistic, 467–71
cartoons, 633–344, 639, 641. *See also* comics
Caso, Alfonso, 615
Castañeda, Antonia, 142
Castañeda, Carlos E., 42, 43–44, 47
castellanización, 478
castellanos, 337
caste structure, 21–22, 32, 61, 62, 262, 338,
    634
castilia, 373
Castillo, Debra, 585, 586
castizos, 318
Catholicism, 224, 233, 261, 278, 280, 342;
    altars and, 298, 303–4; imagery/signifiers
    of, 594, 652; influence of, 328–29, 376,
    420
census data, 54, 55; on education, 100, 489,
    498, 502; on employment, 331, 503; on
    income, 99; on home language, 501–2;
    on labor, 85, 89, 503; on nativity, 95;

on occupations, 98, 331; on population,
    78, 472–73, 502, 504–7, 616, 641;
    Mexican, 618, 630, 632; on migration/
    immigration, 85, 86, 87, 95–97, 465; on
    population, 97, 487; on socioeconomic
    status, 98–100, 467, 482–83, 504; on
    metropolitan areas, 94
Certeau, Michel de, 2
Cervantes, Lorna Dee, 519
Chabram-Dernersesian, Angie, 147, 408, 539
Chamberlain, Samuel E., 44
Chavarria, Jesús, 36–37
Chávez, Angélico, 39
Chávez, César, 51, 258, 416
Chávez, Eusebio, 339
Chávez, Jennie, 423
Chávez, John, 149
Chávez-Cano, Esther, 591
Chávez-Silvermann, 589
Chee, Pablo, 616–17
Chicago, 77, 81, 84–88, 94–98
Chicana movement, 352, 357–60, 365
Chicana politics: and cultural nationalism,
    353–56; development of, 419–20; and
    familism, 354, 417, 419; and feminism,
    358–59, 360–64, 538–44; identity
    and, 321–23, 374, 387, 538, 541;
    MALCS, 356–57; scholarship and,
    544–48; as separatist, 352–53. *See also* El
    Moviemiento; performative politics
Chicana/o studies: and anthropology, 527,
    528, 546; and Asian studies, 616,
    642–43; and community-based research,
    545–46; development of, 1–3, 5, 14–15,
    34, 539; and feminism, 528; limitations
    of, 230; and literature, 446; and
    mestizaje, 559, 615; and muralism, 270;
    and religion, 225, 275, 277, 278; scope
    of, 10–15, 405–6, 548; and sociology,
    314; and traditional curricula, 408, 410.
    See also El Grito
Chicanismo, 197, 210–11, 421, 531, 640
Chicano (term), 19, 322, 346, 347
Chicano Authors (Bruce-Novoa), 434, 438
Chicano historical research/writing, 3–4,
    10–15, 32– 38, 171; on altars, 303;
    anthropological, 533–44; approaches to,
    21, 23–24, 28–29, 31–32, 63–64; border
    studies, 135–138; Chicanas in, 372; on
    colonial era, 40–41; on families, 418; on
    film, 177; on freeways, 524; future of,
    141–48; and gender, 112–113; historical
    narrative, 658–59; on independence era,

42–48; interpretative problems, 111; on literature, 440, 454; need for, 78–80, 107, 108–110, 433, 442; on postwar era, 49–50; religion and, 278–80; and social sciences, 52–56; on theater, 232–33; uses of, 138–140; on women, 419–21. *See also* Chicano press

Chicano historiography, 4, 12, 32–33, 38, 494; assessment of, 107–8

Chicano history: of borderlands, 466–67, 587–88; colonial era, 317; contemporary era, 126–130; immigration, 81; independence era, 42–48, 259, 261–65, 376–78; periodization of, 59–63, 124–126; Spanish colonial era, 24, 317–18, 375–376; Spanish myth, 40–41; twentieth century, 25, 130–135, 270, 379; of urban areas, 512–13

Chicano Moratorium against the Vietnam War, 1

Chicano movement, 21; character of, 139–40, 326, 415; Chicanas and, 352–60, 364, 365, 420–21, 676; and Chicano studies, 405, 407, 410; and critical discourse, 439, 447, 451–53; and cultural maintenance, 117; and cultural nationalism, 114, 176, 205, 211, 534; and familism, 413, 416–19, 677; fracturing of, 149; impact of, 57; and machismo, 423–24; as revolutionary force, 407; and sexuality, 673, 677, 679

Chicano Poetry (Bruce-Novoa), 438

Chicano politics: Aztlán and, 198–216; and cultural nationalism, 176; development of, 138–40, 148–49; *El Grito* and, 529–533; and familism, 422; and feminism, 316, 319–20; history of, 59–63; identity and, 387; and machismo, 424; masculinization of, 323; organizations and, 138; scholarship and, 534–35. *See also* Chicano movement; El Moviemiento; performative politics

"Chief Tahachwee," 516

Chinese Exclusion Act of 1882, 617–18

Chinese immigration/immigrants, 469, 470, 476, 493, 616–39

chingada/chingadas, 598, 602, 606

"Chino, El," 619–21, 628

"Chinos, Los," 624–27

cholo/cholos, 132–33, 134, 187, 209, 683, 688

Choosing Democracy (Campbell), 490

Christians/Christianity, 225, 230, 260, 328, 594, 662; social status of, 337–39;

theology, 276–78. *See also* altars

cinema, 176, 177; cinema barrio, 170, 178, 189; Latin American, 181. *See also* film/films

citizenship, 41, 549, 676; cultural, 674, 689, 695; legislation and, 470; political, 570; racialized, 605, 608; social, 562–67, 676; spatial dynamics of, 676; status and, 338

City of God (Cuadros), 522

Ciudad Juárez, 582, 599, 601, 604, 606

civil rights groups/movements, 21, 114, 345, 484, 529

class consciousness, 112

Classic Stage Company, 390

class structure: anthropology and, 534–35; of blacks, 109; of colonists, 340–41, 375; comparisons by, 20; and critical discourse, 447–48, 454; and culture formation, 130; differentiation within, 111–13, 139–40, 336–37; exploitation/ oppression and, 362–63, 394, 456; feminism and, 351–52, 541; historical analysis and, 142; impact of, 117–18; of laborers, 121; language and, 483, 486–91; lower class, 343–47, 634; in Mexico, 259, 262, 263, 328, 330; middle class, 337, 355; of migrants, 91; and music, 128–29; in nineteenth century, 60, 61; in plays, 392; race and, 123–24, 654; socioeconomic, 145, 185; stratification by, 3, 13, 22, 64, 362; working class, 131–33, 592

Coatlicue, 602

coding, sexual/ethnic, 172, 179, 673, 675–76, 690, 692

code switching, 452, 487, 497

collective experience, 112–13, 227

Collier Burns Act of 1947, 513

Colón, Miriam, 389

colonial art/literature, 38–43, 262

colonial framework/model, 32, 81, 115–18, 534

colonialism, 53, 123, 125; anthropology and, 532, 535; and Chicano oppression, 353; intent of, 203; internal, 115, 139, 329–30, 407, 411, 414; performance and, 391, 394; resistance to, 418. *See also* decolonization

colonias, 61, 63, 123, 591, 600

colonization, 601; effects of, 62, 378, 420; of females/queers, 216; histories of, 57–58, 116; identity and, 316, 318, 326–27, 358; and linguistic development,

colonization (*continued*)
478–82; and machismo, 422–23; social
values, 338–41; of Southwest, 337–38,
466–67
comedy, 176, 179, 237–38, 619–32, 636–37
comics: as borderland, 679–81; commentary
in, 683–85; framing in, 679–81, 682,
685, 688, 692, 695; iconic language,
690; sexuality in, 673–75
community: Aztlán and, 210; concept of, 301–3,
410; creation/production of, 29, 31, 562,
563, 569–70, 571, 607, 608; emphasis
on, 545–46; identity and, 478, 480;
involvement of, 406; transnational, 566
comunidad, 184, 678
conciencia de la mestiza, 320, 321
conciencia de sí, 315, 317, 321, 323, 337
Conciencia y lenguaje en la novela (Calderón),
438
Conferencia de Mujeres por la Raza, 355
conjunto, 128–30, 603–5
Connor, Seymour V., 45
conquest, 124–26, 142, 481; altars and, 304;
Christianity/Catholicism and, 277–78,
328–29, 337; chronicles of, 328; cultural
production and, 338; images of, 260–61,
262–63; narratives of, 183; by U.S., 420
conquistadors, 259, 277, 375
consciousness, 300, 317, 337; community, 30;
differential, 4; Chicana/o, 112, 129, 208,
211, 270, 381, 421–25, 541; Christian/
Catholic, 280; gender, 585; mestiza,
381, 382, 584, 602, 606; oppositional,
223–24, 227, 229; political, 140–41,
320–21, 356, 380; women's, 419. *See also*
self-consciousness
consumerism, 91, 130, 132, 134, 483, 497,
521, 592
"Contrabando y traición" (Los Tigres del
Norte), 603
Coordinating Council for Latin American
Youth of Los Angeles, 127–28
Córdova, Alfred C., 48, 51
Corliss, Richard, 177
corridos, 226, 240, 251, 255, 603–6, 619,
624–28, 634, 638
Cortés, Carlos, 50, 171, 173
Cotera, Martha, 354
cotton economy, 119
Crichton, Kyle, 51
crime, 20, 133, 469, 535. *See also* femicide
criollos, 382, 376, 478, 481
critical discourse, 408

critical theory/thought, 216, 433, 437, 455
crónicas diabólicas de Jorge Ulica, Las
(Rodríguez), 442
Crusade for Justice, 416
Cruz, Migdalia, 391, 392
Crystal Frontier: A Novel in Nine Stories
(Fuentes), 598–602
Cuadros, Gil, 522–23
Cuellar, Jose, 275, 546
cultural aesthetic, 224, 227, 229, 230
cultural discourse, 206, 209, 215, 408
cultural identity: Aztlán and, 198; Chicano
studies and, 147, 223, 535; of Chinese
immigrants, 642; conquest and, 338;
construction of, 215; as dynamic process,
336; Mexican, 423; performance and,
388; plays and, 391; preservation of, 571;
resistance and, 418; Spanish, 343
culturalists, 327, 433, 450, 452, 484, 539
cultural nationalism: Aztlán and, 200, 205,
207; Chicanas and, 325, 353–56, 435;
Chicano movement and, 359, 450,
528, 534; critique of, 535, 546; decline
of, 176; feminism and, 319, 360, 364;
performance and, 323; pre-Columbian
focus of, 270; theater and, 392
culture/cultures: art and, 300; barrio, 182,
187–88, 687; and borderlands, 212, 215,
583–84; consumer, 132, 148; definition
of, 583; feminism and, 351, 355, 358,
363–64, 539; and ideology, 127–30;
immigrant, 337; Indian/indigenous,
259–61, 328, 337–38, 602; language
and, 492–98; literary, 429–32, 450–51,
453–54; maquila, 596; Mexican, 116–17,
223, 326, 354, 598, 615–621, 629, 633;
minority, 485; vs. nature, 309; origin
of Chicano, 19–20, 282; political, 570;
production of, 518, 525; queer, 676, 689;
regional, 24–25, 31; sexual, 675–76, 679;
Spanish, 338; and stereotypes, 53, 58;
syncretic, 29, 37, 39. *See also* American
culture; popular culture
Culture Clash,
curanderas/curanderismo, 322, 392, 393, 394

dada, 267
Darley, Alexander M., 47
Daston, Lorraine, 662
Davalos, Karen Mary, 410–11
Davis, William Heath, 46
Davis, William Wetts Hart, 46
de Alva, Jorge Klor, 205, 210

decolonial imaginary, 4
decolonization, 315, 410–11, 415, 417
deconstruction, 226, 430, 536, 539–41,
    547–48
deindustrialization, 131
de la Cruz, Sor Juana Inez, 534
de la Garza, Rodolfo, 137–38, 143
de la Guerra, Augustias, 47
de la Peña, Terri, 676
de Lara, José Bernardo Gutiérrez, 50
Del Castillo, Adelaida, 353, 560
del Castillo, Richard Griswold, 110, 116,
    118–19, 138, 142
De León, Arnoldo, 110, 116, 122
Delgado, Fray Carlos, 340
delinquency, 128, 133
Deloria, Ella, 543
de Man, Paul, 437, 439
demographics: Chicano/Hispanic, 78–101,
    174–76, 482–83, 496; in education, 546;
    in Midwest, 92–100; in U.S., 465–68,
    475–76
Denver Chicano Youth Liberation
    Conference, 326
depression migration, 81
derogatory terms, 342–46
Derrida, Jacques, 438–39, 549
Desert Blood (Gaspar de Alba), 601, 606–8
de Thomas, Francisco, 46
Detroit, 77, 87, 88, 94, 97–98
de Zubarán, Francisco, 594
día de los muertos, 399
Día de los Vivos (Diaz), 323, 398, 399
"Dialectic of Difference, A: Toward a Theory
    of the Chicano Novel" (Saldívar), 437
Dialectic of Enlightenment, 524
diaspora, 201–2, 212, 480
Diaz, Paul Timothy, 398, 398–99
Díaz, Porfirio, 259, 263, 355, 618
dichos, 226, 250–55
differential consciousness, 4
differentialist racism, 484
diglossia, 477
Discourse in the Novel (Bakhtin), 454
discrimination, 129, 133, 347; class, 20, 410;
    color, 18; as common experience, 139,
    413; economic, 120, 123; labor market,
    89, 180; and language, 484, 489, 503;
    against Latinos/Chicanos, 48, 56, 61–62,
    117, 344; in Mexican literature, 57; in
    the South, 24
Disney, Walt, 410, 516, 517
Disneyland, 410, 516, 518

displaced migration, 81
"destierro de los Chinos, El," 621–24
diversity: of Chicano experience, 12, 56, 113,
    116, 118–21, 318; of Chicano/Latino
    community, 12–13, 30, 53, 143, 512;
    cultural, 10, 547, 549; of families, 491,
    678; linguistic, 466, 476, 477, 480–83,
    493
Dobie, J. Frank, 226, 547
Documentary History of the Mexican American
    (Moquin and Van Doren), 36
Domínguez, Fray Atanasio, 340
Downs, Lila, 606, 609
Downtown (Alfaro), 395, 396
downtown areas, freeways and, 513–15
drama, 233–35, 236. *See also* performance;
    teatro/teatros; theater
dramaturgy, 392
dreams: religious, 276, 281–89, 666

Eagleton, Terry, 408–9, 428, 431, 435, 447,
    451
East Los Angeles, 1, 20, 682; in films, 178,
    182, 184, 187; freeways and, 514–23
Eastside Citizens' Committee Against the
    Freeway, 518
economic factors, 20–21, 29, 465; and
    Chinese migrants, 628, 634, 636–38;
    and exploitation/oppression, 216, 329,
    420, 422–24, 567, 588; and femicide,
    598–600, 607; film and, 174, 175;
    freeways and, 514–15; globalization
    and, 473; historical, 59–62, 206, 341,
    377, 467; and inequity, 118–23, 146,
    185, 330, 535; in Ireland, 480, 483; and
    language, 486, 492, 499; and migration,
    468, 472, 587; and social rights, 565–66
economic identity/status, 352, 356, 379, 420,
    469, 484, 530
economic self-determination, 200, 211
economic studies, 37, 42, 46–49, 52, 54, 142,
    144–45
ecstasy, 277, 280, 285, 293
Edgerton, Robert B., 55
Edmonson, Munro S., 52, 533, 536
education: access to, 353, 361, 447, 470, 565,
    682; attainment in, 489–90, 498, 502;
    bilingual, 478, 485, 489; capitalism and,
    535; of Chicanos/Mexican Americans,
    20, 79, 99–100, 180, 354, 489; and
    immigration, 88; for migrants, 571–72;
    and mobility, 131; muralism and, 228,
    265, 272; reforms in, 447; stratification

education (*continued*)
of, 406; studies of, 36, 53–54; theater
and, 233. *See also* higher education
Edwards, Frank, 378
Ehrenberg, Felipe, 266
El Centro Campesino Cultural, 238
El Circulo Dramatico, 389
*El Grito: A Journal of Contemporary Mexican-
American Thought*, 529–592
Eliade, Mircea, 275, 281–82, 284
Elizondo, Sergio, 212–14, 440
Elliot, Edward F., 514
El Movimiento: Aztlán and, 209; Chicanas
and, 325–32, 419, 421, 425, 678; as
decolonization movement, 415; failures
of, 139–40; *familia* and, 416, 418; and
machimso, 422
El Paso, 116, 120–21, 272, 504–5
El Siglio, 56
El Teatro, 261–262
El Teatro Campesino, 181, 227, 232, 236–39,
270, 388
El Teatro Nacional de Aztlán (TENAZ), 240–41
El TRI, 606
emigration, 30, 32, 56–57, 62, 472
employment, 12, 421, 503; access to, 353, 361,
561, 682; blue/white-collar, 330–31;
immigrant, 469; in maquilas, 588–90;
migration and, 82–84, 89–91, 475, 587;
regional, 24
empowerment, 200, 206, 360–64, 382, 660
Encuentro Femeril, 353, 355
English language, 18, 325; acculturation
and, 336, 488–89; in critical discourse,
452; dominance of, 476, 483, 485, 487;
ethnic labels and, 342, 344; and identity
formation, 379, 381, 482; Irish and, 479;
Spanish and English, 325, 452, 487, 680,
690; usage, 501–4
English-only movements, 180, 181, 392,
484–86, 498
Erde, Sarah, 390
Esbjornson, David, 390
Escalante, Jaime, 184–85, 187
españoles, 337–38, 340-41, 343
españoles mexicanos, 341
ethnic consciousness, 36, 129, 140
ethnic groups: conflict among, 36; contact
among, 59, 60; in Midwest, 79–81;
research on, 110, 112
ethnicism, 409, 474, 483, 493, 499
ethnicity: and bodies, 649, 651–52, 667; and
boundaries, 660; and class/social status,

375, 570; and crime, 20; definition of,
344; depictions of, 186; discourse of,
647, 653, 661; exclusion/oppression and,
356, 484; feminism and, 319, 321, 330,
359; historiography and, 58; inequality
and, 353, 361–62, 365; language and,
486, 489–97; marketing and, 483
ethnic studies, 9–10, 15; 79–80
ethnic terms, 342–46
ethnoaesthetics, 300
ethnography/ethnographers, 224, 298, 394,
533, 536, 567; alternate, 545, 546–47,
548; authority of, 411, 528, 530, 544;
feminist, 542; influences on, 537–38
ethnomania, 383
European culture/history, 263, 267, 383, 445,
465
European immigrants/migration, 24, 81–82,
317–18, 348
Euskera, 500
"Evolution of Chicano Literature, The"
(Paredes), 440
exploitation, 35, 58, 677; of Chicanas, 328,
332; class, 362; economic, 175, 636; of
gendered bodies, 589; labor, 48, 57, 61,
62, 136, 216, 470–71; of Mexicans, 634;
of Native Americans, 517

Fabian, Johannes, 300
Fabrega, Horacio, 55
familia de la raza, la, 364, 414, 622
familism, 354, 412–18, 420–22, 675
family/families: and altars, 229, 298–99,
304–10; American culture and, 130;
changes in, 407; female head of, 590,
599, 607; feminism and, 355, 358–59,
364, 541; gender roles in, 330, 528,
569; heteronormativity and, 685,
695–96; identity and, 382, 665–67;
importance of, 650, 677–78; language
and, 491; machismo and, 424, 540;
metaphorical meaning of, 303; middle
class, 483; migration/immigration and,
88, 89, 91, 567–68; nineteenth-century,
379; patriarchy in, 664; in plays, 389;
research on, 39, 54, 141–42; sexuality
and, 654, 655, 662, 677; and worker
solidarity, 112; world wars and, 62. *See
also* familism
Fanon, Frantz, 111, 202–4
farms/farm labor, 25, 61, 77–78, 89–92, 98,
107, 118–22; exploitation of, 136, 570;
families, 330, 389; murals about, 266,

270. *See also* Teatro Campesino; United Farm Workers
fatalism, 253, 255, 536
Faulk, Odie B., 37, 39, 45
Faulkner, William, 657
Federation for American Immigrant Reform (FAIR), 485
Félix, Charles, 271
femicide, 559, 581; cultural response, 582–83; fictional narratives of, 583, 609
feminists/feminism: in anthropology, 538–44; and art forms, 299; collective experience and, 113; family and, 695; and femicide, 587, 607, 608; and Chicano politics, 316, 319–320; discourse of, 351–66, 528; lesbian, 373, 380, 382, 450, 607, 660; materially based, 534–35; multiracial, 412; political consciousness of, 320, 389; scholarship, 432, 434, 439; and social revolution, 419; and spatial rhetoric, 676–77, 679; third-world, 229; and U.S. feminists, 319
feministas, 354
femmage, 309–10
Fergusson, Erna, 37, 344
fiction, 55, 57, 432, 433, 498, 606–8, 647, 655, 658, 666
Field, Matt, 378
fieldwork, 297, 535–38
Fiesta de los Teatros, 239–40
Figural Language in the Novel (Saldívar), 437
film/films, 13; authenticity of, 180, 182, 183–84, 186–87; femicide and, 583, 587, 606; language and, 495; as localizing discourse, 178–79; market for, 174–76; reviews of, 173–74; as social criticism, 185; and social problems, 177, 187; studies on, 177–78; as text, 171–72
film studies, 13
Fogel, Walter, 54
folk art, 297–302, 309
folklore: definition/meaning of, 226, 248–51, 300, 518; derogatory terms in, 342; about freeways, 410, 513, 522; proverbs and, 224, 226; scholarship on, 55, 298, 300;
folktales, 248–252
Foucault, Michel, 3, 549, 685, 689
Francis, E. K., 51
Freeway Fighters, 518
freeways, 409–10; and culture of progress, 516–22; and identity formation, 522–23; as social dividers, 486, 512–15, 524

Fregoso, Rosa Linda, 147, 434, 677
Freud, Sigmund, 310
"From the Critical Premise to the Product: Critical Modes and Their Application to a Chicano Literary Text" (Sommers), 433
Frontera Collection, 640
Fuentes, Carlos, 275, 559, 583, 586, 598–606
Function of Criticism, The (Eagleton), 494
Fusco, Coco, 322, 394–95

gabacho, 216, 217
Galarza, Ernesto, 23, 49, 130, 137
Gamboa, Erasmo, 136, 144
Gamio, Manuel, 18, 48, 57, 83, 143, 633
García, Alma, 355–56
Garcia, Elena, 421
García, Ignacio, 140
García, Juan, 144
García, Mario T., 1, 110, 116–17, 120–21, 127–29, 135–36
García Andrade, Lilia Alejandra, 582
García Cantú, Gastón, 45
García-Sayán, Diego, 581
Garza Birdwell, Yolanda, 422
Gaspar de Alba, Alicia, 321, 380–82, 584, 589, 601, 606–8, 690
Gates, Henry Luis, Jr., 445
Geertz, Clifford, 299, 300
gender: in Chicano history, 13, 107, 113, 117, 123, 142, 147; and Chicano politics, 389; concepts of, 412–13, 450; and discrimination, 570, 676; and exploitation, 589; and family, 569; and feminism, 540–44; gender-based oppression, 353–56, 519; identities/roles, 130, 214, 216, 316–17, 319–23, 407, 471, 583–84, 606, 685; and identity formation, 585; ignored, 537, 538; labor and, 588–89, 600; as literary/scholarly subject, 394, 539, 667, 673, 679; mestizaje and 615; as segregating factor, 486, 687; stereotypes, 325, 628, 692; stratification of, 361–63
generational differences: acculturation and, 130, 134; and Hispanic/Latino population, 345, 348, 487; impact of, 488; in scholarship, 11, 13, 54, 110, 114, 441. *See also* Mexican American generation
genízaros, 318, 340, 376
gente de razón, 318, 340

geography, 119, 144, 201, 212, 321;
    borderlands, 583, 585, 591
geopolitical boundaries/entities, 226, 228, 394,
    409, 473, 584–85, 679
Gilbert, Fabiola Cabeza de Vaca, 46–47
Gipson, Fred, 46
Glassie, Henry, 302
globalization, 468, 474, 586, 599–600, 603
"Golden Age of Criticism, The" (Mitchell),
    429
Goldfinch, Charles W., 51
Goldman, Shifra, 225, 227–28, 230
Goldsmith, Arnold L., 428
Gomez, Marga, 397
Gómez Peña, Guillermo, 213, 322, 394, 584
Gómez-Quiñones, Juan, 5, 11–12, 140, 209,
    535, 539, 546
Gonzáles, Gilbert, 128
Gonzáles, Rodolfo "Corky," 2, 204, 270, 417
Gonzales, Sylvia, 208, 440
Gonzales-Berry, Erlinda, 440, 656, 666
González, Deena J., 107, 108, 320–21
González, Henry B. 51
González, Nancie, 344
González Echevarría, Roberto, 438
Gordon, Edmund, 545
gorras blancas, 115, 118
"Gracias, América sin fronteras" (Los Tigres
    del Norte), 603
graffiti, 521, 673, 682, 688
Grant, Ulysses S., 44
Great Depression, 84, 126, 129, 379
Great Lakes region, 76–77, 272
Great River: The Rio Grande in North America
    (Horgan), 37
Great Wall of Los Angeles, The (Baca), 518
Grebler, Leo, 55, 345
Greer, Scott A., 52
Gregg, Josiah, 377, 378
Gregg, Robert D., 47
gringo/gringos, 112, 123, 203, 213, 342, 416,
    600
Guardiola, Gloria, 422
guided migration, 91
Guillén, Nicolás, 499
Gulf Dreams (Pérez), 380
Gutiérrez, David, 108
Gutiérrez, Felix F., 496
Gutiérrez, José Angel, 52, 416
Gutiérrez, Ramón A., 144–46, 317–18, 321
Gutiérrez de Lara, José Bernardo, 50
Gutman, Herbert G., 112
Guzmán, Ralph, 49

Hall, Stuart, 171
Hatfield, Charles, 682
hegemony: artistic, 269; cultural/social, 354,
    542, 546, 584; of freeways, 518–22;
    Mexican, 265; in social sciences, 532;
    Spanish, 41
Hernández, Deluvina, 5, 53
Hernandez, Jaime, 560, 673, 682
Hernández, Jorge, 603, 604
Hernández, Luis, 604
Heroes and Saints (Moraga), 389, 391
Herrera-Sobek, María, 605
heterogeneity: Aztlán and, 201; of border
    states, 475–76; class, 22; cultural, 11,
    21, 475; ethnic, 447, 476; of population/
    community, 16, 25, 35, 58, 409, 481; in
    U.S., 472
heteroglossia, 477
heteronormativity, 389, 675–76, 679, 685,
    689–95
heterosexism, 528, 538, 673, 683, 685–86,
    688, 696
heterosexuality, 213, 323, 351, 392, 410, 542,
    544, 673, 676, 677
Hidalgo, Ernesto, 48, 57
hierophany, 282–84
higher education, 490, 10, 352, 356, 539, 405,
    15, 447
Higuera, Prudencia, 47
Hijas de Cuauhtémoc, 355
Hinojosa, Rolando, 658
Hispanic/Hispanics: class divisions, 346;
    diaspora, 202; generic term, 373, 482;
    identity, 213–14, 323; history, 317,
    336–37; political, 140–41; film, 170;
    market, 175; population, 175, 342, 345;
    portrayals of, 177; press, 170, 173–74,
    179–87, 434, 494. *See also* Hispanic
    Hollywood
Hispanic Hollywood, 170, 174–77
hispanista/ hispanism, 227, 259, 261
Hispanos, 24–25, 119
historical research/writing, 1–2, 110, 372–73.
    See also Chicano historical research/
    writing; Chicano history
historiography, 2, 4, 12, 32–33, 38. *See also*
    Chicano historiography
Hobsbawm, Eric, 121, 474, 478–79, 483
Hoffman, Abraham, 49
Hollon, Eugene W., 37
Hollywood: liberalism in, 183–86; stereotyped
    roles, 176–78, 179, 183, 186, 323, 391
Holmes, Jack, 59
home: as folk art, 309; importance of, 416, 421

homeland: borderlands as, 468; mythic, 14, 197–99, 200–1, 202, 211, 213, 215, 382; queer, 679; search for, 231, 371, 380–81, 547

homophobia, 319, 363, 664

homosexuality, 650, 653–54, 656, 661, 667, 676, 678–79, 685

Horgan, Paul, 37

horizon of expectations, 173, 188–89

Horkheimer, Max, 524

House of Bernarda Alba, The (Lorca), 391

housing, 90–91, 130, 132, 485, 515, 565, 677

huelgas. See strikes

Huerta, Jorge A., 225, 226–27, 388, 440

Hunger of Memory (Rodriguez), 147

Hurston, Zora Neale, 543

Hutchinson, Cecil Alan, 39

Iberian culture, 337, 338, 500

identity: Aztlán and, 200–4, 208; of the body, 681, 685; in borderlands, 213; Chicana, 320, 375, 674; civic, 562–63, 567; collective, 352; of colonists, 318, 337, 348; construction/formation of, 3, 11, 13, 134, 147–48, 320, 374, 378–79, 478; corporate, 340; decolonization of, 315; ethnic, 117, 343, 375, 381, 541, 660–61; film and, 180, 184; folklore and, 248, 302; gender, 214, 584; and historical consciousness, 147; hybrid, 214–15; immigration and, 317; indigenous, 201, 228, 615; language and, 492–93; Latino/a, 321–22; mestizo, 640; Mexican, 345; muralism and, 269; national, 2, 101, 376, 410, 465, 616, 633; performance and, 386–87, 392, 394–99; in plays, 389–92; political, 322–23, 539, 541, 658, 659; public space and, 521; scholarship and, 405–6; search/struggle for, 321, 370–73, 376; of self, 19, 200, 317; stereotyping and, 316; transformation of, 585–86, 653. *See also* cultural identity; racial identity; sexual identity

ideology: American, 138, 143, 675–76; Chicano, 542; and culture, 126–130; ethnic, 344; feminist, 319, 351–52, 352; *indigenismo*, 615; literary, 439, 455; maternal, 304; muralism and, 266; nationalist, 354, 364, 619; patriarchal, 605, 664; racist, 123, 148

indigenism/*indigenismo*, 206, 210, 227, 267–68, 615; muralism and, 259–261, 270, 271

Illinois, 76–78, 85, 87–88, 93, 94–99, 506, 568

immigrants: from Asia, 476, 477, 488, 493, 641; from China, 616–39; derogatory terms for, 345–47; educational status of, 99; hostility towards, 465; languages of, 409, 466, 467; legal status of, 91; nativity of, 92–93, 95; number/ population of, 86–88, 90, 92, 94–96, 343, 465–68, 472–73, 502; political, 472; socioeconomic status of, 97–99; unauthorized/undocumented, 378, 465, 470–71, 561–62; wages/working conditions for, 88, 89, 90, 98; women, 471, 569–70

immigration, 23, 77; backlash against, 469–70, 584–85; cultural change and, 130; and human rights, 570–71; impact on Chicano communities, 135–38, 143, 470, 488; impact on Hispanic communities, 124–26, 342–47, 376; during Mexican Revolution, 206; into Mexican Southwest, 118–19; to Mexico, 616–18; to Midwest, 81–100; reasons for, 85, 89, 120–21, 468–69; research on, 48–49, 78–80, 135–38; undocumented, 86–87, 91; and world war, 81, 83–85, 130, 206. *See also* census data; migration

Immigration and Nationality Act of 1965, 85

Immigration and Naturalization Service (INS), 86, 584

Immigration Reform and Control Act of 1986 (Simpson-Rodino), 181

Indian heritage, 18, 30, 173, 214–15, 277–78, 328, 678. *See also* indigenous heritage

Indianness, 652–53, 666

Indians, 205, 318, 472, 477; assimilation of, 60; classification of, 340–41, 376; murals portraying, 259–61, 262, 268; research on, 36, 38, 47; as settlers, 40, 57; Spanish and, 337–40, 374–75; stereotypes of, 516–17; treatment of, 329. *See also* indigenous peoples

indigenism/*indigenismo*: 206, 210, 227, 615; American, 270; of Chicano muralists, 271; of Mexican muralists, 259–64, 270; of South American muralists, 267–68

indigenous heritage, 203, 208, 210–11, 216, 373, 376; and cultural nationalism, 354; languages and, 478, 481; literature and, 654, 664, 666; muralism and, 227–28, 259–61; *teatro*/theater and, 233, 388, 394. *See also* Indian heritage; mestizaje

indigenous identity, 317–18, 321, 323, 374, 482
indigenous peoples: altars of, 304; in Mexico, 615, 633–34; rights of, 199, 200. *See also* Indians
indios, 318, 338
industry, 84, 87, 90, 131, 206, 379. *See also* maquilas/maquiladoras
inequality/inequity: within academia, 545; for Chicanas, 360, 362, 410; and Chicano movement, 10, 116, 124, 146; structural, 134, 535
Inner City Cultural Center, 238, 240
Inquisition, the, 340
Inter-Agency Committee on Mexican American Affairs, 34
Inter-American Commission on Human Rights, 581
Inter-American Court of Human Rights (IACHR), 581
interethnic relations, 59–60, 80
intermarriage, 22, 123, 142, 199, 338, 616, 627–29, 634, 638–39
internal colonialism, 115, 117, 139, 407, 411, 414, 534
internationalism, 176
intolerance, ethnic, 465, 485
Ireland, 479–80, 483
Iron Cages (Takaki), 110
"Is Female to Male as Nature Is to Culture" (Ortner), 309
Islam, 283
Islas, Arturo, 647–49, 650, 655, 657–67

Jaco, Gartley E., 54
James, Henry, 657
Jauss, Hans Robert, 173
Johnson, Dale V., 54
Jones, Jacqueline, 141
Jones, Jessica E., 560
Jones, Michael Owen, 300
Jones, Oakah, 116
"Journey, The" (Martin), 519
"Juárez" (Amos), 608
Judah, Charles, 44

Kanellos, Nicolás, 388, 494
Karno, Marvin, 55
Kearney, Michael, 537, 538
Kendrick, Walter, 428
Kennedy, John F., 55
Kennedy family, 307
Kerber, Linda, 147

Kiev, Ari, 54
kinship, 207, 305, 307, 389, 409, 413, 418, 499, 591, 679
Klinger, Barbara, 172
Kubler, George, 301

La Bamba, 13, 130, 172, 174–75, 179–182
Labarthe, Elyette, 204–5
labor/laborers: agricultural, 24, 77, 89–92, 568; census data on, 85, 98, 331, 503; Chinese, 618; exploitation, 216, 468, 475; history of, 61–62, 120–21, 125; immigrant, 470–72, 566, 569, 573; racism in, 120; research on, 48–49, 52, 112–13, 120–21, 142; rights, 265; secondary labor market, 131; suburbanization of, 132; underground, 85; unions/organizing, 261, 499, 533; women and, 141–42, 583. *See also* maquilas/maquiladoras
labor migration, 82–83, 89–92, 475, 476, 591
labor segmentation theory, 139
Laclau, Ernesto, 216
Lamar, Howard Roberts, 47
Land of Many Frontiers: A History of the American Southwest (Faulk), 37
Langford, J. Oscar, 46
language/languages: artistic, 265, 266; and community, 478–79; and culture, 492–98; discrimination and, 484–85, 489, 503; English, 342; and folklore, 255; identity and, 147, 409, 454, 478, 484; in Ireland, 479–80; in Los Angeles, 476; loss of, 213; of majority/minority, 248, 476, 483, 492; protecting/maintaining, 388, 471, 486–92; research on, 434, 437, 438, 446; stratification of, 483; in U.S., 465–66, 472, 476–77, 501–2. *See also* Spanish language; linguistics
Lara, Oscar, 603
La Raza Unida, 140, 416
La Red, 278
lares, 304
Latin America: Asians in, 616, 641; common market, 566; culture of, 495; sexuality in, 597
Latin Americans, 318: artists, 257, 267, 269; critics, 434; identity and, 345, 347; immigrants, 466, 468, 471, 482, 487, 641; novelists, 391
latinidad, 674
Latino (term/label), 213, 322, 345, 371, 387, 482

Latino/Latinos: Asian-Latinos, 616, 641–42; culture of, 388, 391, 494; diversity among, 488, 491, 493; education of, 489–91, 502; as embodied subject, 394; employment of, 503; in films, 179, 185, 186; and identity, 317, 322–23, 395; incarceration of, 490; media, 495–98; and migration/immigration, 470–71, 480–81; language and, 465–66, 480, 482–86; performance/theatre, 323, 388–89, 392, 394, 396–97; political incorporation and, 144; population of, 211, 409, 467–68, 472–73, 477, 481, 487, 502, 504–6; poverty and, 504

Latino Eligibility Task Force, 490

Latino studies, 387

La Tules, 378–79

Law Number 31, 638–39

Leach, Edmund, 303

League of United Latin American Citizens, 345

Leal, Luis, 204

Lefebvre, Henri, 675

legislation: immigration, 84, 472, 569; labor, 91; Mexican, 581, 638–39

Lerner, Gerda, 141

lesbian/lesbians: depictions of, 685–93; and *familia,* 678; feminism and, 351, 373, 380, 660, 679; identity, 320, 381, 676–77; literature, 213–14, 321, 382–83, 542, 607; scholars, 374, 539

Leyba, Jesús, 416–17

liberal feminism, 319, 360–61

Limón, José, 171, 347, 531, 547

Line Around the Block, A (Gomez), 397

linguistics: and acculturation, 467, 488–89; borders, 321, 381; cartography/mapping, 467–71, 474; code-switching, 487–88; diversity, 479–80, 485; dominance, 376; and ethnicity, 344; and identity, 202, 214, 484; metathesis, 346. *See also* language

Lipsitz, George, 130, 143

literacy, 478

literary criticism, 428, 539–40; and alternative cultures, 432; assumptions of, 430–31; Chicana, 434–36; Chicano, 433–34; general, 449–43; global, 453–56; metacritical, 443–49; schools of, 437–441

"Literary Criticism: The State of the Art" (Kendrick), 428

literary studies, 408, 473

Literary Theory (Eagleton), 428

literature: 1600–1800, 38–41; 1800–1848, 42–45, 494; 1848–1900, 45–47; 1900–1945, 48–49; 1945–1970, 49–50; biography, 50–52; border, 586–87; Chicana, 542, 677; Chicano, 657–61; disability, 648–49; general works, 35–38; immigration, 336–37; lesbian, 542; Mexican, 56–57; methodology, 63–65; on Midwestern Chicanos, 78–81; nationalist, 207; periodization, 59–61; 124–26; scope of, 32–34; social science, 52–56, 420, 422; victimization in, 115; writer's perspective, 58–59

liturgical drama, 233–34

lobos, 318, 340

Locas: The Maggie and Hopey Stories (Hernandez), 673–74, 680, 682, 695

Longeaux y Vásquez, Enriqueta, 421–22

López, Ronald, 49

López Saenz, Lionela, 424

López y Rivas, Gilberto, 57

Lorca, Federico García, 391

Los Angeles: barrios, 521, 678; Chino-Chicano communities in, 641; culture, 143; freeway construction in, 513–15; histories of, 116–19, 127, 143; languages in, 476–77, 502; Latinos in, 504; murals in, 271, 518–19; newspapers, 494; portrayals of, 394, 395, 673; radio/television stations, 496–97; riots in, 49, 127, 488; theater in, 235; theaters in, 495; urbanization in, 512–13, 675. *See also* East Los Angeles; freeways

Los Jaguares, 606

Los Mascarones, 239

Los Teatros de Aztlán, 232, 241

Los Tigres del Norte, 583, 603–6, 608

Love and Rockets (Hernandez), 673

Loving in the War Years (Moraga), 382

Lugo, Alejandro, 586

Lugo, Felix Alfonso, 587

Lugo, José del Carmen, 47

Lummis, Charles Fletcher, 47

machismo, 255, 358, 407, 533, 599; Chicanas and, 326–27, 422–25; and family structure, 540

MacMinn, George, 234–35

Madsen, William, 52, 533, 537

majoritarian institutions, 387

majoritarian stereotypes/labels, 316, 318, 322

Making Face, Making Soul (Anzaldúa), 543, 544
MALCS. *See* Mujeres Activas en Letras y Cambio Social
Malinche, 262, 333, 372, 601–3, 678
Malintzin. *See* Malinche
Manifest Destiny, 60, 197, 201, 467
Manuel, Herschel, 53
maquilas/maquiladoras, 474, 582, 585, 587–93; and beauty pageants, 596–97; culture of, 596–97; literature and, 599–602, 607; music about, 603–6; photography of, 593–94
Marin, Richard "Cheech," 176, 181–82
Margins (de la Peña), 676
Marqués, René, 389
Márquez, Antonio, 649, 657–58
Márquez, Gabriel García, 391, 520
Martin, Andrés, 375
Martin, Patricia Preciado, 519
Martinez, Antonio José, 51
Martinez, Juan, 50
Martinez, Oscar, 116
Marxism, 139, 206
Marxist analysis/criticism, 114, 405, 411, 435, 440, 524
Marxist publications, 174, 185
masculinist binaries, 593, 598, 608
masculinity, 382, 539, 604; attitudes about, 382, 408, 584; and cultural production, 590; iconography of, 601; and privilege, 660; readings of, 606. *See also machismo*
masculinization, 323, 389
Massey, Doreen, 678, 691
Massey, Douglas, 143
matriarchy, 590, 606, 608
Maya/Mayan, 210, 233, 259, 304, 677
Mazatlán, 627–28
Mazón, Mauricio, 110, 116, 127–28, 138
McCloud, Scott, 680
McGlashan, Alan, 279
McKittrick, Myrtle M., 51
McWilliams, Carey, 36
MECHA, 416
media: and femicide, 581; and identity, 482; and immigration, 469–70, 488; mass media, 20, 132, 143, 176; media curriculum, 171, 173; Spanish-language, 13, 497
Meinig, D. W., 37, 59
Mejida, Manuel, 57
Memory Tricks (Gomez), 397
Menéndez, Ramón, 176, 186–87

Messervy, William, 377
mestizaje: Aztlán and, 199; in Chicano studies, 559, 615–16; feminism and, 320; identity and, 377, 382, 632; language and, 481; in literature, 652; in murals, 227, 261–62; in poetry, 210, 214; radical politics and, 322, 324; re-examination of, 640; in religion, 275
mestizo/mestizos, 30, 33, 339; and Aztlán, 209, 212; identity and, 317–18, 371, 374–76, 482; in Mexico, 271, 329, 476, 615; in murals, 259–61; nationalism and, 616, 633, 640; and Revolution, 259, 270; settlers, 38, 40, 59, 199, 344; subjugation of, 328–29; in U.S., 481
Mestizo Nation, 200
metacritical studies, 443–49
Mexican American (label/term), 343, 345, 347, 371
Mexican American generation, 127–29, 130–31, 139
Mexican American People, The (Grebler, Moore, and Guzmán), 55, 345
Mexican Americans: assimilation of, 202, 210, 530; vs. Chicanos, 140; construct of, 227; culture of, 11, 19–21, 532–34; as ethnic group, 16, 18–19, 20; and family, 299; and folklore, 248, 252; identity of, 11, 424, 438; middle class, 547; religions traditions of, 298–99, 304; representations of, 546–47; studies about, 36–37, 48–50, 53, 54–56; social status of, 21–22, 24–25, 535; third-generation, 488, 650; underachievement of, 532; and Vietnam War, 529. *See also* Chicanas; Chicanos
Mexican Americans (Stoddard), 414
Mexican Americans: An Awakening Minority (Servin), 36
Mexican American scholarship, 529–34, 536–37, 544
Mexicano (label/term), 318, 338, 341, 343, 344–45
Mexicanos, 51, 81, 116, 123–24, 376; and Chicanos, 136–38, 487; culture of, 114, 363–64; folklore of, 248–55; and identity, 381; immigration of, 198, 201; in Texas, 475
Mexican Revolution, 62, 239, 624, 627; muralists and, 205–6, 208, 258, 261, 262–63, 265; racial formation and, 633–39

Mexicans: derogatory terms for, 344–45; disdain for, 378; and gold rush, 343

Mexico: Africans in, 615–16; annexation, 353, 377, 420; Chicano ties to, 206–7; Chinese immigrants in, 616–18, 640; colonization by, 24; conditions in, 202; corruption in, 599; critical texts from, 434; cultural heritage of, 354; economic development in, 588, 591, 599–600; ethnic identity in, 375–76; film industry in, 495; influences, 32; loss of northern territories, 376–77; media in, 495; nationalism in, 210; as nation-state, 474; organizing in, 500; politics in, 124, 137, 467, 587–88; popular culture in, 619–39; relations with U.S., 60, 531, 598; religion in, 284; studies about 56–57, 60–61, 116, 206, 567; *teatro* in, 239–40; women in, 328–29, 420, 569. *See also* immigration; femicide; maquiladoras; migration; muralism

Meyers, Frederick, 54

Michigan, 76–77, 78, 85, 93, 94, 96, 97

Midwest: agricultural workers in, 136; blacks in, 110; Chicanos in, 76–100; immigration to, 379

Migrant Souls (Islas), 666

migrant workers, 568, 688, 690; conditions for, 180; and human rights, 571–72; studies on, 35, 49. *See also* immigrants; labor/ laborers

migration: Black, 110; and class status, 375; feminism and, 320, 358; international, 468–69, 500, 564; interregional, 80, 81, 95–96; Mexican, 81–82, 125, 329, 475–76; seasonal, 76, 81–82, 89–91; in Southwest, 61; studies on, 33, 53, 57; undocumented, 86–87; urban, 24, 101, 379. *See also* census data; immigration

Milagro Beanfield War, 179, 182–84

milagros, 306

Milk of Amnesia/Leche de Amnesia (Troyano and Troyano), 396–97, 397

Miller, J. Hillis, 437, 439

Miller, Michael, 345, 346

minority/minorities: academic treatment of, 79, 114; Anglos as, 415; Chicanos as, 57; culture of, 248, 485; language use, 476–498; Latinos as, 481, 483; and political struggle, 140; racial, 14; status/ position of, 20–21, 32, 209; workers, 485

Mirzoeff, Nicholas, 679

Mitchell, David T., 648

Mitchell, Richard, 51

Mitchell, W. J. T., 429

Mittlebach, Frank, 54

mobility, 83–84, 89, 97, 115, 120, 129, 131

Moctezuma, Teódula, 602

modernization, 407, 410, 413–14, 418, 478, 480; in Mexico, 593, 618

modernization theory, 142

Mohanty, Chandra, 605, 608

Molina de Pick, Gracia, 330

Monsiváis, Carlos, 492, 585

Montejano, David, 122, 144–45

Monterde, Francisco, 233

Montoya, José, 210

Montoya, Richard, 393

Moore, Joan, 53, 132

Moquin, Wayne, 36

Moraga, Cherríe, 198–99, 321, 380–82, 389–92, 543, 660–61, 673, 677–78, 695

Morin, Raul, 40

"Morir despacio" (Cardona), 593–94, 597

Morrison, Toni, 275

Movimiento Estudiantil Chicano de Aztlán (MECHA), 416

Muhammad, 283

mujer, la, 325, 352, 355

Mujer, La (mural), 271

Mujeres Activas en Letras y Cambio Social (MALCS), 356–57, 546

"Mujeres de Juárez, Las" (Los Tigres del Norte), 604–5, 608

mulatos, 318, 339, 679

multilingual diversity, 475, 476, 483

multiracial diversity, 392, 406, 475, 481, 486

Muñoz, Carlos, 52, 139–40

Muñoz, José, 396, 658

muralism/muralists: Chicano, 224, 269–72; Mexican, 225, 227–28, 257–58

murals: in California, 271–72; in Caribbean and South America, 267–268; freeways and, 410, 513; indigenism and, 259–260; and international issues, 264–66; in Los Angeles, 518; mestizaje and, 261–62; revolutionary history and, 262–63

murder, 582. *See also* femicide

Murillo, Bartolomé Esteban, 594, 595

music/musicians, 259, 616; depictions of, 271; Mexican, 496, 603; Spanish, 294–95; studies of, 128, 130, 143. See also *conjunto*; corridos; *norteño* music

mutualista organizations, 116

My Family (Nava), 677

NAFTA. *See* North American Free Trade Agreement
narcocorrido, 603
narrative: Chicano, 445; in comics, 695; in criticism, 439; cultural, 648; fictional, 583; in film, 171, 172, 179, 183, 186; historical, 658; in literature, 652, 655–56, 680–81; in murals, 262, 269; in plays, 391–92
National Association of Chicana and Chicano Studies, 546
national consciousness, 210, 336
national identity, 2, 101, 410, 616, 633
nationalism/nationalist: American Indian, 205; Aztlán and, 198–200, 201, 202, 204–5, 207–8, 211; Black, 205; Chicano, 2–4, 11, 112, 212, 362, 388; decline of, 111, 408, 436; economic, 634, 637–38; *El Grito* and, 531–32; and *familia,* 417; feminism and, 319, 363, 420; historical writing, 114, 117, 147; Mexican, 206, 210, 259, 267, 619, 624, 636; proto-nationalism, 478, 493; rhetoric, 140; state power and, 584; student movement, 373; studies of, 44–45; territory and, 677; theater and, 392; third world, 415. *See also* cultural nationalism
nation-states, 409, 473–75, 479, 562–63, 567, 584
Native Americans. *See* Indians
Nava, Gregory, 677
Navarro, Luis, 240
Negrón-Mutaner, Frances, 681
neo-indigenism, 270
New Criticism, 455
new labor history, 112–13
New Mexico: conquest of, 337–38; diversity in, 145; and drama, 234–35; and ethnic identity, 343–44; Hispanics in, 24–25; Indians in, 340; and immigration, 376, 480; industrialization in 141; intermarriage in, 123; media in, 494; and Mexico City, 344; population in, 92, 96, 199, 341, 504–6; and religion, 376; social life in, 144; studies about, 38–39, 42–43, 46–51; women in, 376
New Spain, 31, 40, 59, 124, 227, 277, 467
newspapers, 57, 61; Chicanas and, 435; film criticism in: 171, 174, 178–80; Spanish-language, 171, 174, 178–79, 235, 476, 494–95; theatrical reviews, 235

New York City, 77, 94, 264, 269, 298; Chicano theater in, 388, 391, 396, 397
Nieto-Gómez, Anna, 355, 539
"Niña, La" (Downs), 609
Niño Fidencio, 275
Noriega, Chon A., 13–14, 386
norteño music, 603
North American Free Trade Agreement (NAFTA), 474, 497, 566, 585, 599
Northamericanization, 492
North from Mexico: The Spanish Speaking People of the United States (McWilliams), 35
"No te dejes," 226, 249–50, 253–54
nuevo mexicanos, 318, 338, 344, 374
Nyerere, Julius, 417

occupations, 77, 88, 97–98
Occupied America (Acuña), 111, 115
On the Road: A Search for American Character (Smith), 394
Operation Wetback, 86
oppositional consciousness, 223–24, 227, 229
oppositional discourse, 362
oppression, 124, 147; Aztlán and, 208, 216; Chicanas and, 319, 332, 356, 362–63; class-based, 456; culture and, 518; ethnicity-based, 358; gender-based, 353, 354, 359, 365, 519, 599; and inferiority, 423; language-based, 467, 484–85; plays about, 394; sex-based, 330, 356; social, 415; studies on, 53, 116;
oral history, 63, 64, 435
Orientalism (Said), 454
Orozco, José Clemente, 227, 259–61, 262, 264–66, 268, 272
orquesta music, 128
Ortner, Sherry, 309
Otero, Miguel A., 46
otherness, 5, 281, 284, 411
Our Southwest (Fergusson), 37
Ouspensky, Léonid, 305

pachucos, 62, 128, 132–33, 209
Padilla, Felix, 140
Padilla, Genaro, 124, 146, 207
paganism, 303
Palacio, Vicente Riva, 44
Paredes, Américo, 47, 58, 441, 547; and anthropology, 528, 535–38, 541, 548; and literary history, 440; and proverbs, 224–26;
Paredes, Raymund A., 440–41
Park, Katherine, 662

Parkman, Francis, 378
Partido Liberal Mexicano, 355
Pastores, Los, 234
patria chica, 337
patriarchal binaries, 583, 586, 598
patriarchal codes/ideologies, 673, 683, 685–87, 690, 695
patriarchal society/economy, 587, 588, 591–92, 600, 633, 677
patriarchy, 126, 144, 199, 667; in academia, 538; Aztlán and, 678; Chicanas and, 319–20, 325, 355, 358, 360, 362–64, 528; discourse of, 586, 605; in families, 414, 420, 422, 540; and female workforce, 590; feminism and, 351–52, 541; oppression by, 412
Pattie, James Ohio, 418
Paul, Rodman W., 59
Paz, Octavio, 206–7, 262, 598, 602, 654
Peña, Manuel, 128–29, 138, 143
Peñalosa, Fernando, 11, 53
penates, 304
peninsulars, 341
Perales, Alonso S., 45
Pérez, Emma, 4, 321, 380–82, 542
Peréz de Villagrá, Gaspar, 38, 337
Pérez-Torres, Rafael, 5, 14, 230
performance: Chicana, 232; definition of, 322–23, 387; of folklore, 254–55; essays as, 224, 226; of experience, 227, 228; of gender norms, 569; and identity, 315, 386, 394–95, 399; Latino, 388–89, 392–99; performance studies, 387; of queer sexuality, 664, 696; of the sacred, 230; of self, 397–99; of speech events, 536. See also drama; performing politics; plays; *teatro/teatros*; theater
performance art, 213, 322, 323, 386, 392, 584
performative agency/identities, 323, 537
performative politics, 223–30, 316, 322, 394
performative space, 687
Performing the Border (Biemann), 608–9
periodization, 59–63, 124–26
Pesquera, Beatriz M., 319–20
photography, 593–98
Pike, Albert, 378
Pina, Michael, 201
Pino, Pedro B., 42
Pitt, Leonard, 47
Plan de Santa Barbara, El, 230, 278, 405, 539
Plan Espiritual de Aztlán, El, 3–4, 199–200, 202–3, 209, 416, 615

plays, 232–36, 240. See also drama; *teatro/teatros*; theater
pochos/pochismo, 137, 209, 213, 345–46, 346, 380, 541
polarization, 466, 469
Poleo, Héctor, 268–69
Política indiana (Solórzano y Pereira), 339
political action/activism, 4, 62–63, 139, 202, 257. See also Chicana politics; Chicano politics; performative politics
political economy, 10, 229, 585–89, 600, 604, 608
politics: community and, 561, 562, 570, 572; citizenship and, 563–65, 571; corruption in, 202; family and, 412–13, 416, 418; film and, 178, 182, 184, 187, 189; identity and, 394, 395, 658–59; immigrants and, 330, 570; international, 566; language and, 488–93; Latinos and, 144, 466; Mexicans and, 122, 128, 137, 347; in Mexico, 116, 202, 266, 329, 467, 587; migration/immigration and, 468, 470, 472, 476; and representation, 147, 528, 544; studies of, 36–37; 48–49, 52–53, 58–59; surrogation and, 649; theater and, 388–92, 394–95; in U.S., 32, 267, 341, 465. See also Chicana politics; Chicano politics; performative politics
Ponce, Juan García, 438
popular culture, 134, 178, 410, 516–17, 616, 633
population profiles, 92–93, 465–66, 501–7
Portillo, 606, 608
Portinari, Cándido, 268
postconquest era, 121, 125, 261, 602
poverty, 63, 99–100, 134, 362, 409, 678; of Latinos, 467, 475, 485, 486, 490, 504; in Mexico, 202; studies of, 53, 133
prayer, 300, 306, 308, 605
preconquest era, 122, 125, 227, 233, 259, 304
press, 171, 174, 176, 179; Hispanic: 170, 173–74, 179–87, 434, 494. See also media
Priestly, J. B., 514
Profile of Man and Culture (Ramos), 206
Programa de Industrialización Fronteriza, 587
Programa Nacional Fronterizo (PRONAF), 587
Project Consejo, 417
Proposition 187, 470, 496, 565, 572
Proposition 209, 490
Proposition 227, 489

prostitution, 378, 599, 587

protest/protests, 91, 120–21, 518, 525, 572; against Chinese, 627; corridos as, 226; proverbs as, 255; student, 488

Protest Is Not Enough, 143–44

proverbs, 223, 224–25, 250–55. *See also dichos*

psychohistory, 63–65

Puerto Ricans, 76–81, 92–94, 97, 136, 140, 270–71, 322, 391, 472, 481; census data on, 502–4, 506

Puerto Rican Traveling Theatre, 389

queering, of social norms/spaces, 673, 674, 678–79, 689–90, 692–93

Quetzalcóatl, 259–60, 277–78, 689

Quinto Sol Publishing, 529

Quiroga, José, 681, 685

Quran, the, 283

Rabinal Achi, 233

Rabinow, Paul, 527-28

Race and Class in the Southwest (Barrera), 148

racial groups/minorities, 11, 14, 17–18, 414–15, 417, 450

racial identity, 409, 633, 634, 661

racialized systems/subjects, 372, 394, 398, 516–17, 588, 605, 608, 681

racism: and anti-immigration efforts, 469–70; against blacks, 342; Chicana movement and, 358, 362–63, 374; consequences of, 18, 129, 147, 676; and discrimination, 362; environmental, 389; in historical texts, 46; institutional, 120–22, 131, 184, 485; and language, 484; among Latinos/Mexican Americans, 481, 654; mestizaje and, 615; in Mexican society, 210, 329, 338–39; nationalism and, 112, 114; and oppression/subordination, 146, 356, 358–59; in research, 40, 529–30, 532; and stereotyping, 52, 227; studies on, 45, 110, 145. *See also* discrimination

radio, 476–77, 494–97, 604. *See also* media

Radio: Bordertown (Culture Clash), 394

Radio Mambo (Culture Clash), 394

Rain God, The: as autobiographical, 648; and bodies in relation, 651–54, 661, 666; critical responses, 648; and disability, 661–63; as family narrative, 649, 665, 667; sexuality in, 650, 653, 654; surrogation in, 654–61

raíz olvidada, 615–16

Rambo, Ralph, 51

Ramirez, José Fernando, 43

Ramirez, Manuel, 414

Ramos, Samuel, 206

ranchera music, 496

rasquachismo, 227

rastreo, 598

Raya, Marcos, 272

raza, la, 17, 101, 237, 413, 415, 421–22, 677

"Raza Cósmica, La" (Vasconcelos) 18, 371

Read, Benjamin M., 46

Rebirth of Our Nationality, 272

recordings, spoken-word, 636–37, 639, 640–41

Redford, Robert, 182–83

"Reflections on American 'Left' Literary Criticism" (Said), 428

refugees, political, 472

Regeneración, 355

regeneration, 291–93, 304

Régimen de castas, 338

regionalism, 267, 269

religion, 29, 112, 124, 224–25; in Chicano life, 276; history of, 279–82; ideologies, 651; Islam, 283; in literature, 230, 275; murals and, 260, 270; plays and, 233–35; publications, 185, 190; shamans, 285; Sioux, 282–83; social norms/status and, 338, 348, 376; studies on, 144. *See also* altars; *Bless Me, Ultima*; Catholicism; Christians/Christianity

Religion in Essence and Manifestation (Van der Leeuw), 307

religious creativity, 230, 294

Rendón, Armando, 424

Rengifo, César, 268–69

repatriation program, 49, 84, 180, 469

research: avenues for, 12–13, 17, 22, 28. *See also* Chicano historical research/writing

resistance, 59–61, 114, 147, 176, 201, 533; Aztlán and, 197–98, 208, 216; to colonial status, 415, 418; corridos and, 603, 605; during conquest, 126, 260; debate about, 112; *familia* and, 417; female, 584, 587; forms of, 118, 121; freeways and, 521–22; literature and, 606; movements, 51; muralism and, 265, 269; *teatro* and, 388

Review, 117–18

rights: human, 90, 561, 570–73, 660; civil rights, 122, 345, 416; constitutional, 570; labor, 265; political, 568; reproductive, 355; social, 565–66, 569; women's, 332, 352, 361, 364, 603

Ringgold, Jenny Parks, 46

Rio Grande, 50, 341, 376, 381

Rios-Bustamante, Antonio, 178
Rivera, Diego, 227, 257–68, 270–72
Rivera, Feliciano, 34
Rivera, Jaime Sena, 53
Rivera, José, 391–92
Rivera, Tomás, 440, 658
Rives, George L., 44
Roach, Joseph, 654–55, 659
Road to Tamazunchale, The (Arias), 520
Robinson, Cecil, 440
rockera, 603
Rodríguez, Juan, 440, 442, 452
Rodríguez, Ralph E., 649, 696
Rodriguez, Richard, 146–48, 488, 493
Rodríguez, Roberto, 389
Rodríguez, Sylvia, 547
Rodríguez Monegal, Emir, 438
Rojas, Carlos A., 346
Rolando Hinojosa Reader, The (Saldívar), 434
Román, David, 322–23
Romano-V., Octavio Ignacio, 50, 528, 529–31, 533–34, 539, 543–44
Romo, Ricardo, 110
Rosaldo, Michele Z., 540
Rosaldo, Renato, 135–36, 225, 544, 546, 548, 674, 676, 689
Rowbatham, Sheila, 419, 423
Rueda, Emma
rural areas, 62; Chicanos/Mexican Americans in, 22, 23, 91, 93, 146, 270; labor in, 33, 267; migration from, 24–25, 35, 101, 379, 468; poverty in, 132; undocumented workers in, 471; vs. urban areas, 22–24, 61, 88
Russel y Rodríguez, Mónica, 547

Sabogal, José, 268
sacred knowledge, 285, 288–89
sacredness, 224–25, 229–30, 279; of body, 655; family and, 299; hierophany, 282–84; in literature, 275–76, 286–94, 656; specialists, 284–85; of violence, 654, 659–60. *See also* altars
Sacred Pipe, The, 282–83
Safran, William, 202
Said, Edward W., 408, 429, 436, 454–56
saints, 304–8, 601
Salazar, Rubén, 1, 258
Saldana-Portillo, Maria Josefina, 615, 640
Saldívar, José David, 437, 439, 603, 657–58
Saldívar, Ramón, 437, 438, 605
Salinas, Ric, 393
Salvadorans, 476, 482, 499, 506

Samora, Julian, 49
Sánchez, George I., 35, 48–49, 53, 107, 108, 532
Sánchez, Marta E., 434, 653, 657–58
Sánchez, Pedro, 51
Sánchez, Rosaura, 409, 434, 440, 667
Sánchez Lamego, Miquel A., 44
Sánchez Orozco, Alejandra, 606
San Diego, 337, 388, 394, 466, 476, 503; census data on, 504; immigrants and, 471, 475, 562; and literary criticism, 440
San Diego State College, 34
San Diego State University, 204
Sandoval, Chela, 4, 223
San Francisco Mime Troupe, 236
Santa Barbara, 116, 118, 235, 343, 494; and literary criticism, 437, 440
Santa Fe, 374, 375, 377–78; census data on, 505
Santibañez, Enrique, 48, 57
Saragoza, Alex, 12–13
Saunders, Lyle, 35, 52
Schapiro, Miriam, 309
Schmidt, Fred, 54
Scott, James, 521
Scott, Joan, 113,
secondary labor market, 131, 547
segregation, 18, 21, 117, 122, 480, 547; housing, 85; job, 120; redevelopment and, 678; school, 129
Segura, Denise A., 319–21
Selective Bibliography for the Study of Mexican American History, 34
self-consciousness, political, 321, 374, 380
Seminar on Immigration, Racism, and Racial Discrimination, 572
semiotics, 172, 299, 428
separatism, 224, 352–53
Servin, Manuel P., 34, 49
sexism, 147, 328, 330, 332, 687; critical discourse and, 456; in Mexico, 329; perpetuation of, 395
racism/classism, 356, 362–63; sex-roles and, 419–20
sexual economy, 586, 587, 589, 600, 605, 683
sexual identity/orientation: borderlands and, 211, 214; 666, 679; Chicano research and, 372, 380, 406; community and, 389; construction of, 320–22; ethnic identity and, 395; feminism and, 365; of Mexican male, 628, 654, 690; and sex-roles, 407, 412–13, 41, 422, 424; stereotyping and, 316–17, 323

sexual idioms, 378–79
sexuality/sexualities: ambiguous, 673;
     American culture and, 130, 132;
     centrality of, 538, 540–44; and disability,
     650; family and, 678; feminism and,
     539; gay, 647–48, 650; intersectionality
     and, 559; in Latin America, 597;
     in literature, 648, 661, 673–74; and
     maquila labor, 592; patriarchal control
     of, 325, 596–97; queer, 664, 673, 676,
     677; race/ethnicity and, 653–54, 660,
     667; and rape/murder, 597; space and,
     674. *See also* homosexuality; *virgen-puta*
Sexuality of Latinas, The, 480
sexualized/sexual body, 216, 560, 598, 651,
     653–55, 661–66; production/regulation
     of space and, 674–75, 678
sexual norms/ideologies, 675–76, 677, 683,
     688, 696
sexual oppression/domination, 319, 329, 330,
     394; of undocumented women, 561; and
     shamans, 280, 285, 286–89, 293
Shrunken Head of Pancho Villa, The (Valdez),
     236
Sierra, Justo, 44
Siguenza, Herbert, 393
Singletary, Otis A., 45
Sioux religion, 282–83, 28
Siqueiros, David Alfaro, 227, 261, 263–68,
     271–72
Smith, Anna Deavere, 434–436, 394
Smith, George W., 44
Smith, Justin, 44, 45
Snyder, Sharon L., 648
social change, 1, 9, 111, 130, 176, 225, 265,
     409–10
social history, 108, 110–17, 128, 132–33, 146,
     380
socialism, 264
social realism, 268, 269
society: acceptance into, 128, 327; American,
     114, 124–25, 127, 135, 143, 204; art
     and, 300; Catholic, 594; Chicano,
     28–30; colonial/colonized, 318, 423;
     criticism and, 444; diversification of,
     564; dominant/majority, 79, 110, 269,
     330–32, 407, 414–15, 417–18, 421, 676;
     Euro-American, 209; and gender, 147;
     Indian, 277; liberal democratic, 563;
     mestizo, 615; metro/suburban, 514, 524;
     Mexican, 120, 210, 328–30, 598; New
     Mexican, 340–41; patriarchal, 591–92,
     600, 667; restructuring of, 364–65;

Spanish, 338, 340; stratified, 348, 362,
     536; *tejano*, 116, 122–23; women and,
     352, 420, 425. *See also* Chicano society
Society of Castes, 338
socioeconomic status: barriers, 687; of
     Chicanos, 124, 522; of Chicanas, 357,
     360, 523, 673, 687; effects of, 134, 143;
     language and, 485–86; of Mexican
     Americans, 20, 24, 130, 132; in Mexico,
     328; in Midwest, 97
socioeconomics: research on, 12, 39, 55, 145;
socioeconomic systems, 199, 328
sociolinguistics, 224, 299, 405
sociology, 5, 16, 53, 412, 534
Soja, Edward, 675, 678
Sollors, Werner, 660
Solórzano y Pereira, Juan de, 339
Sommers, Joseph, 433
Song of Unity, 271
Sosa Riddell, Adaljiza, 315–17, 318–19,
     320–21, 419–20
South America, 92–94, 267–69, 271–72, 472,
     481, 488, 520; census data on, 502–5
South Texas, 122, 128, 145–46, 171, 345, 346,
     547. *See also* altars
Southwest: Anglo-Chicano relations in, 21;
     capitalism and, 125; diversity in, 466;
     economy of, 130–32; Mexican labor in,
     83–85; history of, 40–41, 45, 59–62;
     intermarriage in, 616; language use in,
     487, 494–98; and migration, 24, 82,
     95–96; populations of, 92–93, 119,
     146, 468, 481; research on, 37–57, 79,
     141–42; reterritorialization of, 409, 467;
     Spanish in, 317–18, 480; social status/
     categorizations in, 122, 338–42, 375–76
Southwest: Old and New (Hollon), 37
*Southwest: Three Peoples in Geographical
     Change*
     (Meinig), 37
"Soy Chicana Primero" (Longeaux y Vásquez),
     421–22
space: conceptual, 321; cultural, 187, 228,
     409, 497, 679; organization of, 475;
     production of, 678; regulation of, 675,
     677; and sexuality, 674, 675, 682–88;
     structured/constructed, 673, 681
"Space of Chicano Literature, The" (Bruce-
     Novoa), 438
Spain: altars in, 304; colonization by, 337,
     343, 347–48, 466–67; drama and, 233–
     35, 391; history of, 264–65; relationship
     with, 376; social status/categorizations

in, 338. *See also* New Spain

Spanish American Alliance of Tucson, 345

Spanish language: and cultural production, 493–94; and ethnic identity, 343–44, 374–76, 481, 482, 541; and English, 379, 381, 452, 499; geopolitics of, 409; loss/ maintenance of, 199, 484–92; media, 171, 174, 178, 476–77, 494–98; number of speakers, 480, 501–2; and prejudice, 654; and racialization, 681; slang, 682; status and, 685; translation of, 536–37

Spanish myth, 40–41

Spanish-speaking/origin population: census data on, 92–100, 501–7; diversity of, 145; history of, 337–343, 615; location of, 118–19, 480; as majority, 477; in Metro areas, 483–84; in Midwest, 76–78, 568; occupations of, 330–331; in popular culture, 633; studies on, 35–59, 79–80; subordination of, 120

spatialization, 679

Spence, Louise, 171

Spiro, Melford E., 418

Spivak, Gayatri, 383

Stam, Robert, 171

Stand and Deliver, 175, 176, 184–88

Standard metropolitan statistical areas (SMSAs), 94

Stearns, Peter N., 114

stereotypes, 316, 318, 322; ethnic, 60, 516–17; in film, 176–78, 179, 183, 186, 323, 391; gender, 325, 628, 692; racist, 52, 227; sexual identity, 316–17, 323

Stern, Alexandra Minna, 615, 640

Stevens, Jacqueline, 675

Stikes, Melvin P., 54

Stoddard, Ellwyn, 414

St. Paule, Irma, 390

stratification: of education, 406; of gender, 361–63; of Hispanics, 336; of language, 483; of society, 348, 362, 483, 536

Street of the Sun, The (Rivera), 391

strikes, 84, 120, 421; agricultural, 49, 236–38, 416; depictions of, 263–64

students: and Chicano studies, 5, 108; and college admission, 417, 529; delinquency, 128, 133; dropouts, 489; in El Movimiento, 139; and identity, 134, 345; and language use, 476, 484, 485, 487, 488–90, 493, 503; and political movements, 373; and *teatros*, 232

Stuff (Fusco and Bustamante), 395

subcultures, 20–21, 24, 59, 337

submissiveness, 327, 422–23, 599, 583, 586, 594, 598, 606

subordination, 60, 109, 352, 422; gender, 351, 353, 356, 419; in labor force, 139; language and, 478; and literary production, 446; maquilas and, 597; origins of, 146–47, 414–15; responses to, 120–24, 361–64, 423, 678

suburbanization, 132, 512–13

Sun Belt, 131, 140

surrogation, 654–60, 665

surumatos, 346

symbolism, 303–4, 692

Szombati-Fabian, Ilona, 300

taggers, 521

Tamayo, Rufino, 227, 262

Tanguma, Leo, 272

Taylor, Diana, 387

Taylor, Paul S., 48

teatro/teatros, 176, 181, 226, 233–35. *See also* El Teatro Campesino; El Teatro Nacional de Aztlán

tejano/tejanos: class divisions, 129; identity and, 318, 338, 344–45, 375; influence of, 93; and Mexican control, 119; and Mexican culture, 116; music, 128; and popular culture, 619; social life of, 123;

telenovelas, 391

television, 171, 224, 298, 476, 493, 495, 497

Tennery, Thomas D., 44

Texas: border culture and, 117; capitalism and, 145; census data for, 95–96, 504–6; history of, 337, 341–42, 345; languages in, 476, 497; Mexicans in, 475; Mexican Americans in, 24; and migration, 83, 88, 89, 379; murals in, 272; populations in, 92; school revolt, 416; studies on, 39, 41–44, 50–51, 116. *See also* altars; South Texas

Texas-Mexican Conjunto, The (Peña), 128

Tharp, Roland G., 414

theater: Chicano, 226–27, 323; and identity, 322–23; Spanish-language, 234, 494, 495. *See also* drama; performance; *teatro/ teatros*

Theatre of the Golden Era in California (MacMinn), 234

theme parks. *See* Disneyland

theology, 224, 225, 276–78

Third Woman, 434–35

Third World, 205, 213, 229, 270, 415, 435, 472, 477

This Bridge Called My Back, 435, 543
Thompson, Rosemarie Garland, 648
Tijerina, Reyes López, 51, 281
Tirado, Miguel David, 49, 52, 418
Tireman, Lloyd S., 53
Todo los gatos (Fuentes), 602
transnational corporations/industry, 474, 475, 483, 499, 641
Treaty of Guadalupe Hidalgo, 44, 125
Tropicana, Carmelita, 322, 394–96, 396
Troyano, Alina, 322, 395–96
Troyano, Ela, 396
Trujillo, Carla, 542
Tujunga Wash, 518
Turner, Kay F., 225–26, 229
Twitchell, Ralph E., 43, 47
Two Undiscovered Amerindians Visit (Gómez Peña and Fusco), 394

UCLA Chicano Studies Research Center, 1, 640
UCLA Mexican American Study Project, 22, 79
ujamaa, 417
underclass, 133, 185
undocumented migration/immigration, 86–87, 91, 378, 465, 470–71, 561–62
United Nations Population Fund, 468
United States: annexation of Mexico, 353, 377, 420; diversity in, 476–77; economy of, 131, 468–69; migrant/immigrant labor in, 76–78, 82–100, 470–73; muralism in, 267–69, 270; intolerance/racism in, 21, 46, 378, 414, 465, 469; relations with Mexico, 56, 531, 598. *See also* U.S.-Mexican War
U.S. Census Bureau data, 82–100, 331, 501–7
U.S. Commission on Civil Rights, 79
U.S.-Mexican War, 30, 60, 341, 342
U.S.-Mexico border, 107, 212, 475, 487, 484, 677. *See also* border/borders; borderlands
University of California, Davis, 416, 488
University of California, Santa Barbara, 447–448
University of California Latino Eligibility Task Force, 490
University of New Mexico, 417
urban areas: employment in, 469; ethnic composition of, 88, 476; growth of, 24; history of, 110, 116; migration to, 379, 468; redevelopment of, 678, 687; vs. rural areas, 22–24, 61, 88; Spanish-origin population in, 93; white flight, 513. *See also* maquilas/maquiladoras; suburbanization
urbanization, 35, 111, 128, 132, 145, 210, 413, 419, 675
Ureta, Teodoro Nuñez, 268

Vaca, Nick C., 53, 529–34
Valadés, José C., 44
Valdés, Dennis, 136
Valdez, Daniel, 271
Valdez, Diana Washington, 582
Valdez, Luis, 175–76, 179–81, 227–28, 232, 236–41, 270, 373, 389
Valens, Ritchie, 130, 173
Vallejo, Mariano Guadalupe, 47, 51, 467
value systems, 19, 25, 188; Anglo, 122; Anglo vs. Mexican American, 532–33; colonial, 316; and *dichos*, 252–55; family, 416; heteronormative, 685; literary, 451, 454; merchant, 377; religious/spiritual, 278, 284, 310; traditional, 364, 414; universal, 188; Western, 667
Van de Leeuw, Gerardus, 280–81
Van Doren, Charles, 36
Vasconcelos, José, 206, 371, 615, 633, 640
Velásquez, Isabel, 608–9
vendidas, 354, 541
victimization, 115–17, 126, 147, 388
Vidal, Mirta, 424
Vietnam War, 85, 528–29, 532
Vigil, Diego, 593
Vigil, James Diego, 132
Villa, Raúl, 675, 678, 682, 687
Villanueva, Tino, 346
virgen-puta, 597–98, 602, 608
Virgin Mary. *See* Virgin of Guadalupe
Virgin of Guadalupe, 284, 288, 297–98, 304, 305–8, 329, 598, 678, 685
Virgin of Juárez, 583
visual arts/artists, 223, 606. *See also* muralism/muralists; murals

Waiting in the Wings (Moraga), 695
Wallerstein, Immanuel, 117
Warner, Michael, 674, 675–76, 678, 685, 689, 695
Watt, W. Montgomery, 283
Webb, James Josiah, 42, 378
Weber, David J., 43, 116, 119–20, 122
Weber, Devra, 107
Weinberg, Albert K., 44
Welch, Reginal, 484
wet-heads, 341

Where the Air Is Clean (Moctezuma), 602
Williams, Raymond, 430, 433
Wilson, Tamar Diana, 588–89
Wilson, William J., 133
With His Pistol in His Hand (Paredes), 50
With the Ears of Strangers (Robinson), 440
Wolf, Eric, 39
Wollenberg, Charles, 49
women: choices for, 134; history of, 141–42,
    147; in Mexico, 328–29, 337–39;
    objectified, 683; rights of, 332; status
    of, 123; in workforce, 130. *See also*
    Chicanas; feminism
Women, Resistance and Revolution
    (Rowbatham), 419
women's movement, 332, 351–56, 358–60
women's studies, 9–10
Woodman, Lyman L., 51
Woods, Frances Jerome, 52
workers. *See* labor/laborers; migrant workers
World, the Text, and the Critic, The (Said), 504
World Conference Against Racism, 571
World War I: and immigration, 84–85;
    muralism during, 264, 267, 270

World War II: effect on families, 62; and
    immigration/migration, 25, 83–85,
    379; impact of, 138; labor and, 379;
    muralism during, 261, 265, 269; and
    racial attitudes, 22; relocation camps,
    493; sociocultural consequences of, 127,
    140, 143; and socioeconomic change,
    128, 130–34
Wright, Richard, 14

Yale Critics, The (Martin, Arac, and Godzich),
    439
Yarbro-Bejarano, Yvonne, 227, 389, 440
Ybarra-Frausto, Tomás, 227
Young Girl and Her Future, A (Cardona), 594,
    596
Young Girl at Work, A (Cardona), 594, 595

Zabre, Teja, 43
Zapata, Emiliano, 207, 258, 260, 263, 266
Zapotecs, 538
Zavella, Patricia, 141–42, 143, 541–42, 547
Zoot Suit (Valdez), 175
zoot-suit riots, 49, 116, 127, 469
Zoot-Suit Riots, The (Mazon), 127